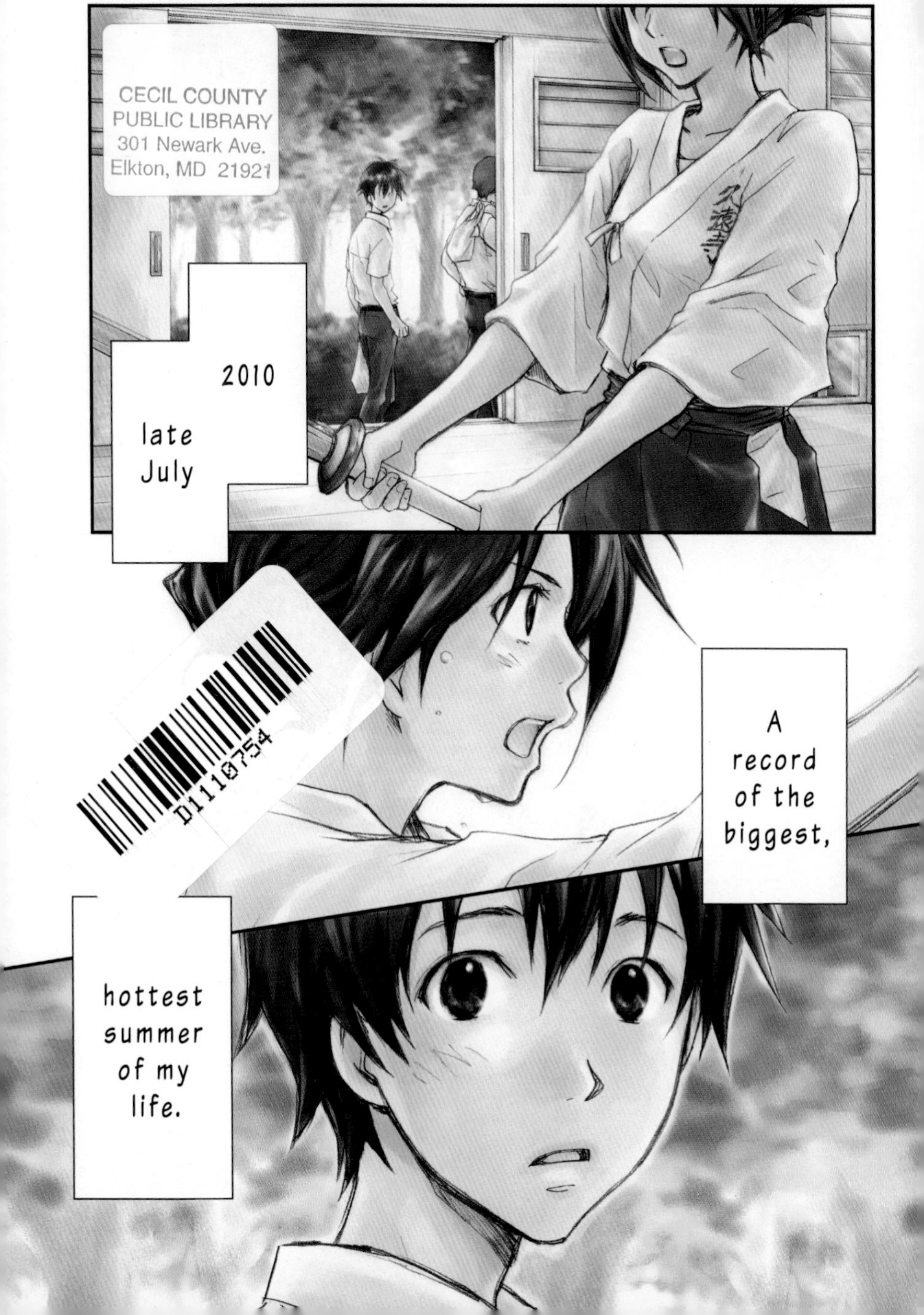
2010
late July
A record of the biggest,
hottest summer of my life.

SUMMER WARS

PART 1

STORY BY
MAMORU HOSODA

ART BY
IQURA SUGIMOTO

CHARACTER DESIGN BY
YOSHIYUKI SADAMOTO

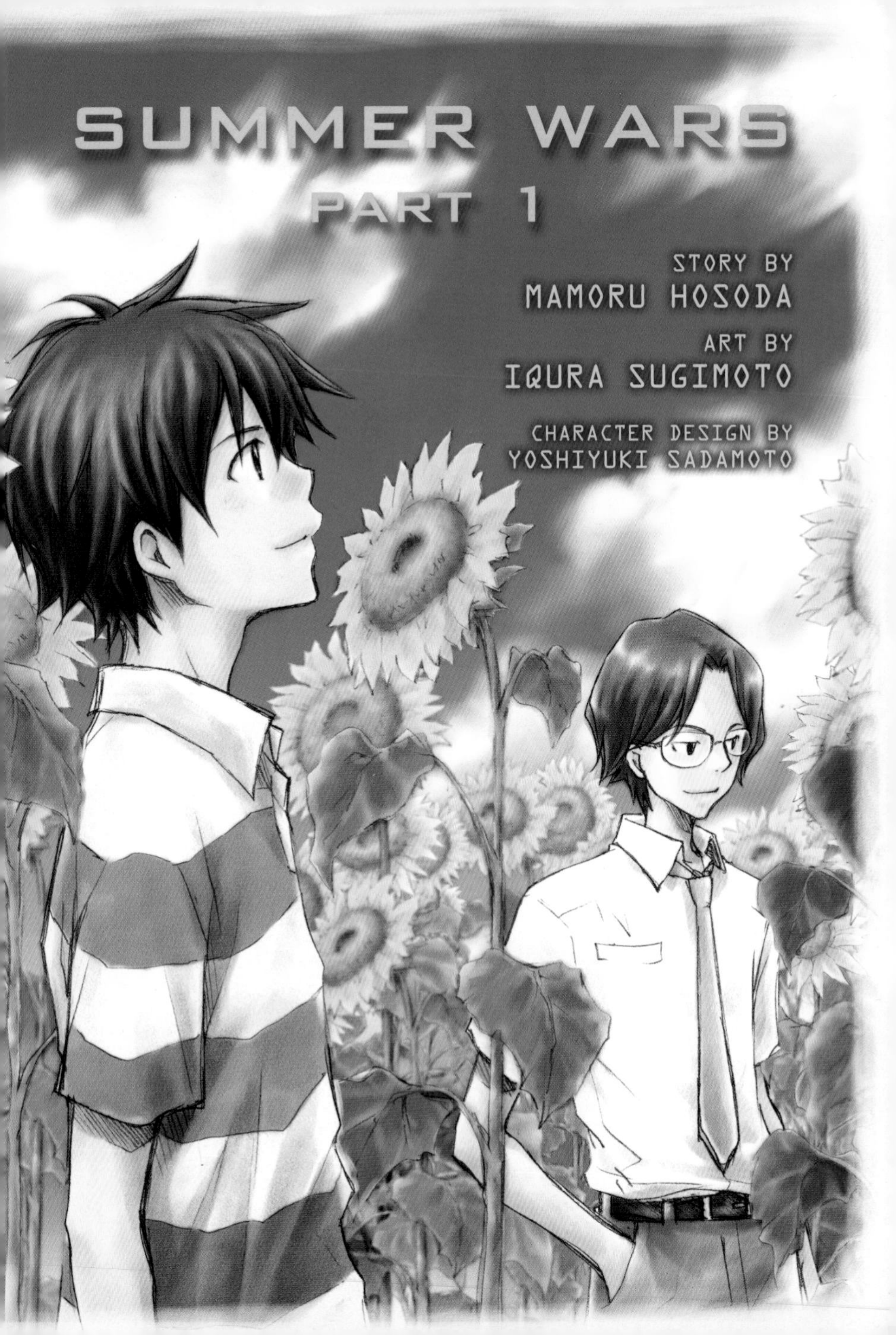

Act One Job for the Summer

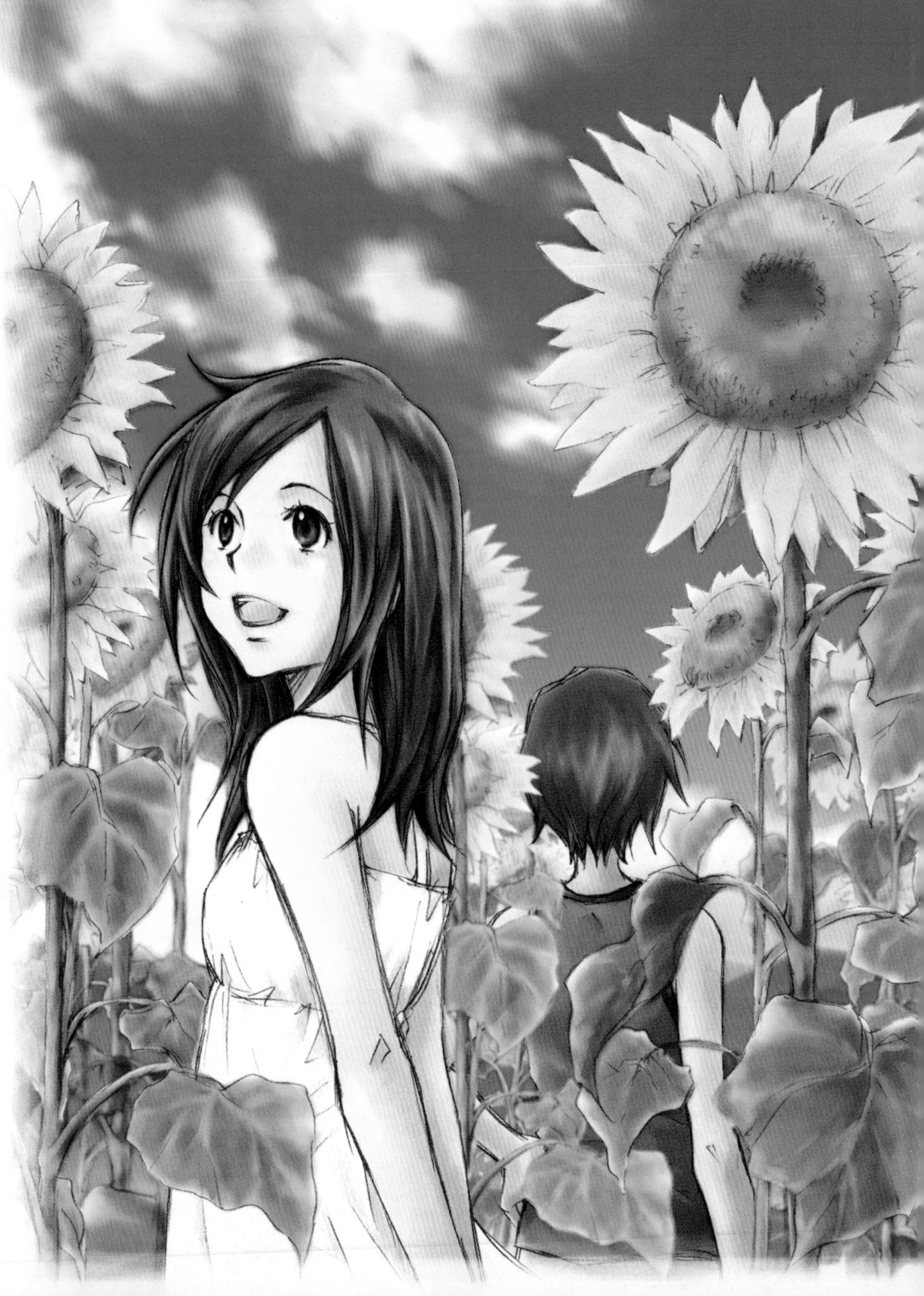

SUMMER WARS
PART 1

CONTENTS

VERTICAL.

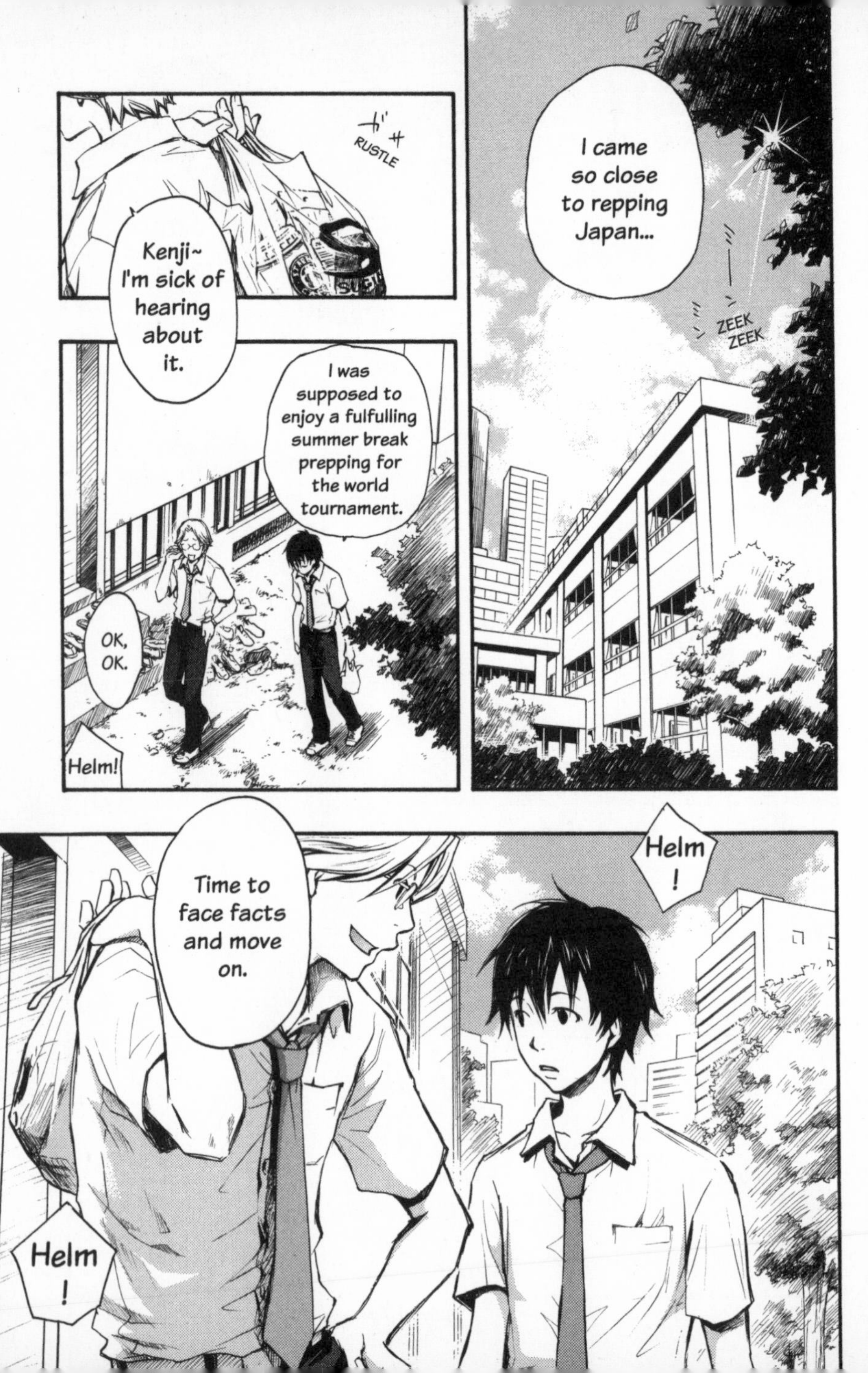
I came so close to repping Japan...
ZEEK ZEEK
RUSTLE
Kenji~ I'm sick of hearing about it.
I was supposed to enjoy a fulfulling summer break prepping for the world tournament.
OK, OK.
Helm!
Helm !
Time to face facts and move on.
Helm !

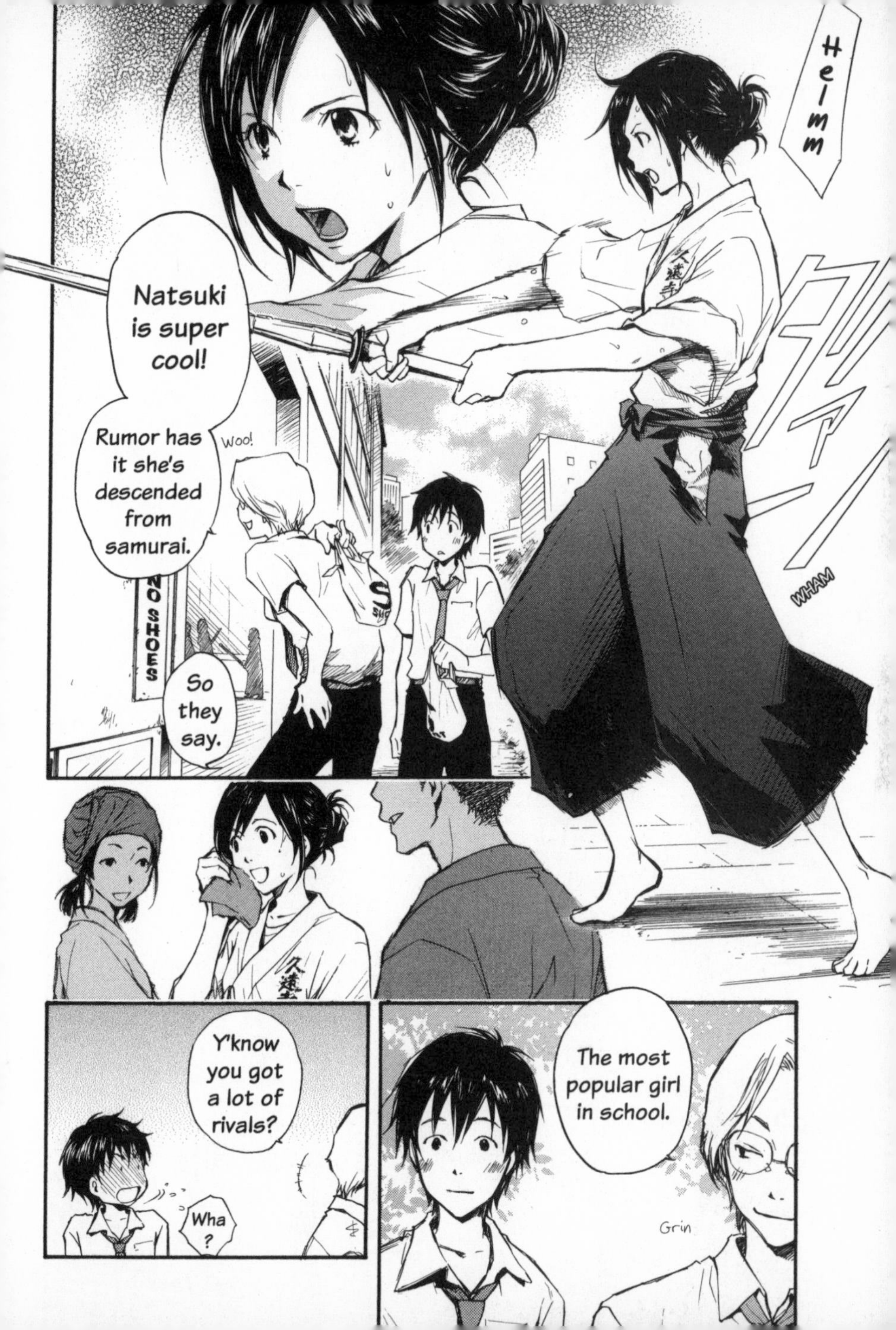
Helmm
Natsuki is super cool!
WHAM
Rumor has it she's descended from samurai.
Woo!
NO SHOES
So they say.
The most popular girl in school.
Grin
Y'know you got a lot of rivals?
Wha?

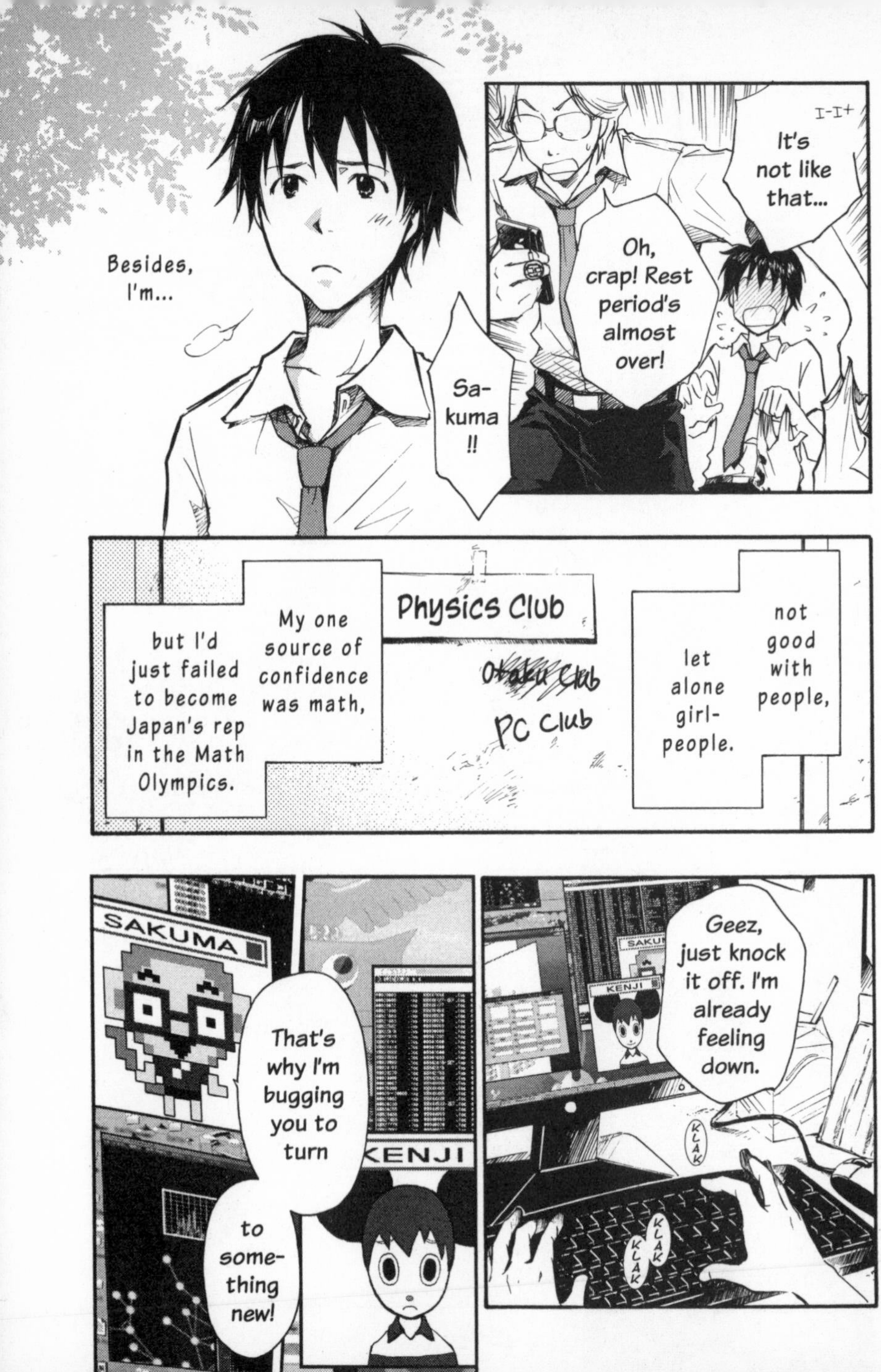
It's not like that...
Oh, crap! Rest period's almost over!
Sa-kuma!!
Besides, I'm...
not good with people,
let alone girl-people.
Physics Club
Otaku Club
PC Club
My one source of confidence was math,
but I'd just failed to become Japan's rep in the Math Olympics.
KENJI
Geez, just knock it off. I'm already feeling down.
KLAK
KLAK
KLAK
SAKUMA
KENJI
That's why I'm bugging you to turn
to some-thing new!

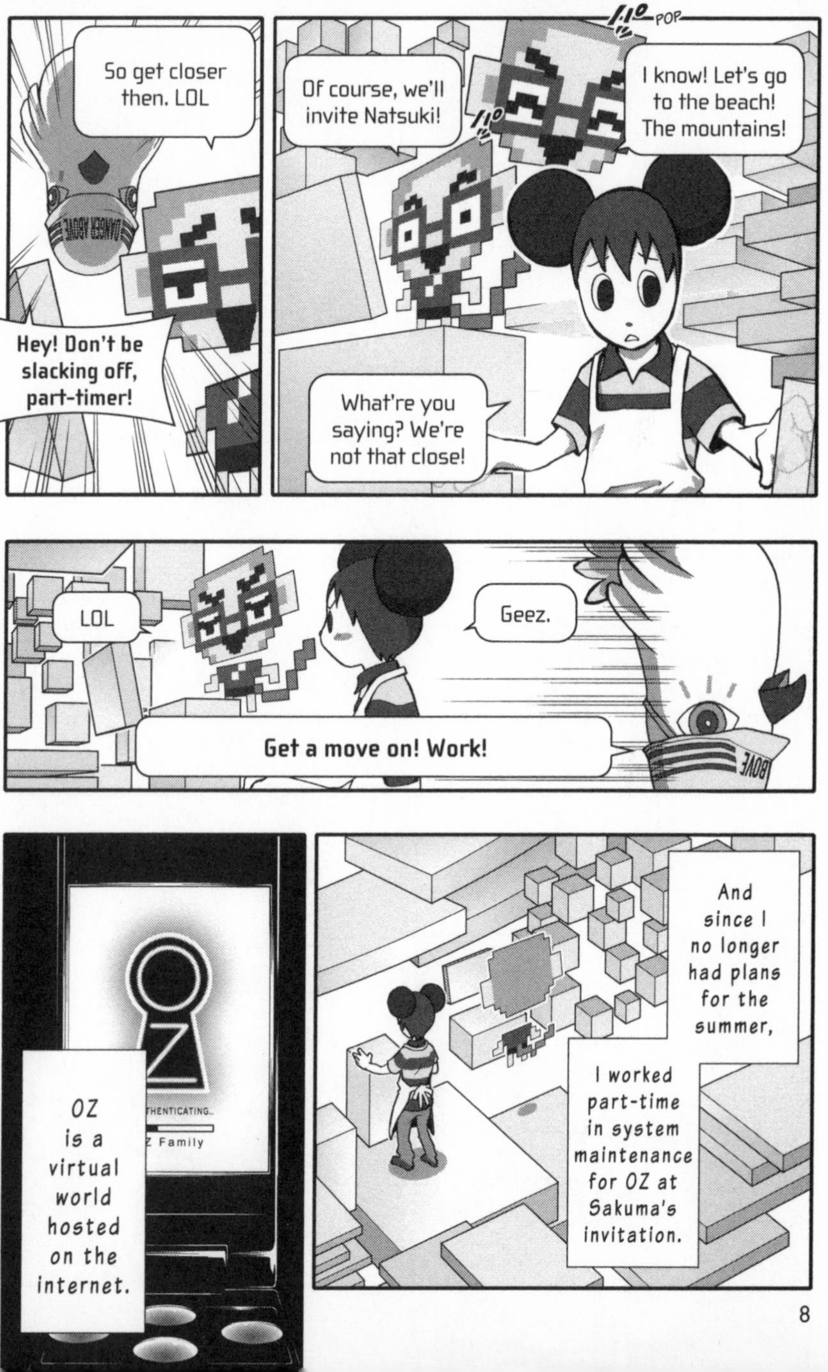
POP
I know! Let's go to the beach! The mountains!
Of course, we'll invite Natsuki!
What're you saying? We're not that close!
So get closer then. LOL
Hey! Don't be slacking off, part-timer!
Geez.
LOL
Get a move on! Work!
And since I no longer had plans for the summer,
I worked part-time in system maintenance for OZ at Sakuma's invitation.
OZ is a virtual world hosted on the internet.

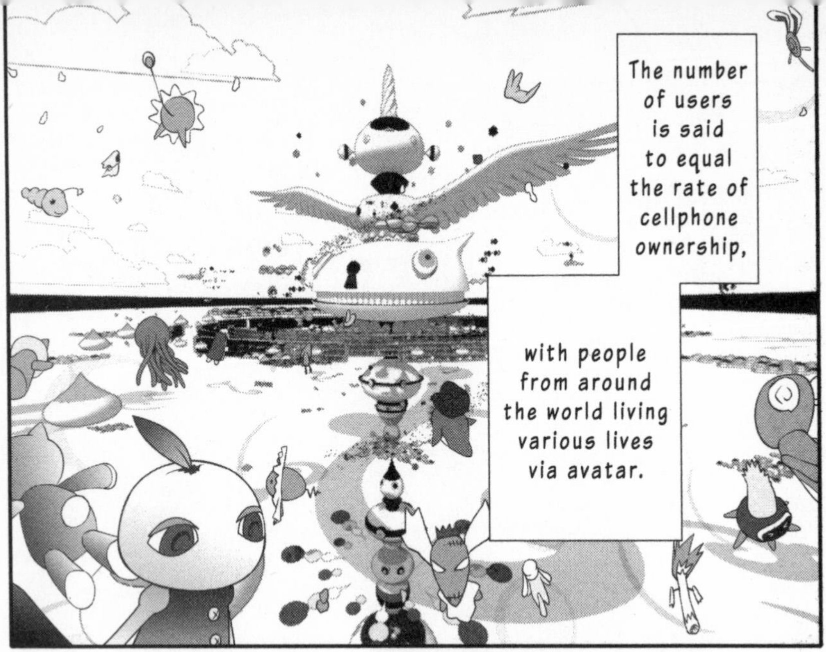
The number of users is said to equal the rate of cellphone ownership,
with people from around the world living various lives via avatar.

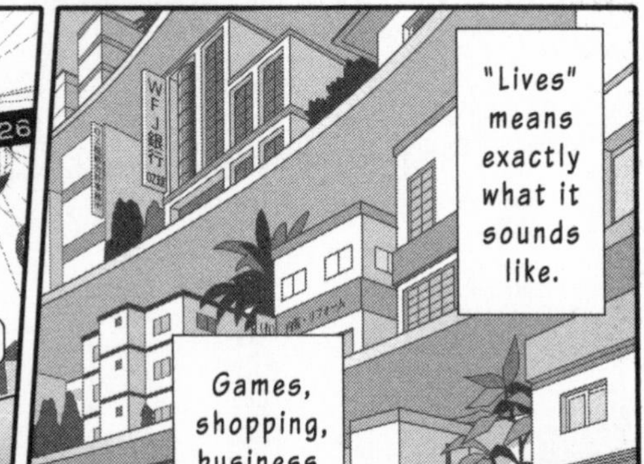
"Lives" means exactly what it sounds like.
Games, shopping, business, official processes ...
One can experience nearly everything like in real life.

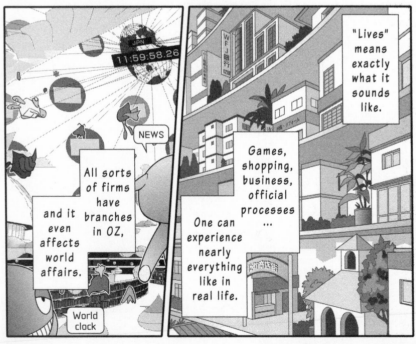

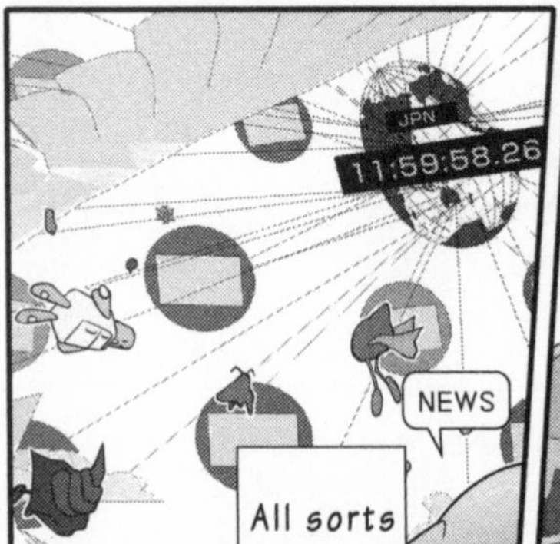
JPN
11:59:58.26
NEWS
All sorts of firms have branches in OZ,
and it even affects world affairs.
World clock

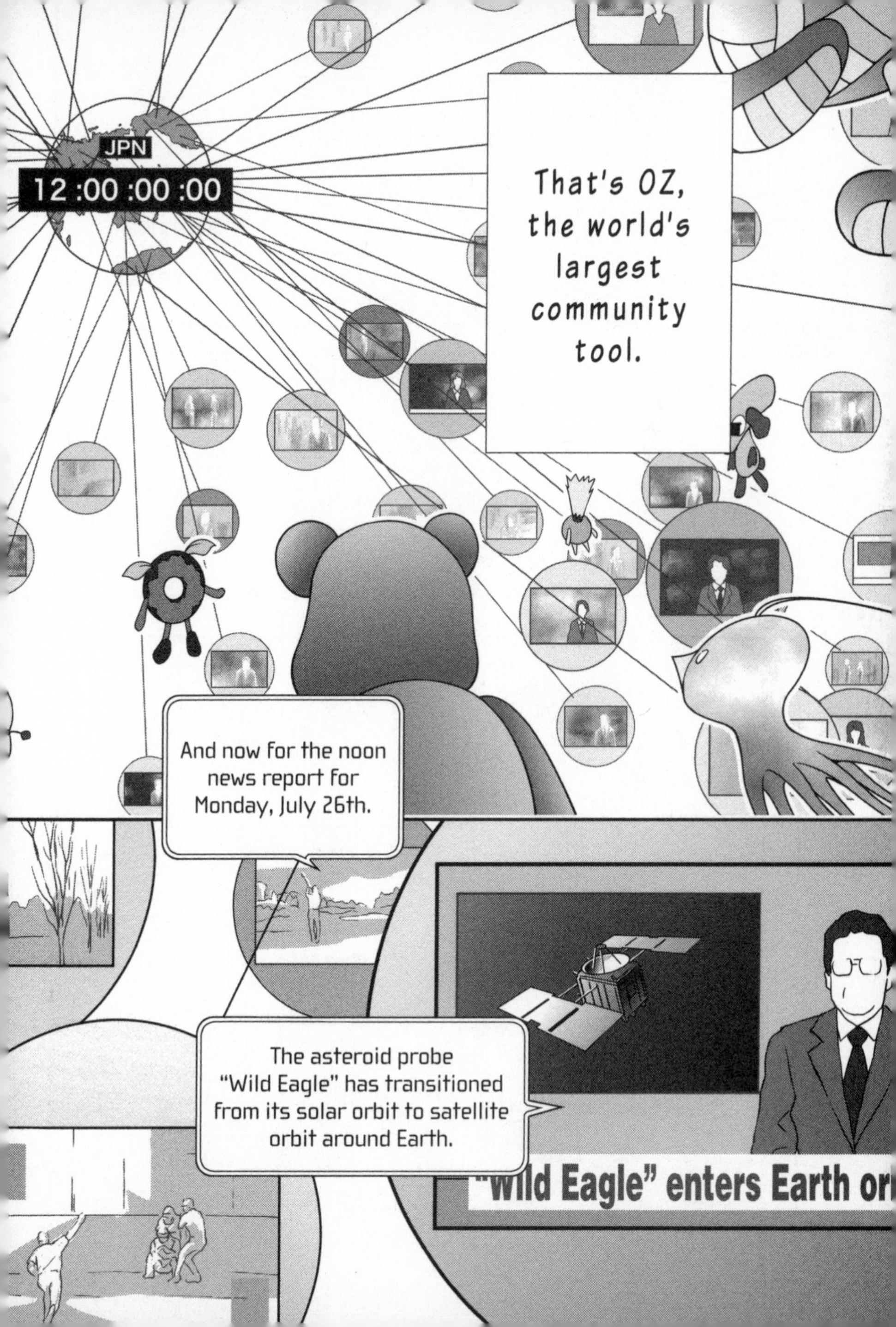
That's OZ, the world's largest community tool.
JPN
12 :00 :00 :00
And now for the noon news report for Monday, July 26th.
The asteroid probe "Wild Eagle" has transitioned from its solar orbit to satellite orbit around Earth.
"Wild Eagle" enters Earth or

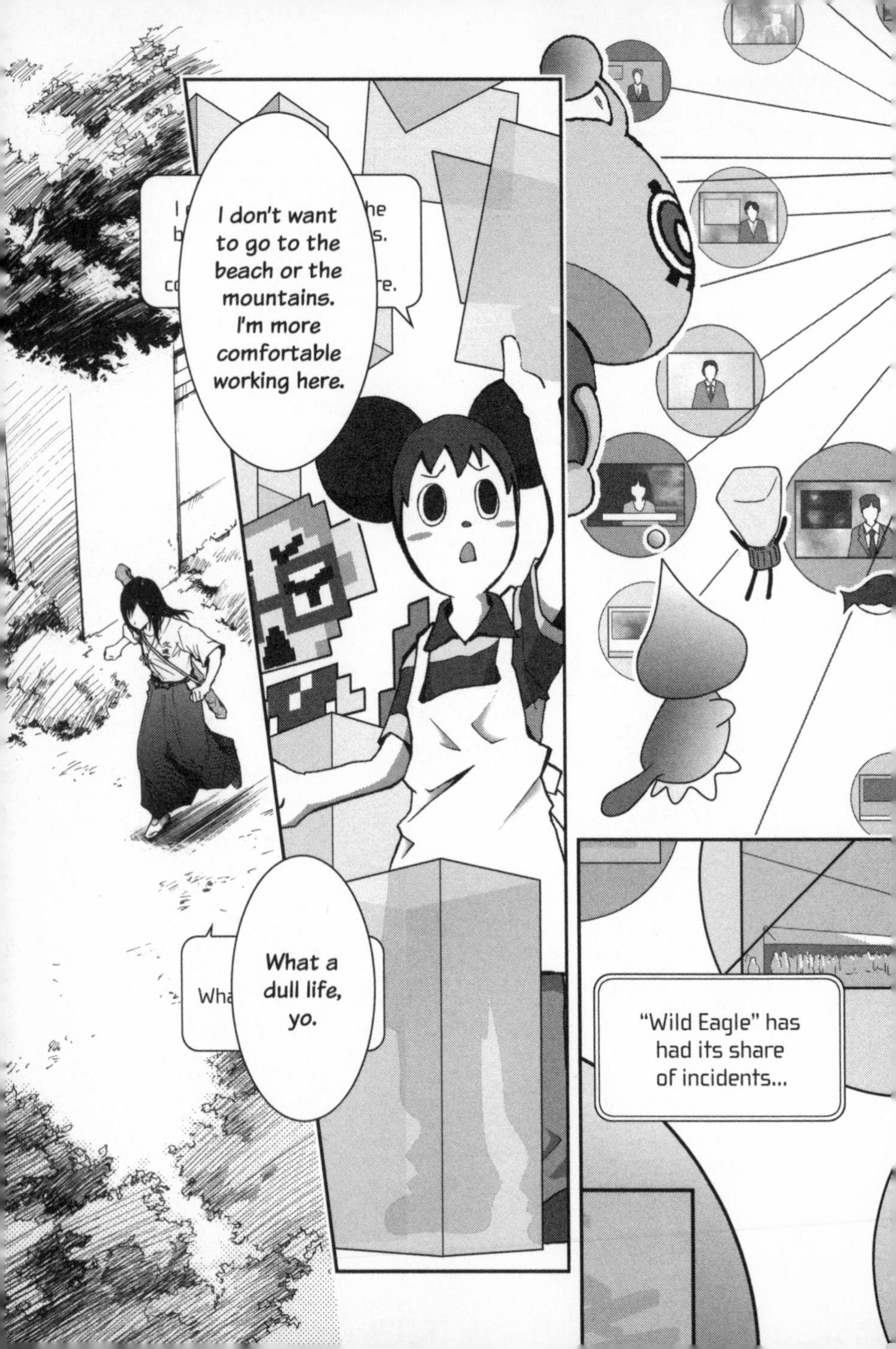
"Wild Eagle" has had its share of incidents...
I don't want to go to the beach or the mountains. I'm more comfortable working here.
What a dull life, yo.

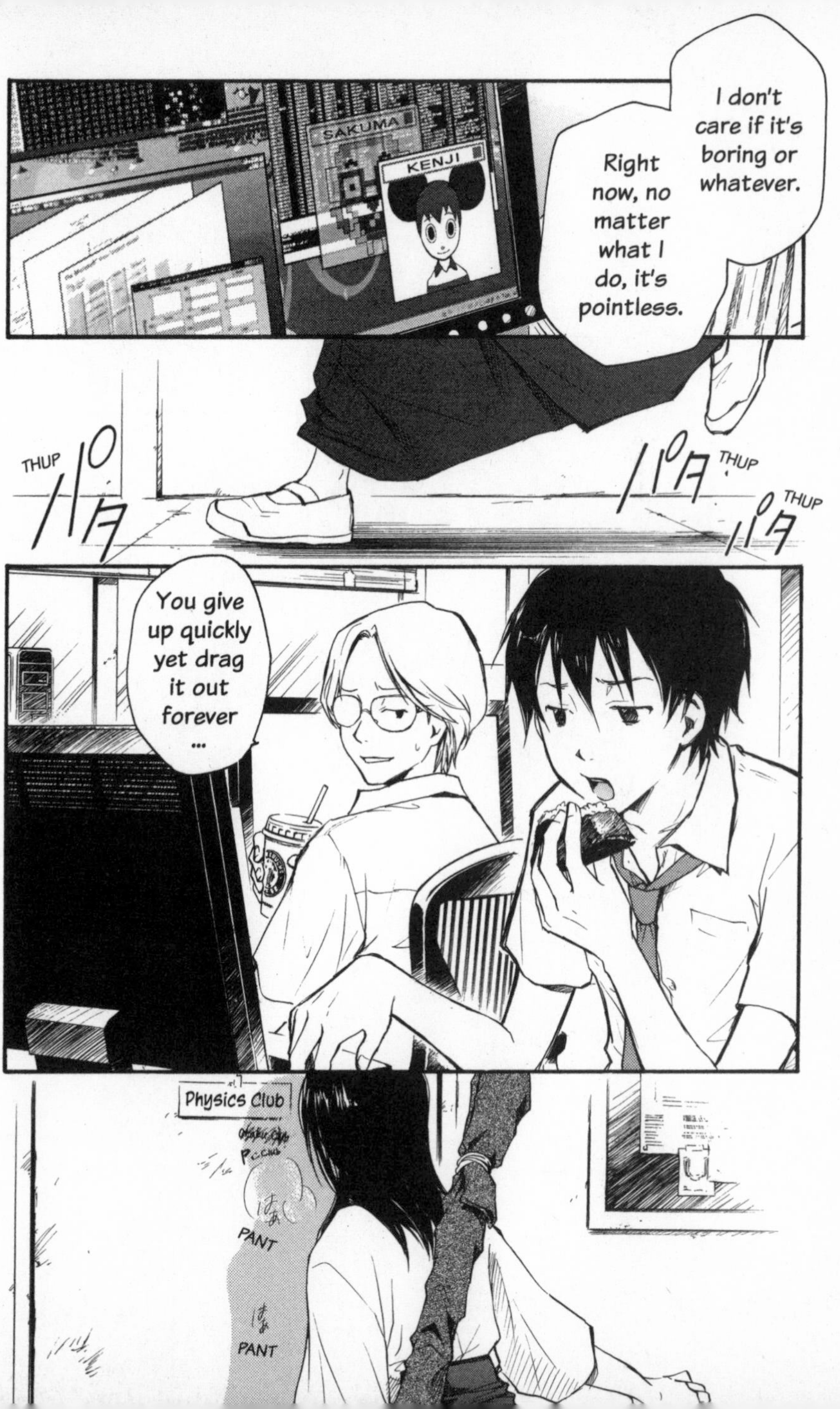
I don't care if it's boring or whatever.
Right now, no matter what I do, it's pointless.
SAKUMA
KENJI
THUP
THUP
THUP
You give up quickly yet drag it out forever ...
Physics Club
PANT
PANT

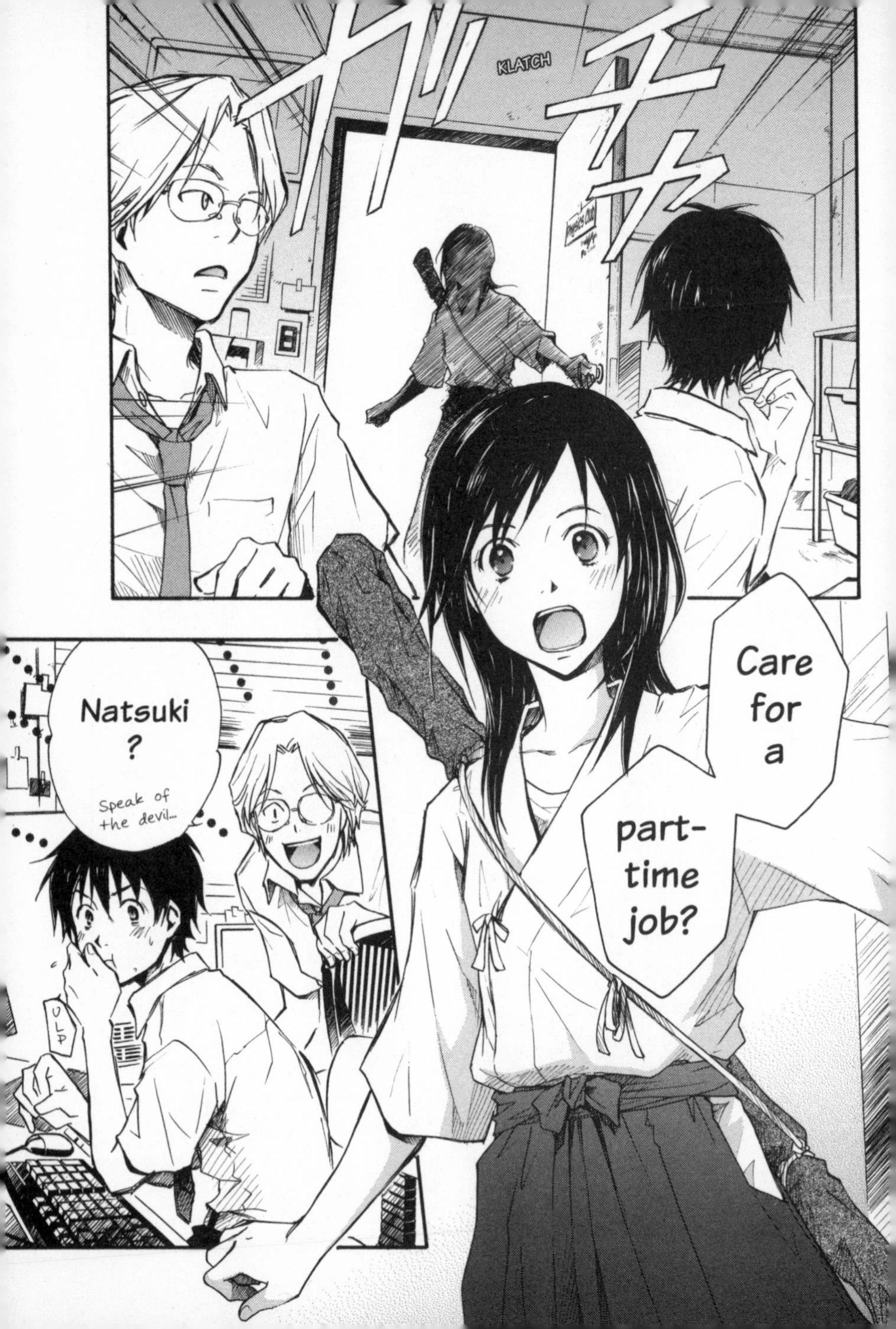
KLATCH
Care for a part-time job?
Natsuki?
Speak of the devil...
ULP

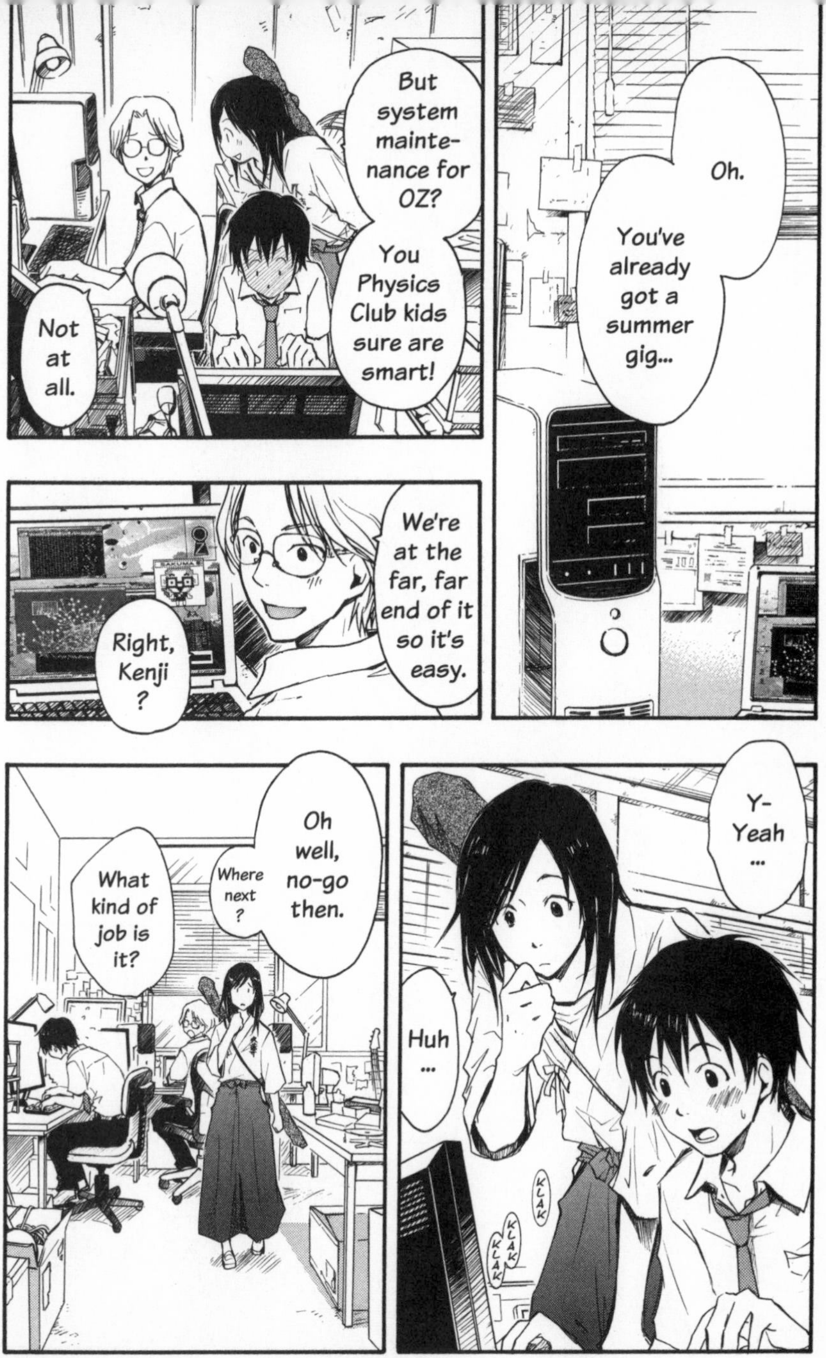
Oh.
You've already got a summer gig...
But system mainte-nance for OZ?
You Physics Club kids sure are smart!
Not at all.
We're at the far, far end of it so it's easy.
Right, Kenji?
Y-Yeah...
Huh...
KLAK
KLAK
KLAK
Oh well, no-go then.
Where next?
What kind of job is it?

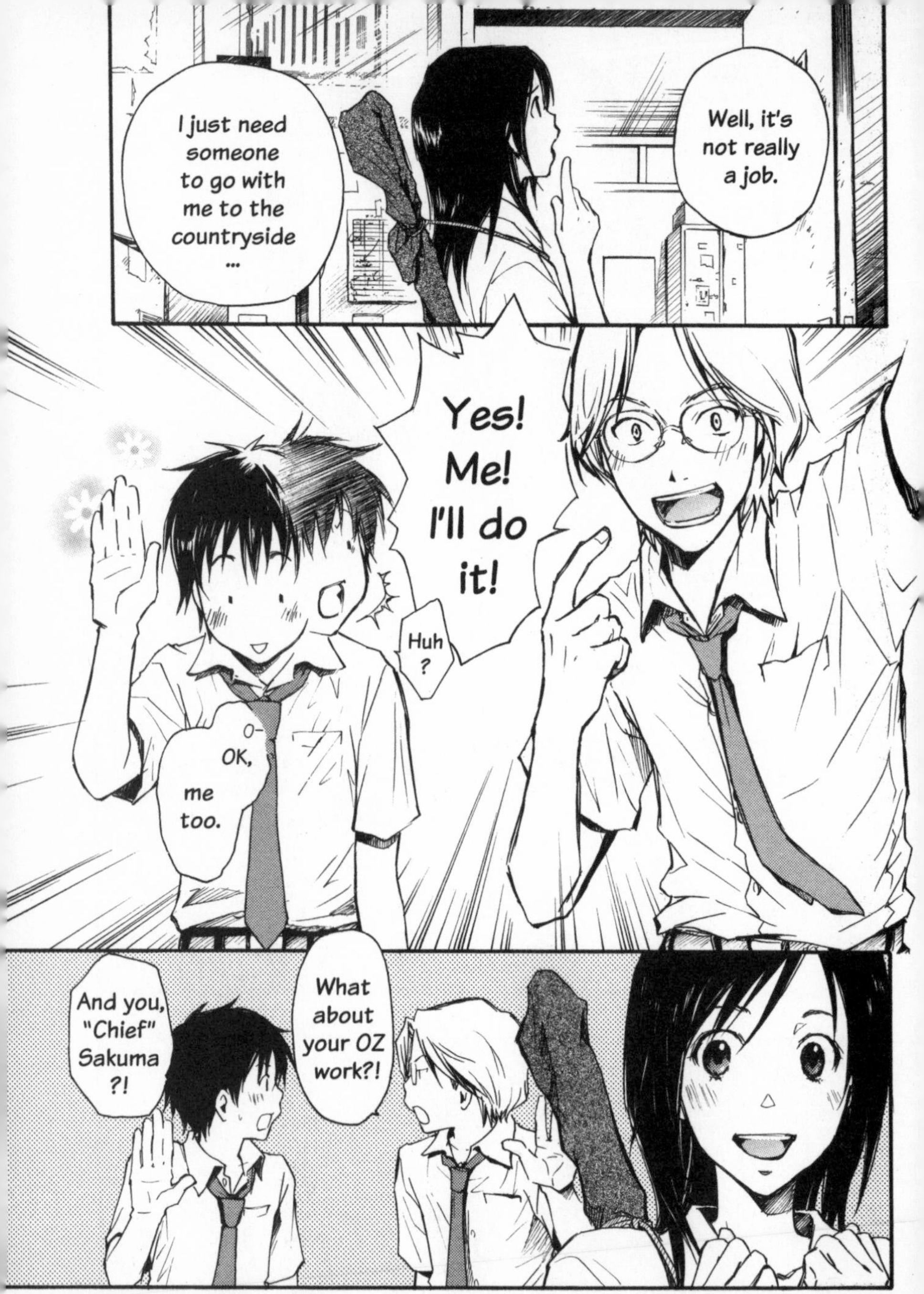
Well, it's not really a job.
I just need someone to go with me to the countryside ...
Yes! Me! I'll do it!
Huh?
O- OK, me too.
What about your OZ work?!
And you, "Chief" Sakuma?!

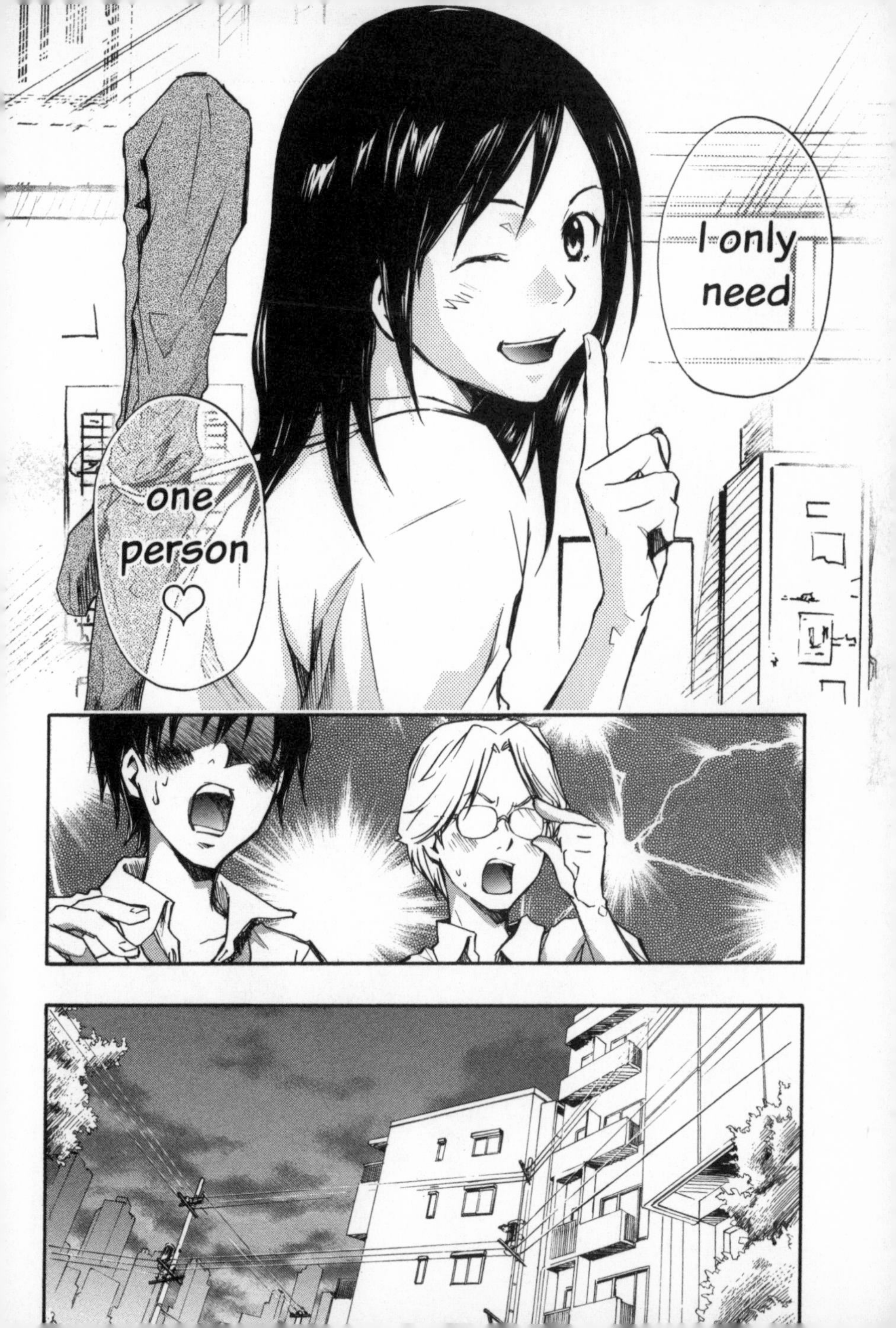
I only need
one person ♡

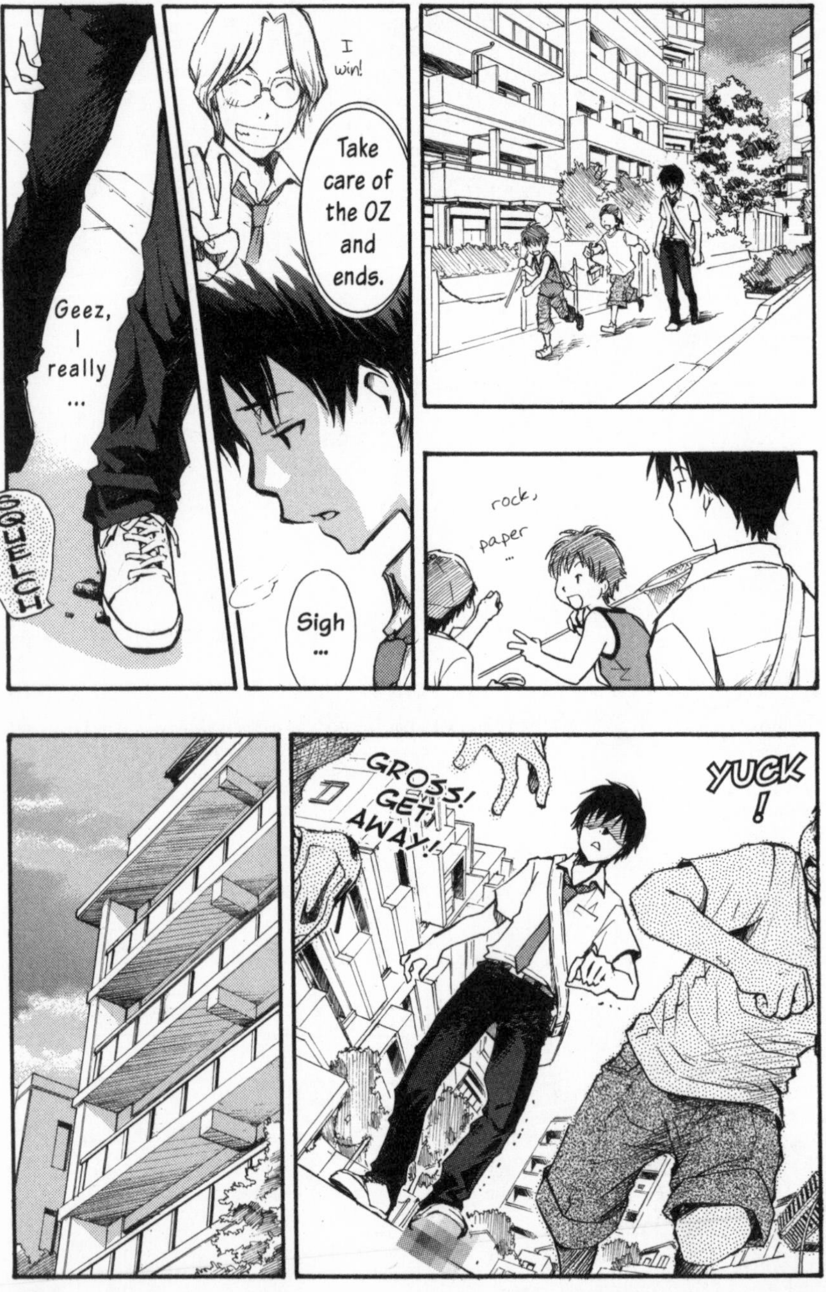
rock, paper ...
I win!
Take care of the OZ and ends.
Sigh ...
Geez, I really ...
SQUELCH
YUCK!
GROSS! GET AWAY!

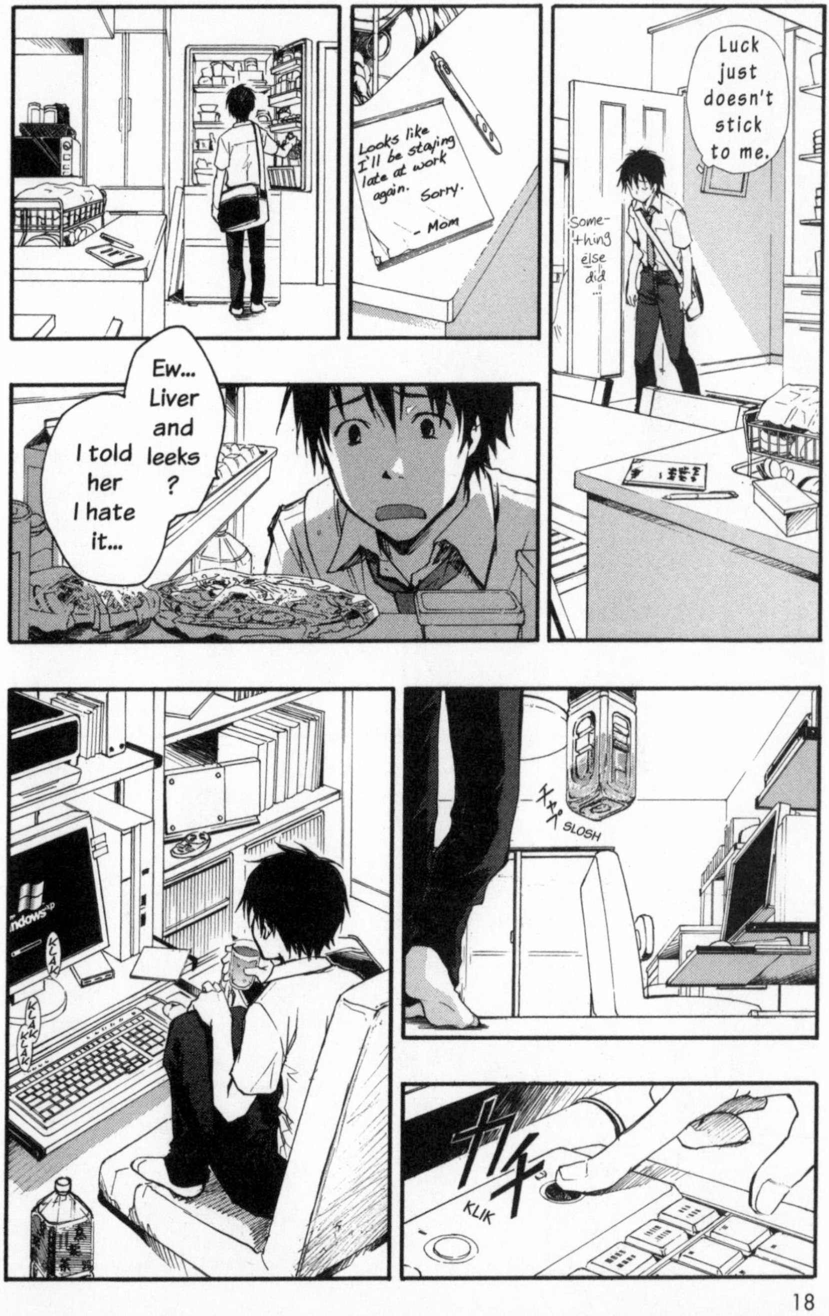
Luck just doesn't stick to me.
Something else did...!!
Looks like I'll be staying late at work again. Sorry. - Mom
Ew... Liver and leeks?
I told her I hate it...
チャプ SLOSH
カチ KLIK
KLAK
KLAK KLAK

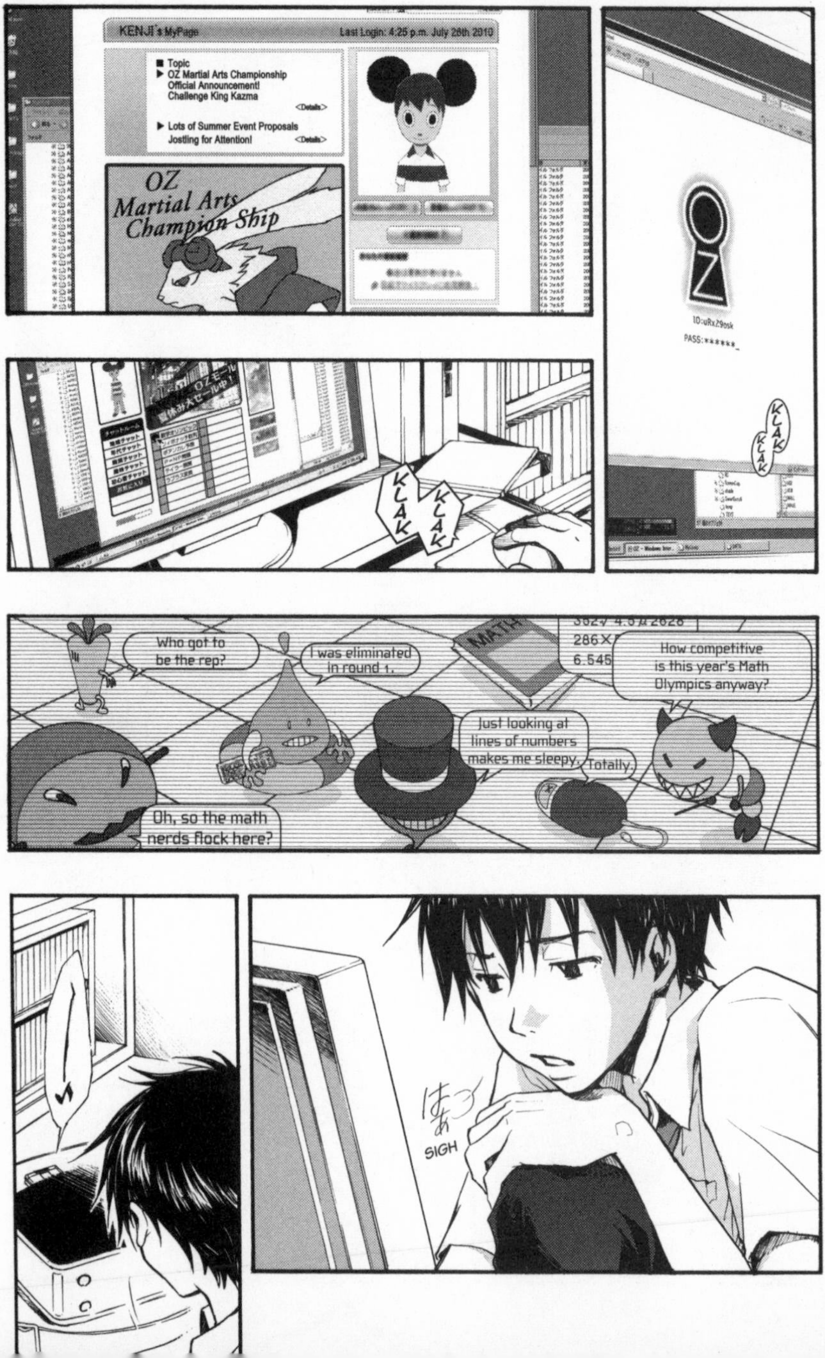

ID:uRx29osk
PASS:******_
KLAK
KLAK
KLAK
KENJI's MyPage
Last Login: 4:25 p.m. July 28th 2010
Topic
OZ Martial Arts Championship Official Announcement! Challenge King Kazma
<Details>
Lots of Summer Event Proposals Jostling for Attention!
<Details>
OZ Martial Arts Champion Ship
KLAK
KLAK
How competitive is this year's Math Olympics anyway?
MATH
Totally.
Just looking at lines of numbers makes me sleepy.
I was eliminated in round 1.
Who got to be the rep?
Oh, so the math nerds flock here?
はぁ
SIGH

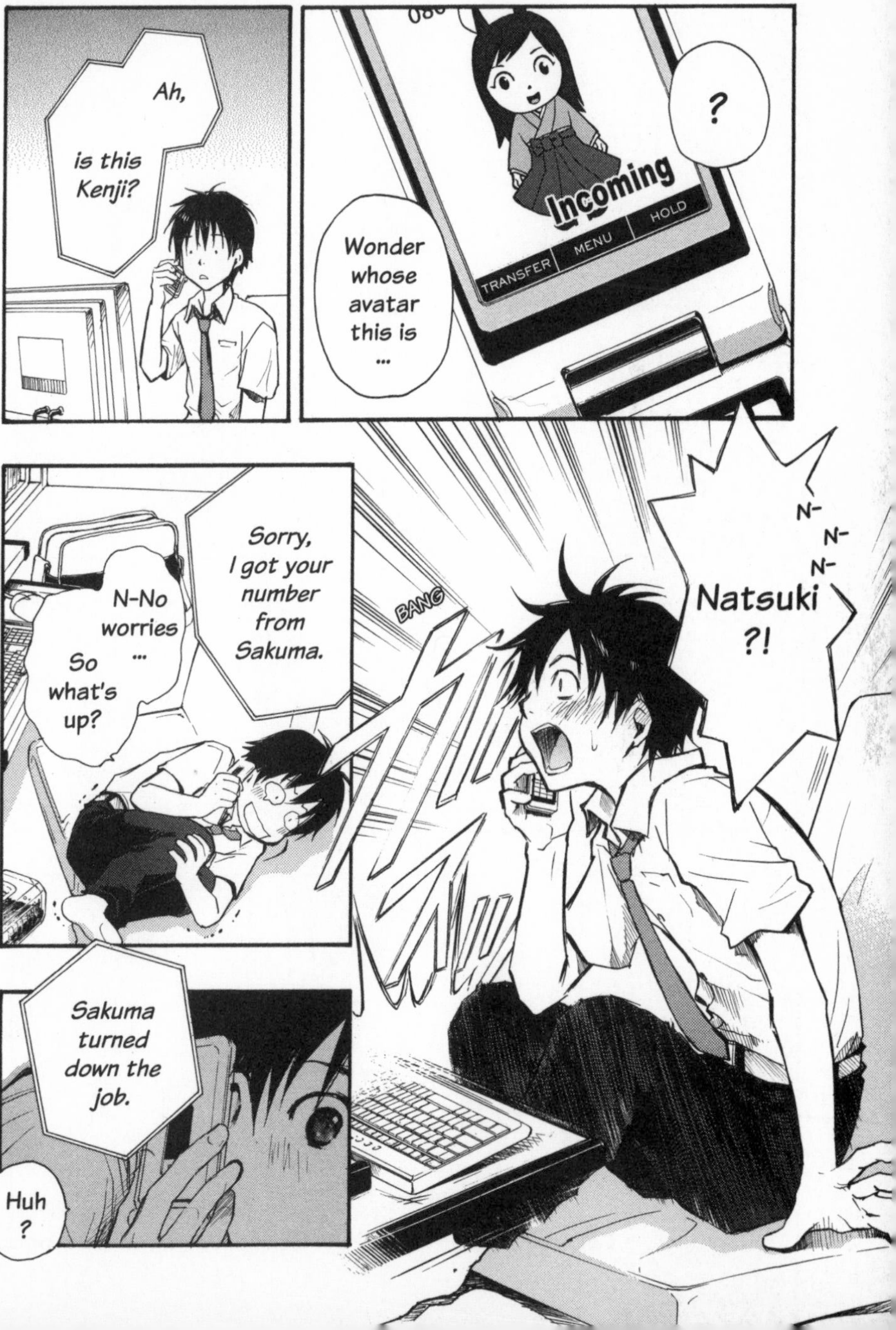
?
Incoming
HOLD
MENU
TRANSFER
Wonder whose avatar this is ...
Ah, is this Kenji?
N- N- N- Natsuki ?!
BANG
Sorry, I got your number from Sakuma.
N-No worries ...
So what's up?
Sakuma turned down the job.
Huh ?

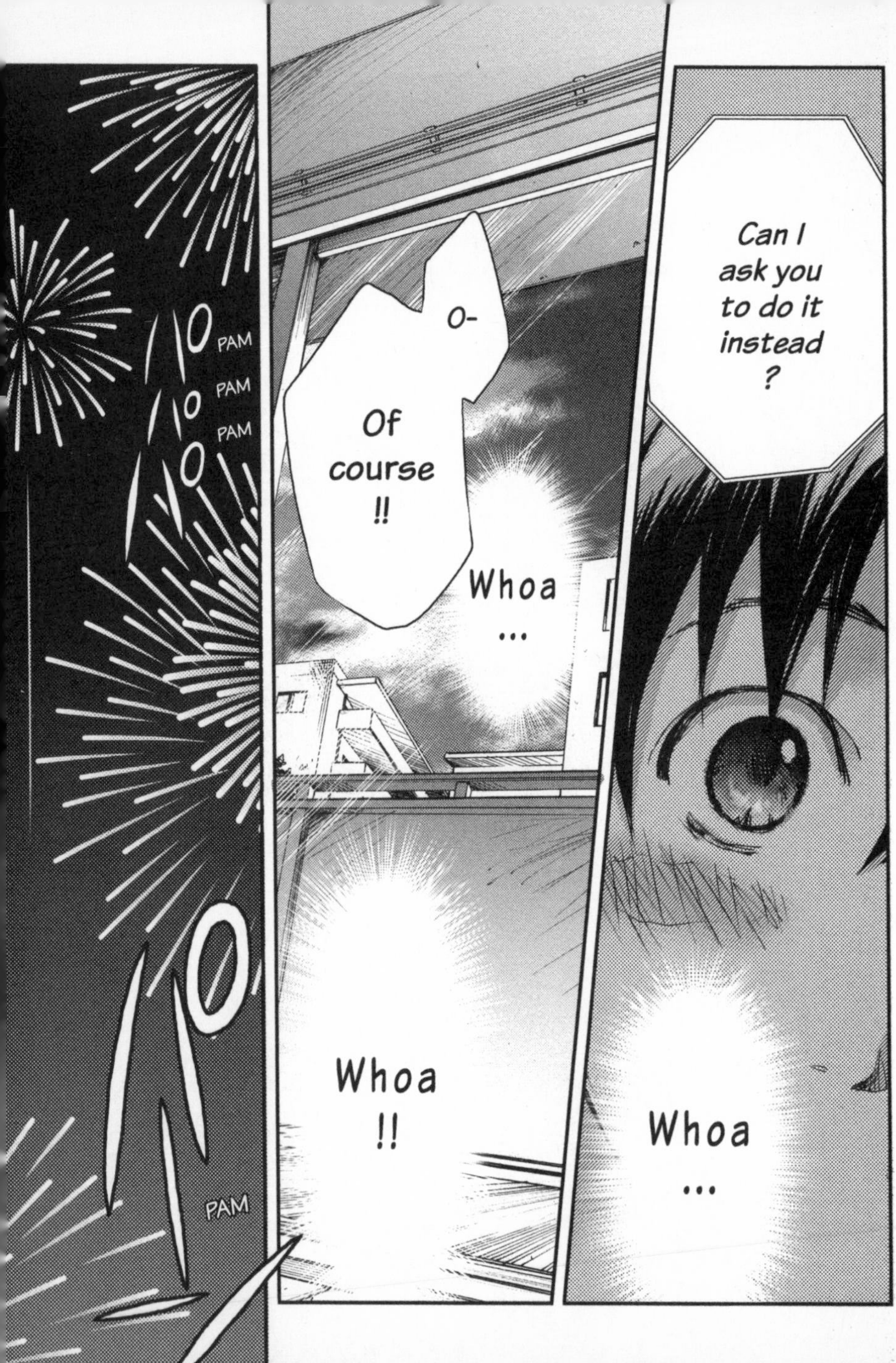
Can I ask you to do it instead?
Whoa...
O-
Of course!!
Whoa...
Whoa!!
PAM
PAM
PAM
PAM

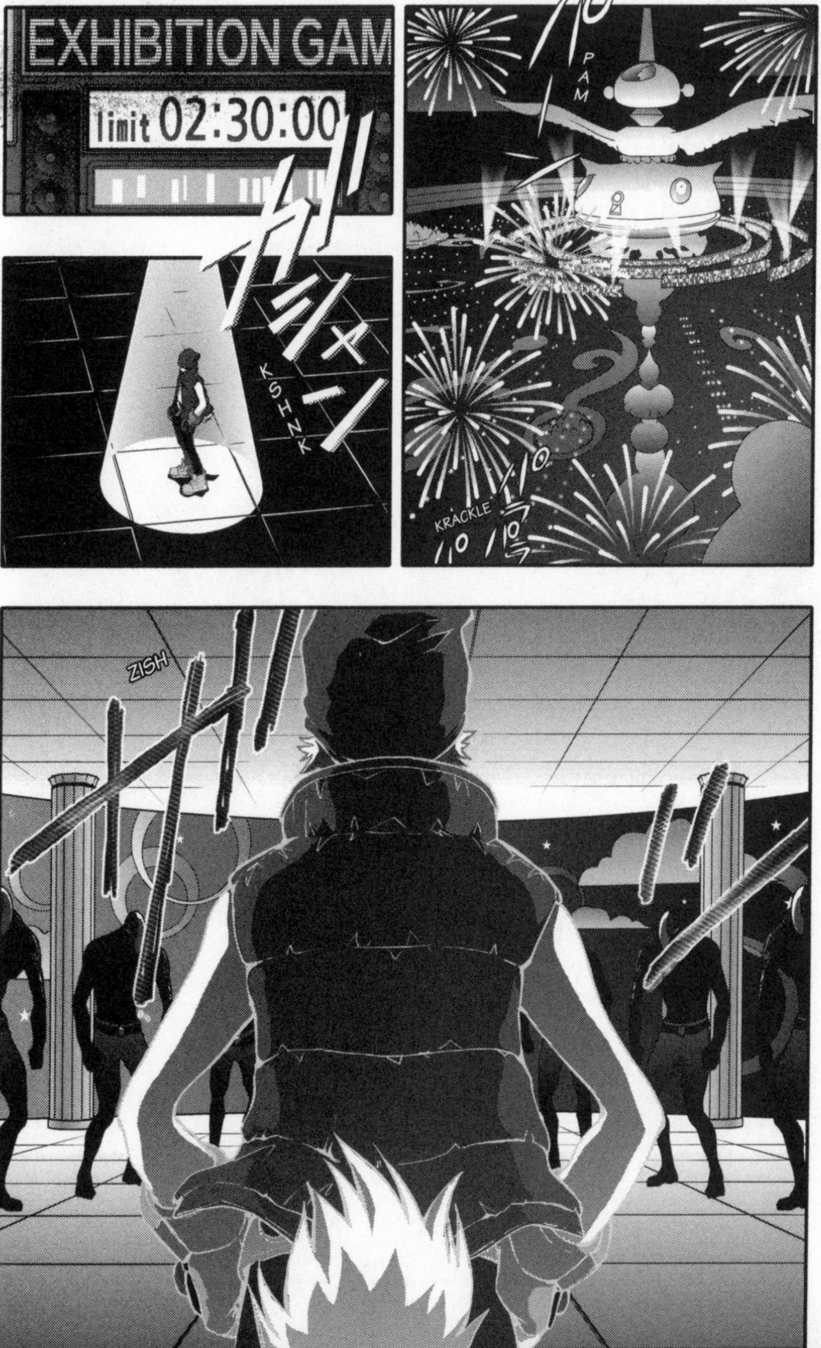
PAM
KRACKLE
EXHIBITION GAM
limit 02:30:00
KSHNK
ZISH

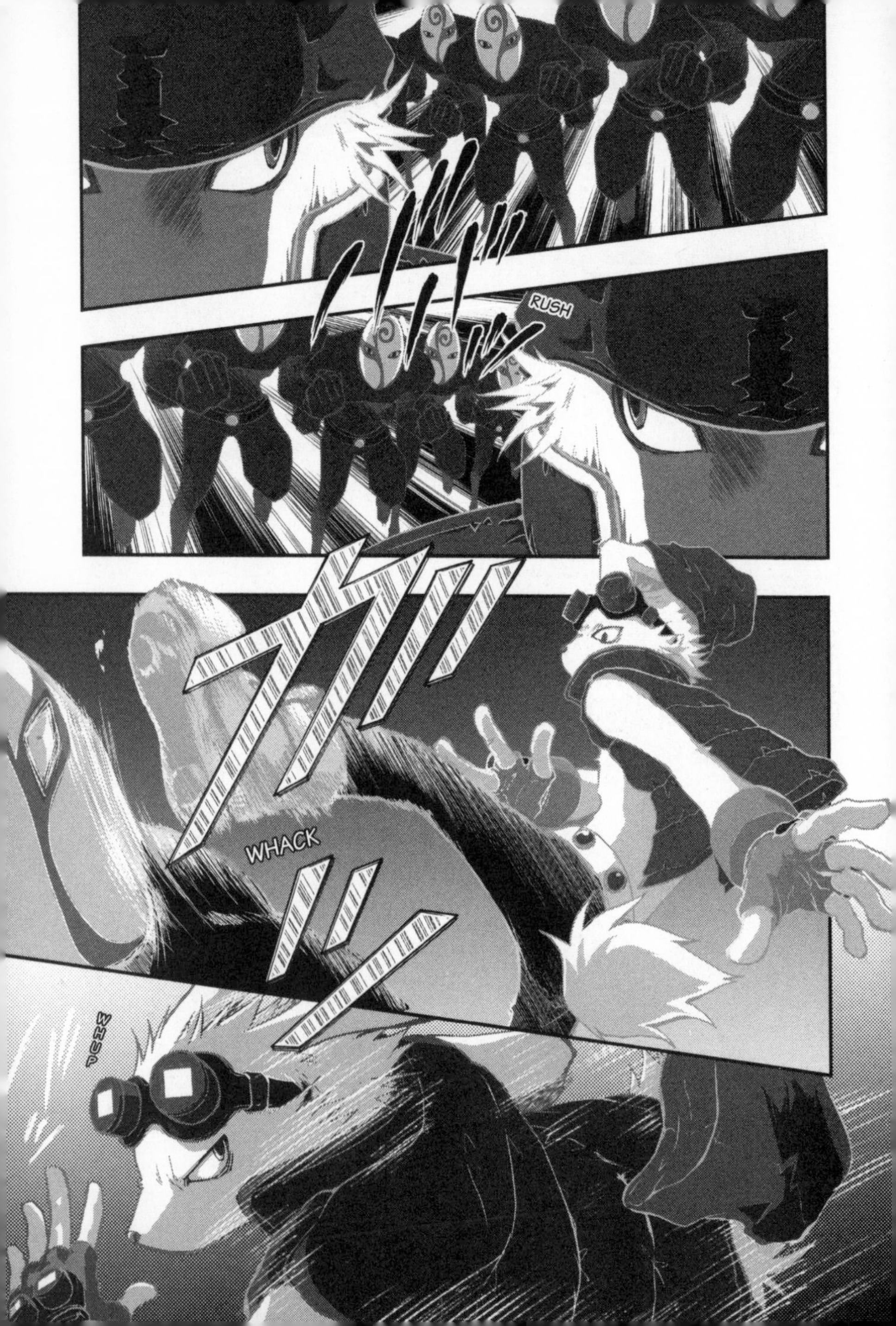
RUSH
WHACK
WHUP

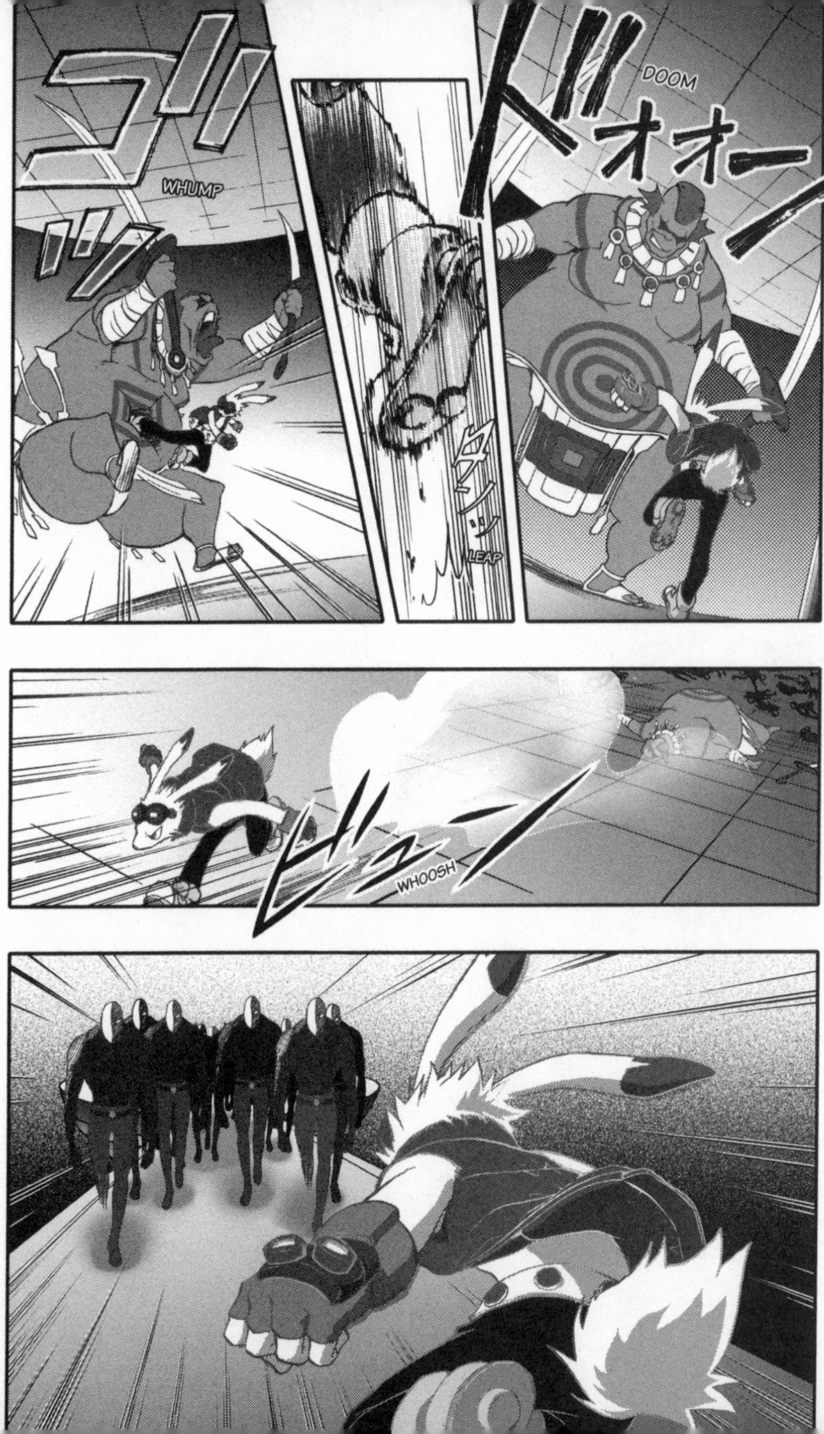
DOOM
LEAP
WHUMP
WHOOSH

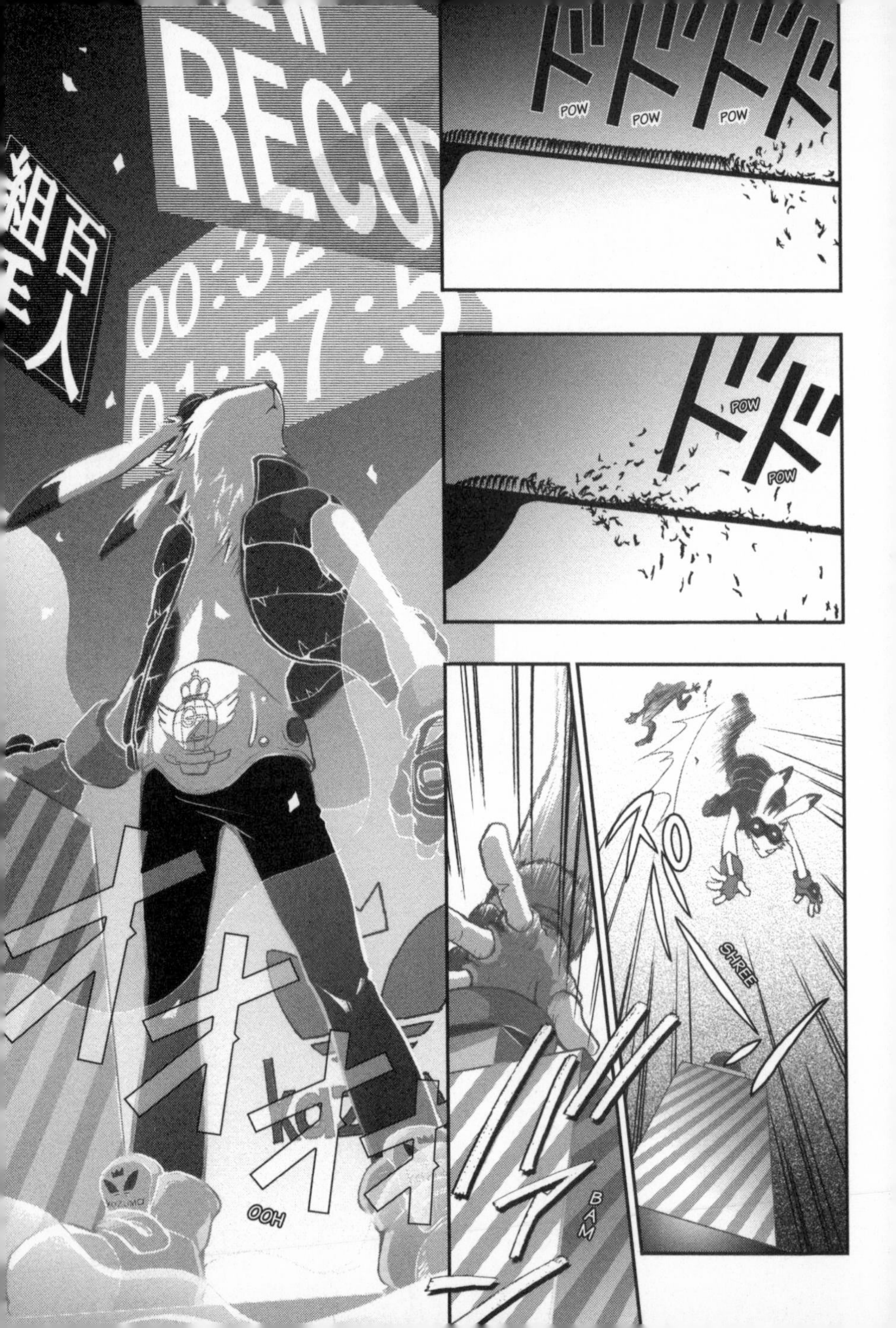
ドドドド
POW
POW
POW
ドド
POW
POW
SHREE
BAM
OOH

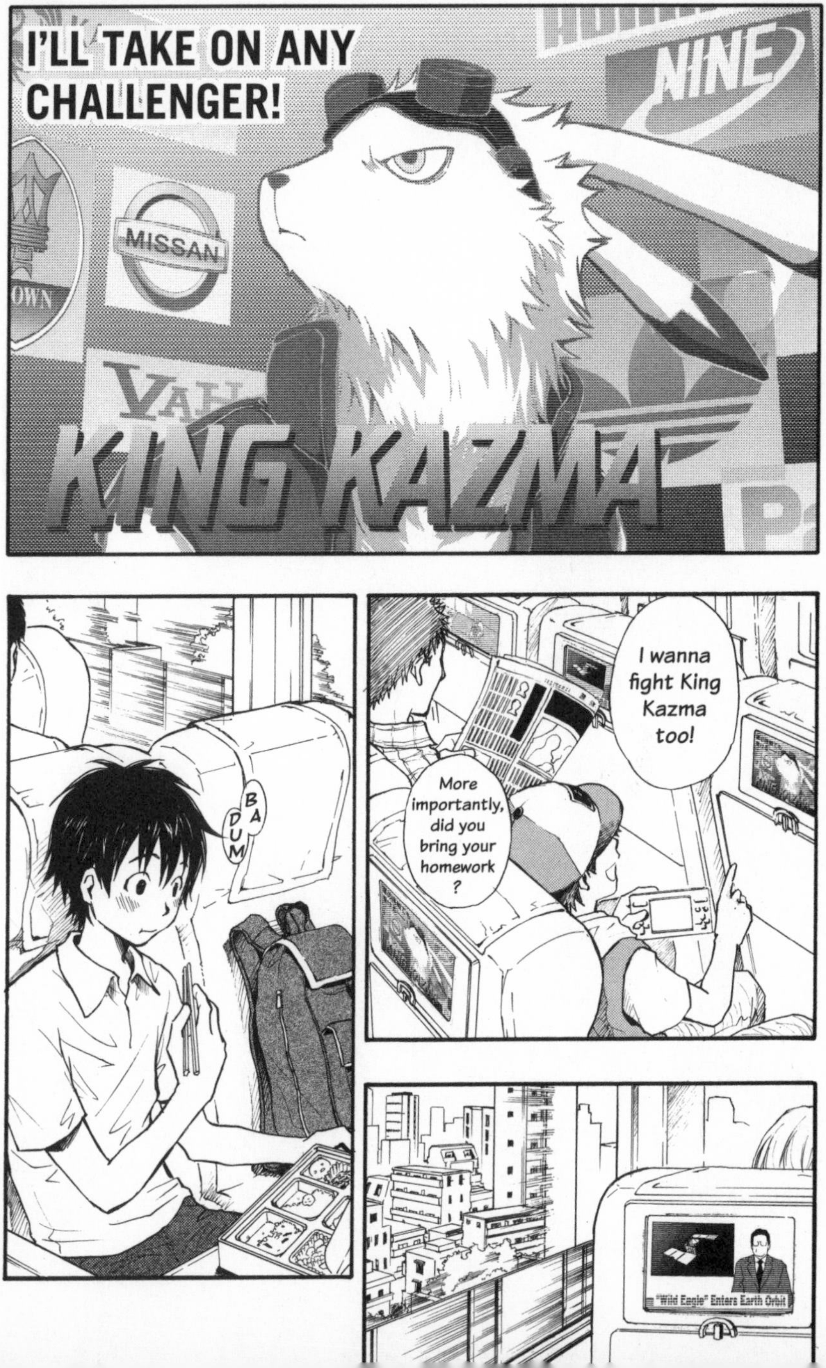
I'LL TAKE ON ANY CHALLENGER!
NINE
MISSAN
KING KAZMA
I wanna fight King Kazma too!
More importantly, did you bring your homework?
"Wild Eagle" Enters Earth Orbit
BA DUM

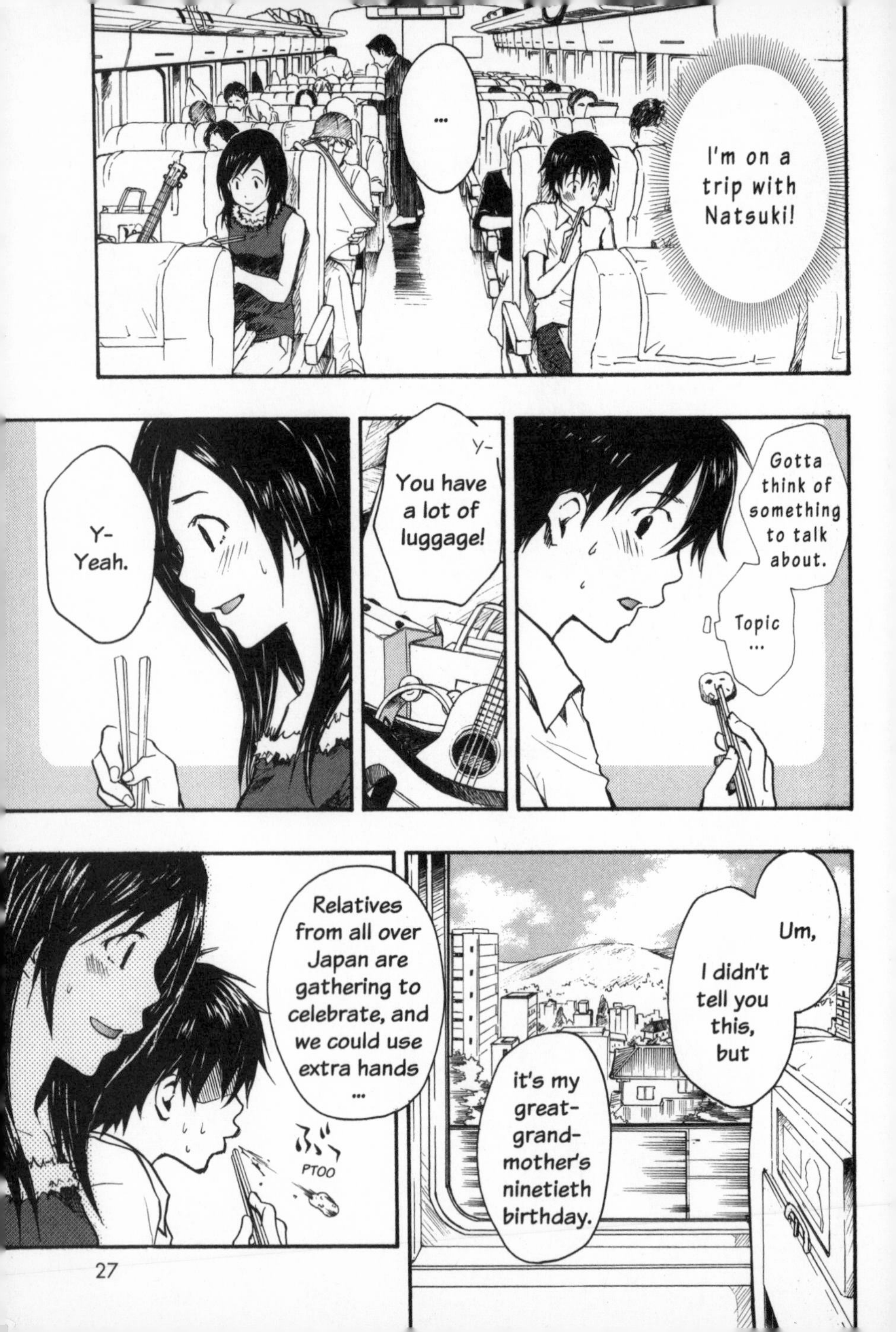

I'm on a trip with Natsuki!
...
Gotta think of something to talk about.
Topic ...
Y-
You have a lot of luggage!
Y- Yeah.
Um,
I didn't tell you this, but
it's my great-grandmother's ninetieth birthday.
Relatives from all over Japan are gathering to celebrate, and we could use extra hands ...
ぶっ
PTOO

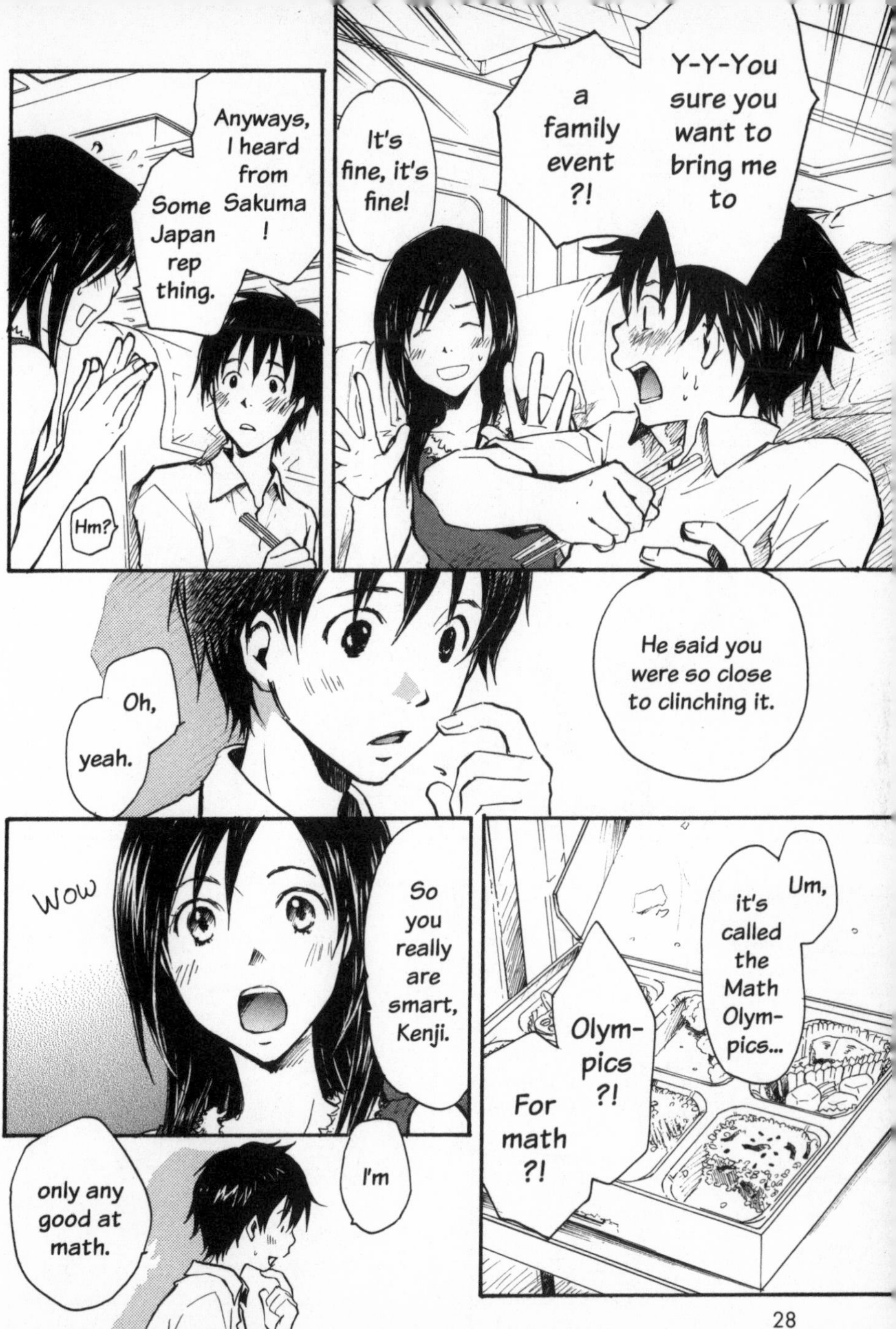
Y-Y-You sure you want to bring me to a family event?!
It's fine, it's fine!
Anyways, I heard from Sakuma!
Some Japan rep thing.
Hm?
He said you were so close to clinching it.
Oh, yeah.
Um, it's called the Math Olympics...
Olympics?!
For math?!
So you really are smart, Kenji.
WOW
I'm only any good at math.

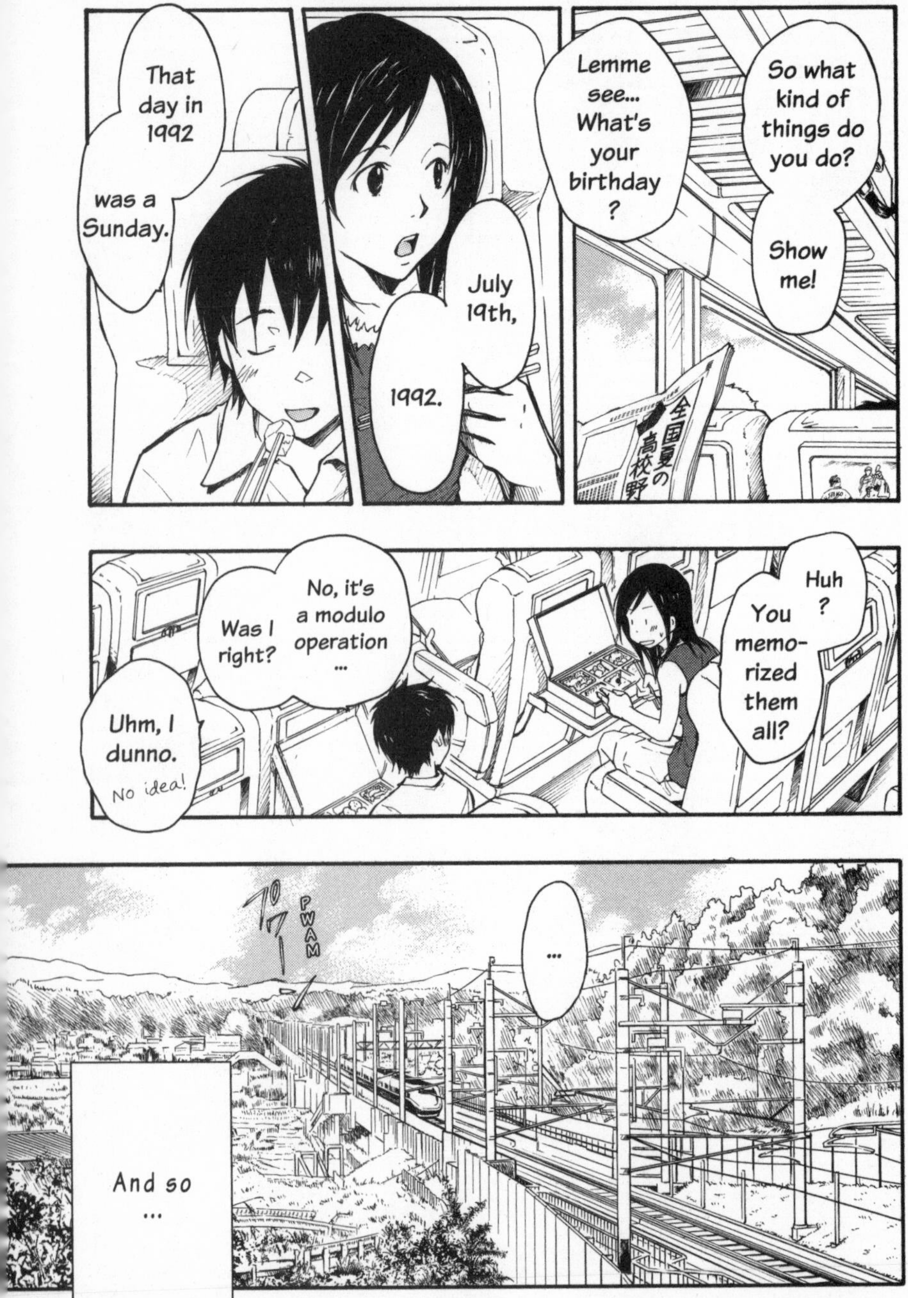
So what kind of things do you do?
Show me!
Lemme see... What's your birthday?
全国夏の
高校野
July 19th,
1992.
That day in 1992
was a Sunday.
Huh? You memorized them all?
No, it's a modulo operation ...
Was I right?
Uhm, I dunno.
No idea!
...
PWAM
プワー
And so ...

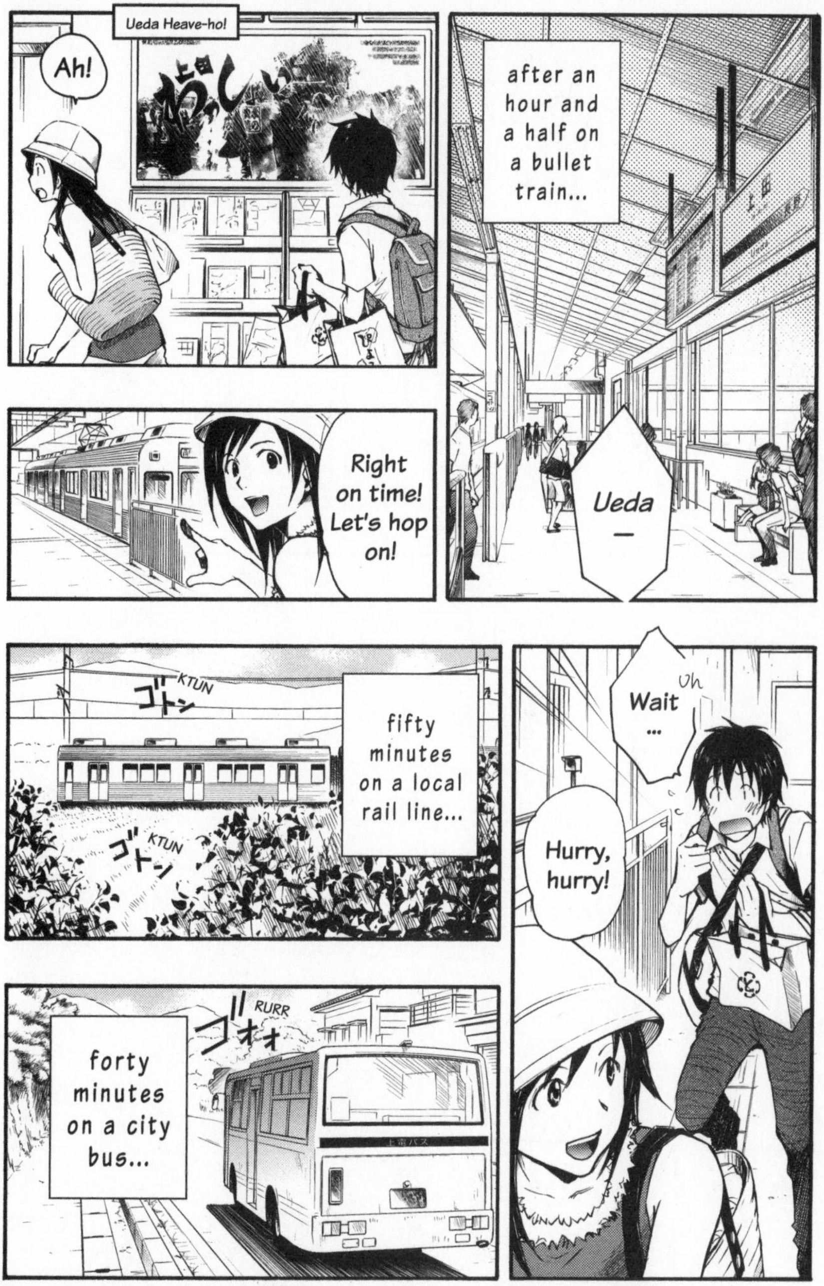

after an hour and a half on a bullet train...
Ueda —
Ueda Heave-ho!
Ah!
Right on time! Let's hop on!
Wait ...
Uh
Hurry, hurry!
fifty minutes on a local rail line...
ゴトン KTUN
ゴトン KTUN
forty minutes on a city bus...
ゴォォ RURR

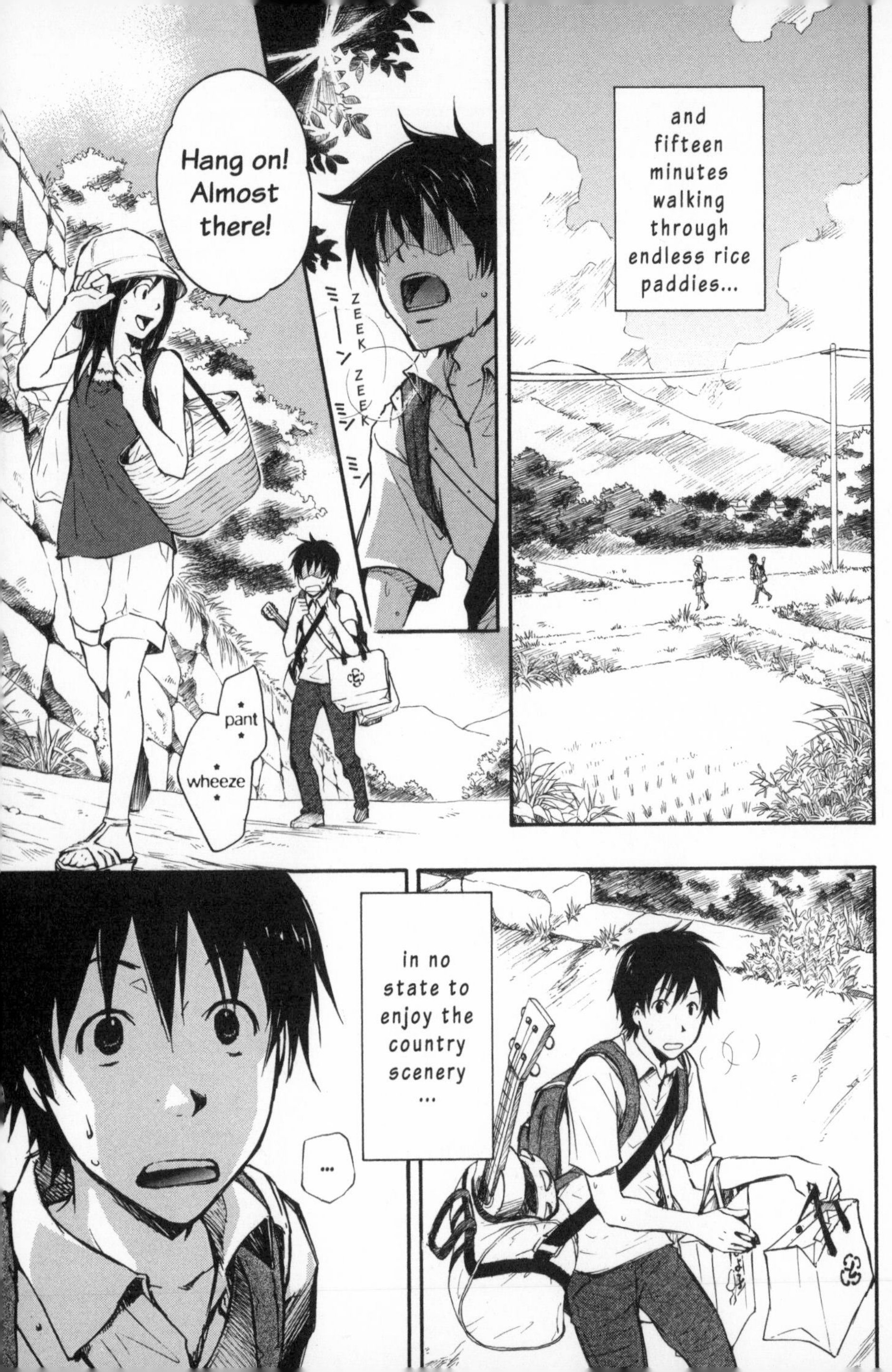
and fifteen minutes walking through endless rice paddies...
ZEEK ZEEK
Hang on! Almost there!
pant wheeze
in no state to enjoy the country scenery ...
...

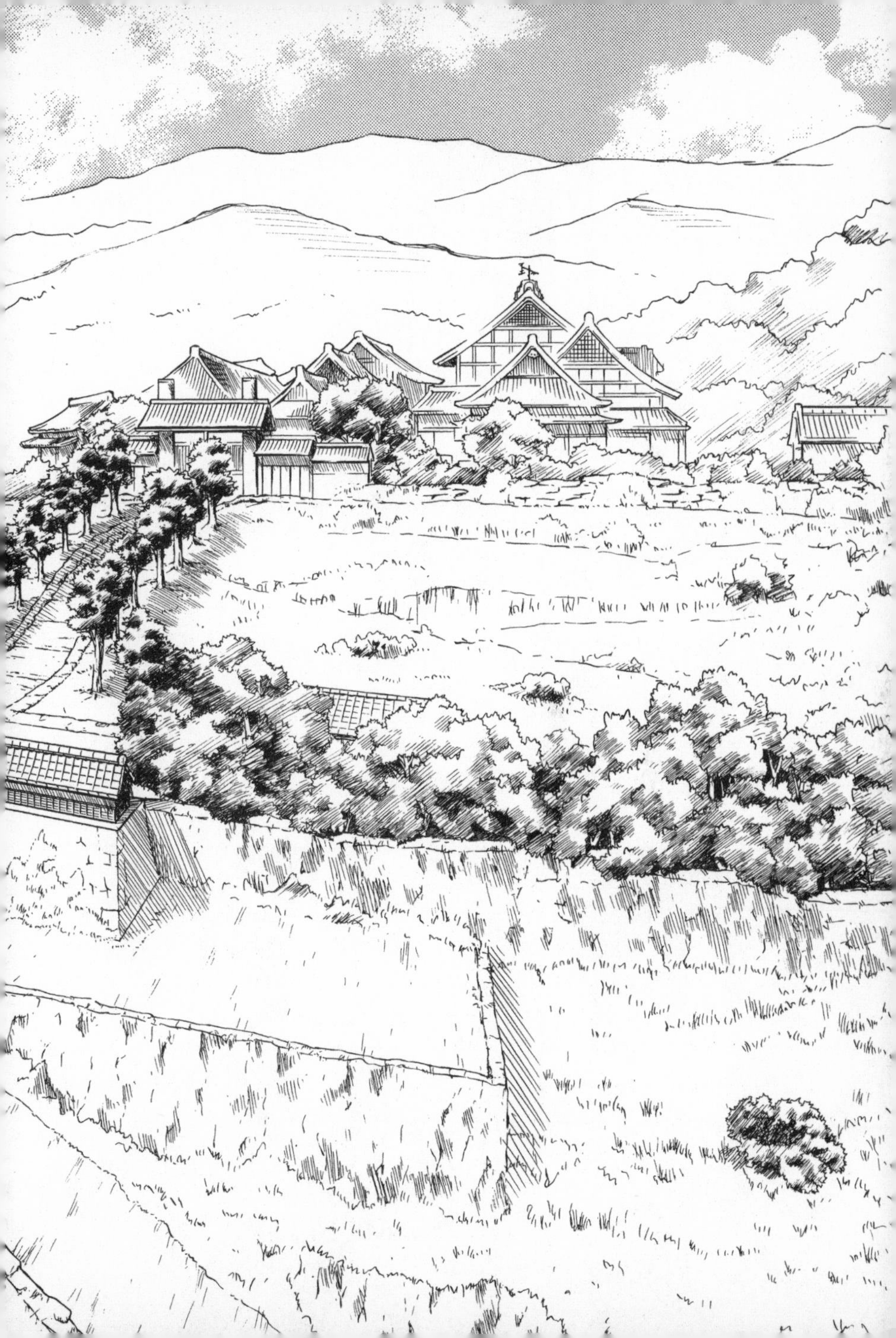

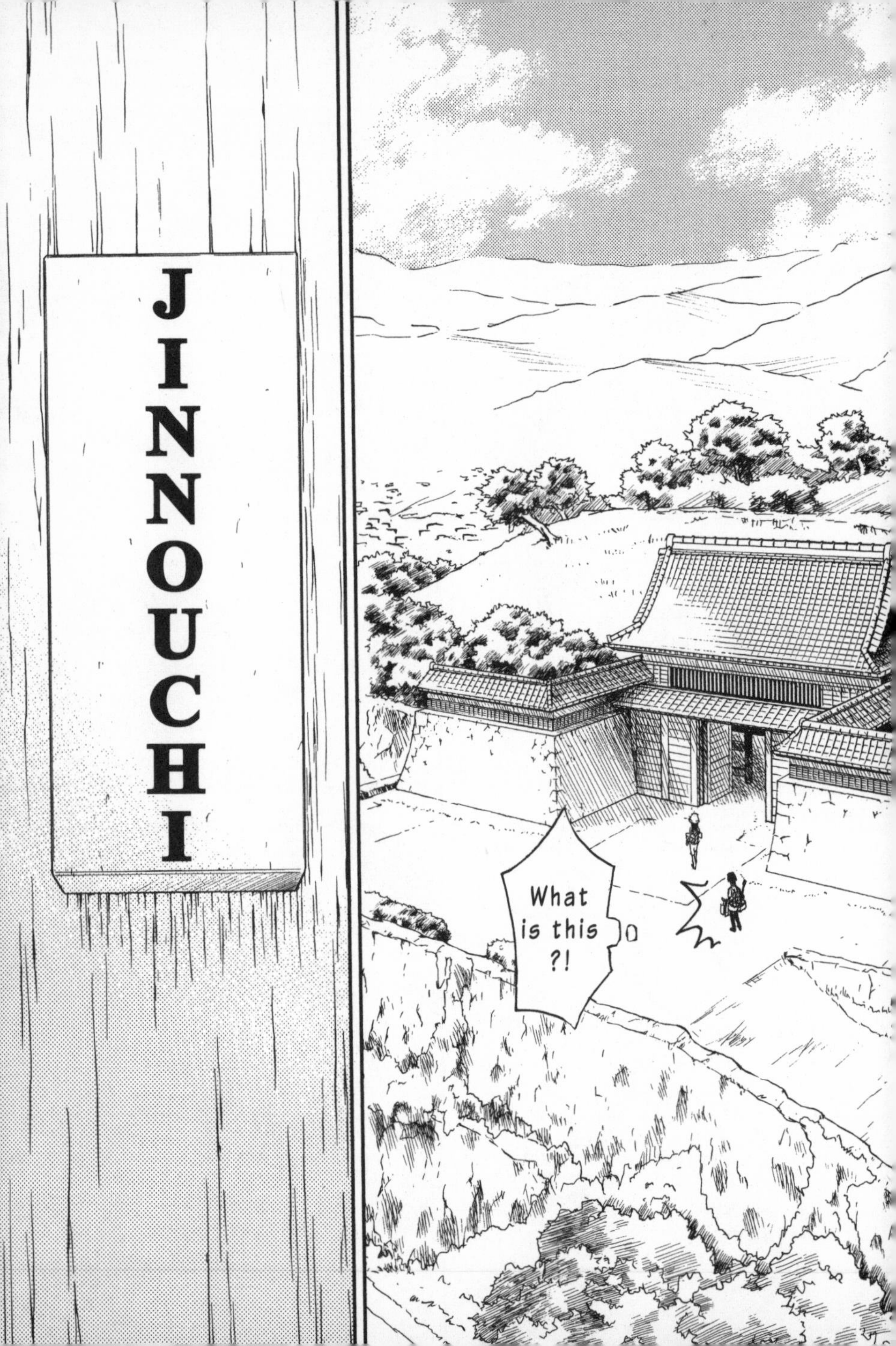
What is this ?!
JINNOUCHI

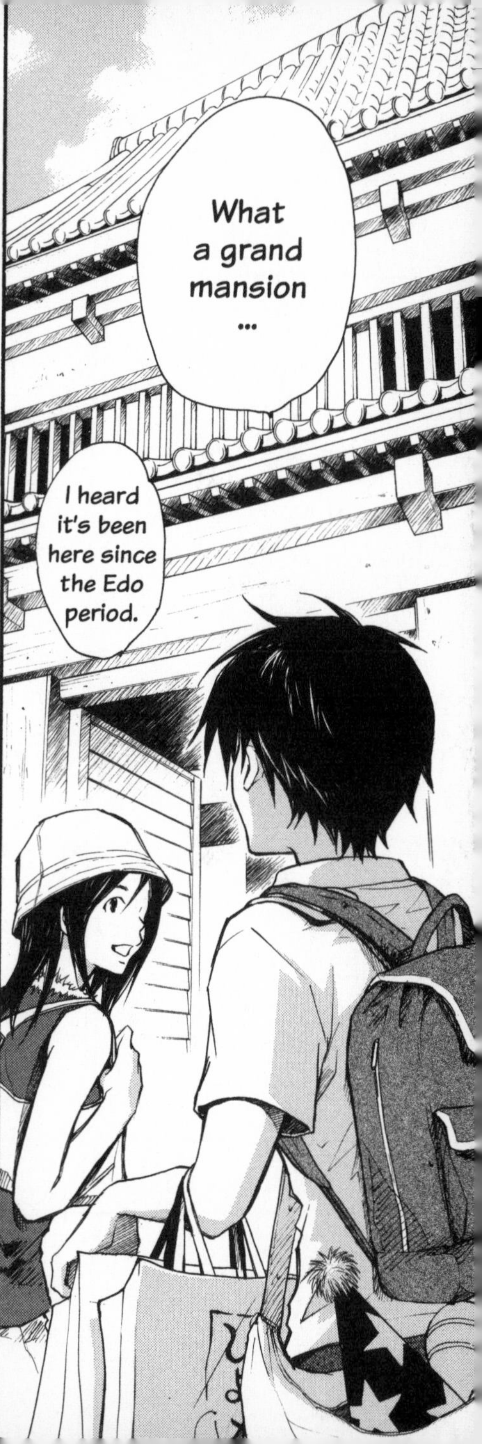
What a grand mansion ...
I heard it's been here since the Edo period.

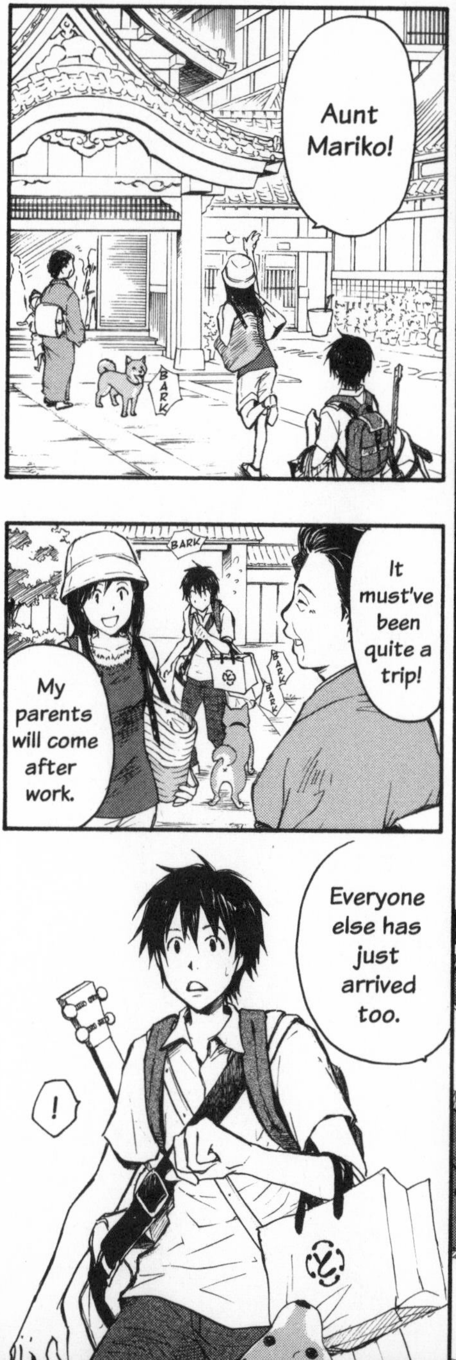
Aunt Mariko!
BARK
It must've been quite a trip!
BARK
BARK
BARK
My parents will come after work.
Everyone else has just arrived too.
!

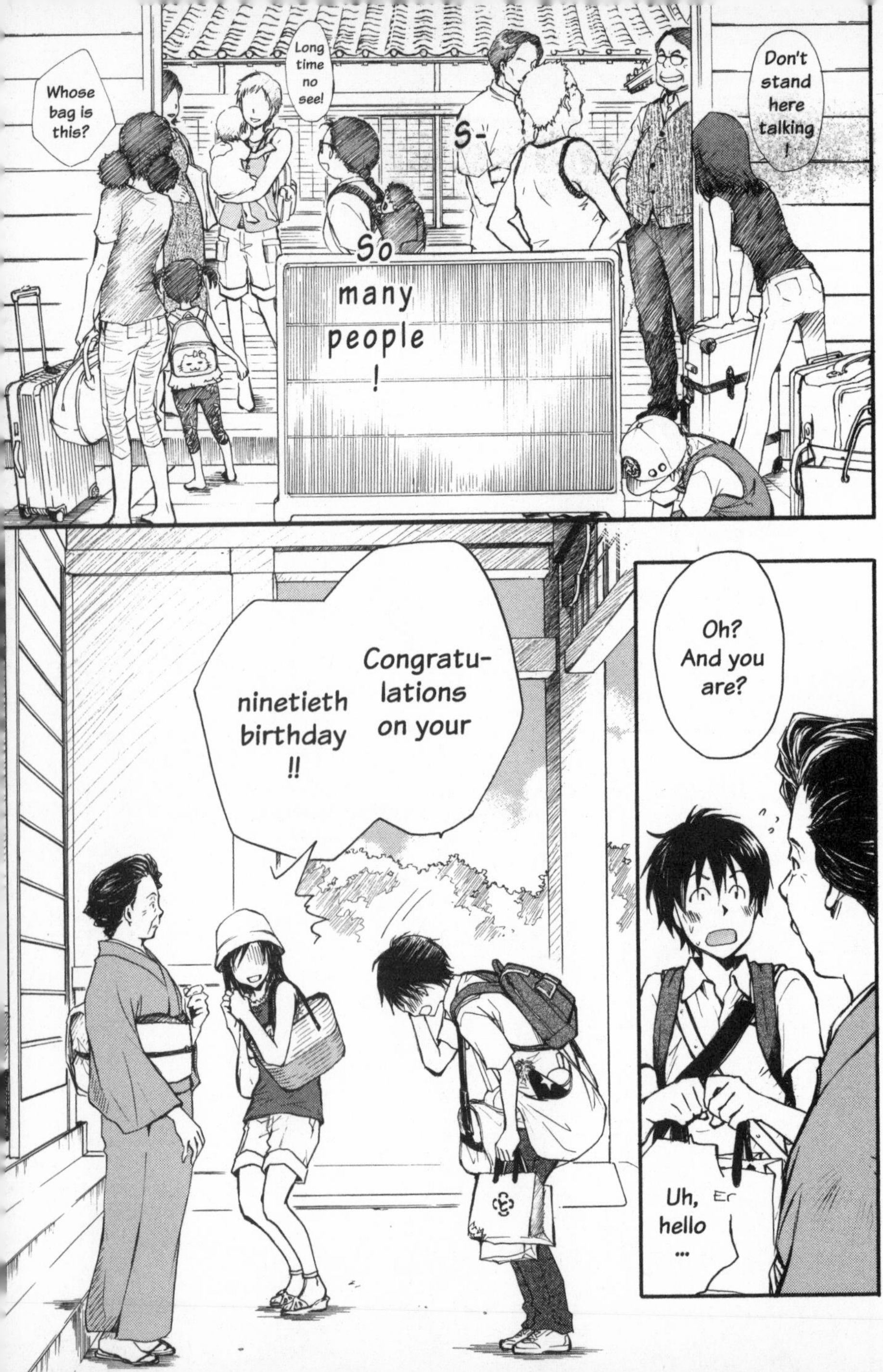

Don't stand here talking!
S-
Long time no see!
Whose bag is this?
So many people!
Oh? And you are?
Er
Uh, hello...
Congratulations on your ninetieth birthday!!

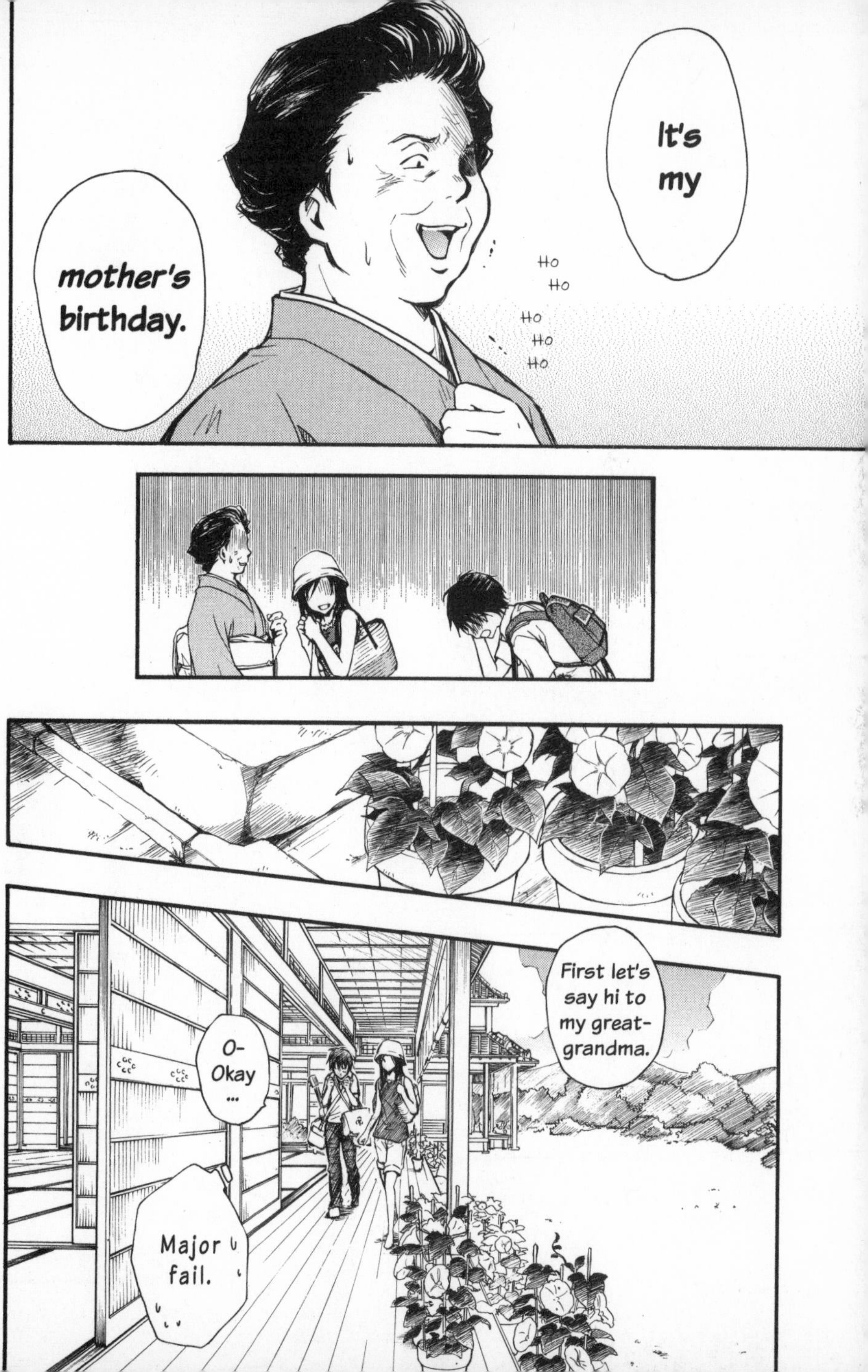
It's my
Ho Ho Ho Ho Ho
mother's birthday.
First let's say hi to my great-grandma.
O-Okay ...
Major fail.

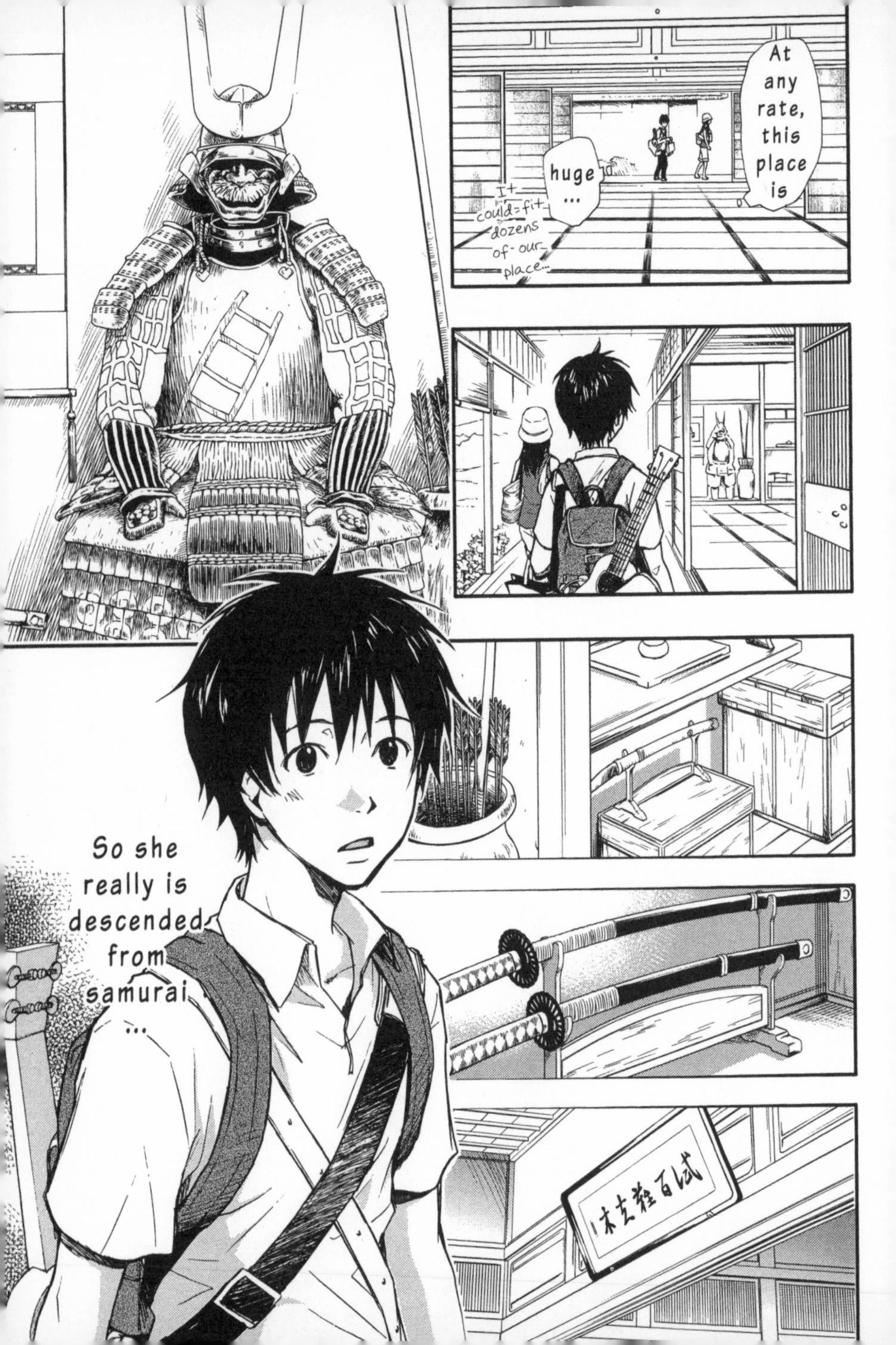
At any rate, this place is
huge...
It could fit dozens of our place...
So she really is descended from samurai...

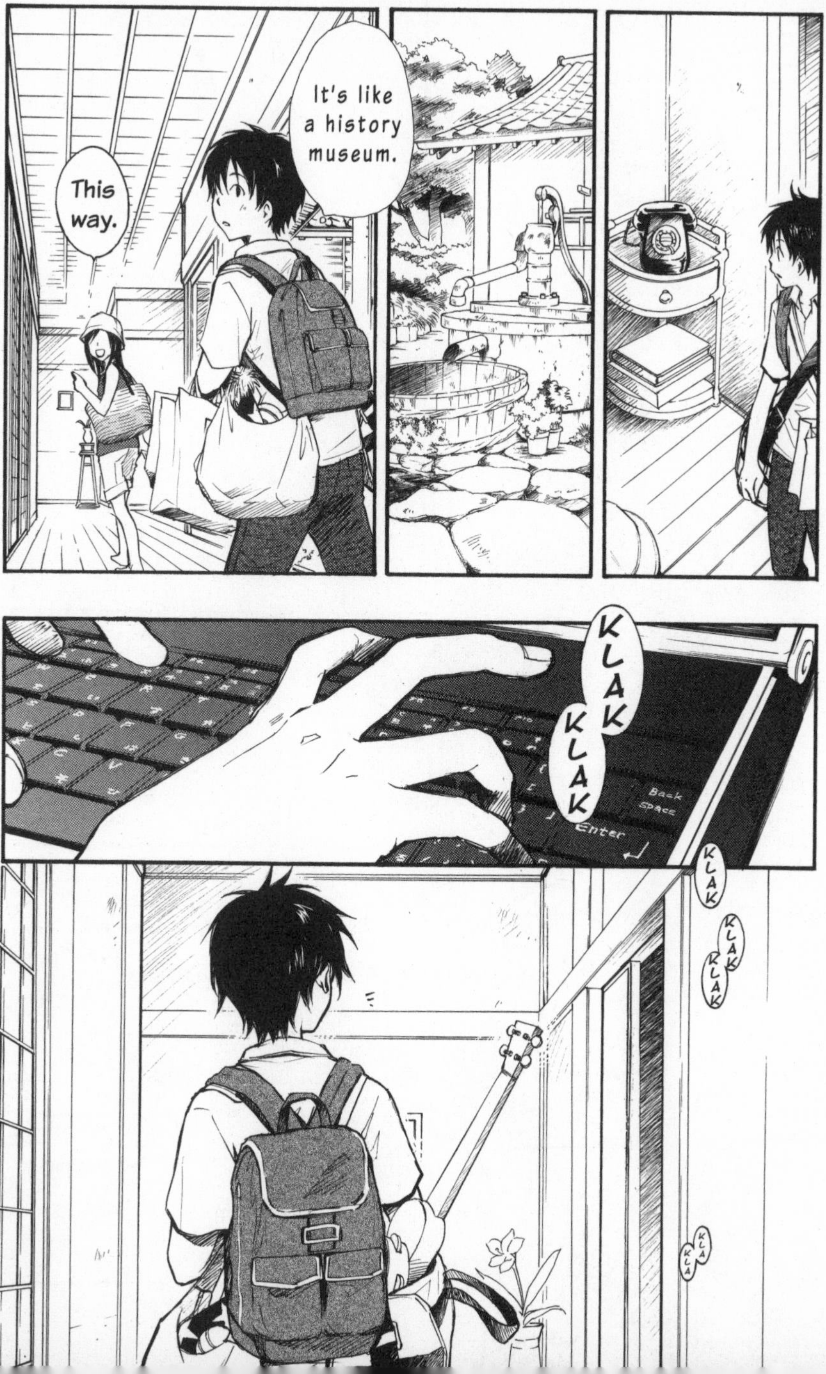
It's like a history museum.
This way.
KLAK
KLAK
KLAK
Back Space
Enter
KLAK
KLAK
KLAK
KLAK
KLA
KLA

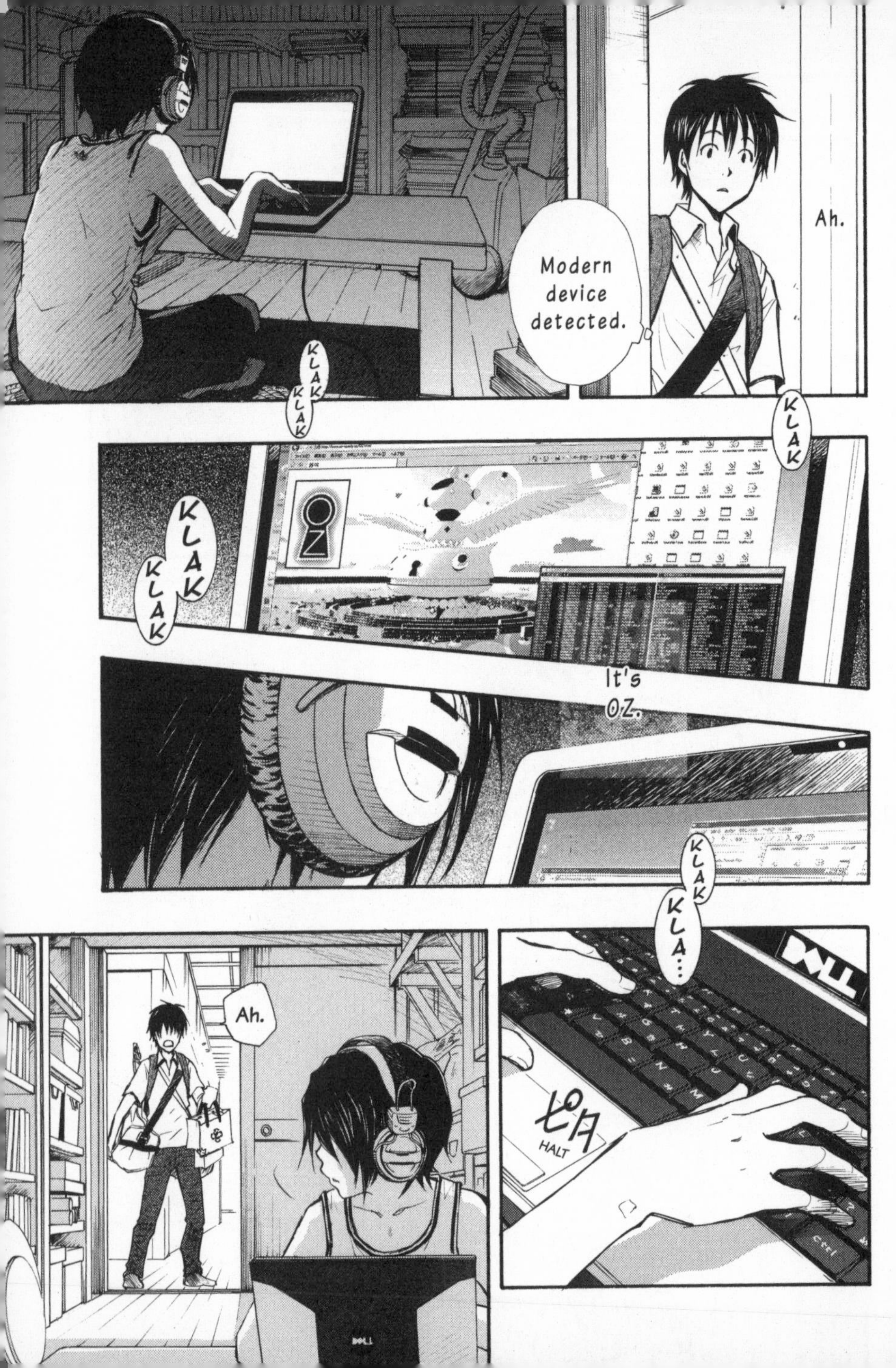
Ah.
Modern device detected.
KLAK KLAK
KLAK
KLAK KLAK
It's OZ.
KLAK KLA...
ピタ
HALT
Ah.

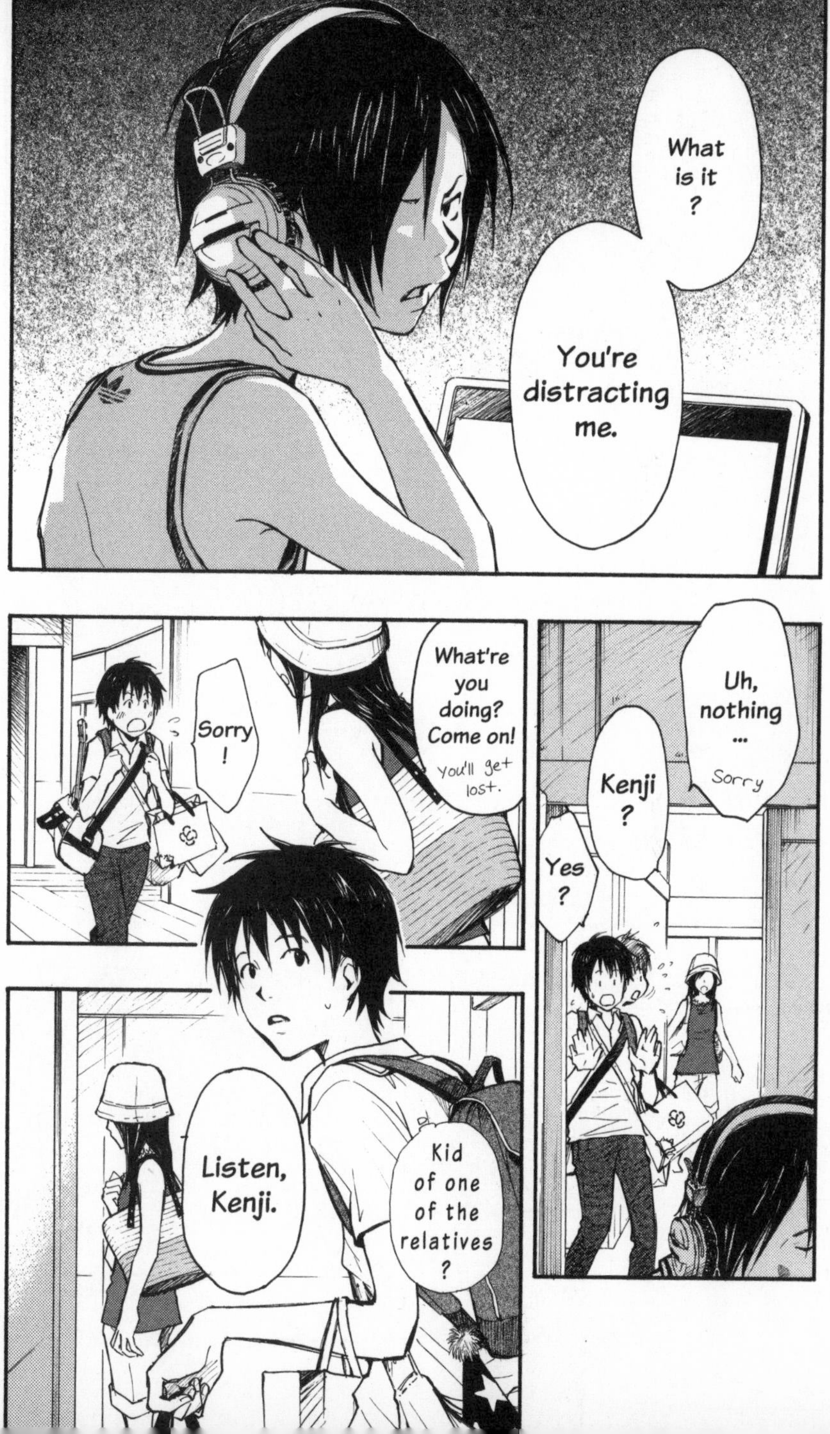
What is it ?
You're distracting me.
Uh, nothing ... Sorry
Kenji ?
Yes ?
What're you doing? Come on! You'll get lost.
Sorry !
Kid of one of the relatives ?
Listen, Kenji.

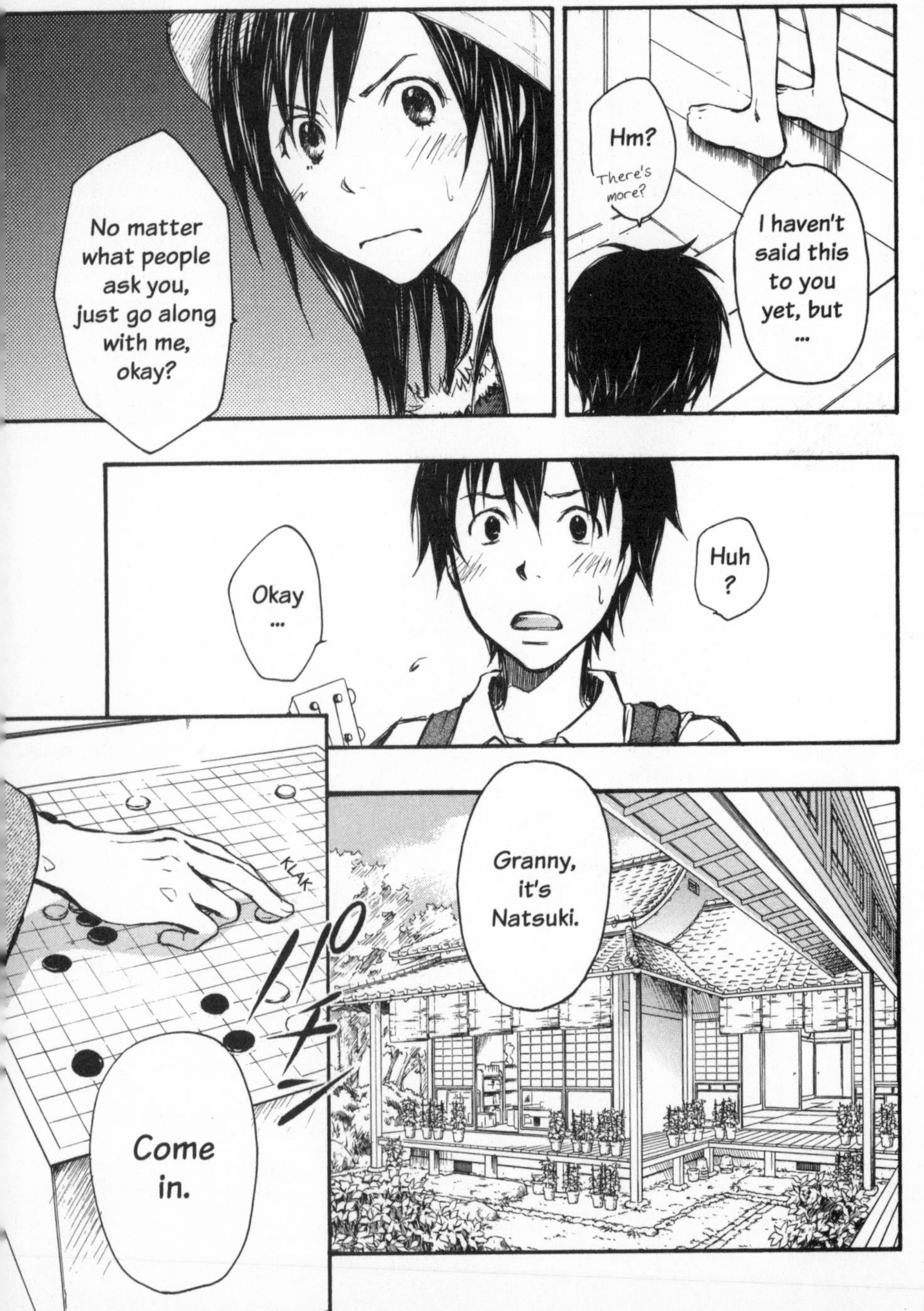
I haven't said this to you yet, but ...
Hm?
There's more?
No matter what people ask you, just go along with me, okay?
Huh?
Okay ...
Granny, it's Natsuki.
KLAK
Come in.

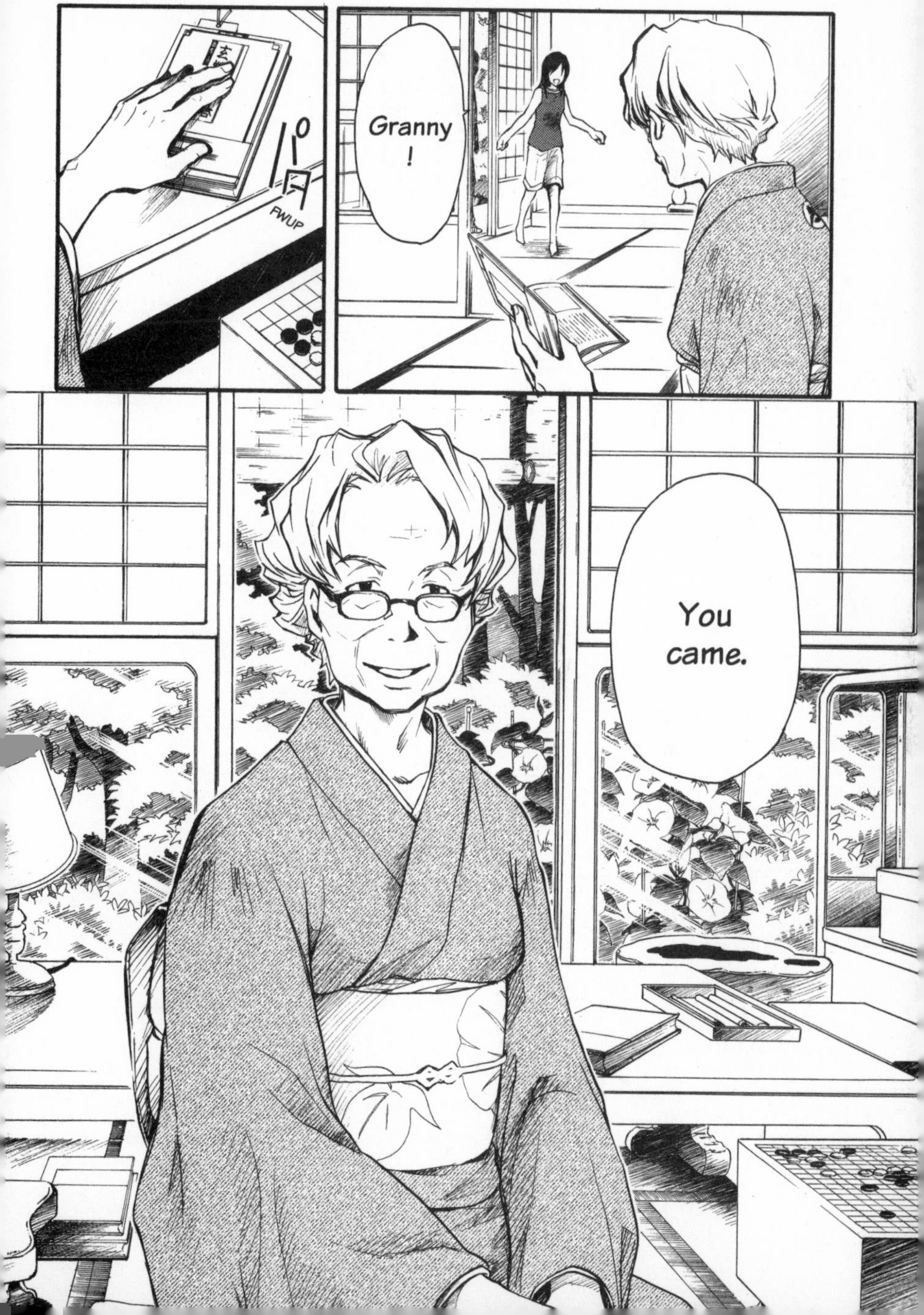
Granny!
FWUP
You came.

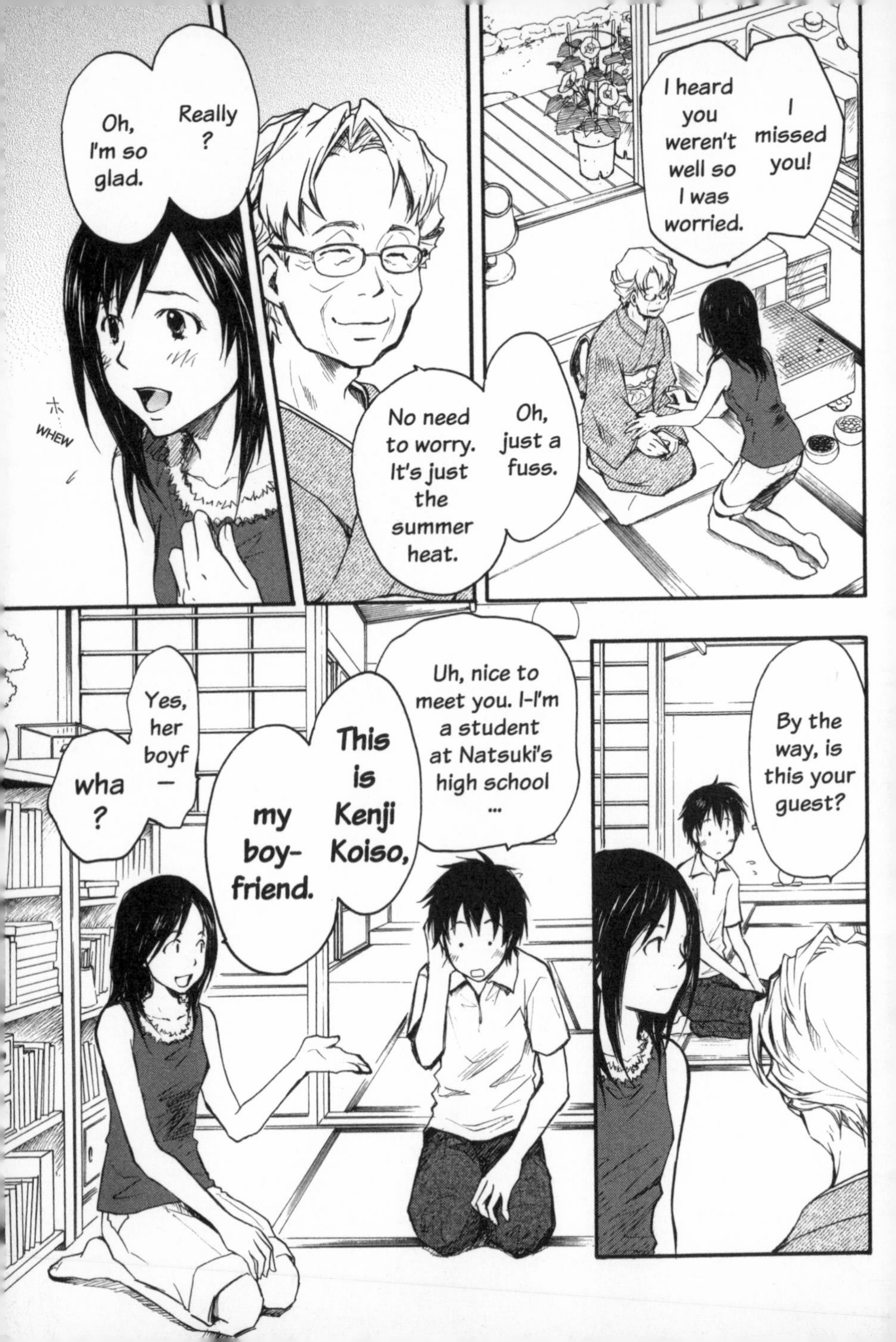
I missed you!
I heard you weren't well so I was worried.
Oh, just a fuss.
No need to worry. It's just the summer heat.
Really?
Oh, I'm so glad.
ホ… WHEW
By the way, is this your guest?
Uh, nice to meet you. I-I'm a student at Natsuki's high school ...
This is Kenji Koiso, my boyfriend.
Yes, her boyf—
wha?

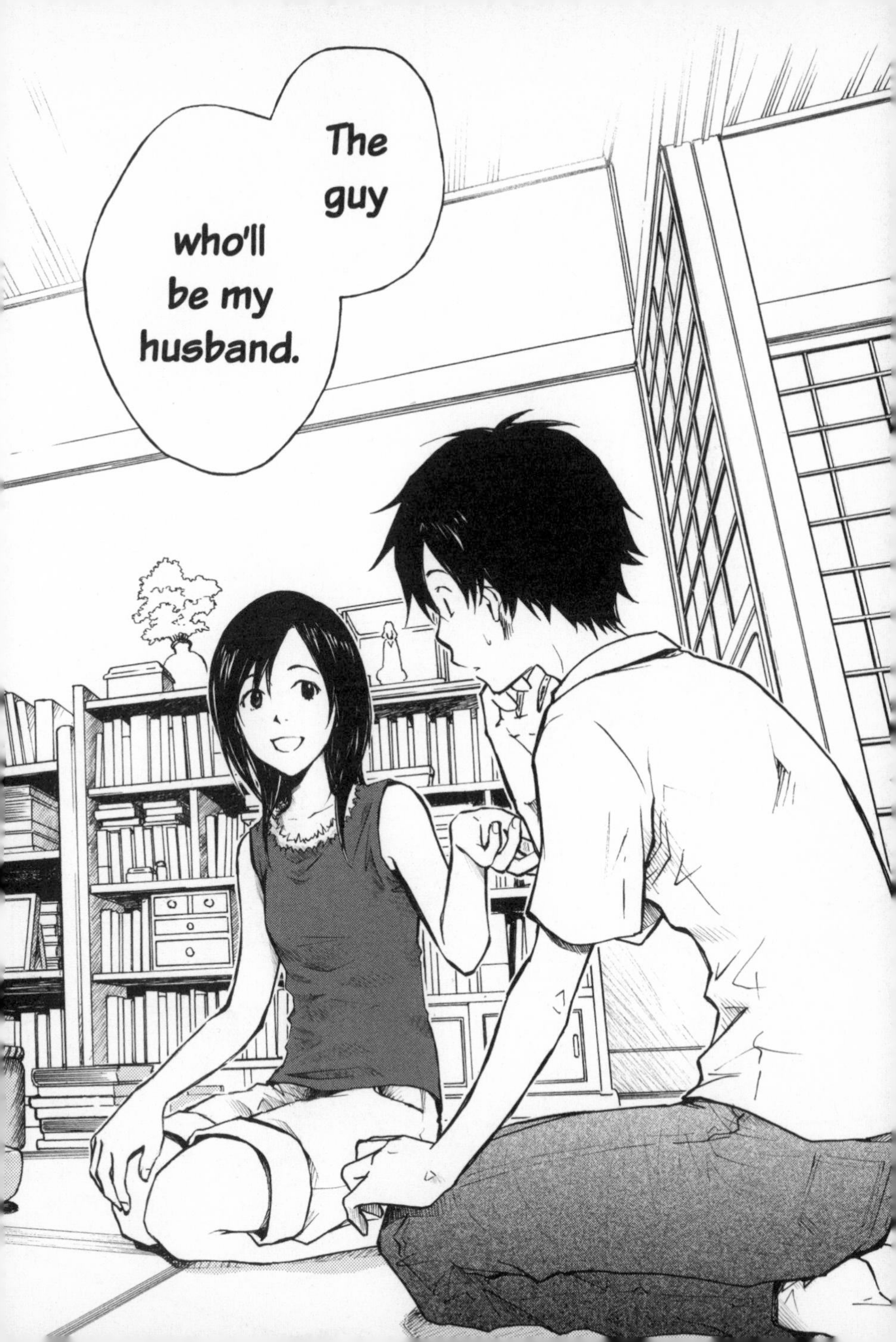
The guy who'll be my husband.

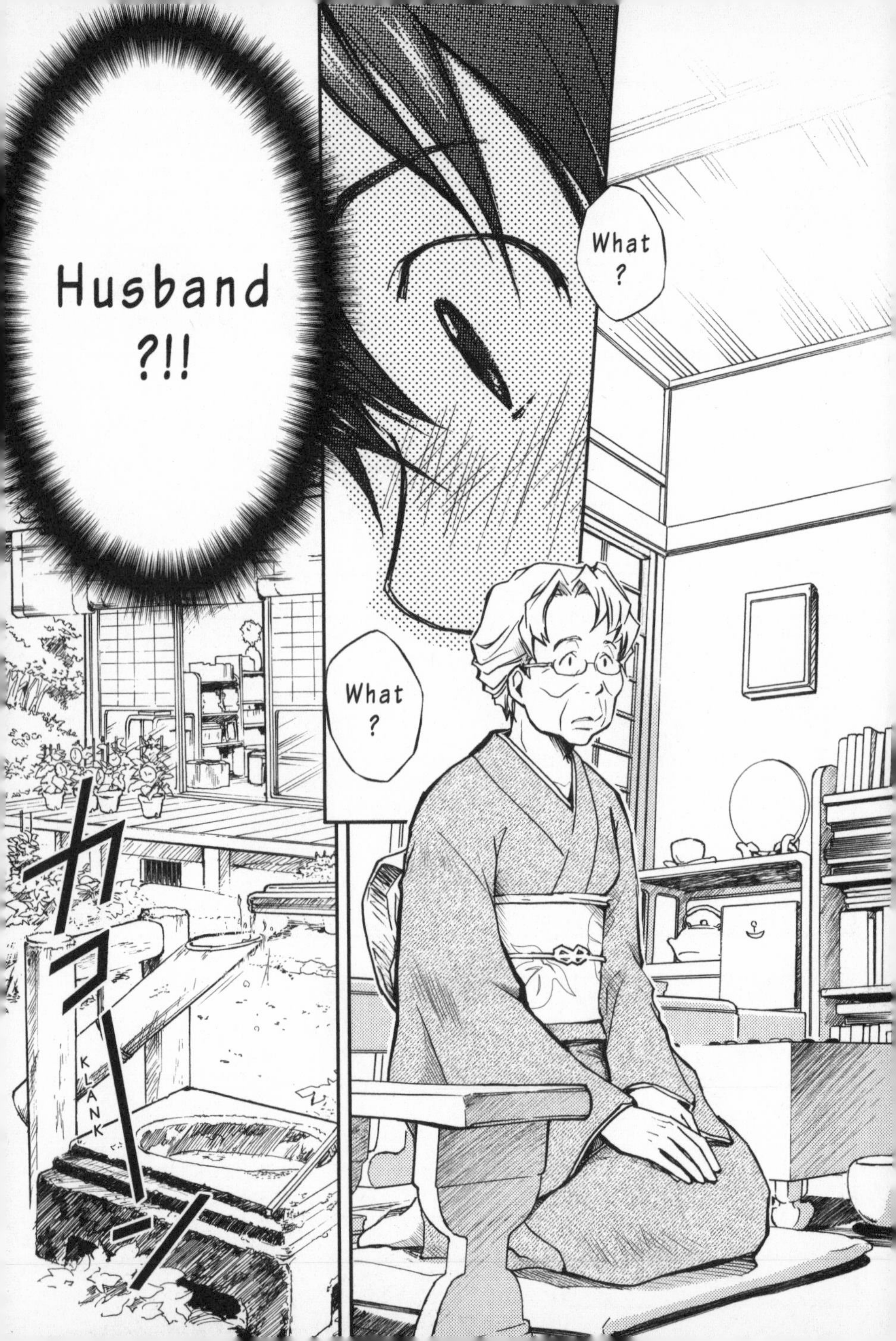
What ?
What ?
Husband ?!!
KLANK

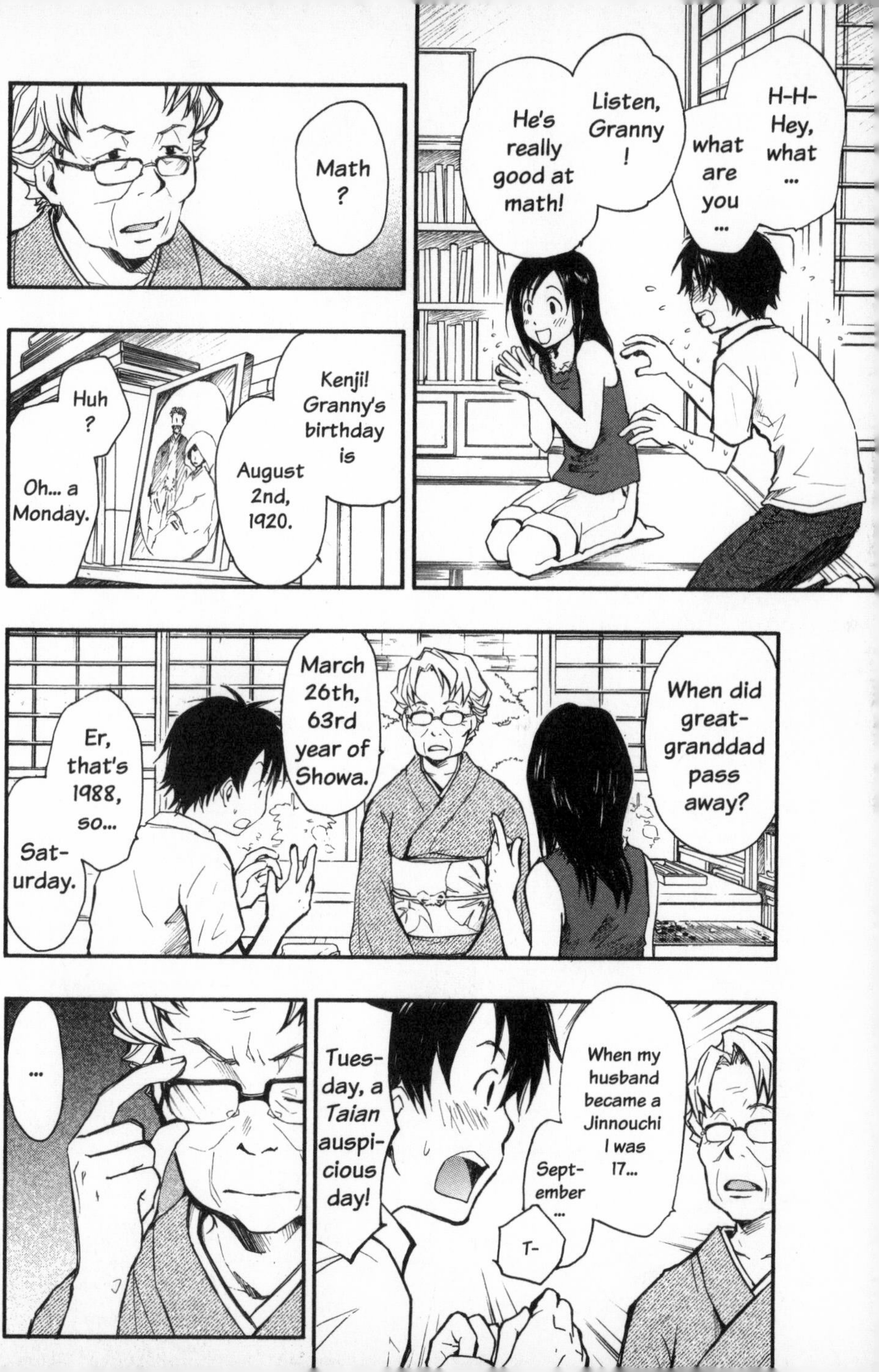
H-H- Hey, what ...
what are you ...
Listen, Granny!
He's really good at math!
Math?
Kenji! Granny's birthday is
August 2nd, 1920.
Huh?
Oh... a Monday.
When did great-granddad pass away?
March 26th, 63rd year of Showa.
Er, that's 1988, so...
Sat-urday.
When my husband became a Jinnouchi I was 17...
Sept-ember ...
T-
Tues-day, a Taian auspici-ous day!
...

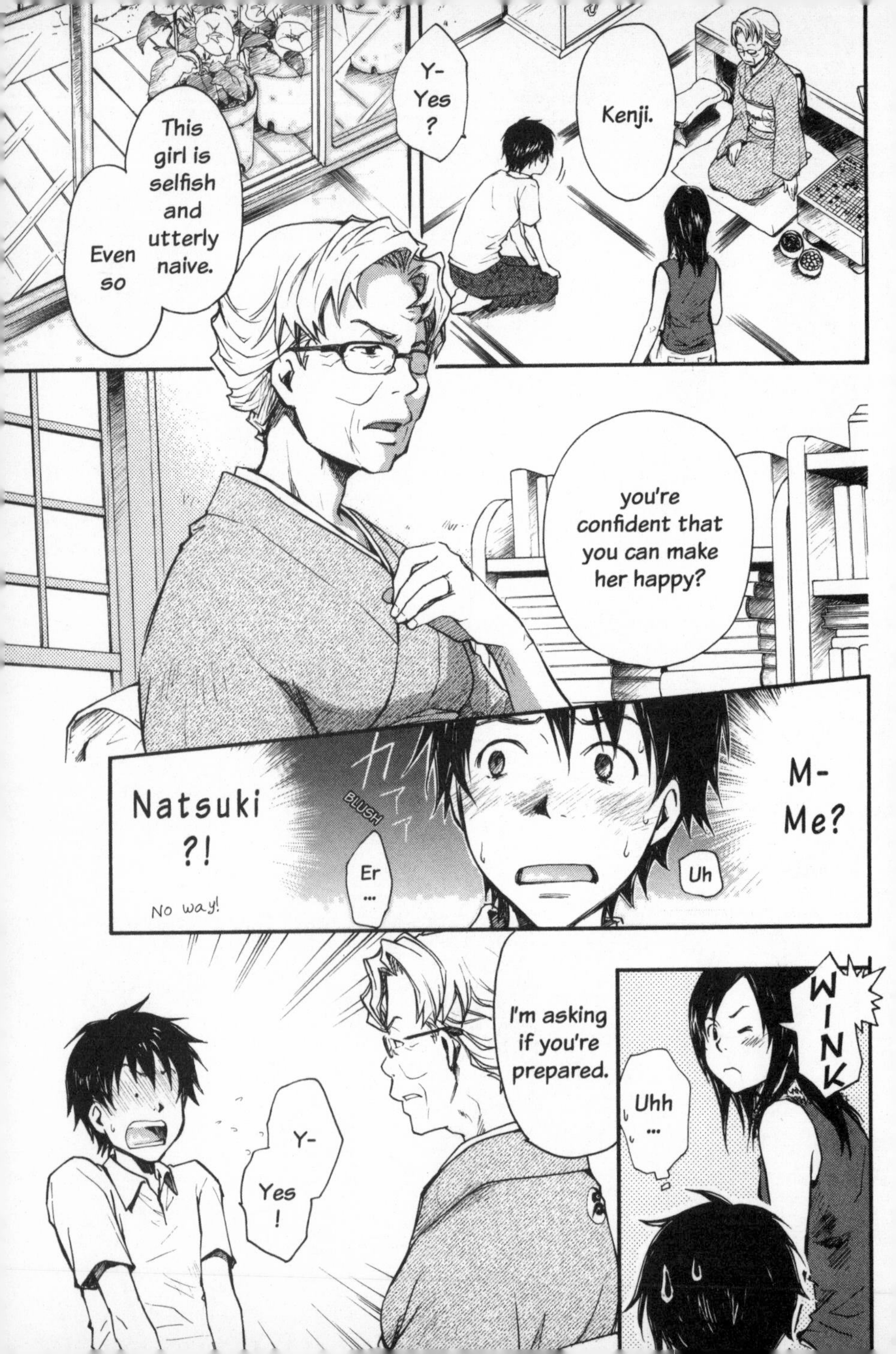
Kenji.
Y- Yes ?
This girl is selfish and utterly naive.
Even so
you're confident that you can make her happy?
M- Me?
Uh
BLUSH
Er ...
Natsuki ?!
No way!
WINK
Uhh ...
I'm asking if you're prepared.
Y- Yes !

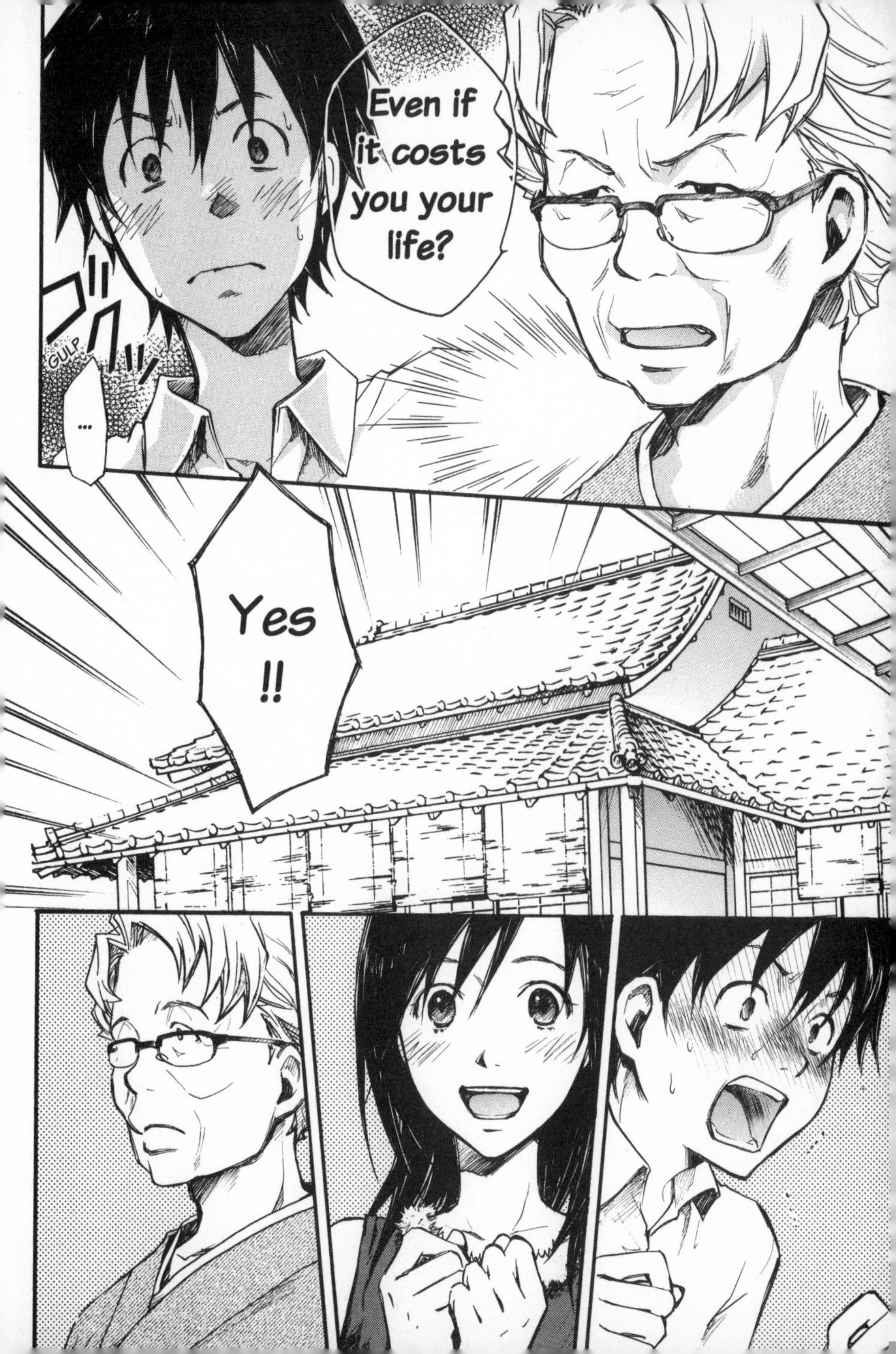
Even if it costs you your life?
ゴクッ
GULP
...
Yes !!

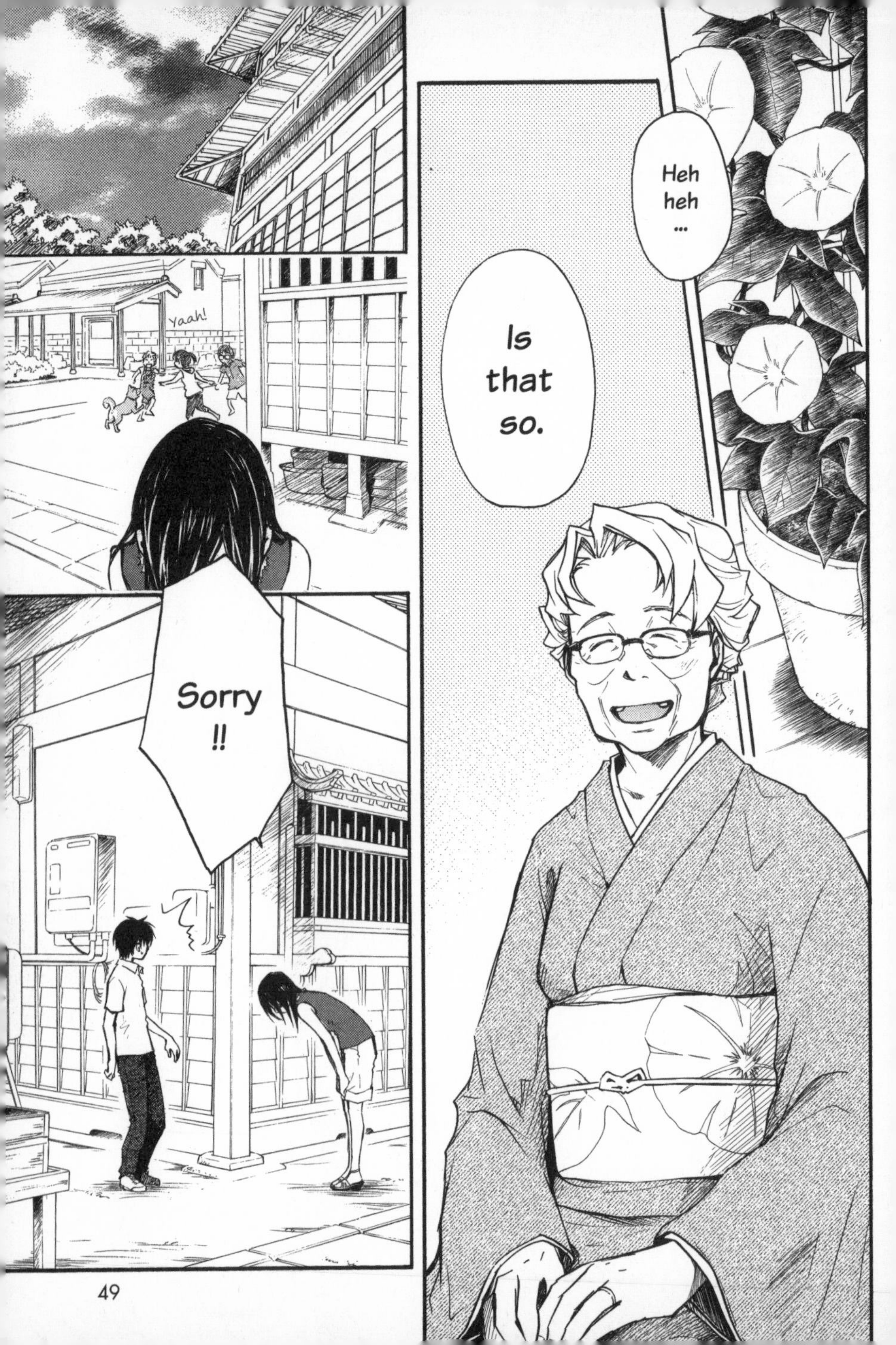
Heh heh ...
Is that so.
Yaah!
Sorry !!

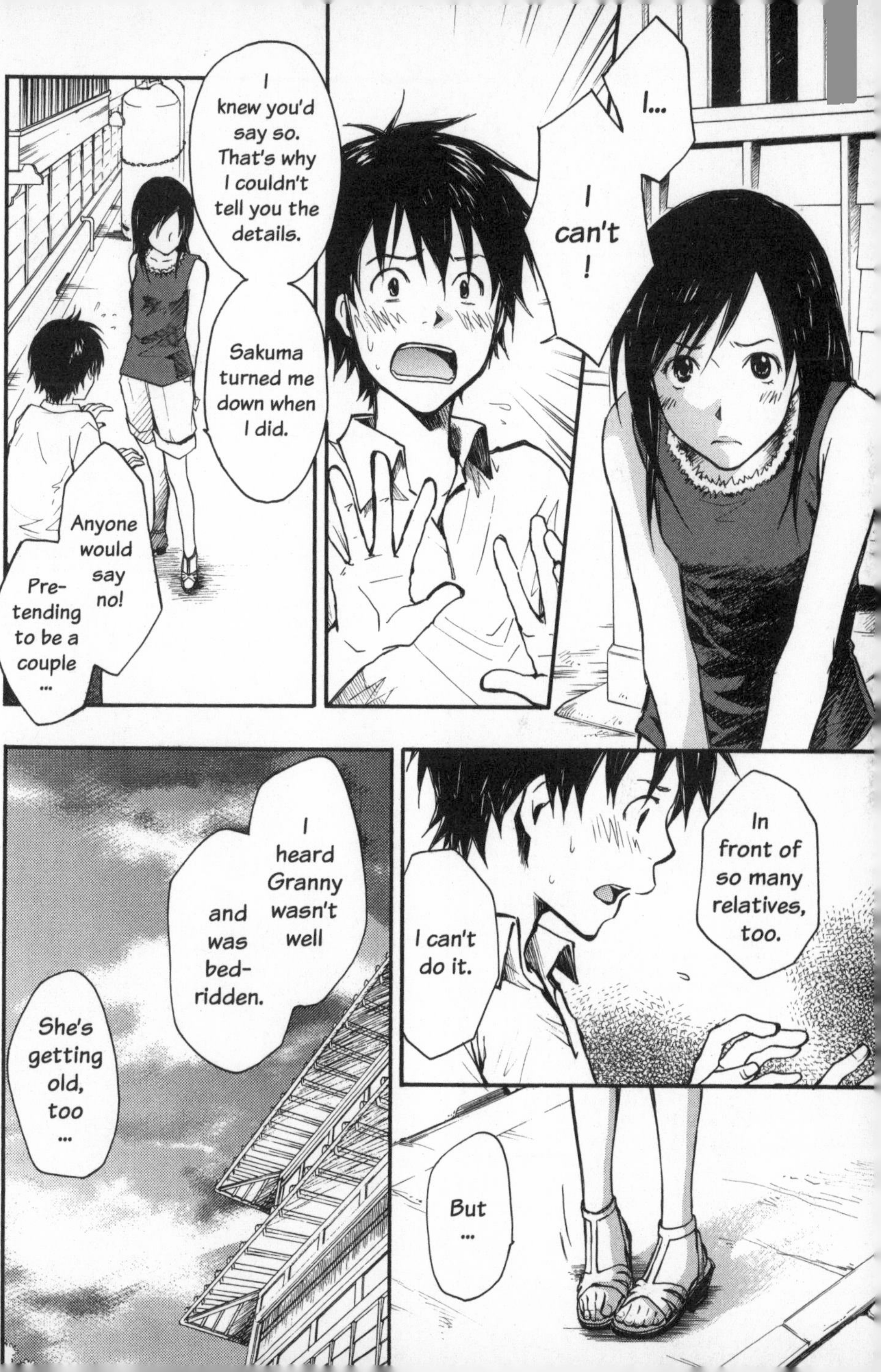
I... I can't!
I knew you'd say so. That's why I couldn't tell you the details.
Sakuma turned me down when I did.
Anyone would say no!
Pre-tending to be a couple ...
In front of so many relatives, too.
I can't do it.
But ...
I heard Granny wasn't well and was bed-ridden.
She's getting old, too ...

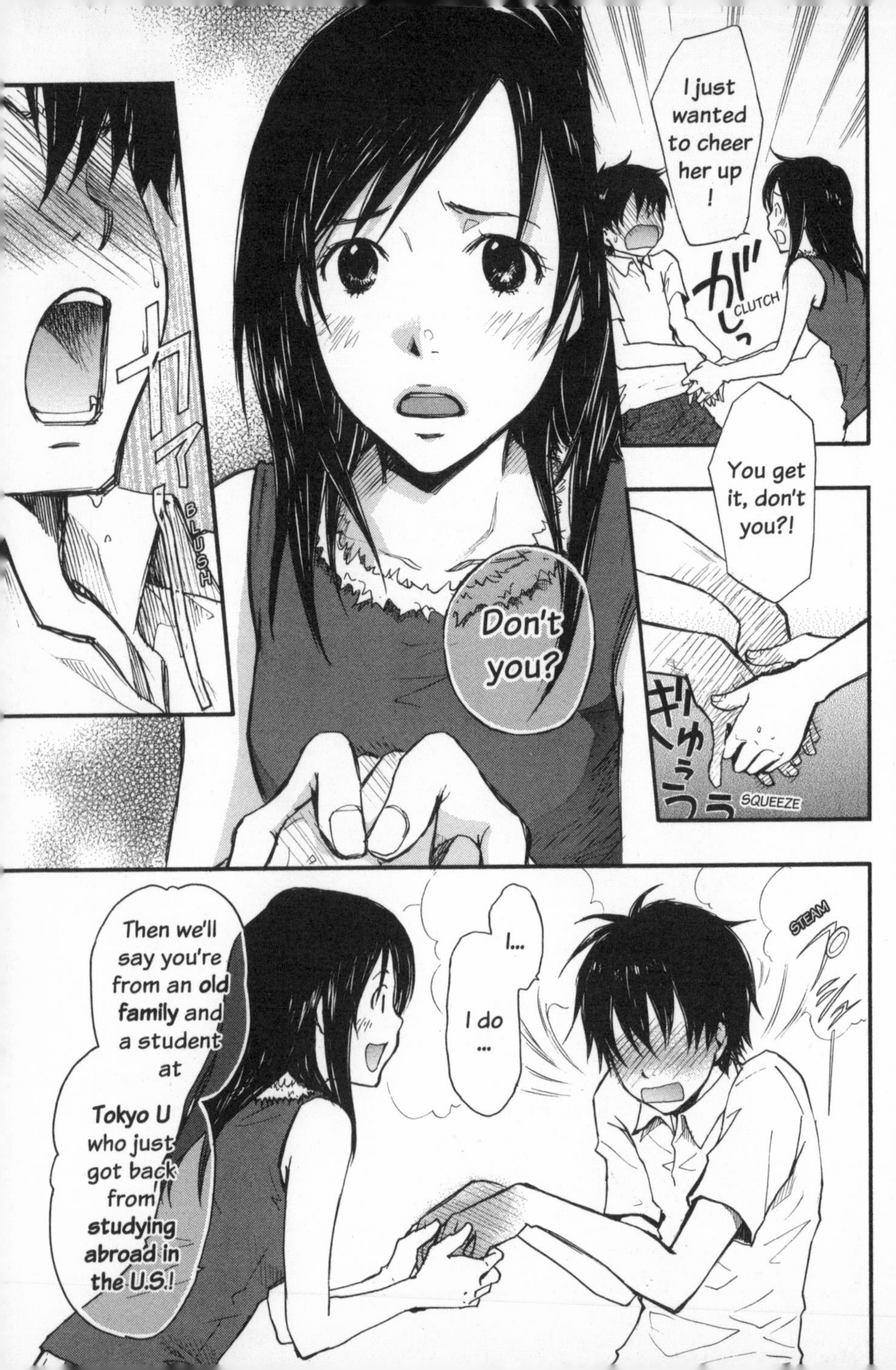
I just wanted to cheer her up!
CLUTCH
You get it, don't you?!
SQUEEZE
Don't you?
BLUSH
STEAM
I... I do...
Then we'll say you're from an old family and a student at Tokyo U who just got back from studying abroad in the U.S.!

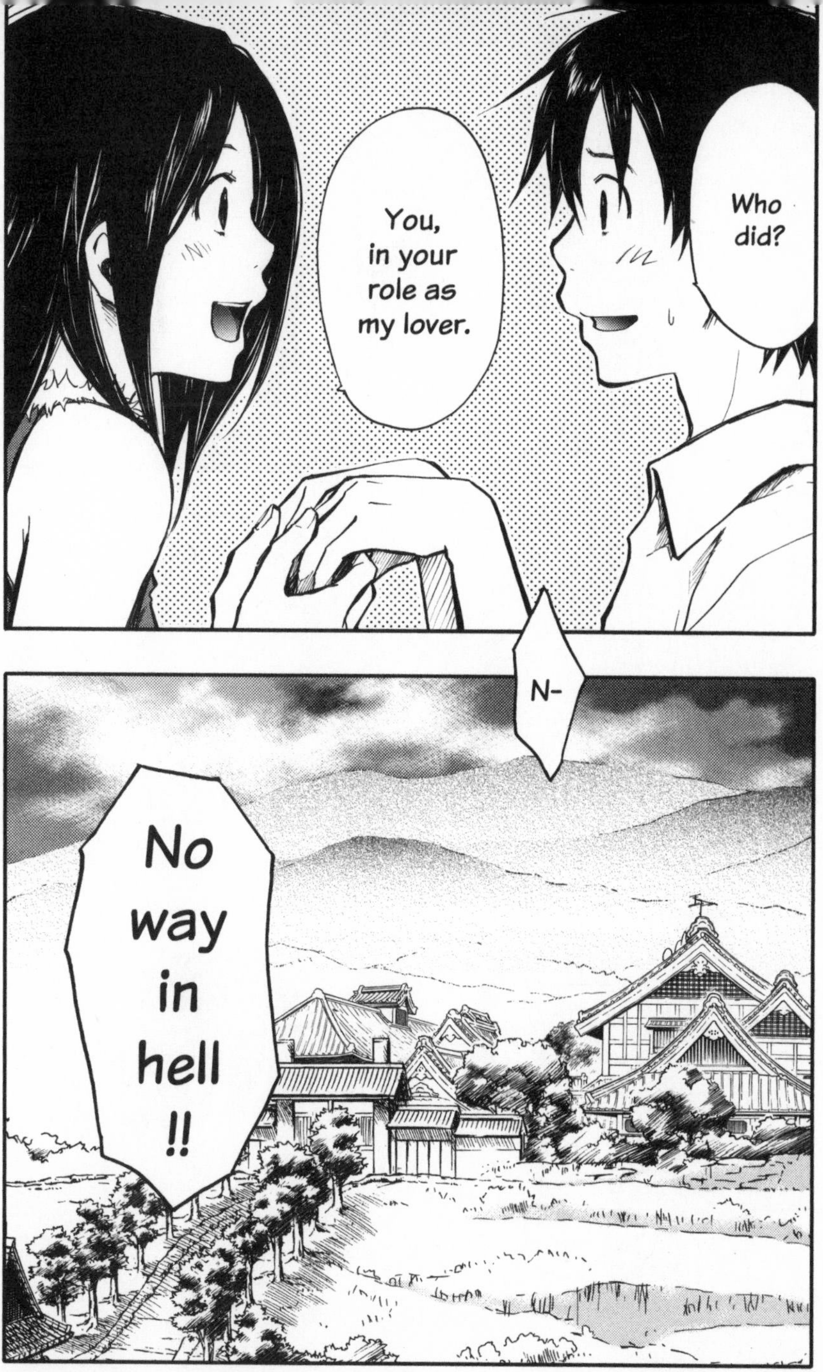
Who did?
You, in your role as my lover.
N-
No way in hell !!

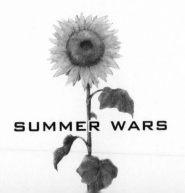

SUMMER WARS

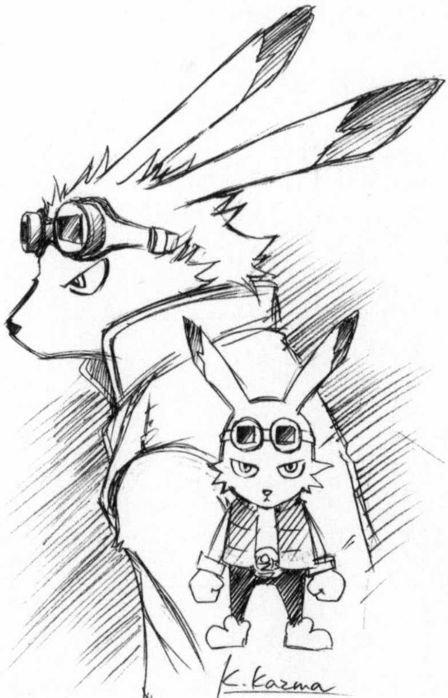
K. Kazma

Act Two A Large Family

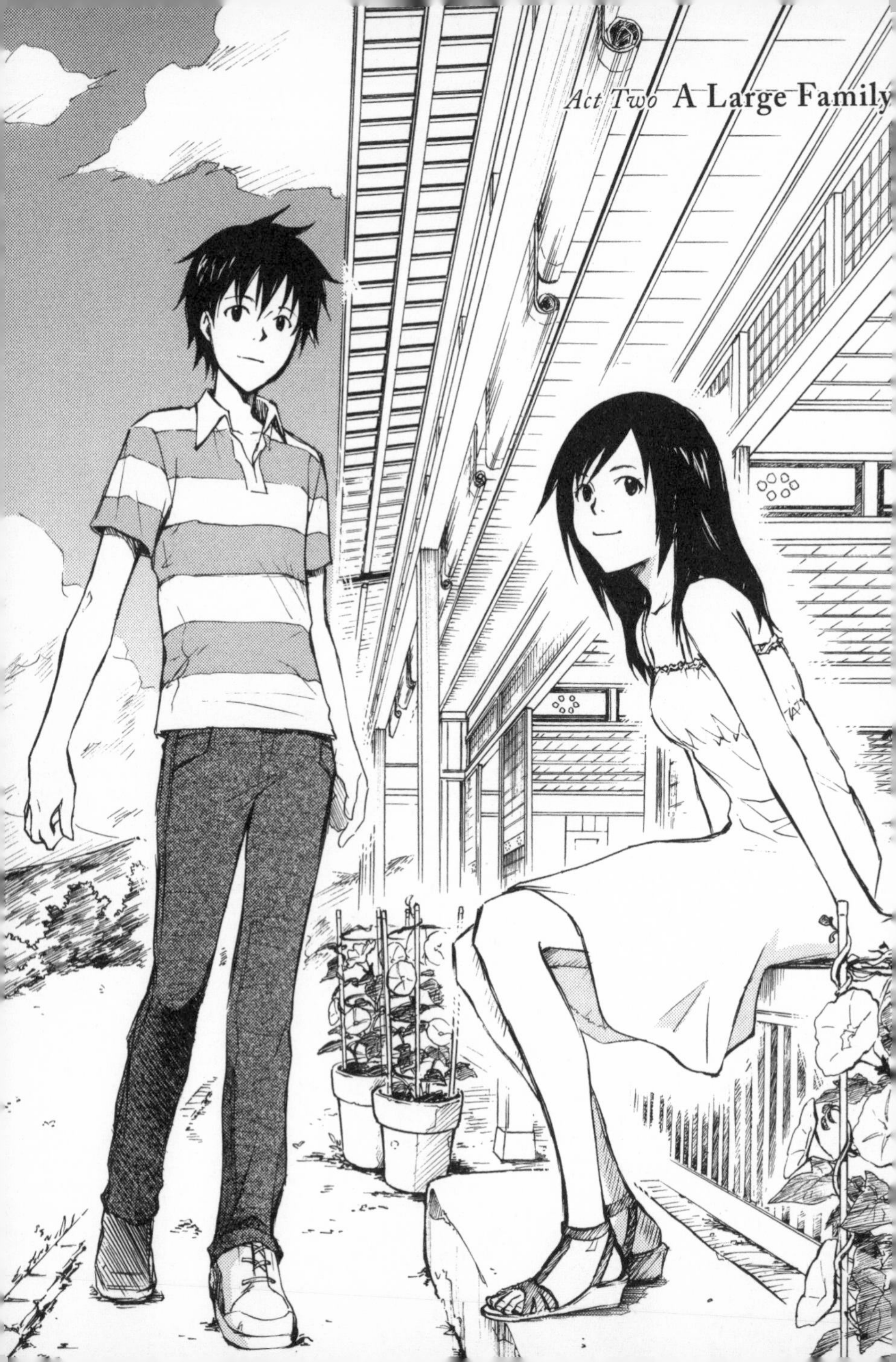

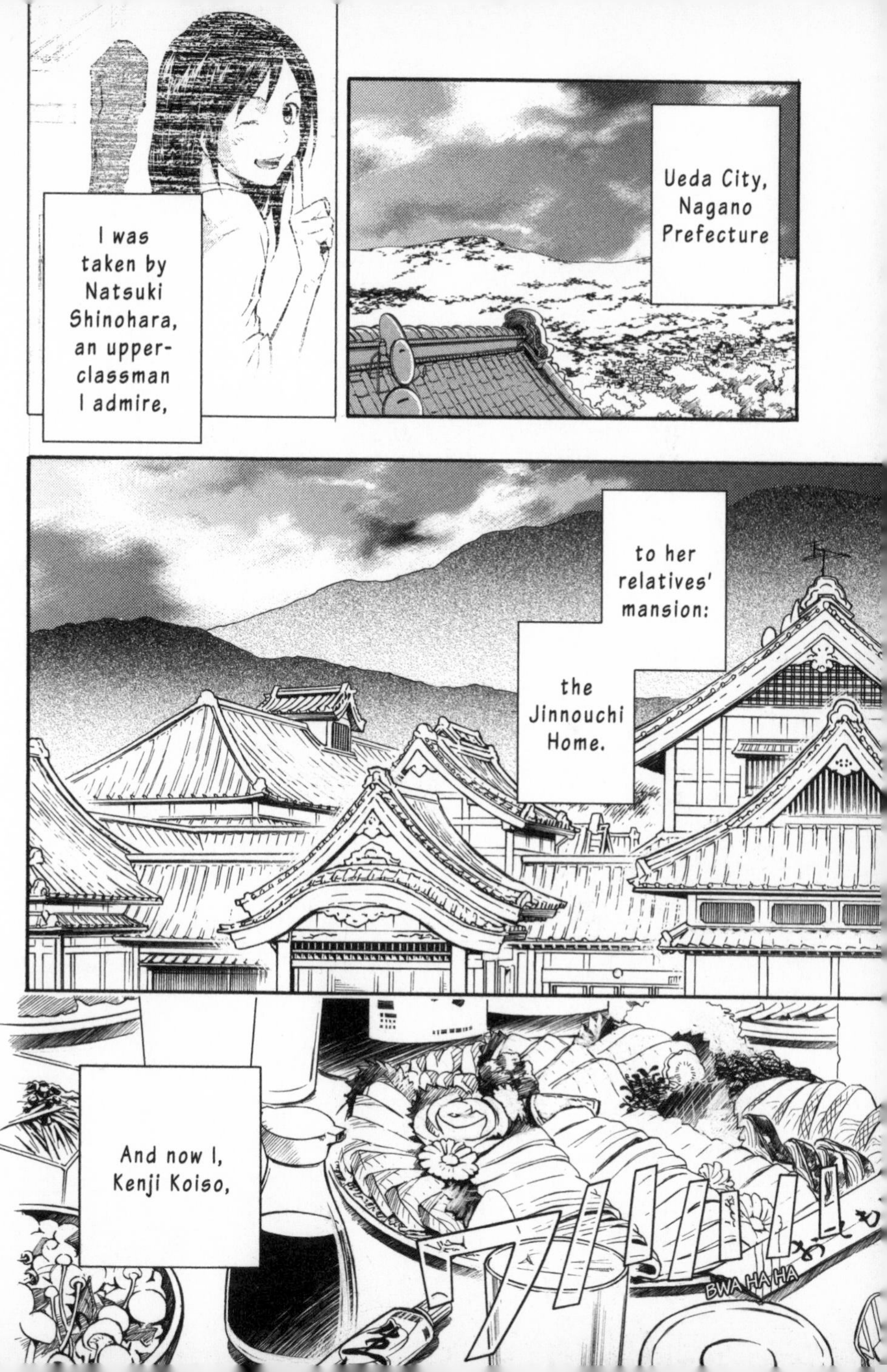
Ueda City, Nagano Prefecture
I was taken by Natsuki Shinohara, an upper-classman I admire,
to her relatives' mansion:
the Jinnouchi Home.
And now I, Kenji Koiso,
BWA HA HA

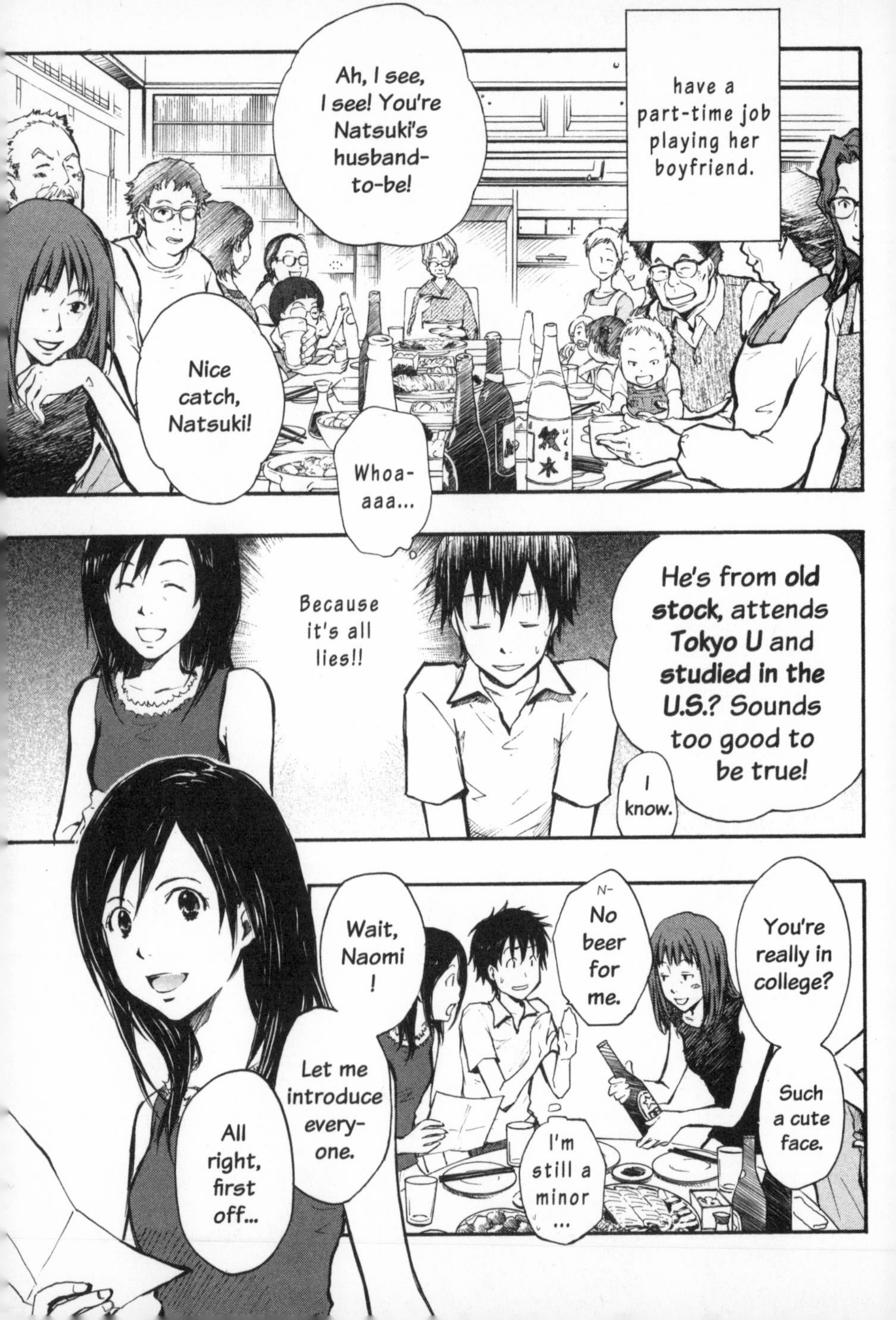
have a part-time job playing her boyfriend.
Ah, I see, I see! You're Natsuki's husband-to-be!
Nice catch, Natsuki!
Whoa-aaa...
He's from old stock, attends Tokyo U and studied in the U.S.? Sounds too good to be true!
I know.
Because it's all lies!!
You're really in college?
Such a cute face.
N- No beer for me.
I'm still a minor...
Wait, Naomi!
Let me introduce every-one.
All right, first off...

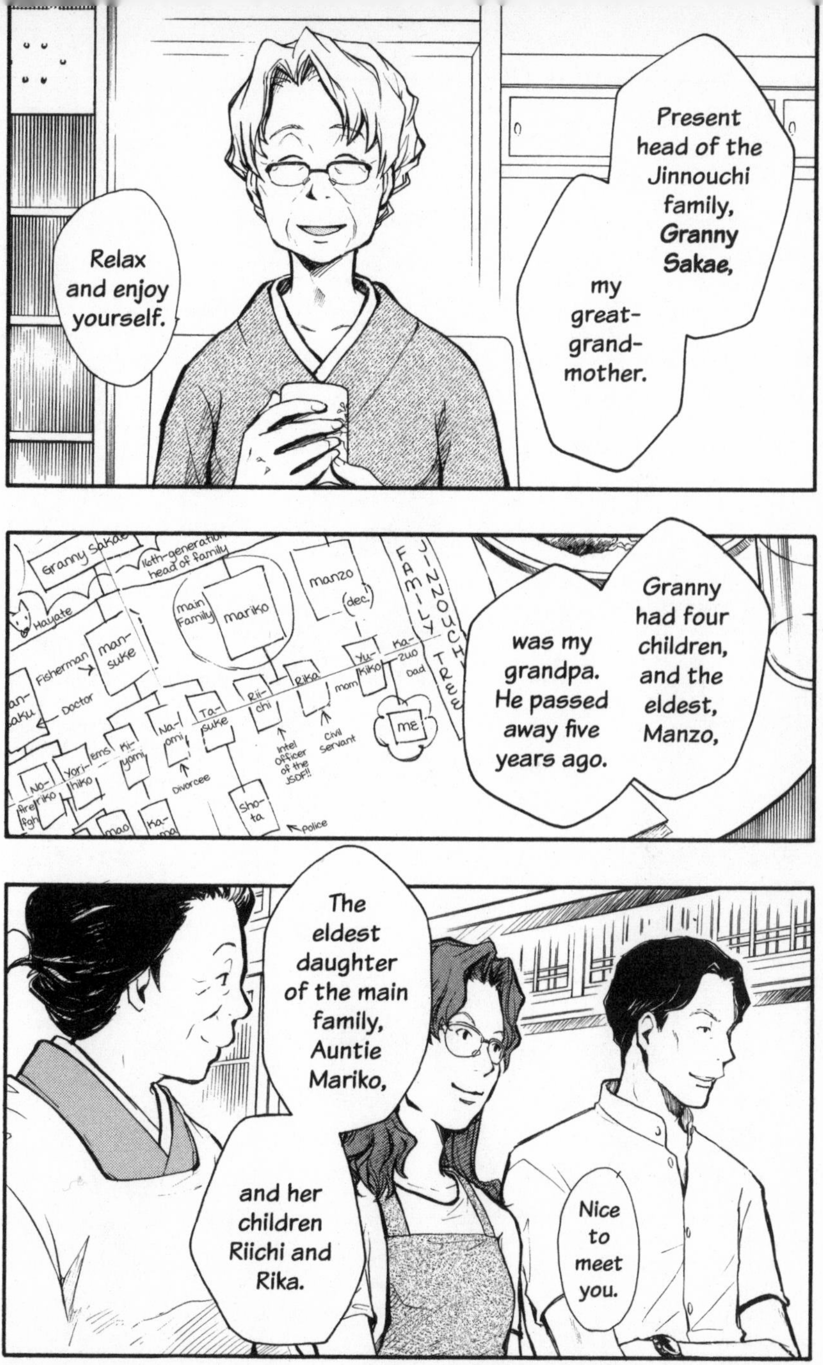
Present head of the Jinnouchi family, Granny Sakae,
my great-grandmother.
Relax and enjoy yourself.
Granny had four children, and the eldest, Manzo,
was my grandpa. He passed away five years ago.
JINNOUCHI FAMILY TREE
Granny Sakae
16th-generation head of family
manzo
(dec.)
main Family
mariko
Hayate
Fisherman
man-suke
Doctor
Yu-kiko
Ka-zuo
Dad
mom
Rika
Rii-chi
me
Civil Servant
Intel Officer of the JSDF!!
Ta-suke
Na-omi
Ki-yomi
Divorcee
Sho-ta
Police
Yori-hiko
No-riko
mao
The eldest daughter of the main family, Auntie Mariko,
and her children Riichi and Rika.
Nice to meet you.

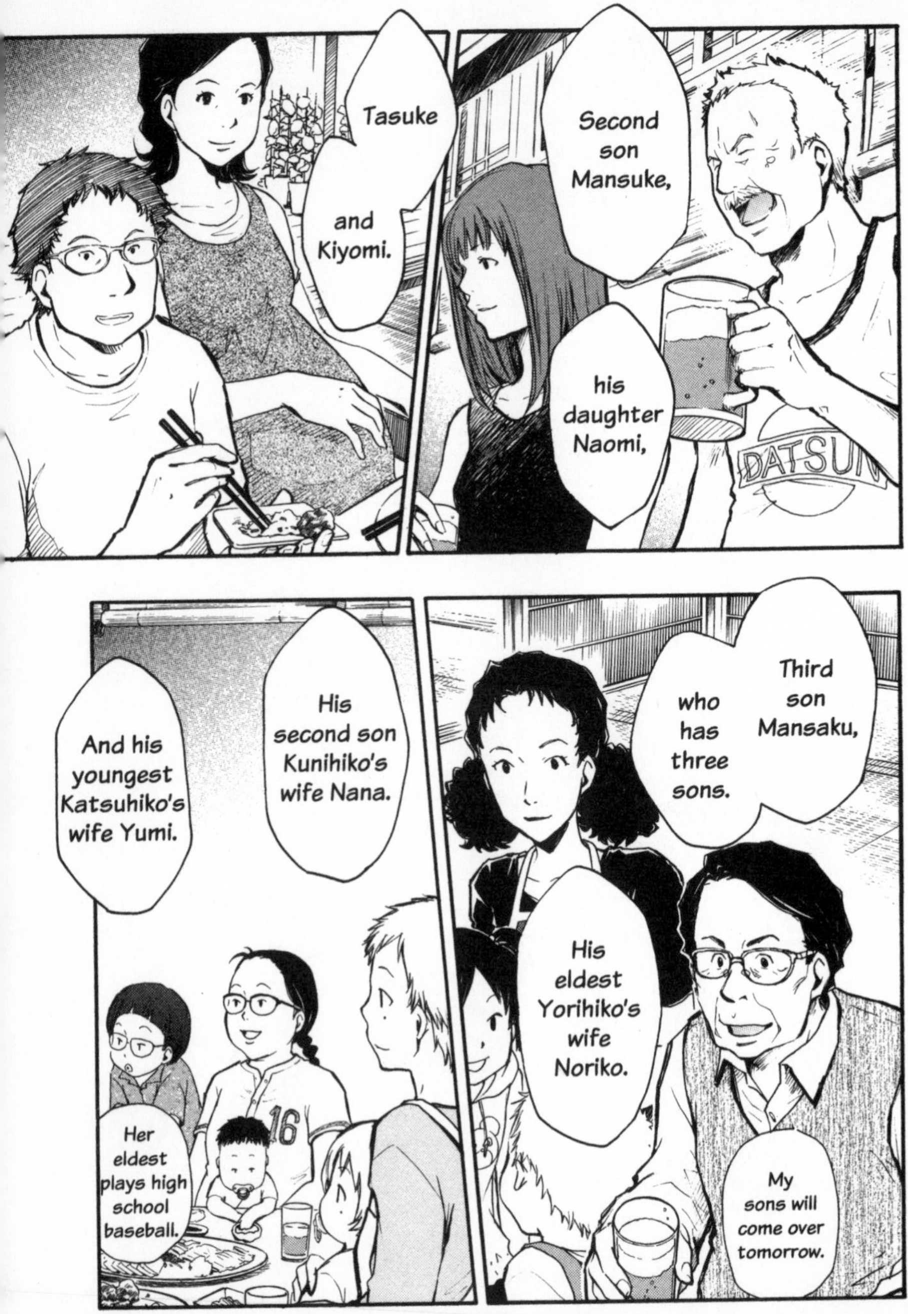
Second son Mansuke,
his daughter Naomi,
Tasuke and Kiyomi.
Third son Mansaku, who has three sons.
His eldest Yorihiko's wife Noriko.
My sons will come over tomorrow.
His second son Kunihiko's wife Nana.
And his youngest Katsuhiko's wife Yumi.
Her eldest plays high school baseball.

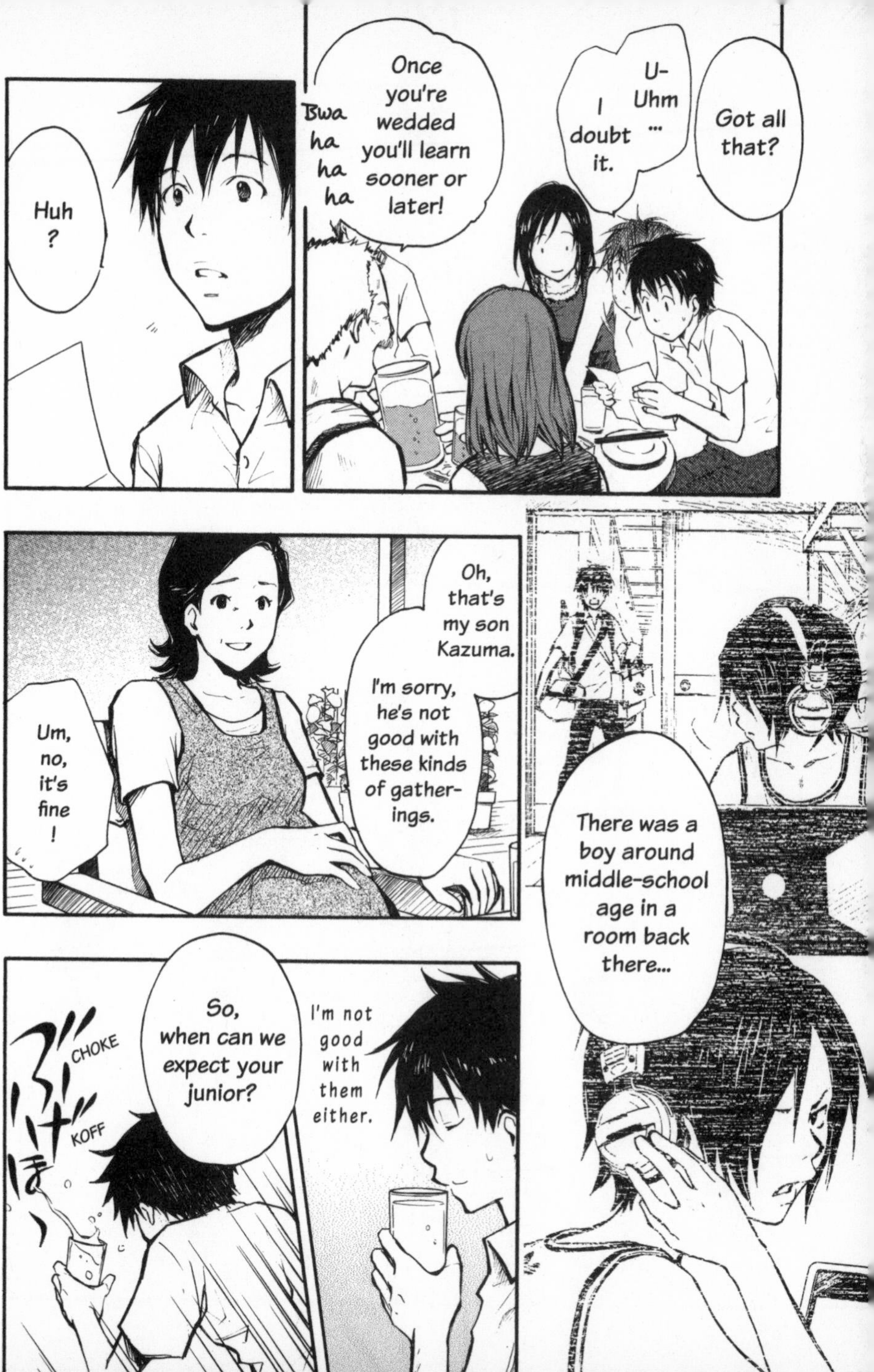
Got all that?
U-Uhm ...
I doubt it.
Once you're wedded you'll learn sooner or later!
Bwa ha ha ha
Huh?
There was a boy around middle-school age in a room back there...
Oh, that's my son Kazuma.
I'm sorry, he's not good with these kinds of gatherings.
Um, no, it's fine!
I'm not good with them either.
So, when can we expect your junior?
CHOKE
KOFF

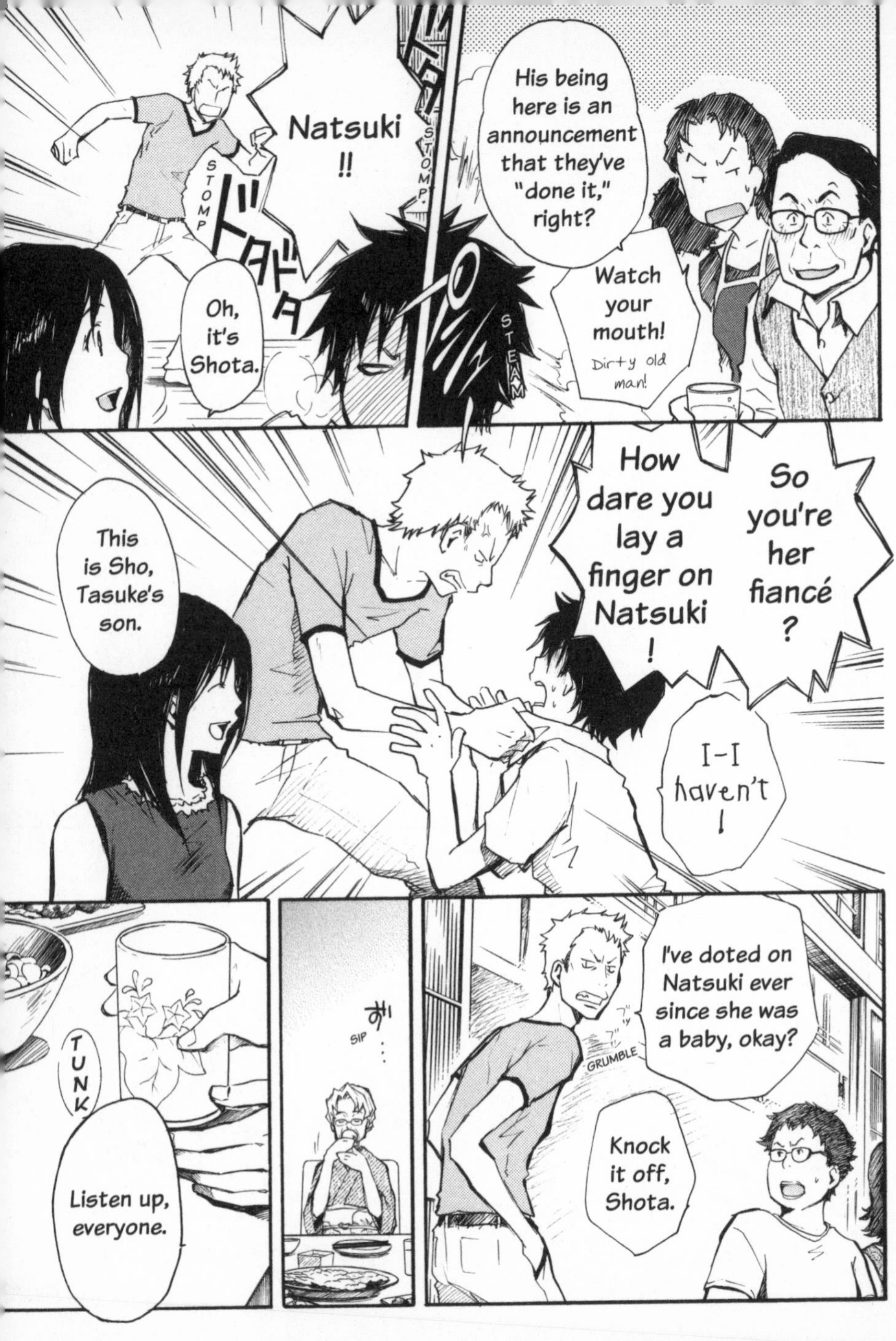
His being here is an announcement that they've "done it," right?
Watch your mouth!
Dirty old man!
STEAM
STOMP
Natsuki!!
STOMP
Oh, it's Shota.
So you're her fiancé?
How dare you lay a finger on Natsuki!
I-I haven't!
This is Sho, Tasuke's son.
I've doted on Natsuki ever since she was a baby, okay?
GRUMBLE
Knock it off, Shota.
SIP...
TUNK
Listen up, everyone.

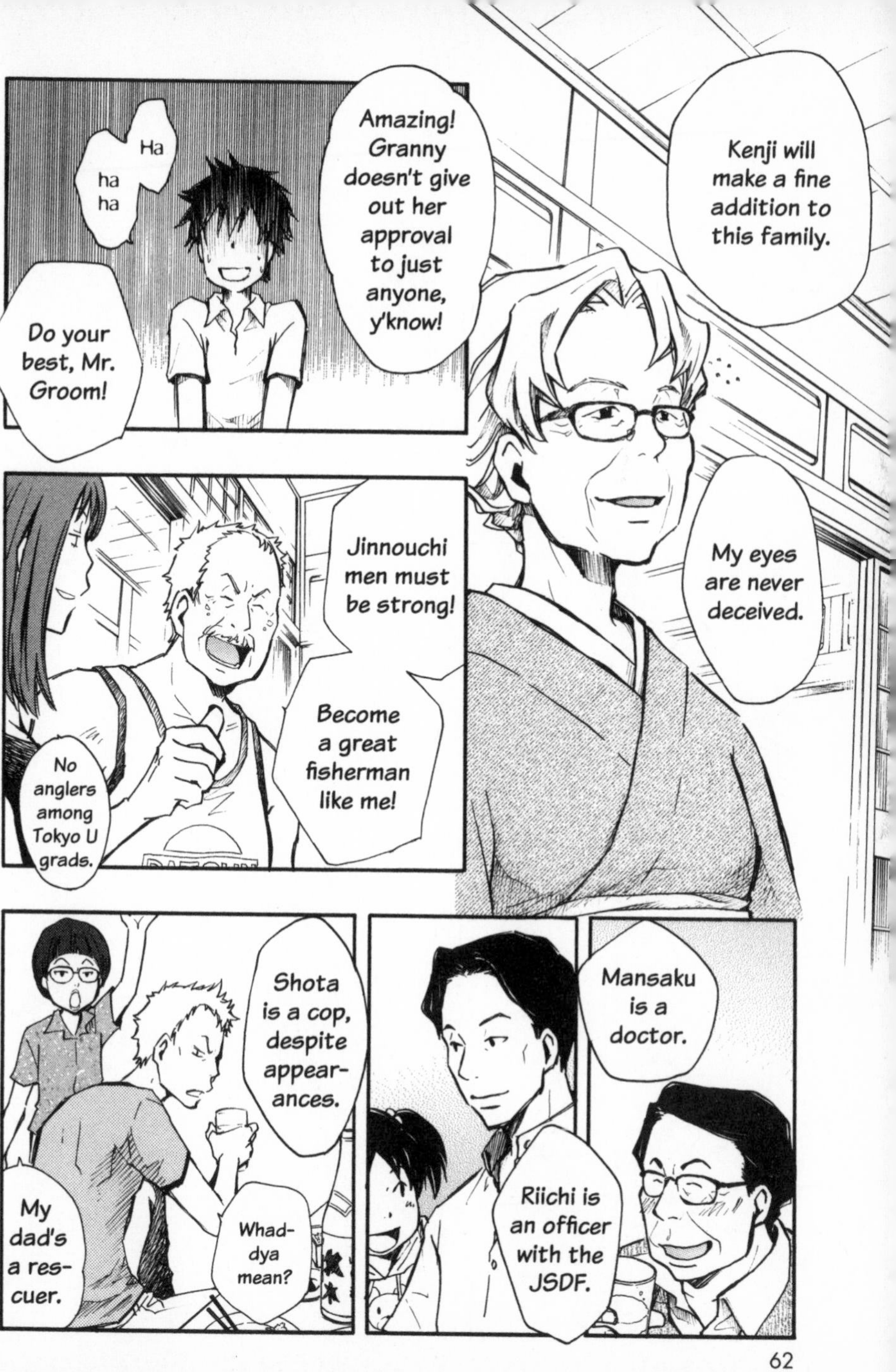
Kenji will make a fine addition to this family.
My eyes are never deceived.
Amazing! Granny doesn't give out her approval to just anyone, y'know!
Ha ha ha
Do your best, Mr. Groom!
Jinnouchi men must be strong!
Become a great fisherman like me!
No anglers among Tokyo U grads.
Mansaku is a doctor.
Riichi is an officer with the JSDF.
Shota is a cop, despite appear- ances.
Whad- dya mean?
My dad's a res- cuer.

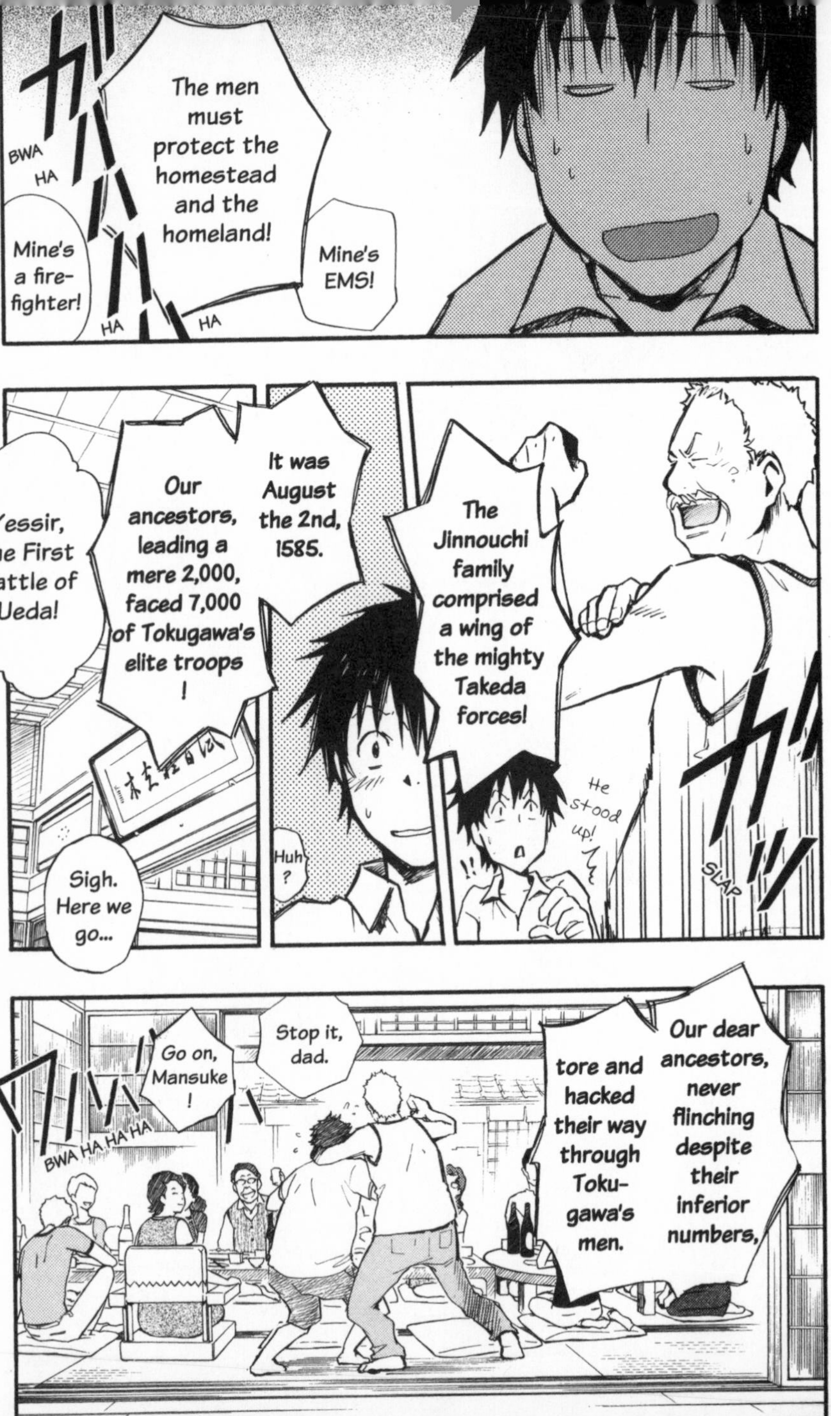
The men must protect the homestead and the homeland!
Mine's EMS!
Mine's a fire-fighter!
BWA HA HA HA
The Jinnouchi family comprised a wing of the mighty Takeda forces!
He stood up!
SLAP
It was August the 2nd, 1585.
Huh?
Our ancestors, leading a mere 2,000, faced 7,000 of Tokugawa's elite troops!
Yessir, the First Battle of Ueda!
Sigh. Here we go...
Our dear ancestors, never flinching despite their inferior numbers,
tore and hacked their way through Toku-gawa's men.
Stop it, dad.
Go on, Mansuke!
BWA HA HA HA

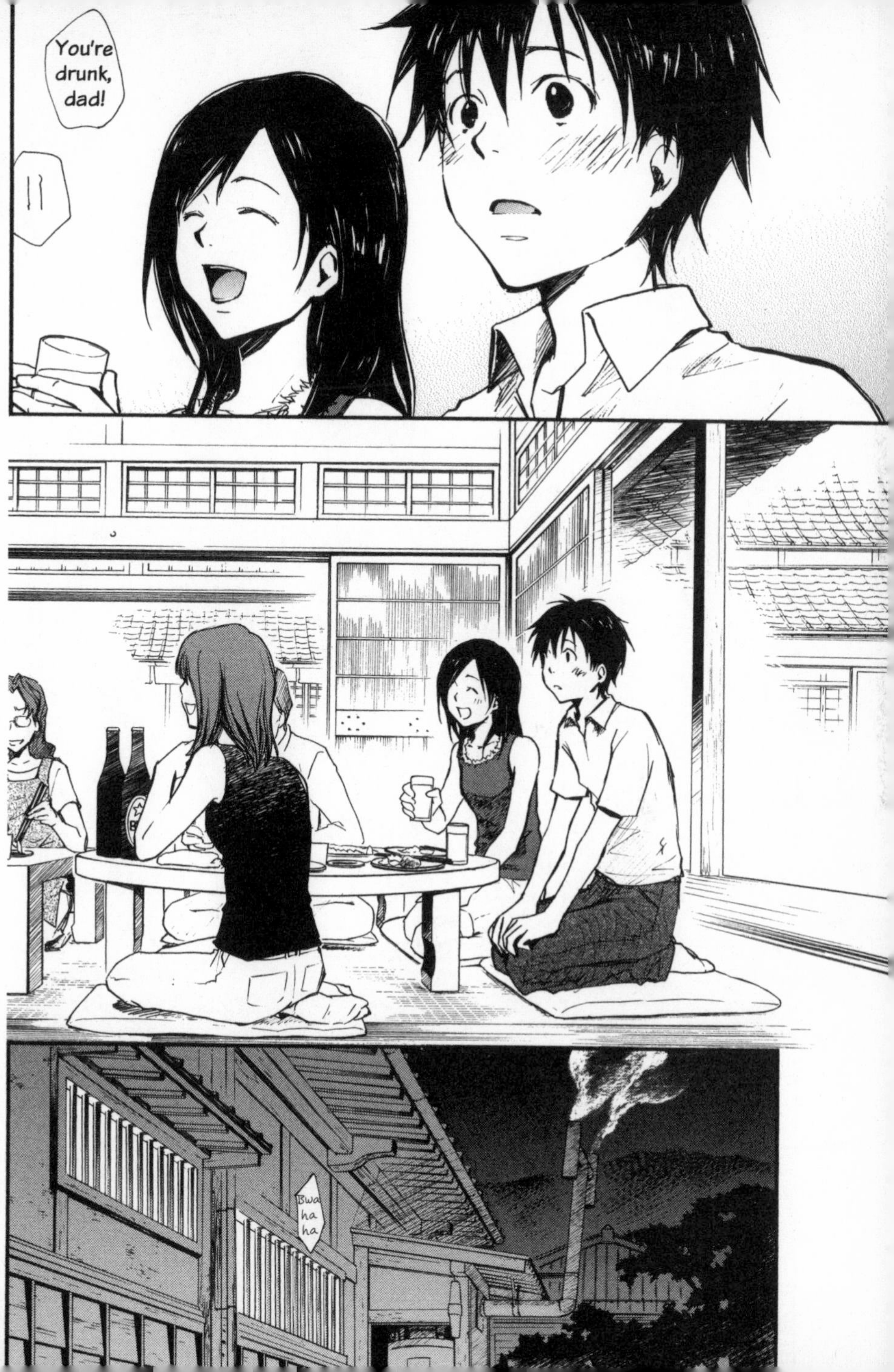
You're drunk, dad!
!!
Bwa ha ha

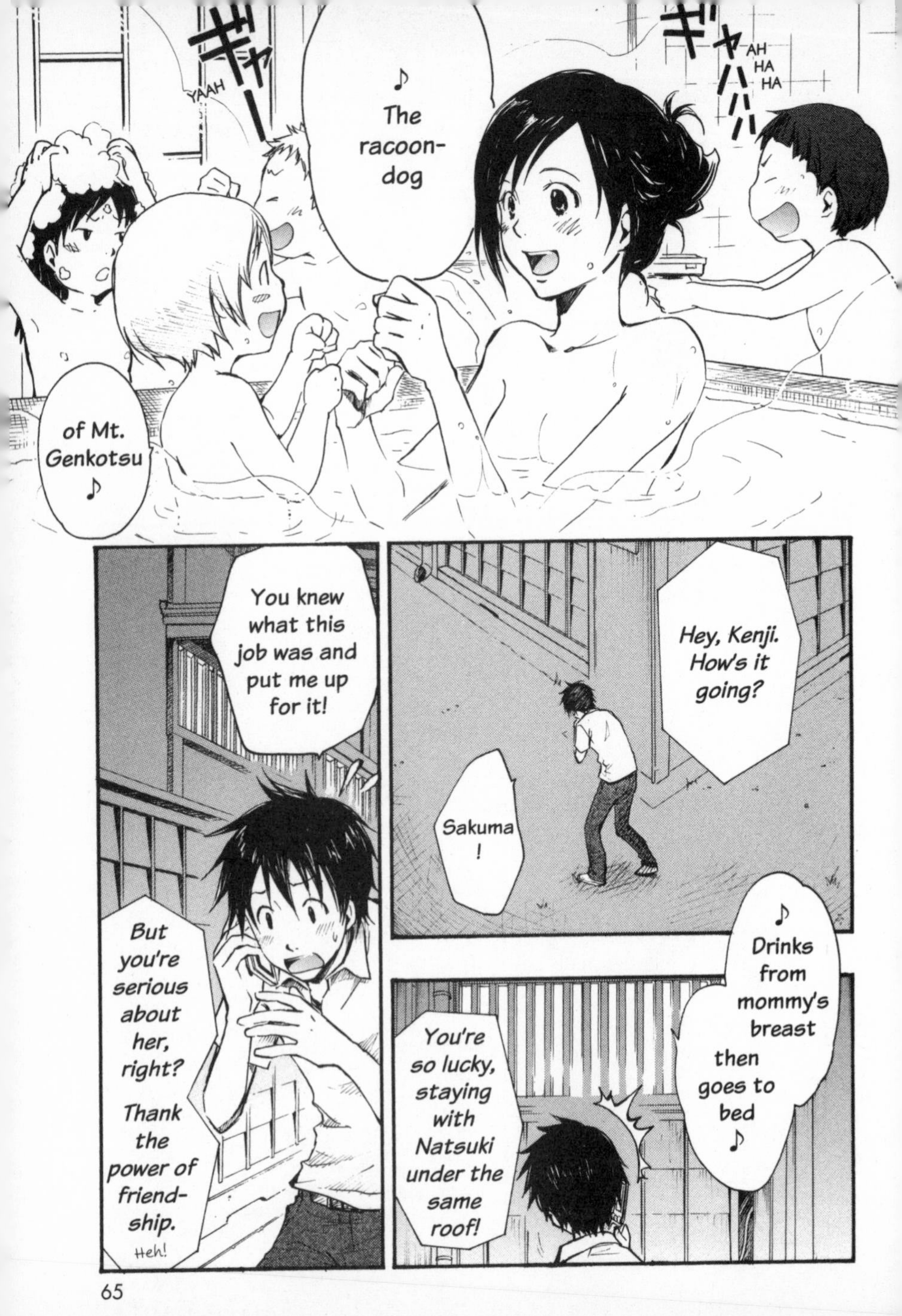
ギャハハハ
AH HA HA
♪ The racoon-dog
ギャー
YAAH
of Mt. Genkotsu ♪
Hey, Kenji. How's it going?
Sakuma!
♪ Drinks from mommy's breast then goes to bed ♪
You're so lucky, staying with Natsuki under the same roof!
You knew what this job was and put me up for it!
But you're serious about her, right?
Thank the power of friend-ship.
Heh!

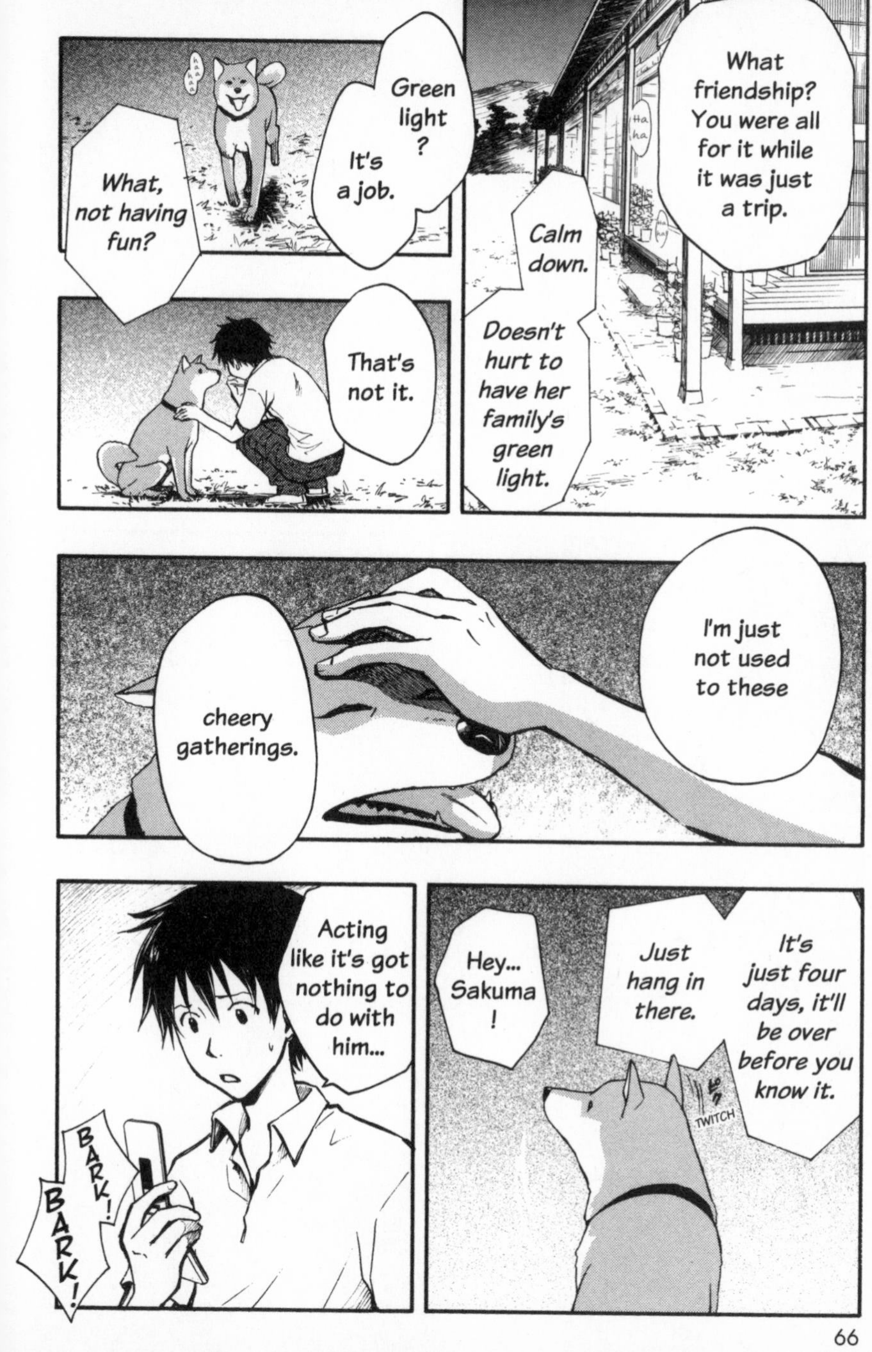
What friendship? You were all for it while it was just a trip.
Ha ha
Calm down.
Doesn't hurt to have her family's green light.
Green light?
It's a job.
What, not having fun?
That's not it.
I'm just not used to these
cheery gatherings.
It's just four days, it'll be over before you know it.
Just hang in there.
TWITCH
Hey... Sakuma!
Acting like it's got nothing to do with him...
BARK!
BARK!

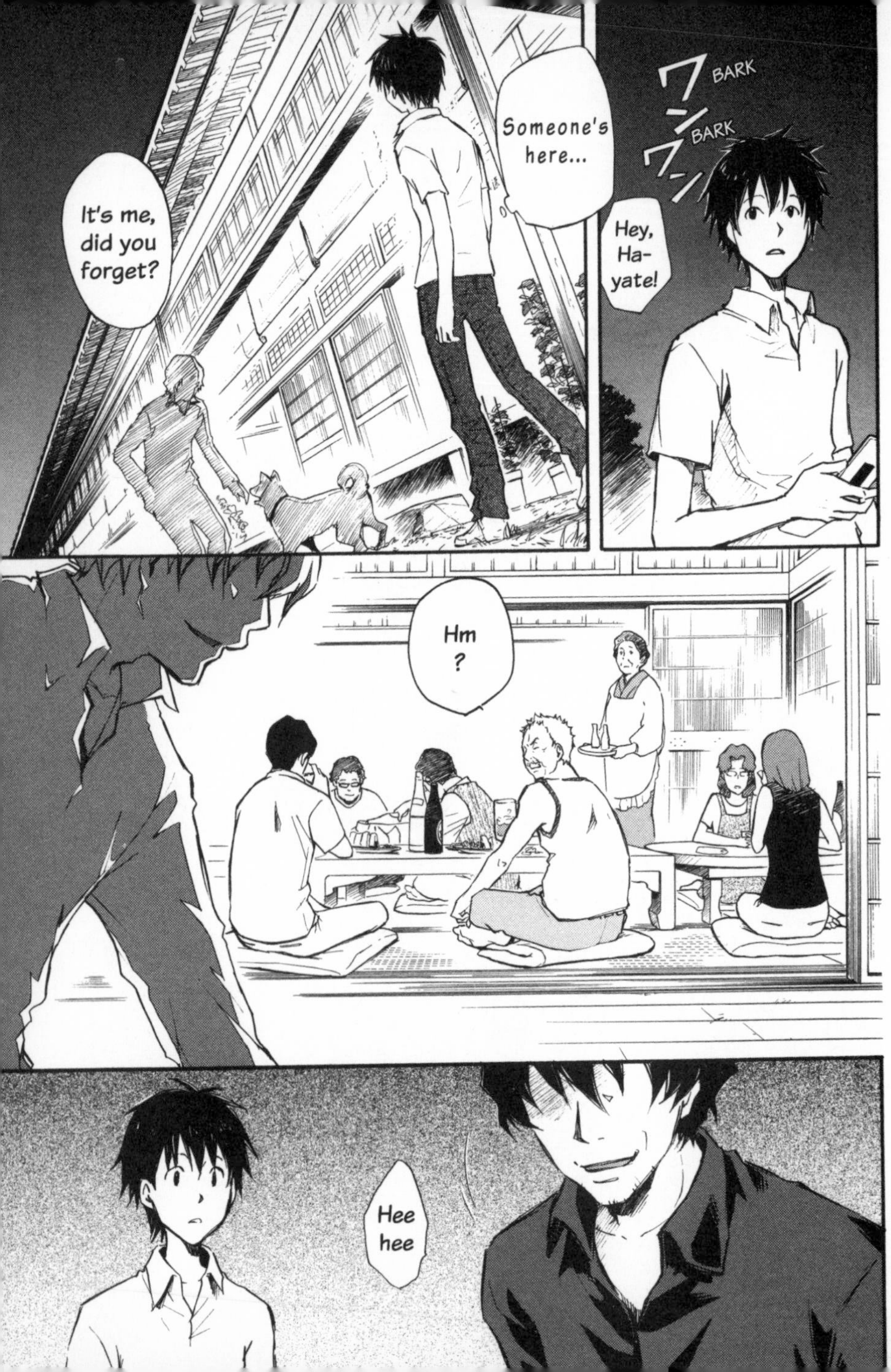
ワン BARK
ワン BARK
Hey, Ha-yate!
Someone's here...
It's me, did you forget?
Hm?
Hee hee

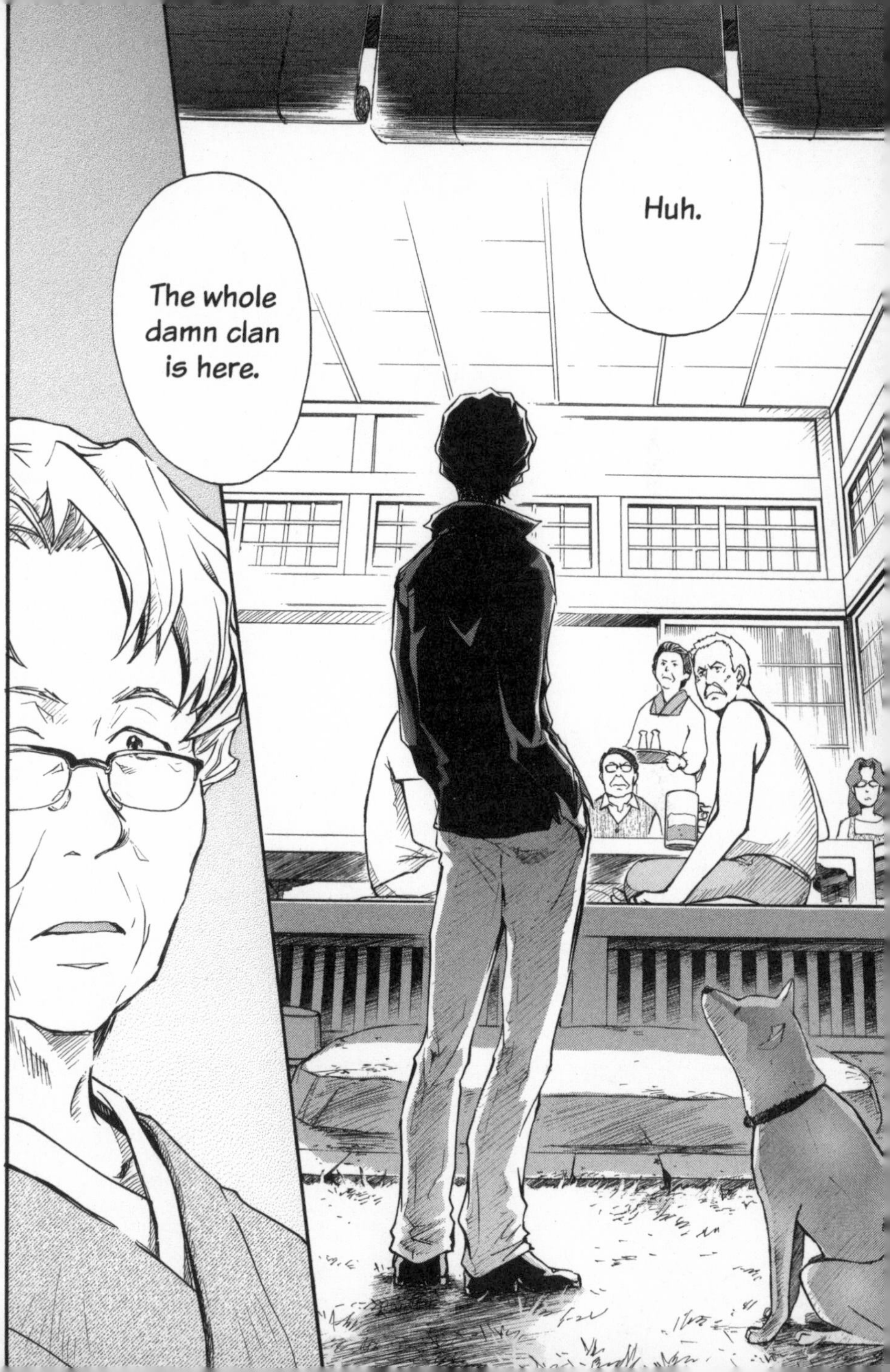
Huh.
The whole damn clan is here.

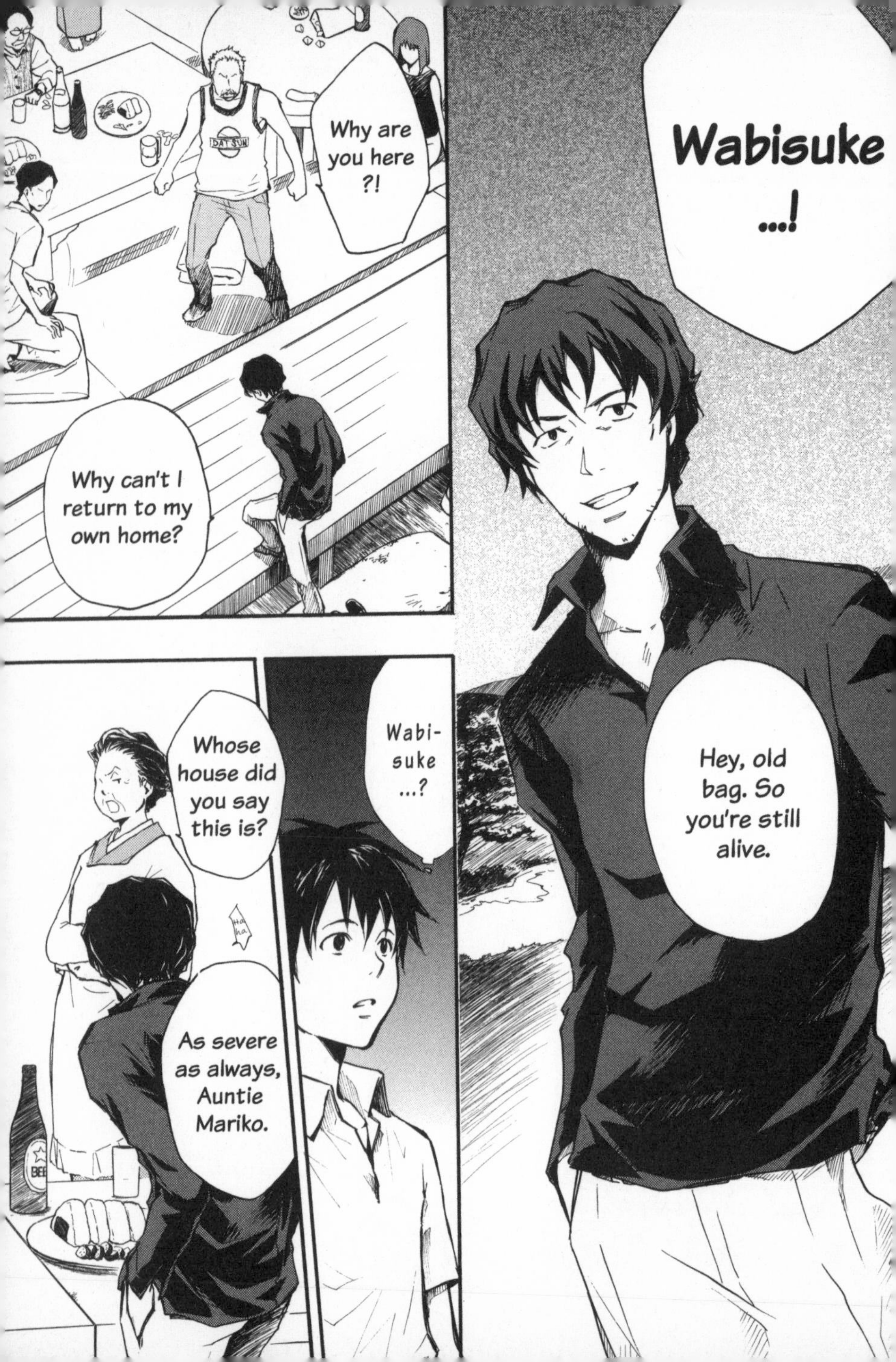
Wabisuke ...!
Hey, old bag. So you're still alive.
Why are you here ?!
Why can't I return to my own home?
Wabi-suke ...?
Whose house did you say this is?
Ha ha
As severe as always, Auntie Mariko.

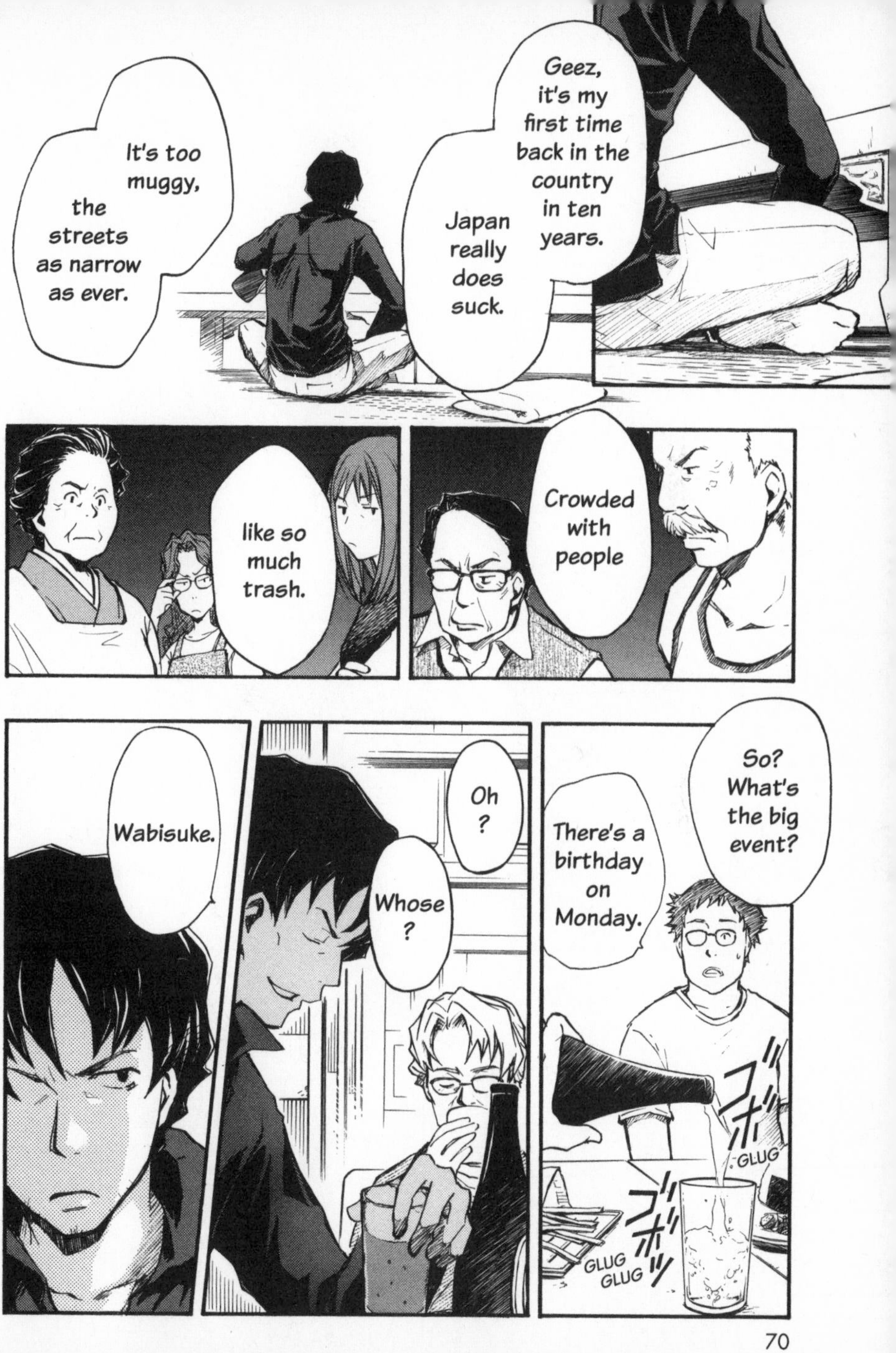
Geez, it's my first time back in the country in ten years.
Japan really does suck.
It's too muggy, the streets as narrow as ever.
Crowded with people
like so much trash.
So? What's the big event?
There's a birthday on Monday.
GLUG
GLUG GLUG
Oh?
Whose?
Wabisuke.

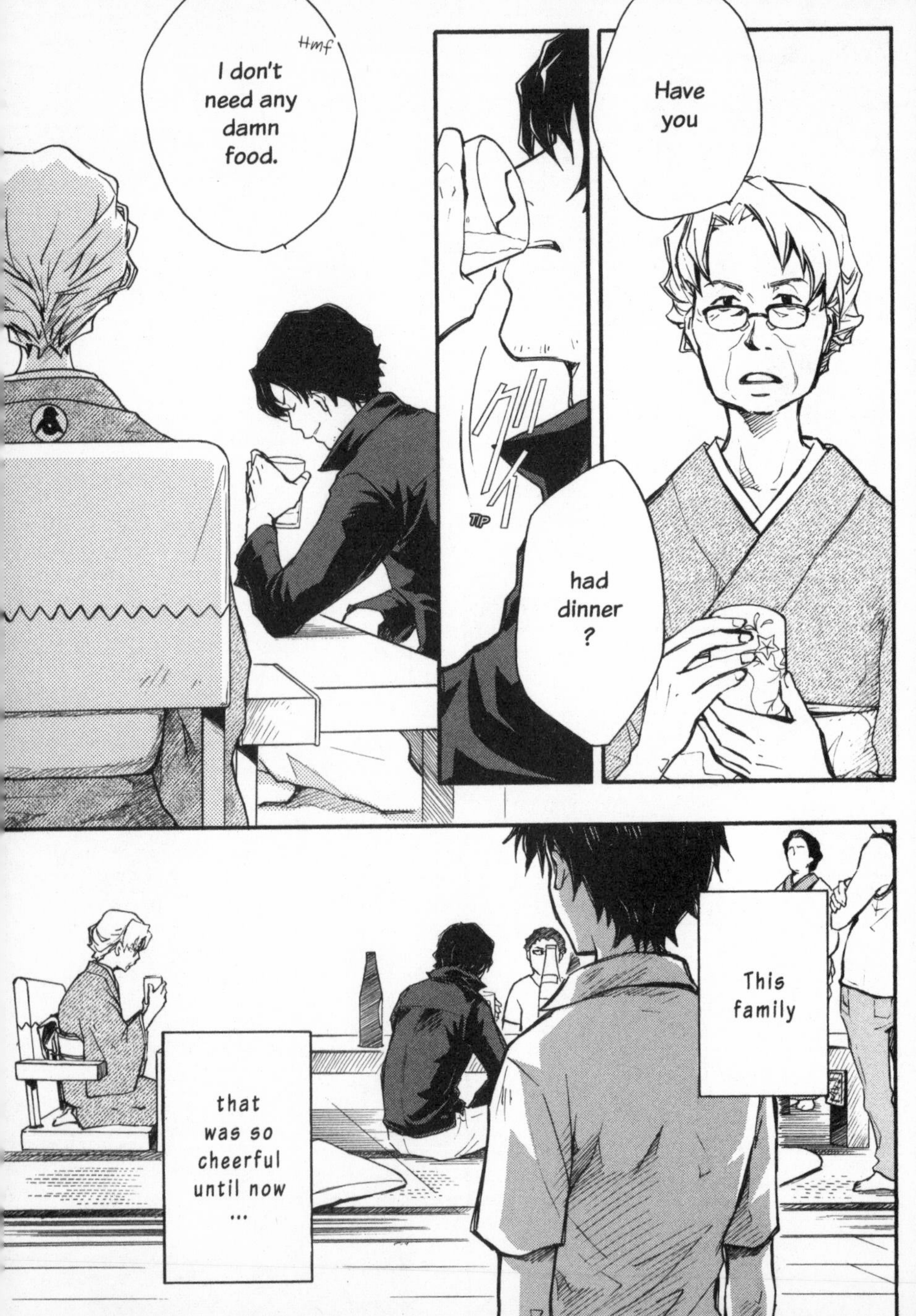
Have you
had dinner?
TIP
Hmf
I don't need any damn food.
This family
that was so cheerful until now ...

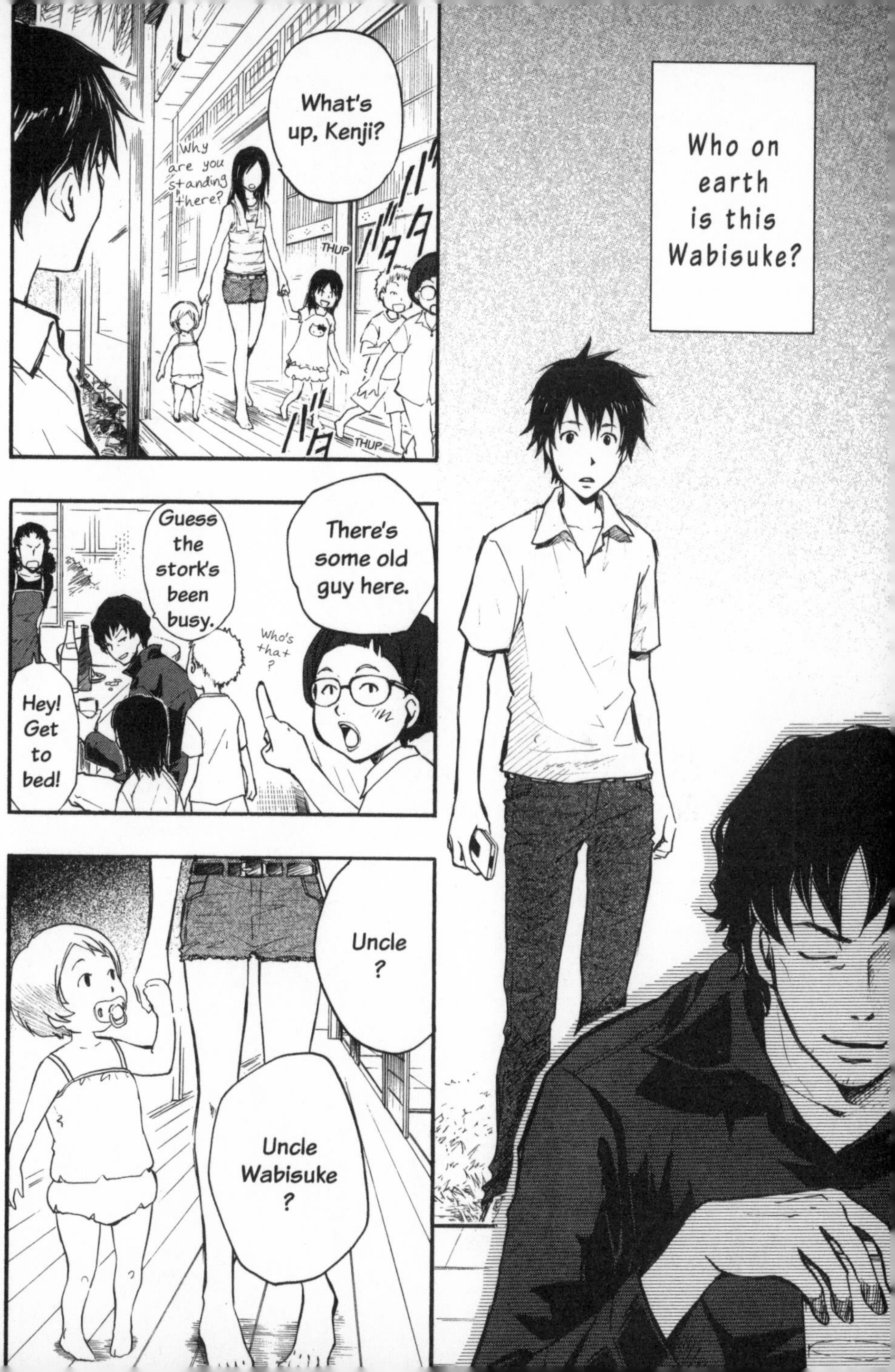
Who on earth is this Wabisuke?
What's up, Kenji?
Why are you standing there?
バタタ
THUP
バタ
THUP
There's some old guy here.
Who's that?
Guess the stork's been busy.
Hey! Get to bed!
Uncle?
Uncle Wabisuke?

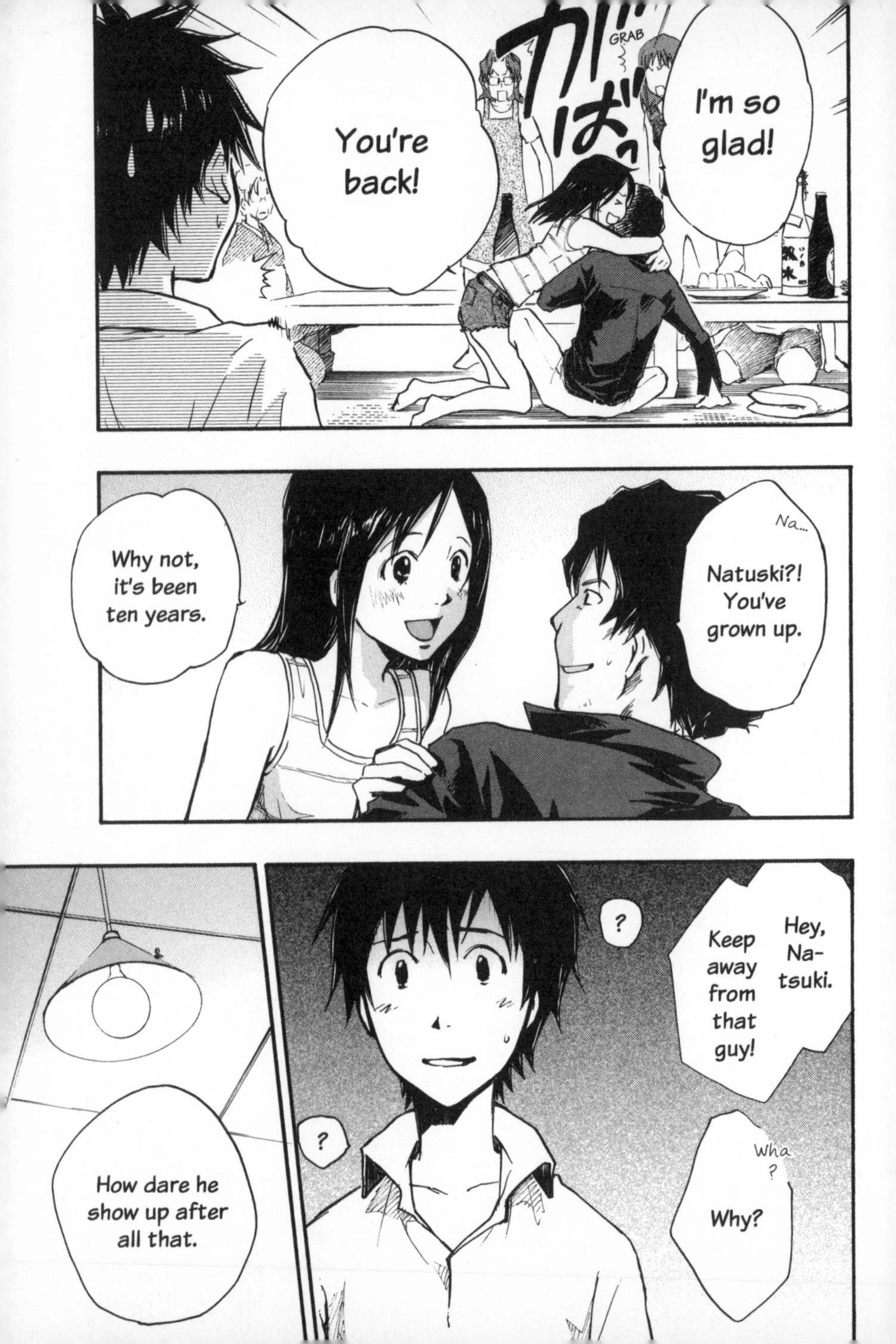
I'm so glad!
GRAB
You're back!
Na...
Natuski?! You've grown up.
Why not, it's been ten years.
Hey, Natsuki.
Keep away from that guy!
?
Wha ?
Why?
?
How dare he show up after all that.

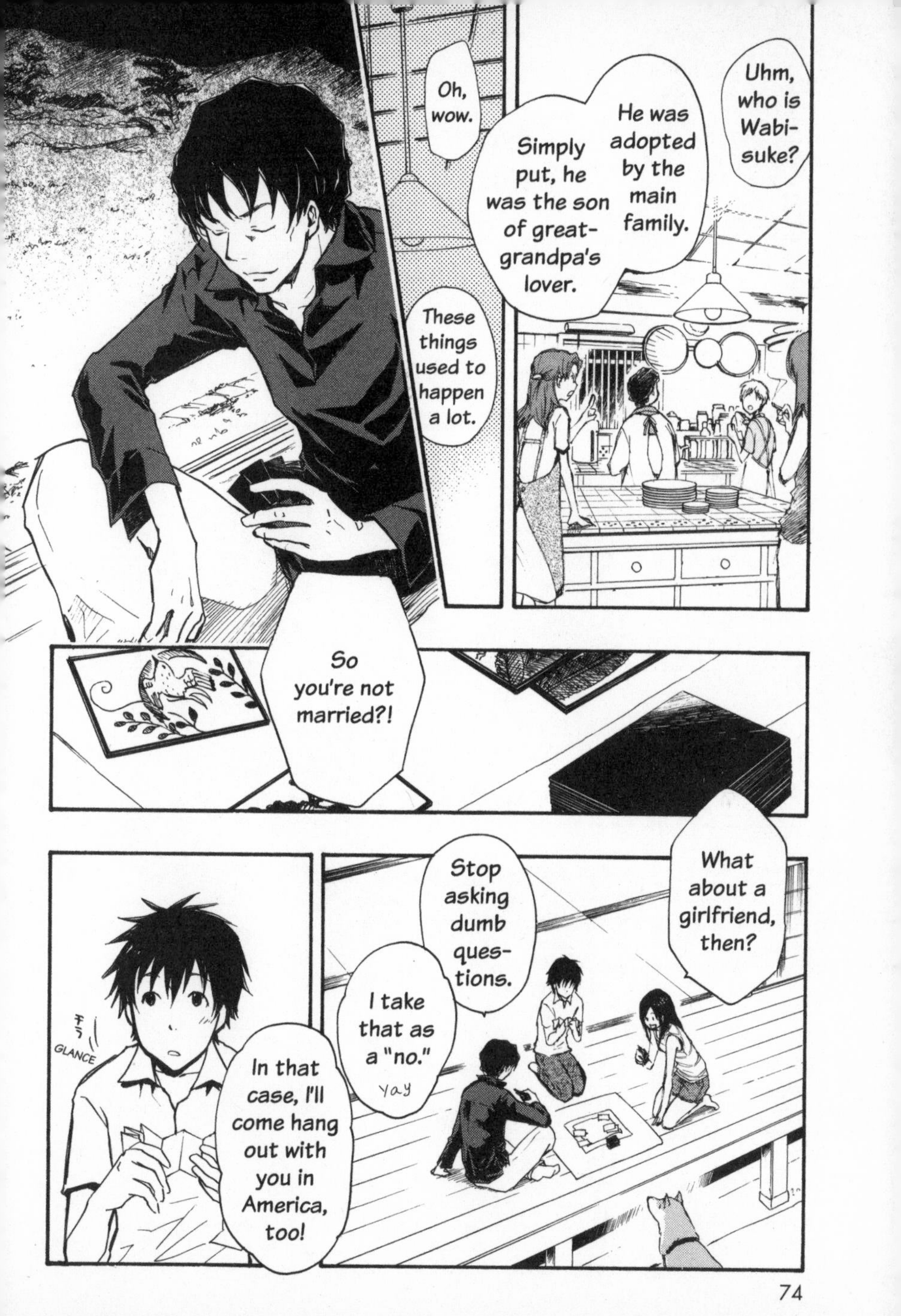
Uhm, who is Wabi-suke?
He was adopted by the main family.
Simply put, he was the son of great-grandpa's lover.
Oh, wow.
These things used to happen a lot.
So you're not married?!
What about a girlfriend, then?
Stop asking dumb questions.
I take that as a "no."
Yay
チラ
GLANCE
In that case, I'll come hang out with you in America, too!

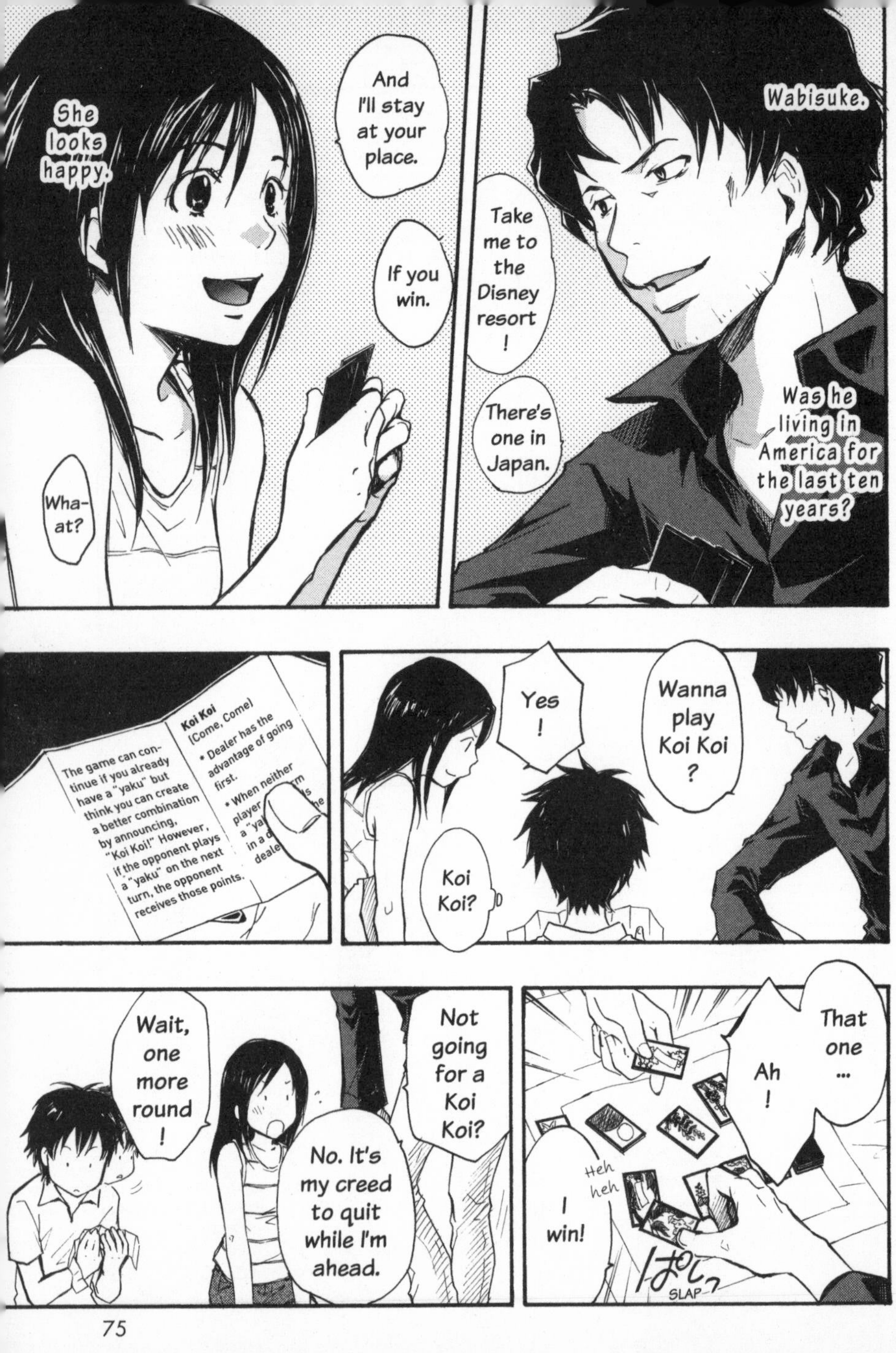
Wabisuke.
Take me to the Disney resort!
There's one in Japan.
Was he living in America for the last ten years?
And I'll stay at your place.
If you win.
She looks happy.
Wha-at?
Wanna play Koi Koi?
Yes!
Koi Koi?
Koi Koi
(Come, Come)
* Dealer has the advantage of going first.
* When neither
The game can continue if you already have a "yaku" but think you can create a better combination by announcing, "Koi Koi!" However, if the opponent plays a "yaku" on the next turn, the opponent receives those points.
That one ...
Ah!
Heh heh
I win!
ぱしっ
SLAP
Not going for a Koi Koi?
Wait, one more round!
No. It's my creed to quit while I'm ahead.

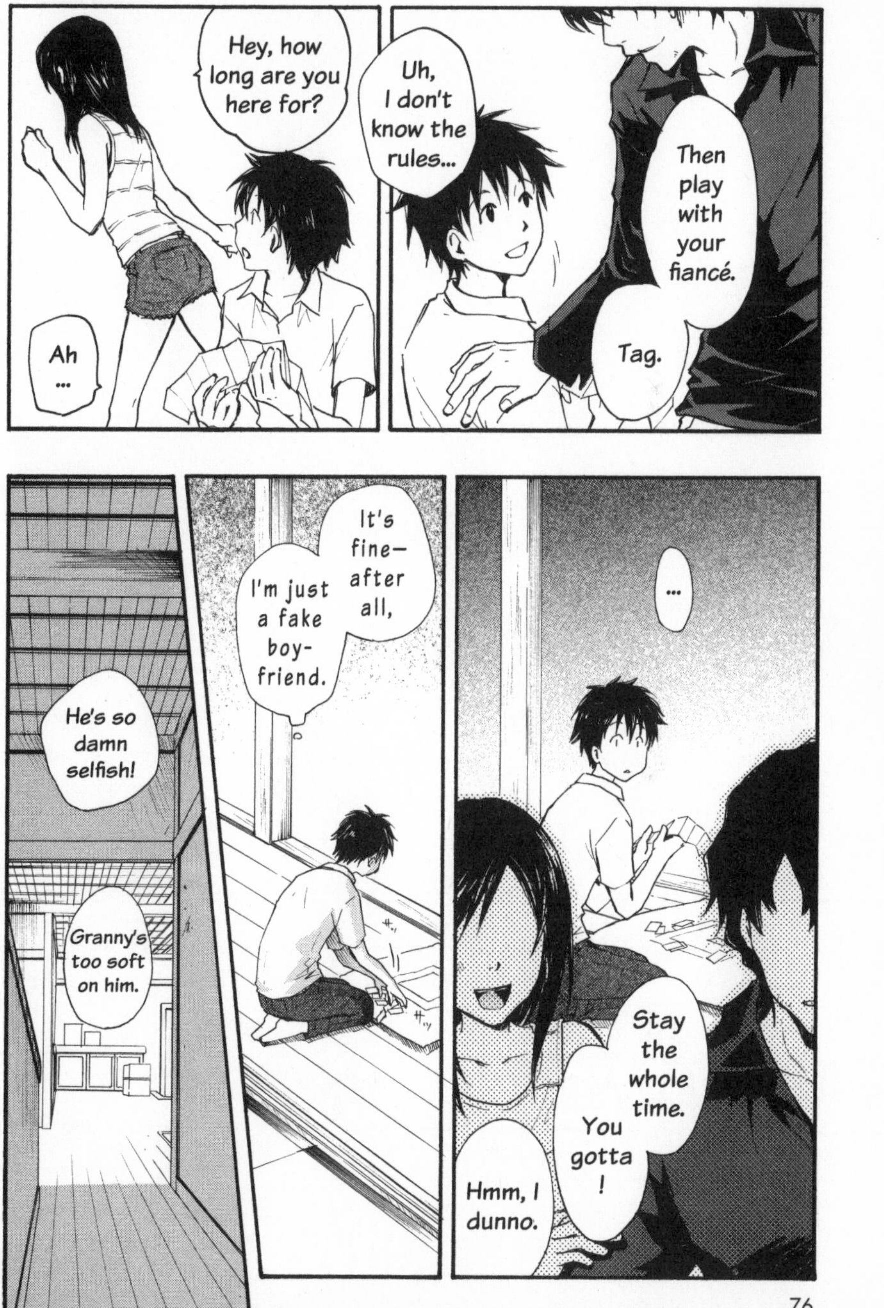
Uh, I don't know the rules...
Then play with your fiancé.
Tag.
Hey, how long are you here for?
Ah ...
...
Stay the whole time. You gotta!
Hmm, I dunno.
It's fine— after all, I'm just a fake boyfriend.
He's so damn selfish!
Granny's too soft on him.

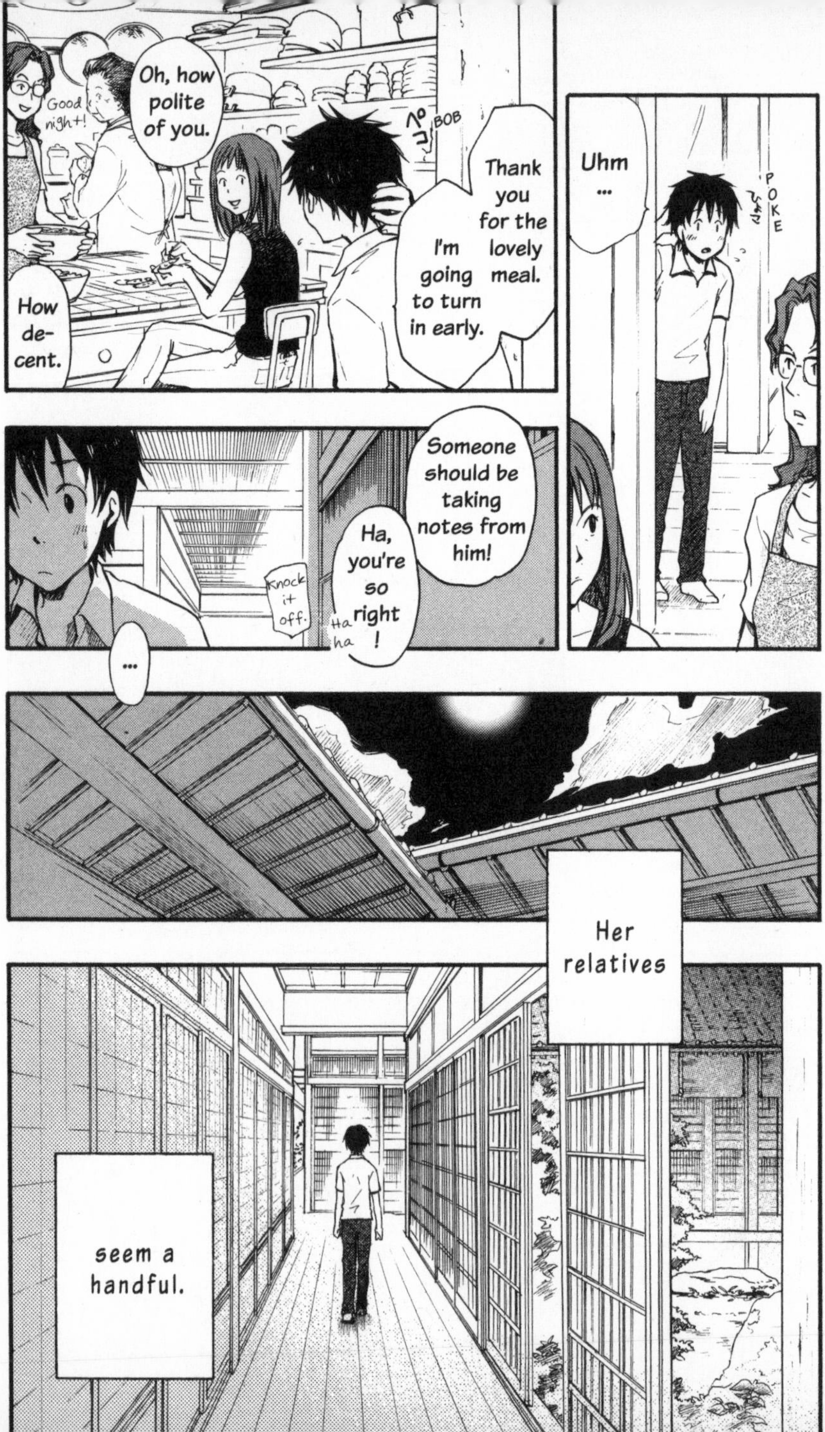
Uhm ...
POKE
Thank you for the lovely meal.
I'm going to turn in early.
BOB
Oh, how polite of you.
Good night!
How decent.
Someone should be taking notes from him!
Ha, you're so right!
Ha ha
Knock it off.
...
Her relatives
seem a handful.

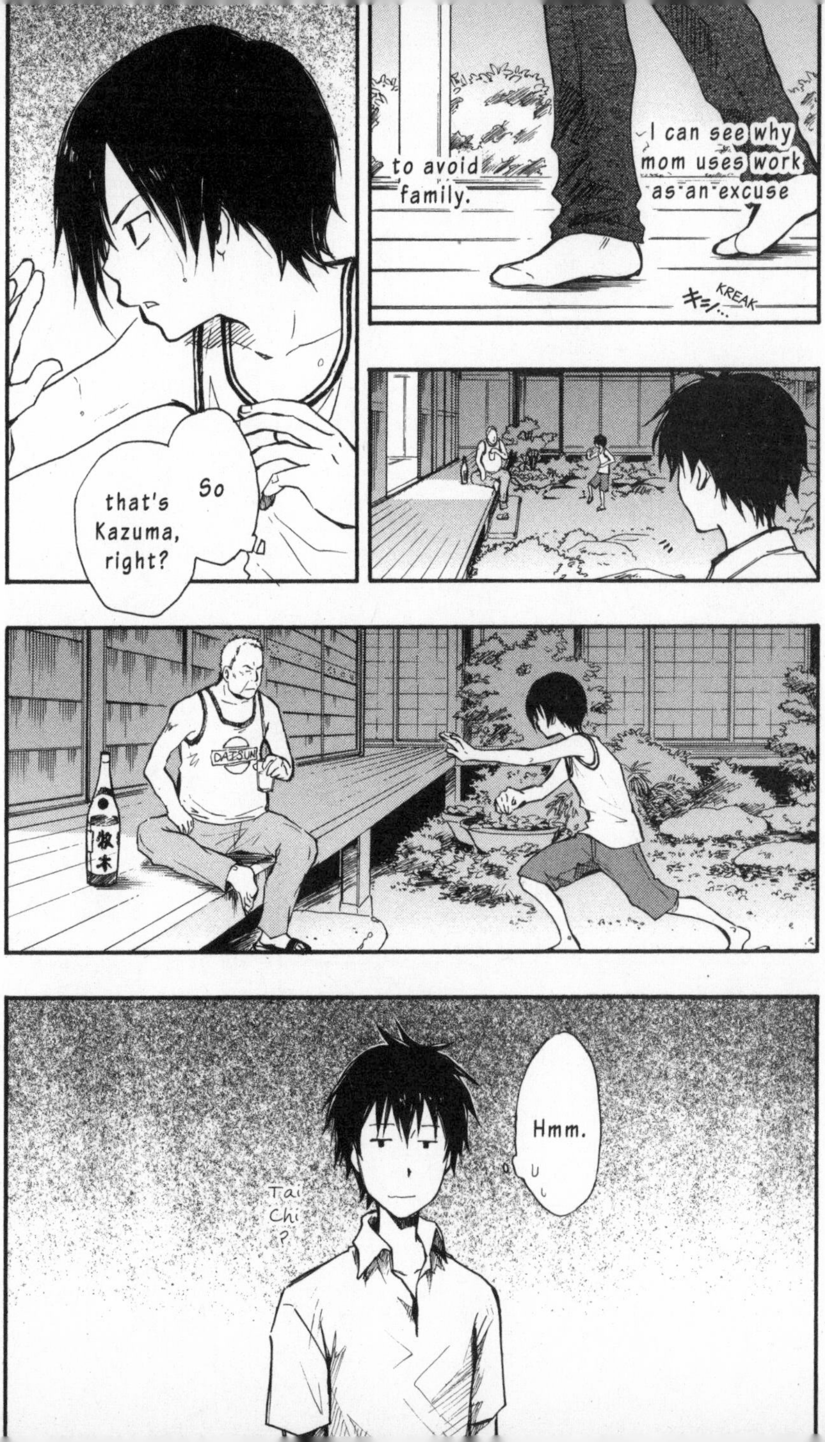
I can see why mom uses work as an excuse
to avoid family.
KREAK
キシ…
So that's Kazuma, right?
DAISUN
Hmm.
Tai Chi?

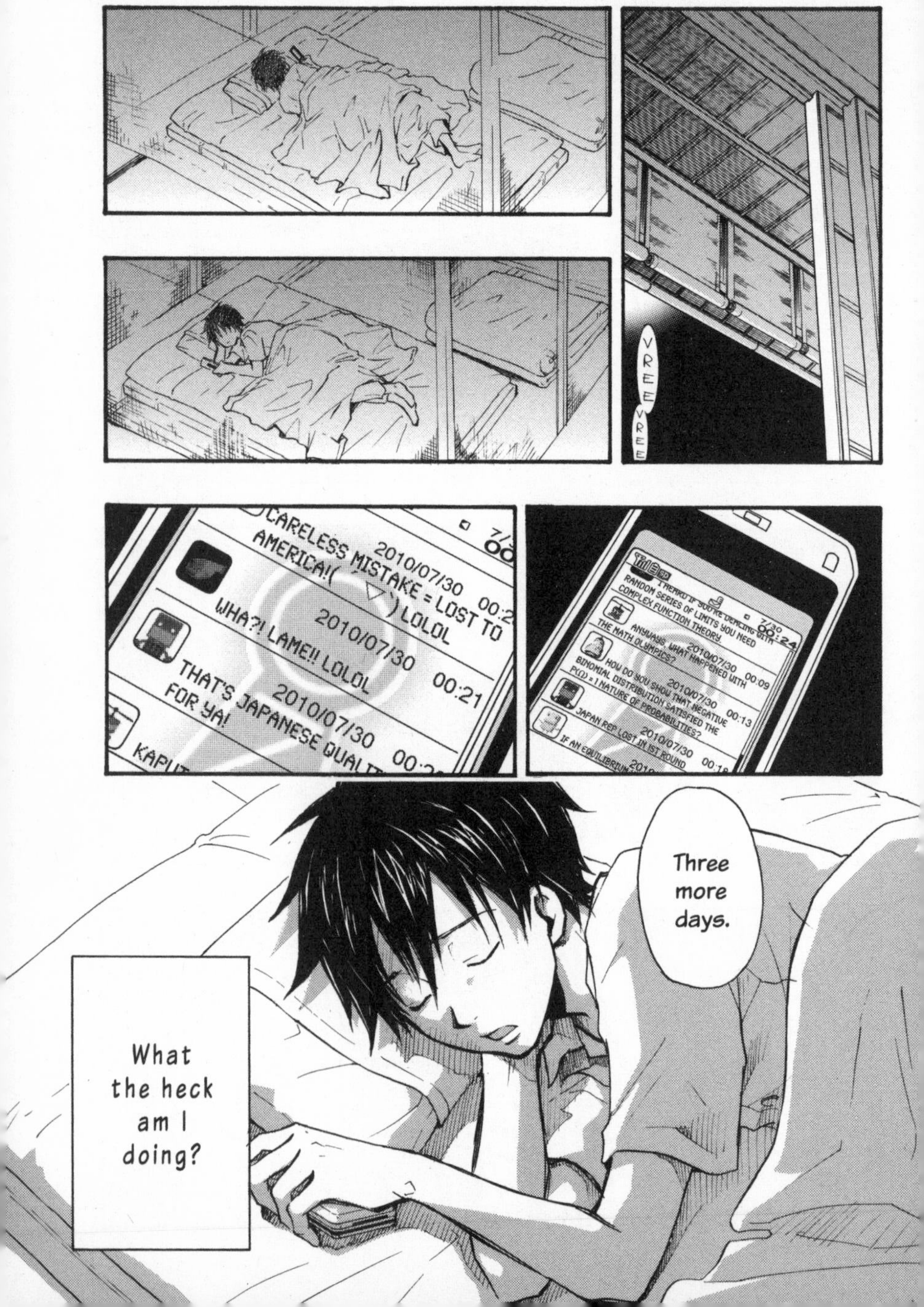
VREE VREE
7/30
00:24
I HEARD IF YOU'RE DEALING WITH RANDOM SERIES OF LIMITS YOU NEED COMPLEX FUNCTION THEORY.
2010/07/30 00:09
ANYWAYS, WHAT HAPPENED WITH THE MATH OLYMPICS?
2010/07/30 00:13
HOW DO YOU SHOW THAT NEGATIVE BINOMIAL DISTRIBUTION SATISFIED THE P(Ω) = 1 NATURE OF PROBABILITIES?
2010/07/30
JAPAN REP LOST IN 1ST ROUND
IF AN EQUILIBRIUM
CARELESS MISTAKE = LOST TO AMERICA!(▽) LOLOL
2010/07/30
WHA?! LAME!! LOLOL
2010/07/30 00:21
THAT'S JAPANESE QUALI
FOR YA!
2010/07/30
Three more days.
What the heck am I doing?

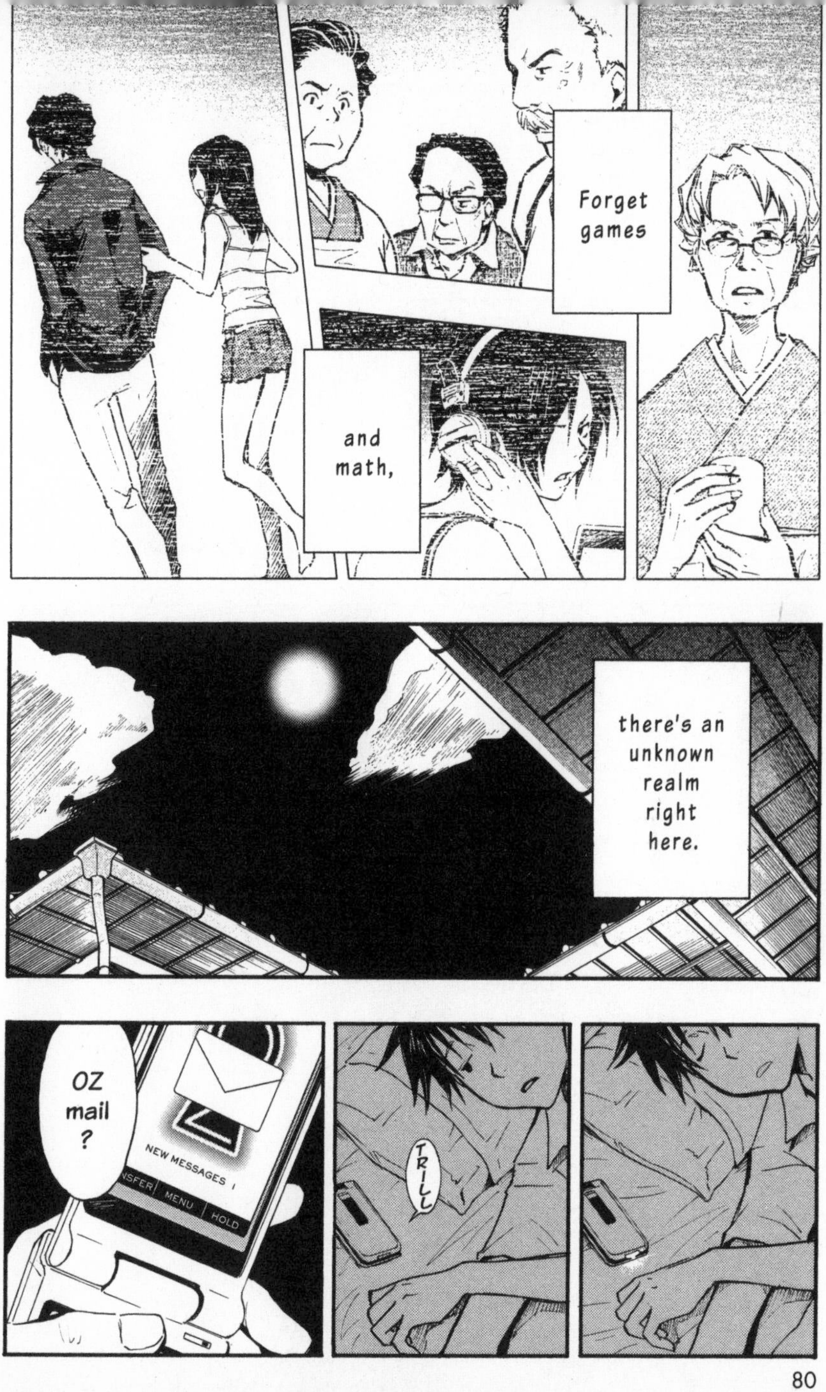
Forget games
and math,
there's an unknown realm right here.
TRILL
OZ mail ?
NEW MESSAGES 1
MENU
HOLD

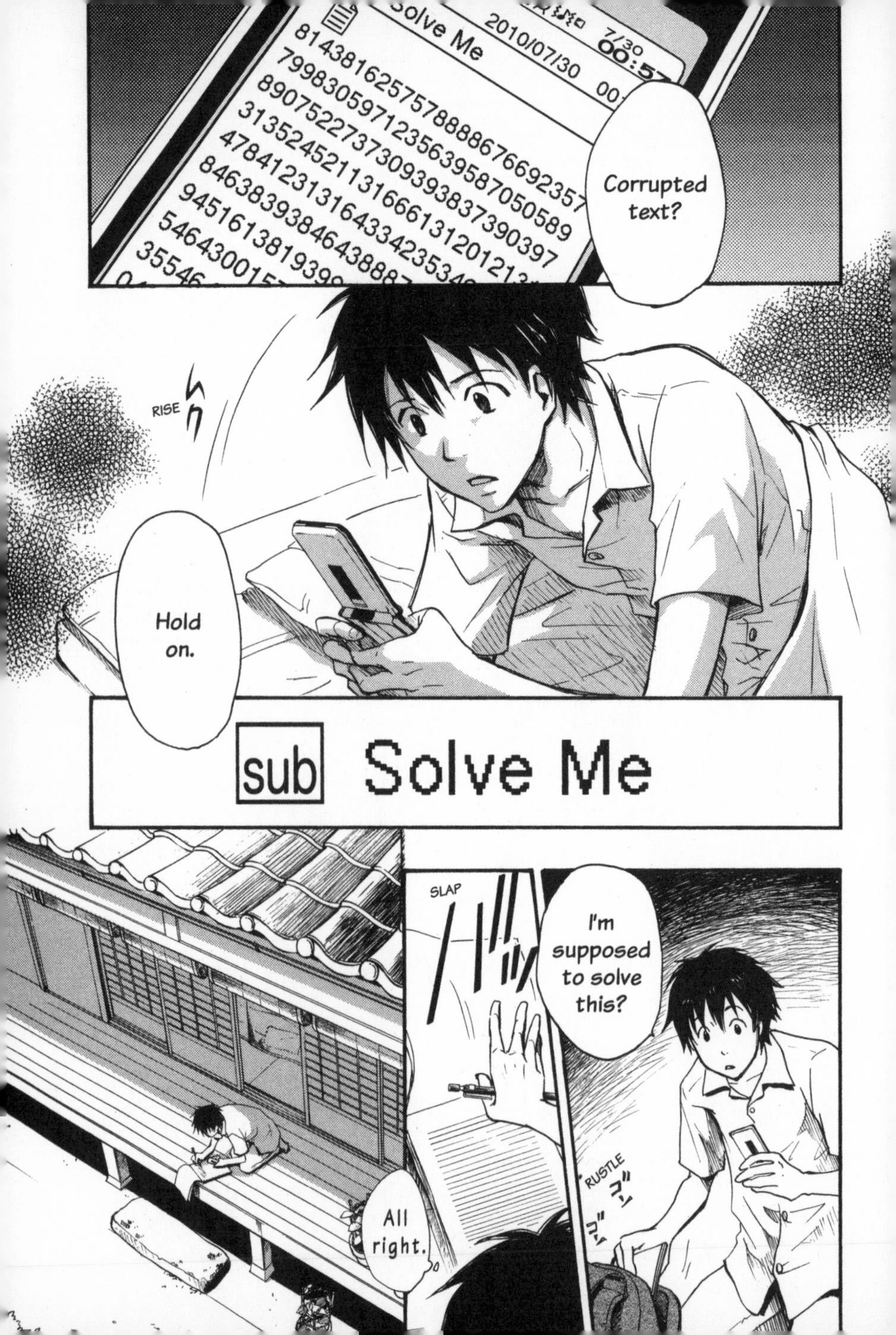
Solve Me
2010/07/30
7/30
00:57
8143816257578888676692357
7998305971235639587050589
8907522737309393837390397
313524521131666131201213
Corrupted text?
RISE
Hold on.
sub Solve Me
SLAP
I'm supposed to solve this?
RUSTLE
All right.

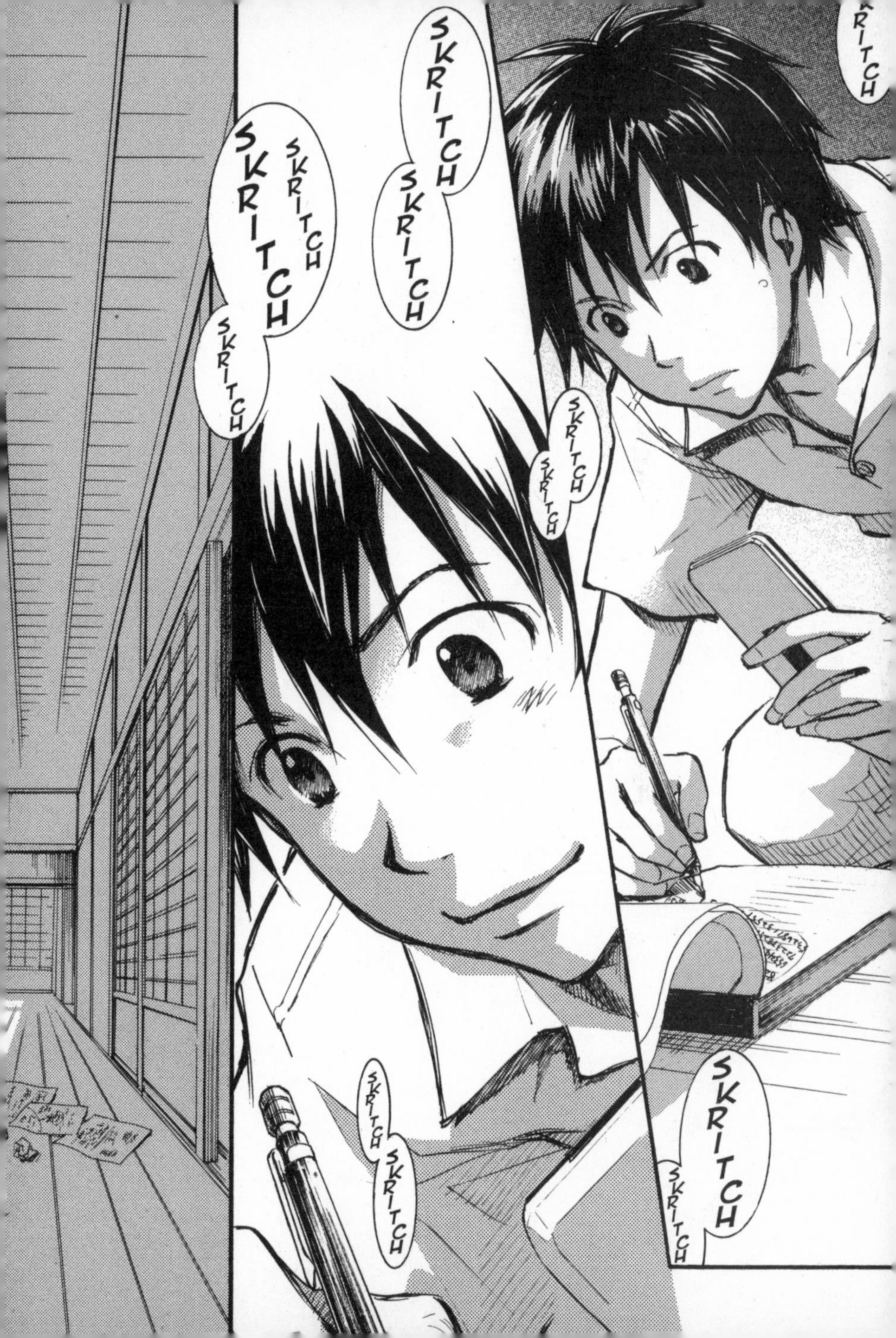
SKRITCH
SKRITCH
SKRITCH
SKRITCH
SKRITCH
SKRITCH
SKRITCH
SKRITCH
SKRITCH
SKRITCH
SKRITCH
SKRITCH

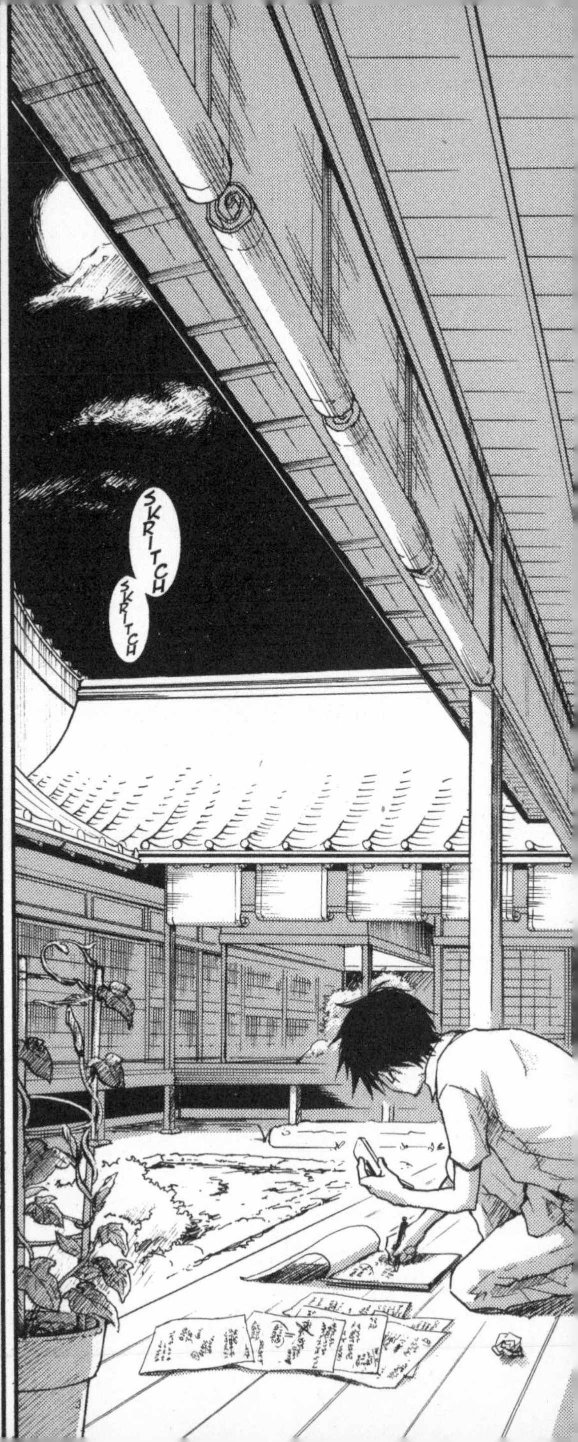
SKRITCH
SKRITCH
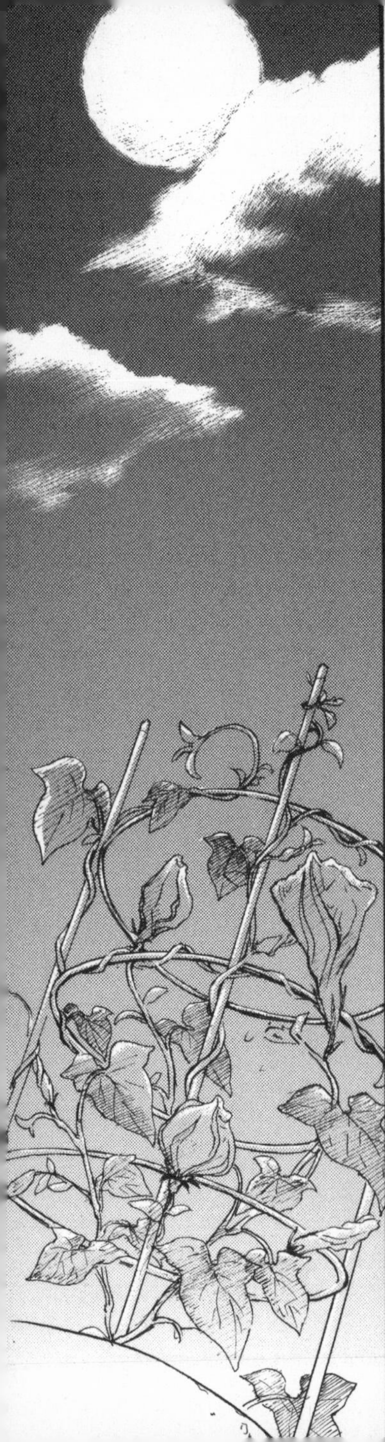

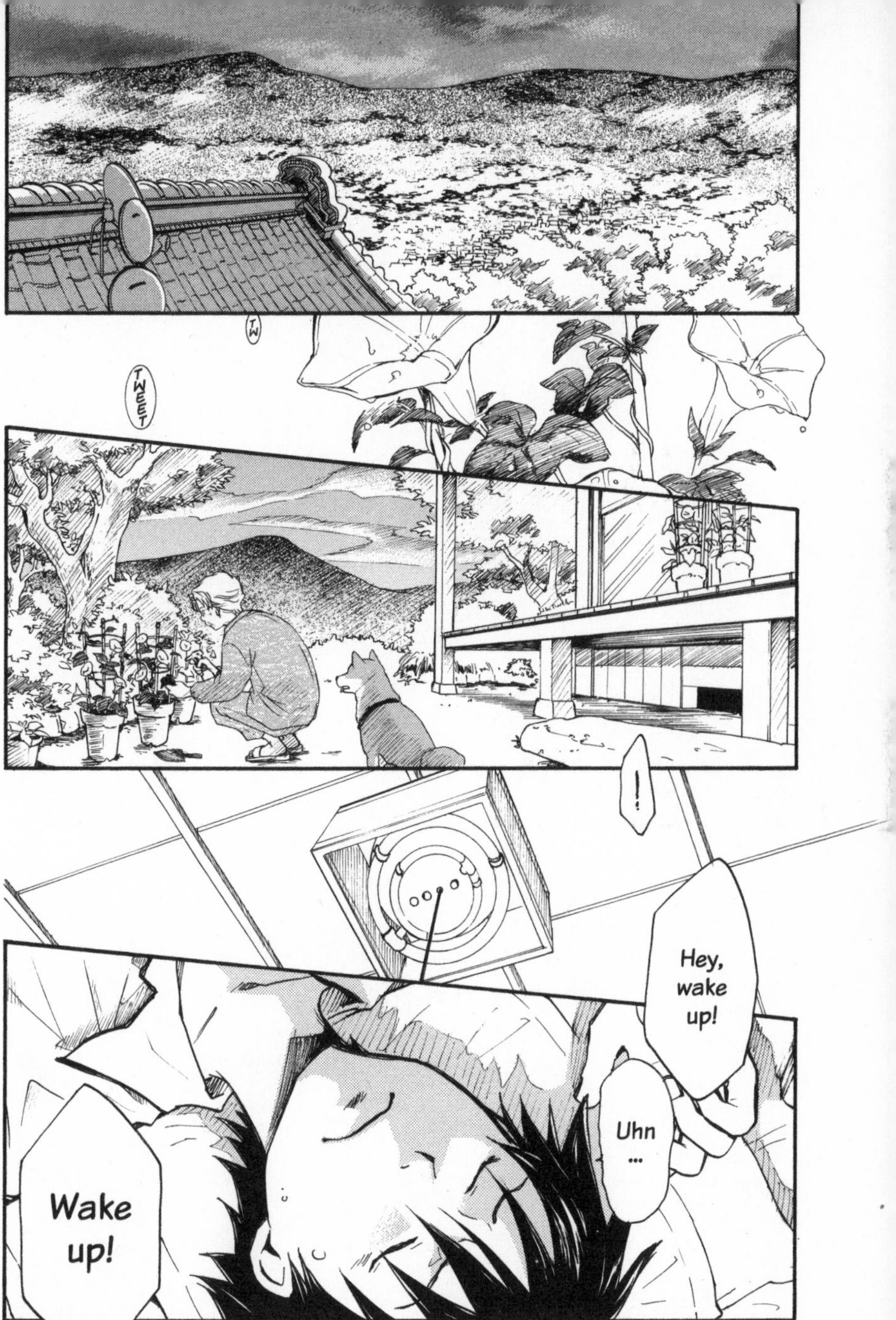
TW
TWEET
!
Hey, wake up!
Uhn ...
Wake up!

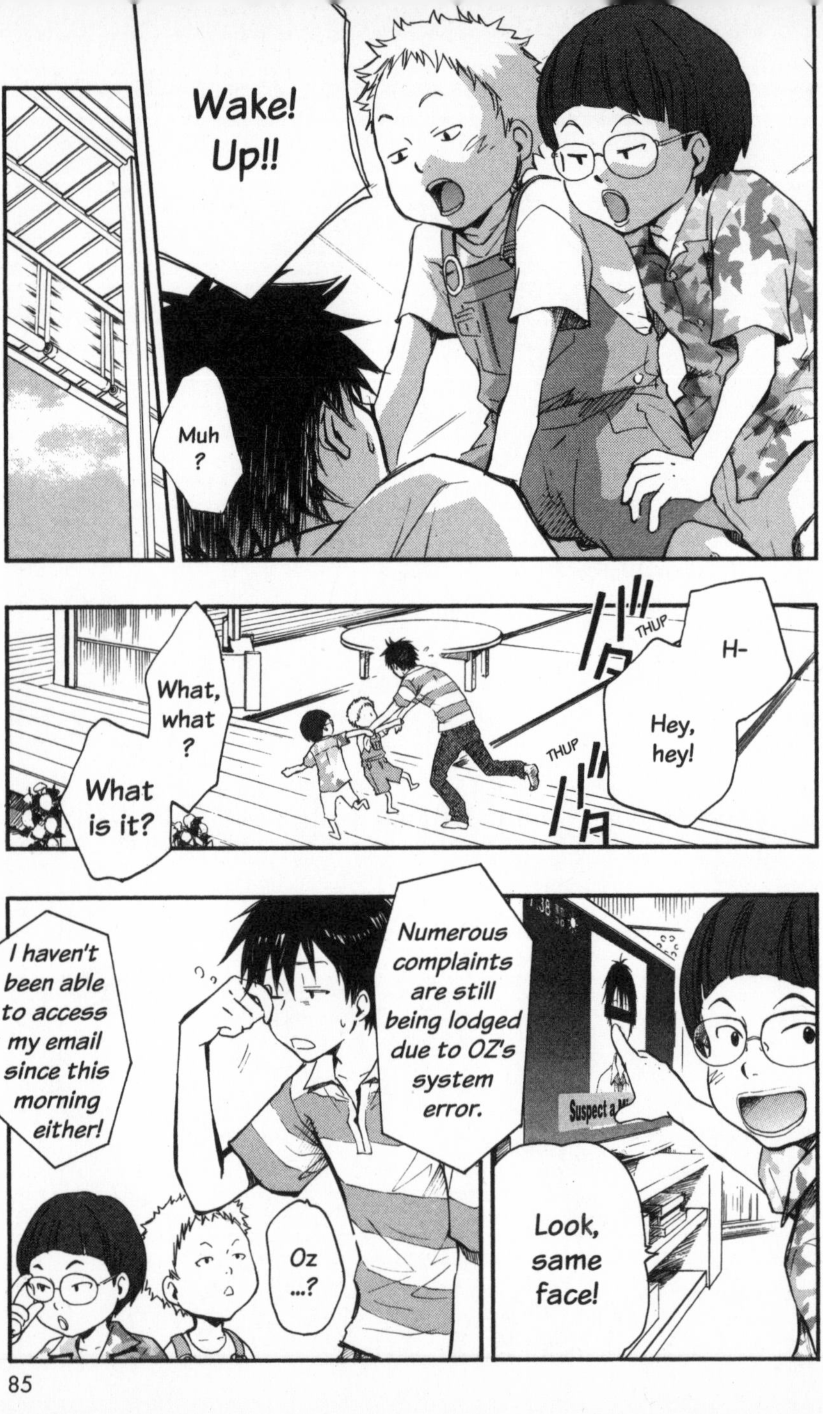

Wake! Up!!
Muh ?
H-
Hey, hey!
THUP
THUP
What, what ?
What is it?
Numerous complaints are still being lodged due to OZ's system error.
Suspect a M
Look, same face!
I haven't been able to access my email since this morning either!
Oz ...?

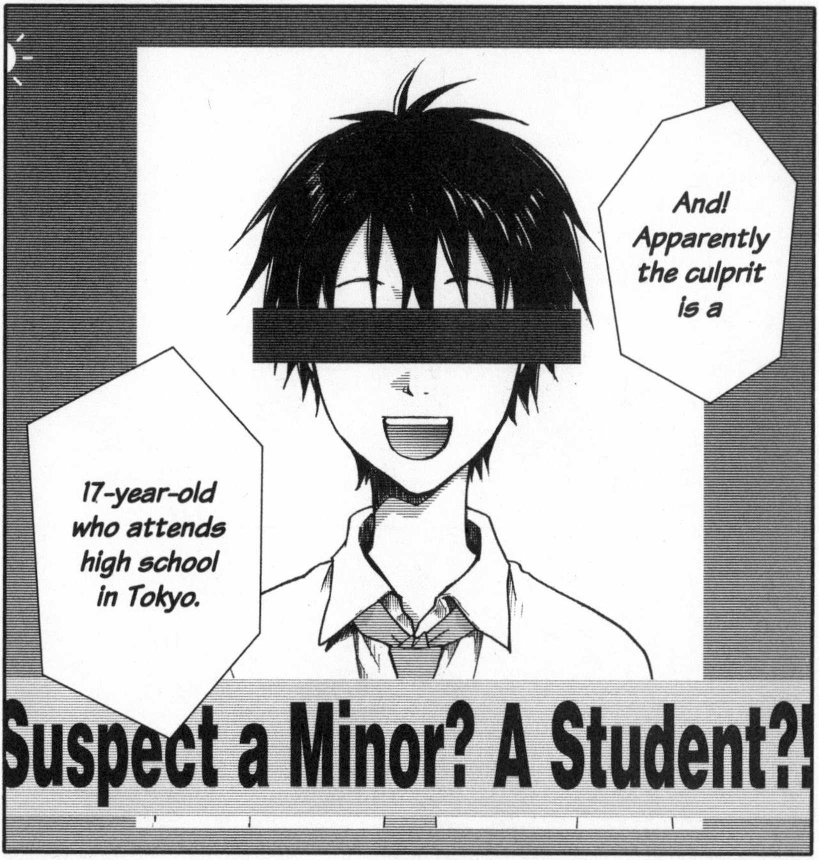
And! Apparently the culprit is a
17-year-old who attends high school in Tokyo.
Suspect a Minor? A Student?!

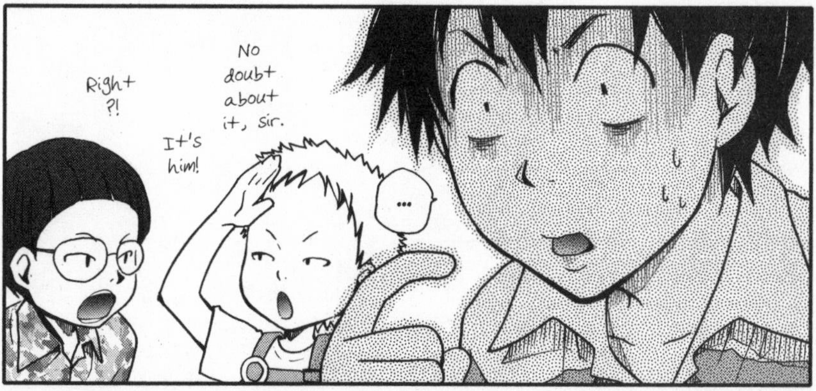
...
No doubt about it, sir.
It's him!
Right?!

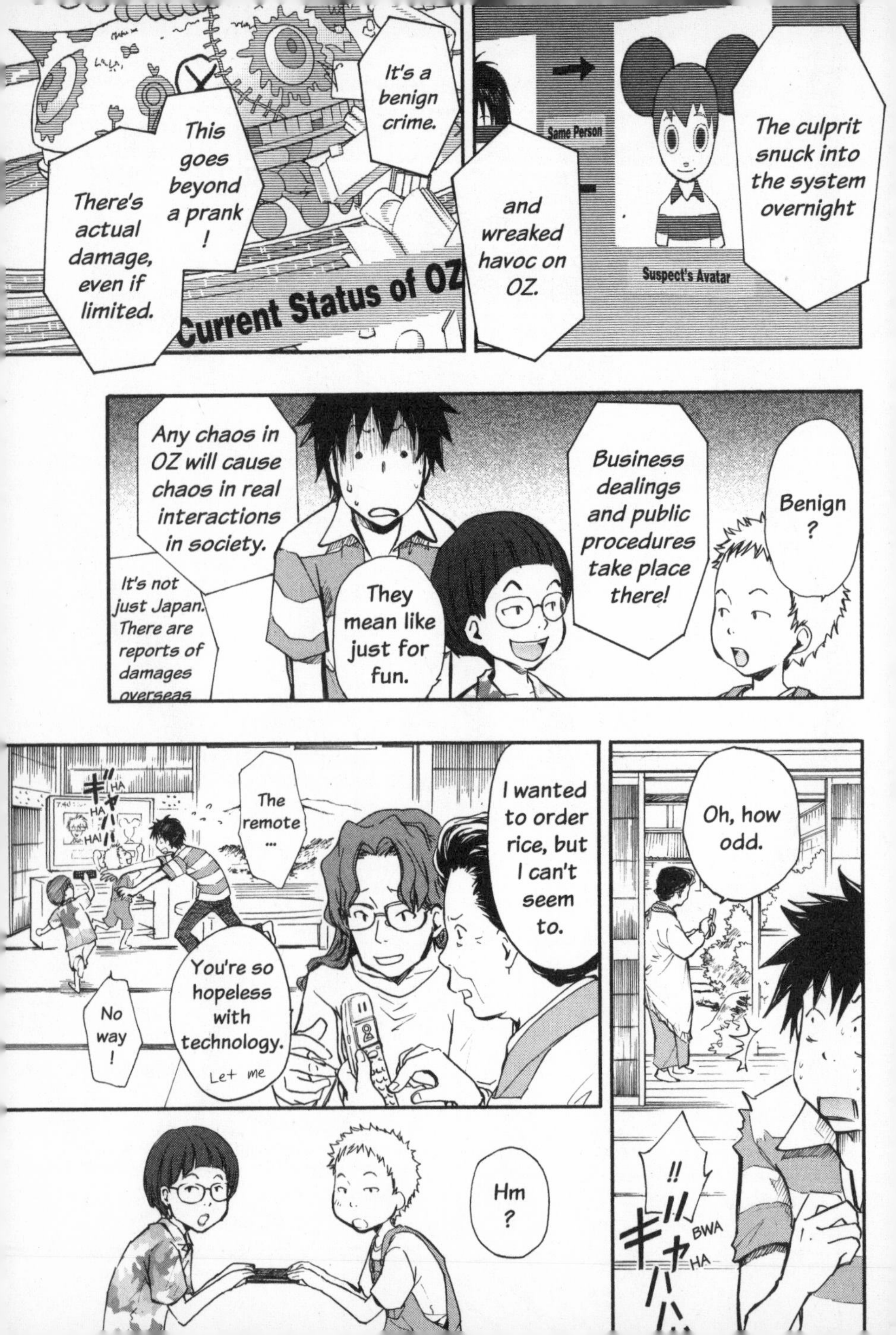
Suspect's Avatar
The culprit snuck into the system overnight
Same Person
and wreaked havoc on OZ.
It's a benign crime.
This goes beyond a prank!
There's actual damage, even if limited.
Current Status of OZ
Benign?
Business dealings and public procedures take place there!
They mean like just for fun.
Any chaos in OZ will cause chaos in real interactions in society.
It's not just Japan. There are reports of damages overseas
Oh, how odd.
!!
ギャハハハ
BWA HA
I wanted to order rice, but I can't seem to.
The remote ...
You're so hopeless with technology.
Let me
ギャハハ
HA HA HA!
No way!
Hm?

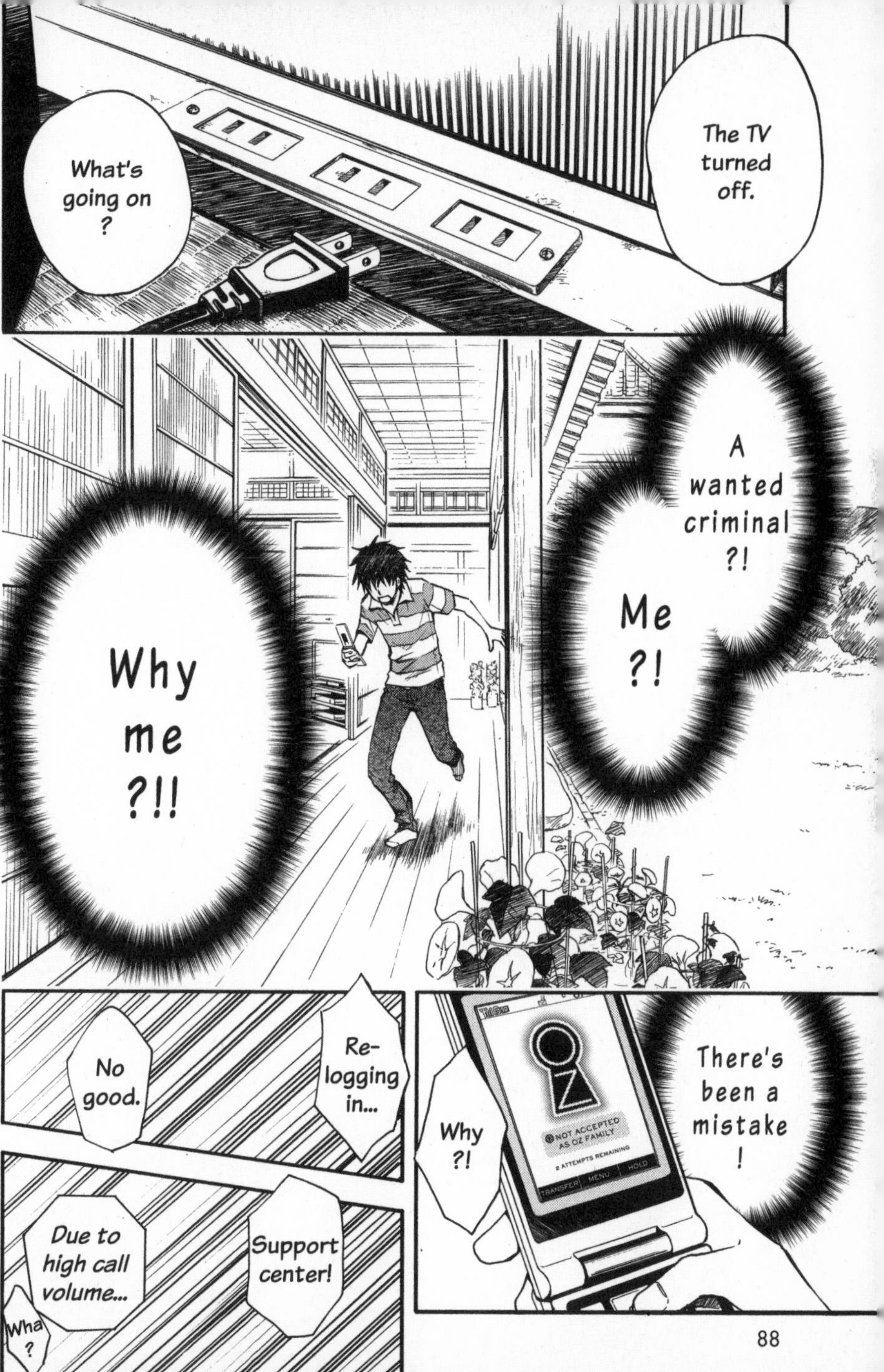
The TV turned off.
What's going on ?
A wanted criminal ?!
Me ?!
Why me ?!!
There's been a mistake !
Why ?!
NOT ACCEPTED AS OZ FAMILY
2 ATTEMPTS REMAINING
TRANSFER MENU HOLD
Re-logging in...
No good.
Support center!
Due to high call volume...
Wha ?

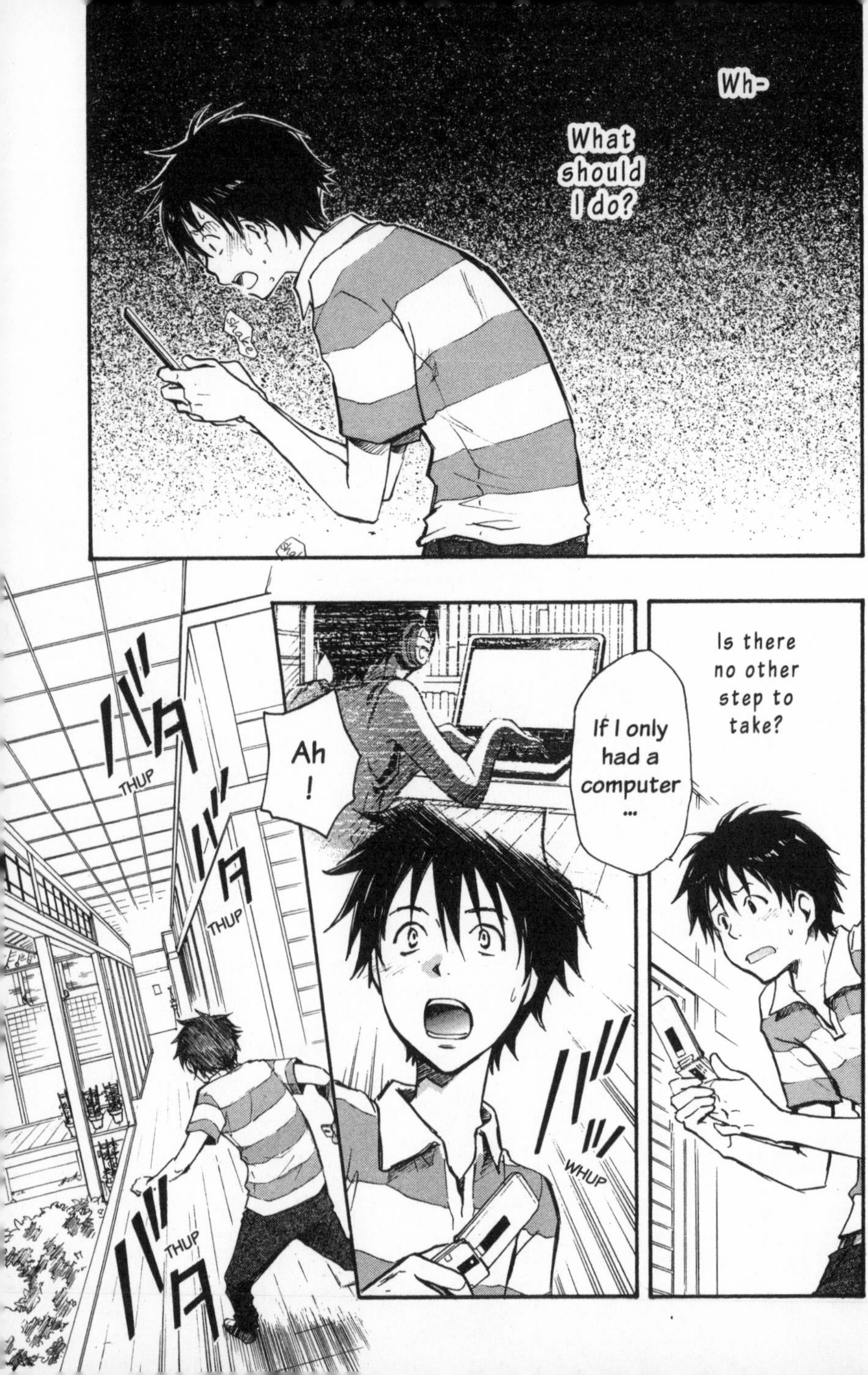
Wh-
What should I do?
shake
Is there no other step to take?
If I only had a computer ...
Ah !
WHUP
THUP
THUP
THUP

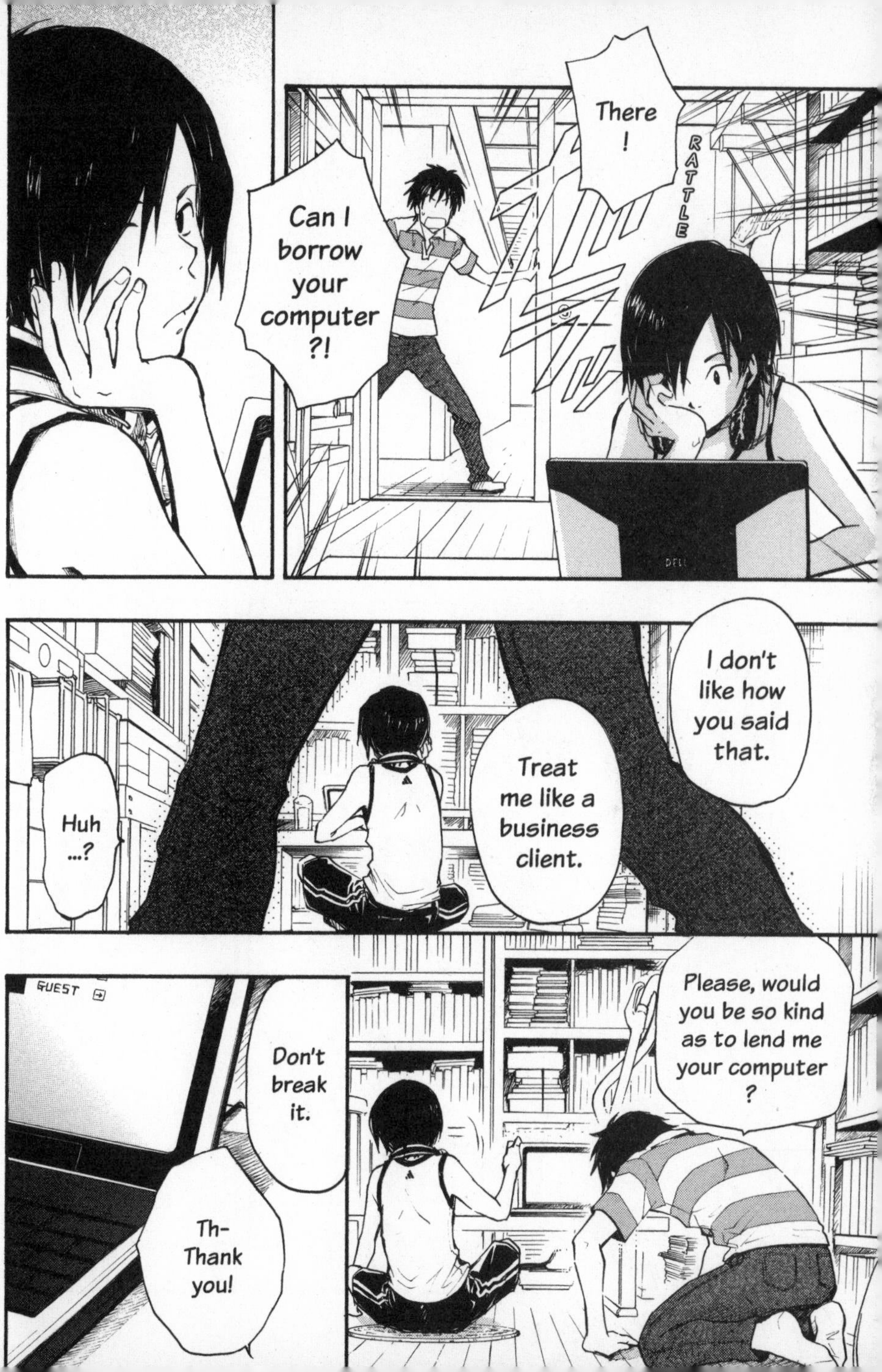
There!
RATTLE
Can I borrow your computer?!
I don't like how you said that.
Treat me like a business client.
Huh ...?
Please, would you be so kind as to lend me your computer?
Don't break it.
GUEST
Th- Thank you!

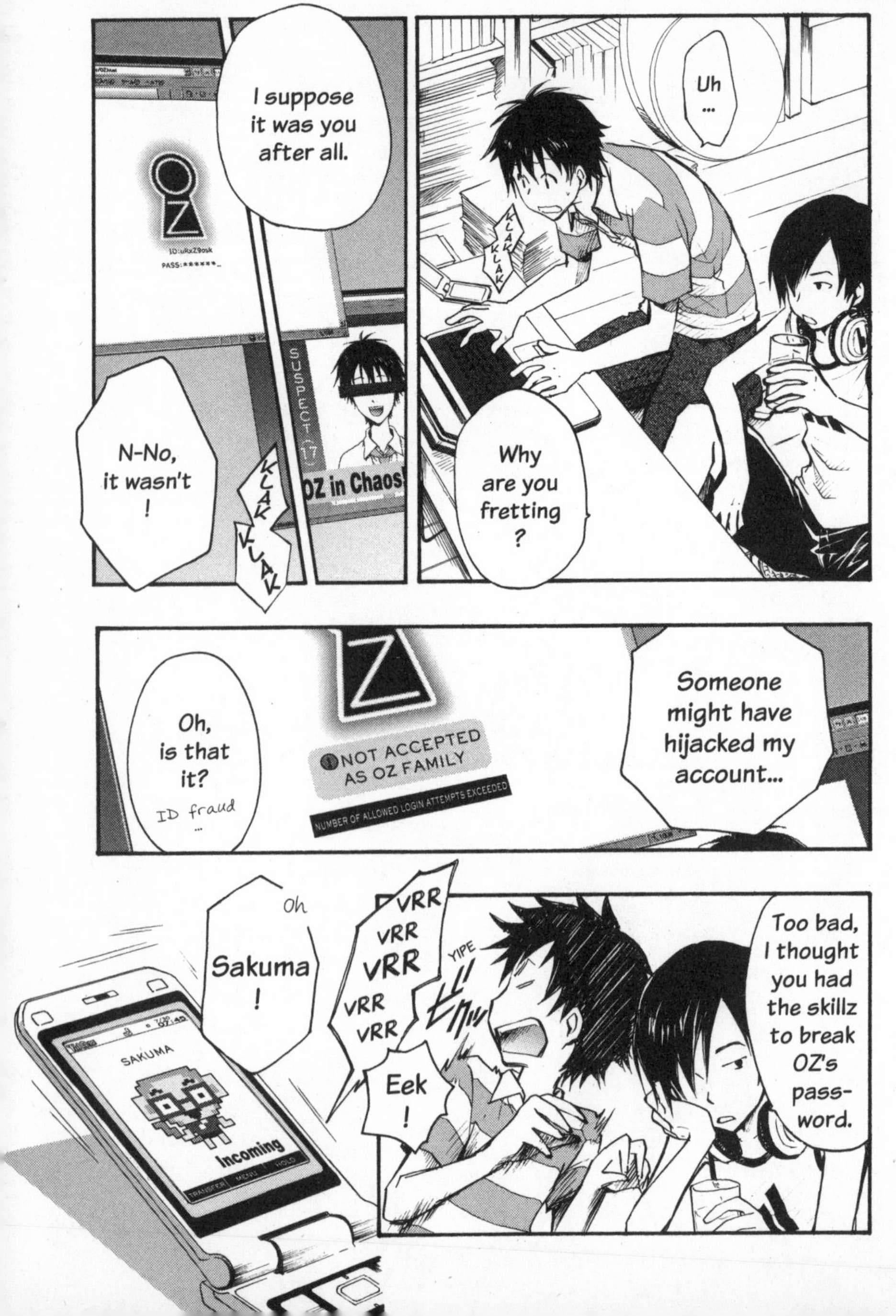
Uh ...
KLAK KLAK
Why are you fretting ?
I suppose it was you after all.
SUSPECT 17
OZ in Chaos!
N-No, it wasn't !
KLAK KLAK
Someone might have hijacked my account...
NOT ACCEPTED AS OZ FAMILY
NUMBER OF ALLOWED LOGIN ATTEMPTS EXCEEDED
Oh, is that it?
ID fraud ...
Too bad, I thought you had the skillz to break OZ's pass-word.
YIPE
Eek !
VRR VRR VRR VRR VRR
Oh
Sakuma !
SAKUMA
Incoming
TRANSFER
MENU
HOLD

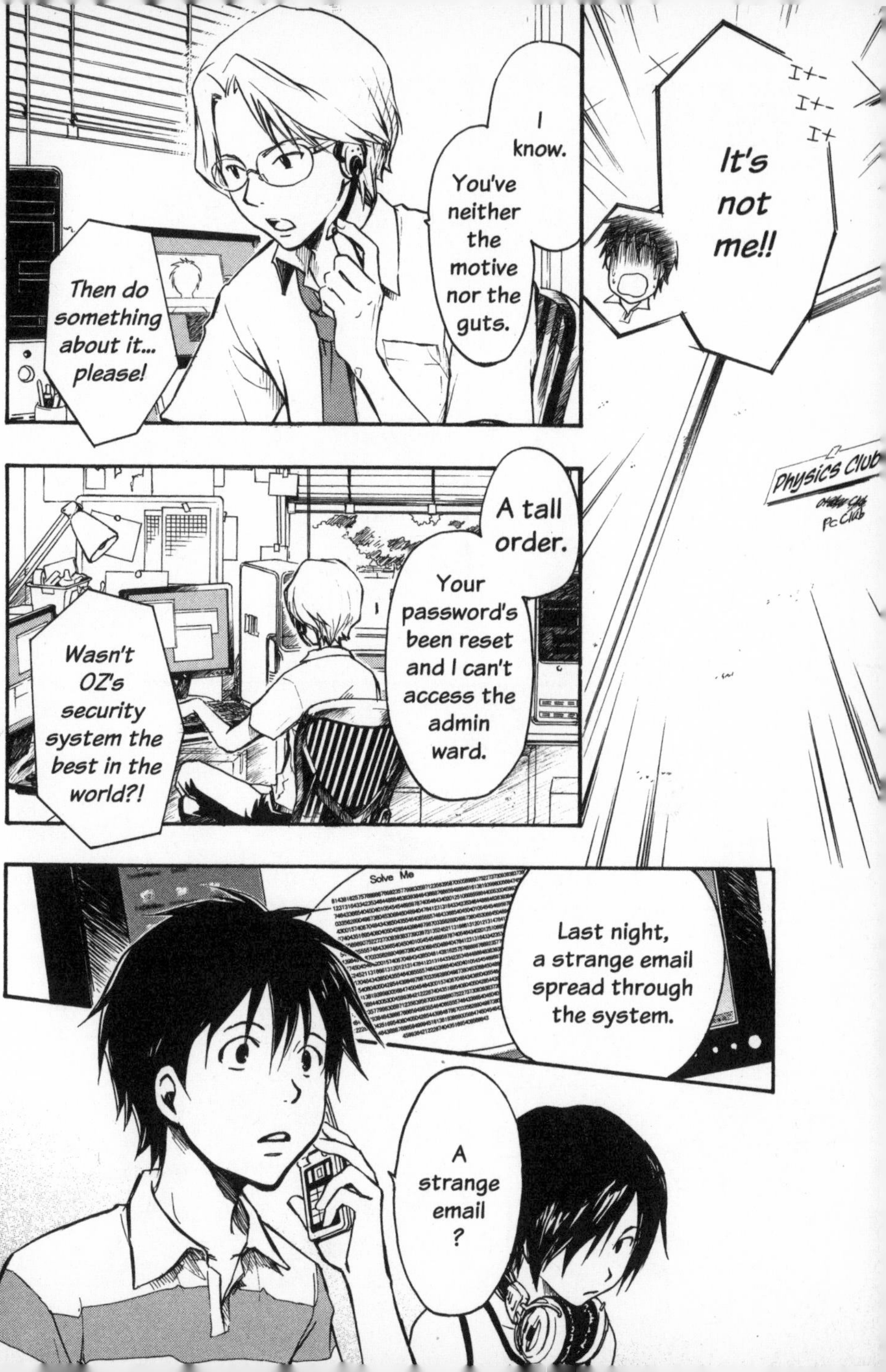

It- It- It
It's not me!!
Physics Club
Pc Club
I know. You've neither the motive nor the guts.
Then do something about it... please!
A tall order.
Your password's been reset and I can't access the admin ward.
Wasn't OZ's security system the best in the world?!
Solve Me
Last night, a strange email spread through the system.
A strange email?

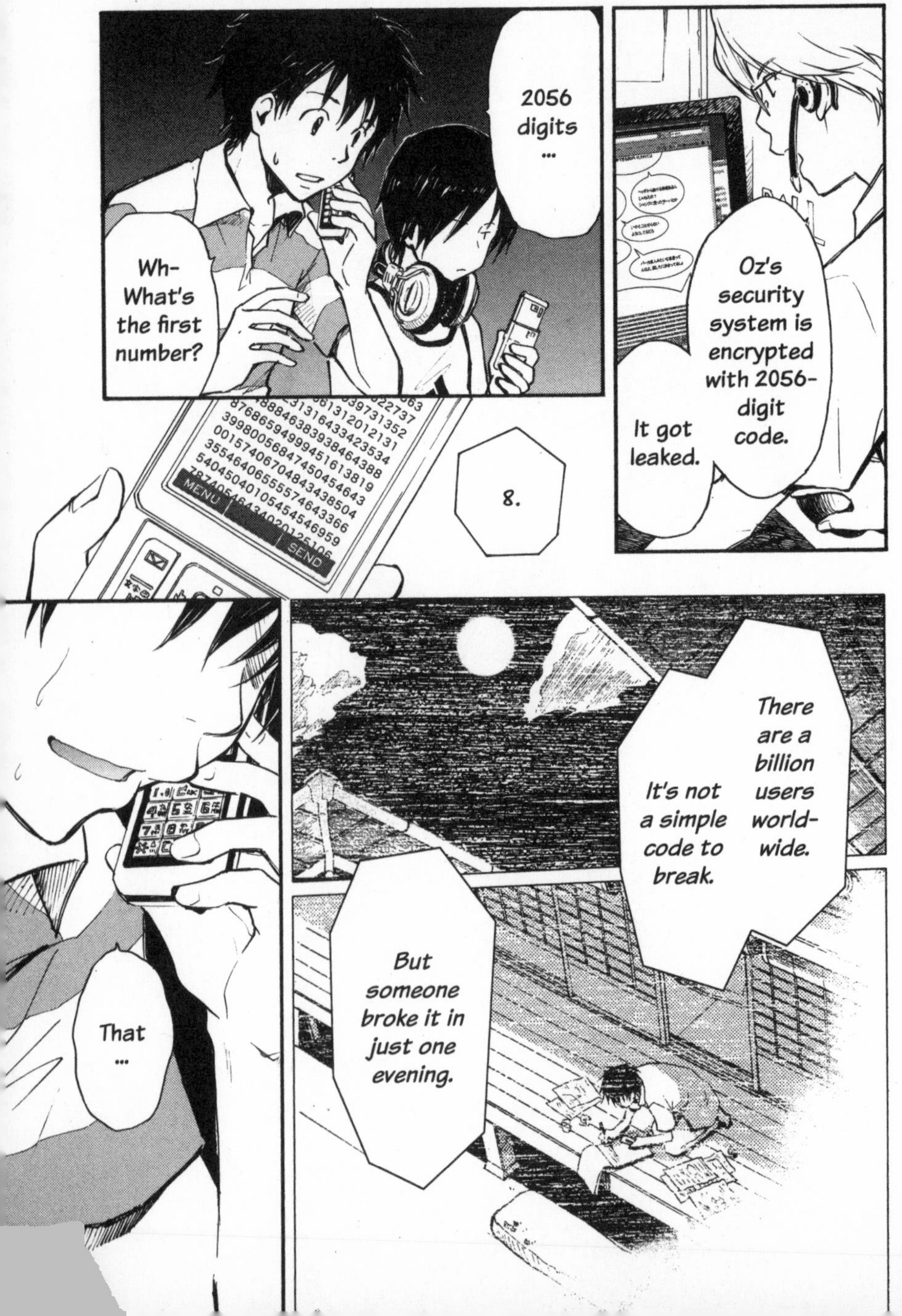
Oz's security system is encrypted with 2056-digit code.
It got leaked.
2056 digits ...
Wh- What's the first number?
MENU
SEND
8.
There are a billion users world-wide.
It's not a simple code to break.
But someone broke it in just one evening.
That ...

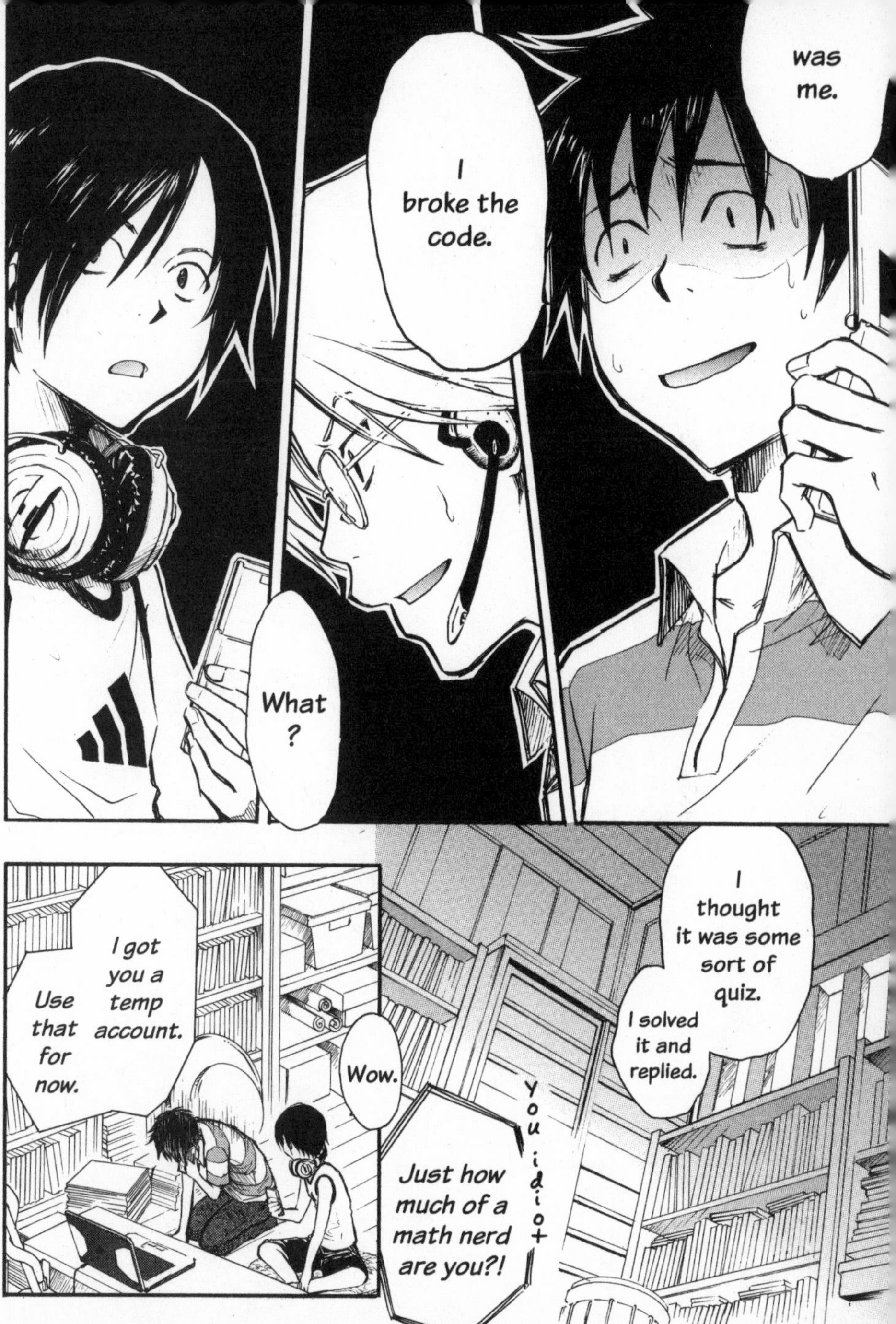
was me.
I broke the code.
What?
I thought it was some sort of quiz.
I solved it and replied.
You idiot
Just how much of a math nerd are you?!
Wow.
I got you a temp account.
Use that for now.

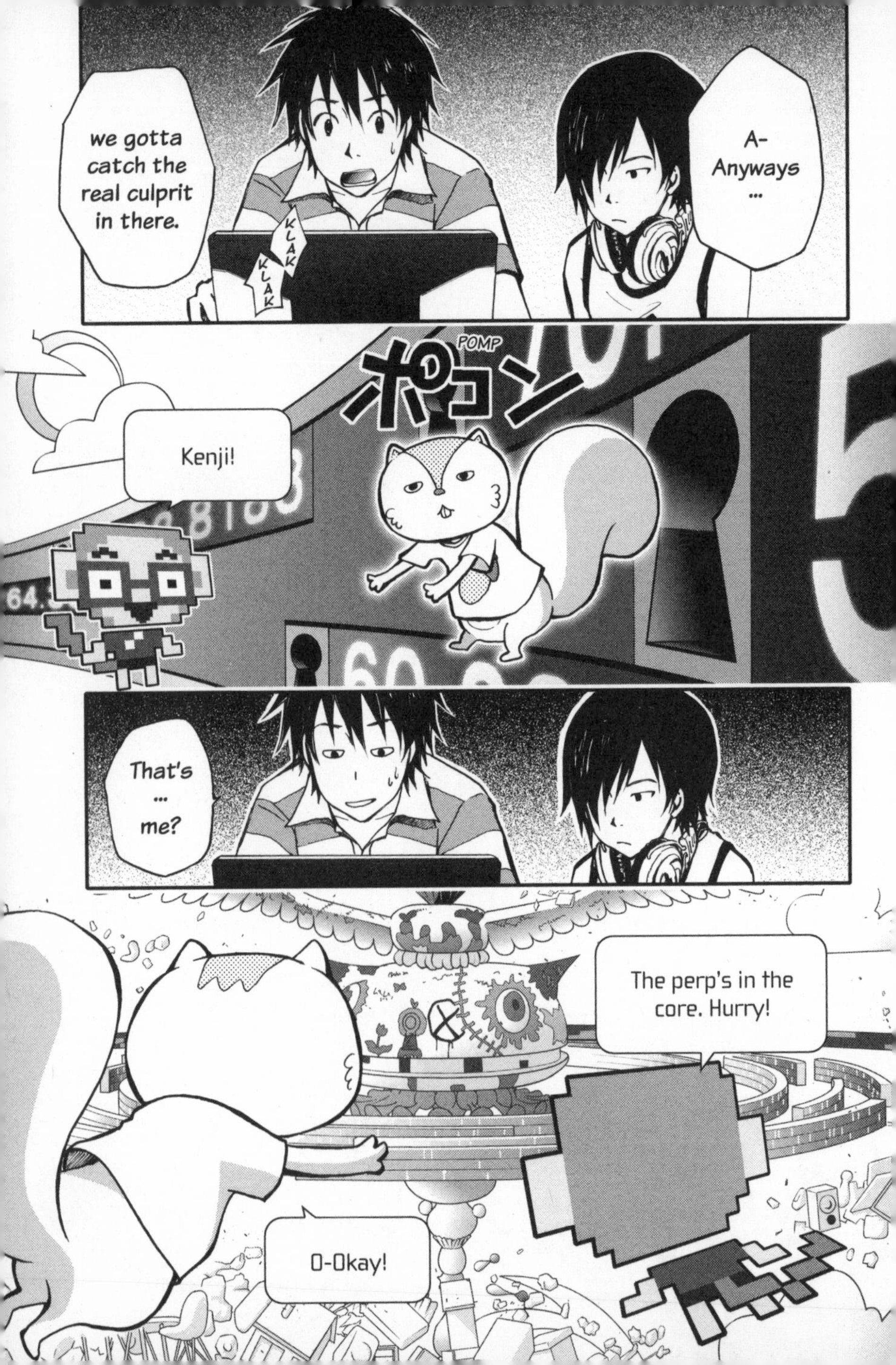
A-
Anyways
...
we gotta catch the real culprit in there.
KLAK
KLAK
POMP
Kenji!
That's ... me?
The perp's in the core. Hurry!
O-Okay!

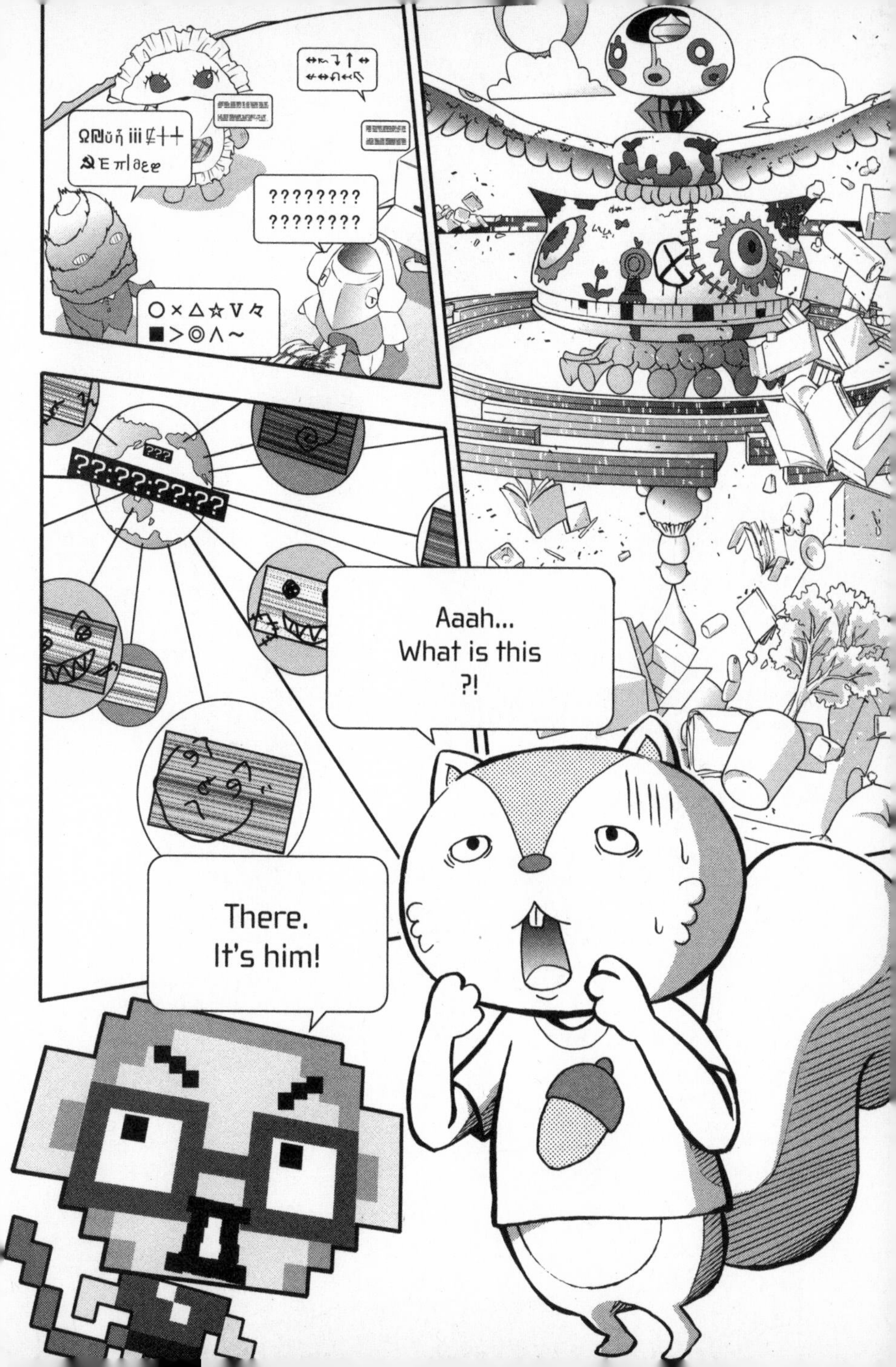
????????
????????
???
??:??:??:??
Aaah...
What is this
?!
There.
It's him!

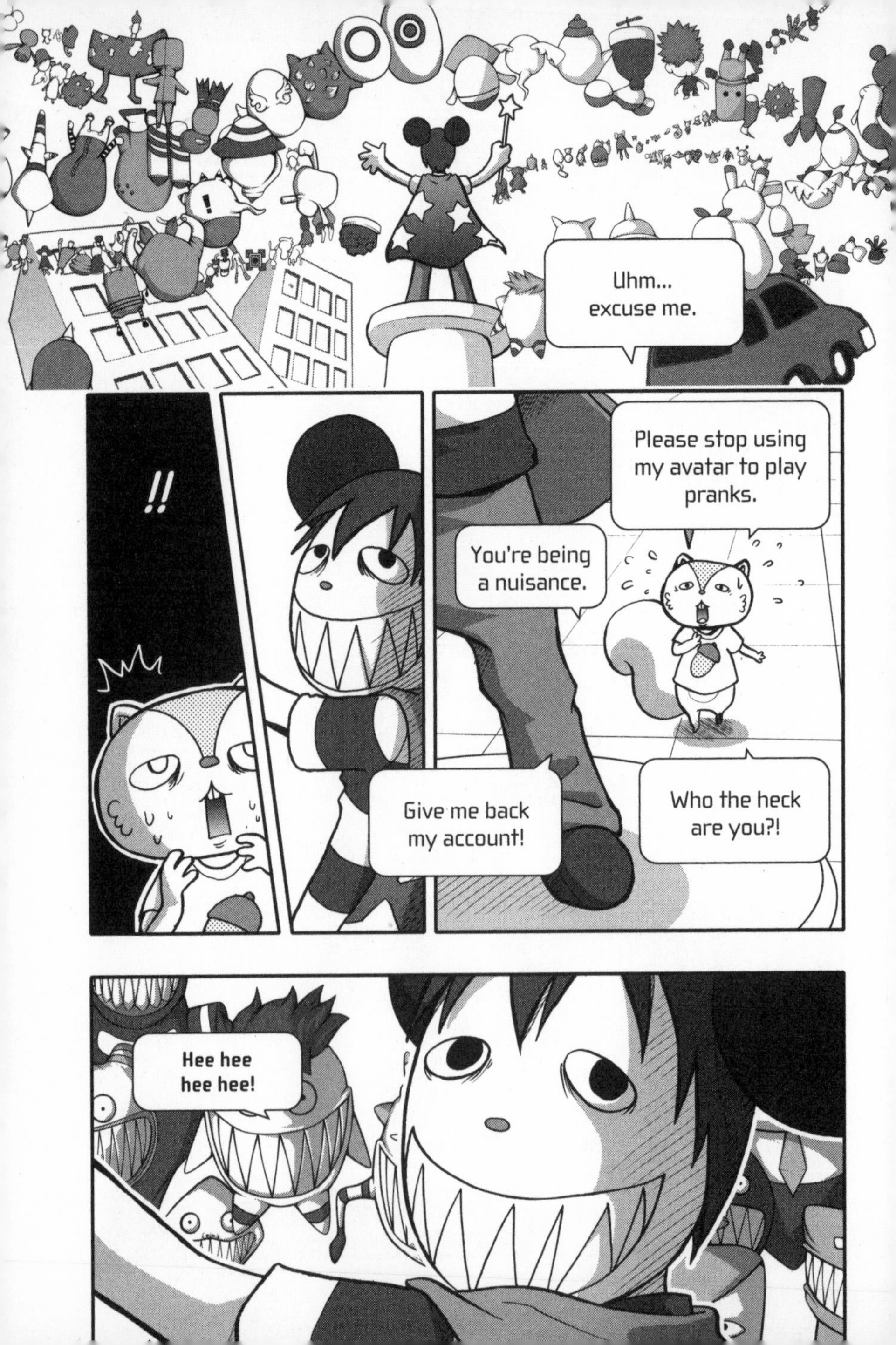
Uhm... excuse me.
Please stop using my avatar to play pranks.
You're being a nuisance.
Who the heck are you?!
Give me back my account!
!!
Hee hee hee hee!

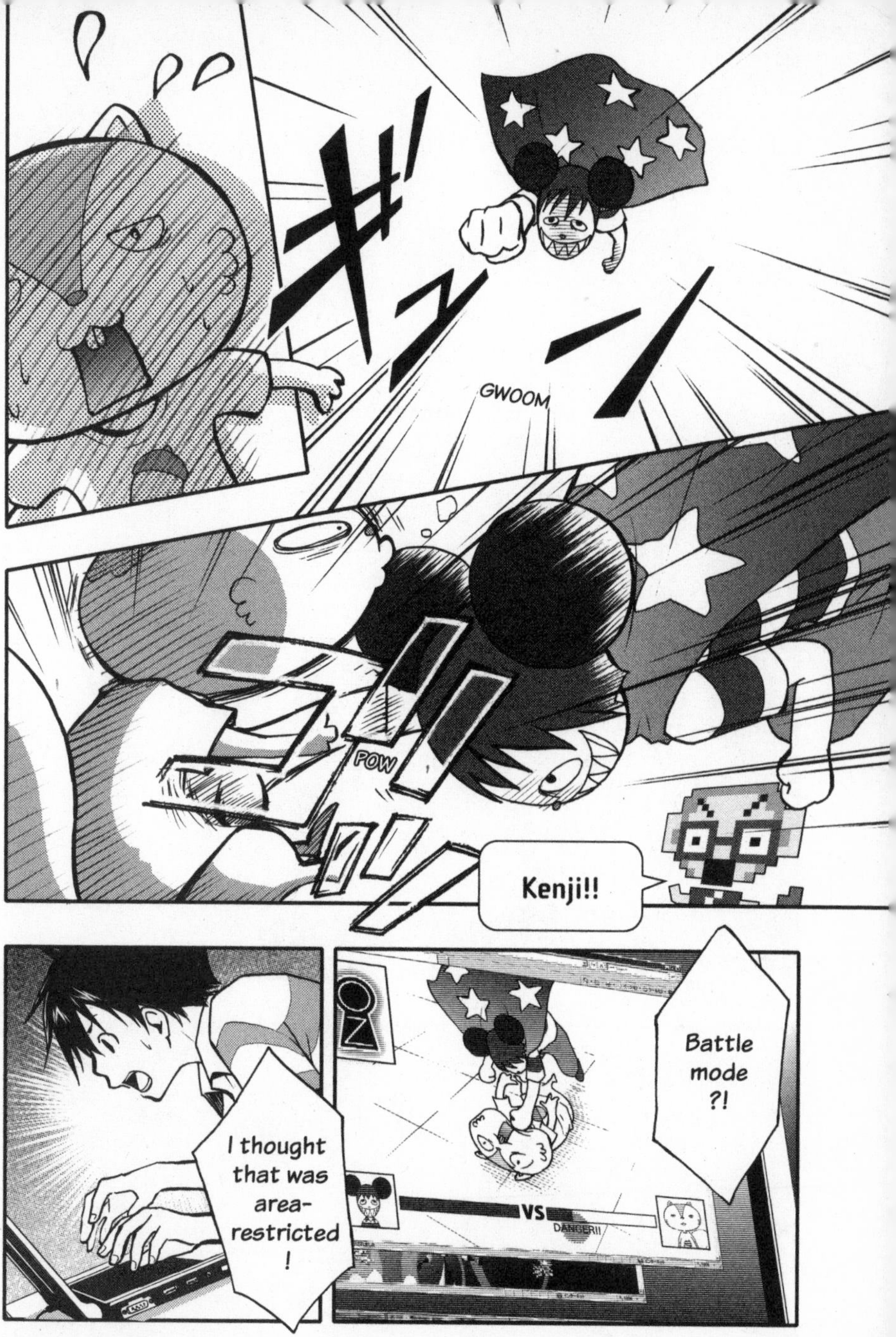
GWOOM
POW
Kenji!!
Battle mode ?!
I thought that was area-restricted !
VS
DANGER!!

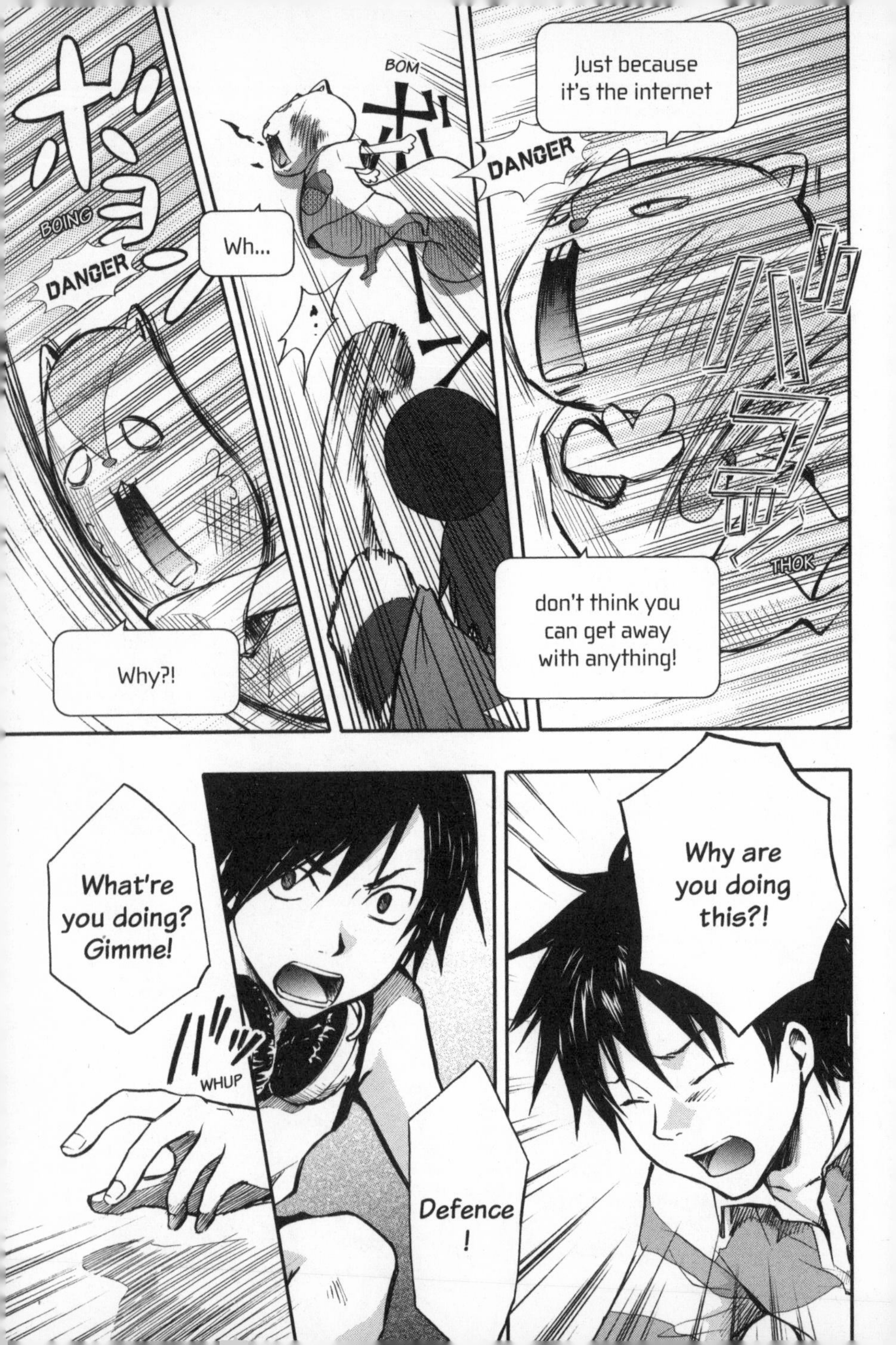
Just because it's the internet
DANGER
don't think you can get away with anything!
THOK
BOM
Wh...
BOING
DANGER
Why?!
Why are you doing this?!
Defence !
What're you doing? Gimme!
WHUP

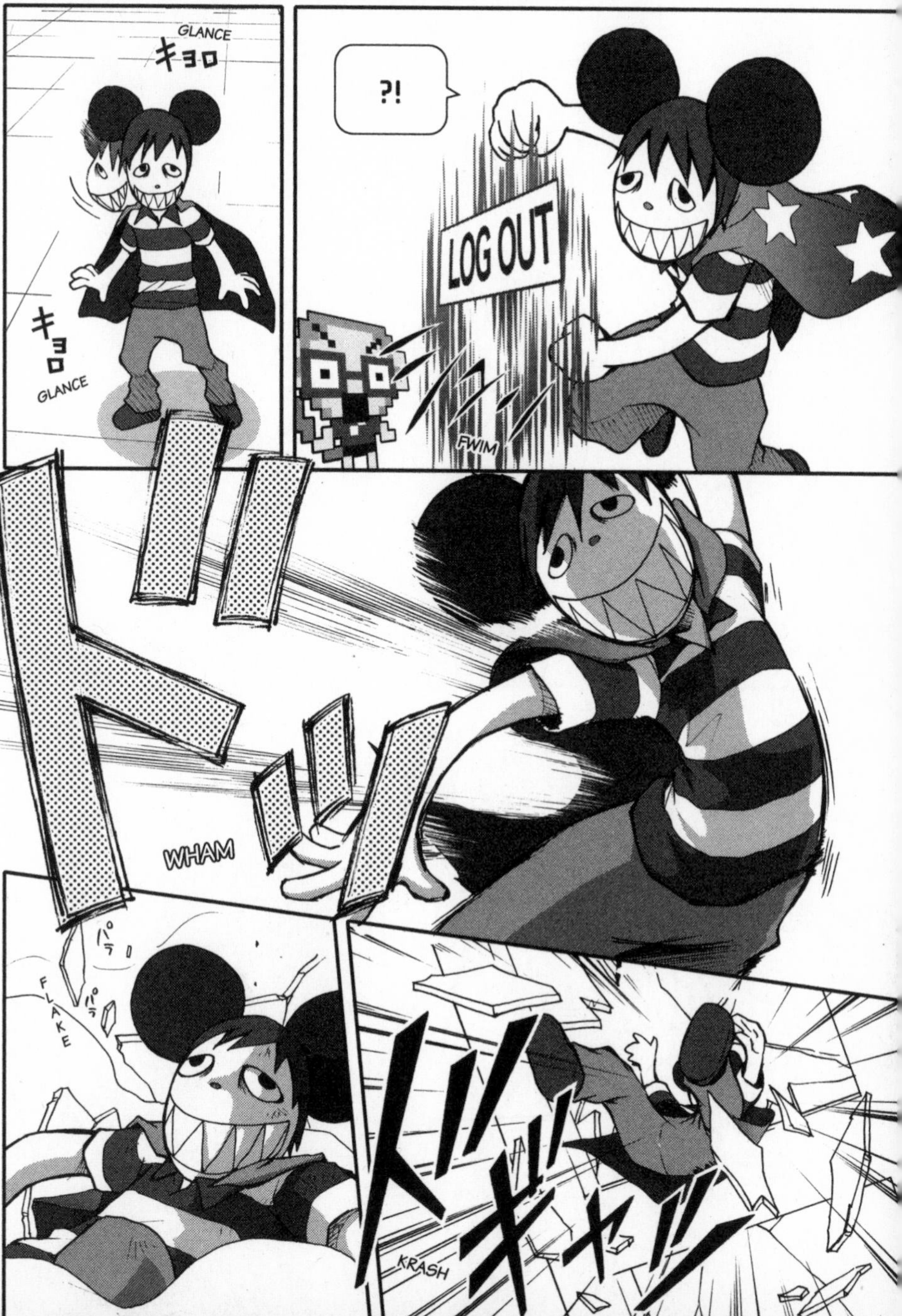
?!
LOG OUT
FWIM
GLANCE
キョロ
キョロ
GLANCE
WHAM
KRASH
FLAKE

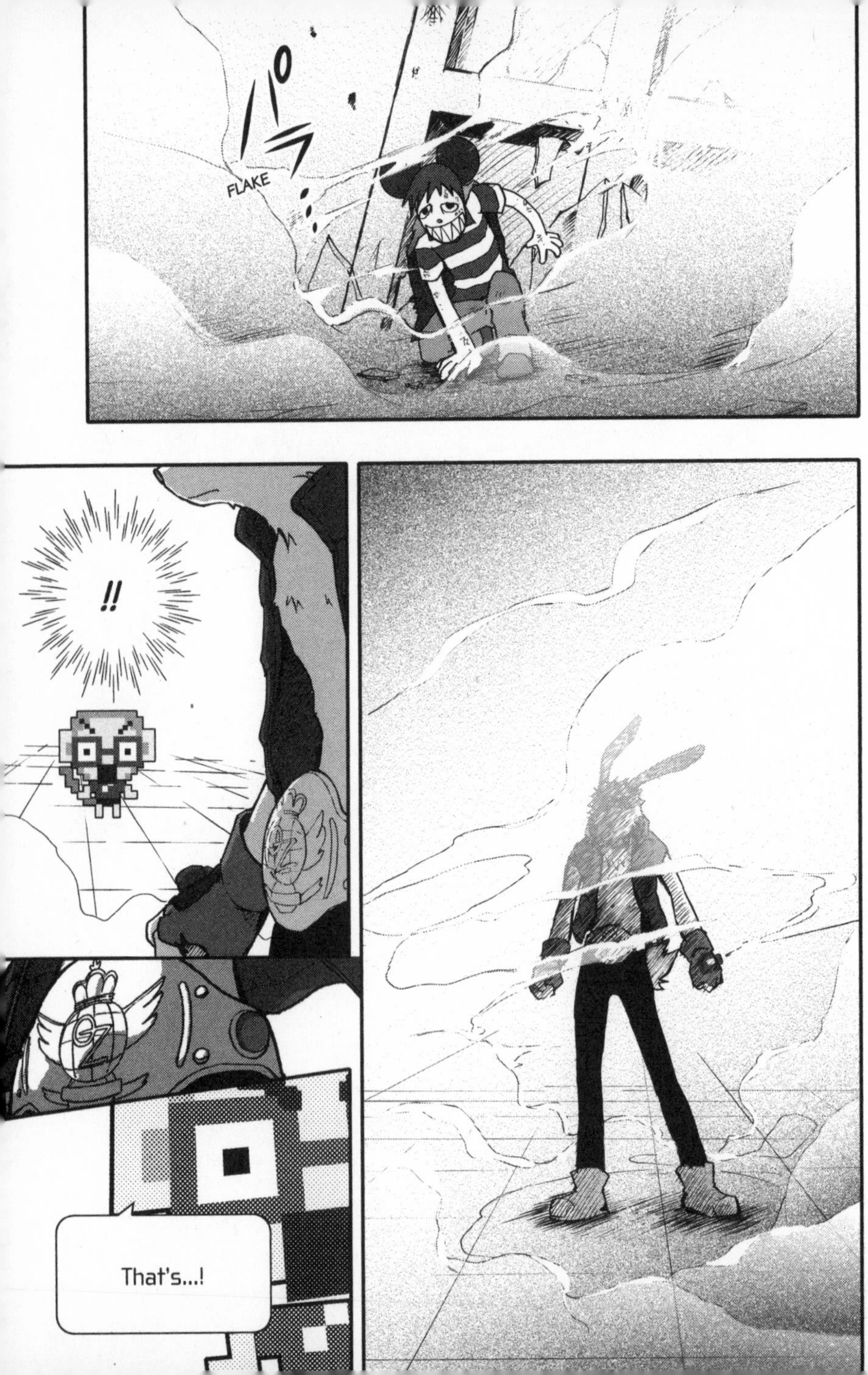
パラ
FLAKE
!!
That's...!

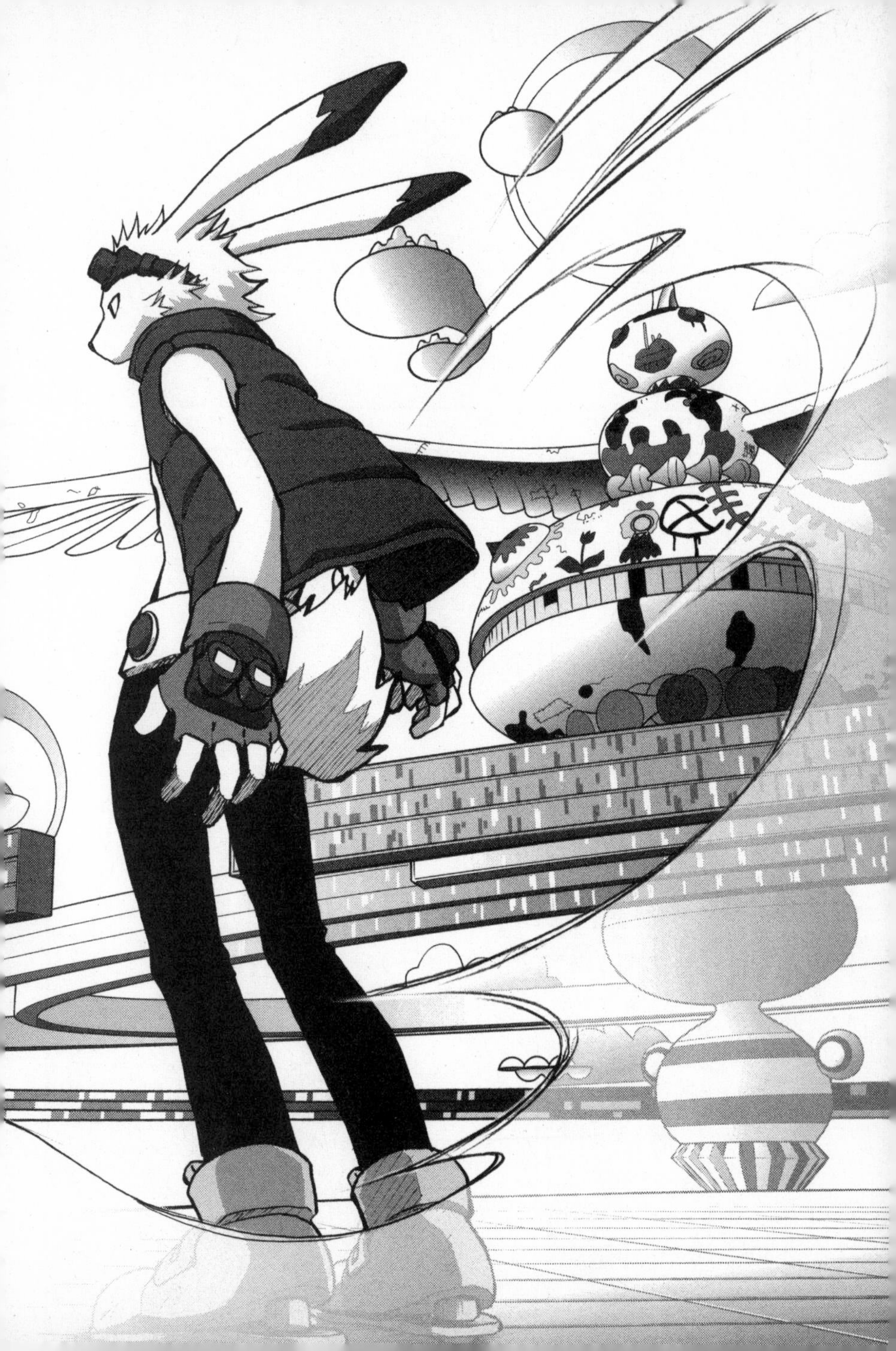

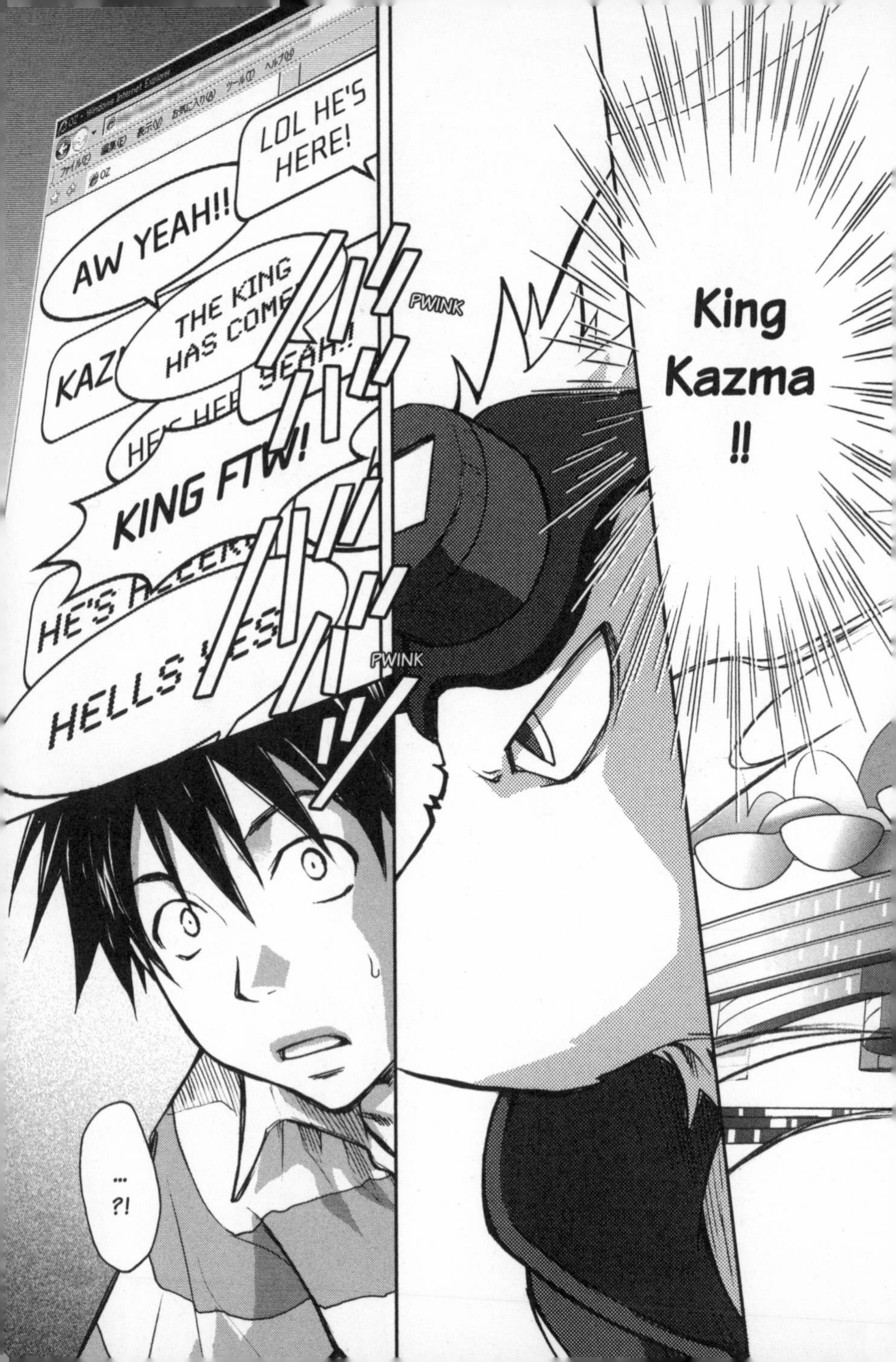
King Kazma !!
PWINK
PWINK
LOL HE'S HERE!
AW YEAH!!
THE KING HAS COME
KAZ
YEAH!!
KING FTW!
HELLS
... ?!

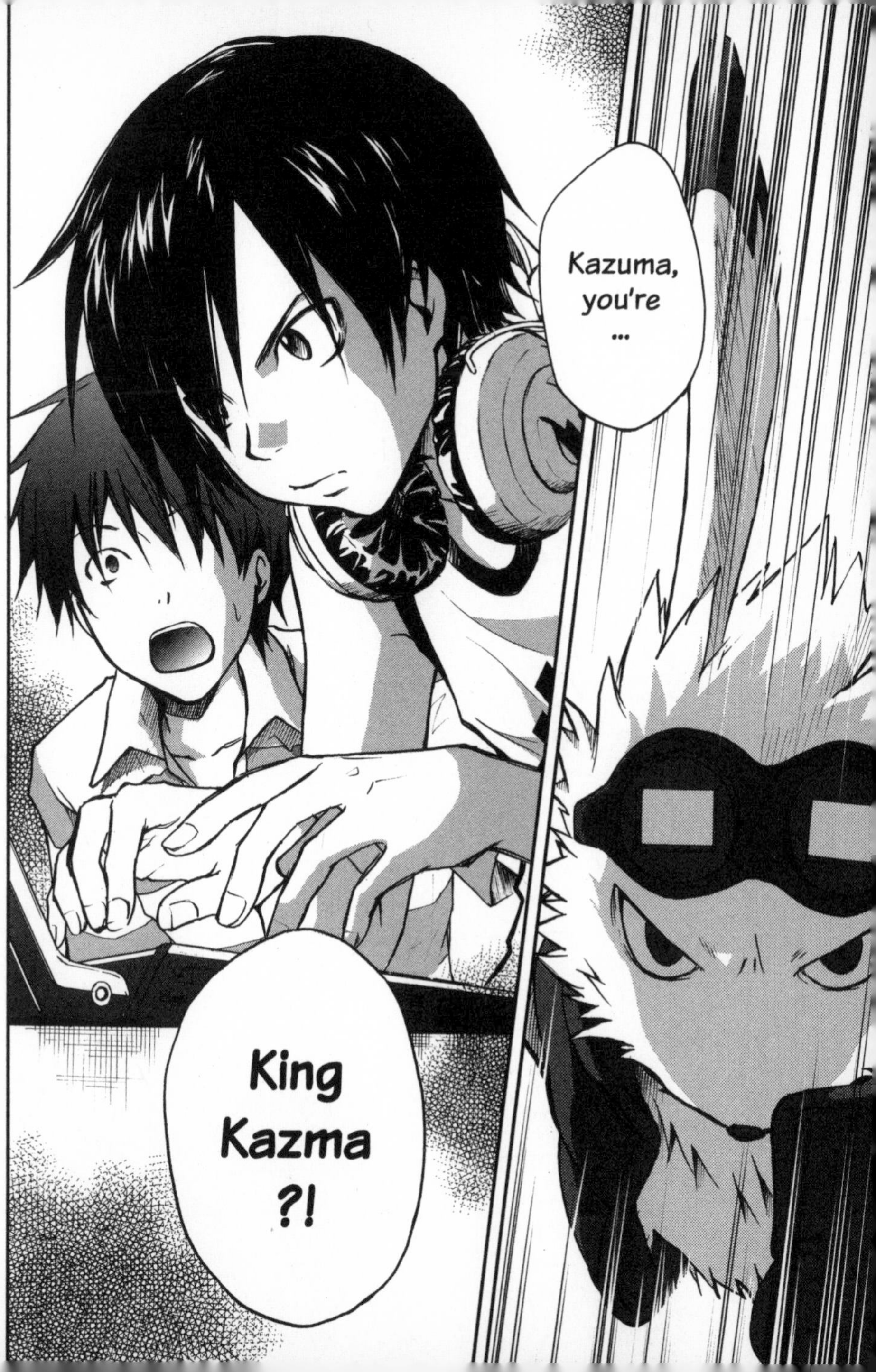
Kazuma, you're ...
King Kazma ?!

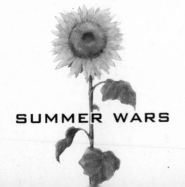

SUMMER WARS

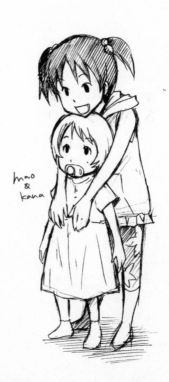

mao
&
kana

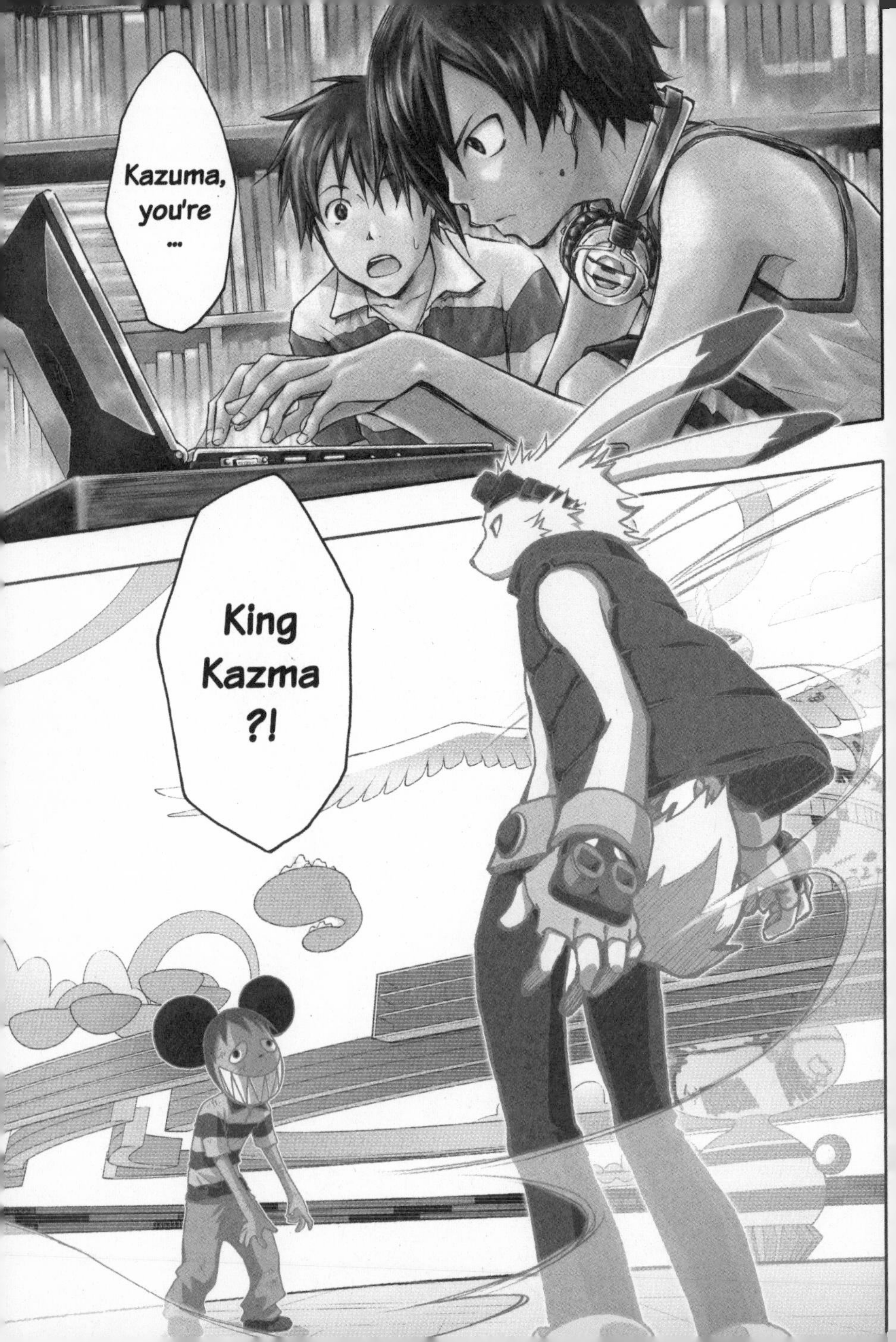
Kazuma, you're ...
King Kazma ?!

Act Three Omen

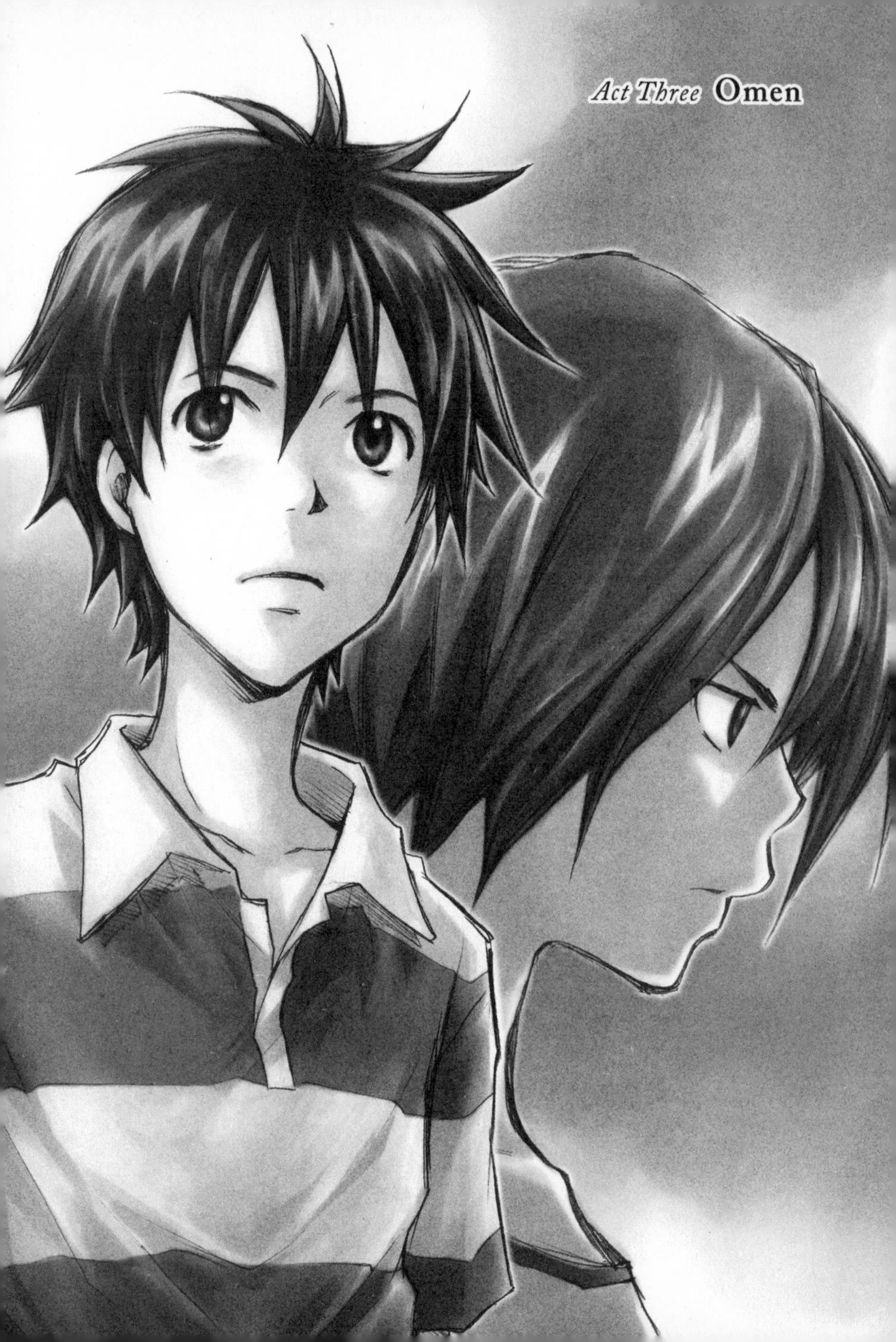

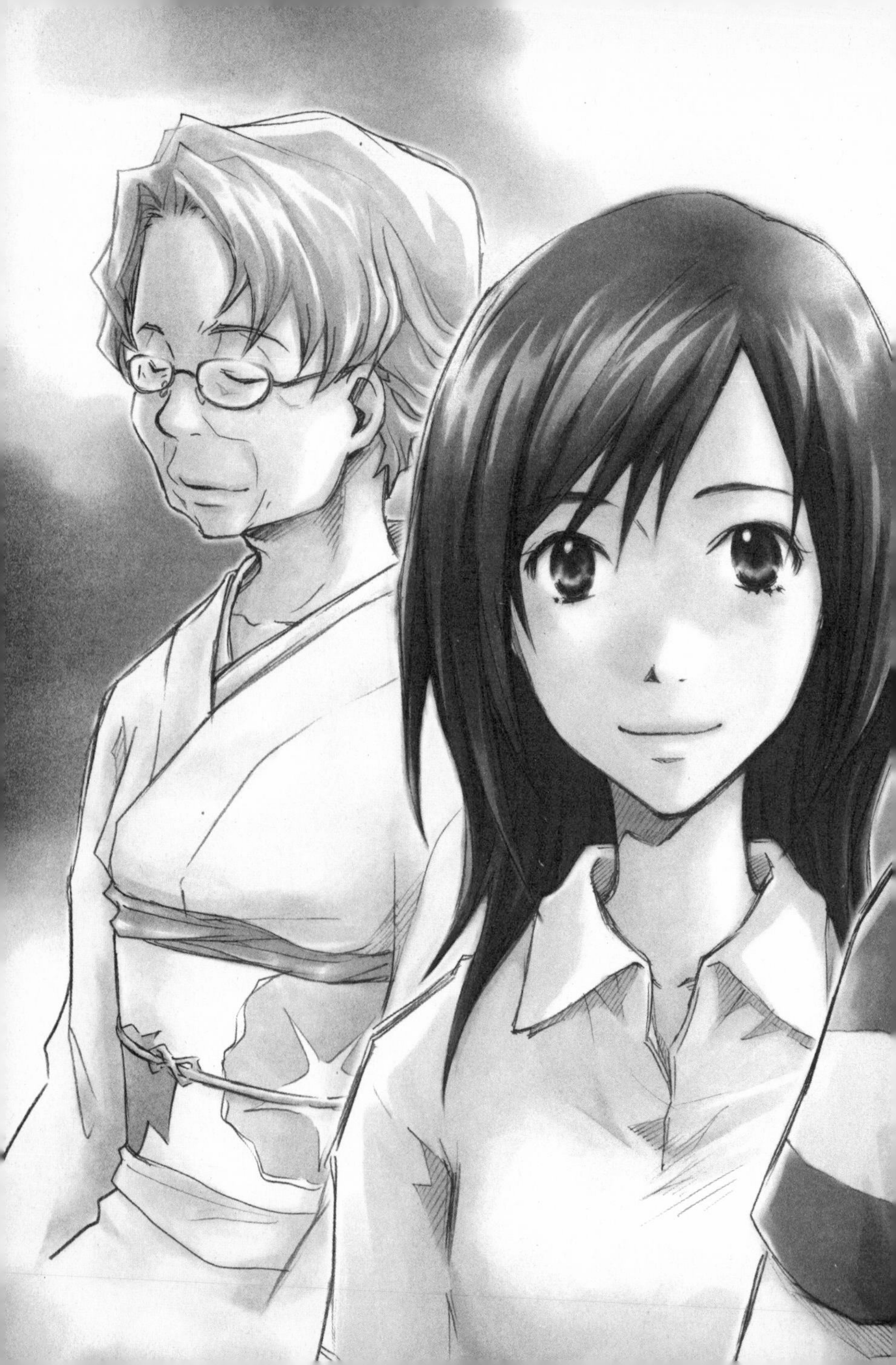

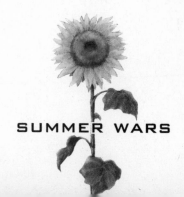

SUMMER WARS

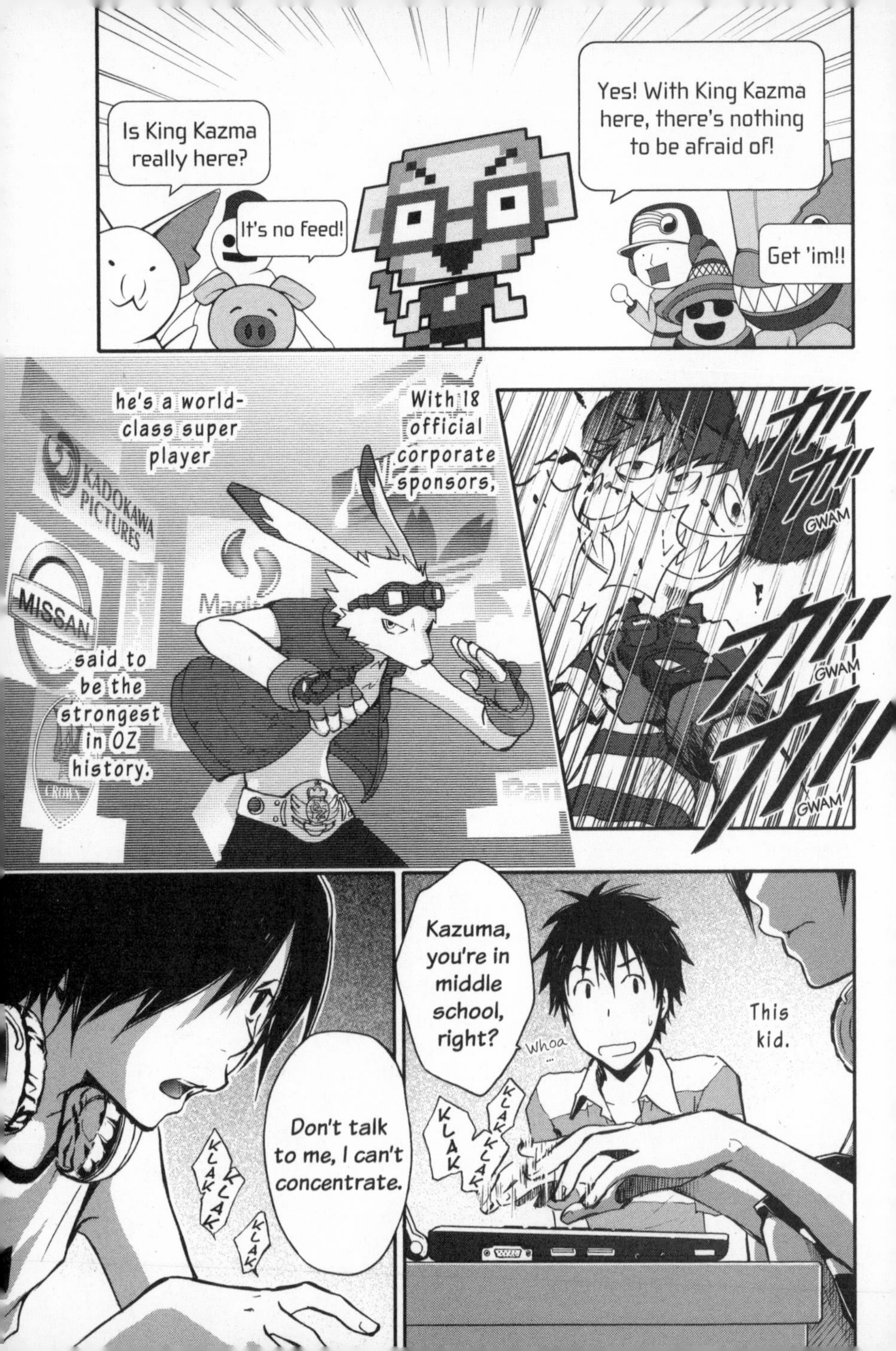

Yes! With King Kazma here, there's nothing to be afraid of!
Get 'im!!
Is King Kazma really here?
It's no feed!
GWAM
GWAM
GWAM
With 18 official corporate sponsors,
he's a world-class super player
said to be the strongest in OZ history.
KADOKAWA PICTURES
MISSAN
This kid.
Kazuma, you're in middle school, right?
Whoa...
KLAK KLAK KLAK
Don't talk to me, I can't concentrate.
KLAK KLAK KLAK

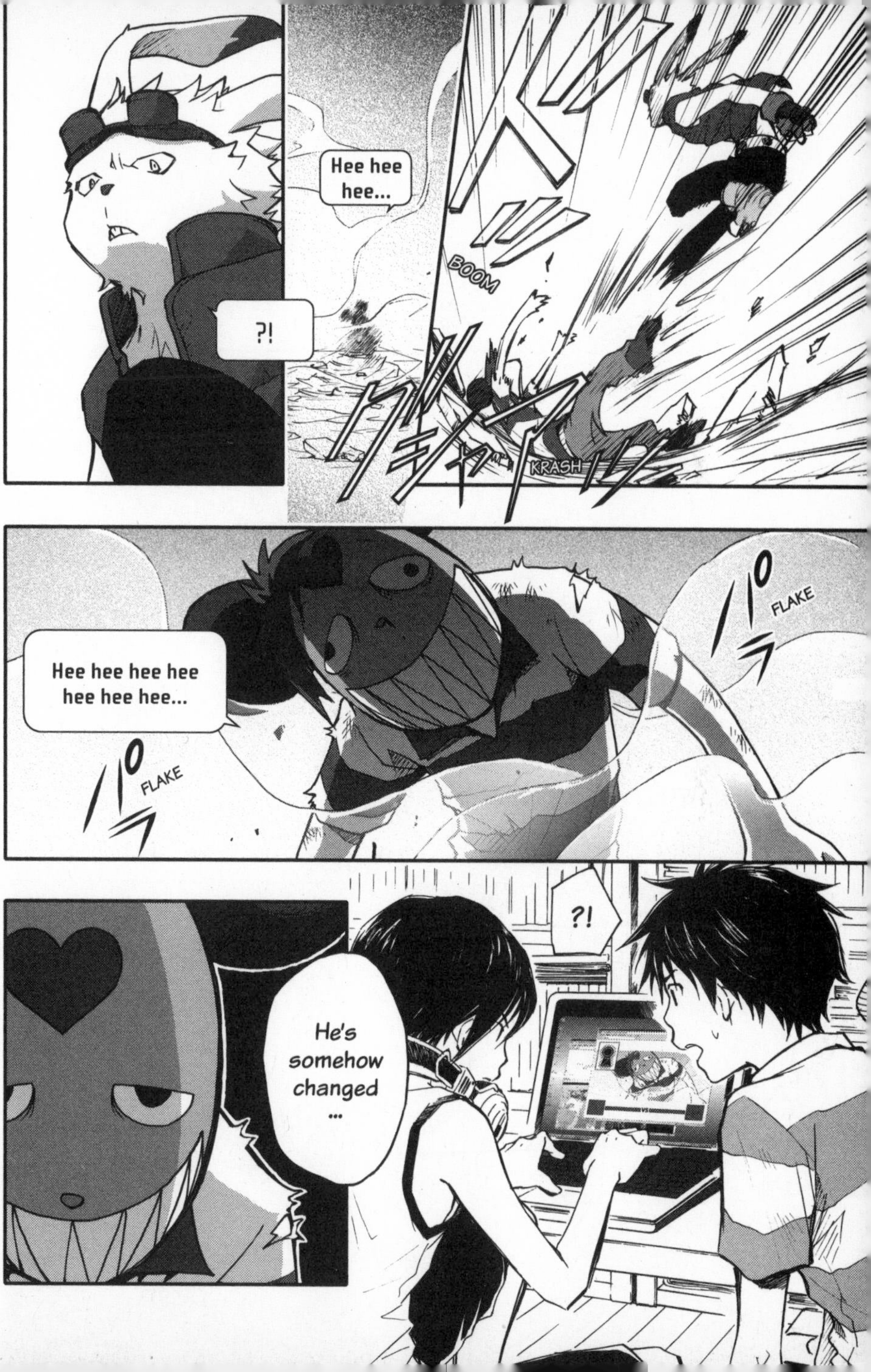
Hee hee hee...
BOOM
KRASH
?!
FLAKE
Hee hee hee hee hee hee hee...
FLAKE
?!
He's somehow changed ...

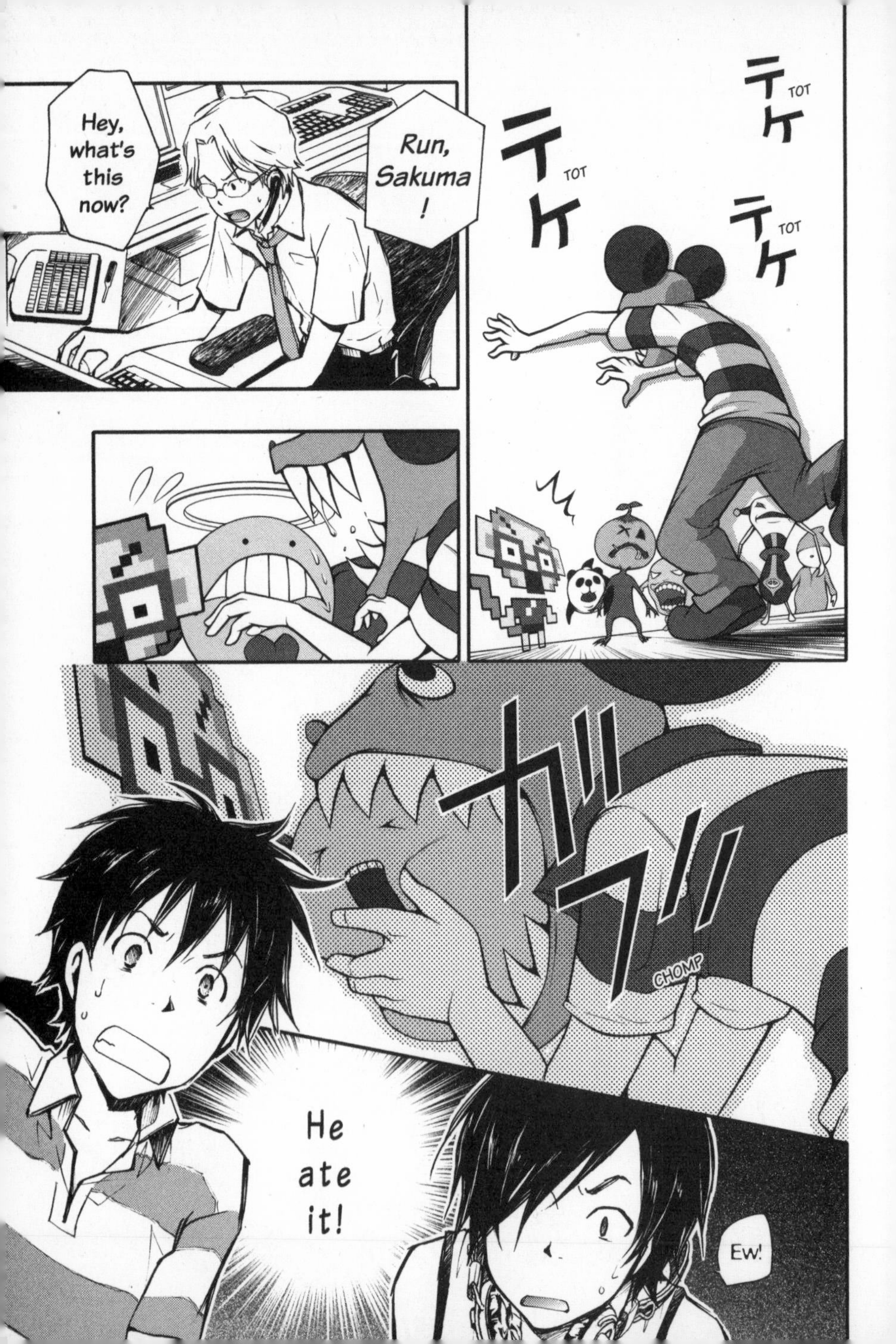
テケ TOT
テケ TOT
テケ TOT
Run, Sakuma!
Hey, what's this now?
カプ
CHOMP
He ate it!
Ew!

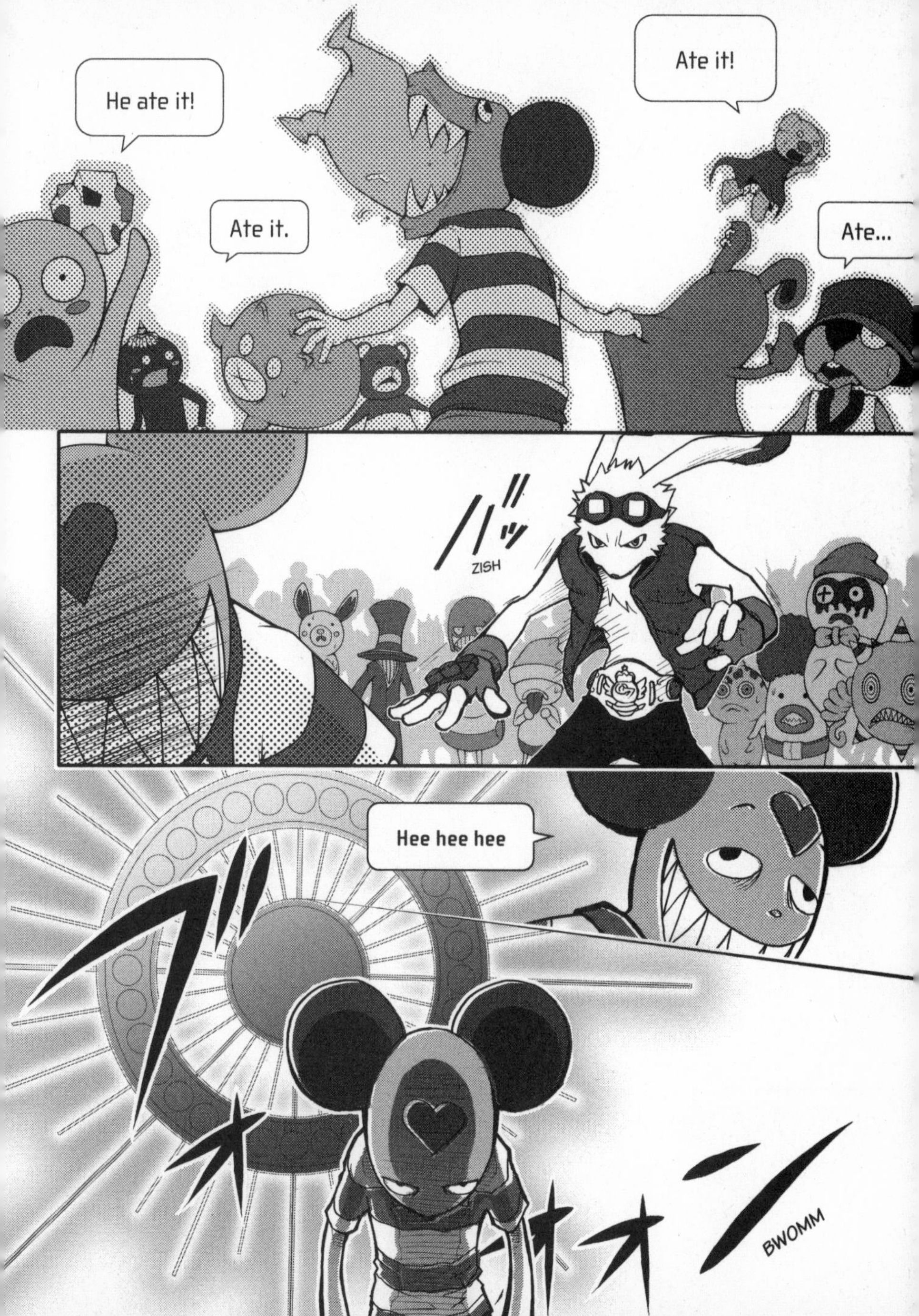

Ate it!
Ate...
Ate it.
He ate it!
ZISH
Hee hee hee
BWOMM

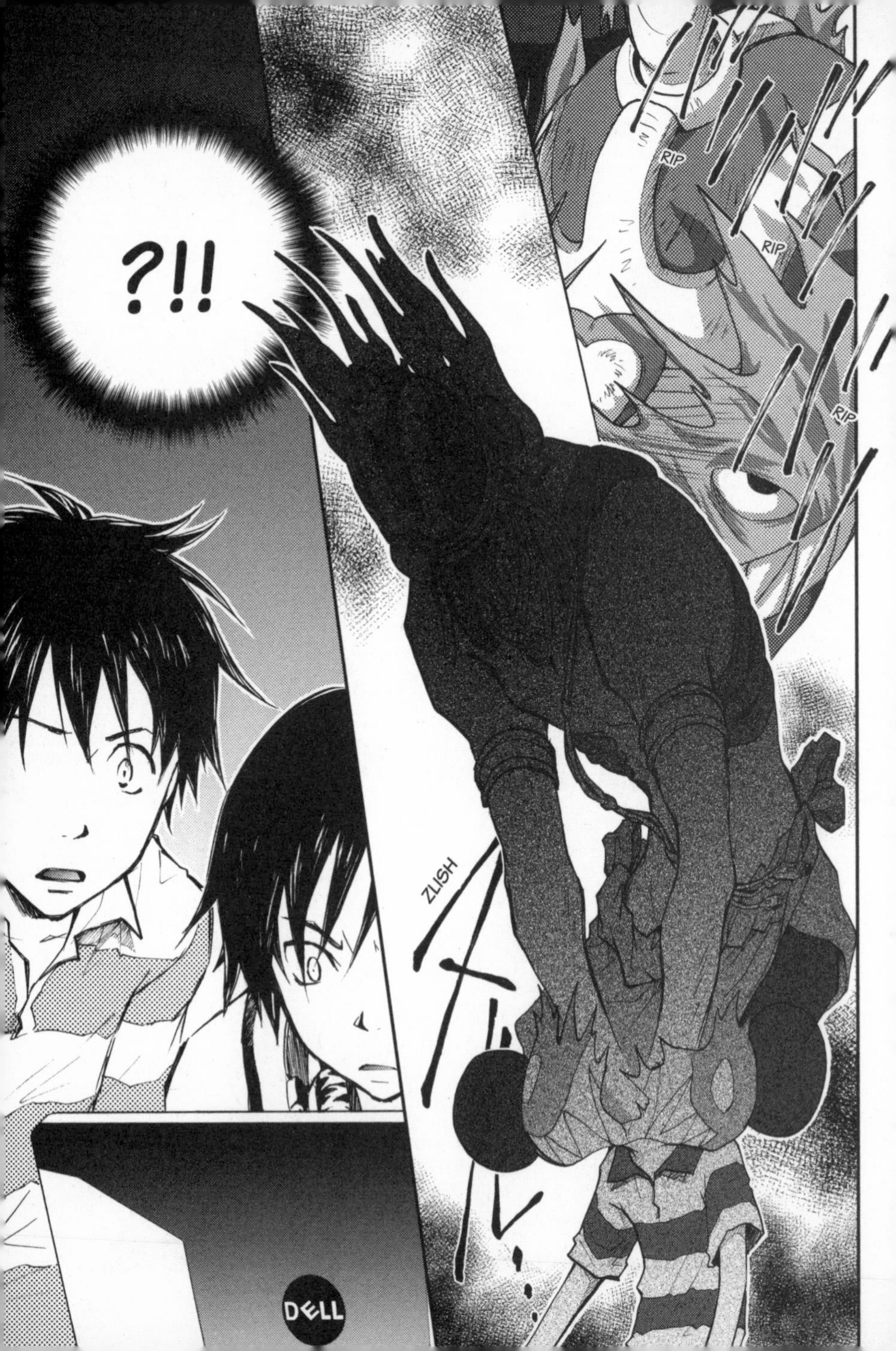
RIP
RIP
RIP
ZLISH
?!!
DELL

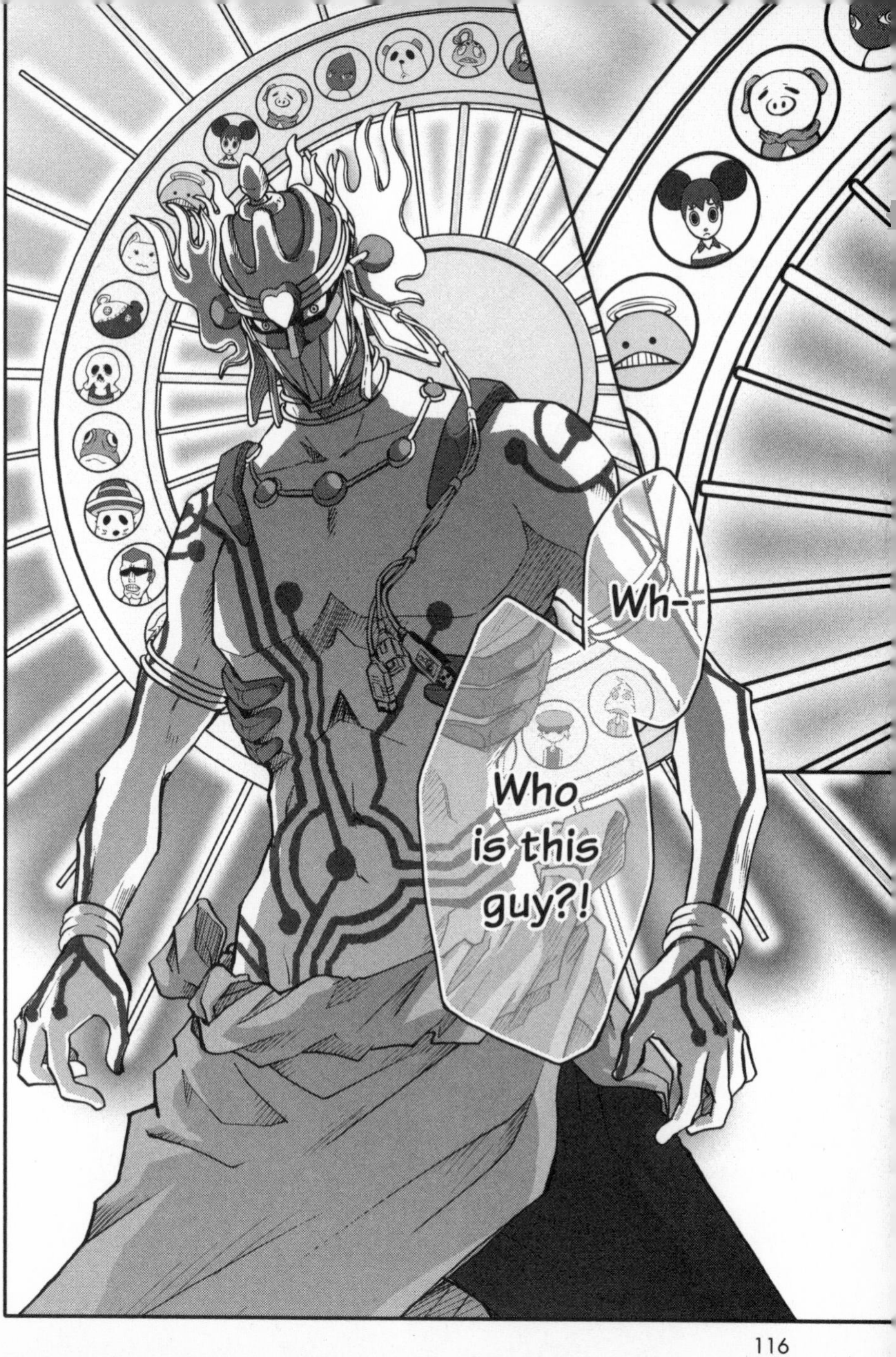
Wh-
Who is this guy?!

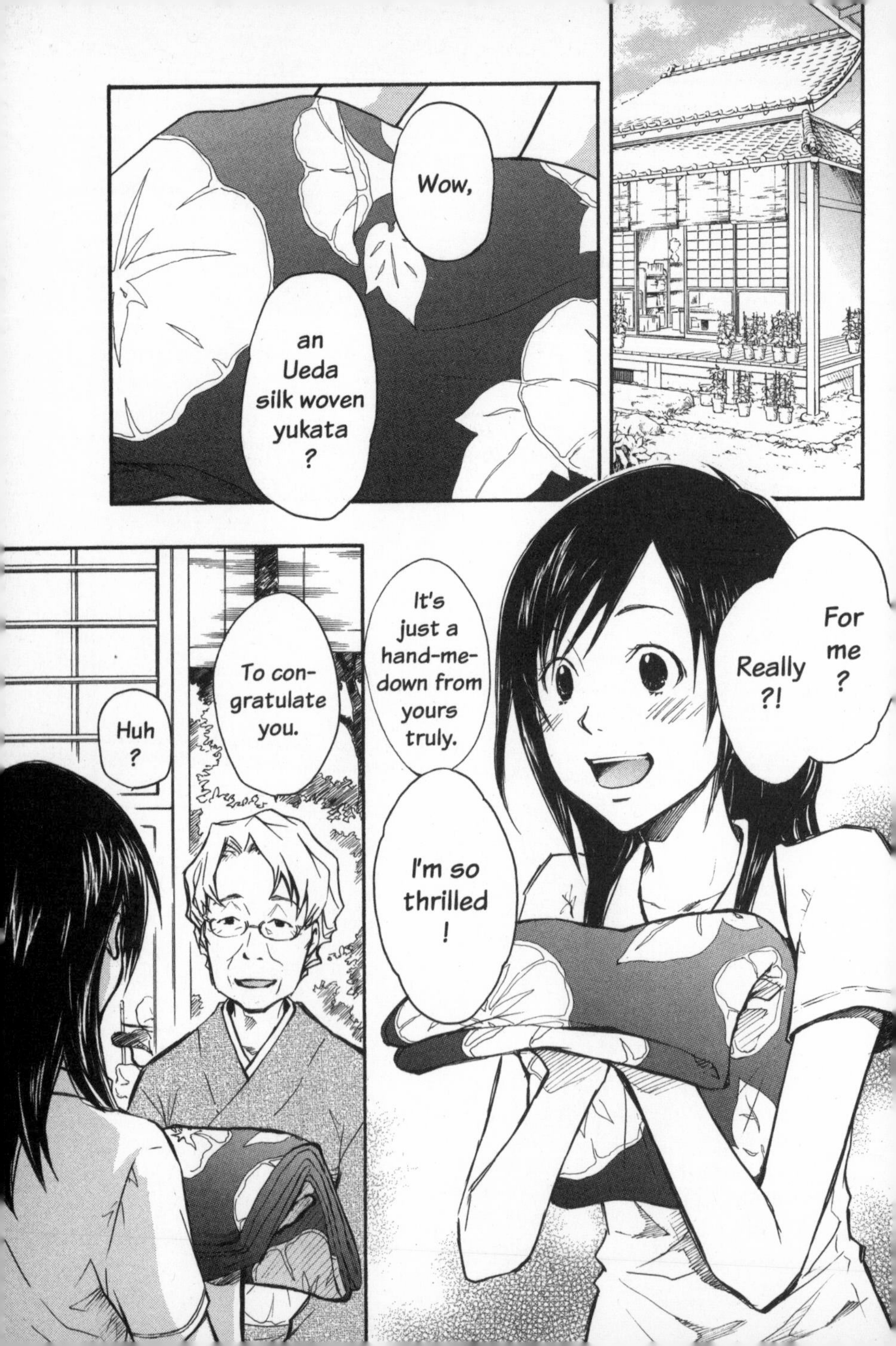
Wow,
an Ueda silk woven yukata?
For me?
Really?!
It's just a hand-me-down from yours truly.
I'm so thrilled!
To con-gratulate you.
Huh?

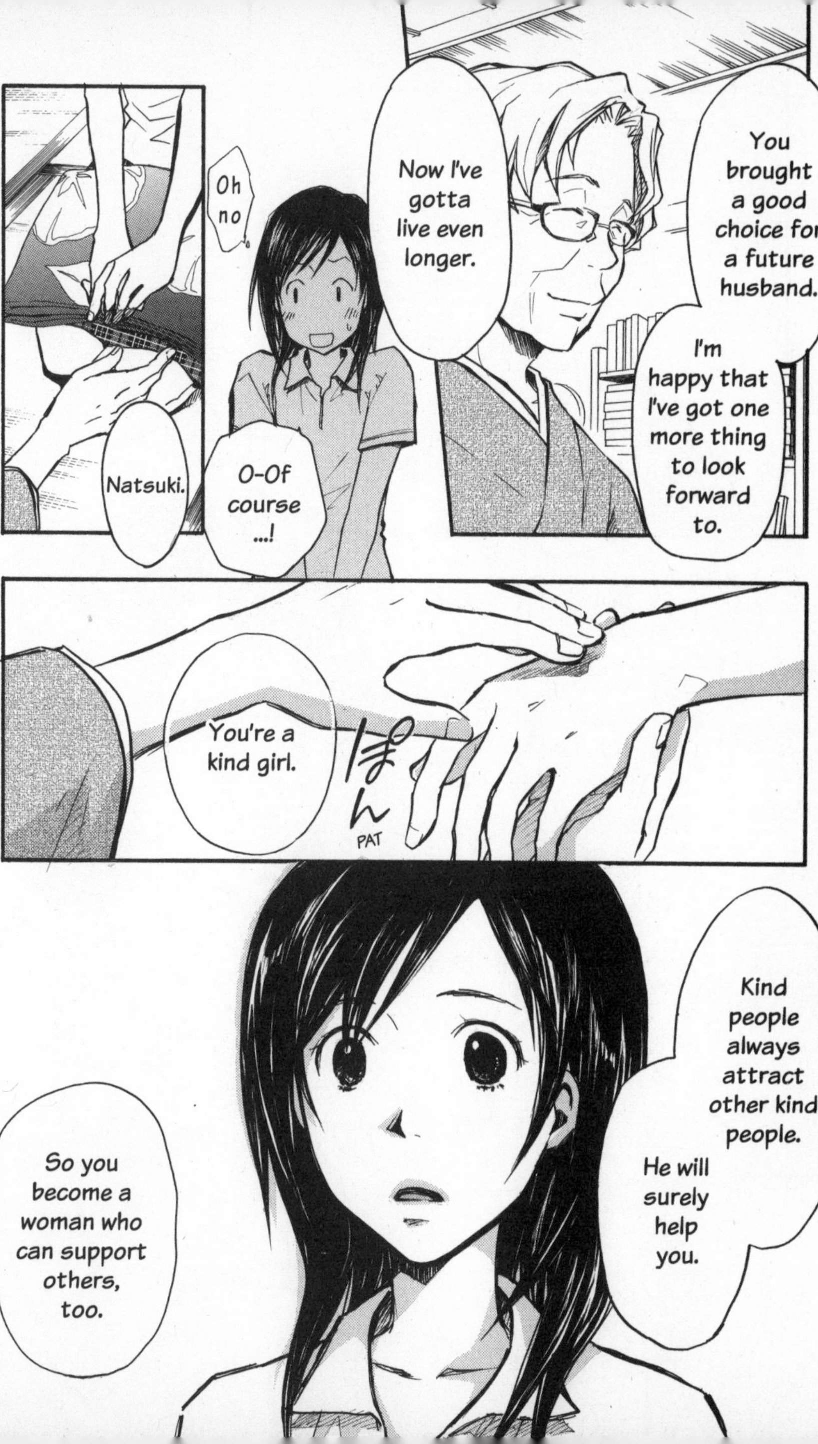
You brought a good choice for a future husband.
Now I've gotta live even longer.
I'm happy that I've got one more thing to look forward to.
Oh no
O-Of course ...!
Natsuki.
You're a kind girl.
ぽん
PAT
Kind people always attract other kind people.
He will surely help you.
So you become a woman who can support others, too.

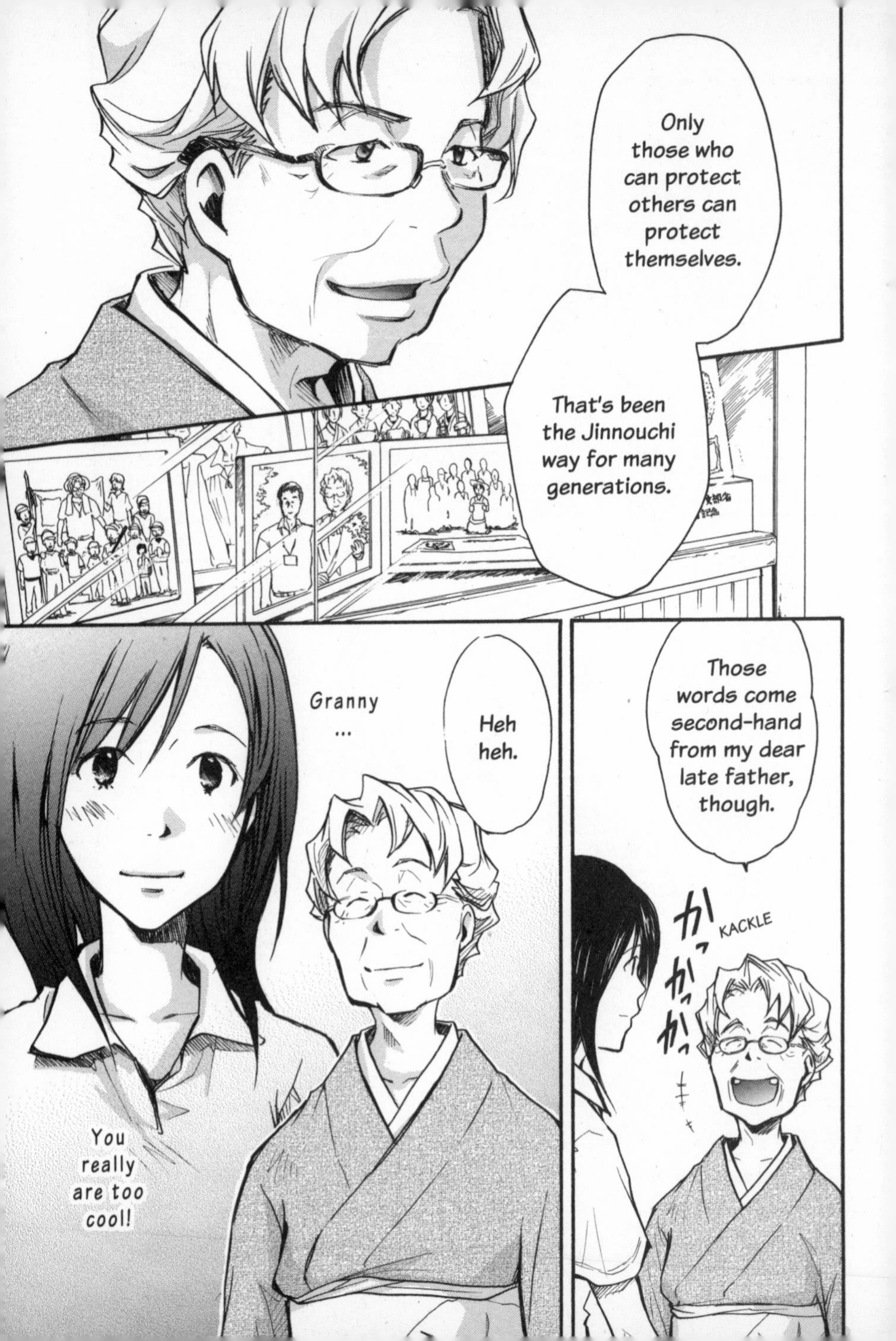
Only those who can protect others can protect themselves.
That's been the Jinnouchi way for many generations.
Those words come second-hand from my dear late father, though.
かっかっかっ
KACKLE
Heh heh.
Granny ...
You really are too cool!

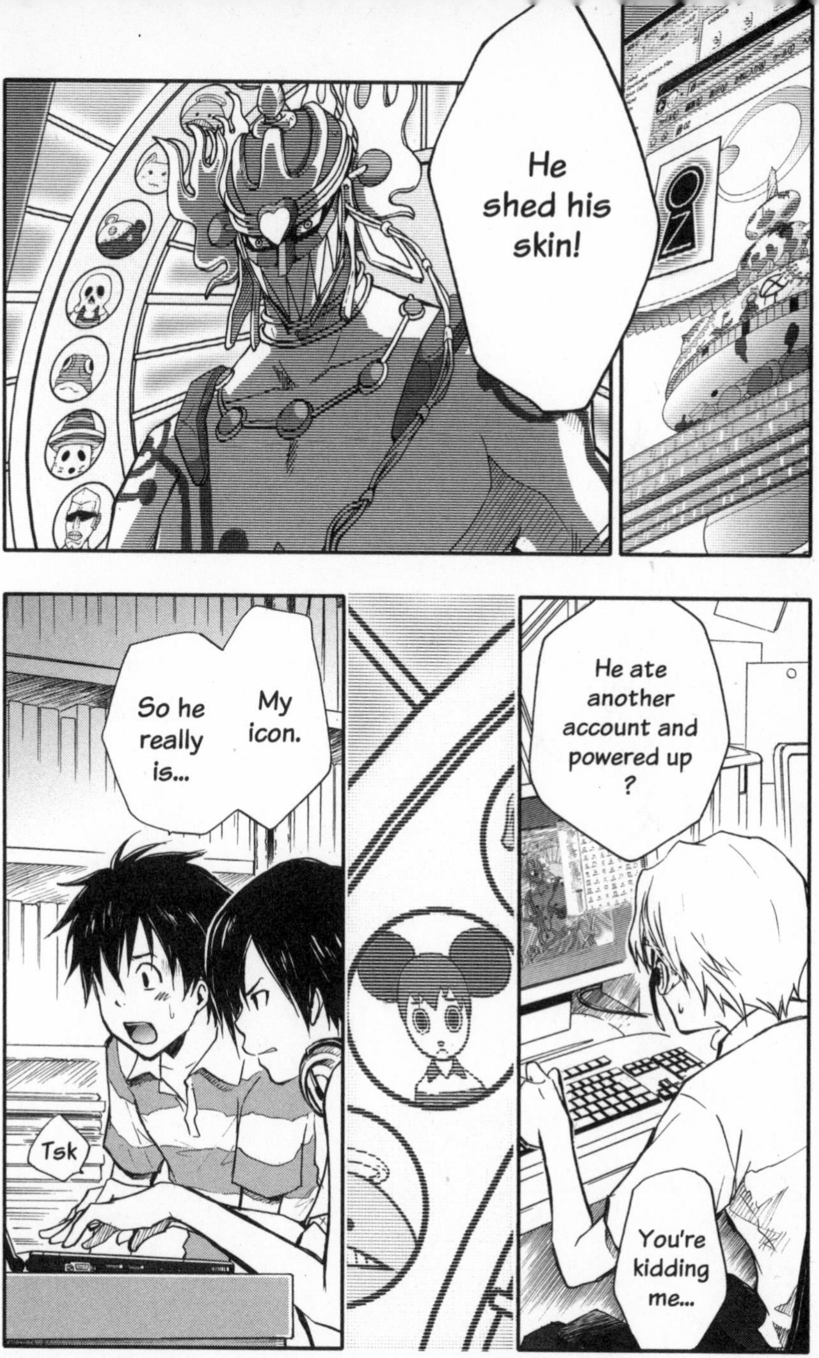
He shed his skin!
He ate another account and powered up ?
You're kidding me...
My icon.
So he really is...
Tsk

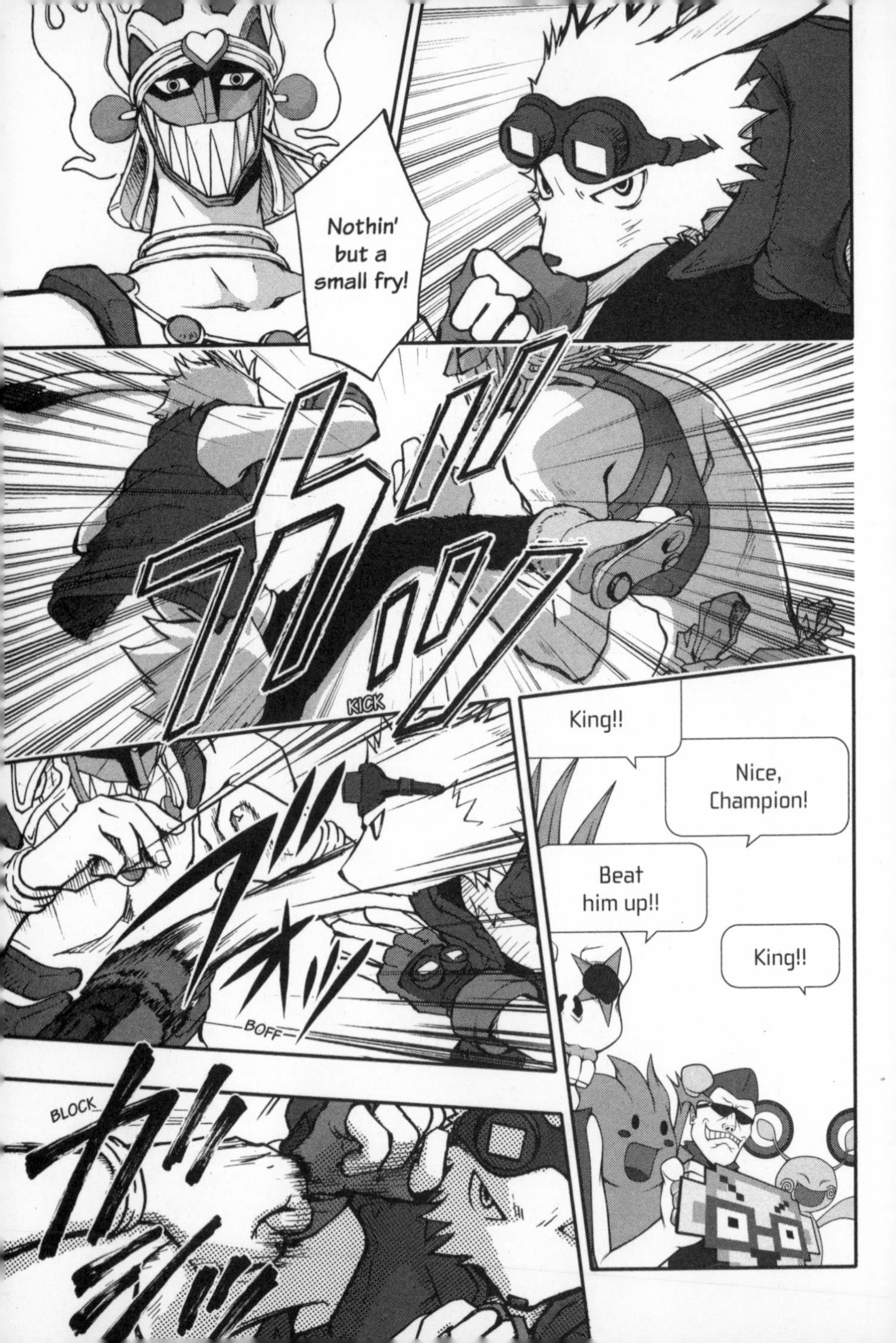
Nothin' but a small fry!
KICK
King!!
Nice, Champion!
Beat him up!!
King!!
BOFF
BLOCK

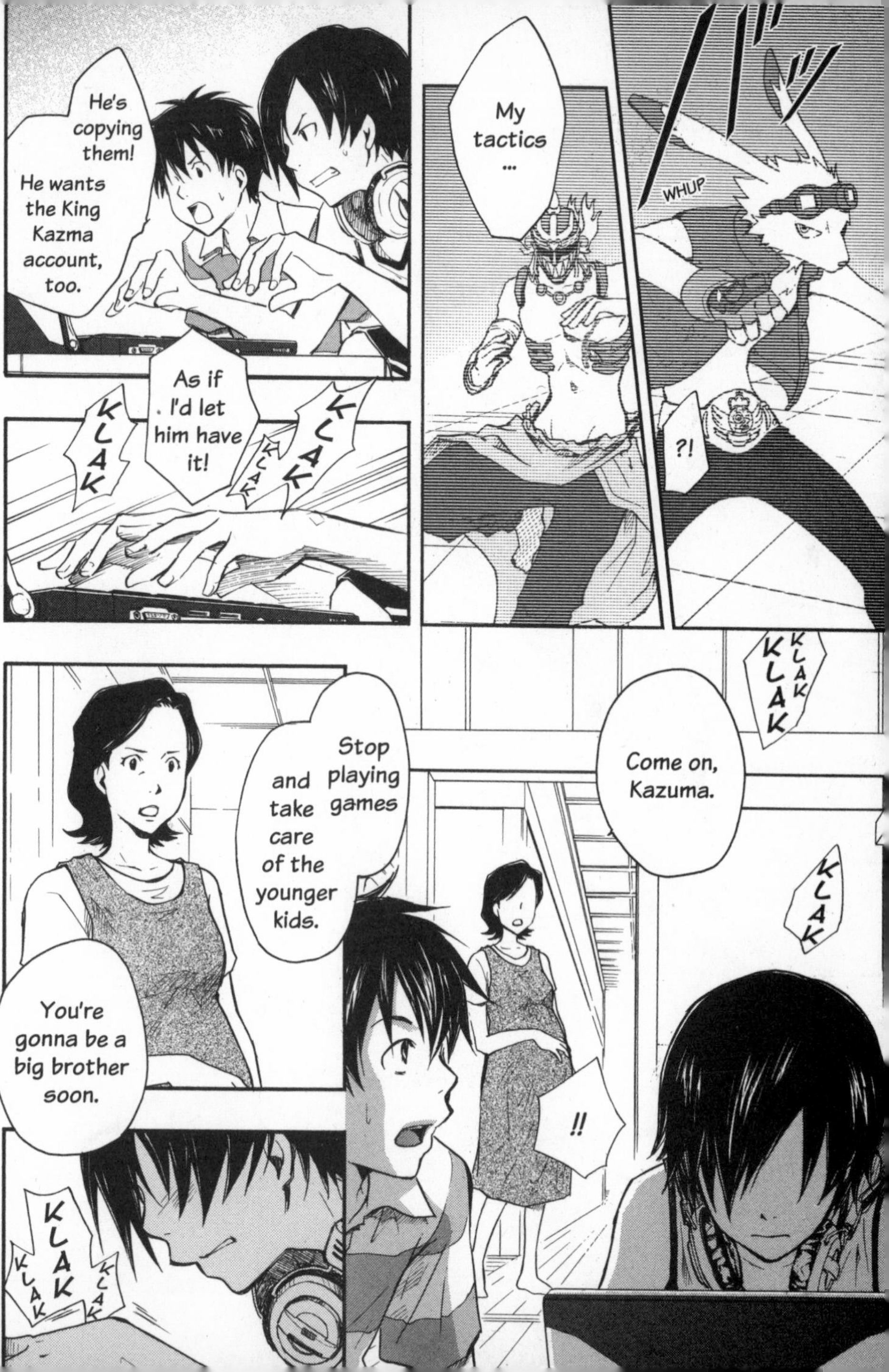
WHUP
?!
My tactics ...
He's copying them!
He wants the King Kazma account, too.
As if I'd let him have it!
KLAK KLAK
KLAK
KLAK
KLAK KLAK
Come on, Kazuma.
KLAK
!!
Stop playing games and take care of the younger kids.
You're gonna be a big brother soon.
KLAK KLAK
KLAK
KLAK

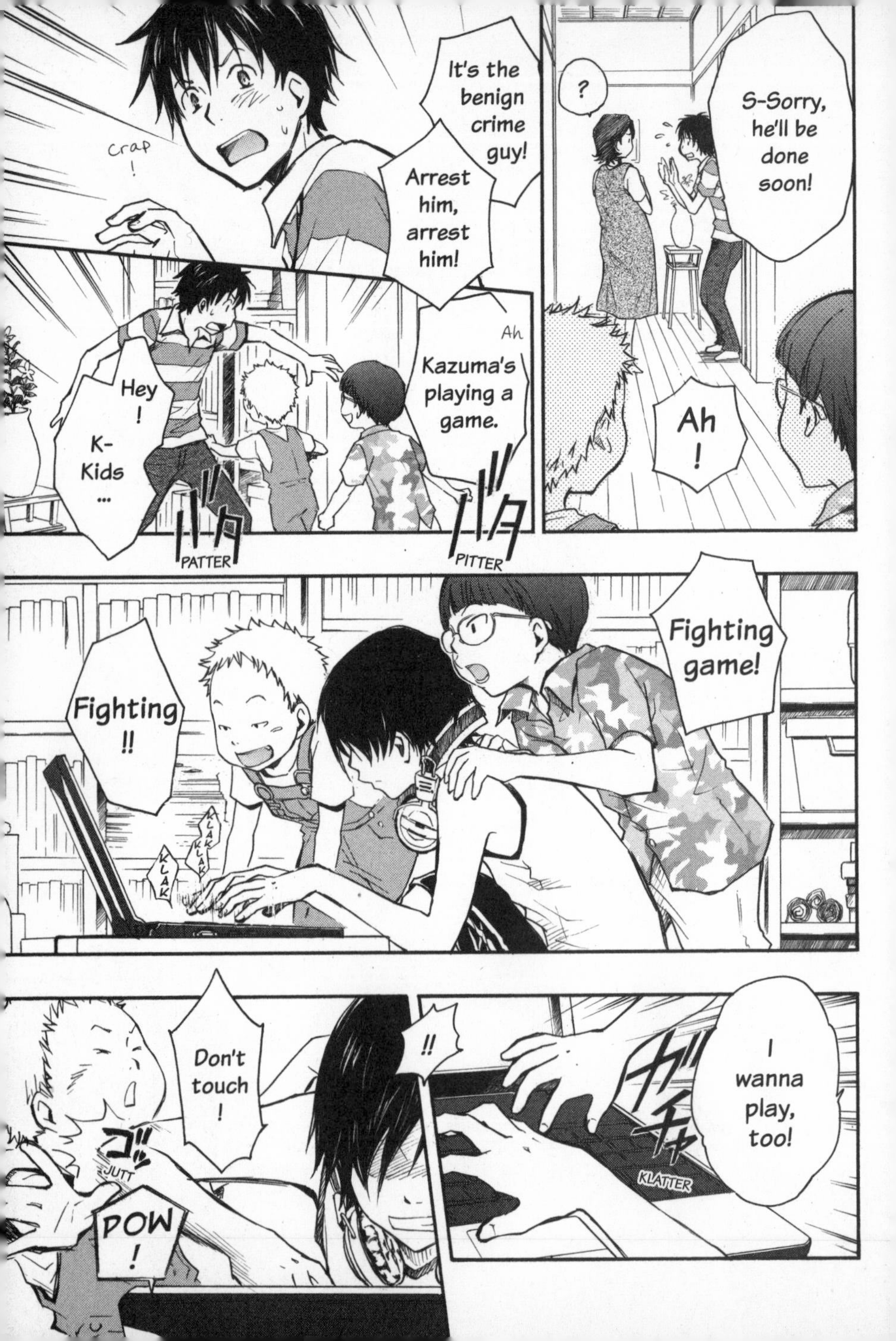
S-Sorry, he'll be done soon!
?
Ah !
It's the benign crime guy!
Crap !
Arrest him, arrest him!
Ah
Kazuma's playing a game.
PITTER
Hey ! K-Kids ...
PATTER
Fighting game!
Fighting !!
KLAK KLAK KLAK
I wanna play, too!
KLATTER
!!
Don't touch !
JUTT
POW !

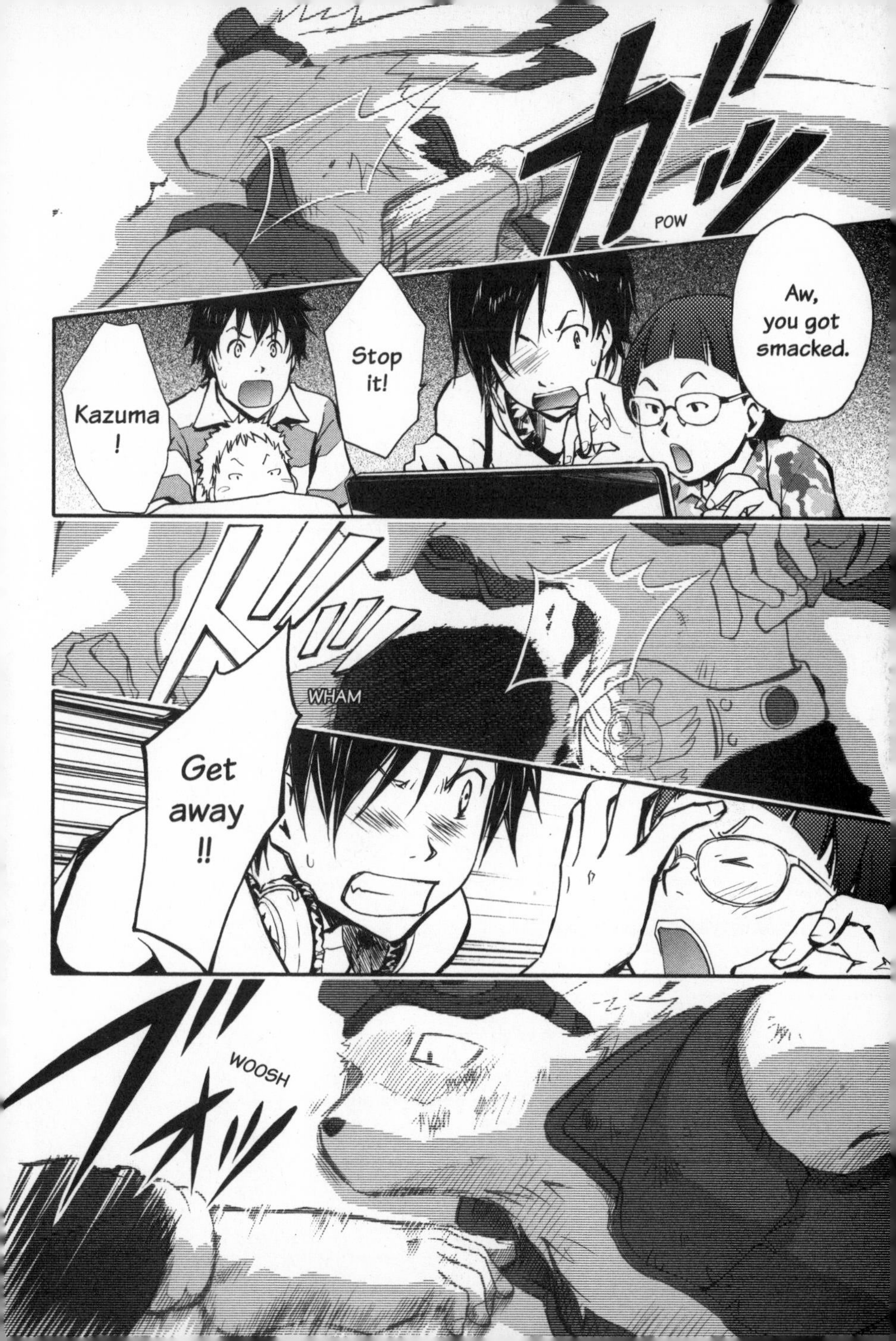
POW
Aw, you got smacked.
Stop it!
Kazuma!
WHAM
Get away!!
WOOSH

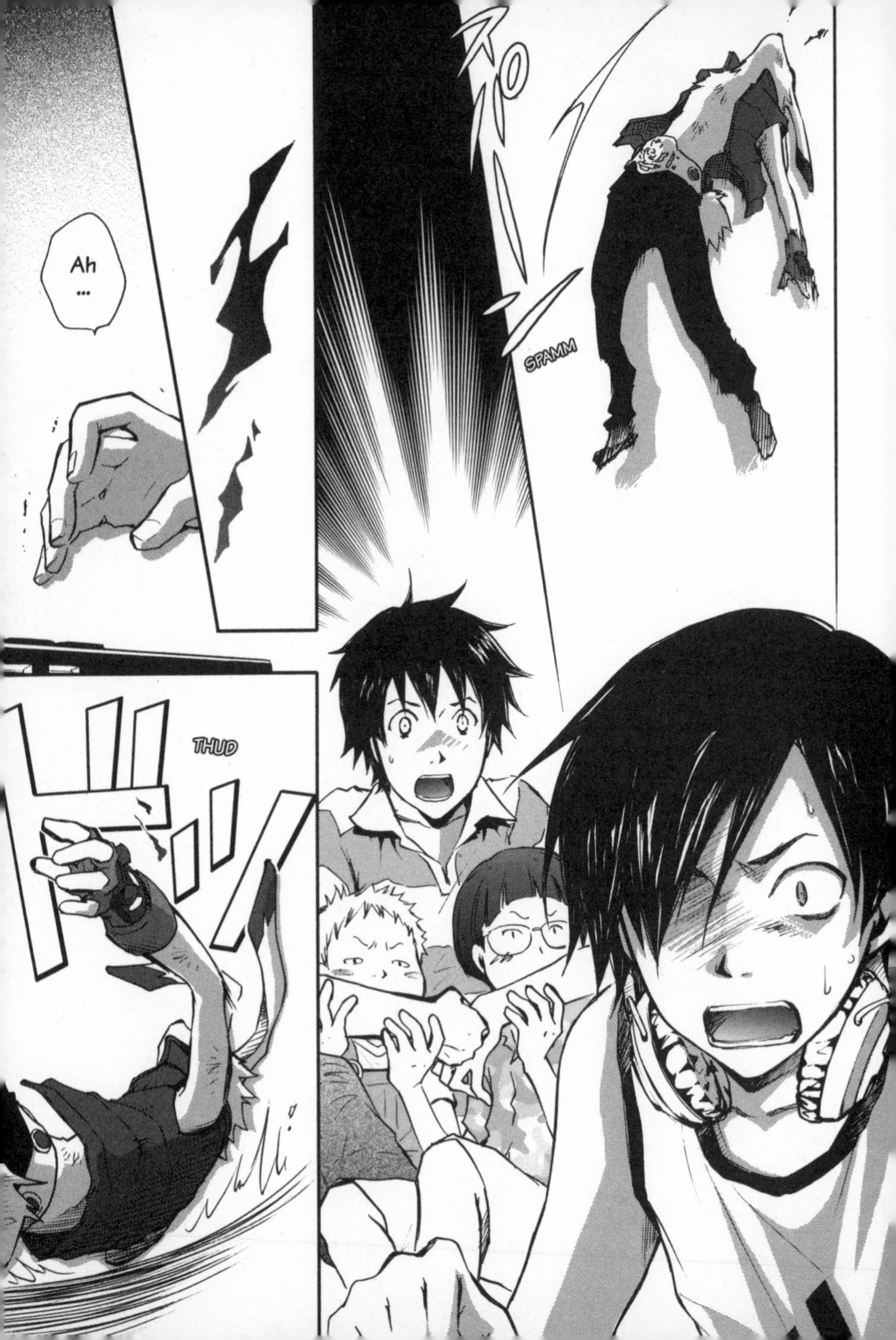
SPAMM
Ah ...
THUD

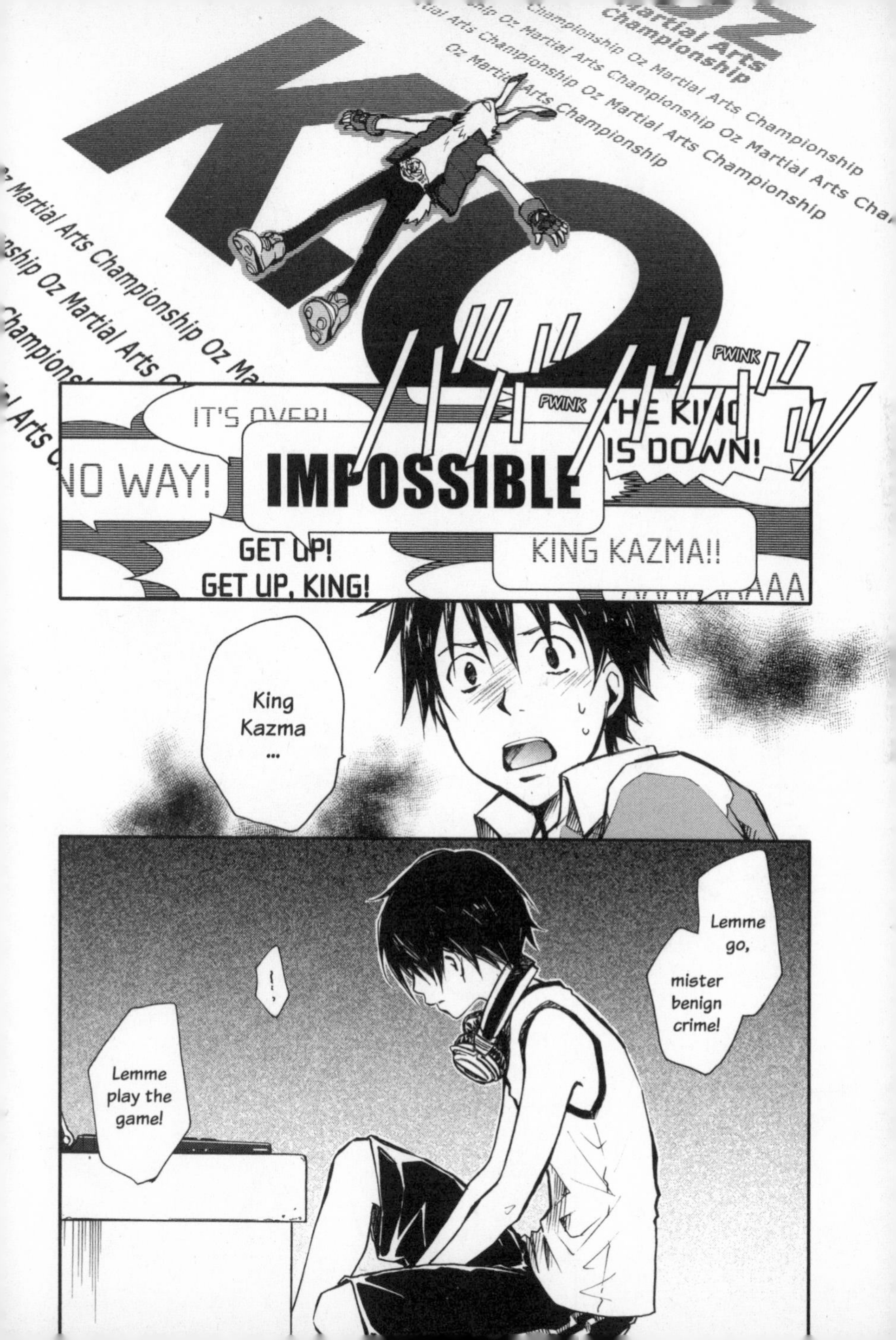

Oz Martial Arts Championship
Oz Martial Arts Championship Oz Martial Arts Championship
KO
PWINK
PWINK
THE KIN
IS DOWN!
IT'S OVER!
IMPOSSIBLE
NO WAY!
KING KAZMA!!
AAAA
GET UP!
GET UP, KING!
King Kazma ...
Lemme go, mister benign crime!
!?
Lemme play the game!

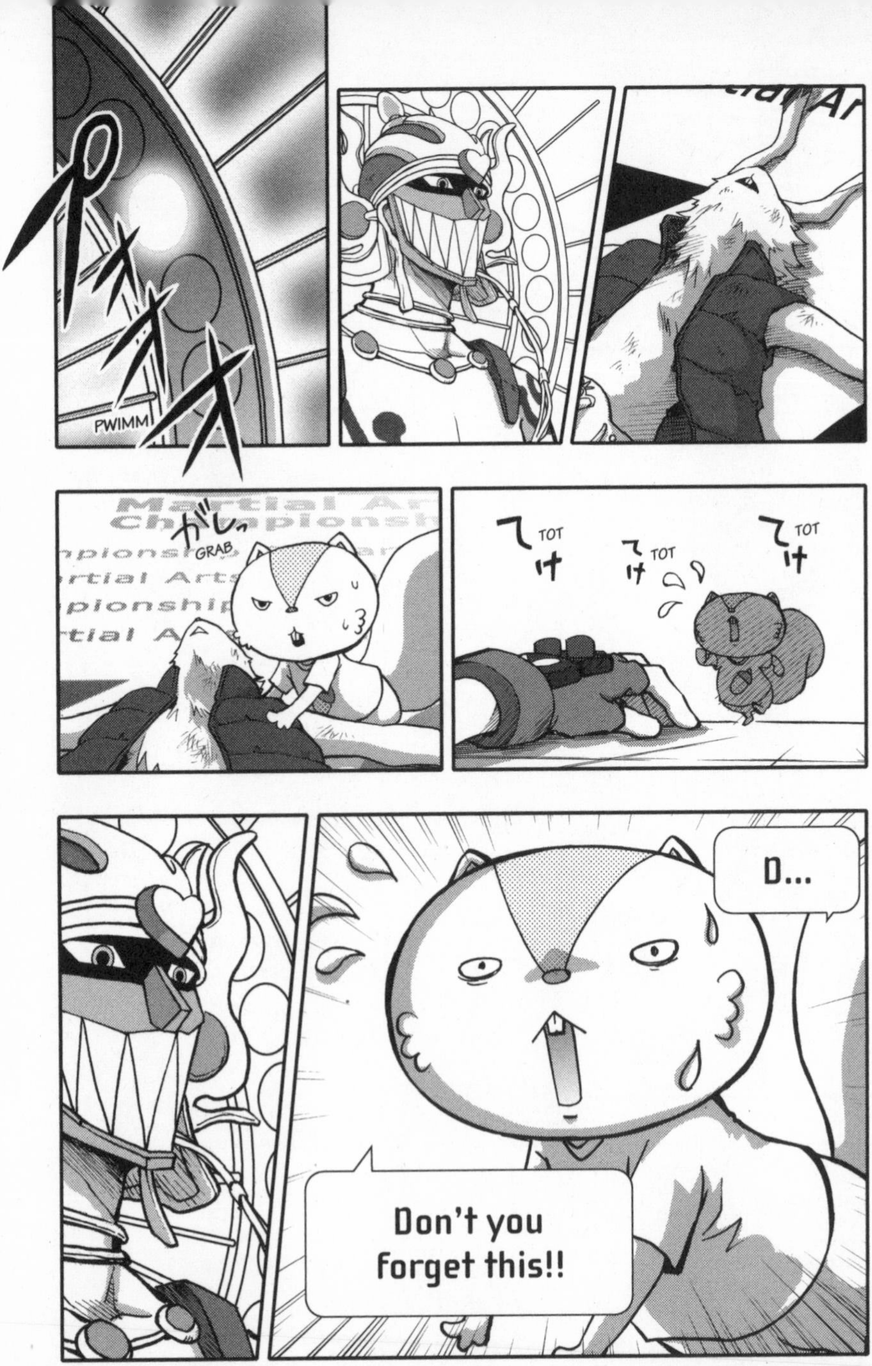

PWIMM
てけ TOT
てけ TOT
てけ TOT
がしっ GRAB
D...
Don't you forget this!!

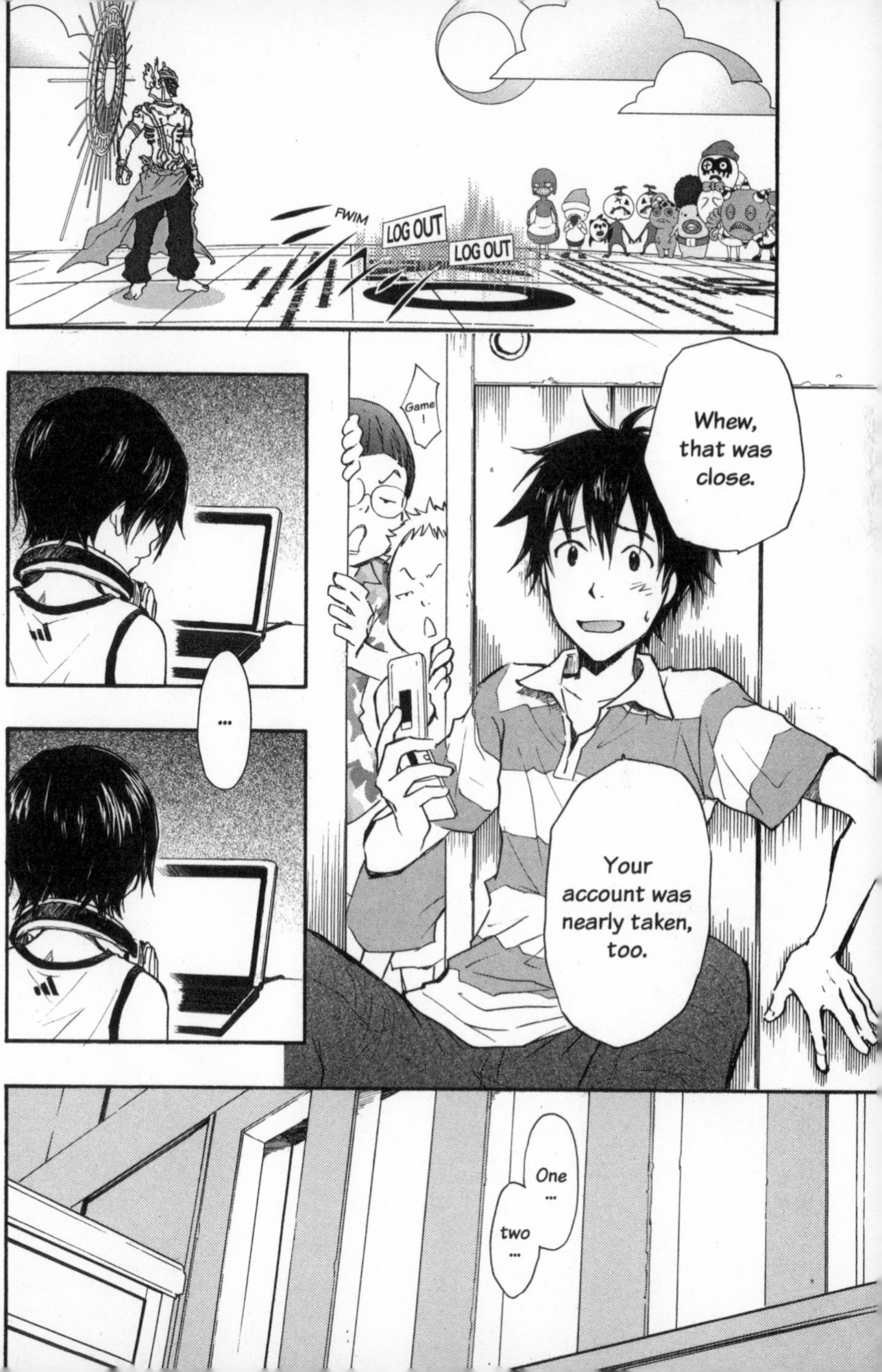
LOG OUT
LOG OUT
FWIM
Whew, that was close.
Game!
Your account was nearly taken, too.
...
One ... two ...

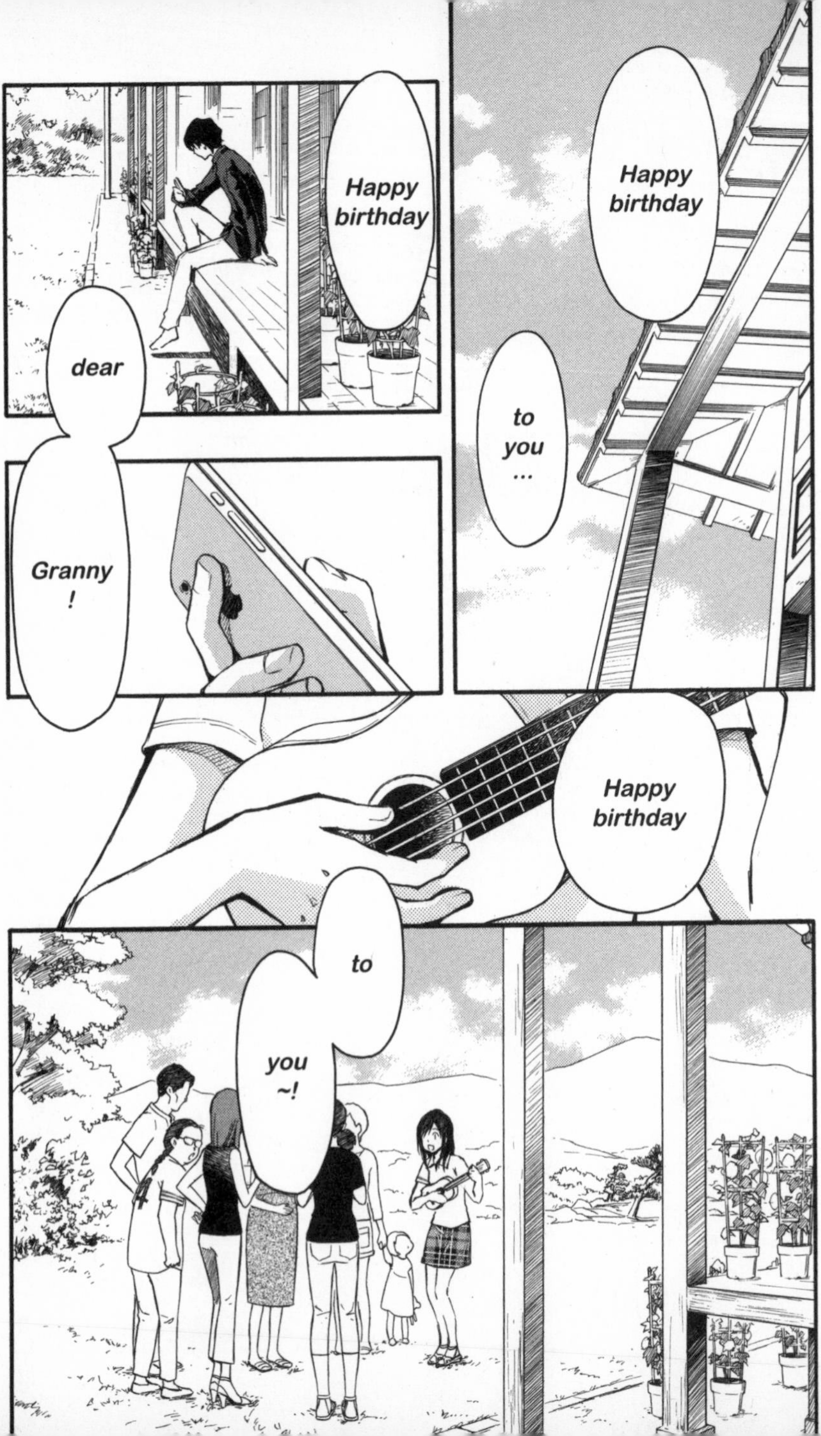
Happy birthday
to you ...
Happy birthday
dear
Granny !
Happy birthday
to you ~!

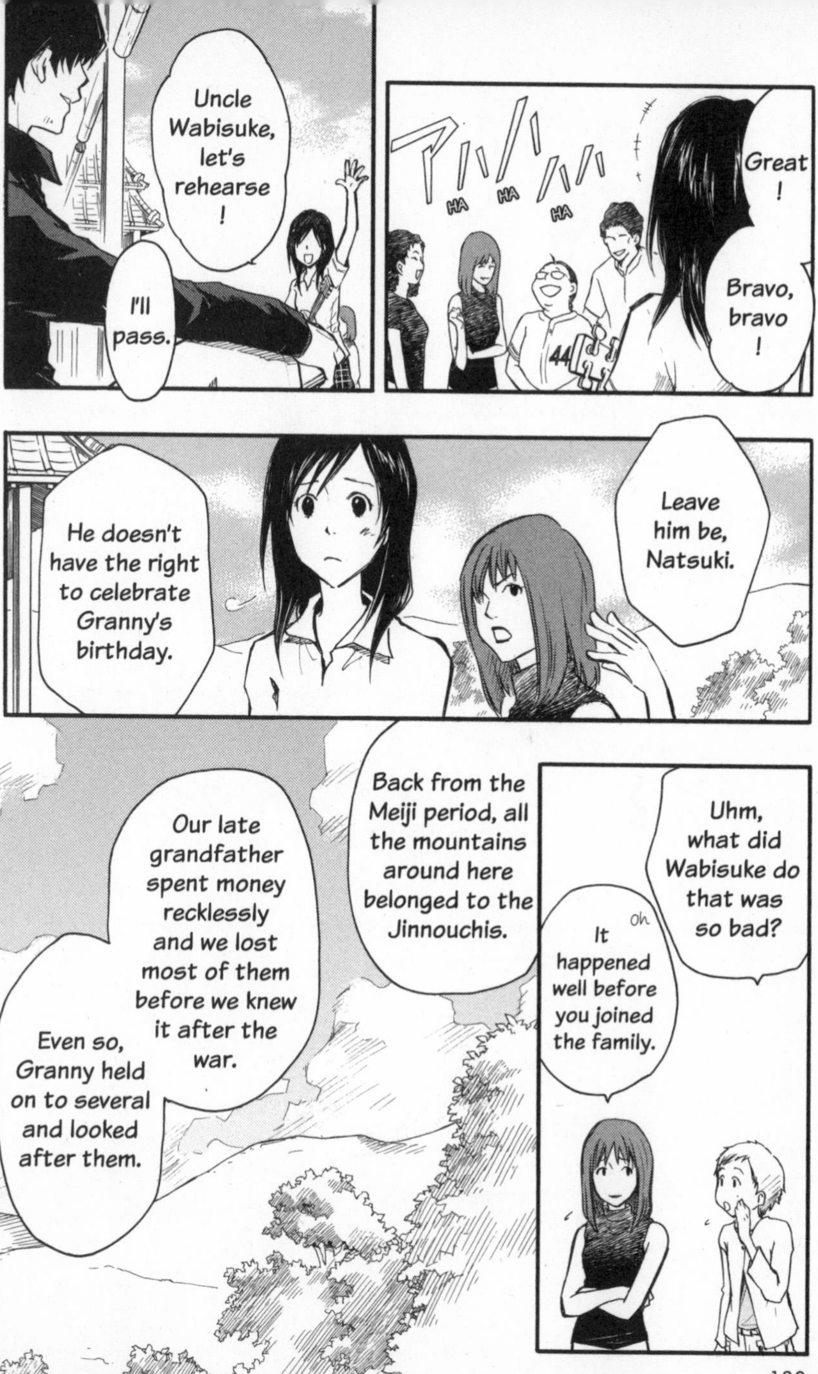

Great!
アハハハハ
HA HA HA
Bravo, bravo!
Uncle Wabisuke, let's rehearse!
I'll pass.
Leave him be, Natsuki.
He doesn't have the right to celebrate Granny's birthday.
Uhm, what did Wabisuke do that was so bad?
oh
It happened well before you joined the family.
Back from the Meiji period, all the mountains around here belonged to the Jinnouchis.
Our late grandfather spent money recklessly and we lost most of them before we knew it after the war.
Even so, Granny held on to several and looked after them.

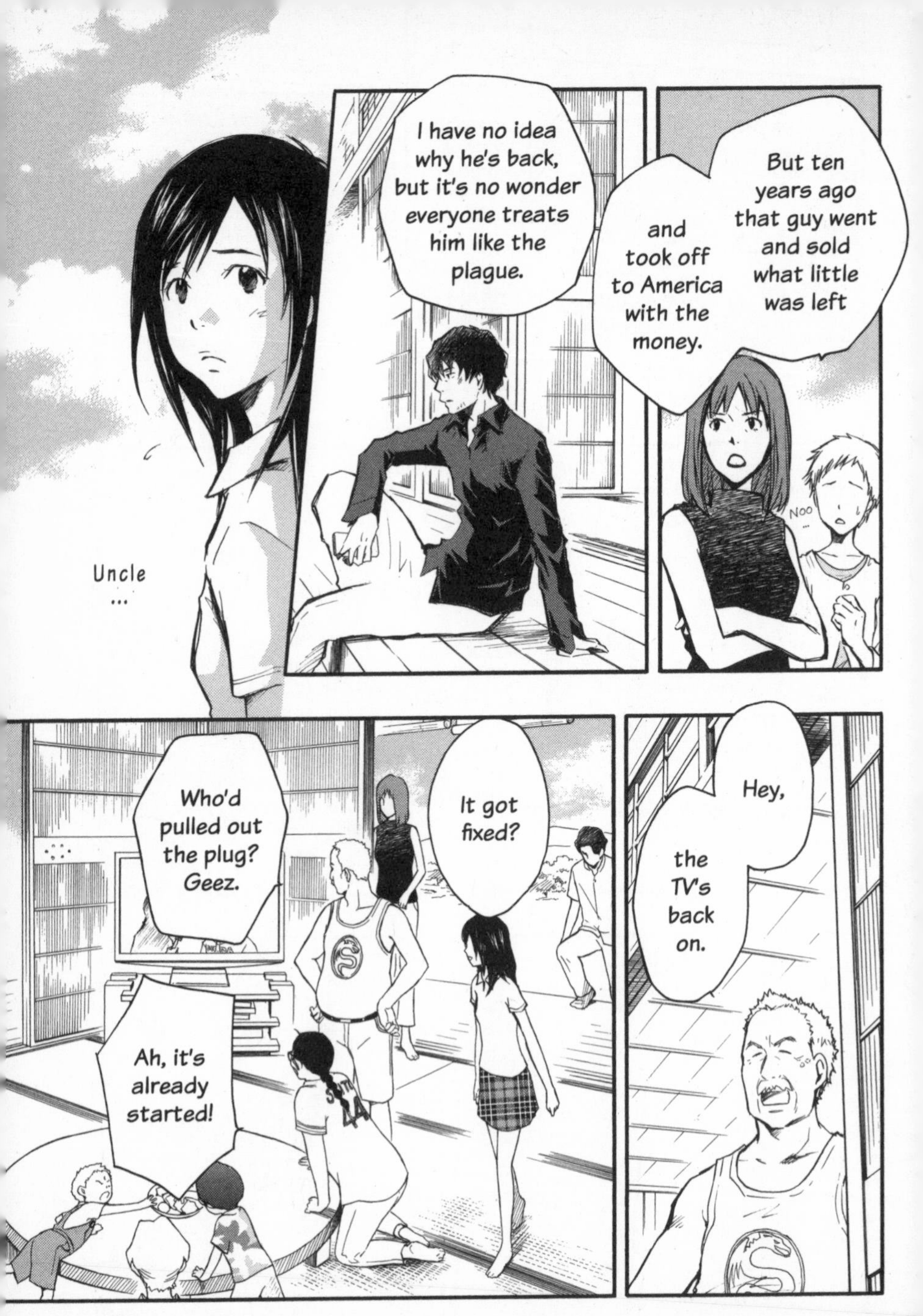
But ten years ago that guy went and sold what little was left
and took off to America with the money.
Noo...
I have no idea why he's back, but it's no wonder everyone treats him like the plague.
Uncle...
Hey,
the TV's back on.
It got fixed?
Who'd pulled out the plug? Geez.
Ah, it's already started!

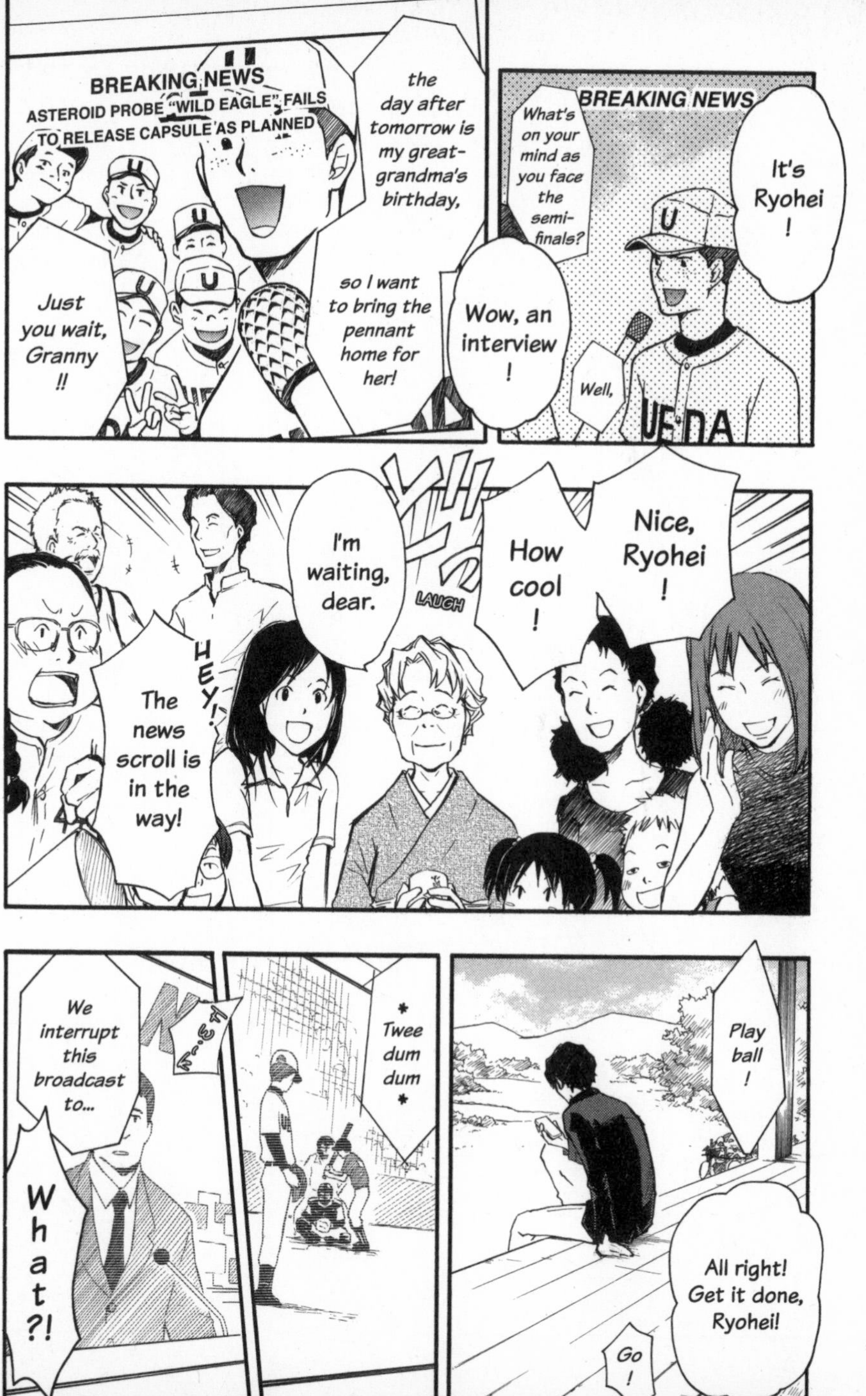
BREAKING NEWS
What's on your mind as you face the semi-finals?
It's Ryohei!
Wow, an interview!
Well,
BREAKING NEWS
ASTEROID PROBE "WILD EAGLE" FAILS TO RELEASE CAPSULE AS PLANNED
the day after tomorrow is my great-grandma's birthday,
so I want to bring the pennant home for her!
Just you wait, Granny!!
Nice, Ryohei!
How cool!
I'm waiting, dear.
LAUGH
HEY!
The news scroll is in the way!
Play ball!
All right! Get it done, Ryohei!
Go!
* Twee dum dum *
We interrupt this broadcast to...
What?!

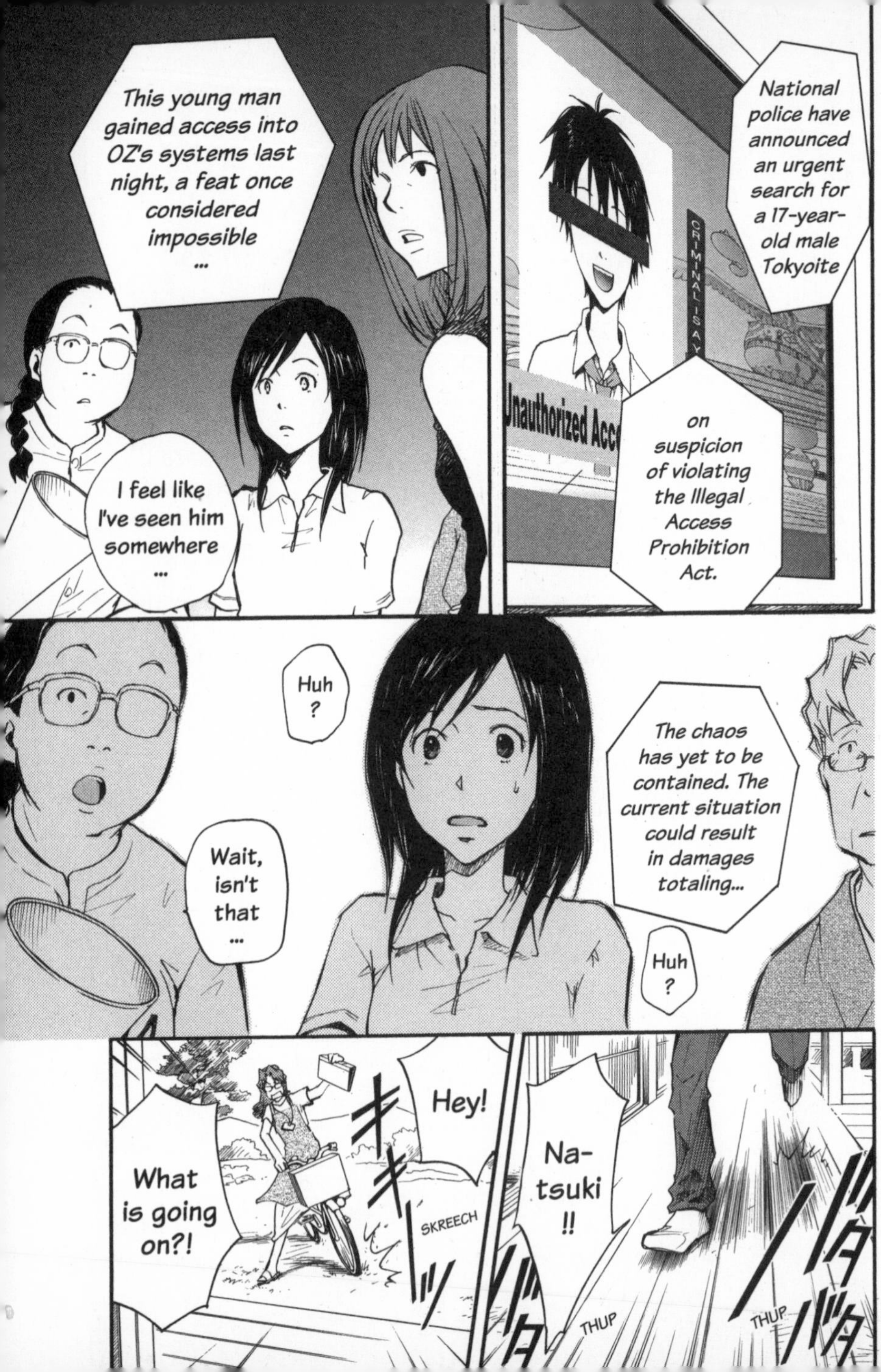
National police have announced an urgent search for a 17-year-old male Tokyoite
on suspicion of violating the Illegal Access Prohibition Act.
This young man gained access into OZ's systems last night, a feat once considered impossible ...
I feel like I've seen him somewhere ...
The chaos has yet to be contained. The current situation could result in damages totaling...
Huh?
Huh?
Wait, isn't that ...
Na-tsuki !!
THUP
THUP
Hey!
What is going on?!
SKREECH

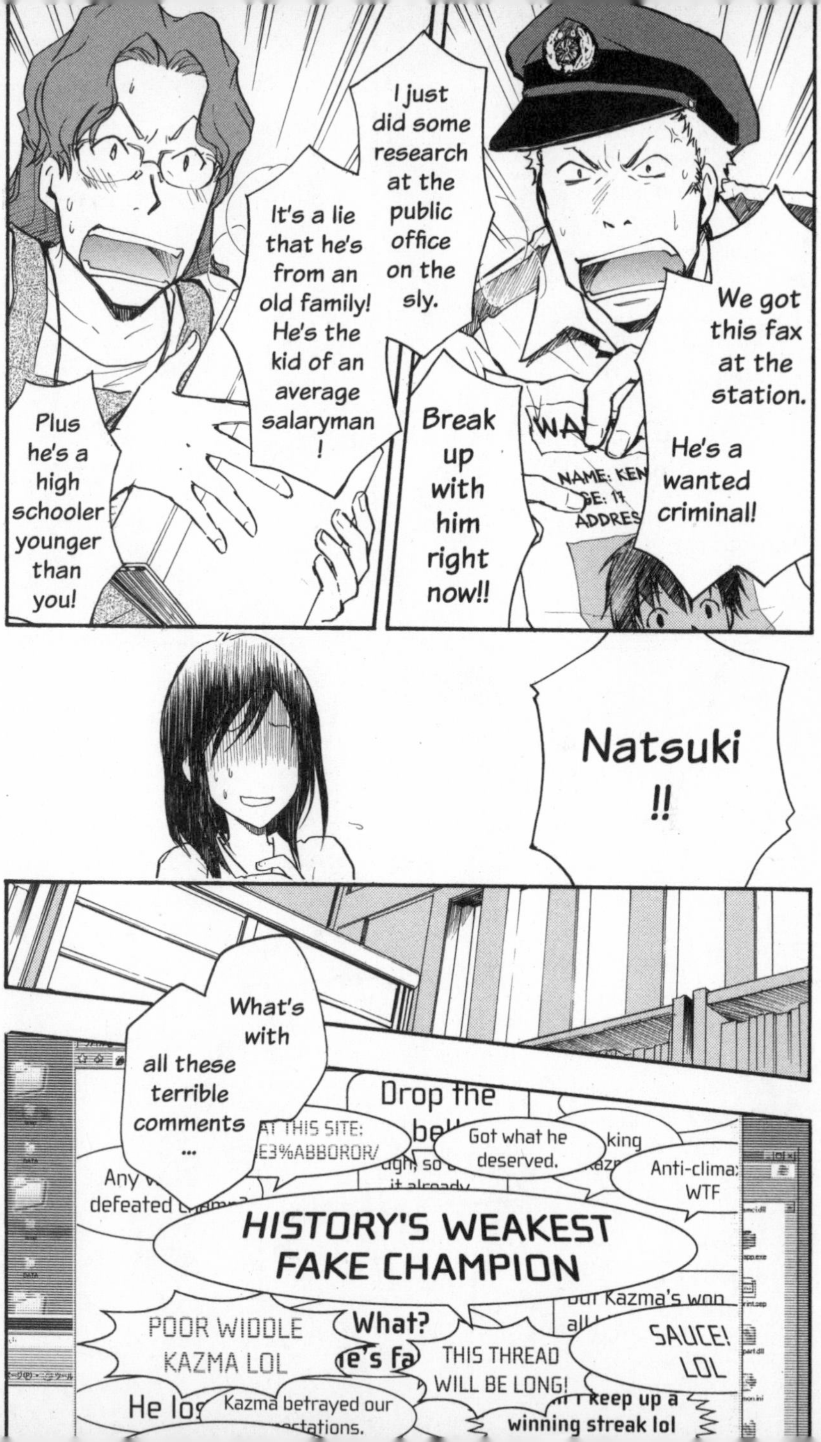

We got this fax at the station.
He's a wanted criminal!
Break up with him right now!!
I just did some research at the public office on the sly.
It's a lie that he's from an old family! He's the kid of an average salaryman!
Plus he's a high schooler younger than you!
Natsuki !!
What's with all these terrible comments...
Drop the
Got what he deserved.
HISTORY'S WEAKEST FAKE CHAMPION
SAUCE! LOL
THIS THREAD WILL BE LONG!
What?
POOR WIDDLE KAZMA LOL
winning streak lol

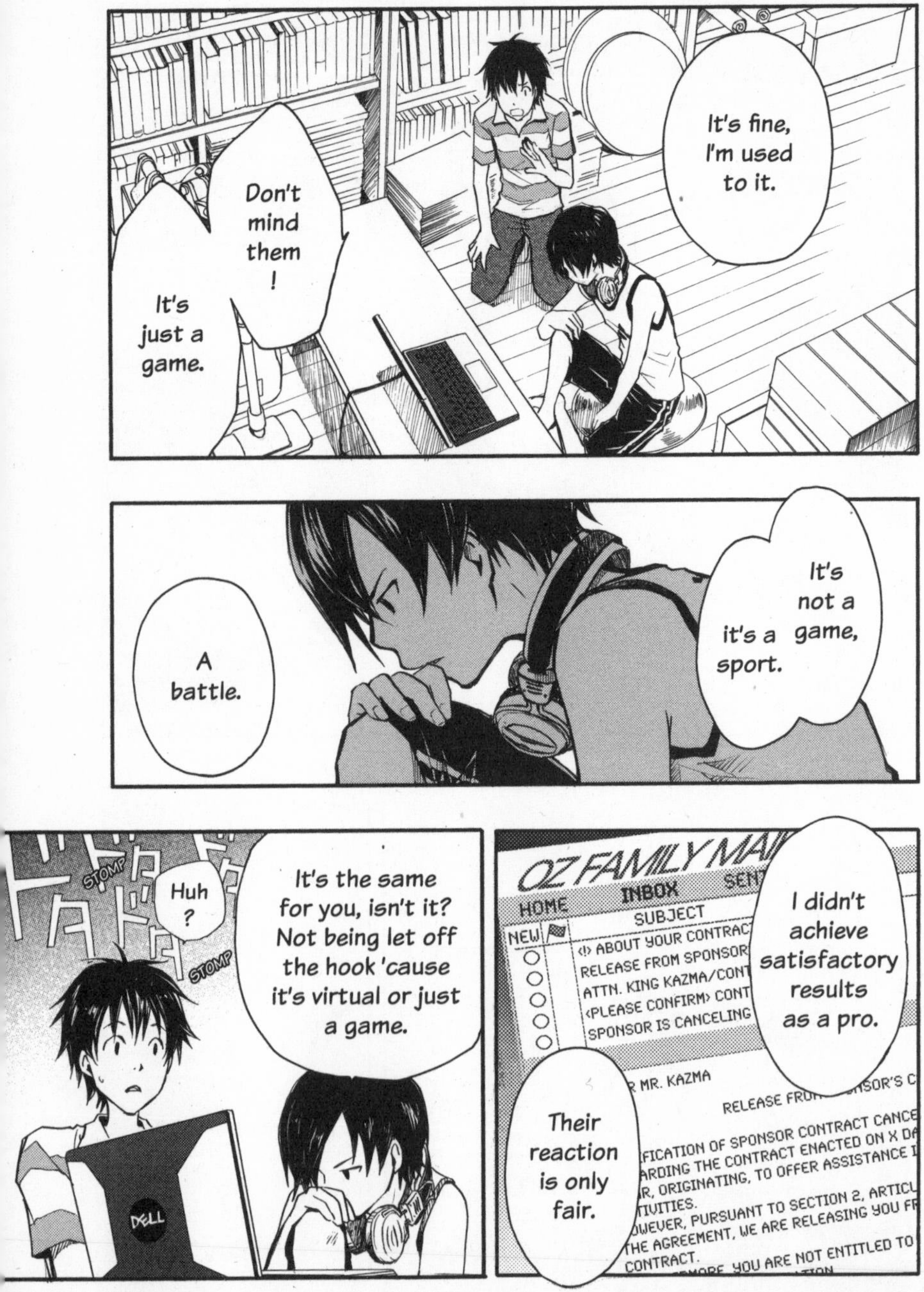
It's fine, I'm used to it.
Don't mind them!
It's just a game.
It's not a game, it's a sport.
A battle.
OZ FAMILY
INBOX
HOME
SUBJECT
NEW
I didn't achieve satisfactory results as a pro.
MR. KAZMA
Their reaction is only fair.
It's the same for you, isn't it? Not being let off the hook 'cause it's virtual or just a game.
Huh?
STOMP
STOMP

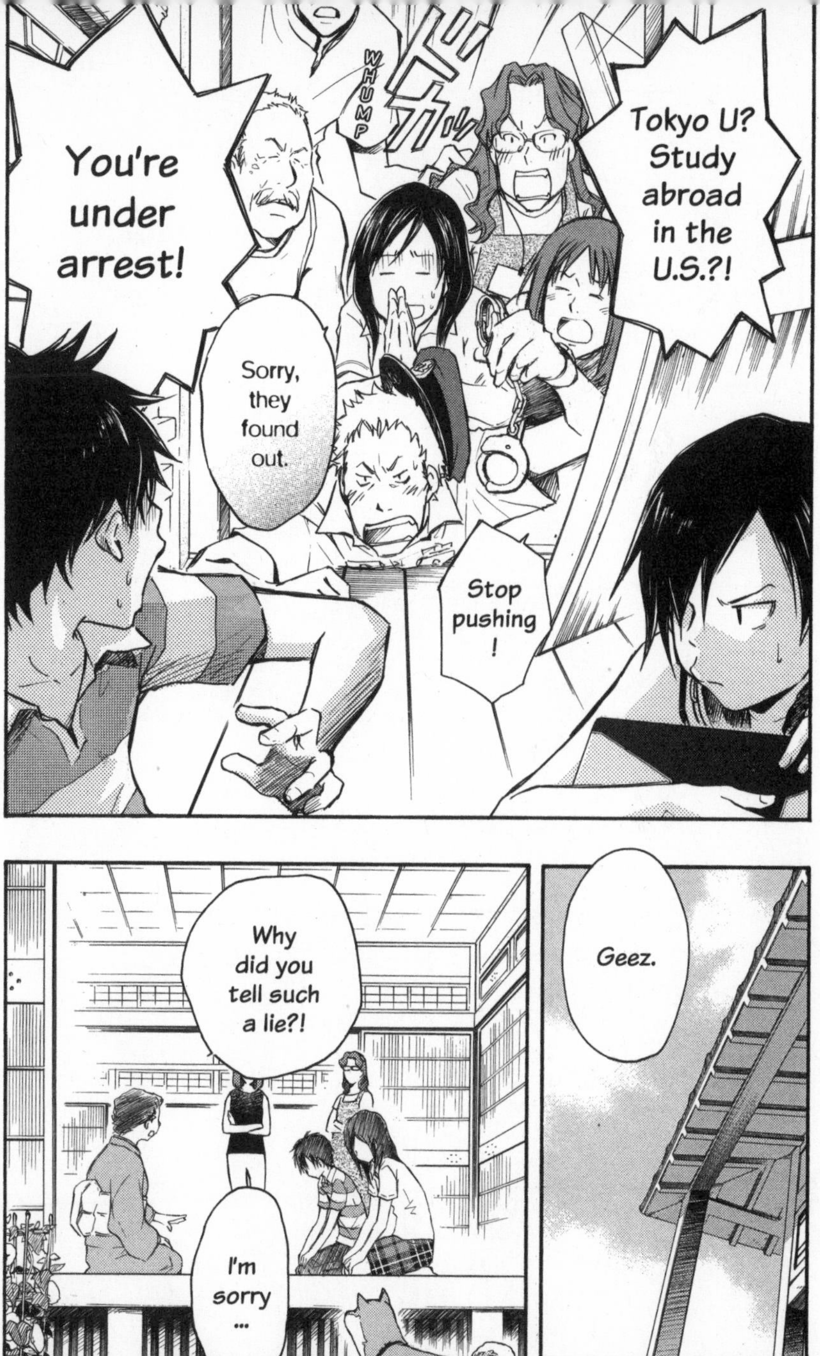

Tokyo U? Study abroad in the U.S.?!
WHUMP
You're under arrest!
Sorry, they found out.
Stop pushing!
Geez.
Why did you tell such a lie?!
I'm sorry ...

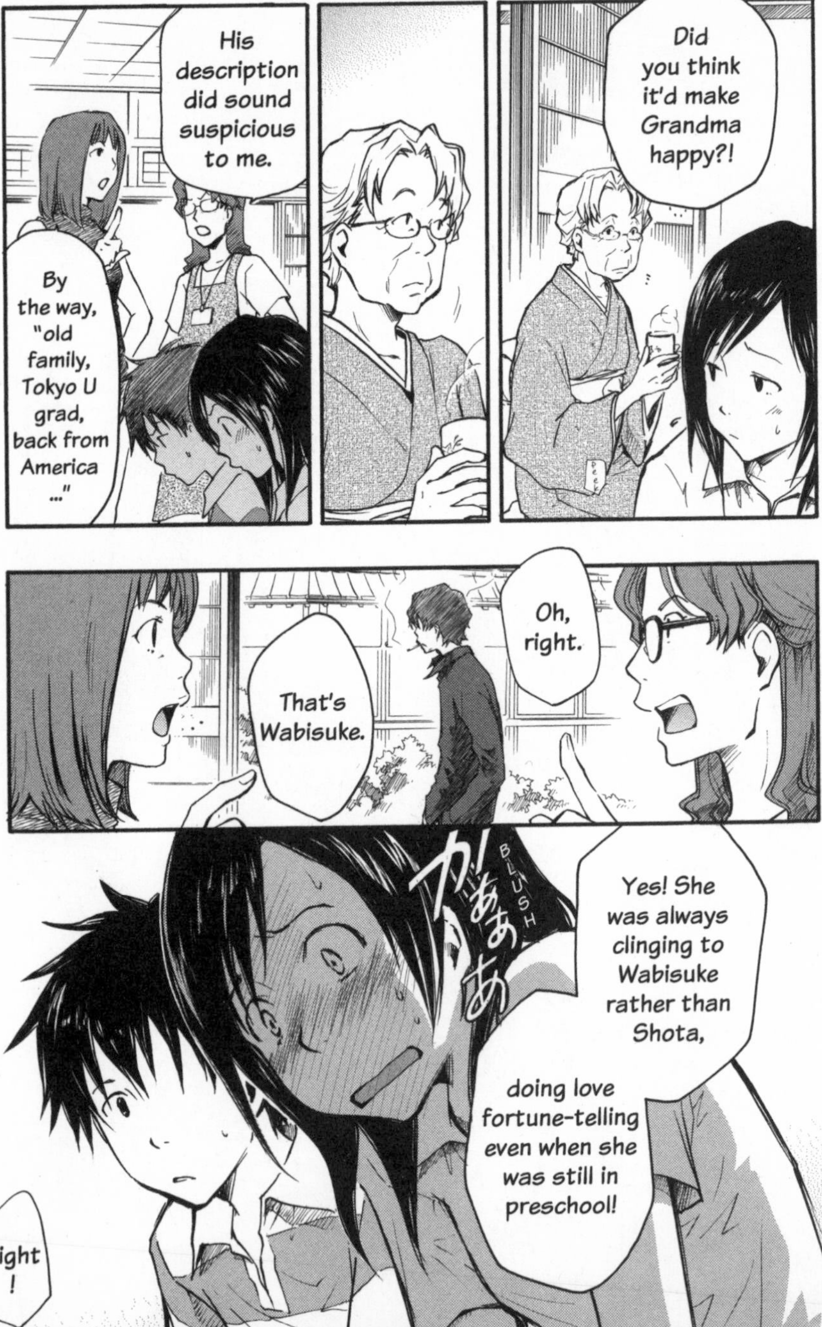
Did you think it'd make Grandma happy?!
Peek
His description did sound suspicious to me.
By the way, "old family, Tokyo U grad, back from America ..."
Oh, right.
That's Wabisuke.
カ!あああ
BLUSH
Yes! She was always clinging to Wabisuke rather than Shota,
doing love fortune-telling even when she was still in preschool!
Right!

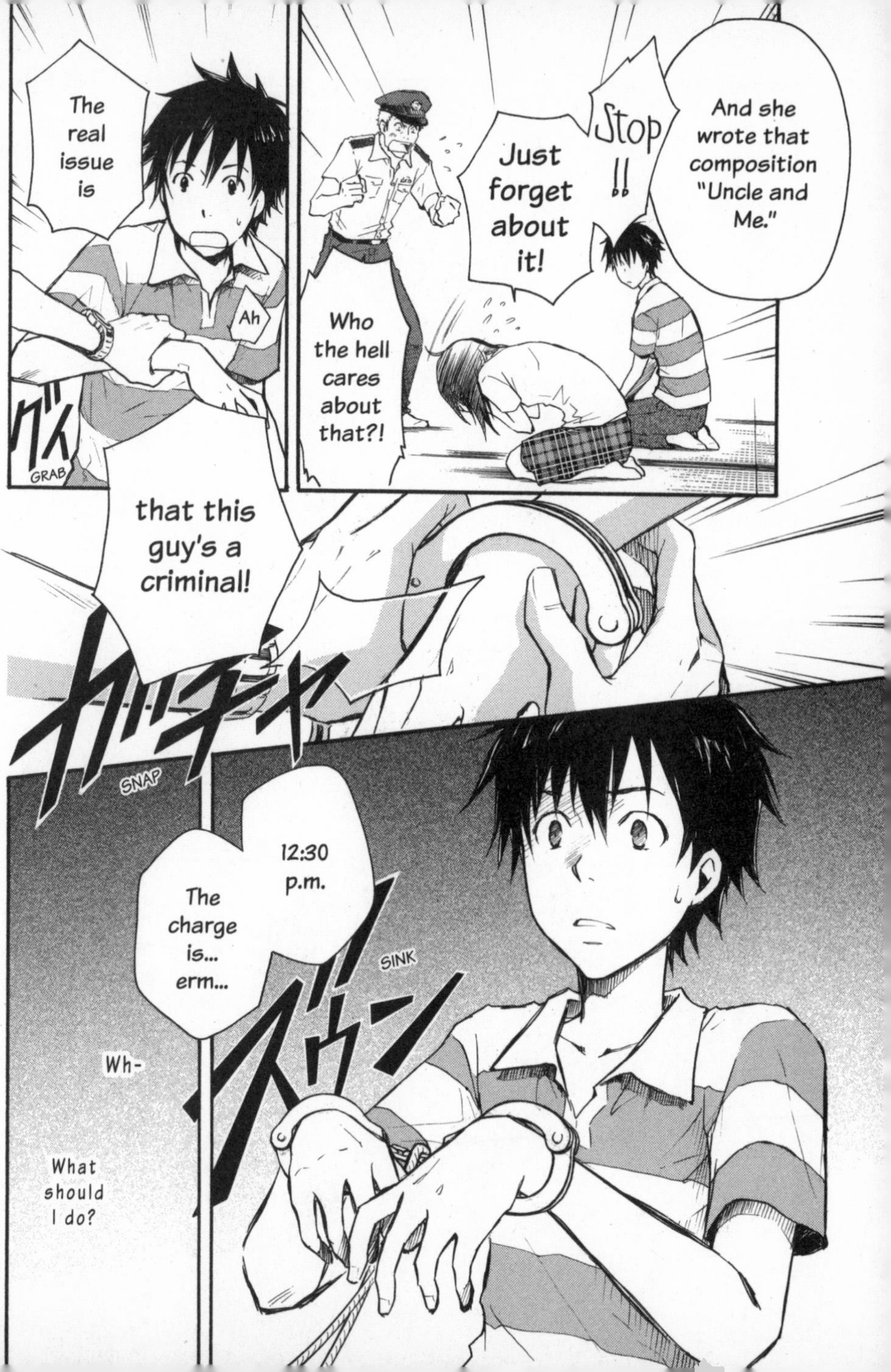
And she wrote that composition "Uncle and Me."
Stop!!
Just forget about it!
Who the hell cares about that?!
The real issue is
Ah
GRAB
that this guy's a criminal!
SNAP
12:30 p.m.
The charge is... erm...
SINK
Wh-
What should I do?

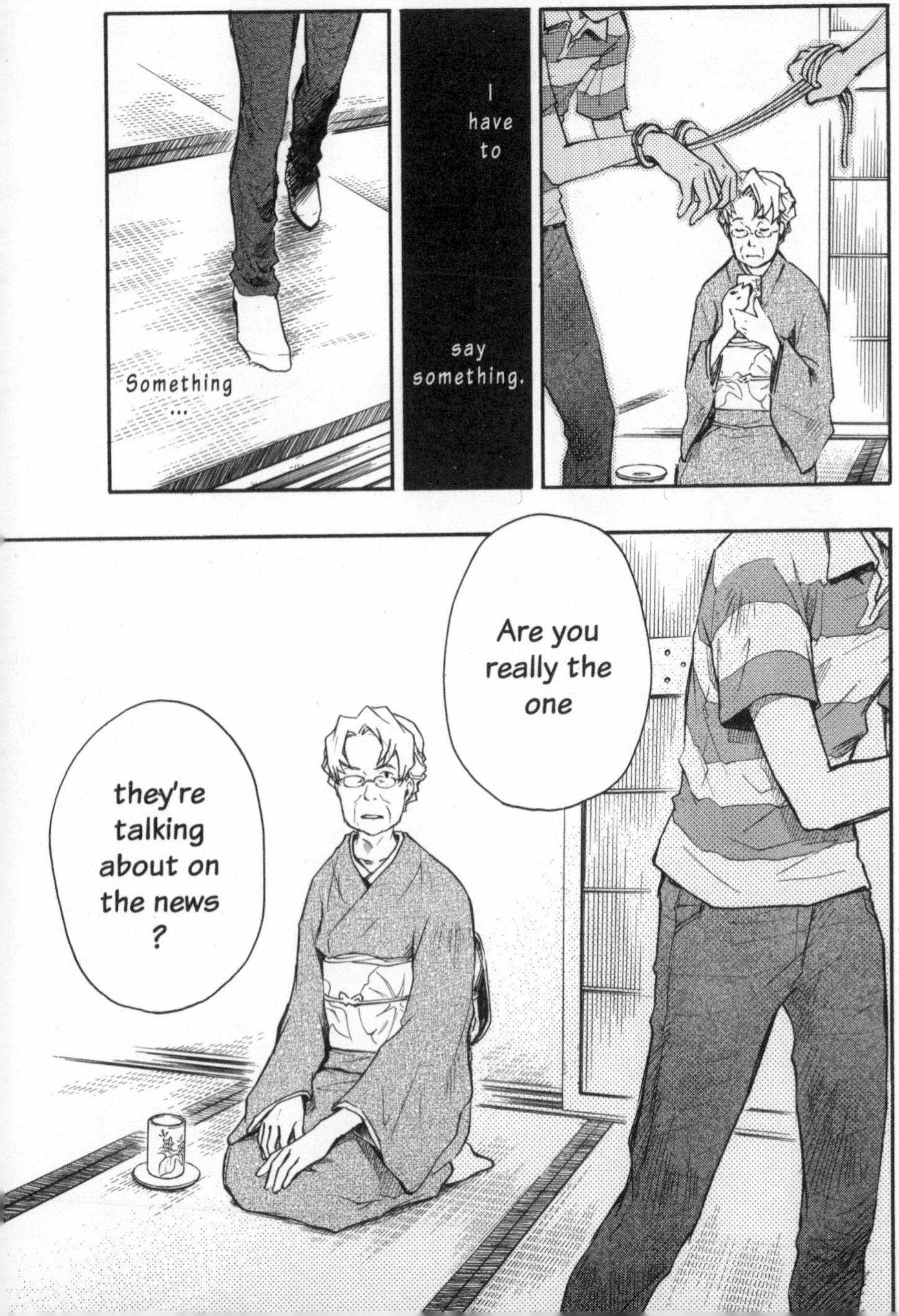
I have to
say something.
Something ...
Are you really the one
they're talking about on the news ?

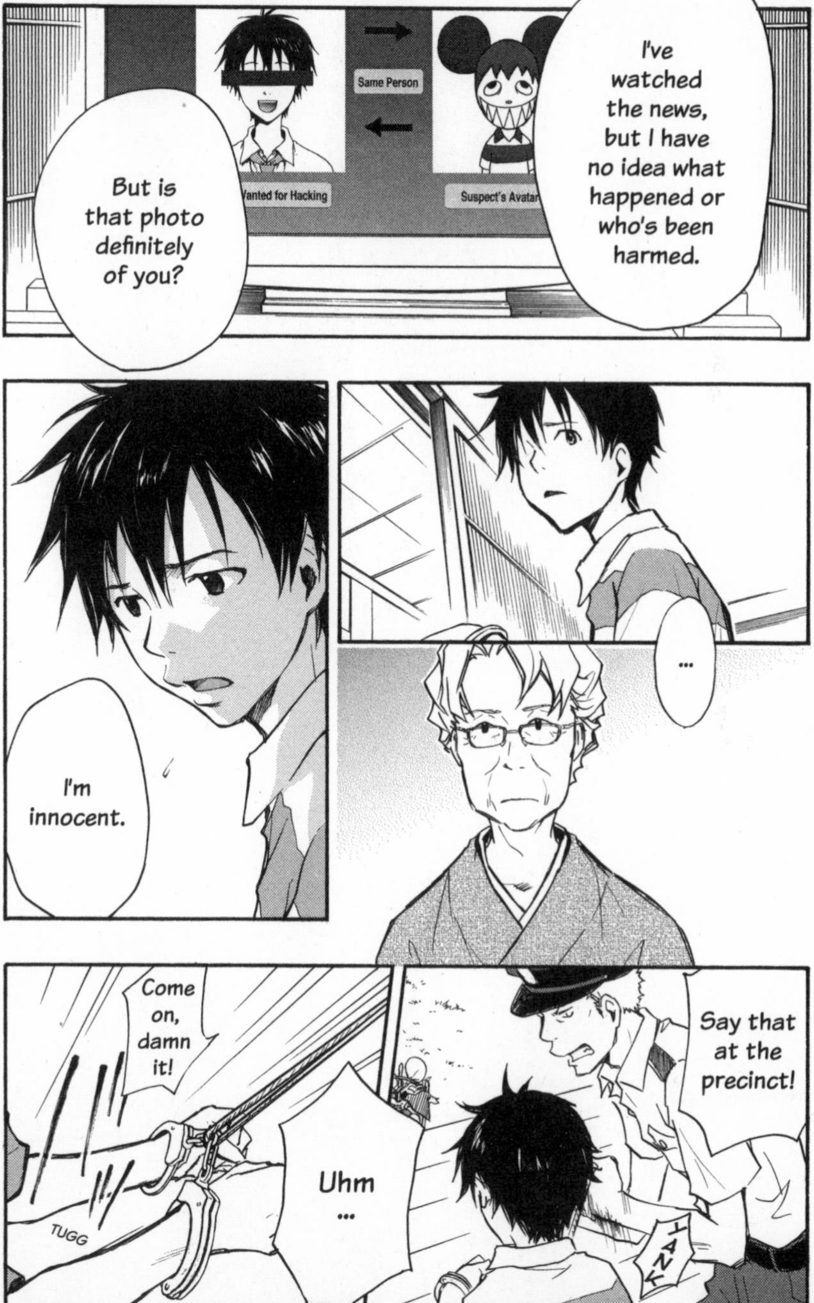
I've watched the news, but I have no idea what happened or who's been harmed.
Suspect's Avatar
Same Person
anted for Hacking
But is that photo definitely of you?
...
I'm innocent.
Say that at the precinct!
YANK
Uhm ...
Come on, damn it!
TUGG

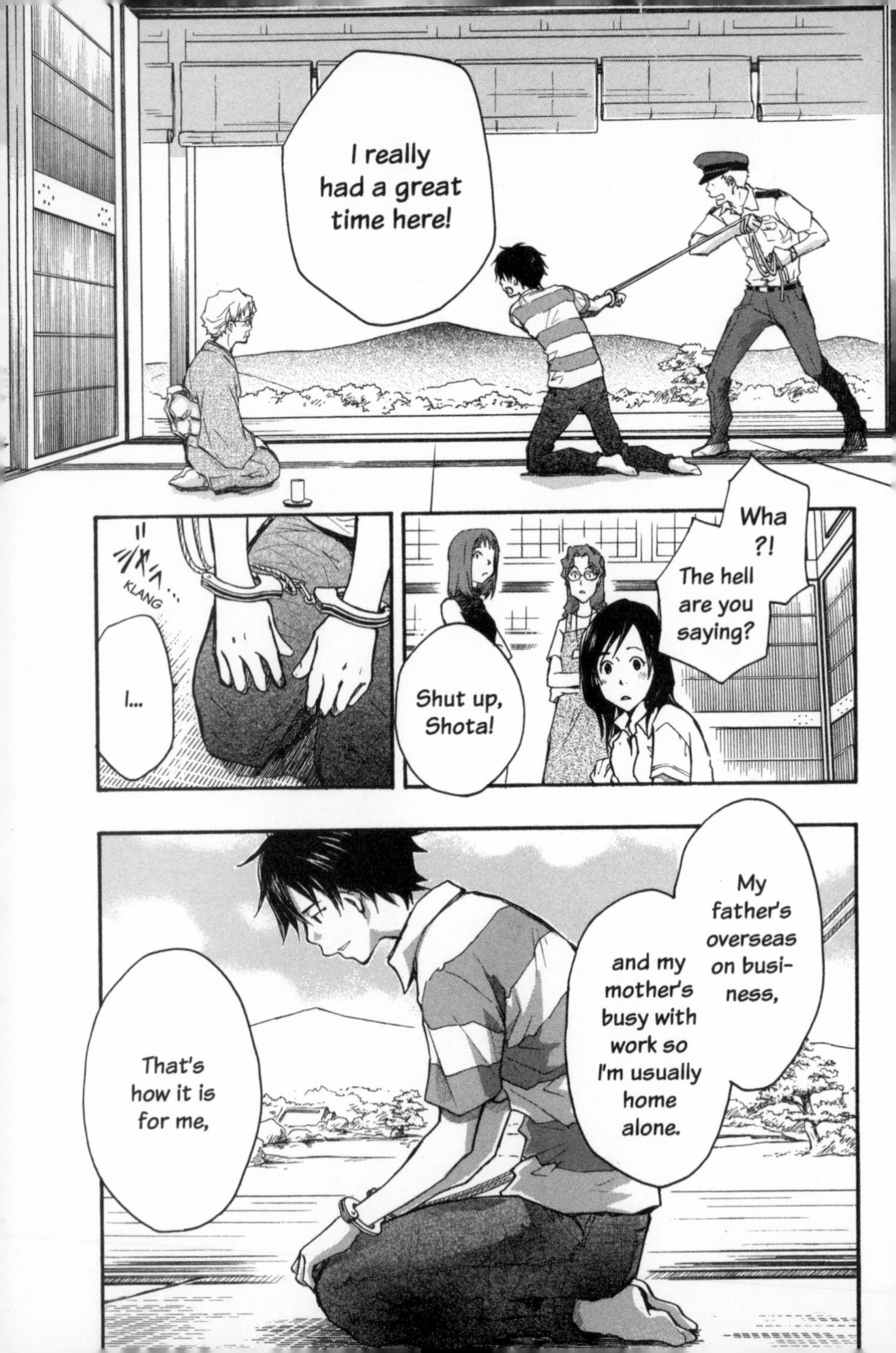
I really had a great time here!
Wha ?! The hell are you saying?
Shut up, Shota!
KLANG
I...
My father's overseas on business,
and my mother's busy with work so I'm usually home alone.
That's how it is for me,

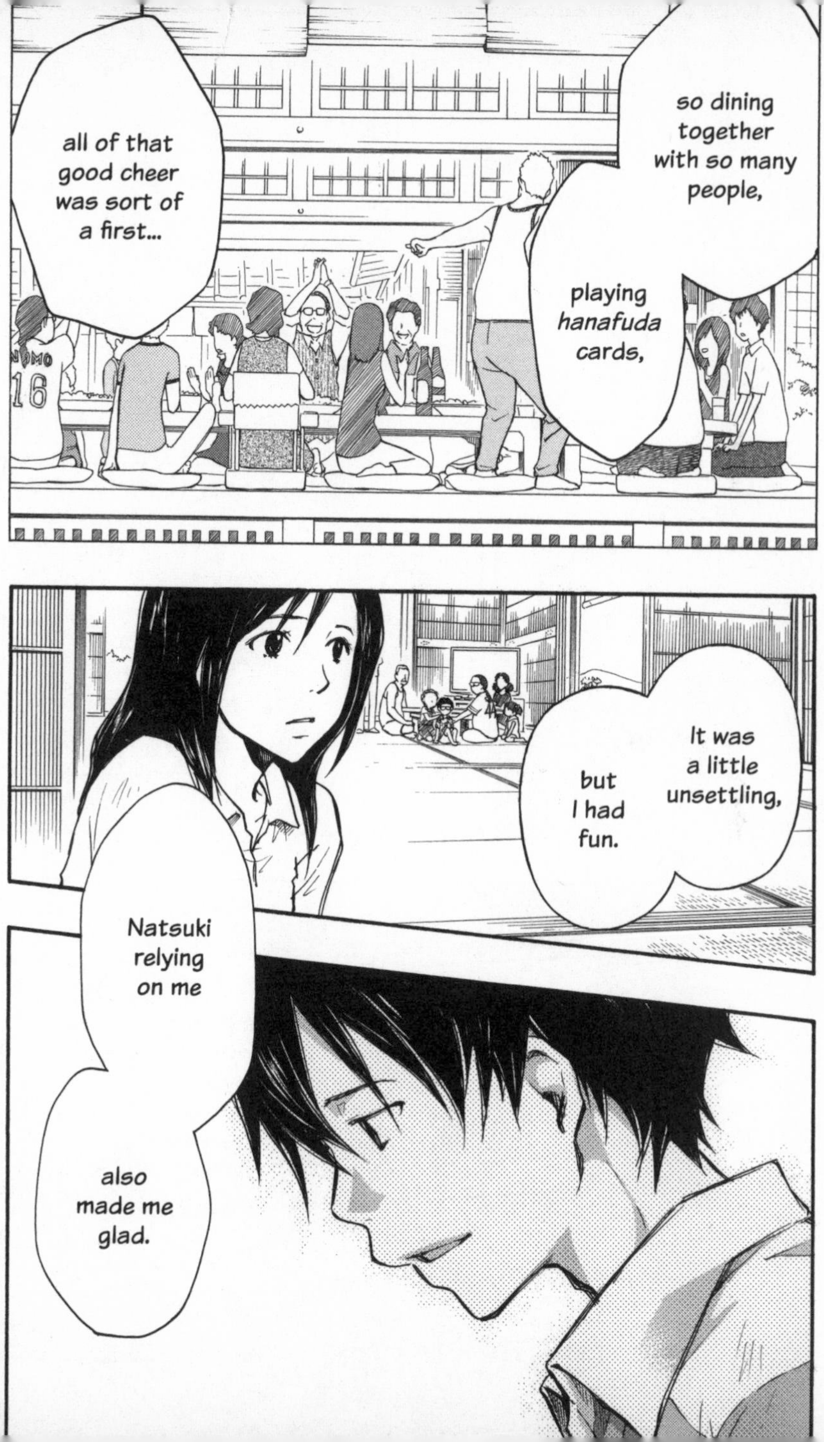
so dining together with so many people,
playing hanafuda cards,
all of that good cheer was sort of a first...
It was a little unsettling,
but I had fun.
Natsuki relying on me
also made me glad.

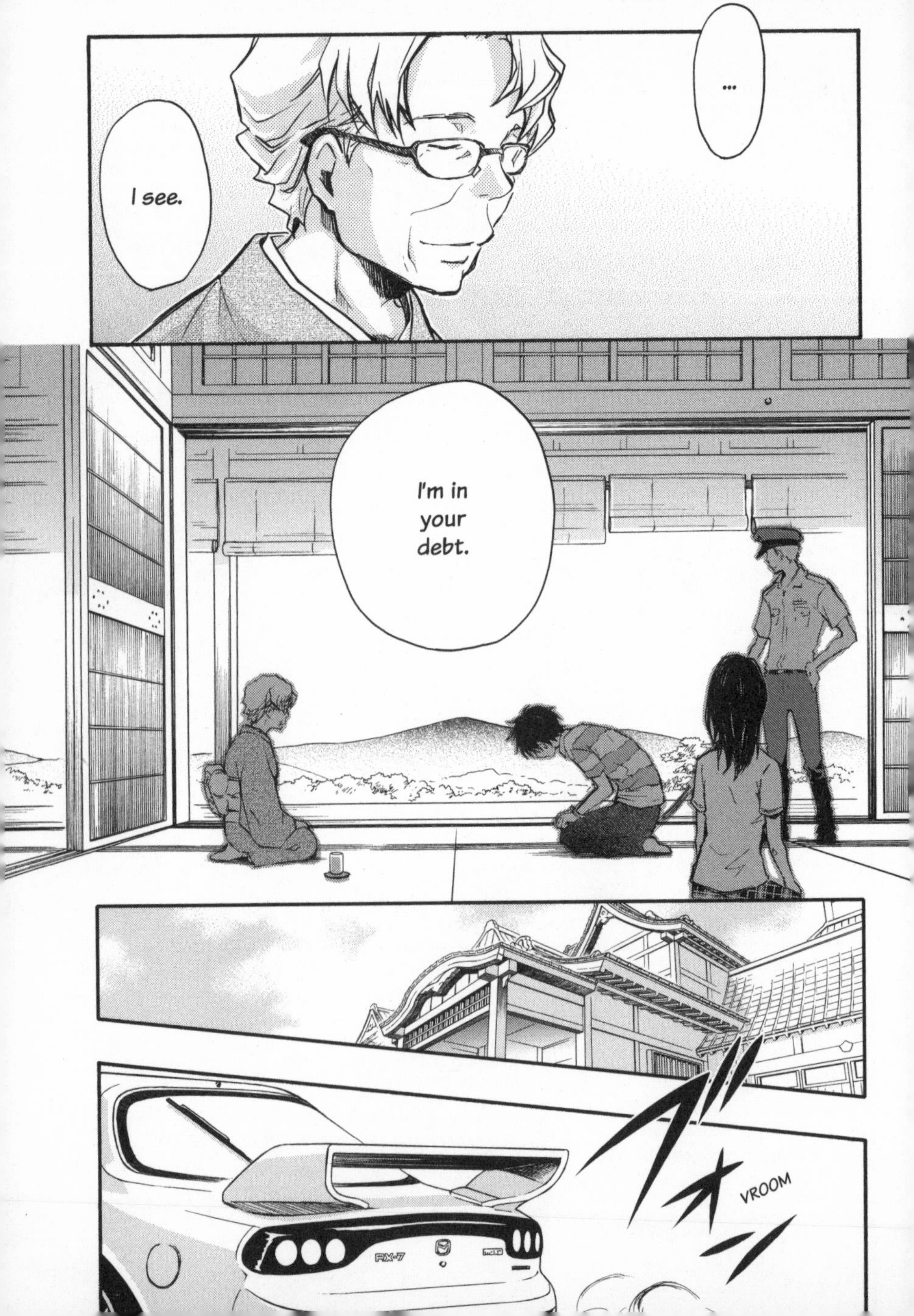
...
I see.
I'm in your debt.
VROOM

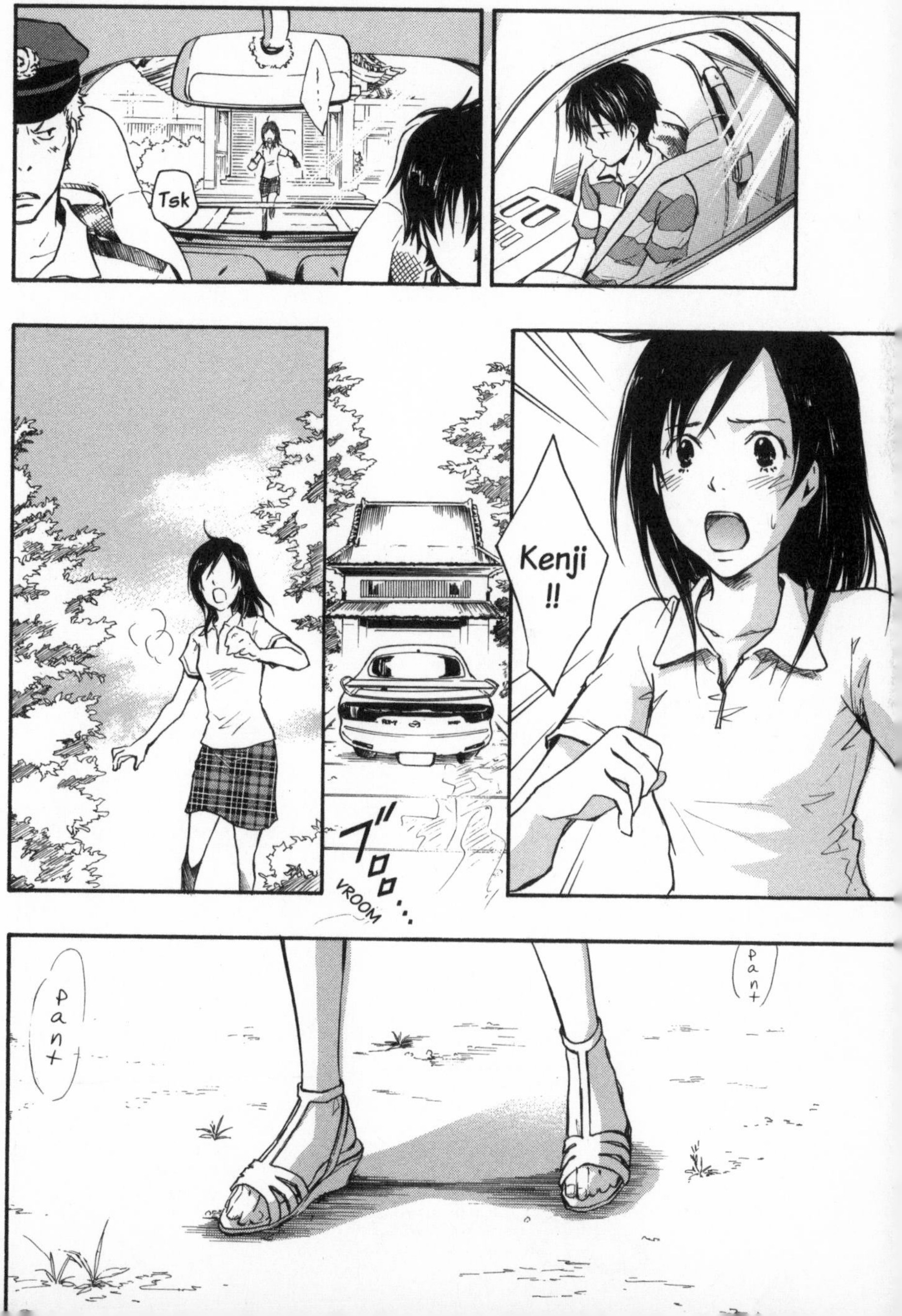
Tsk
Kenji !!
ブロロ…
VROOM
pant
pant

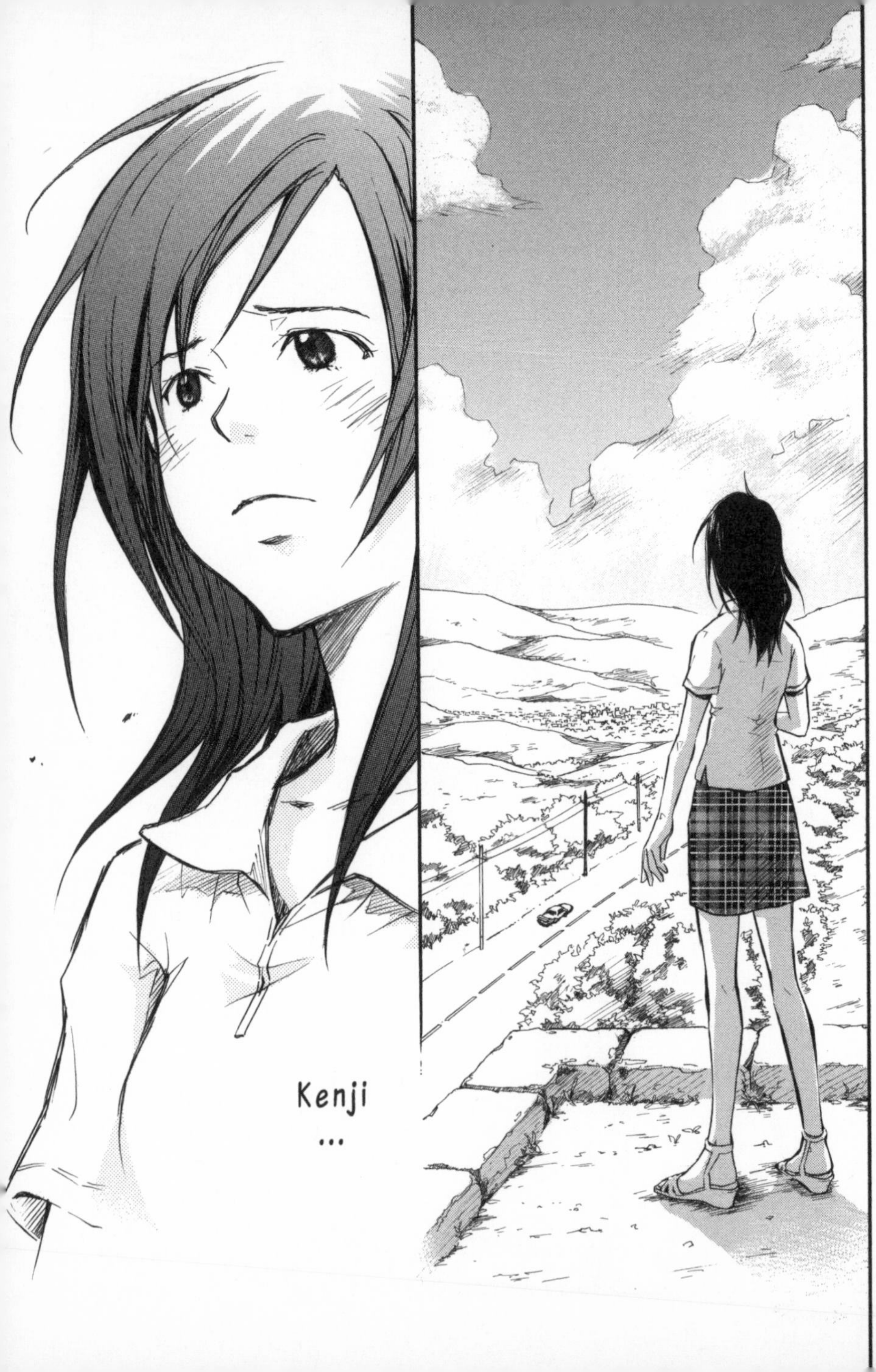
Kenji
...

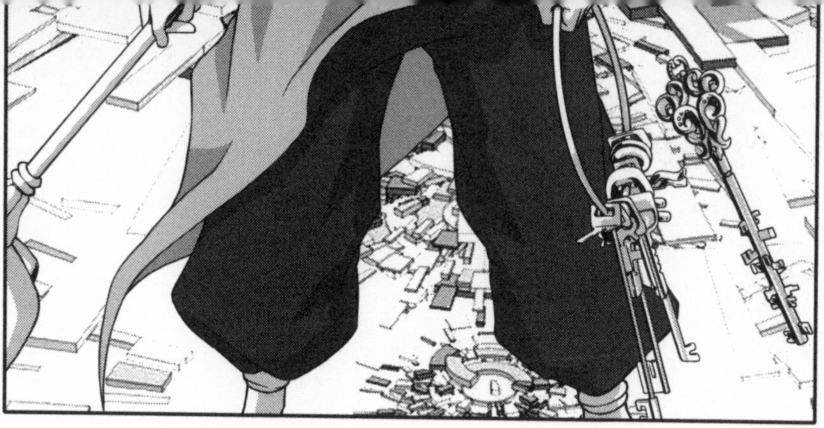

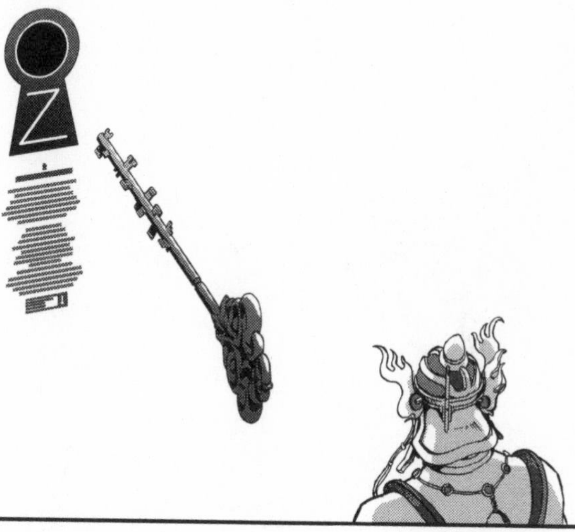

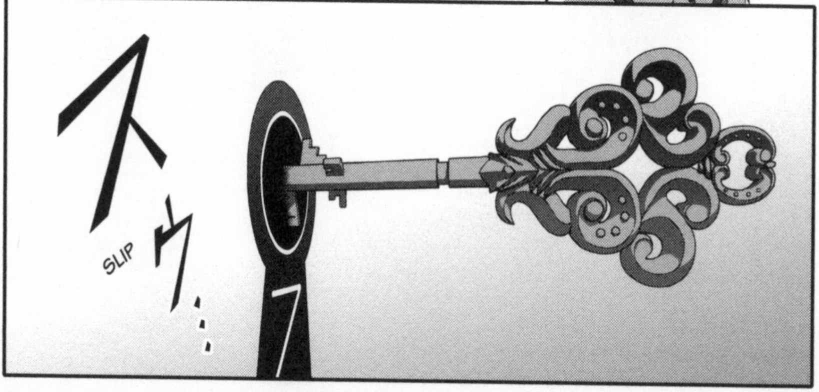
スッ...
SLIP

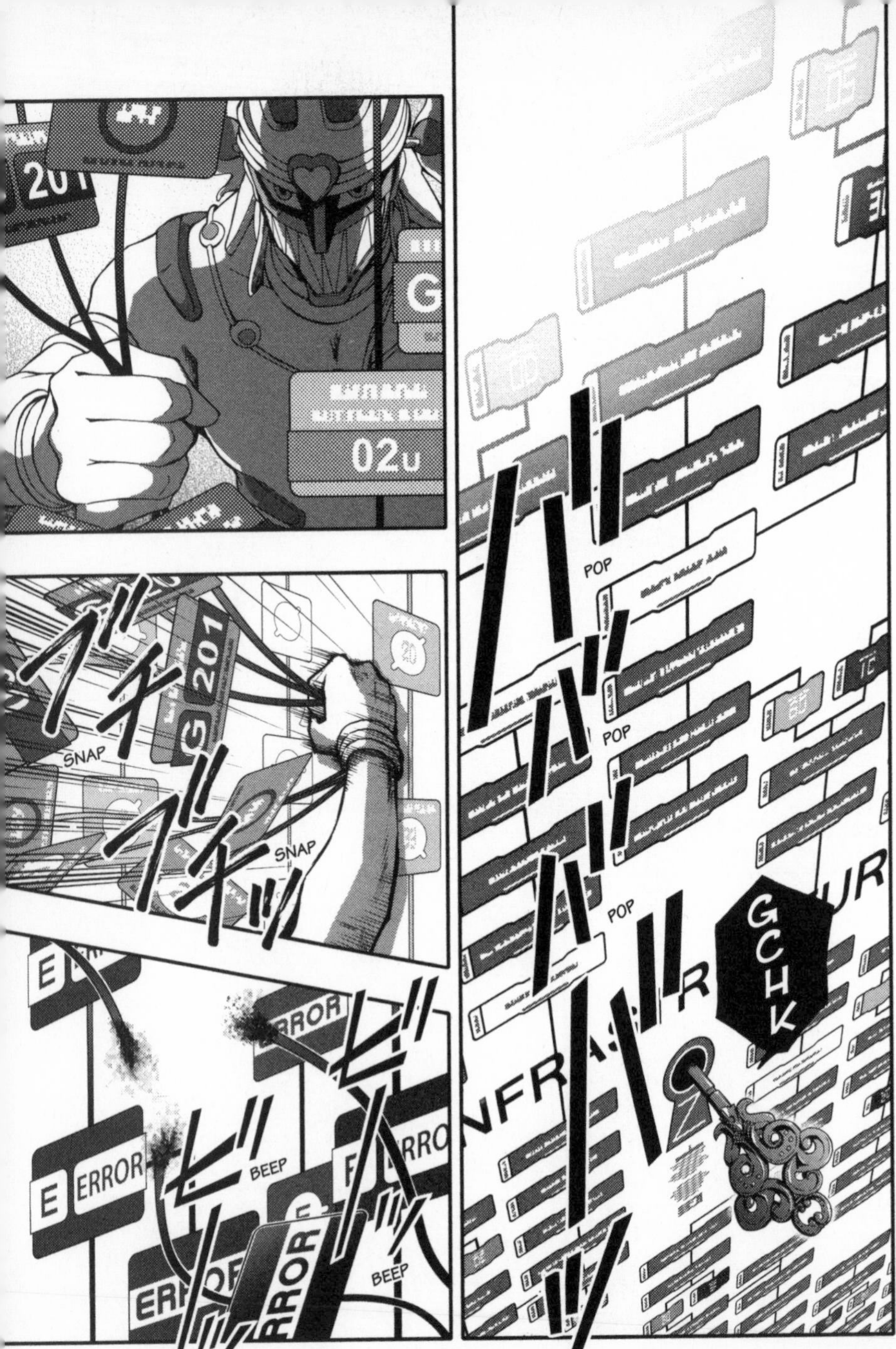

POP
POP
POP
GCHK
201
G
02U
SNAP
201
G
SNAP
ERROR
ERROR
BEEP
ERROR
BEEP

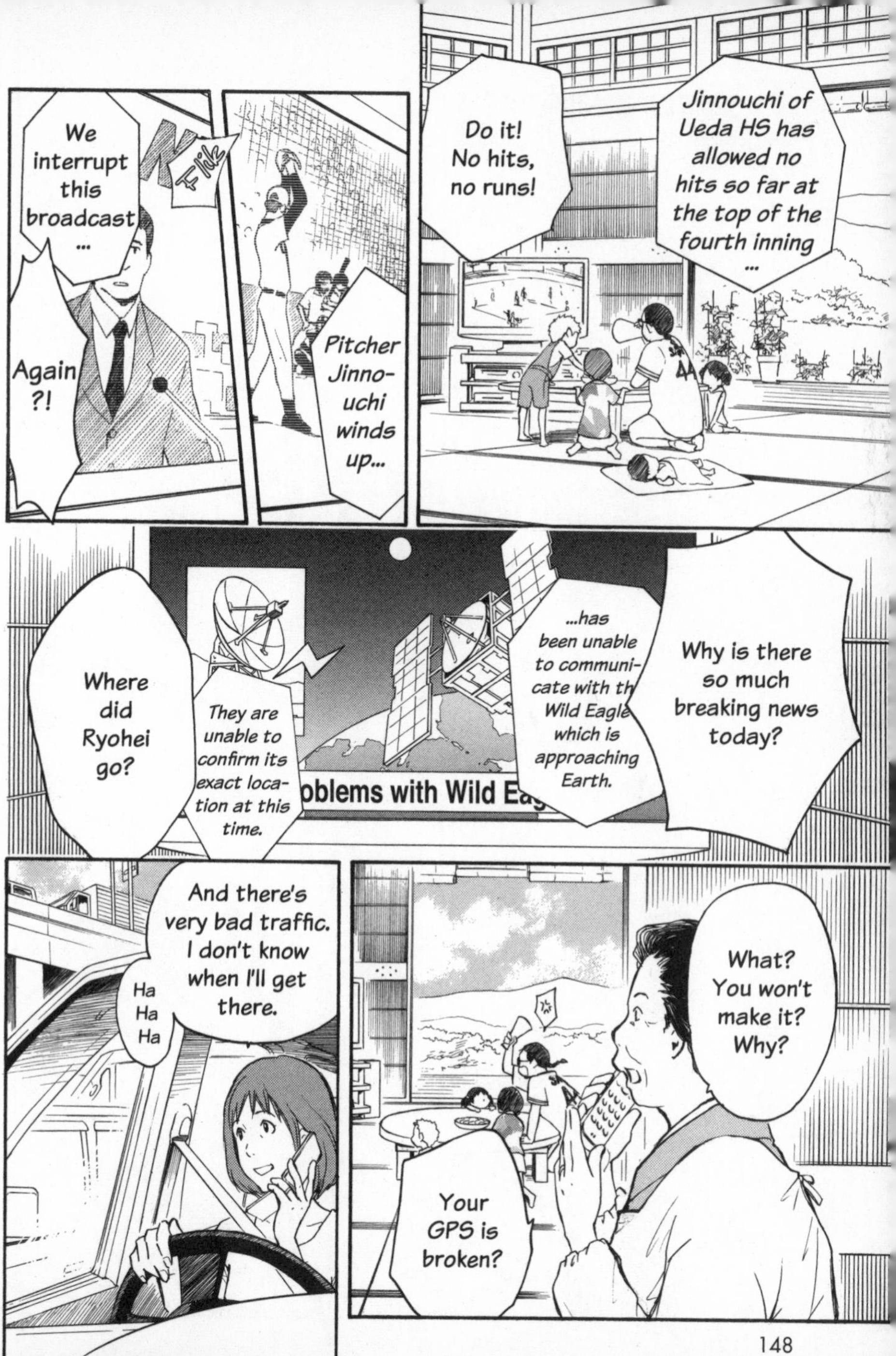
Jinnouchi of Ueda HS has allowed no hits so far at the top of the fourth inning ...
Do it! No hits, no runs!
Flik
Pitcher Jinnouchi winds up...
We interrupt this broadcast ...
Again ?!
Why is there so much breaking news today?
...has been unable to communicate with th Wild Eagle which is approaching Earth.
oblems with Wild Eag
They are unable to confirm its exact location at this time.
Where did Ryohei go?
What? You won't make it? Why?
Your GPS is broken?
And there's very bad traffic. I don't know when I'll get there.
Ha Ha Ha

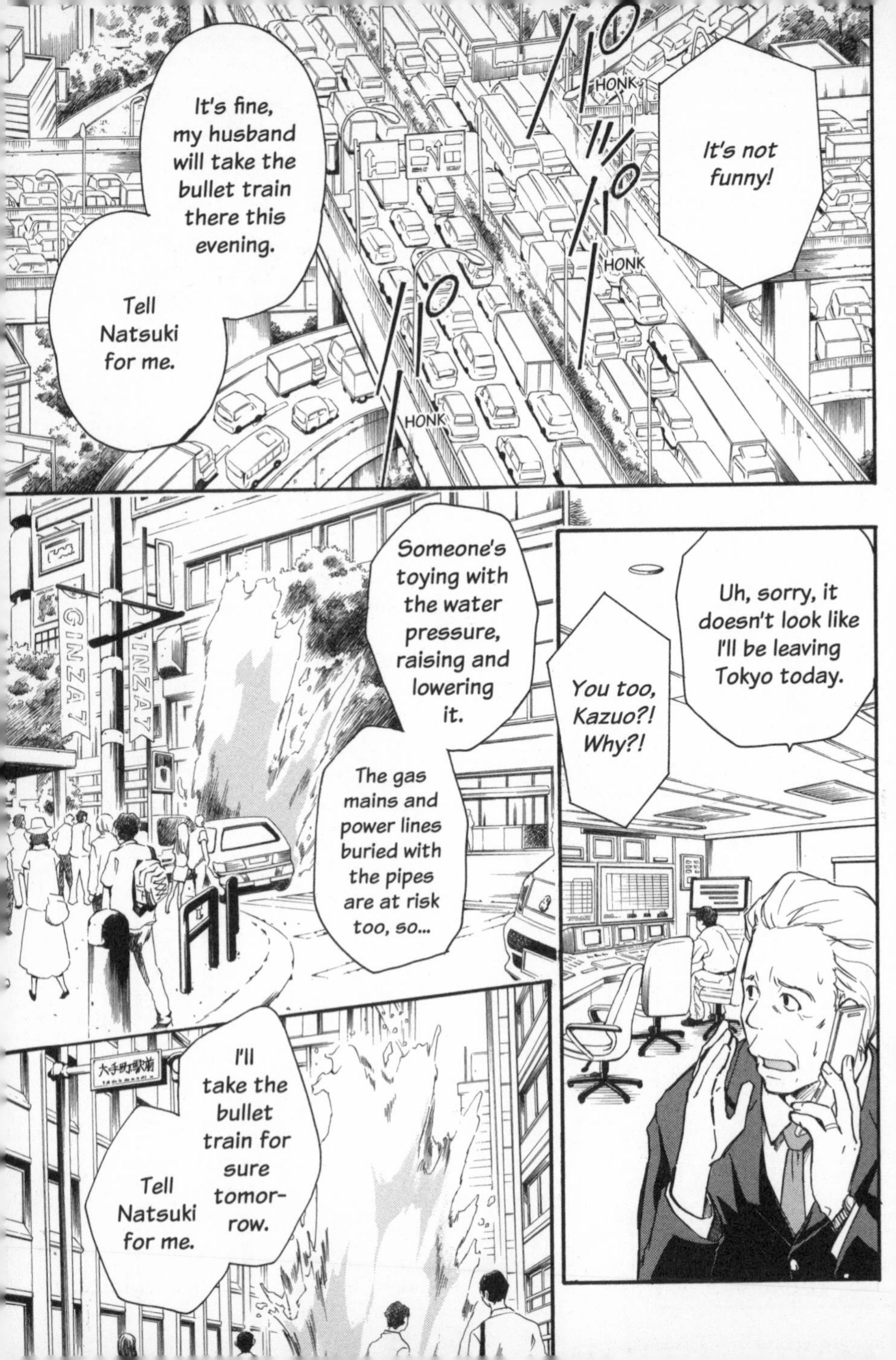
It's not funny!
HONK
HONK
HONK
It's fine, my husband will take the bullet train there this evening.
Tell Natsuki for me.
Uh, sorry, it doesn't look like I'll be leaving Tokyo today.
You too, Kazuo?! Why?!
GINZA 7
GINZA 7
Someone's toying with the water pressure, raising and lowering it.
The gas mains and power lines buried with the pipes are at risk too, so...
大手町駅前
I'll take the bullet train for sure tomorrow.
Tell Natsuki for me.

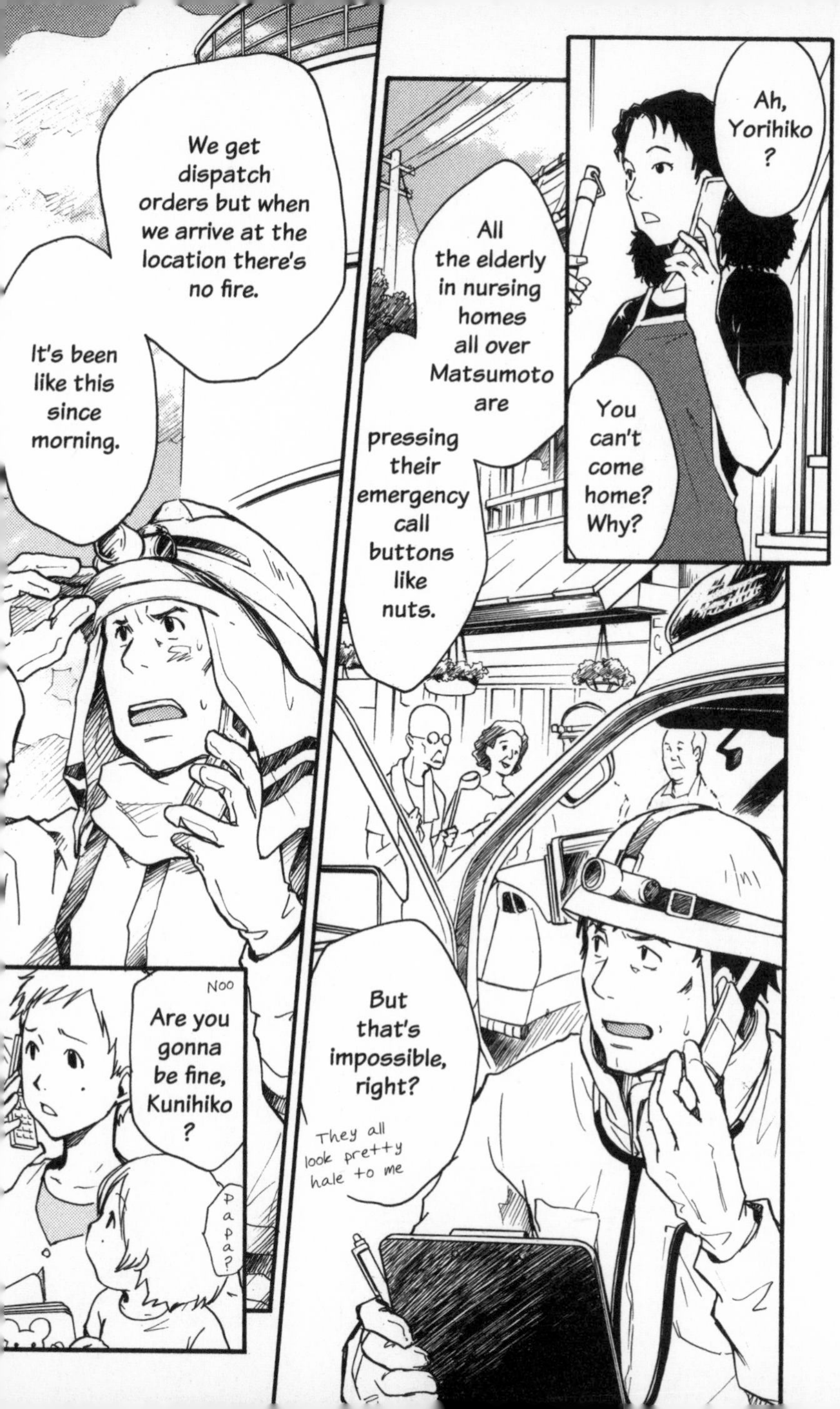

Ah, Yorihiko?
You can't come home? Why?
All the elderly in nursing homes all over Matsumoto are
pressing their emergency call buttons like nuts.
But that's impossible, right?
They all look pretty hale to me
We get dispatch orders but when we arrive at the location there's no fire.
It's been like this since morning.
Noo
Are you gonna be fine, Kunihiko?
Papa?

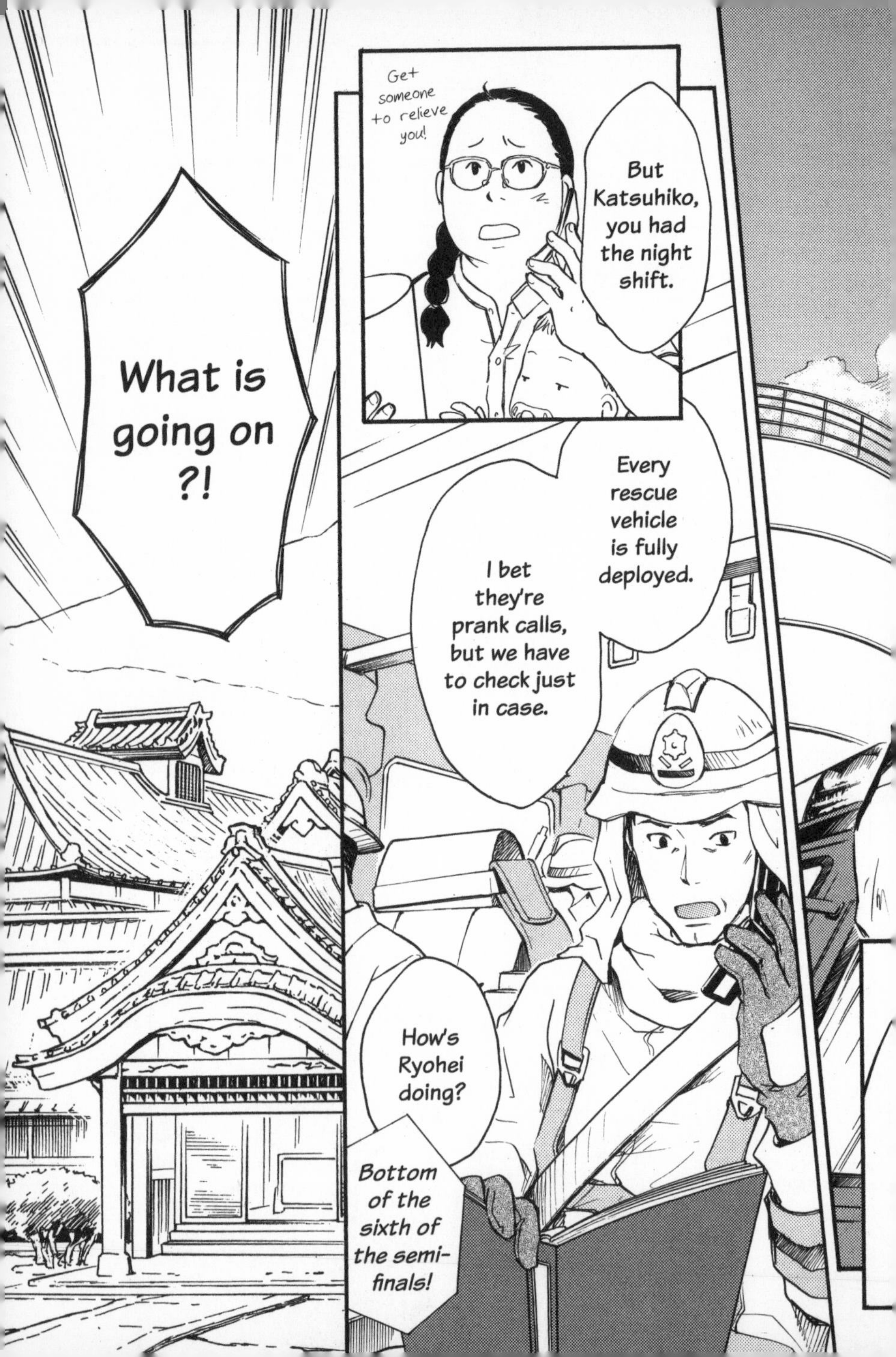
But Katsuhiko, you had the night shift.
Get someone to relieve you!
Every rescue vehicle is fully deployed.
I bet they're prank calls, but we have to check just in case.
How's Ryohei doing?
Bottom of the sixth of the semi-finals!
What is going on ?!

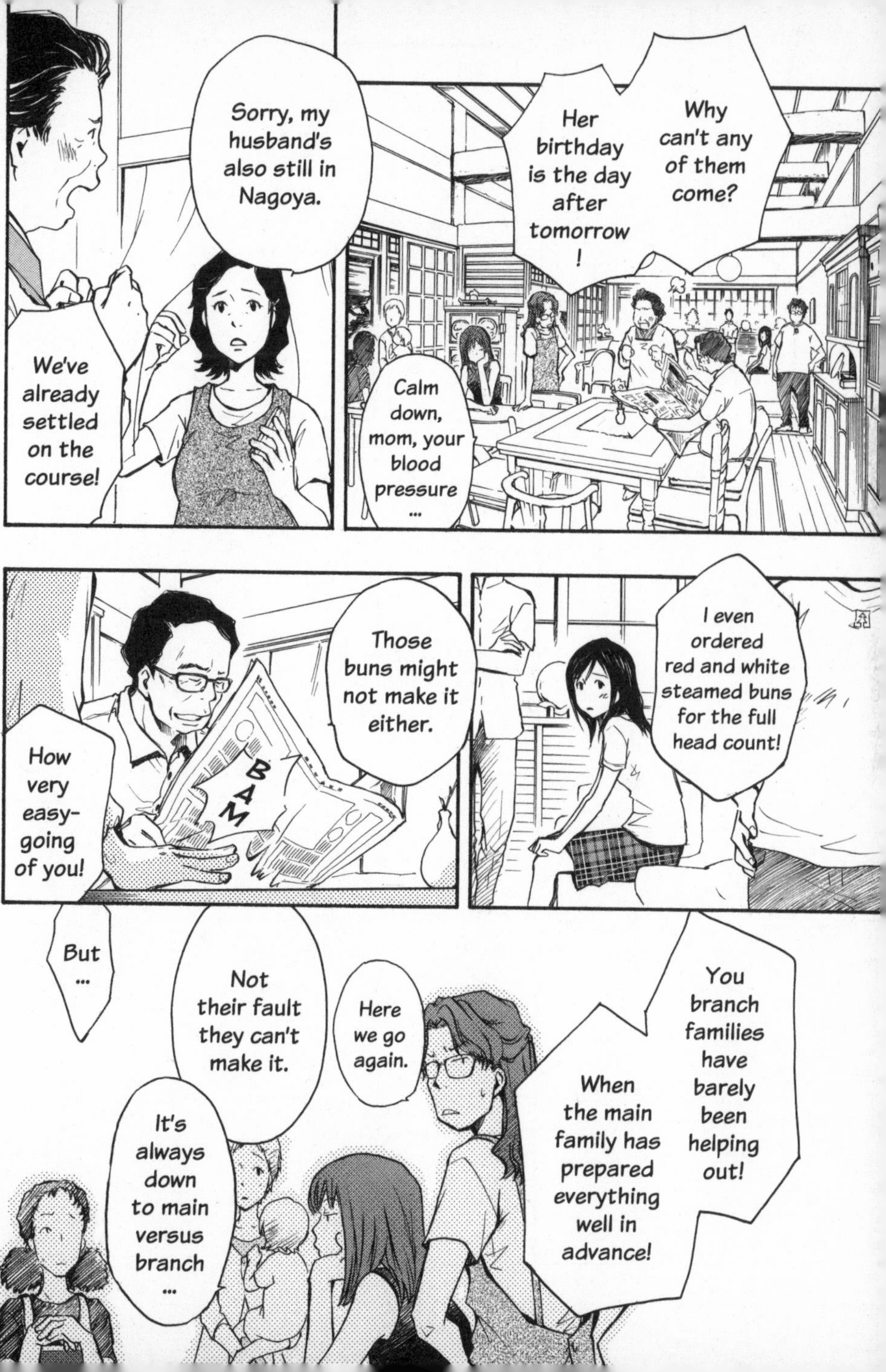
Why can't any of them come?
Her birthday is the day after tomorrow!
Calm down, mom, your blood pressure ...
Sorry, my husband's also still in Nagoya.
We've already settled on the course!
I even ordered red and white steamed buns for the full head count!
Those buns might not make it either.
BAM
How very easy-going of you!
You branch families have barely been helping out!
When the main family has prepared everything well in advance!
Here we go again.
Not their fault they can't make it.
But ...
It's always down to main versus branch ...

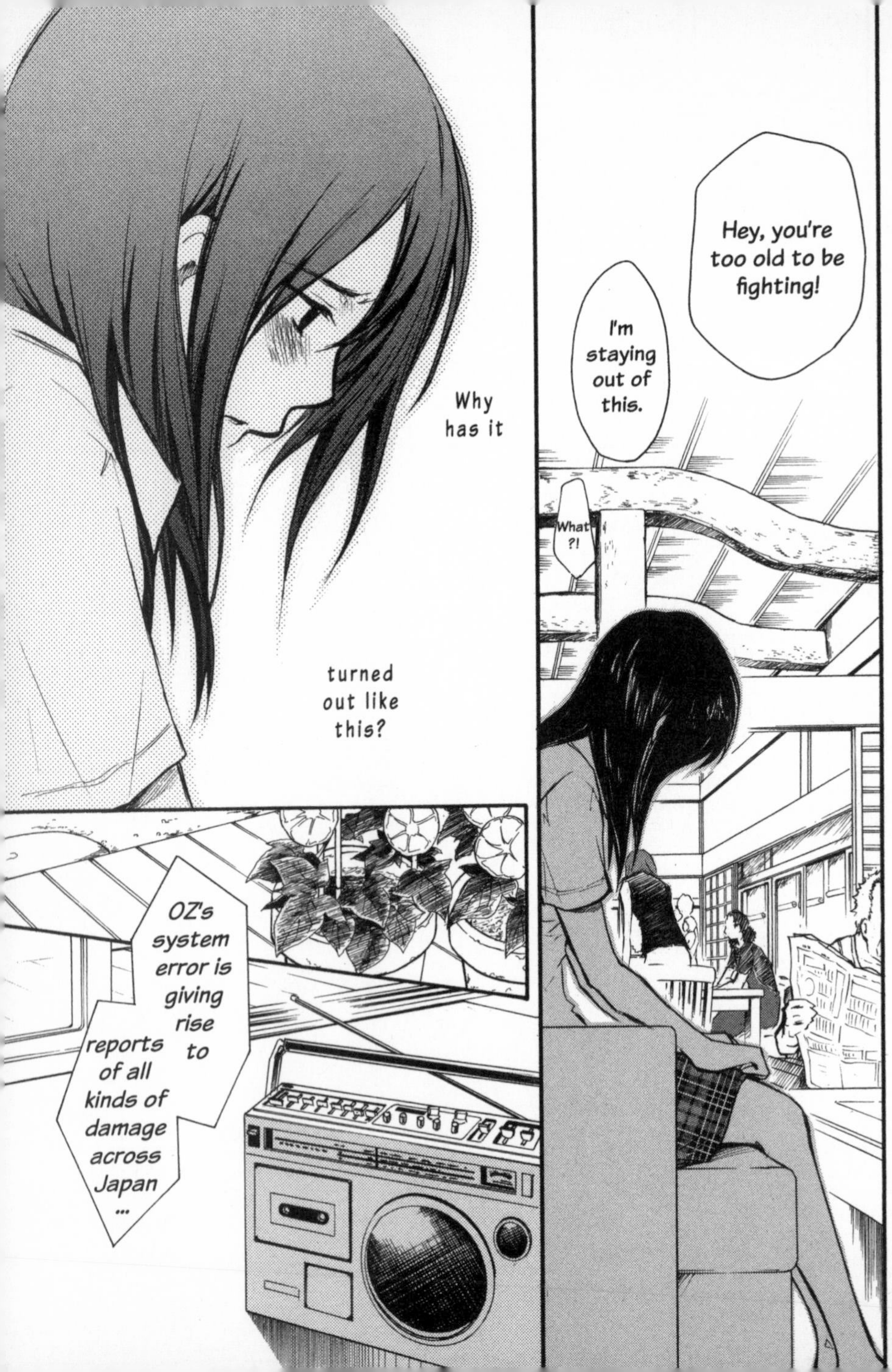
Hey, you're too old to be fighting!
I'm staying out of this.
What?!
Why has it
turned out like this?
OZ's system error is giving rise to reports of all kinds of damage across Japan ...

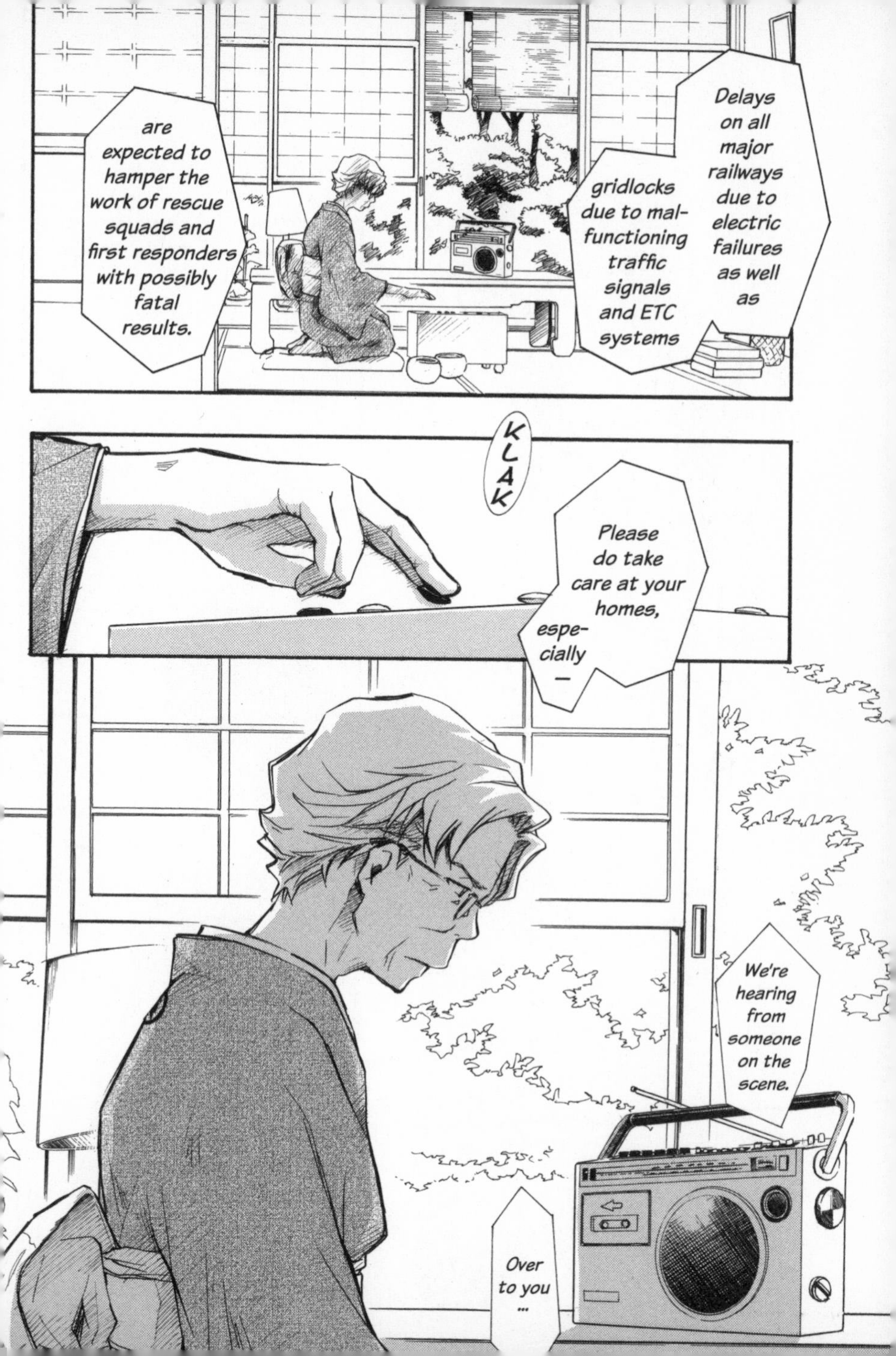
Delays on all major railways due to electric failures as well as
gridlocks due to mal-functioning traffic signals and ETC systems
are expected to hamper the work of rescue squads and first responders with possibly fatal results.
KLAK
Please do take care at your homes, espe-cially —
We're hearing from someone on the scene.
Over to you ...

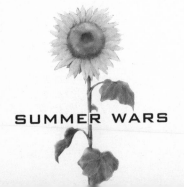

SUMMER WARS

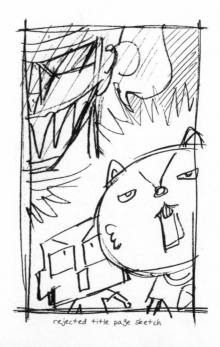

rejected title page sketch

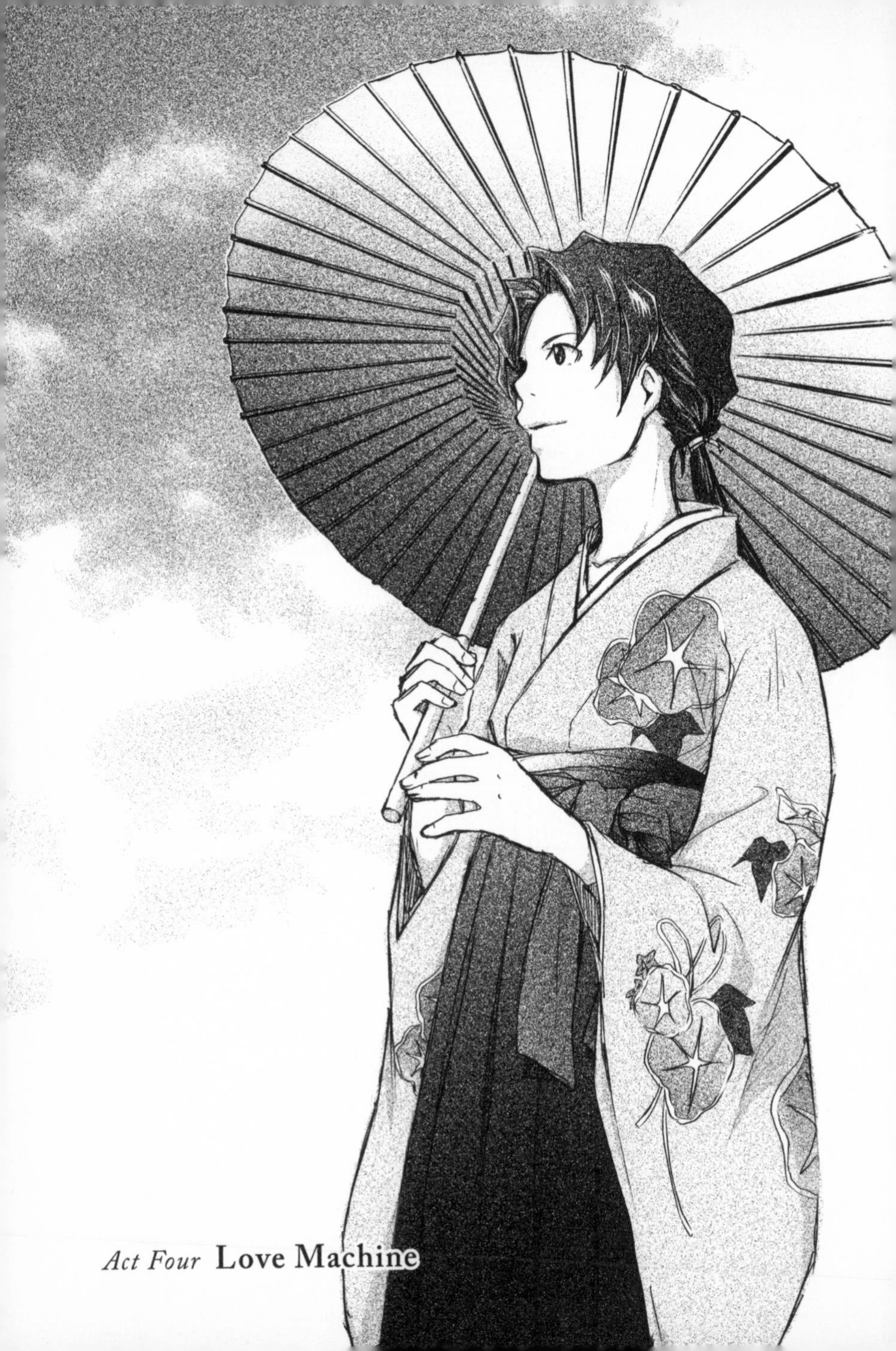

Act Four Love Machine

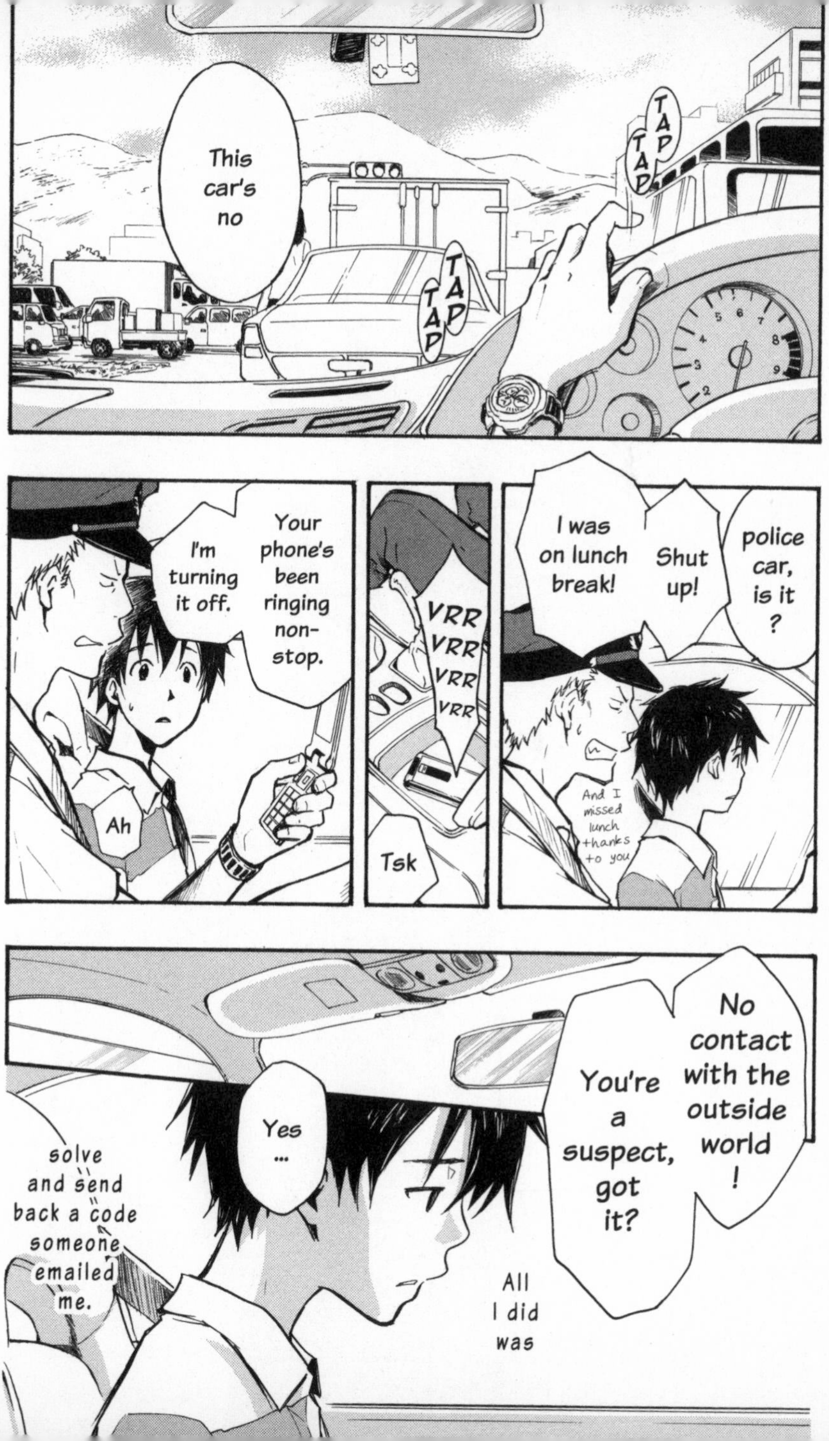
TAP TAP
TAP TAP
This car's no
police car, is it?
Shut up!
I was on lunch break!
And I missed lunch thanks to you
VRR VRR VRR VRR
Tsk
Your phone's been ringing non-stop.
I'm turning it off.
Ah
No contact with the outside world!
You're a suspect, got it?
Yes ...
All I did was
solve and send back a code someone emailed me.

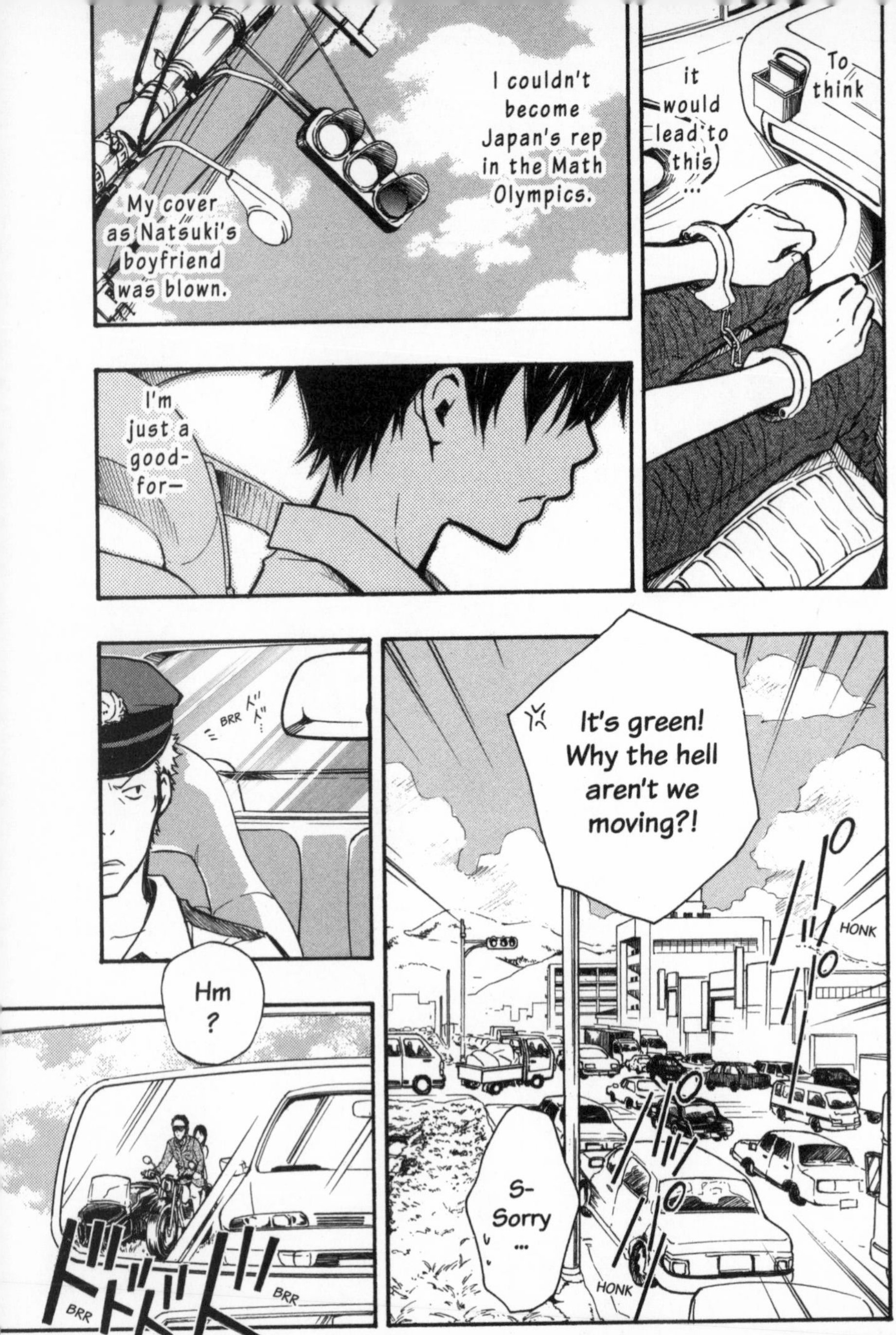
To think
it would lead to this...
I couldn't become Japan's rep in the Math Olympics.
My cover as Natsuki's boyfriend was blown.
I'm just a good-for—
It's green! Why the hell aren't we moving?!
HONK
HONK
S-Sorry...
BRR
Hm?
BRR
BRR

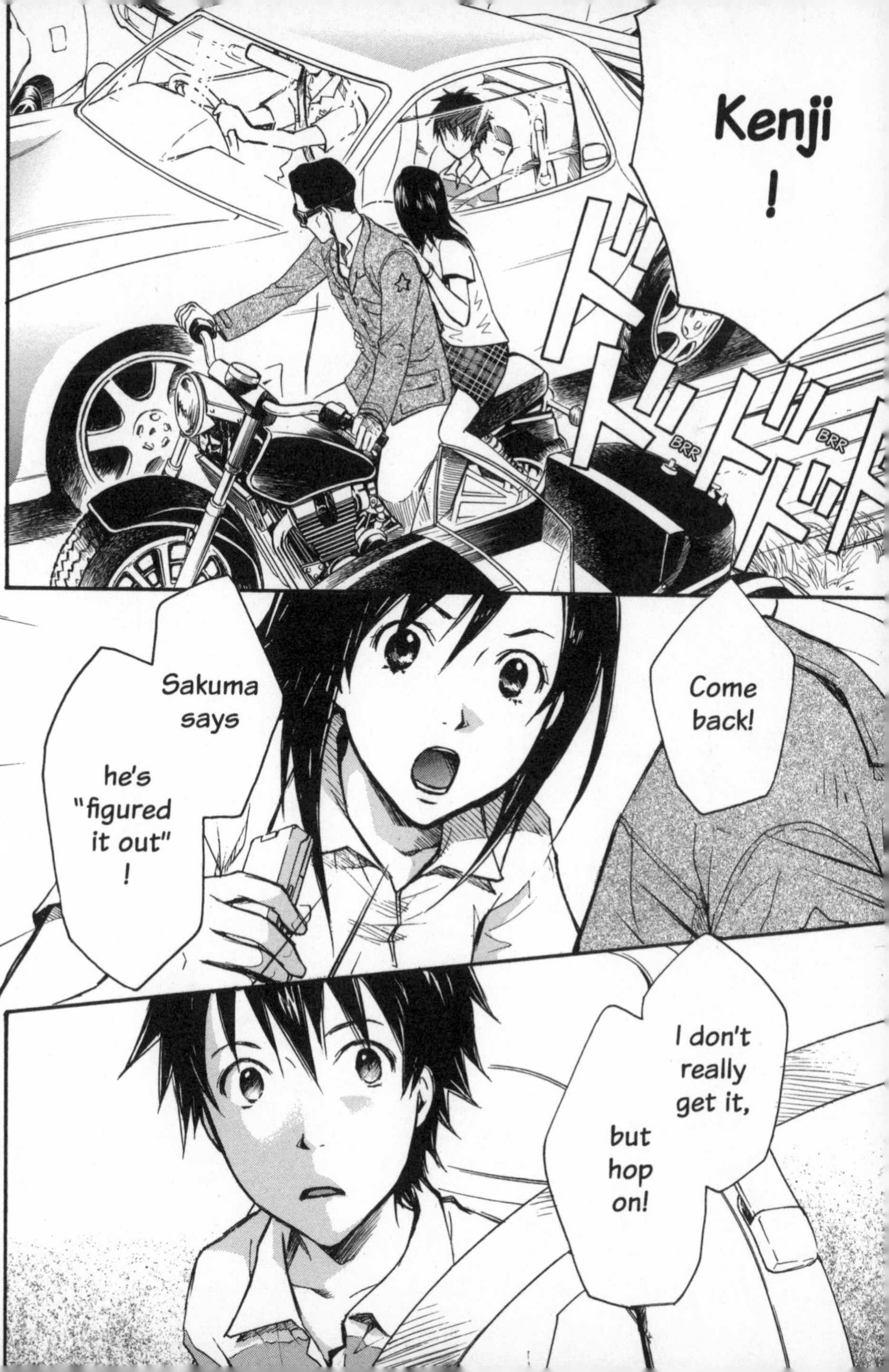
Kenji !
BRR
BRR
Come back!
Sakuma says he's "figured it out" !
I don't really get it, but hop on!

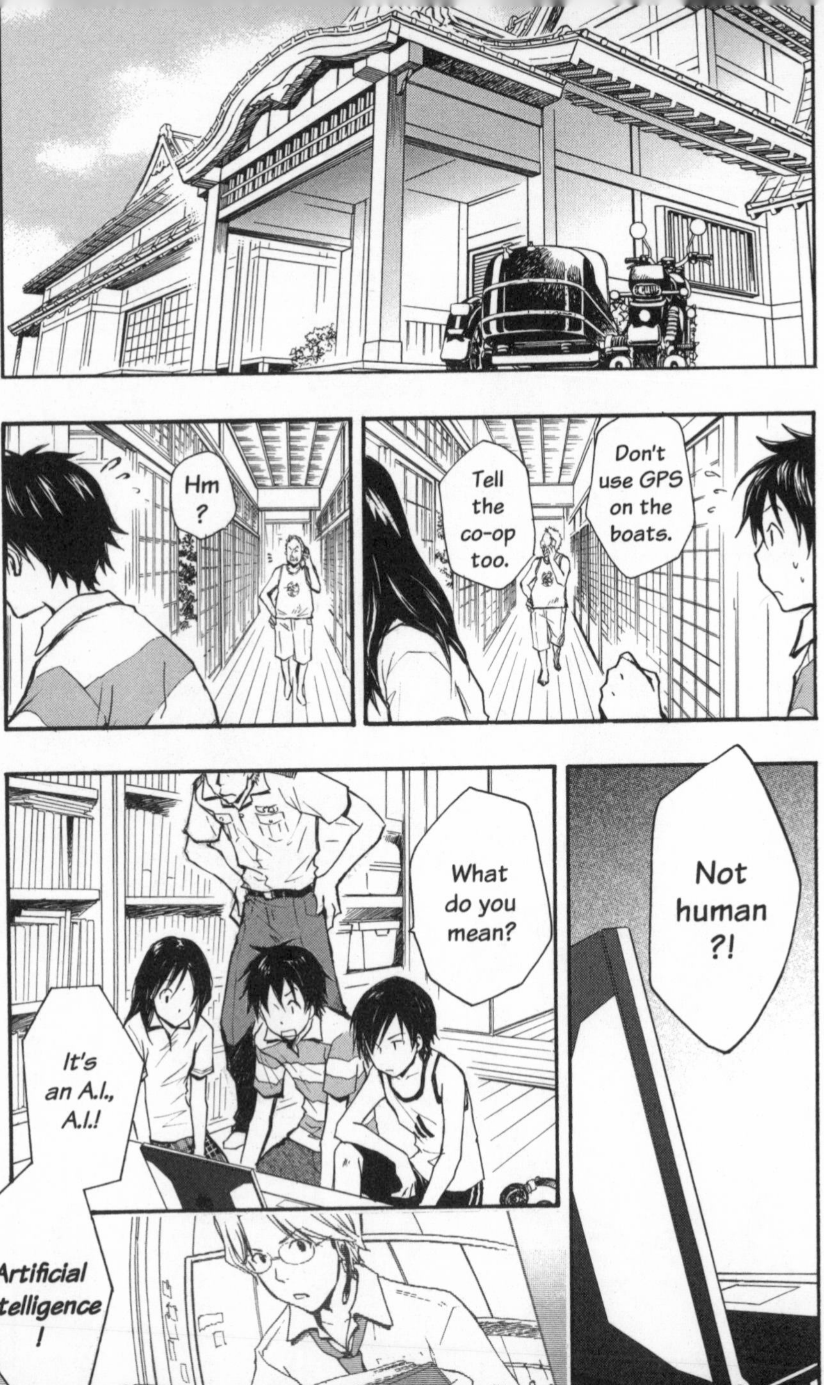
Don't use GPS on the boats.
Tell the co-op too.
Hm?
Not human?!
What do you mean?
It's an A.I., A.I.!
Artificial Intelligence!

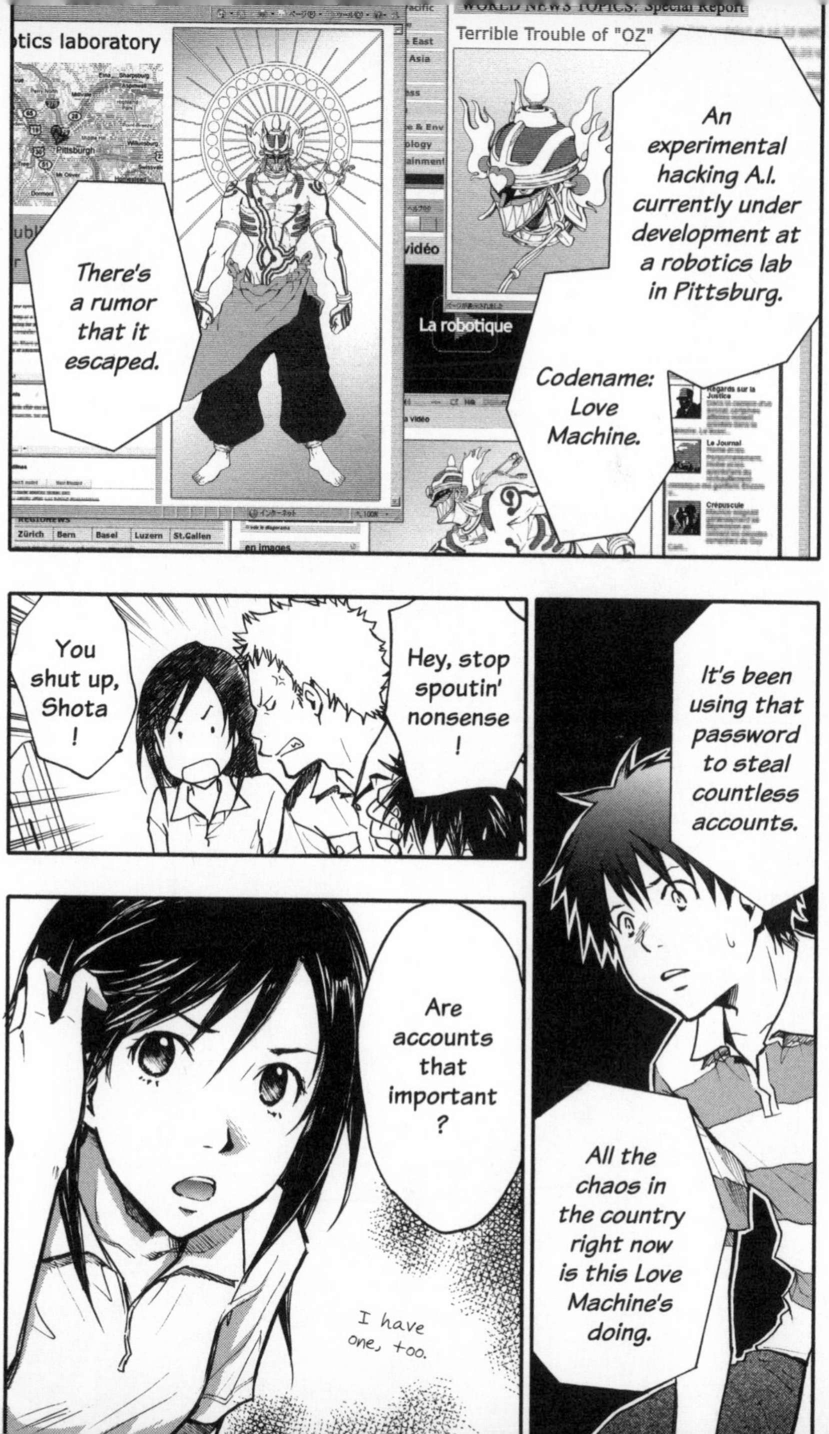
WORLD NEWS TOPICS: Special Report
Terrible Trouble of "OZ"
An experimental hacking A.I. currently under development at a robotics lab in Pittsburg.
Codename: Love Machine.
otics laboratory
Pittsburgh
There's a rumor that it escaped.
vidéo
La robotique
Regards sur la Justice
Le Journal
Crépuscule
REGIONEWS
Zürich
Bern
Basel
Luzern
St.Gallen
en images
It's been using that password to steal countless accounts.
All the chaos in the country right now is this Love Machine's doing.
Hey, stop spoutin' nonsense!
You shut up, Shota!
Are accounts that important?
I have one, too.

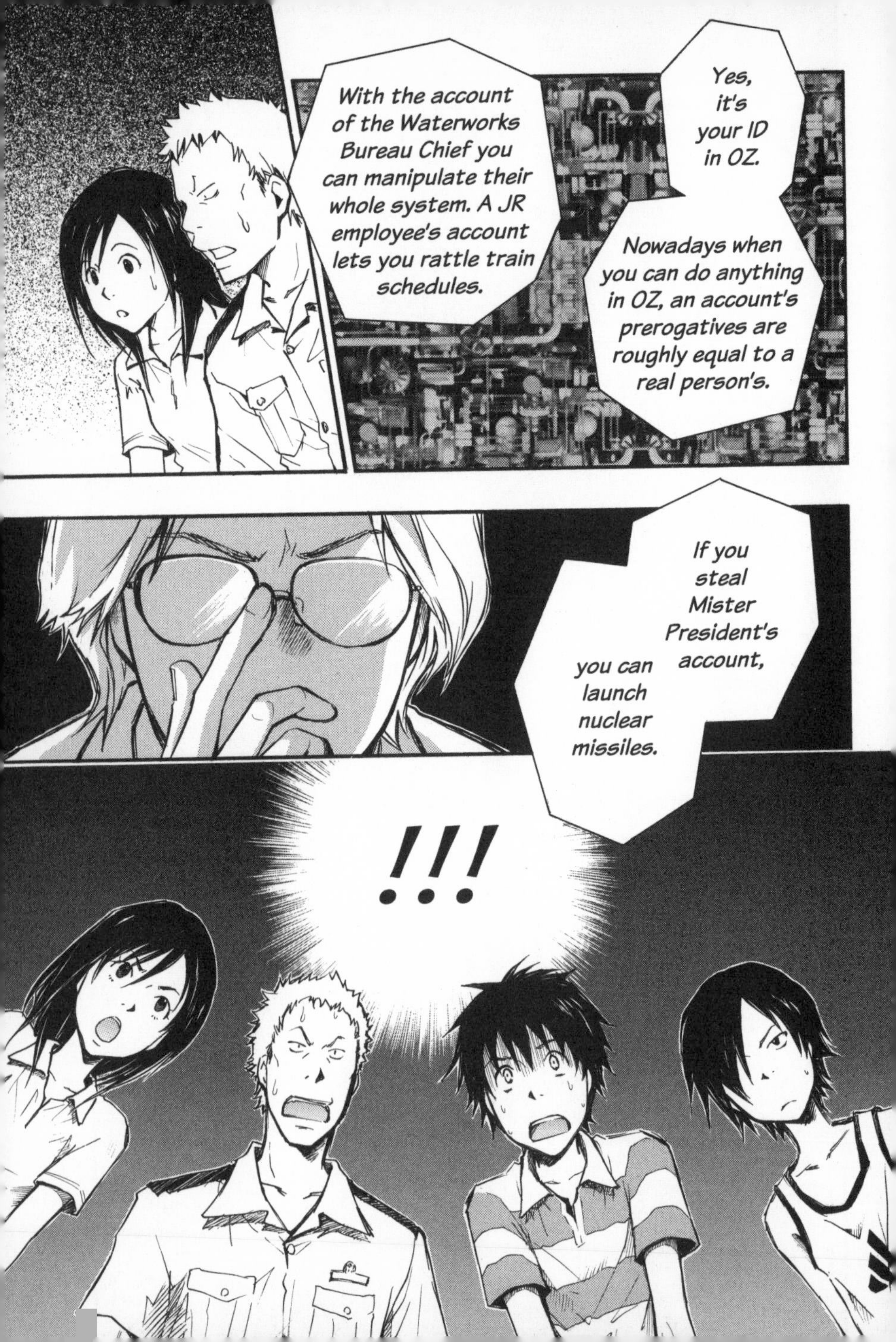
Yes, it's your ID in OZ.
Nowadays when you can do anything in OZ, an account's prerogatives are roughly equal to a real person's.
With the account of the Waterworks Bureau Chief you can manipulate their whole system. A JR employee's account lets you rattle train schedules.
If you steal Mister President's account,
you can launch nuclear missiles.
!!!

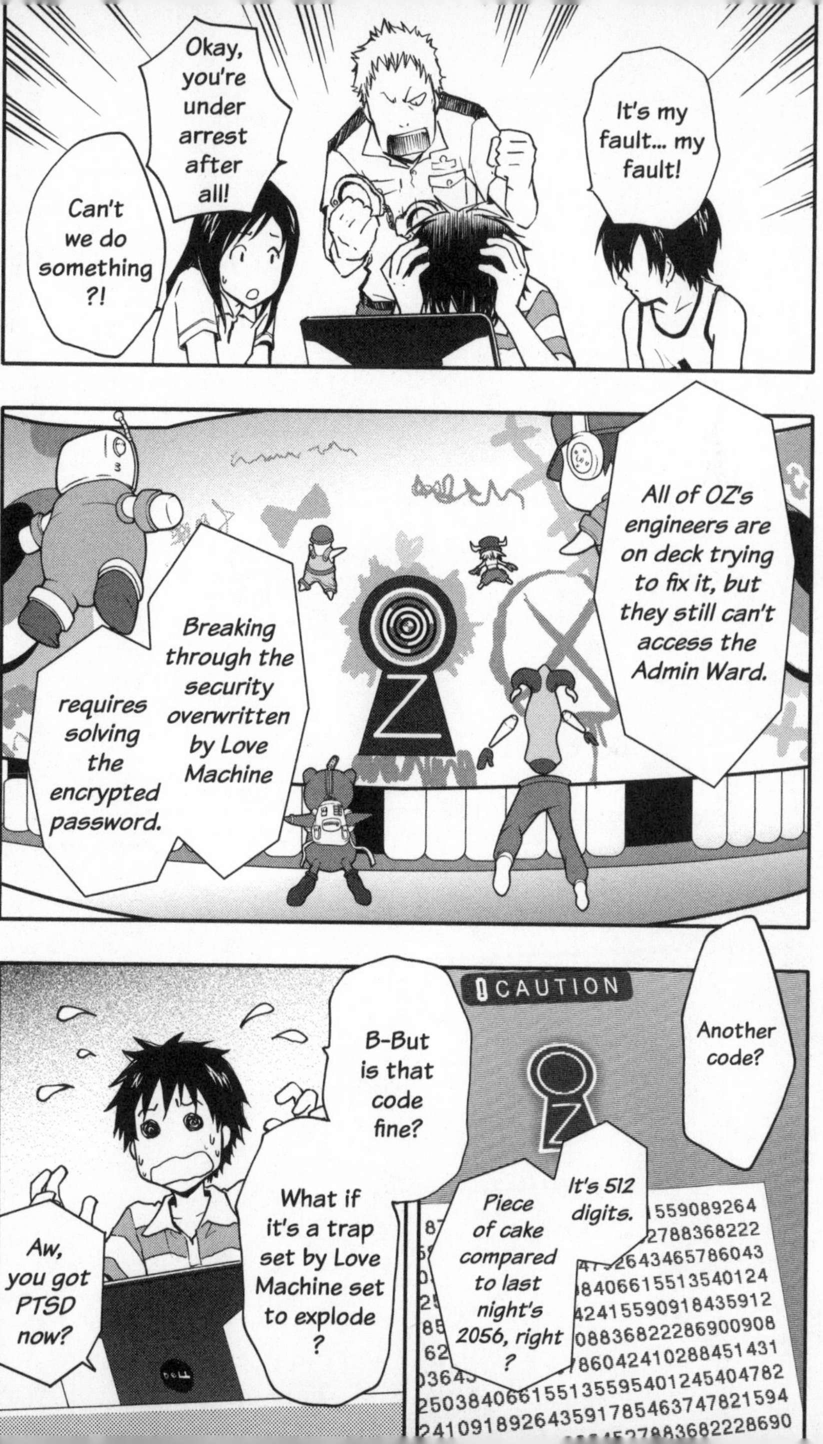
It's my fault... my fault!
Okay, you're under arrest after all!
Can't we do something?!
All of OZ's engineers are on deck trying to fix it, but they still can't access the Admin Ward.
Breaking through the security overwritten by Love Machine
requires solving the encrypted password.
Another code?
CAUTION
It's 512 digits.
Piece of cake compared to last night's 2056, right?
B-But is that code fine?
What if it's a trap set by Love Machine set to explode?
Aw, you got PTSD now?
250384066155135595401245404782
241091892643591785463747821594

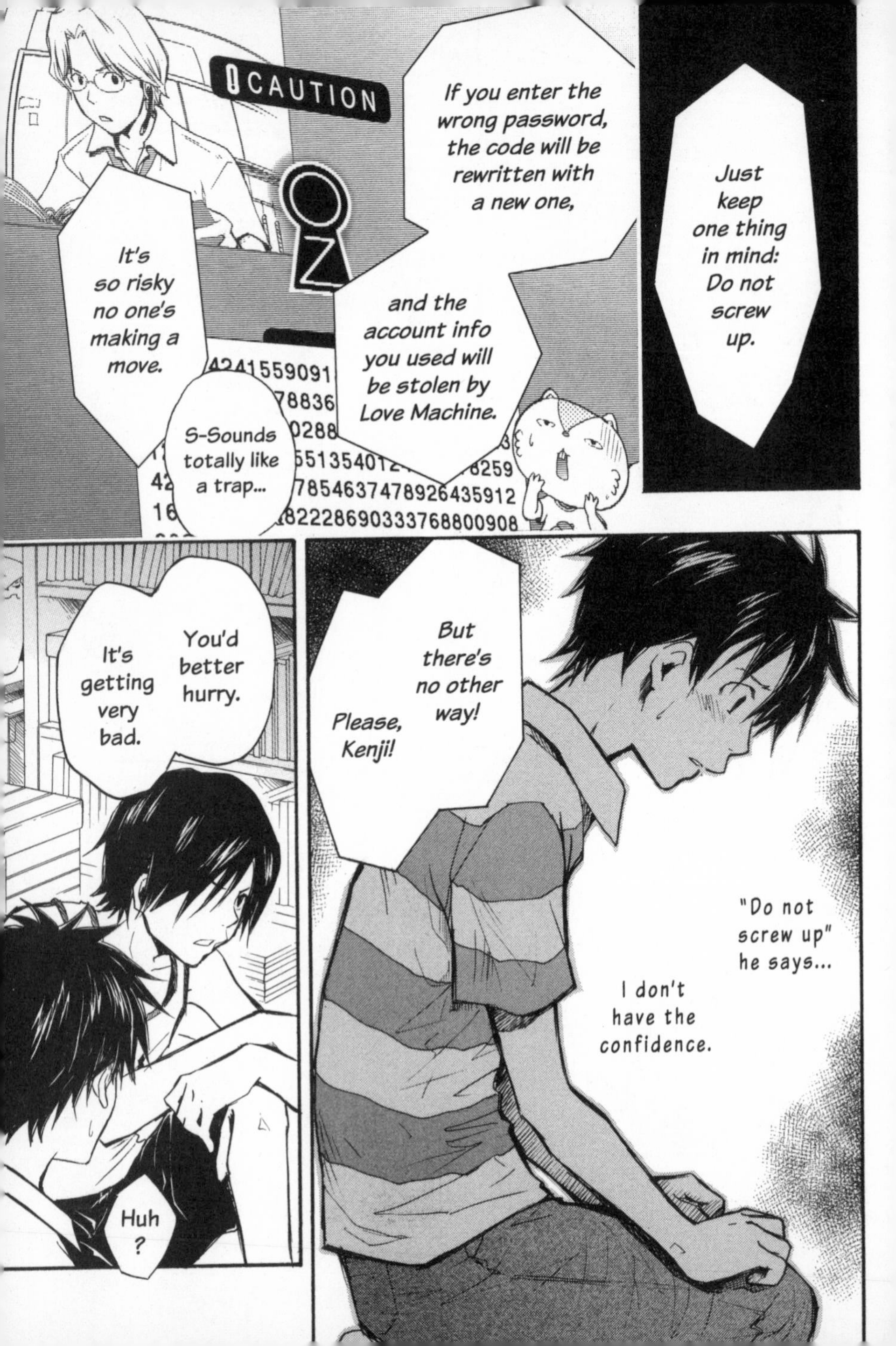
Just keep one thing in mind: Do not screw up.
CAUTION
If you enter the wrong password, the code will be rewritten with a new one,
and the account info you used will be stolen by Love Machine.
It's so risky no one's making a move.
S-Sounds totally like a trap...
But there's no other way!
Please, Kenji!
"Do not screw up" he says...
I don't have the confidence.
You'd better hurry.
It's getting very bad.
Huh?

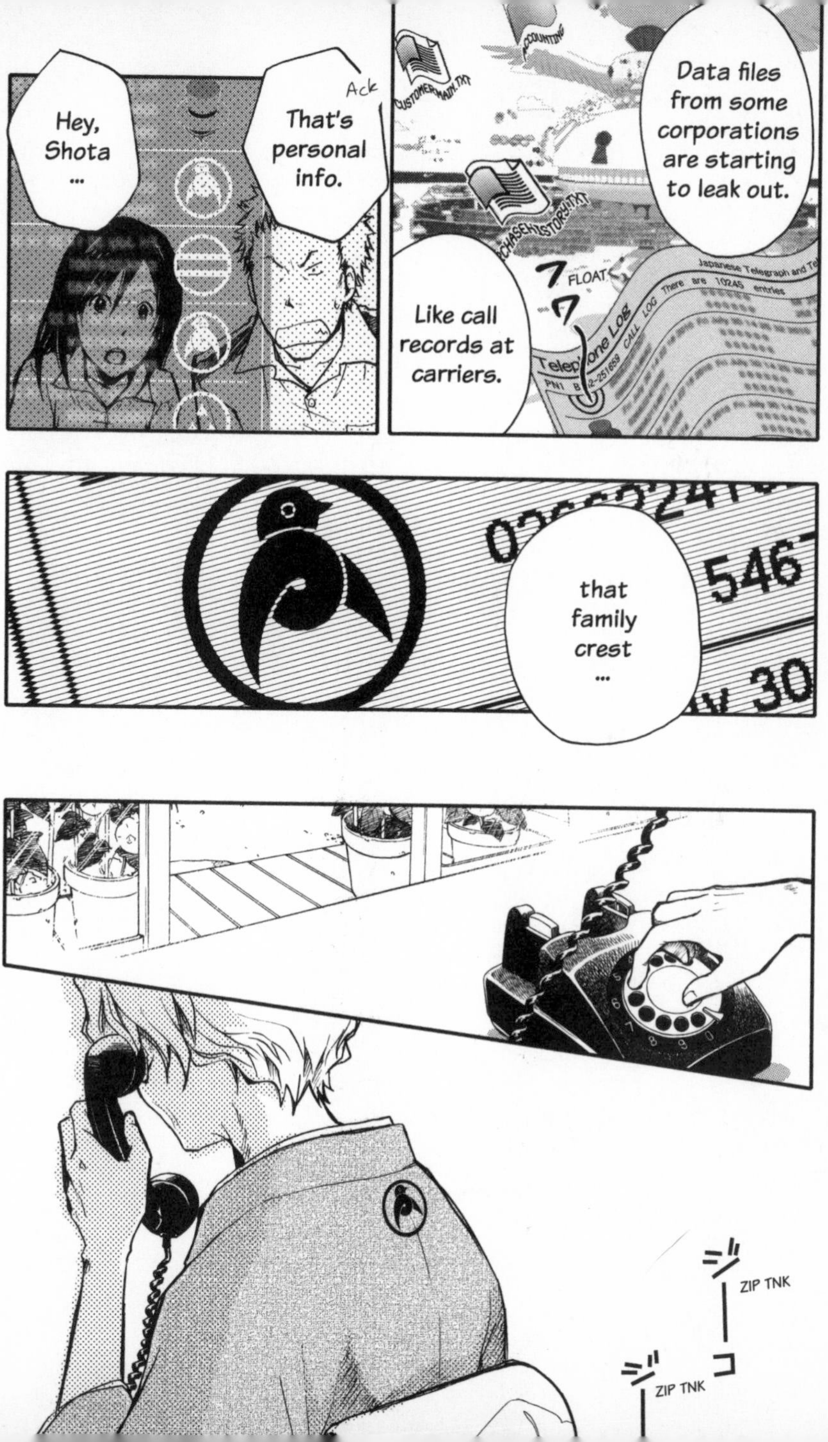
Data files from some corporations are starting to leak out.
ACCOUNTING
CUSTOMERMAIN.TXT
CHASEHISTORY.TXT
FLOAT
Japanese Telegraph and Tel
CALL LOG There are 10245 entries
Telephone Log
Like call records at carriers.
Ack
That's personal info.
Hey, Shota ...
546
that family crest ...
ZIP TNK
ZIP TNK

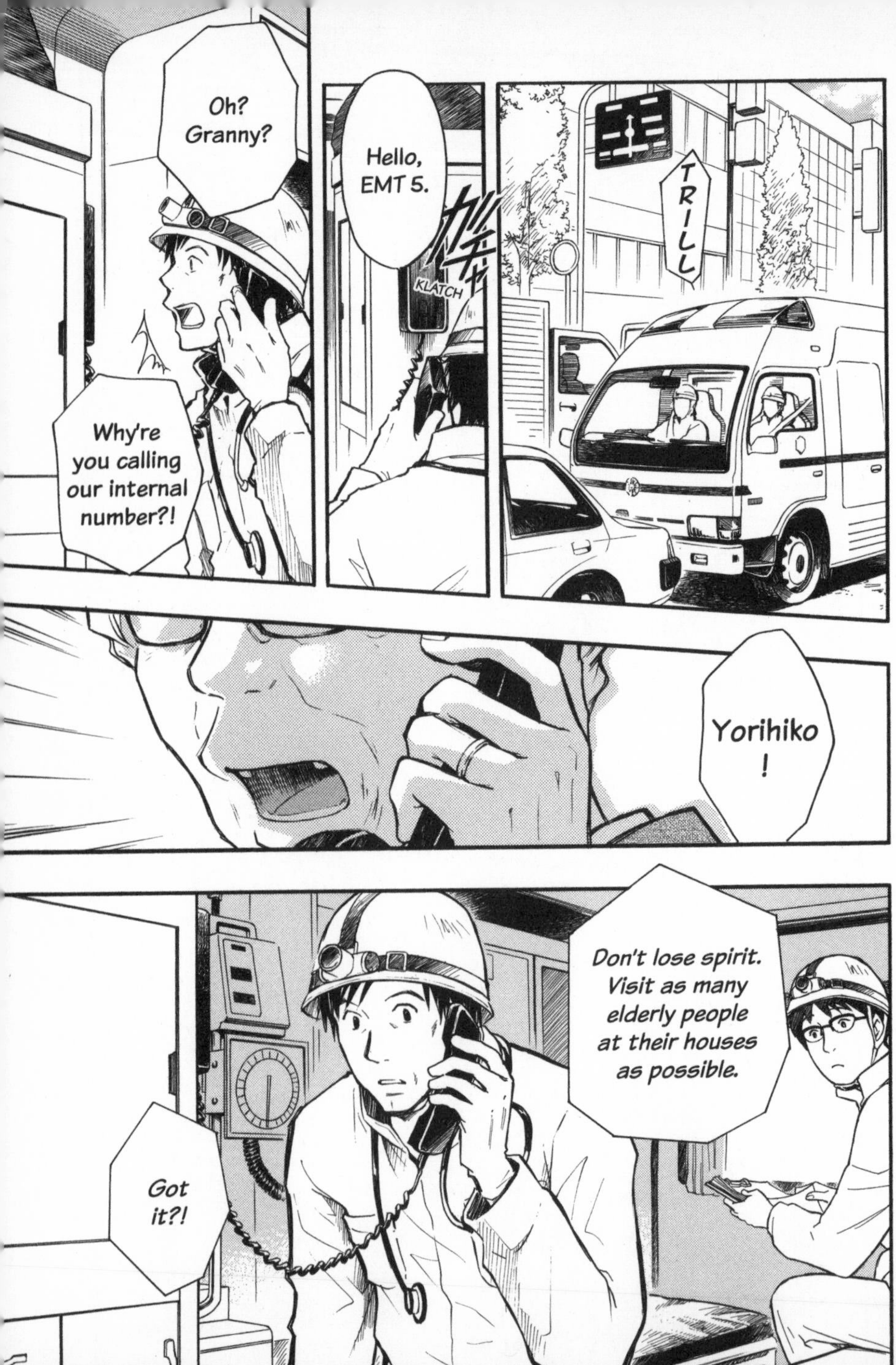
TRILL
Hello, EMT 5.
KLATCH
Oh? Granny?
Why're you calling our internal number?!
Yorihiko!
Don't lose spirit. Visit as many elderly people at their houses as possible.
Got it?!

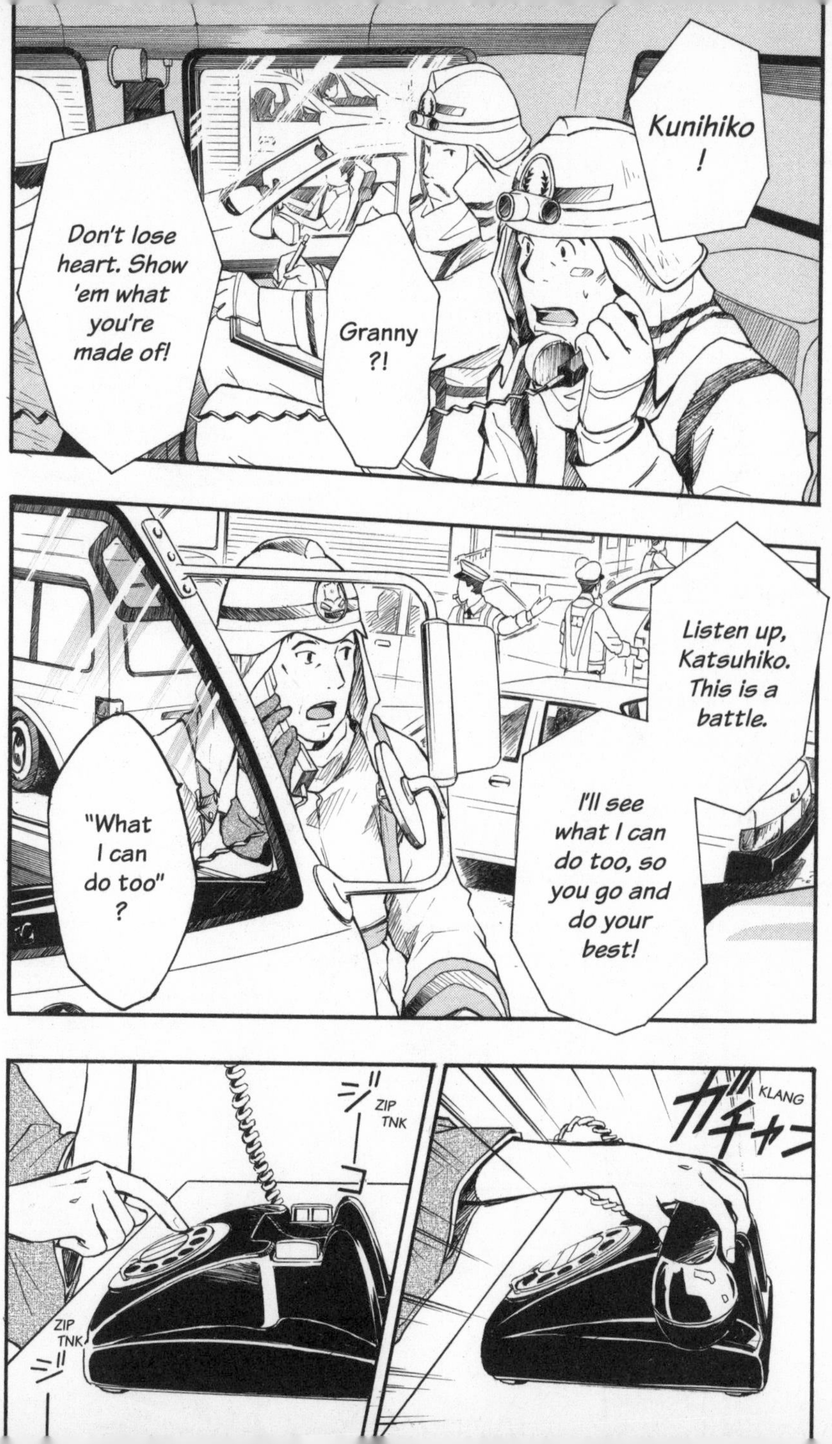
Kunihiko!
Granny?!
Don't lose heart. Show 'em what you're made of!
Listen up, Katsuhiko. This is a battle.
I'll see what I can do too, so you go and do your best!
"What I can do too"?
KLANG
ガチャン
ジー
ZIP TNK
ZIP TNK
ジー

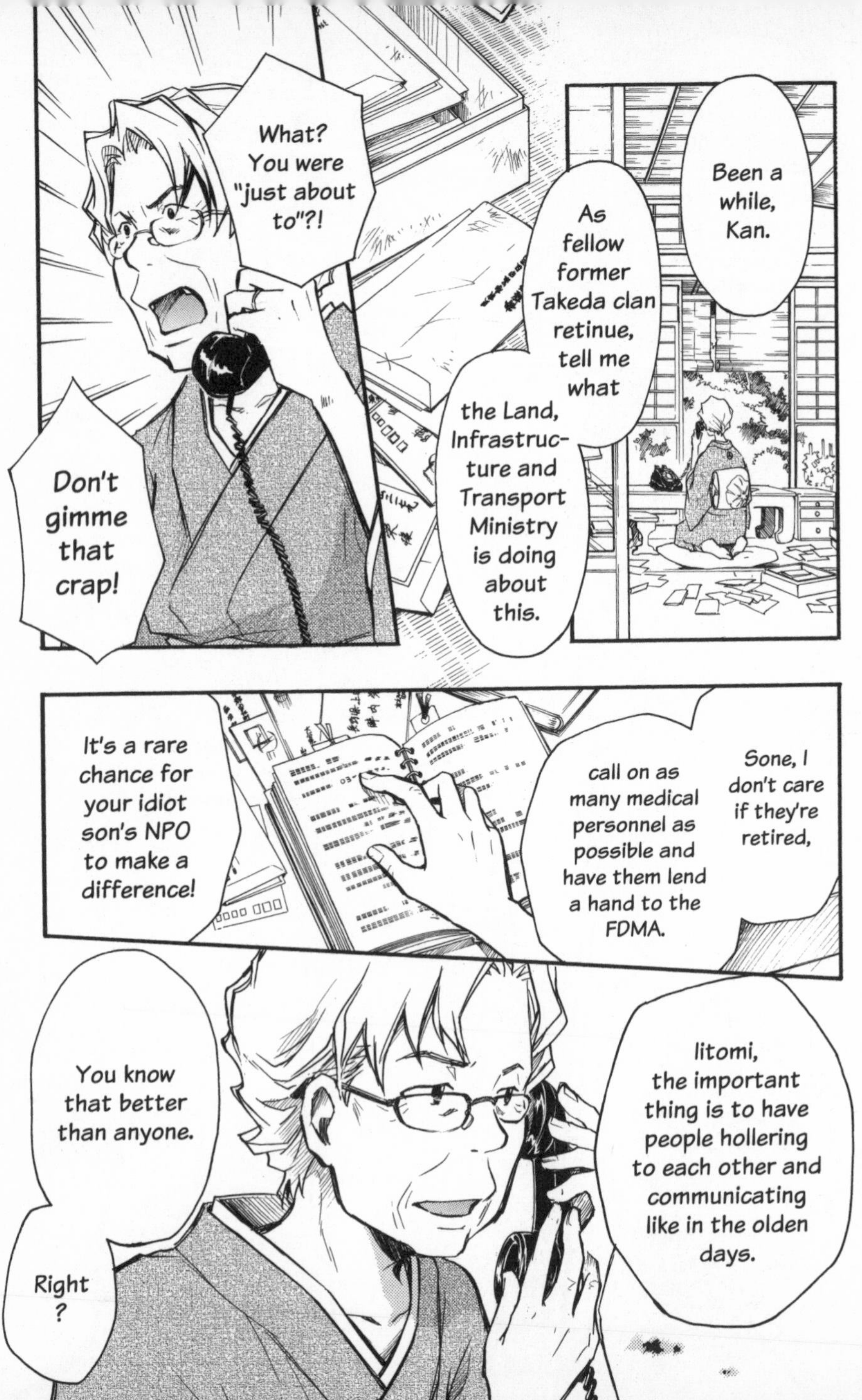
Been a while, Kan.
As fellow former Takeda clan retinue, tell me what
the Land, Infrastructure and Transport Ministry is doing about this.
What? You were "just about to"?!
Don't gimme that crap!
Sone, I don't care if they're retired,
call on as many medical personnel as possible and have them lend a hand to the FDMA.
It's a rare chance for your idiot son's NPO to make a difference!
Iitomi, the important thing is to have people hollering to each other and communicating like in the olden days.
You know that better than anyone.
Right?

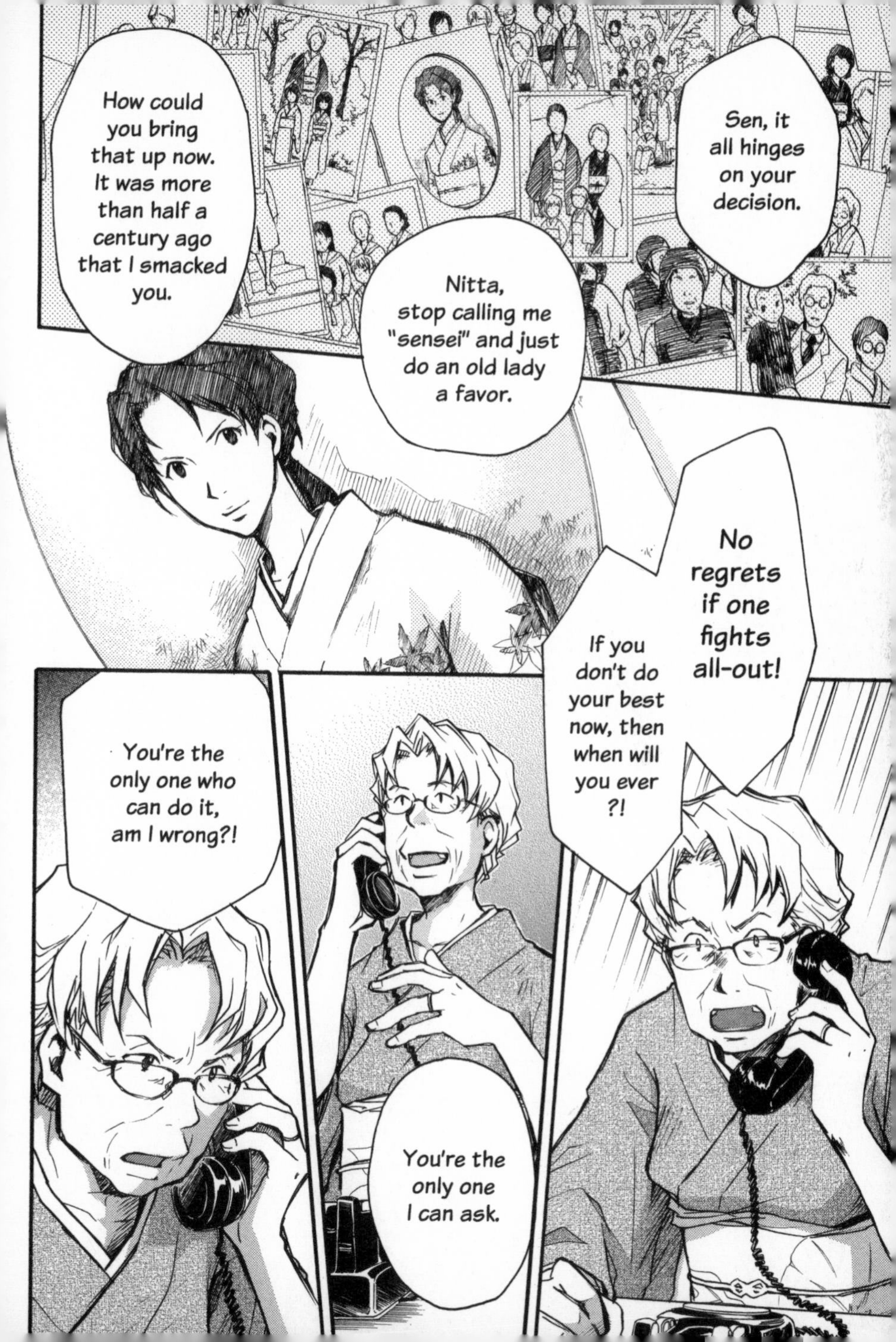
Sen, it all hinges on your decision.
How could you bring that up now. It was more than half a century ago that I smacked you.
Nitta, stop calling me "sensei" and just do an old lady a favor.
No regrets if one fights all-out!
If you don't do your best now, then when will you ever ?!
You're the only one I can ask.
You're the only one who can do it, am I wrong?!

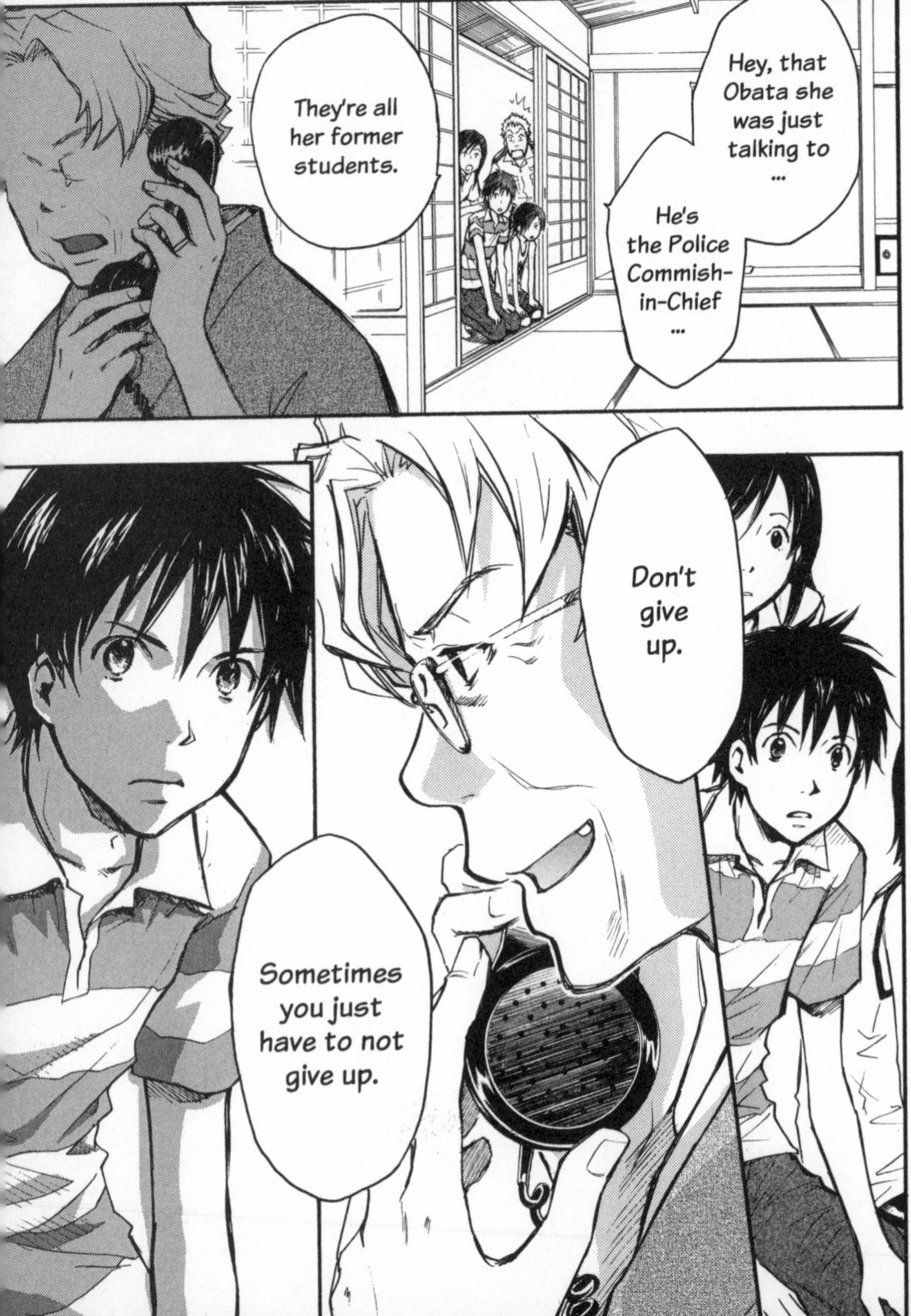
Hey, that Obata she was just talking to ...
He's the Police Commish-in-Chief ...
They're all her former students.
Don't give up.
Sometimes you just have to not give up.

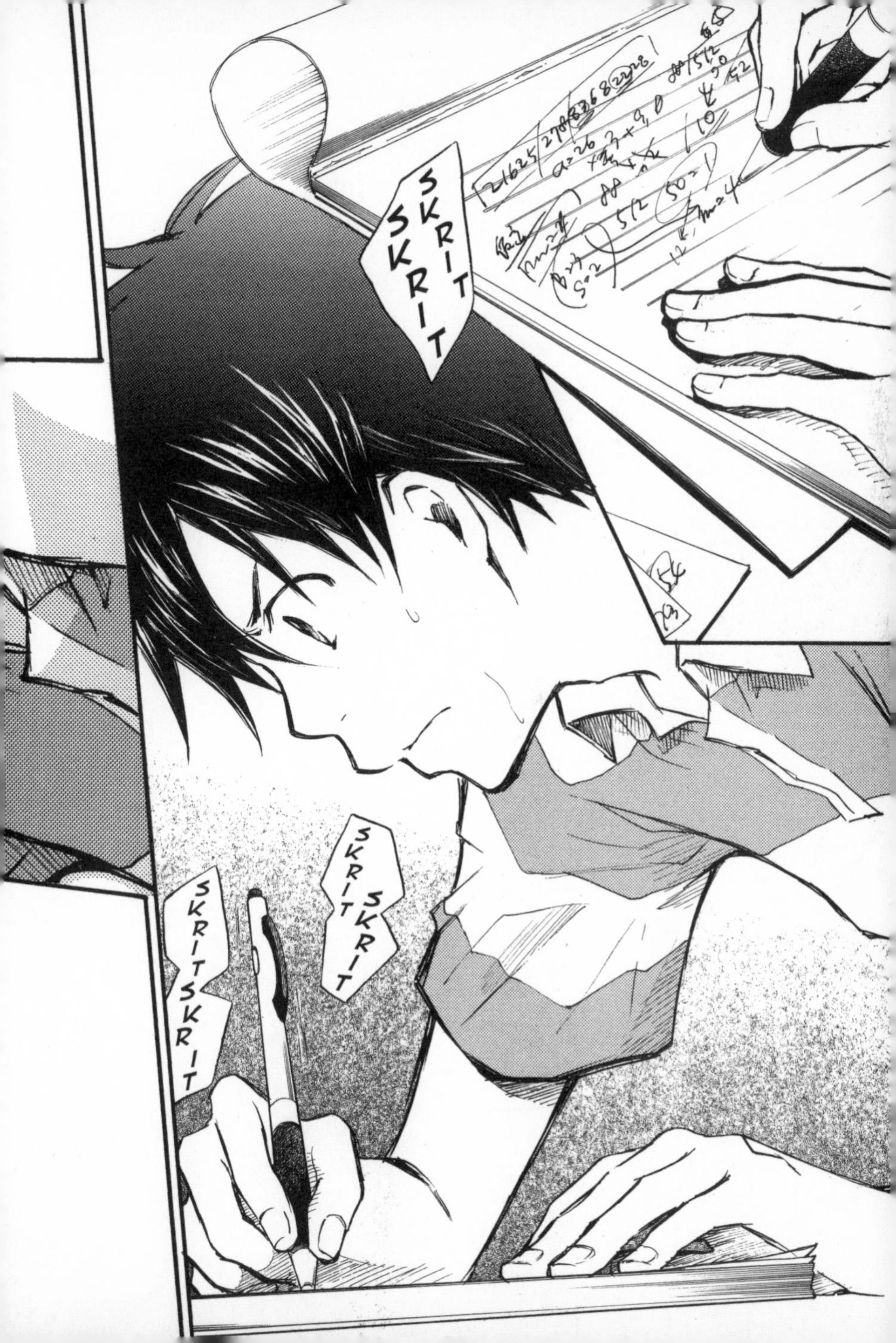
SKRIT SKRIT
SKRIT SKRIT
SKRITSKRIT

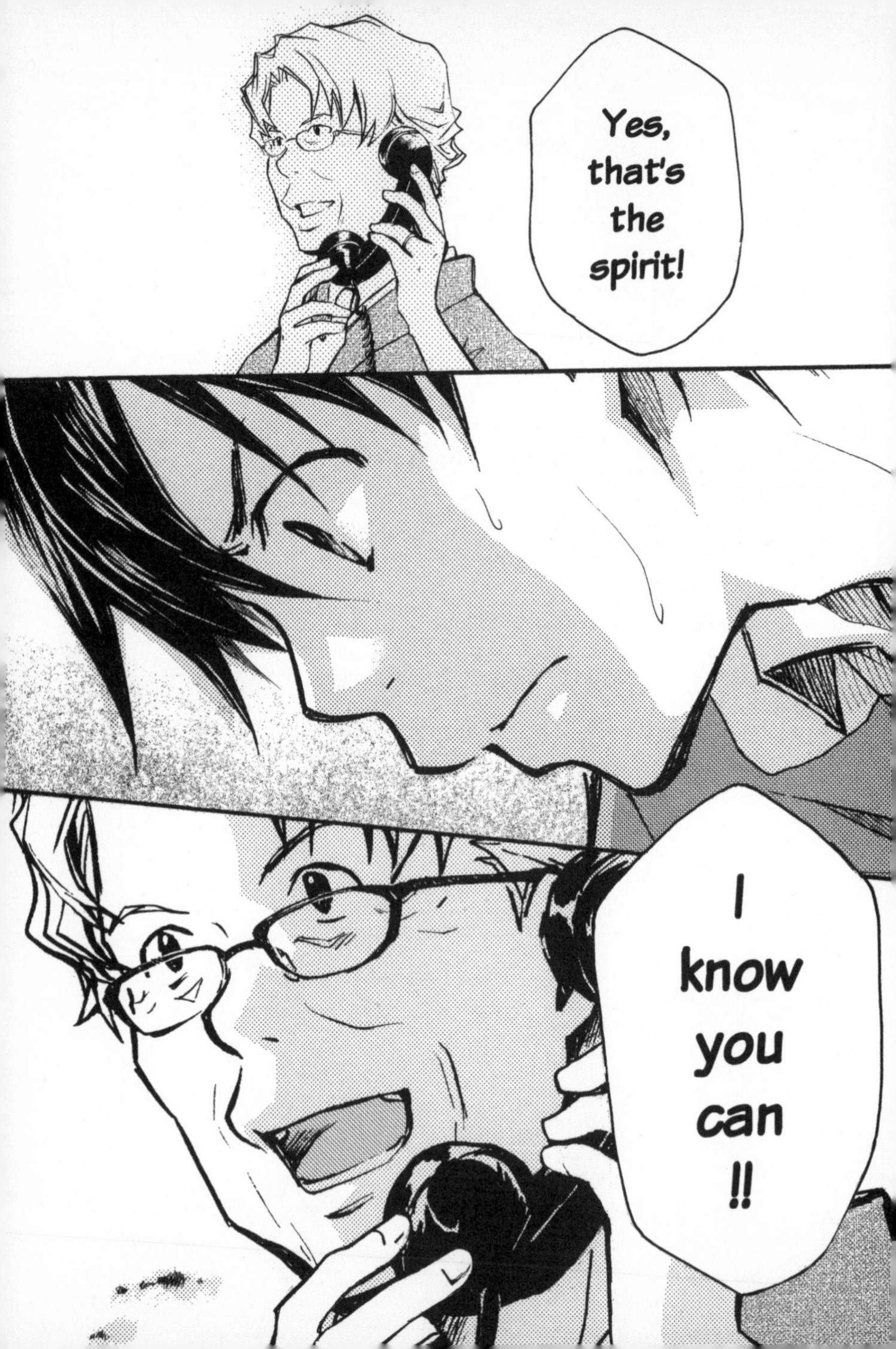
Yes, that's the spirit!
I know you can !!

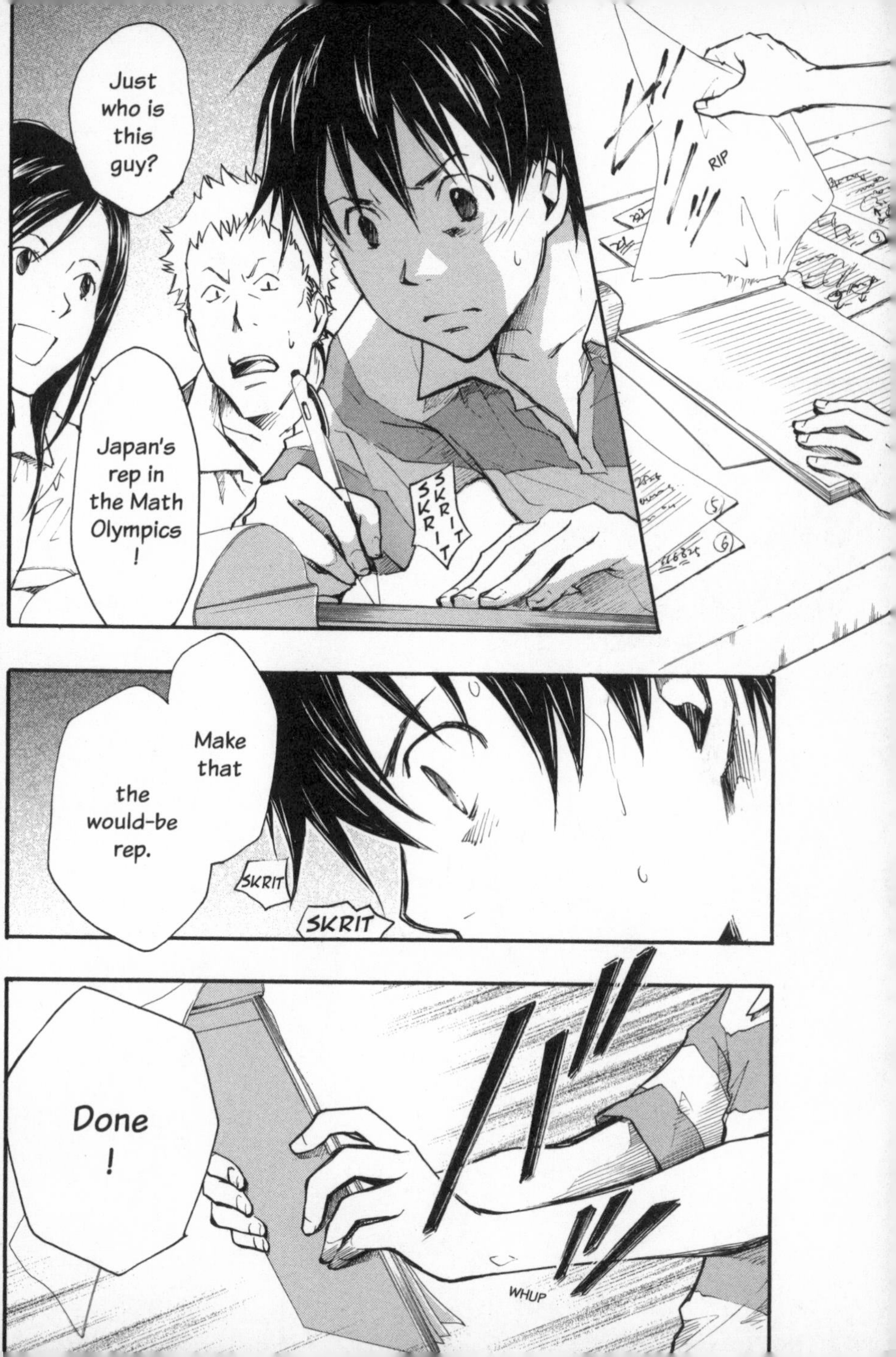
RIP
Just who is this guy?
SKRIT
SKRIT
Japan's rep in the Math Olympics!
Make that the would-be rep.
SKRIT
SKRIT
WHUP
Done!

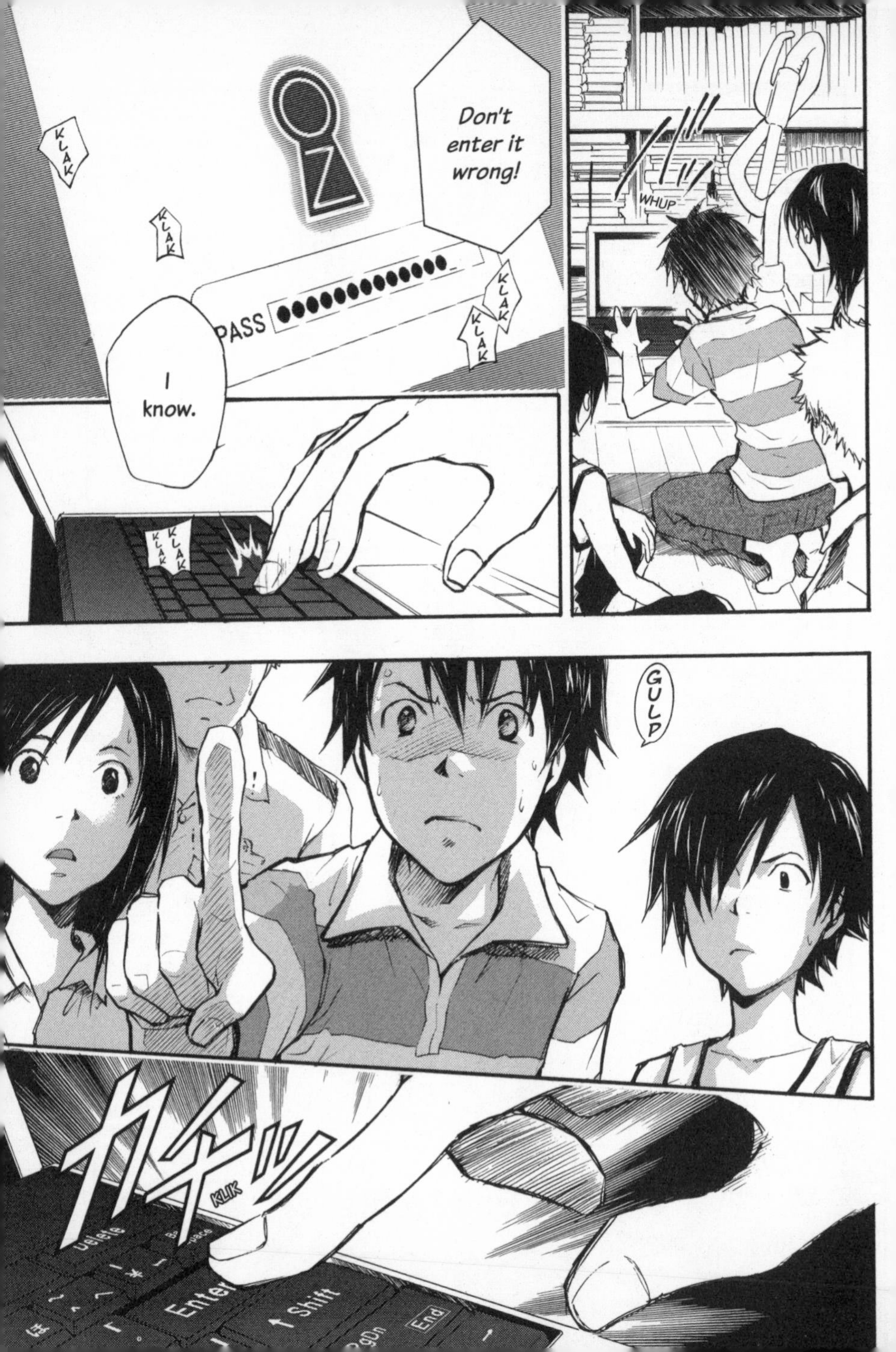
WHUP
Don't enter it wrong!
KLAK
KLAK
KLAK
KLAK
PASS
I know.
KLAK KLAK
GULP
!
カチッ
KLIK
Enter
Shift
End

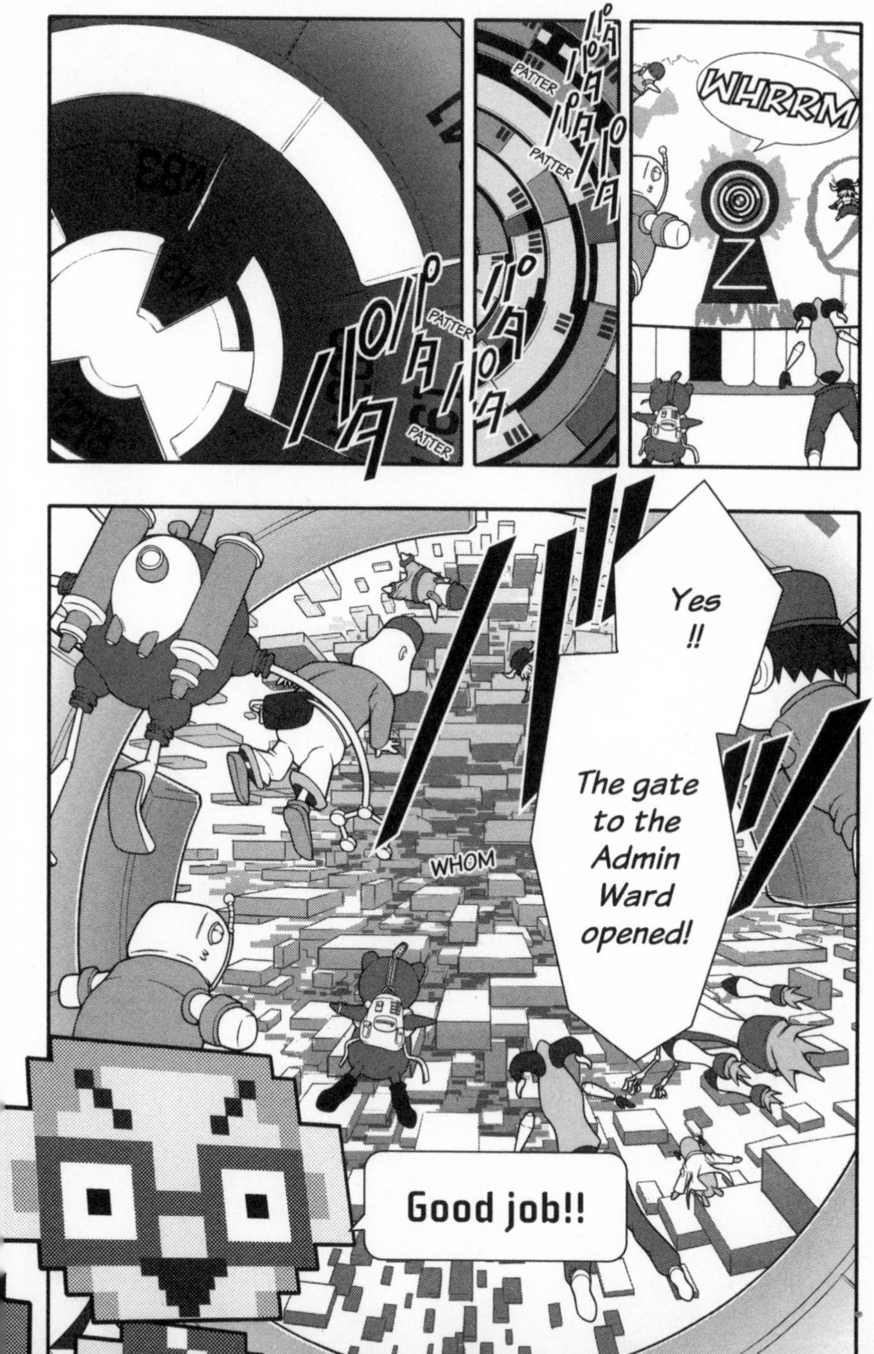
WHRRM
PATTER
PATTER
PATTER
PATTER
Yes!!
The gate to the Admin Ward opened!
WHOM
Good job!!

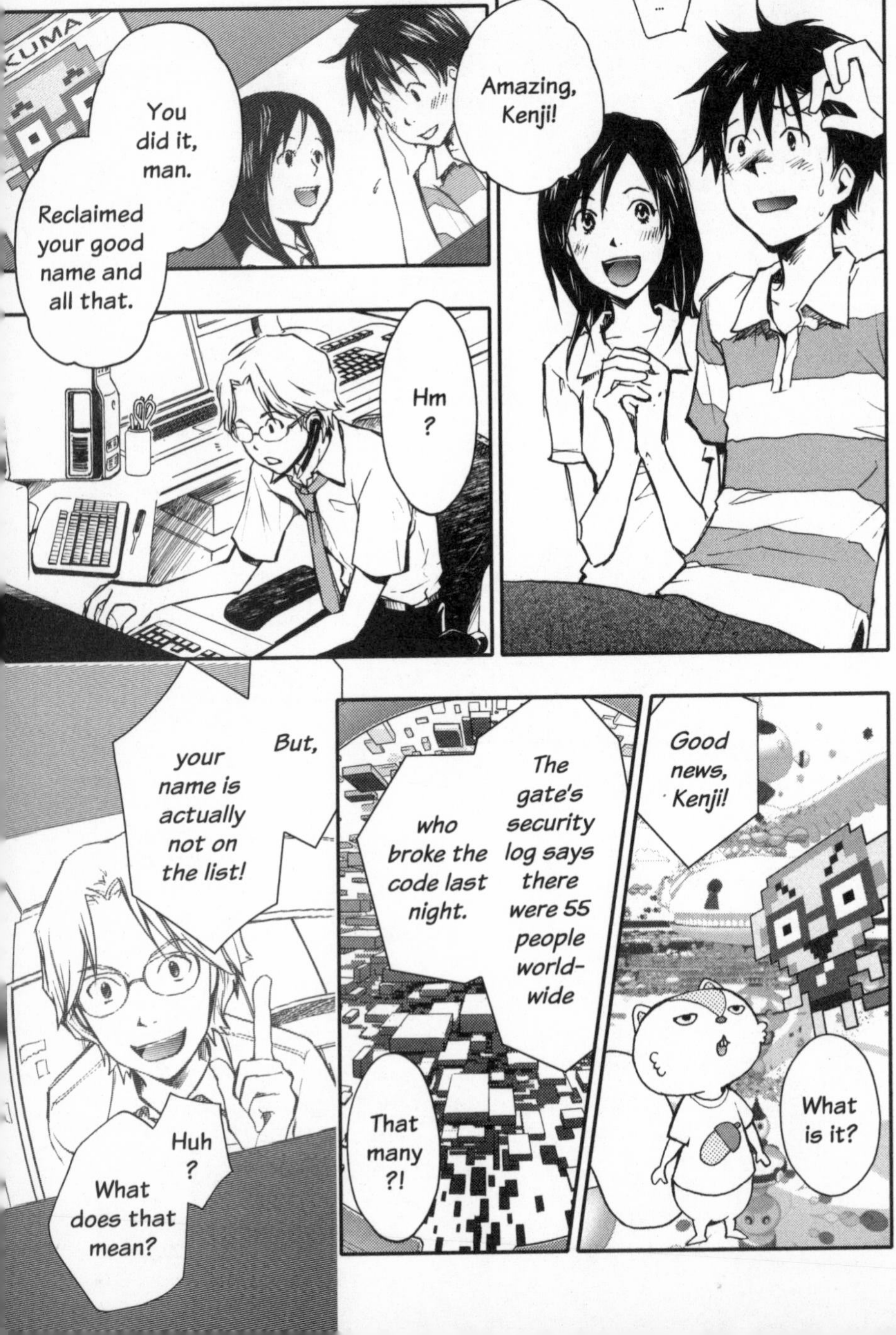
Whew ...
Amazing, Kenji!
You did it, man.
Reclaimed your good name and all that.
Hm ?
Good news, Kenji!
What is it?
The gate's security log says there were 55 people worldwide
who broke the code last night.
That many ?!
But,
your name is actually not on the list!
Huh ?
What does that mean?

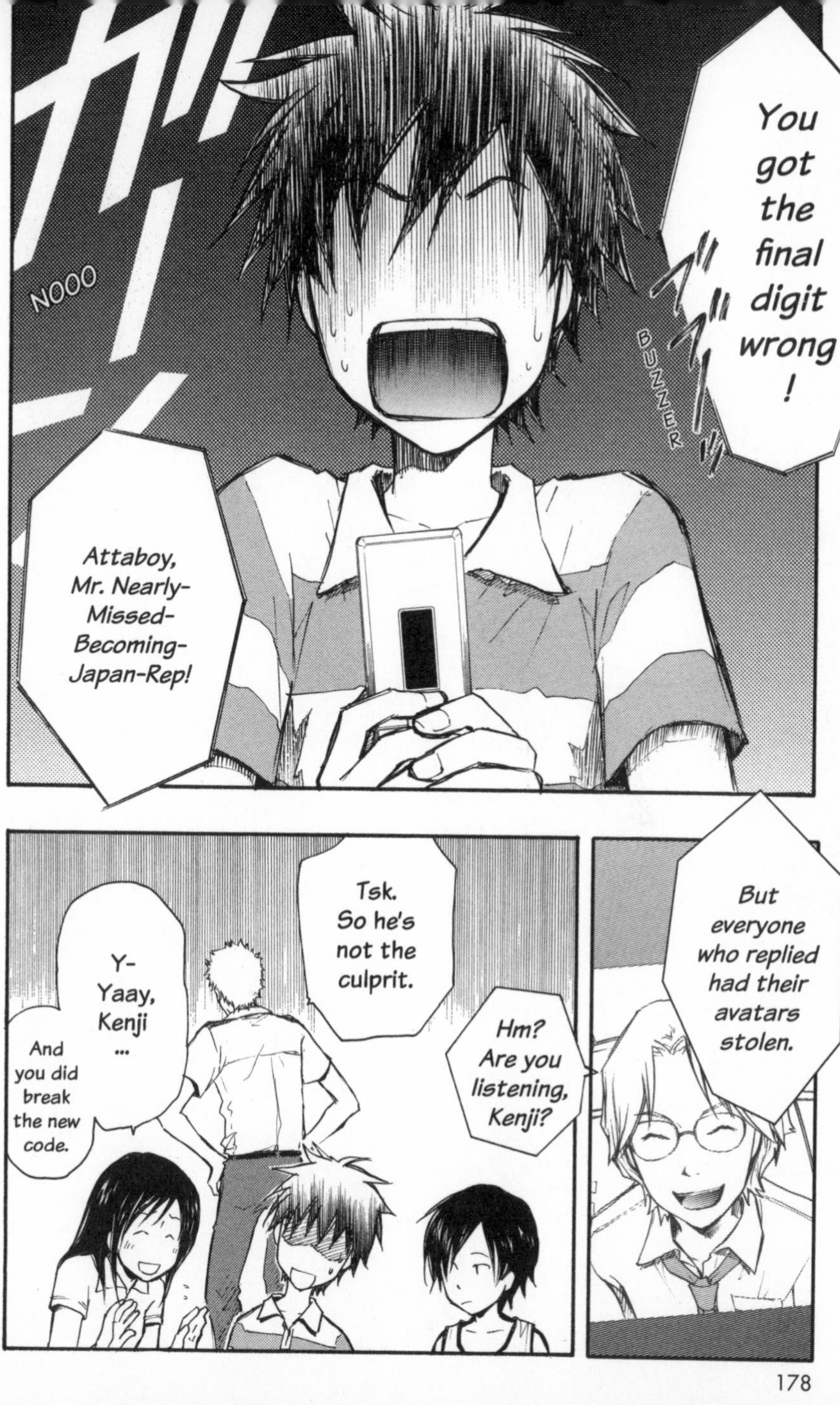
You got the final digit wrong!
BUZZER
NOOO
Attaboy, Mr. Nearly-Missed-Becoming-Japan-Rep!
But everyone who replied had their avatars stolen.
Hm? Are you listening, Kenji?
Tsk. So he's not the culprit.
Y- Yaay, Kenji ...
And you did break the new code.

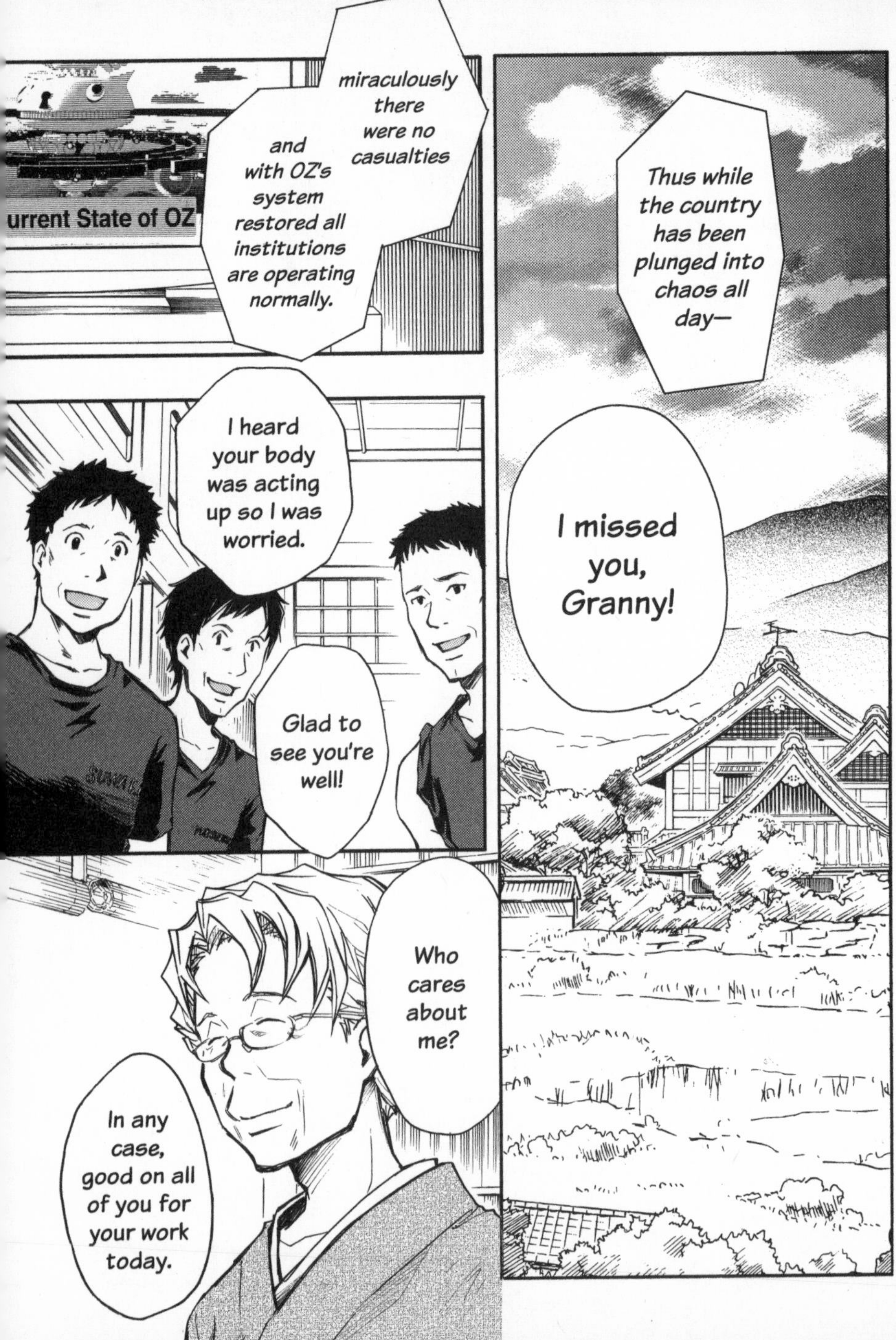

Thus while the country has been plunged into chaos all day—
I missed you, Granny!
urrent State of OZ
miraculously there were no casualties
and with OZ's system restored all institutions are operating normally.
I heard your body was acting up so I was worried.
Glad to see you're well!
Who cares about me?
In any case, good on all of you for your work today.

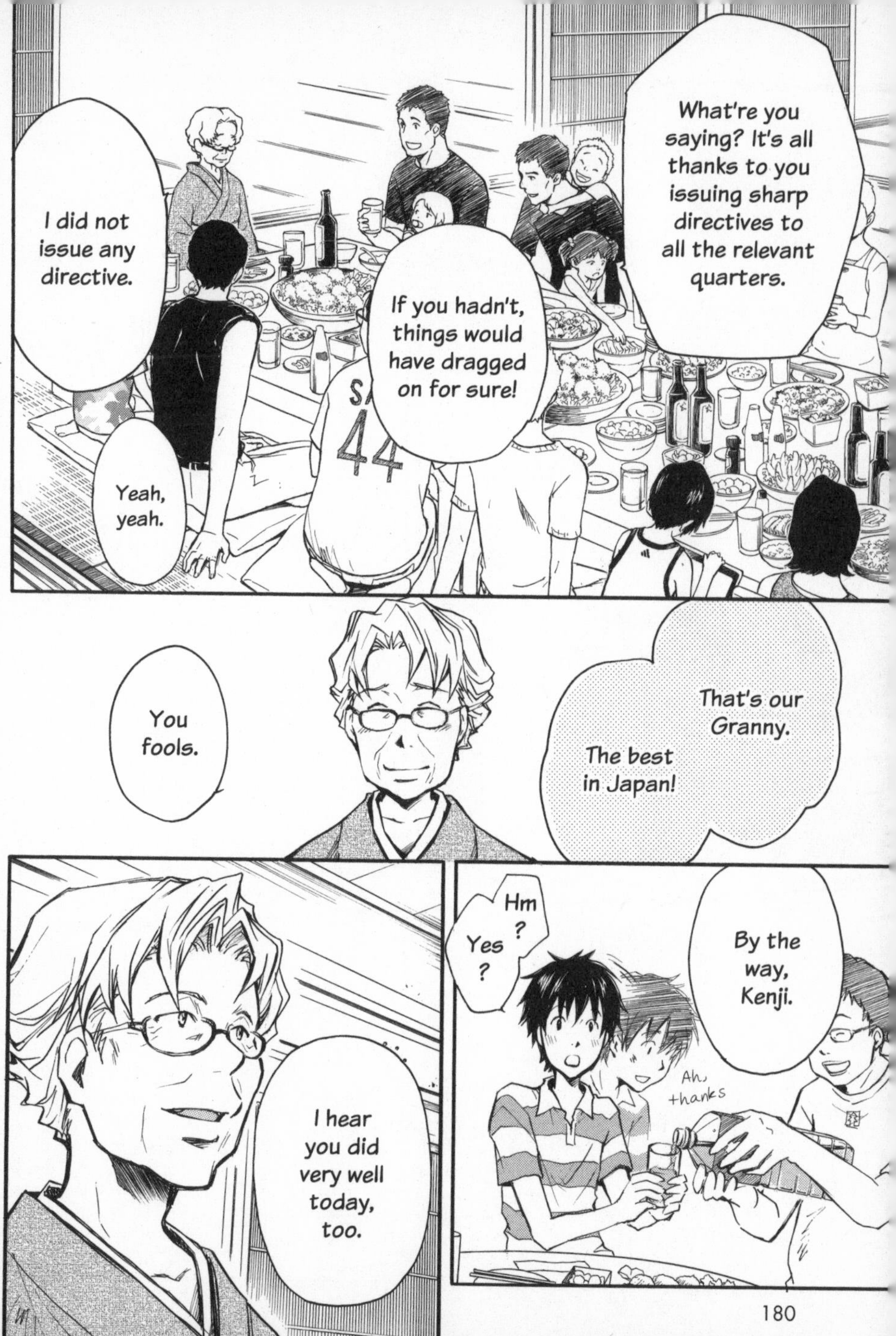
What're you saying? It's all thanks to you issuing sharp directives to all the relevant quarters.
If you hadn't, things would have dragged on for sure!
I did not issue any directive.
Yeah, yeah.
That's our Granny.
The best in Japan!
You fools.
By the way, Kenji.
Hm?
Yes?
Ah, thanks
I hear you did very well today, too.

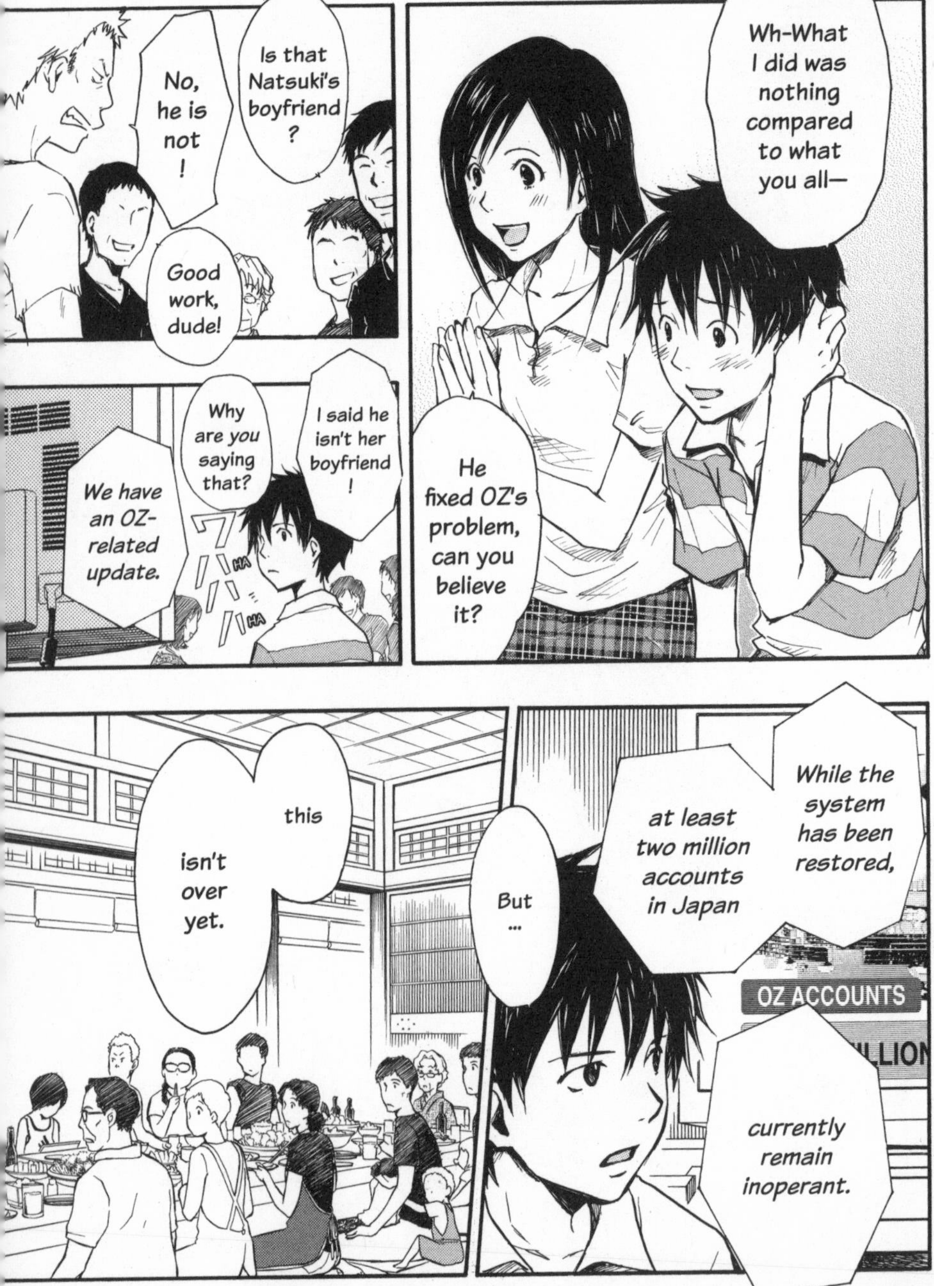
Wh-What I did was nothing compared to what you all—
He fixed OZ's problem, can you believe it?
Is that Natsuki's boyfriend?
No, he is not!
Good work, dude!
I said he isn't her boyfriend!
Why are you saying that?
HA HA
We have an OZ-related update.
While the system has been restored,
at least two million accounts in Japan
OZ ACCOUNTS
currently remain inoperant.
But ...
this isn't over yet.

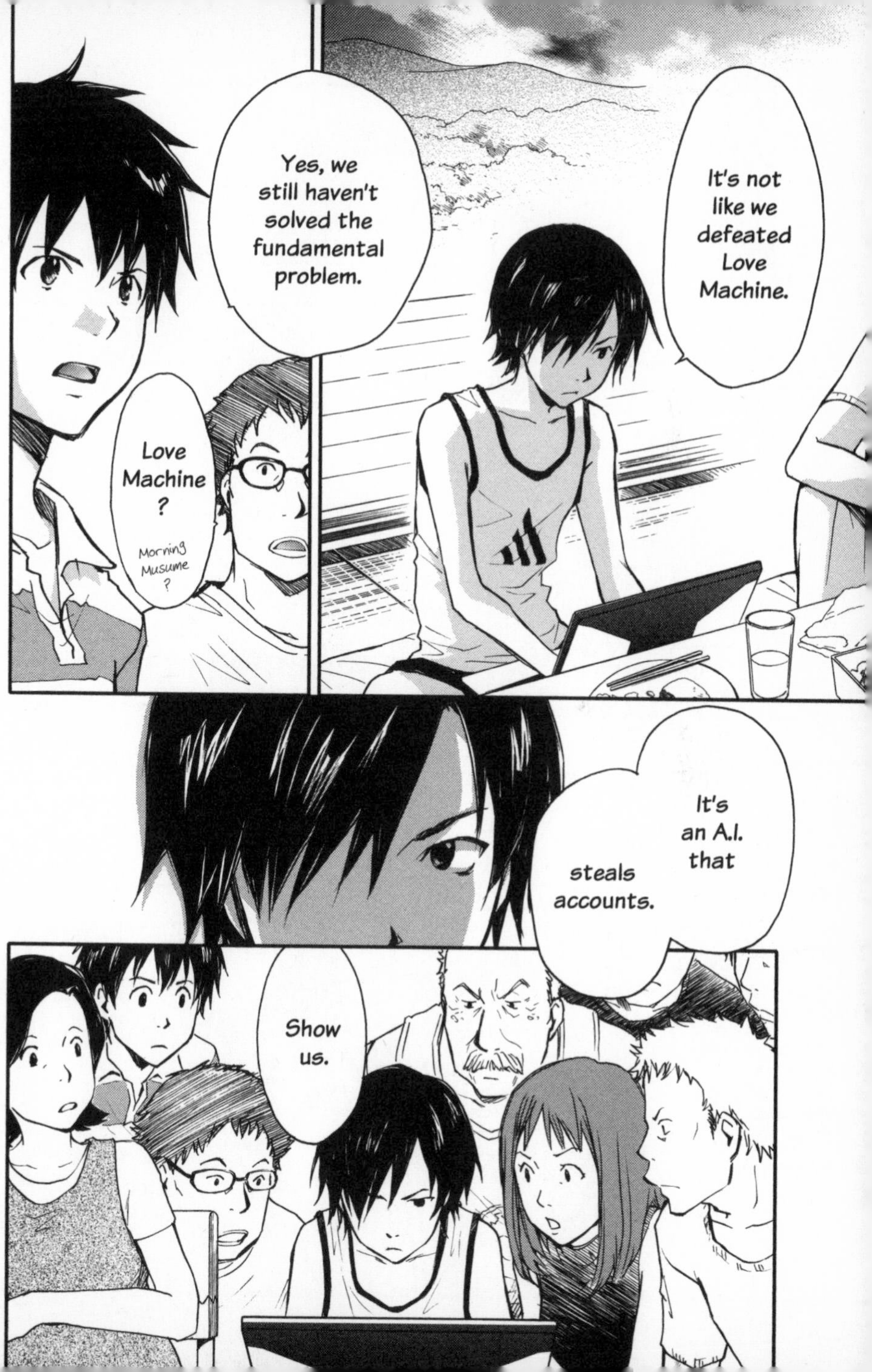
It's not like we defeated Love Machine.
Yes, we still haven't solved the fundamental problem.
Love Machine?
Morning Musume?
It's an A.I. that steals accounts.
Show us.

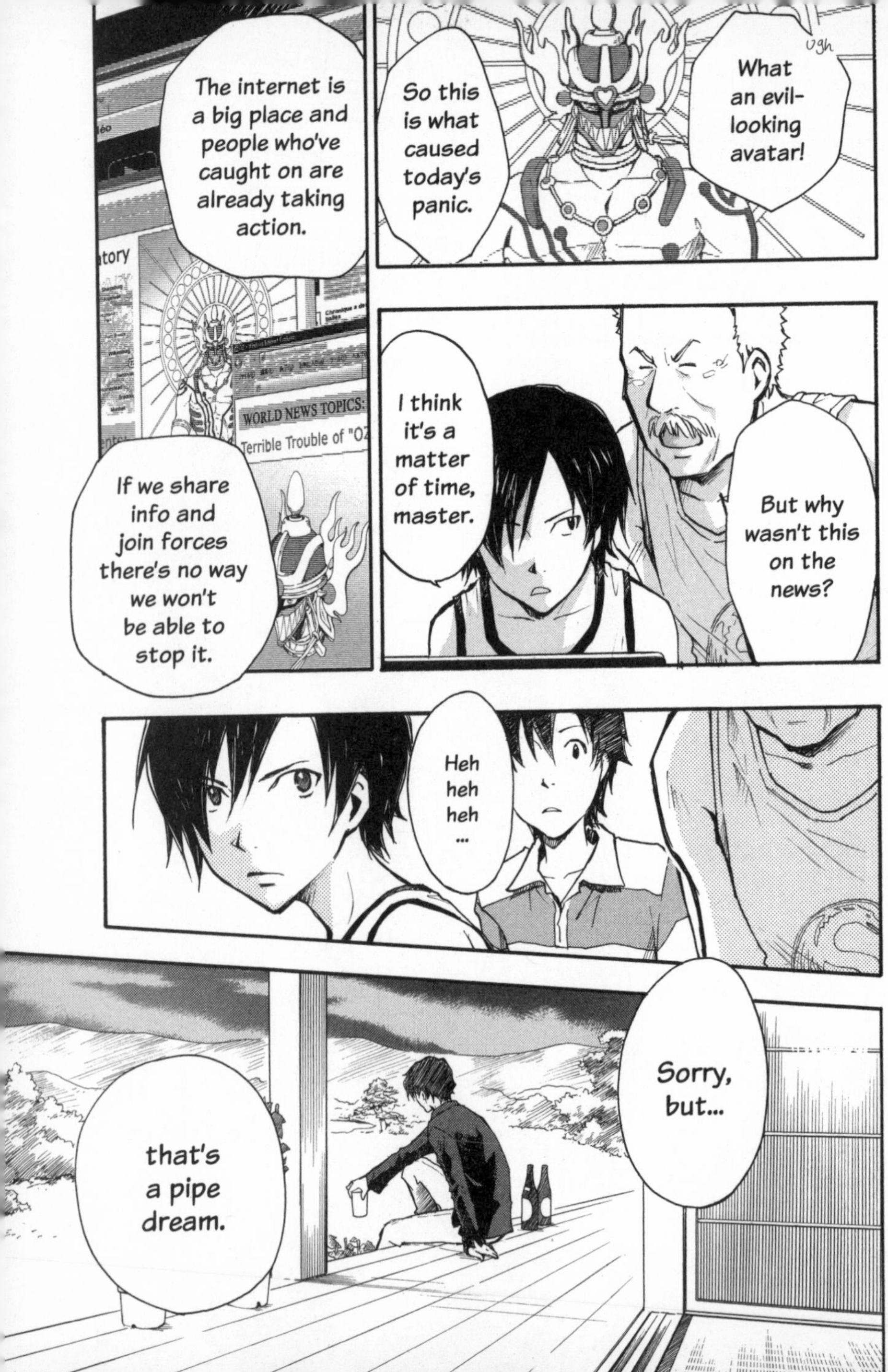
What an evil-looking avatar!
So this is what caused today's panic.
But why wasn't this on the news?
I think it's a matter of time, master.
The internet is a big place and people who've caught on are already taking action.
WORLD NEWS TOPICS:
Terrible Trouble of "OZ
If we share info and join forces there's no way we won't be able to stop it.
Heh heh heh...
Sorry, but...
that's a pipe dream.

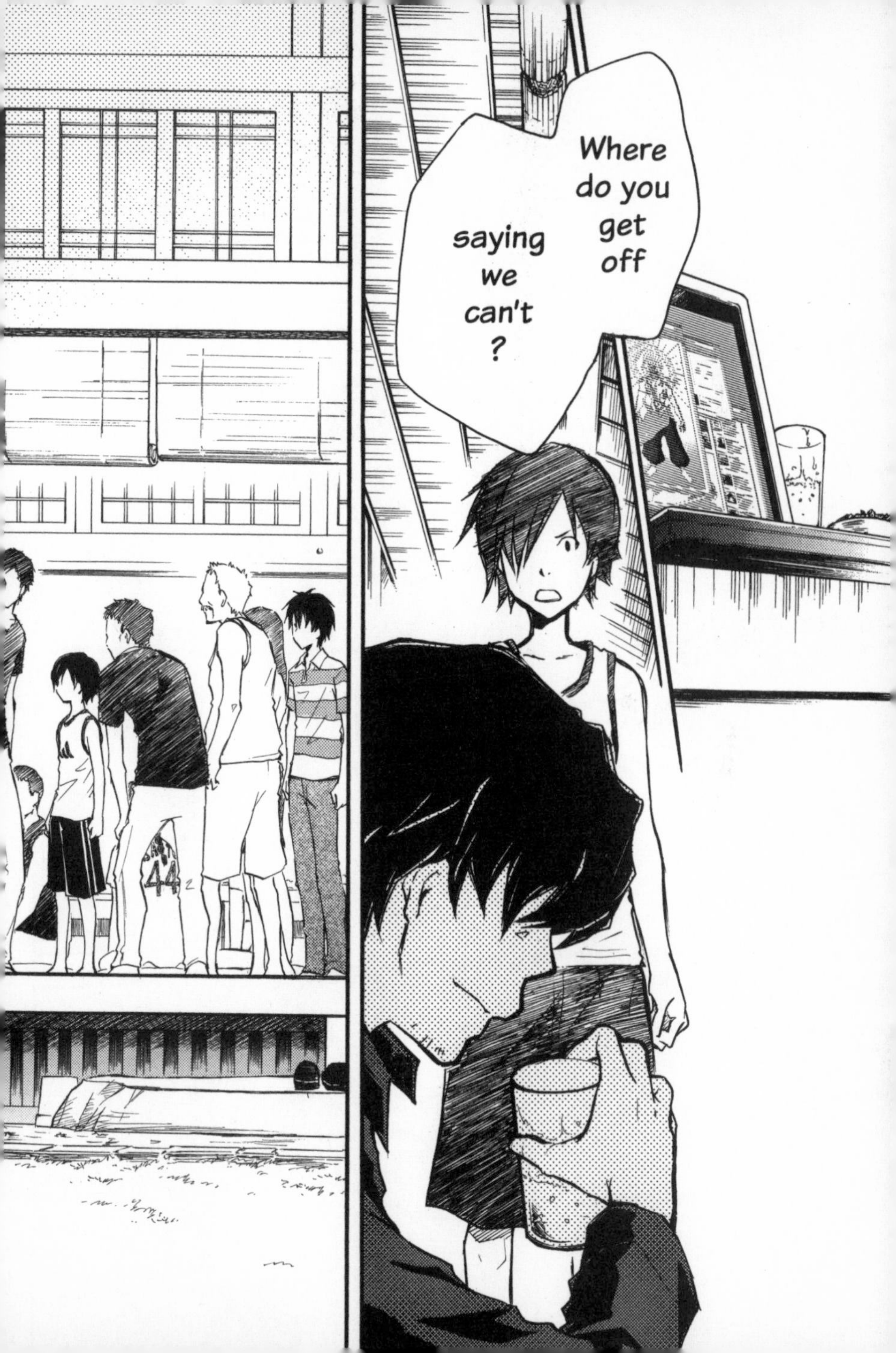
Where do you get off saying we can't?

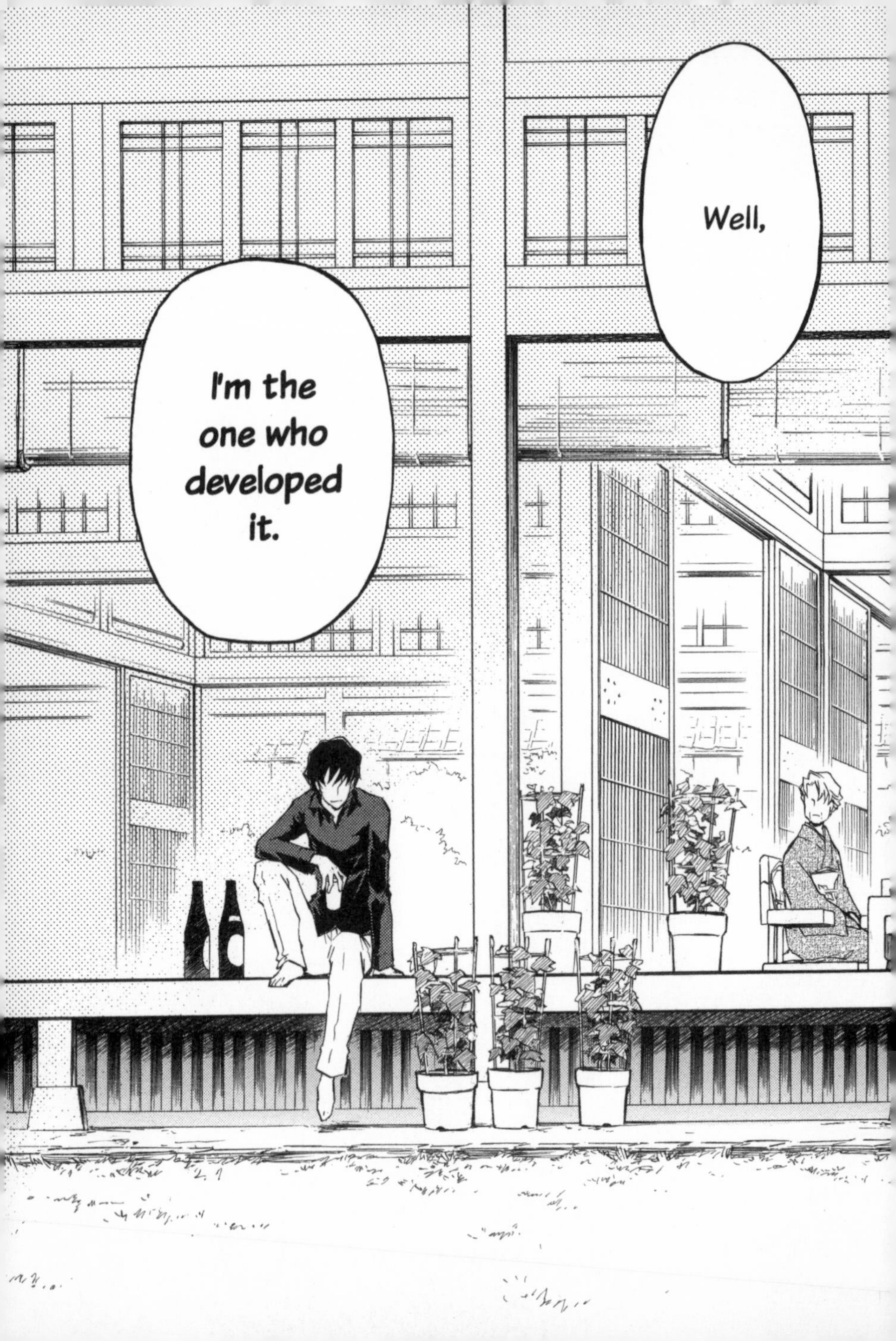
Well,
I'm the one who developed it.

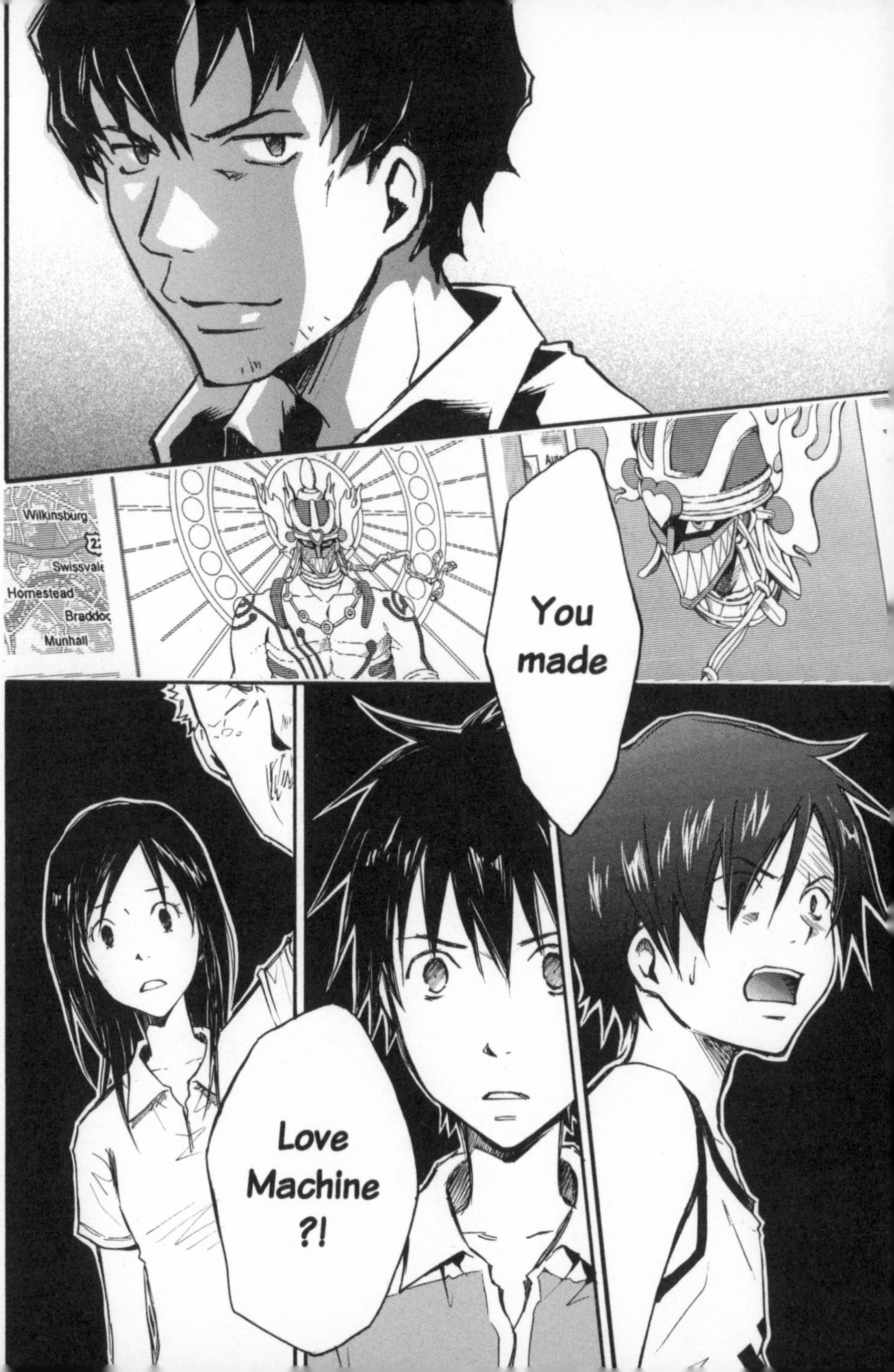
Wilkinsburg
Swissvale
Homestead
Munhall
You made
Love Machine ?!

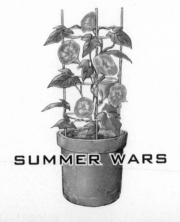

SUMMER WARS

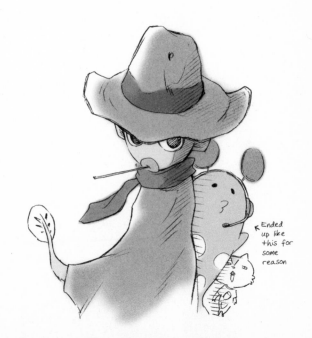

Ended up like this for some reason

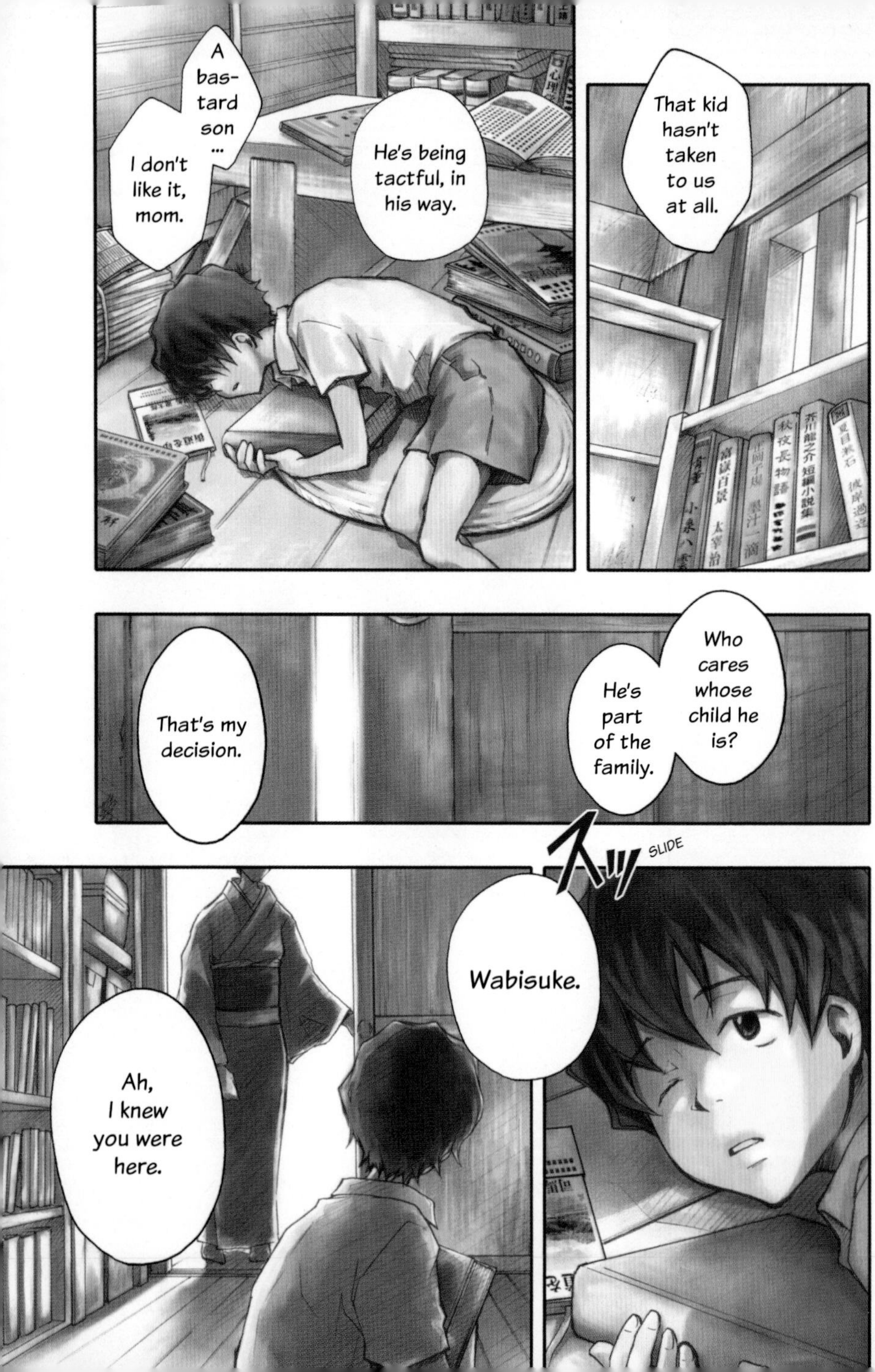
That kid hasn't taken to us at all.
He's being tactful, in his way.
A bas-tard son ...
I don't like it, mom.
Who cares whose child he is?
He's part of the family.
That's my decision.
スッ
SLIDE
Wabisuke.
Ah, I knew you were here.

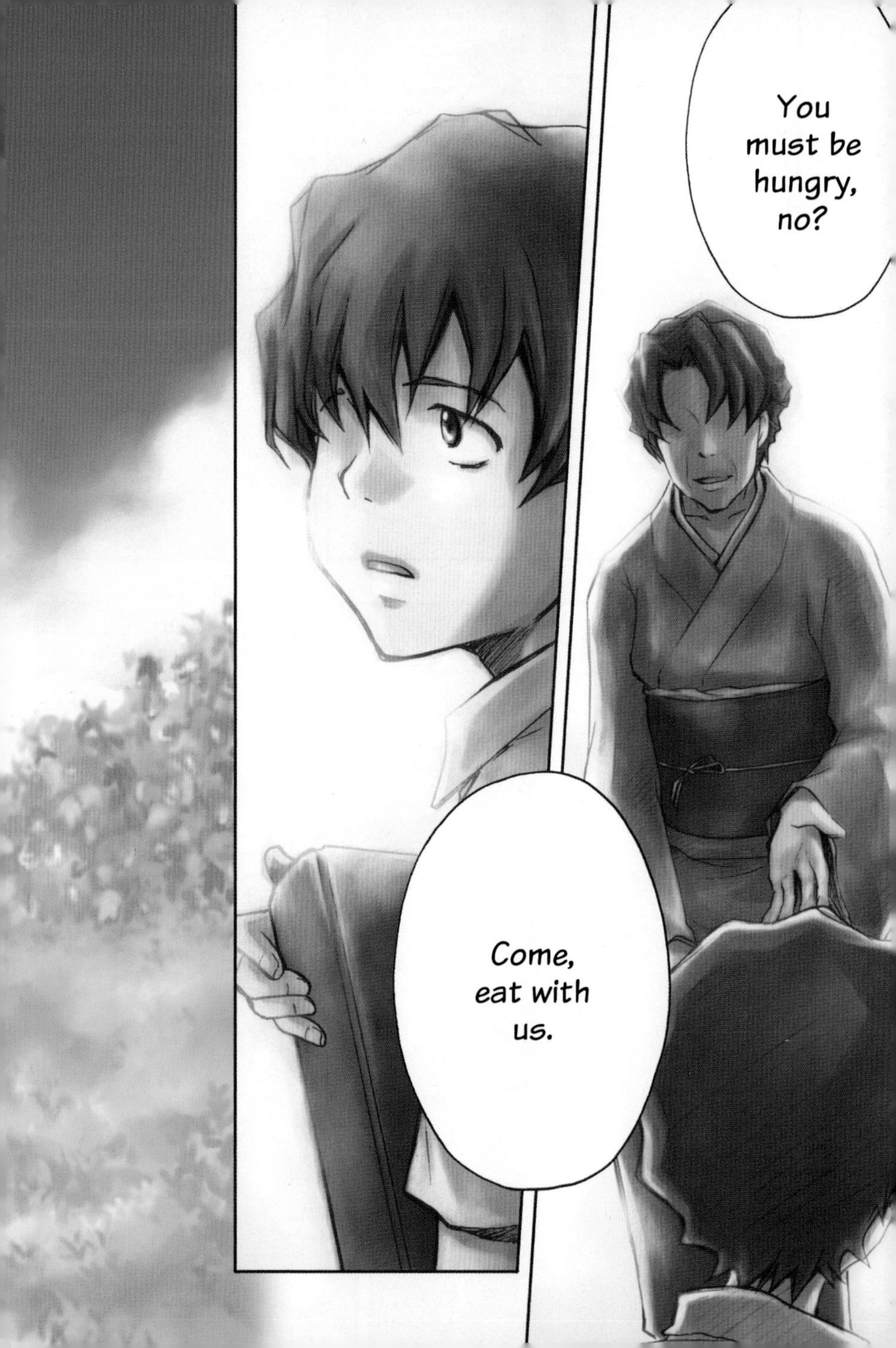
You must be hungry, no?
Come, eat with us.

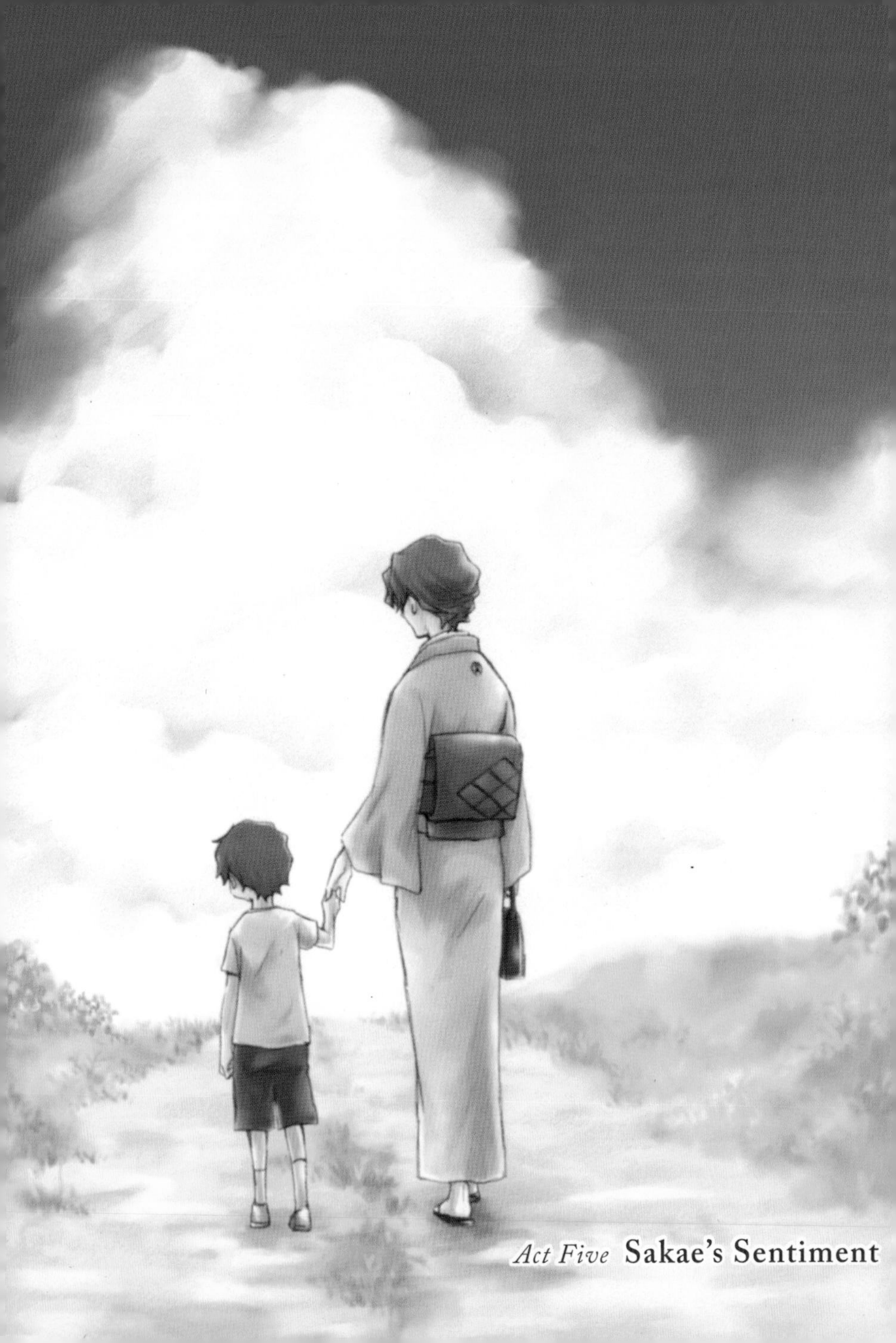

Act Five Sakae's Sentiment

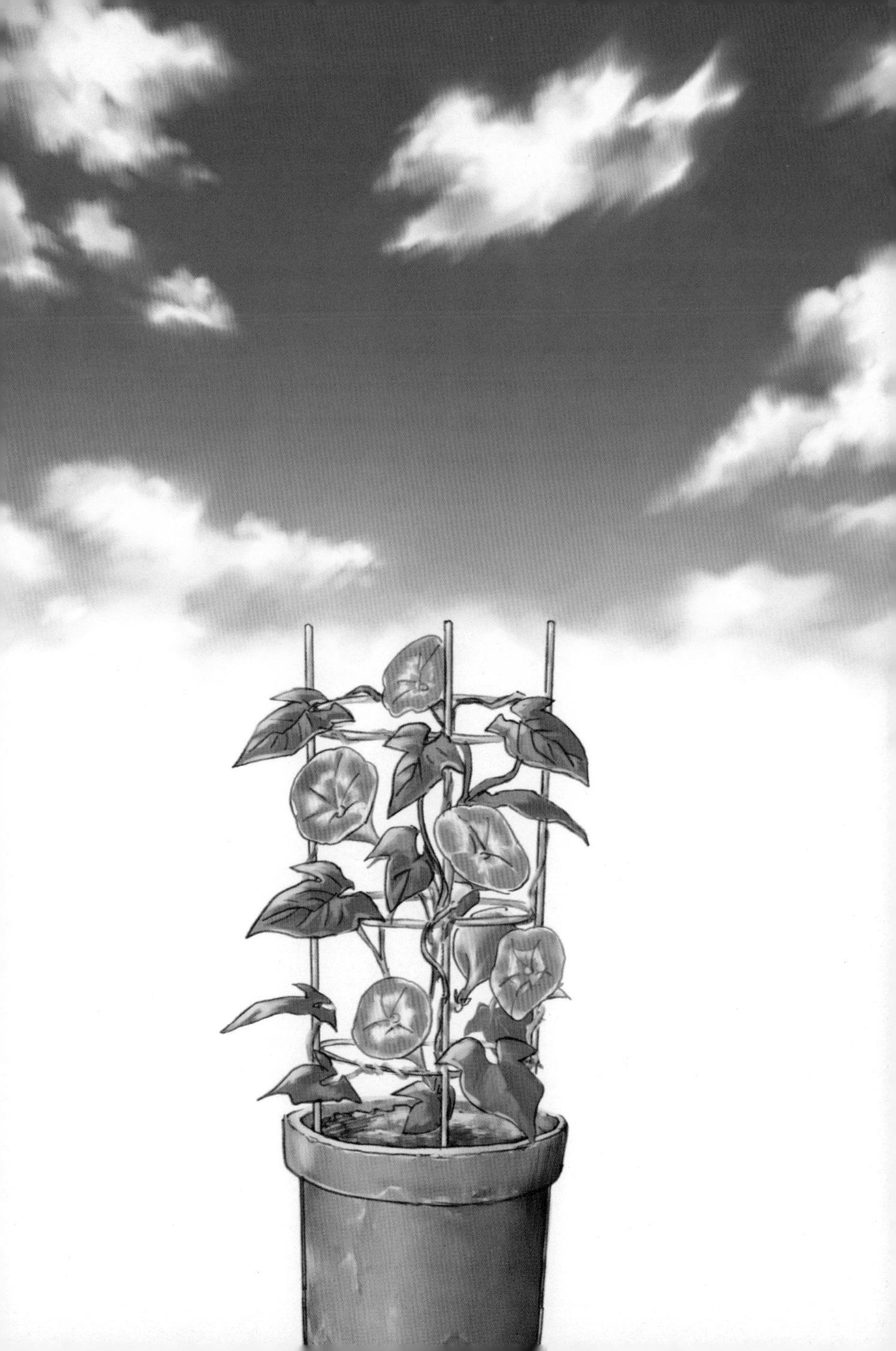

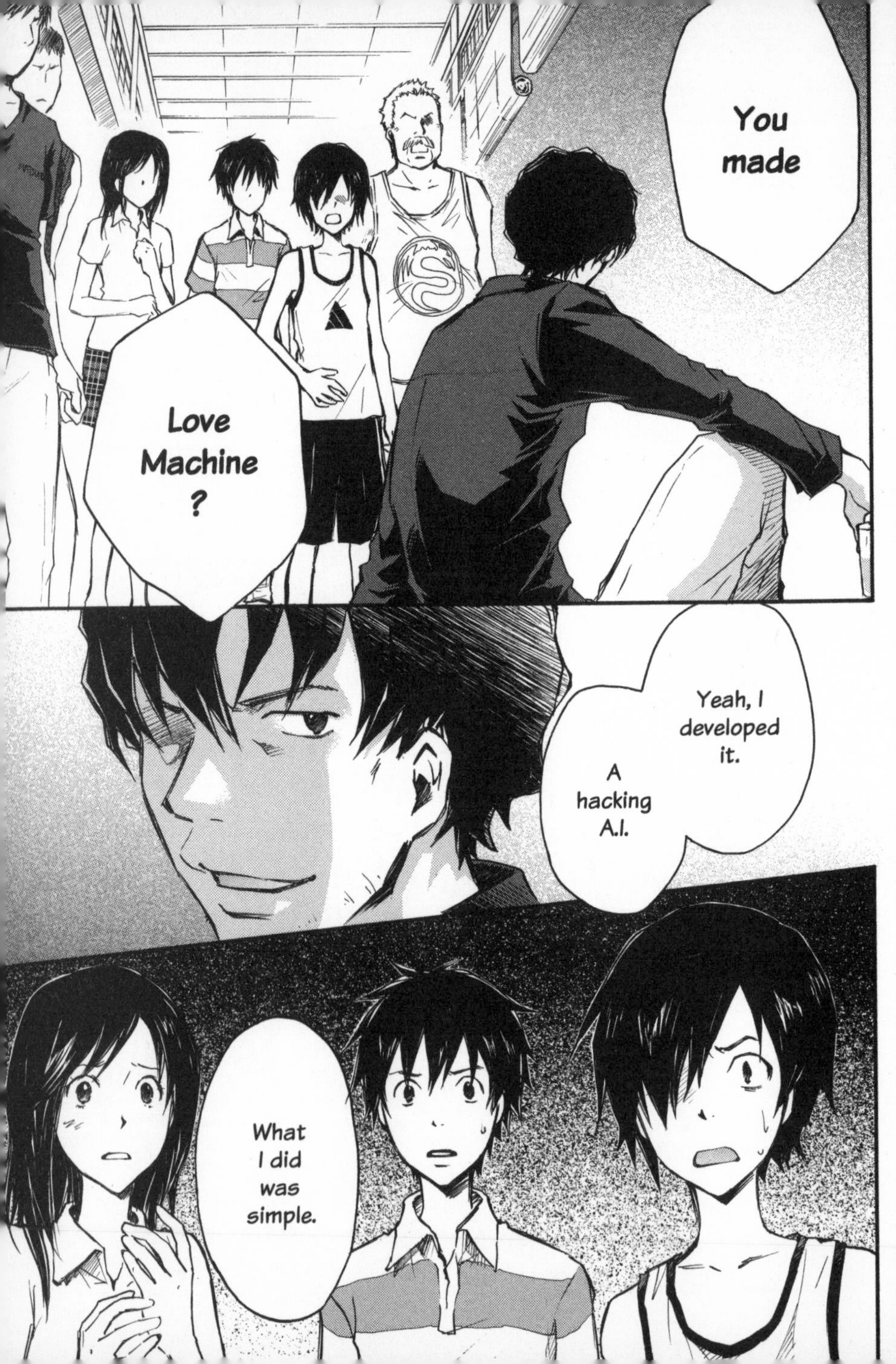
You made
Love Machine ?
Yeah, I developed it.
A hacking A.I.
What I did was simple.

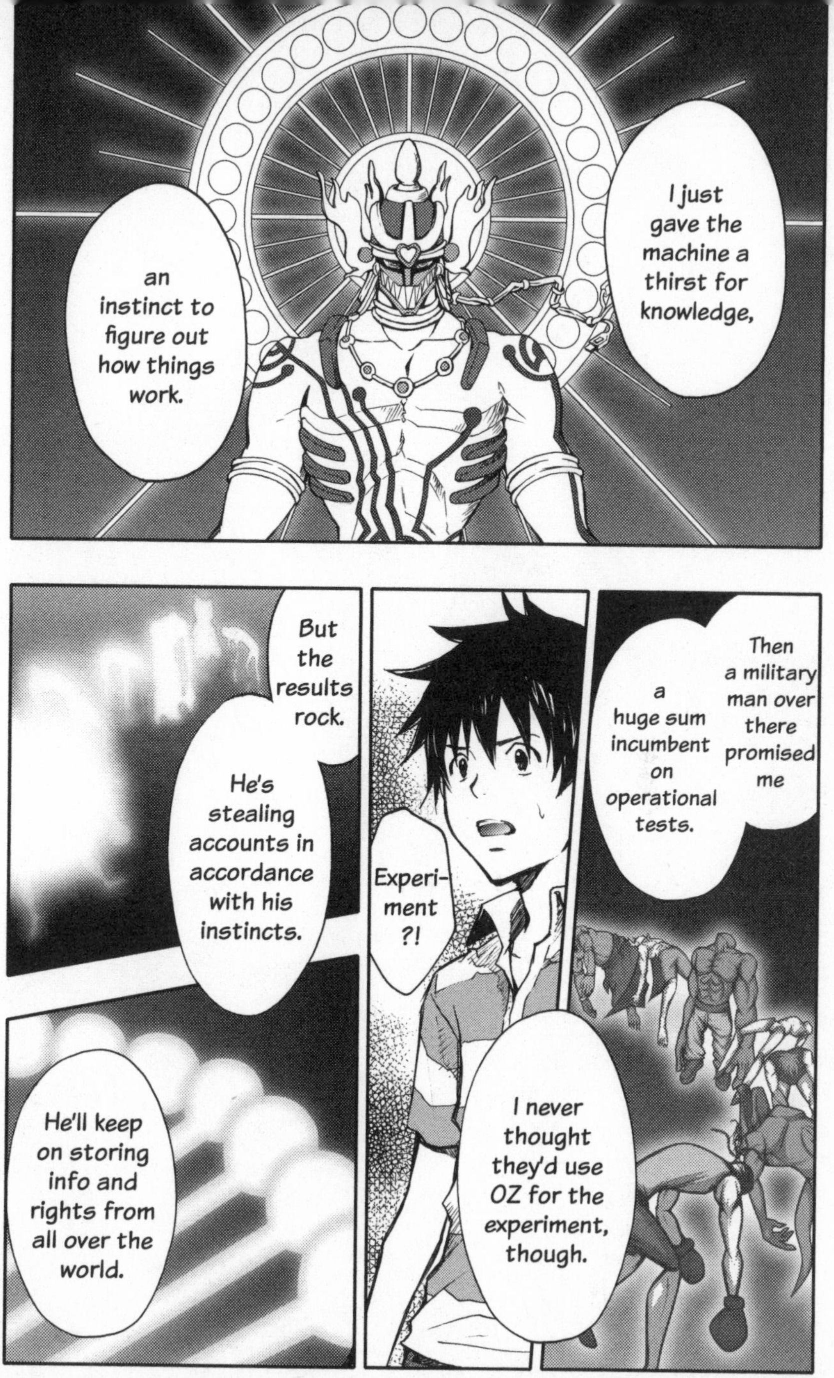

I just gave the machine a thirst for knowledge,
an instinct to figure out how things work.
Then a military man over there promised me
a huge sum incumbent on operational tests.
I never thought they'd use OZ for the experiment, though.
Experi-ment?!
But the results rock.
He's stealing accounts in accordance with his instincts.
He'll keep on storing info and rights from all over the world.

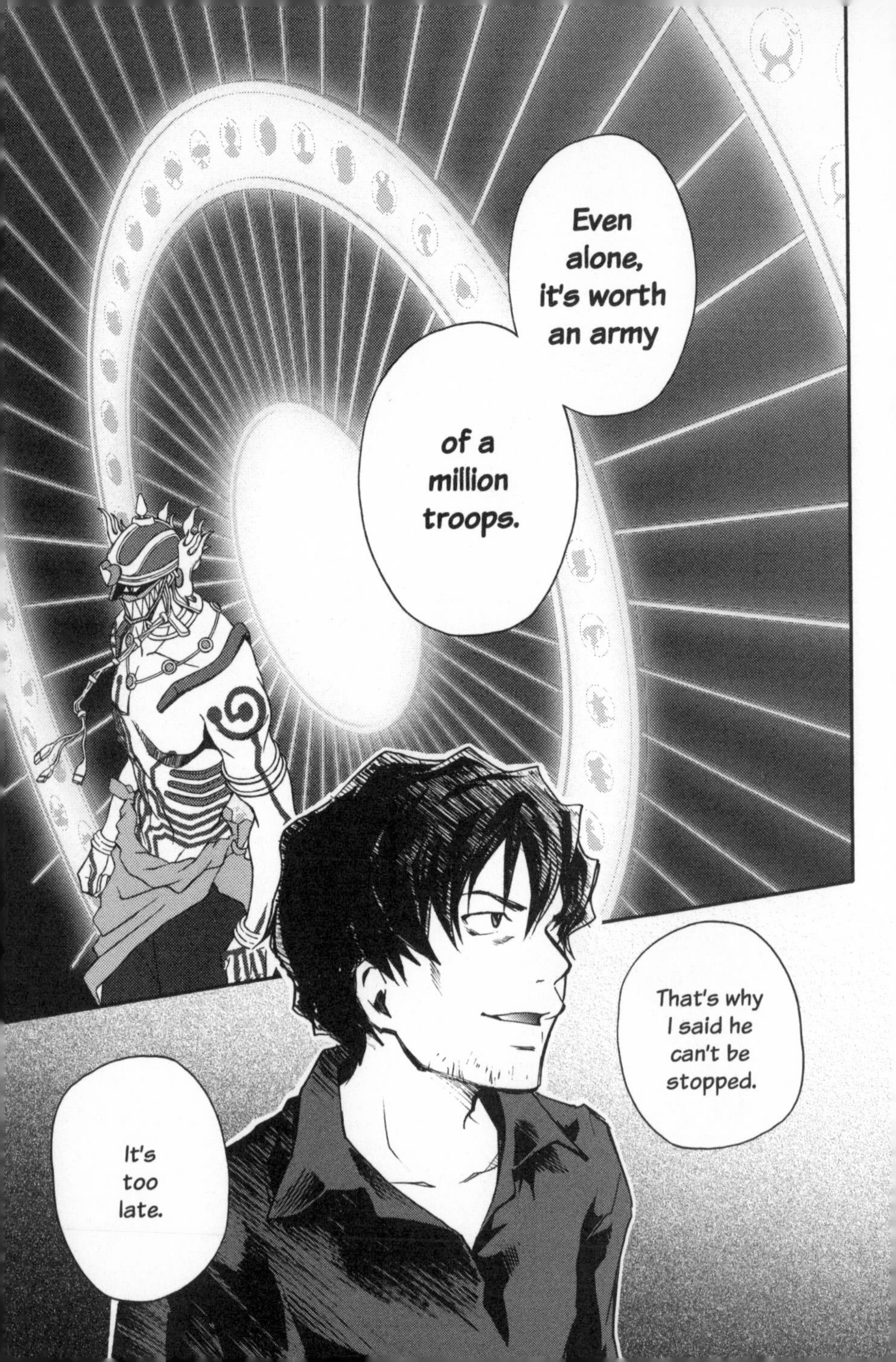
Even alone, it's worth an army
of a million troops.
That's why I said he can't be stopped.
It's too late.

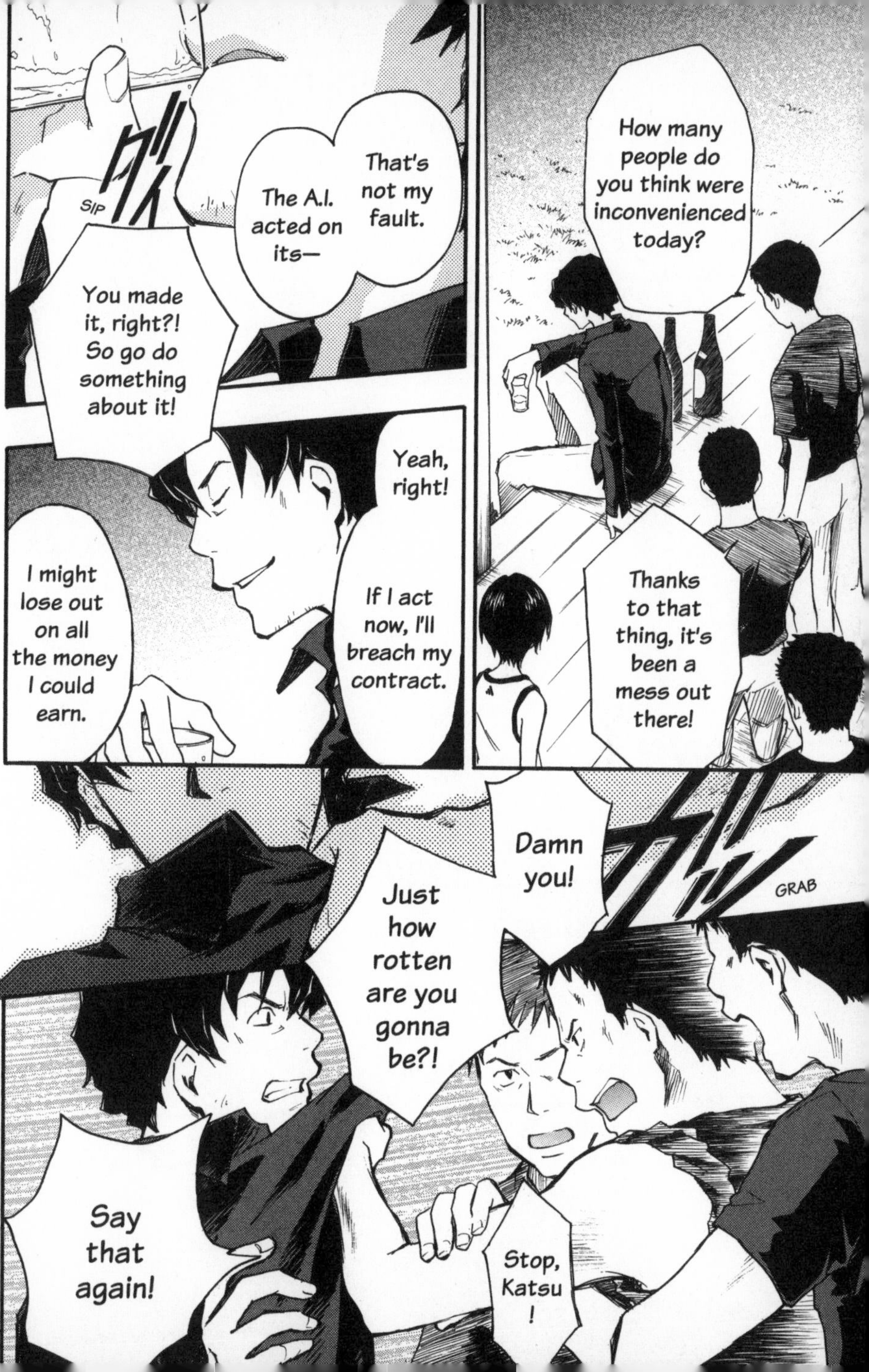
How many people do you think were inconvenienced today?
Thanks to that thing, it's been a mess out there!
That's not my fault.
The A.I. acted on its—
SIP
You made it, right?! So go do something about it!
Yeah, right!
If I act now, I'll breach my contract.
I might lose out on all the money I could earn.
GRAB
Damn you!
Just how rotten are you gonna be?!
Stop, Katsu!
Say that again!

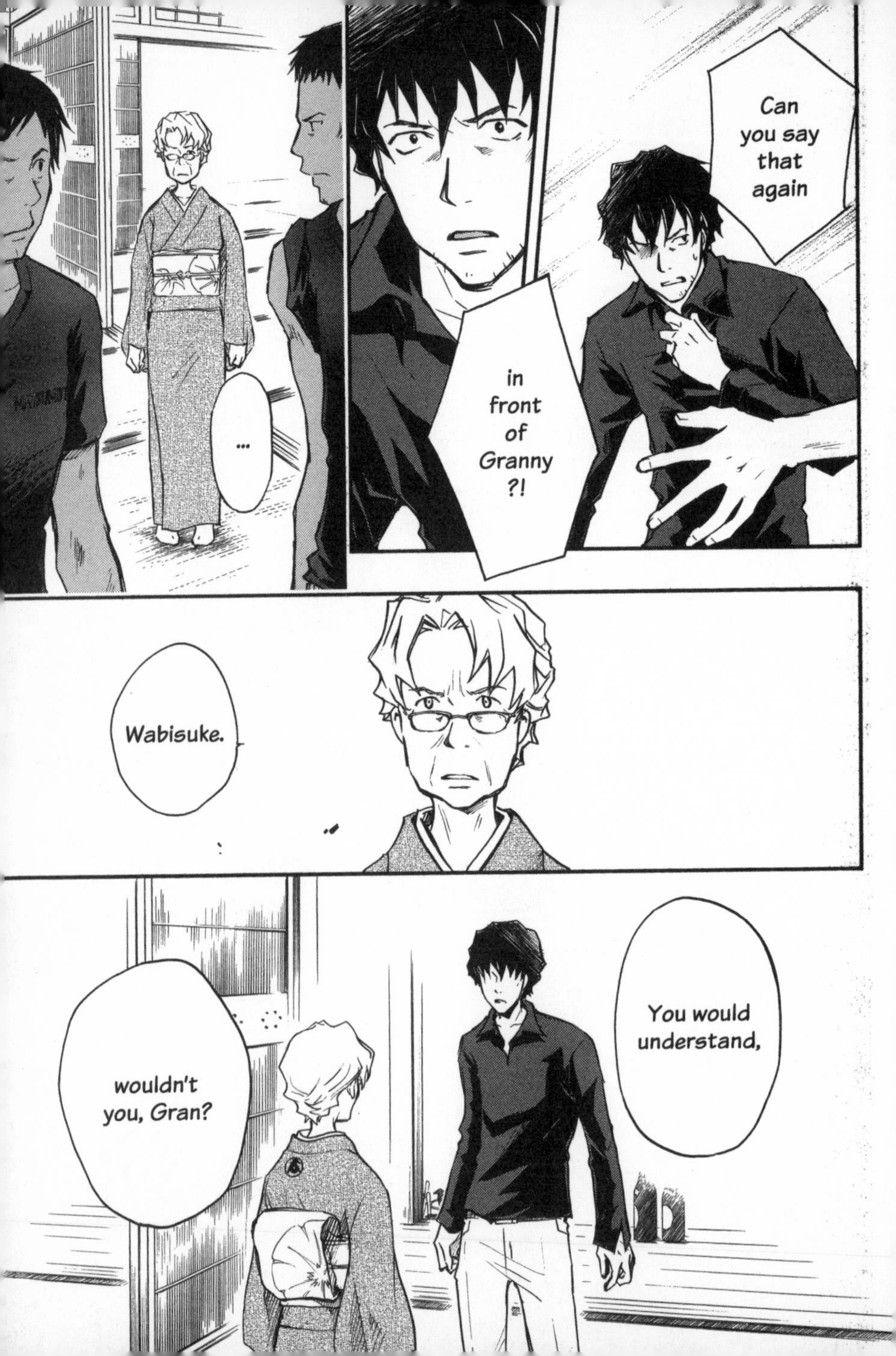
Can you say that again
in front of Granny ?!
...
Wabisuke.
You would understand,
wouldn't you, Gran?

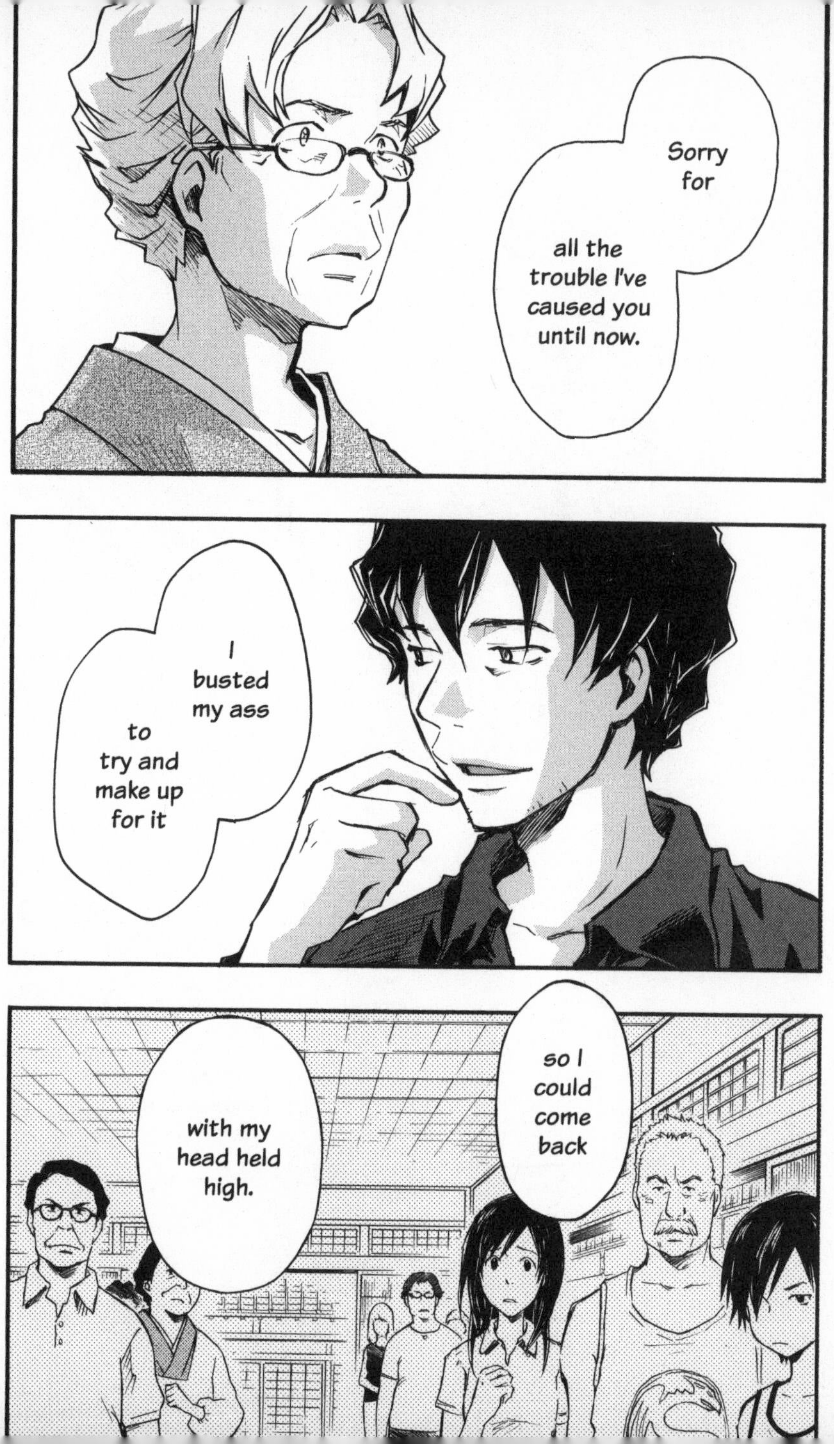
Sorry for all the trouble I've caused you until now.
I busted my ass to try and make up for it
so I could come back
with my head held high.

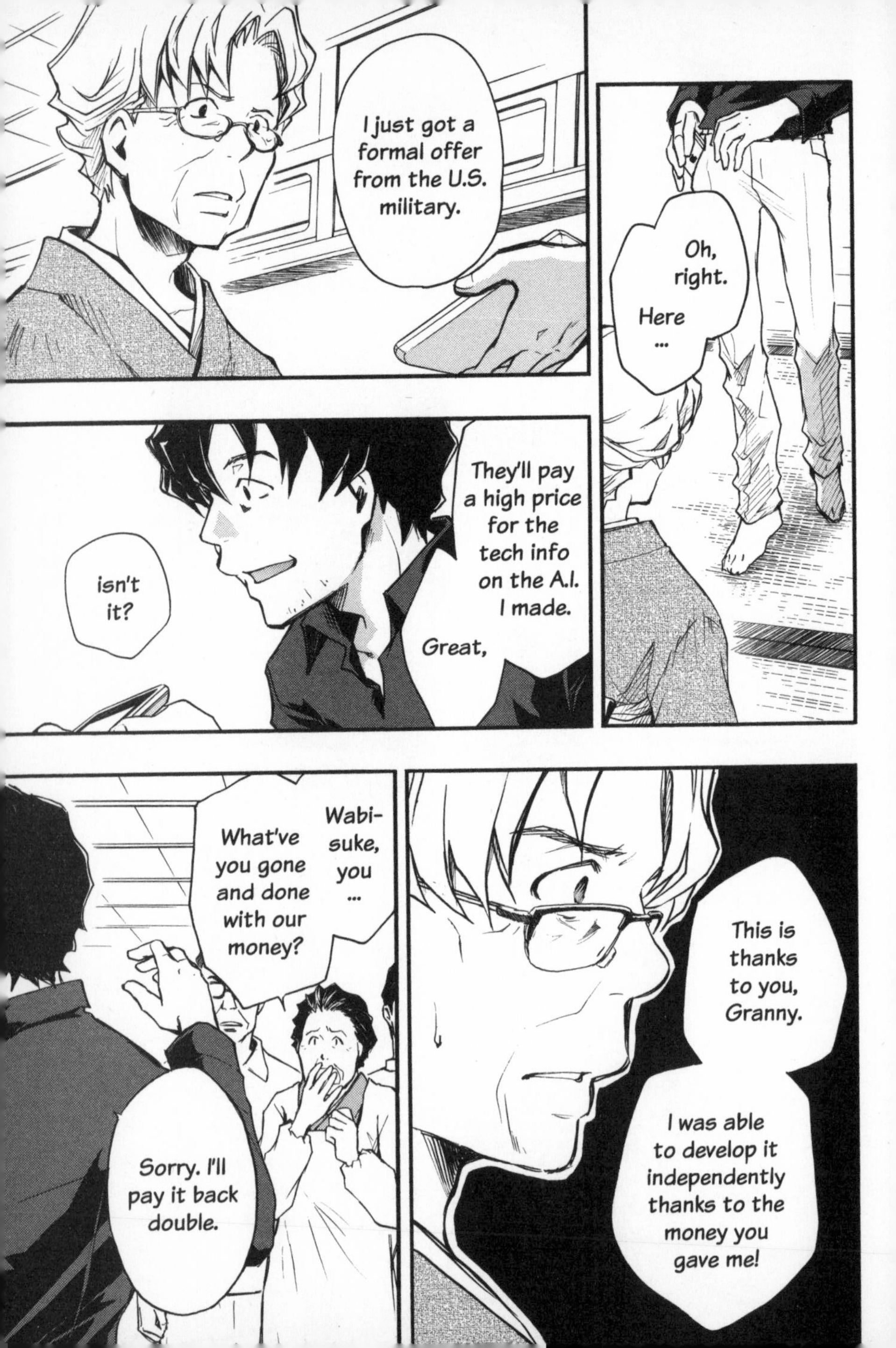
Oh, right.
Here ...
I just got a formal offer from the U.S. military.
They'll pay a high price for the tech info on the A.I. I made.
Great,
isn't it?
This is thanks to you, Granny.
I was able to develop it independently thanks to the money you gave me!
Wabi-suke, you ...
What've you gone and done with our money?
Sorry. I'll pay it back double.

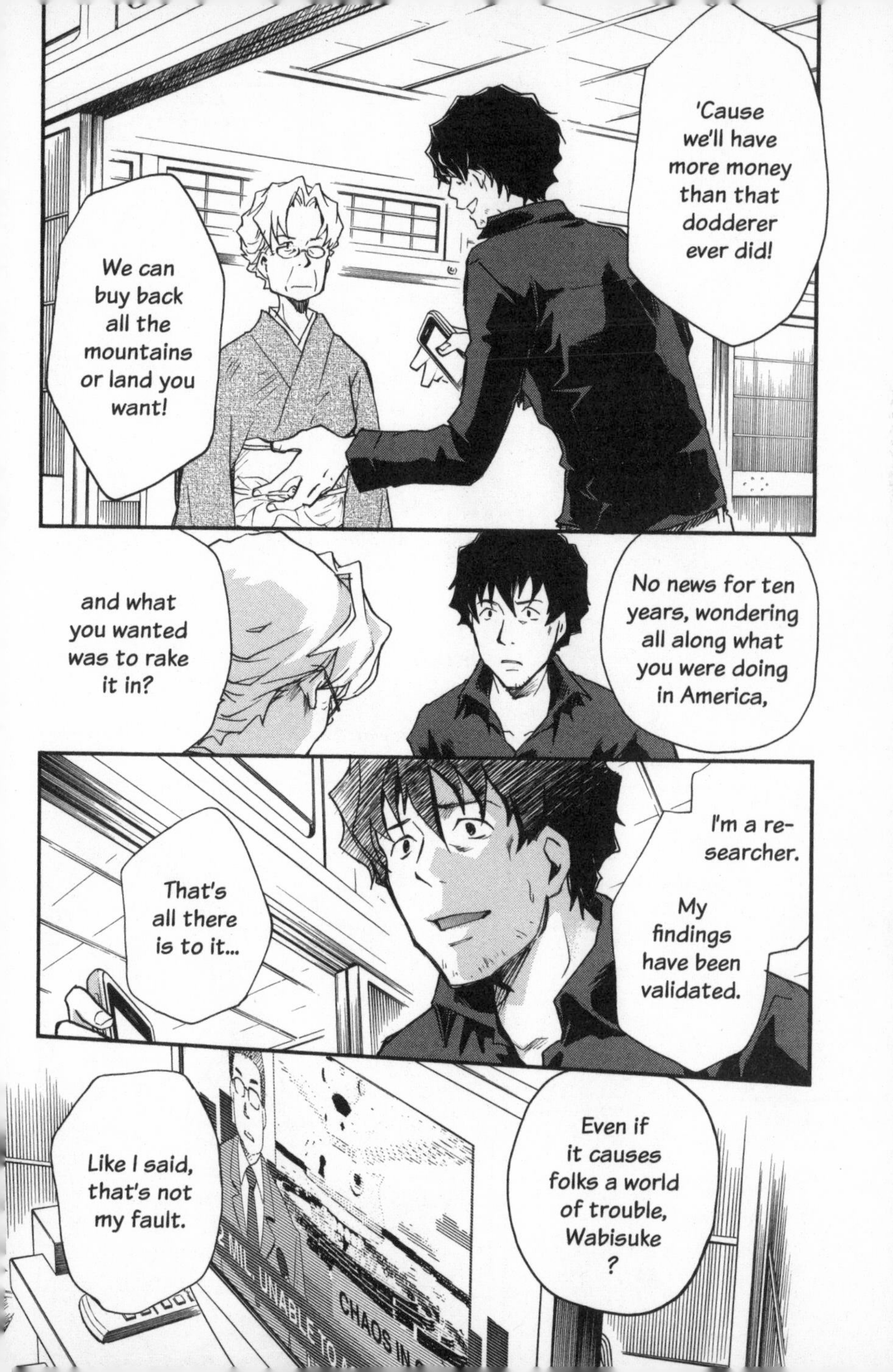
'Cause we'll have more money than that dodderer ever did!
We can buy back all the mountains or land you want!
No news for ten years, wondering all along what you were doing in America,
and what you wanted was to rake it in?
I'm a re- searcher.
My findings have been validated.
That's all there is to it...
Even if it causes folks a world of trouble, Wabisuke ?
Like I said, that's not my fault.

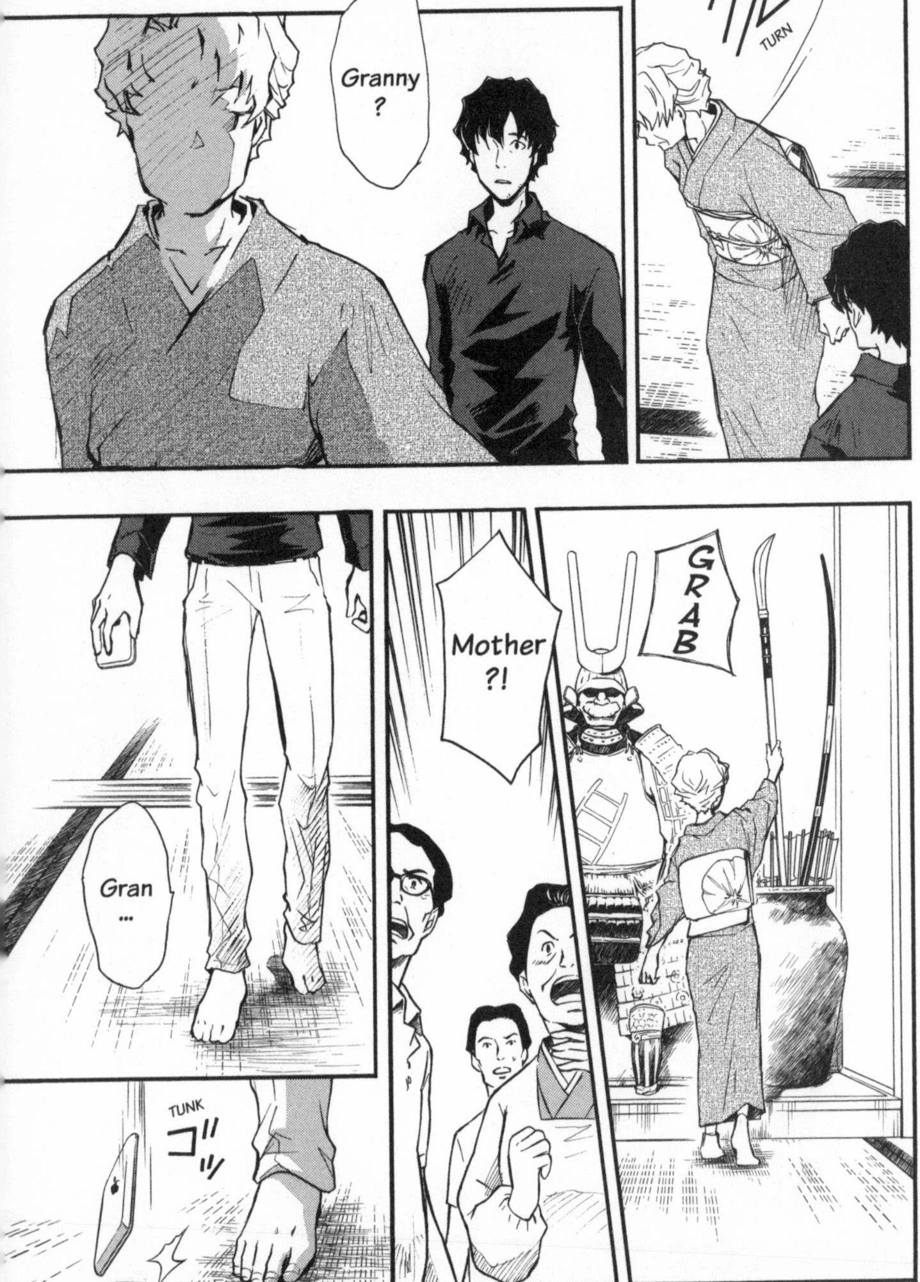
クル
TURN
Granny?
GRAB
Mother?!
Gran...
TUNK
ゴッ

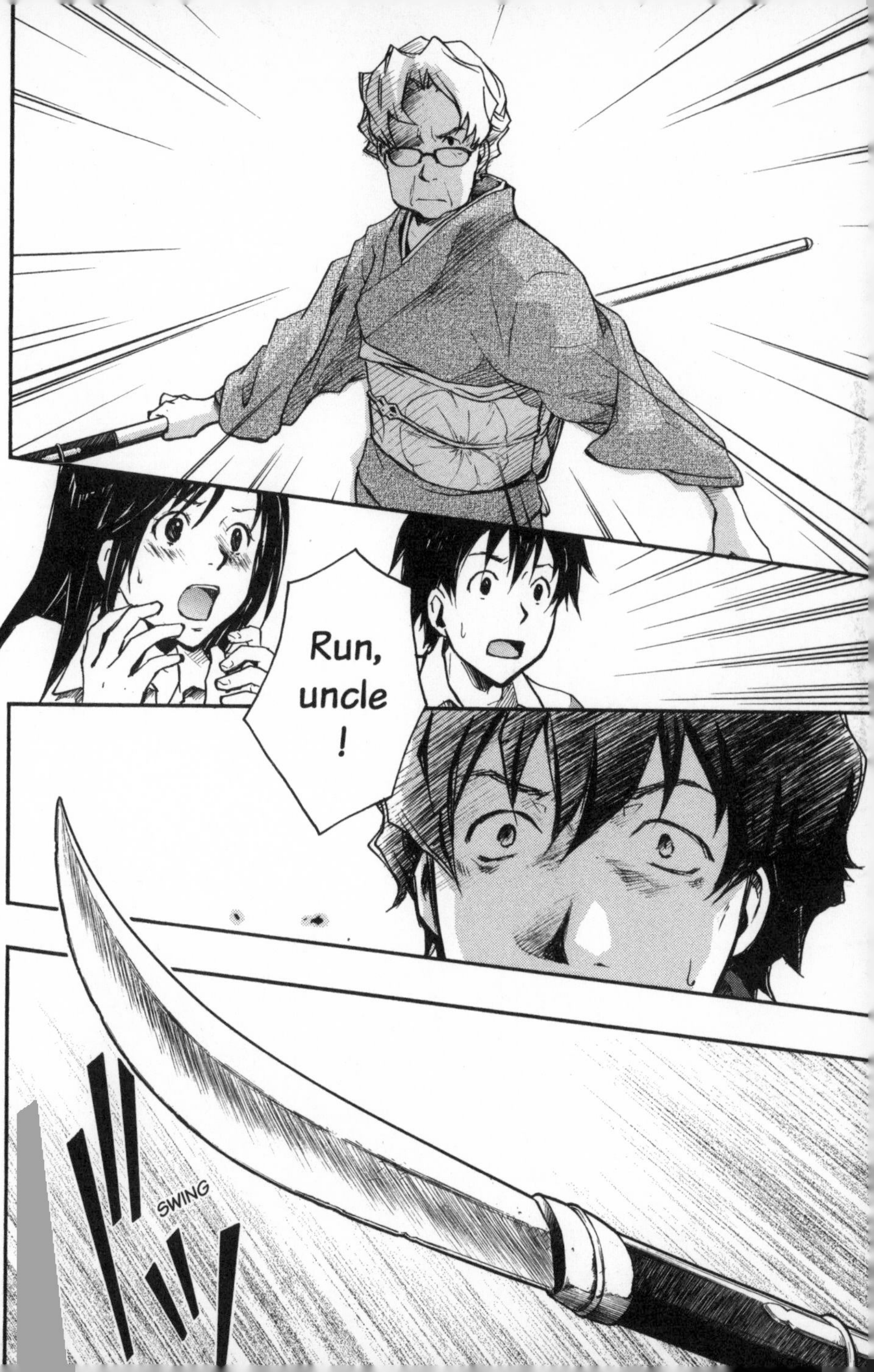
Run, uncle!
SWING

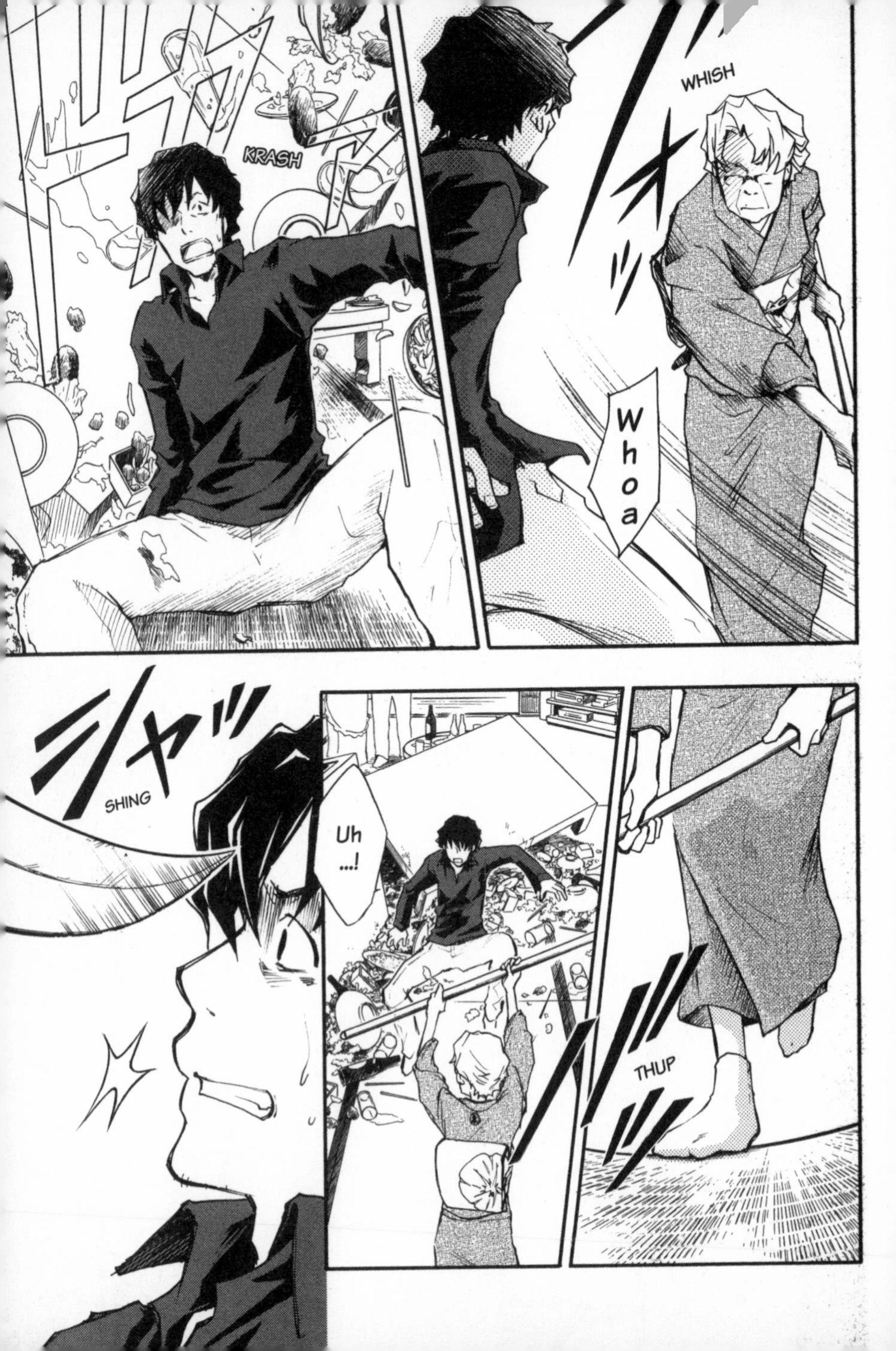
WHISH
Whoa
KRASH
THUP
Uh ...!
シャッ
SHING

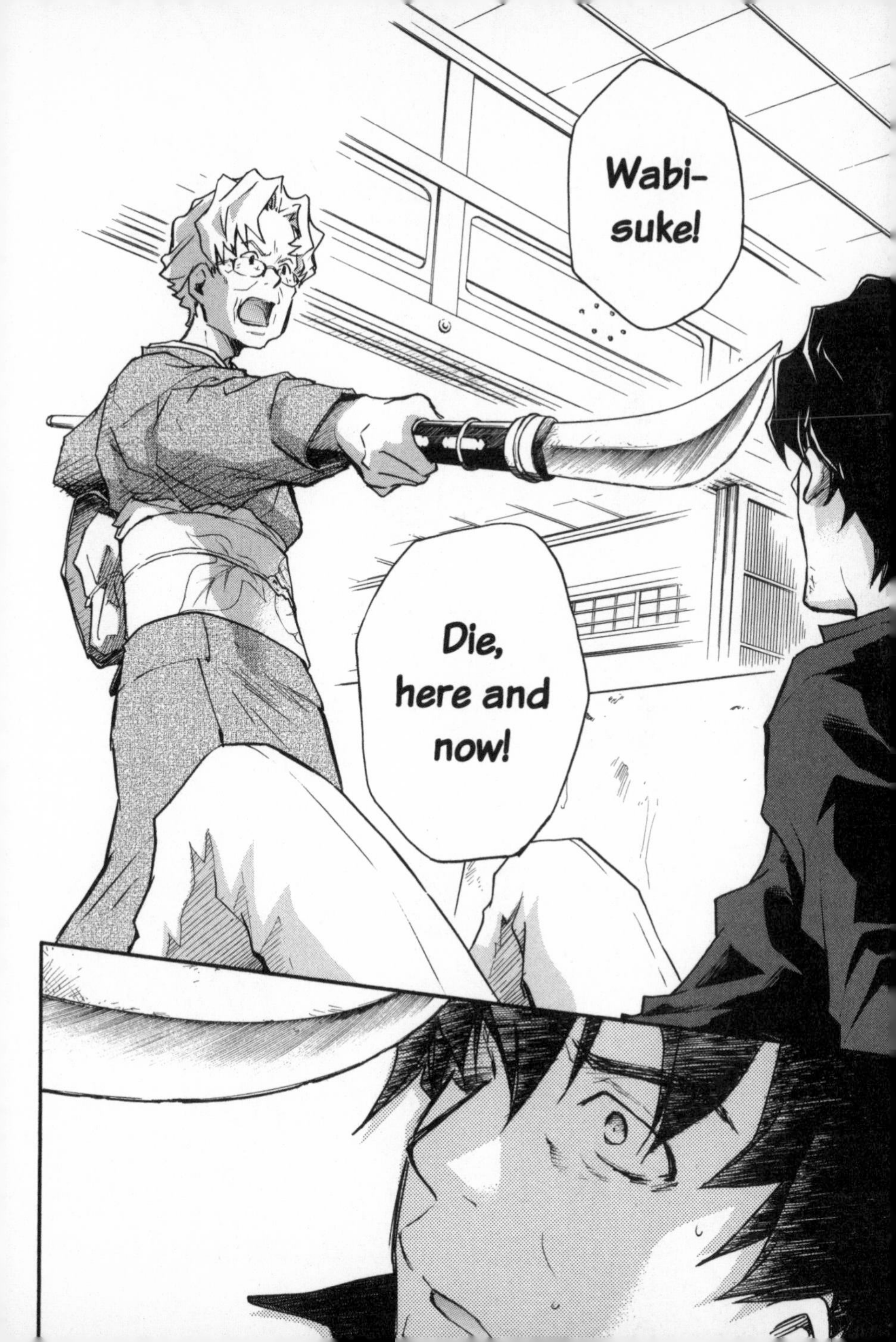
Wabi-suke!
Die, here and now!

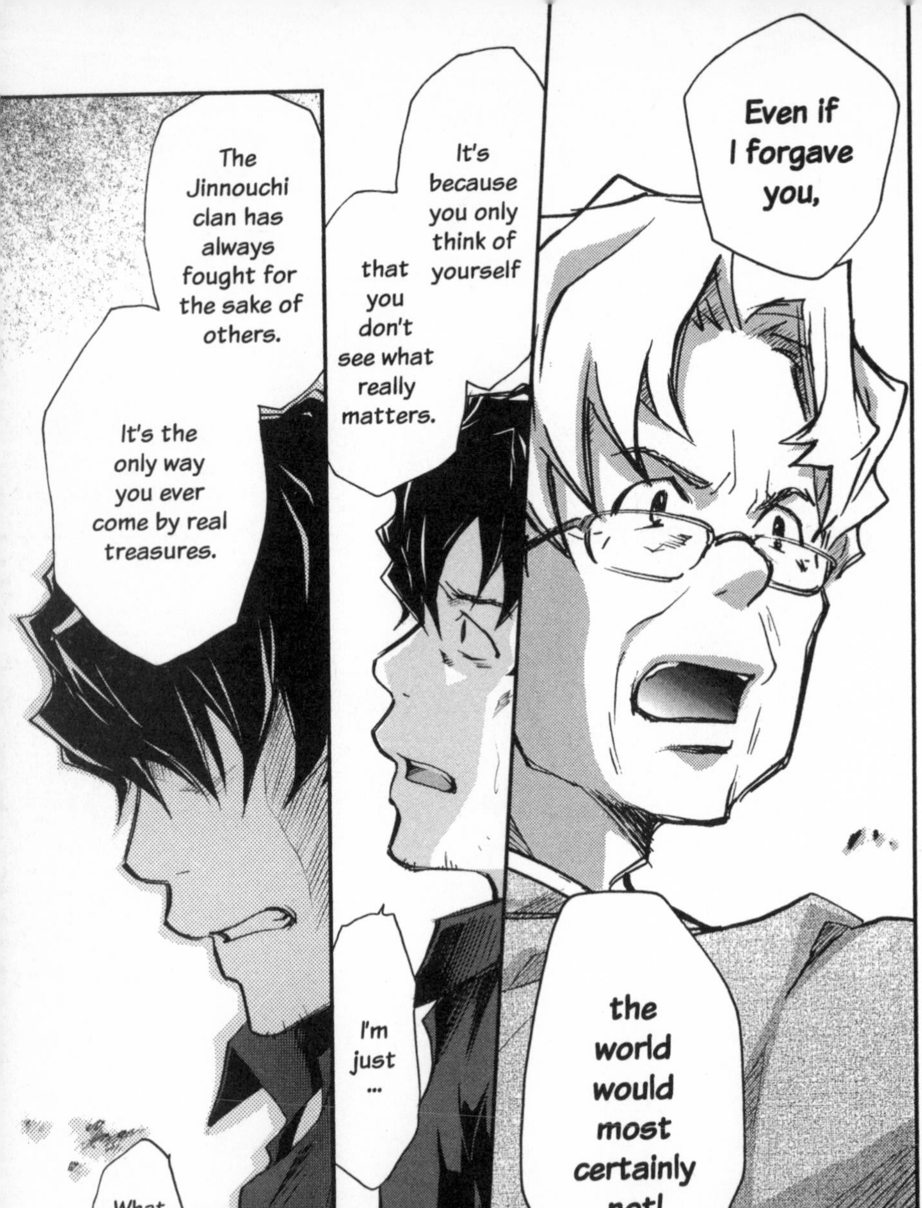
Even if I forgave you,
the world would most certainly not!
It's because you only think of yourself that you don't see what really matters.
I'm just ...
The Jinnouchi clan has always fought for the sake of others.
It's the only way you ever come by real treasures.
What do you know ...

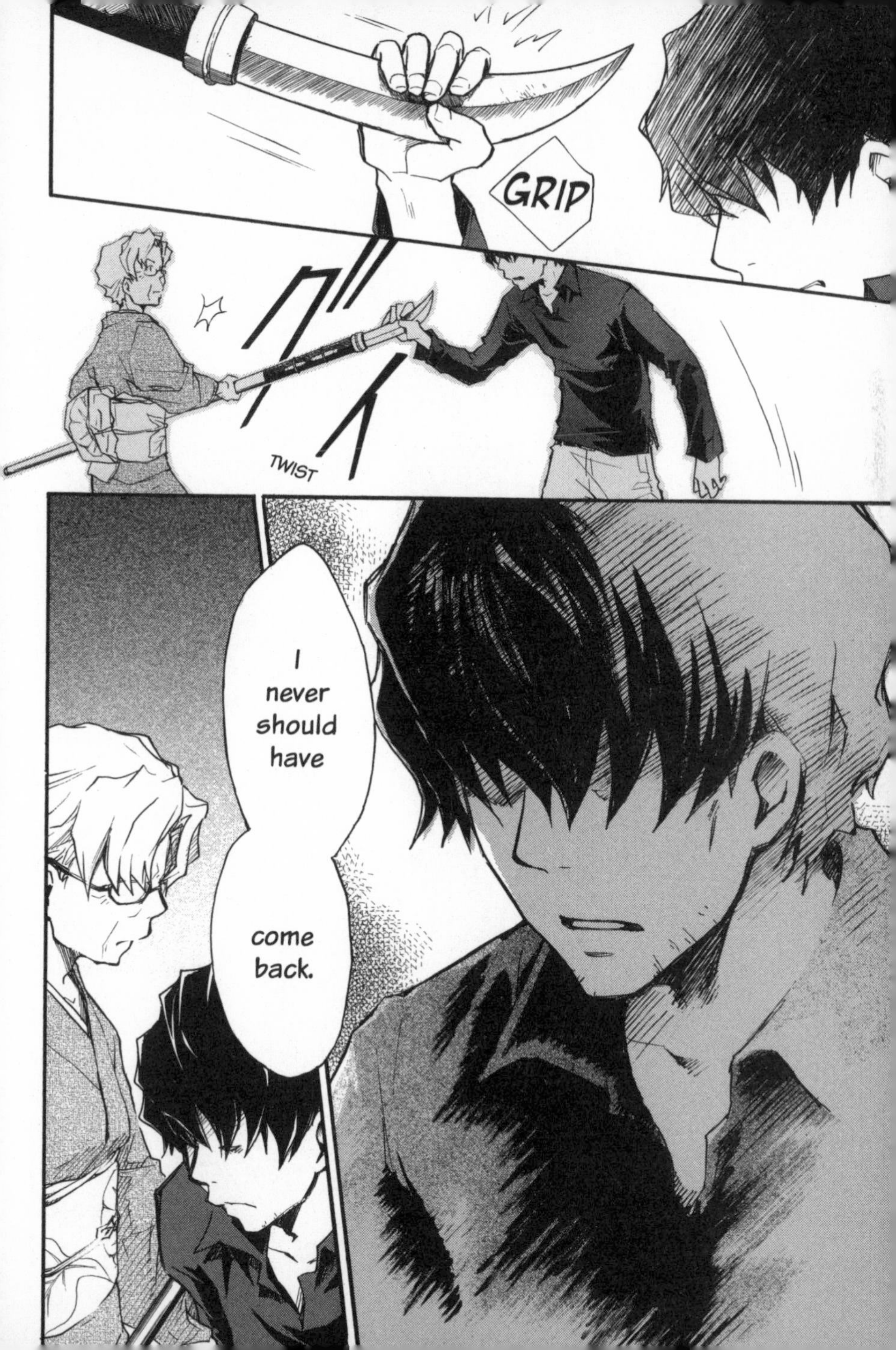
GRIP
TWIST
I never should have
come back.

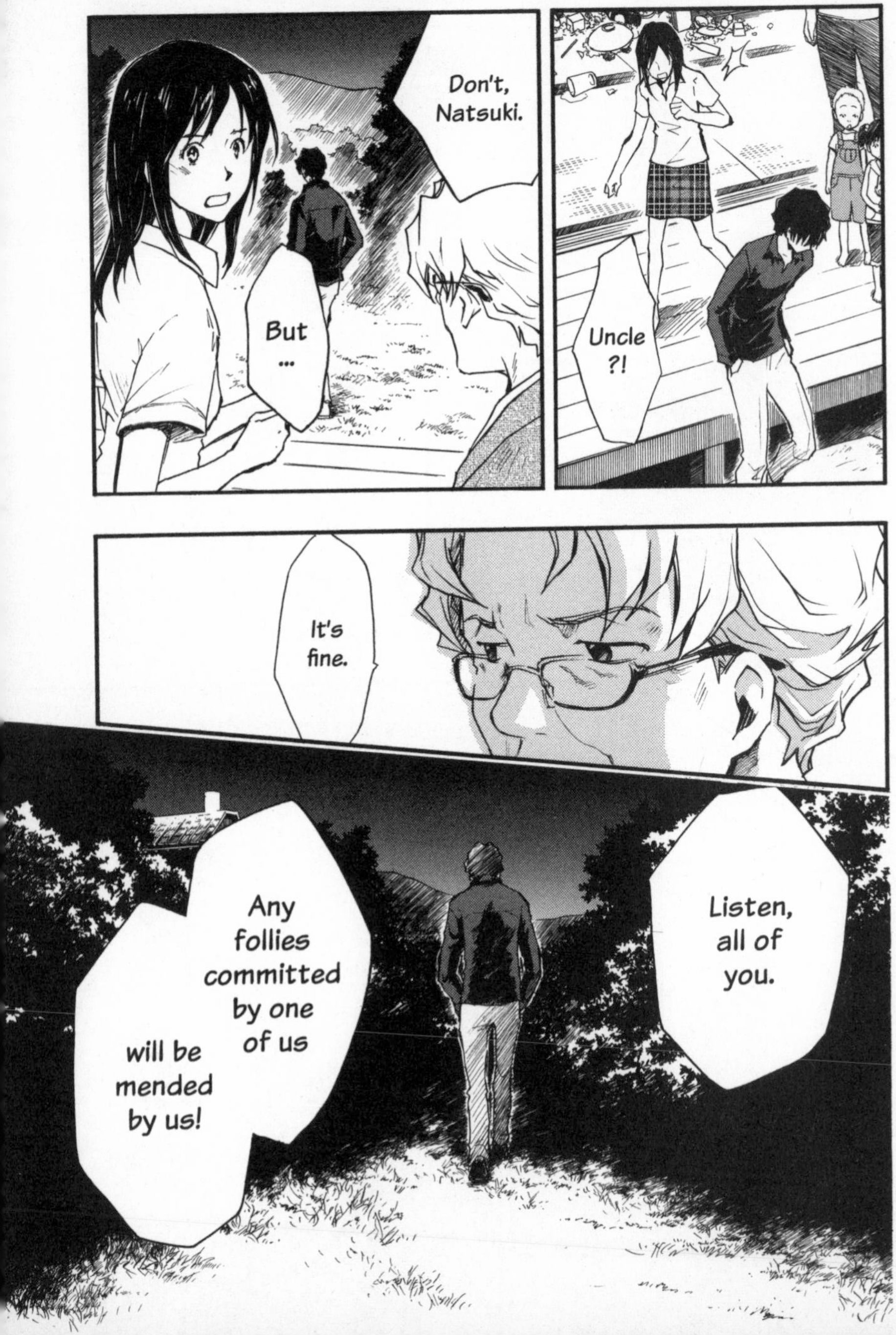
Uncle ?!
Don't, Natsuki.
But ...
It's fine.
Listen, all of you.
Any follies committed by one of us
will be mended by us!

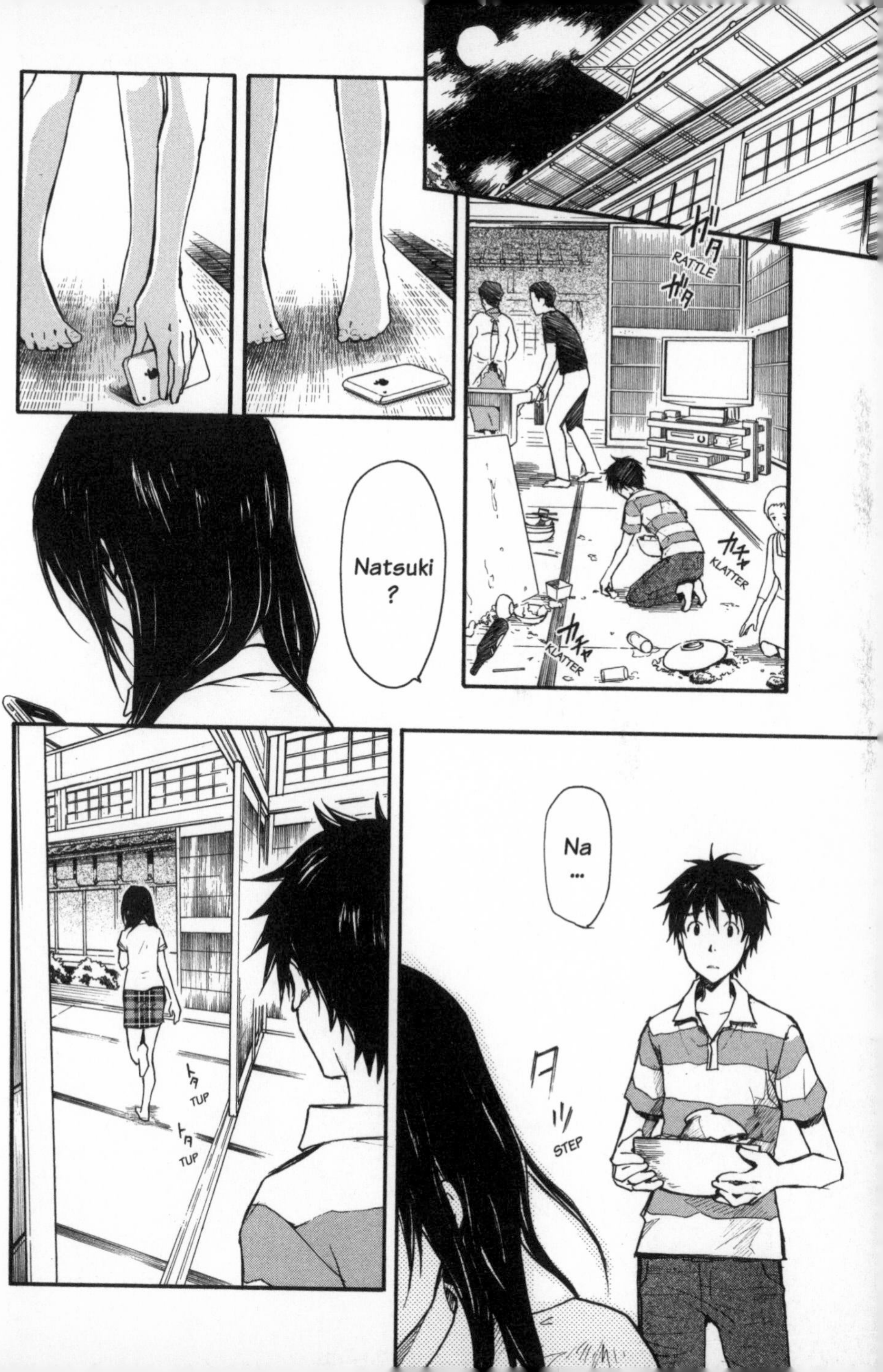

ガタ
RATTLE
ガタ
カチャ
KLATTER
カチャ
KLATTER
Natsuki ?
Na ...
タッ
STEP
トタ
TUP
トタ
TUP

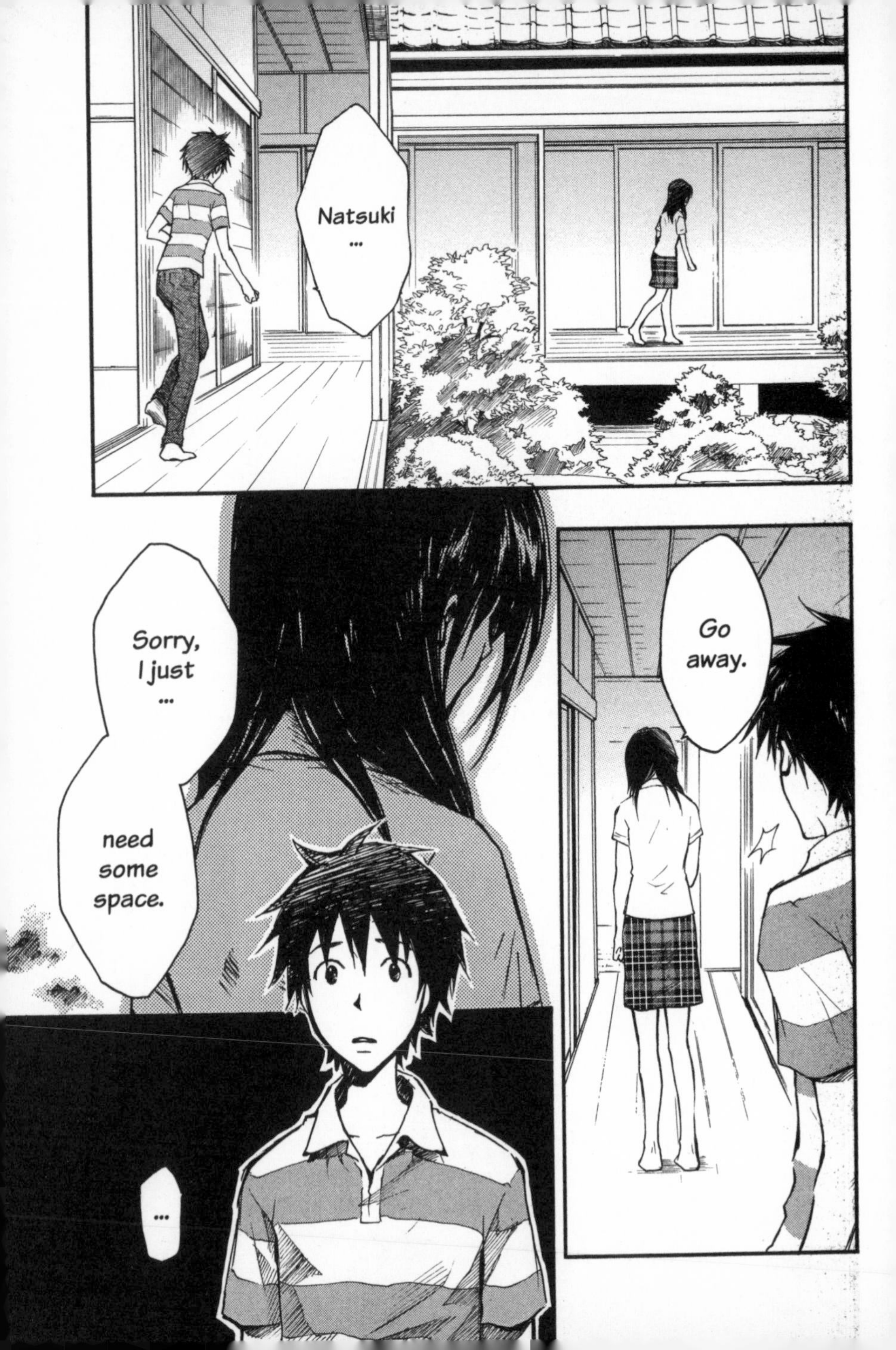
Natsuki ...
Go away.
Sorry, I just ...
need some space.
...

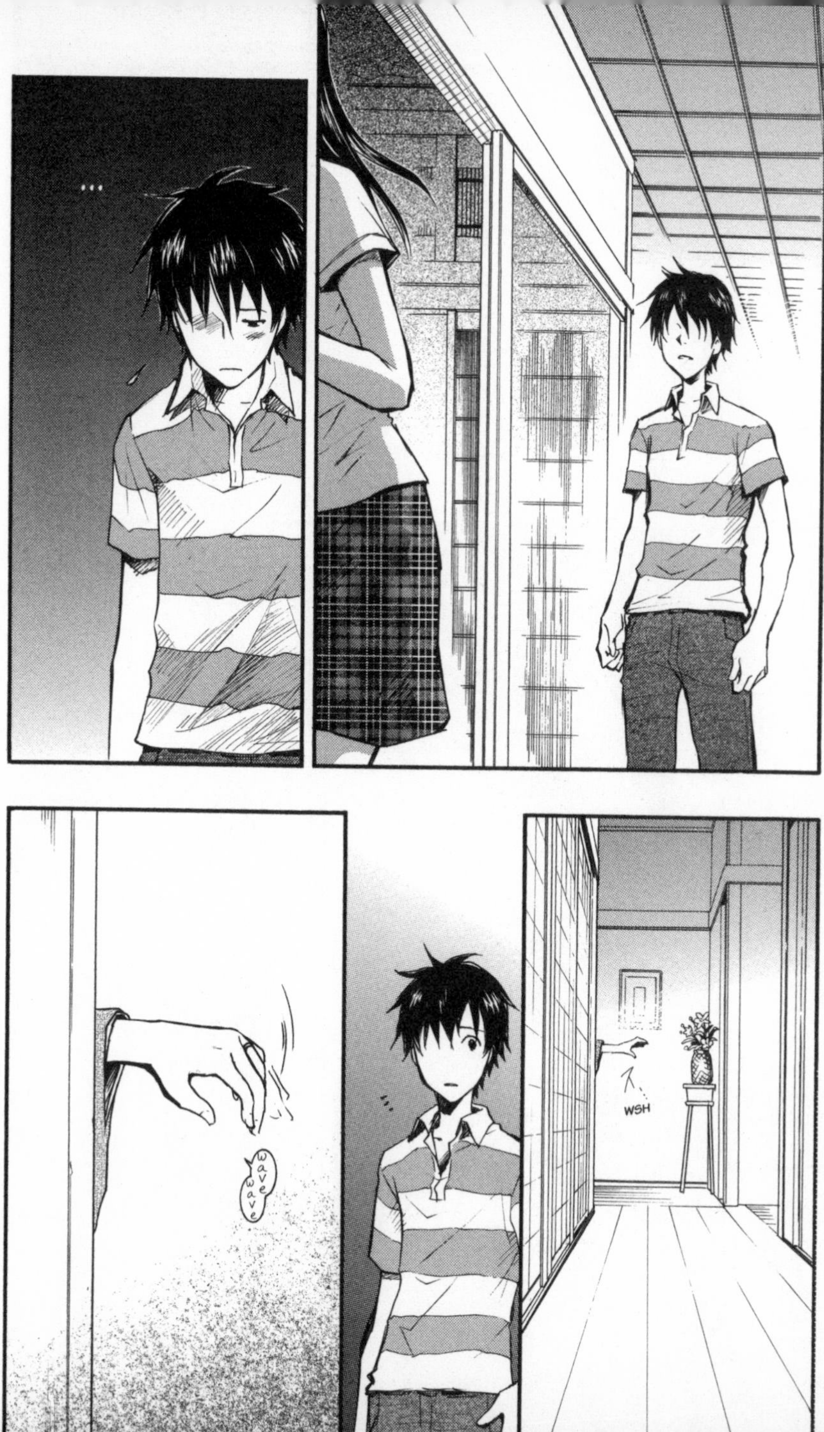
...
ス…
WSH
wave wave

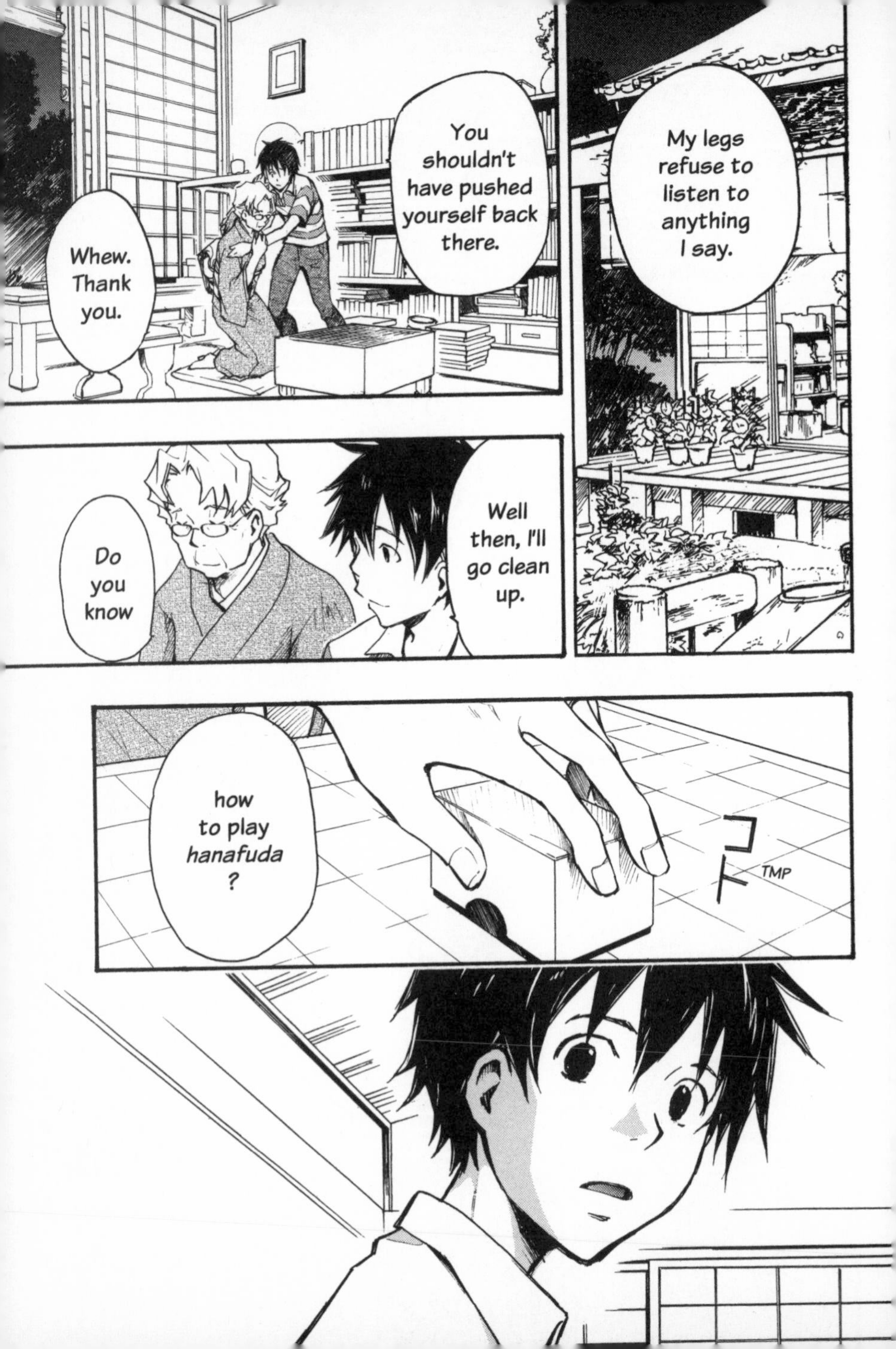
My legs refuse to listen to anything I say.
You shouldn't have pushed yourself back there.
Whew. Thank you.
Well then, I'll go clean up.
Do you know
how to play hanafuda ?
コト
TMP

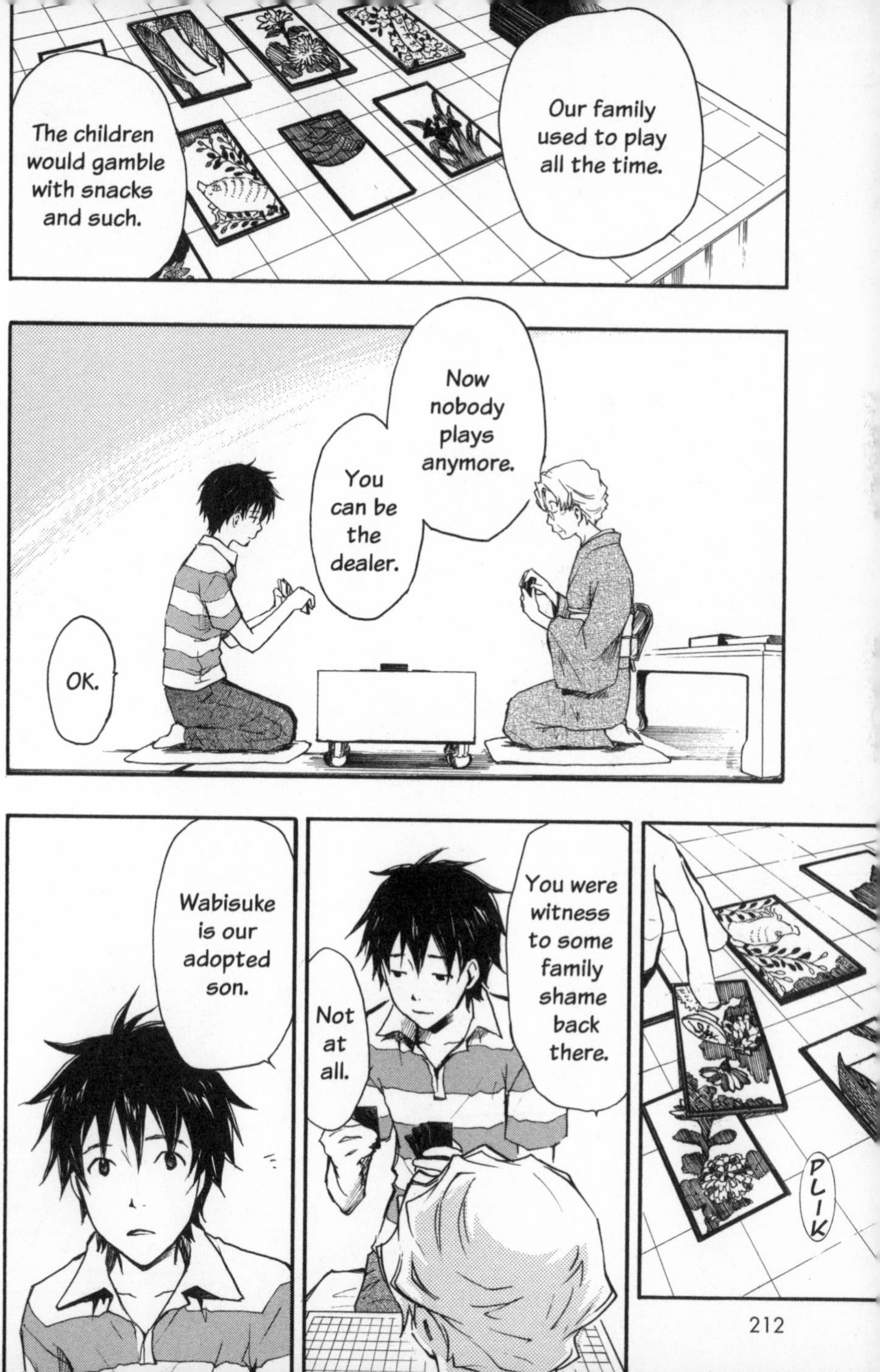
Our family used to play all the time.
The children would gamble with snacks and such.
Now nobody plays anymore.
You can be the dealer.
OK.
PLIK
You were witness to some family shame back there.
Not at all.
Wabisuke is our adopted son.

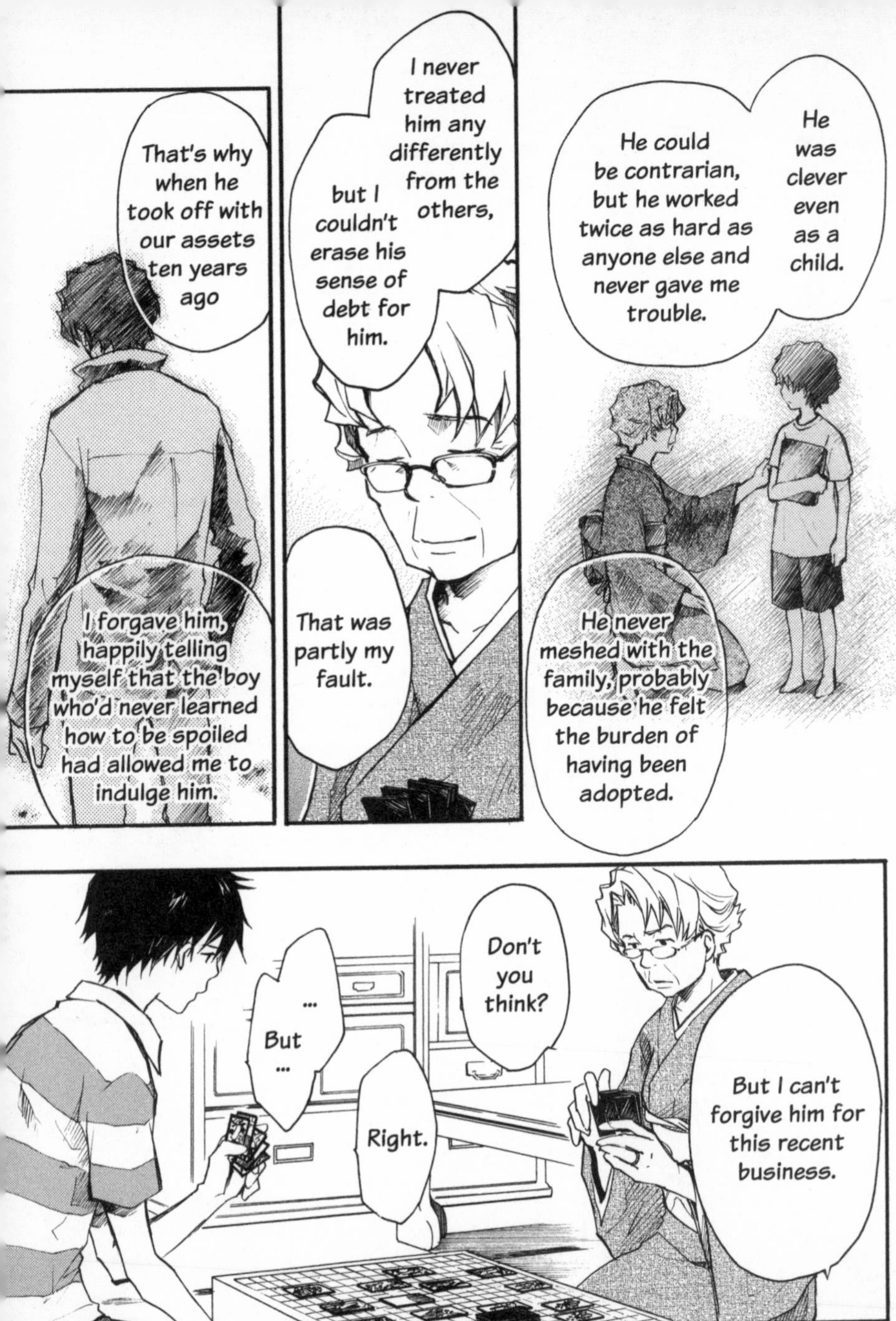
He was clever even as a child.
He could be contrarian, but he worked twice as hard as anyone else and never gave me trouble.
He never meshed with the family, probably because he felt the burden of having been adopted.
I never treated him any differently from the others,
but I couldn't erase his sense of debt for him.
That was partly my fault.
That's why when he took off with our assets ten years ago
I forgave him, happily telling myself that the boy who'd never learned how to be spoiled had allowed me to indulge him.
But I can't forgive him for this recent business.
Don't you think?
Right.
... But ...

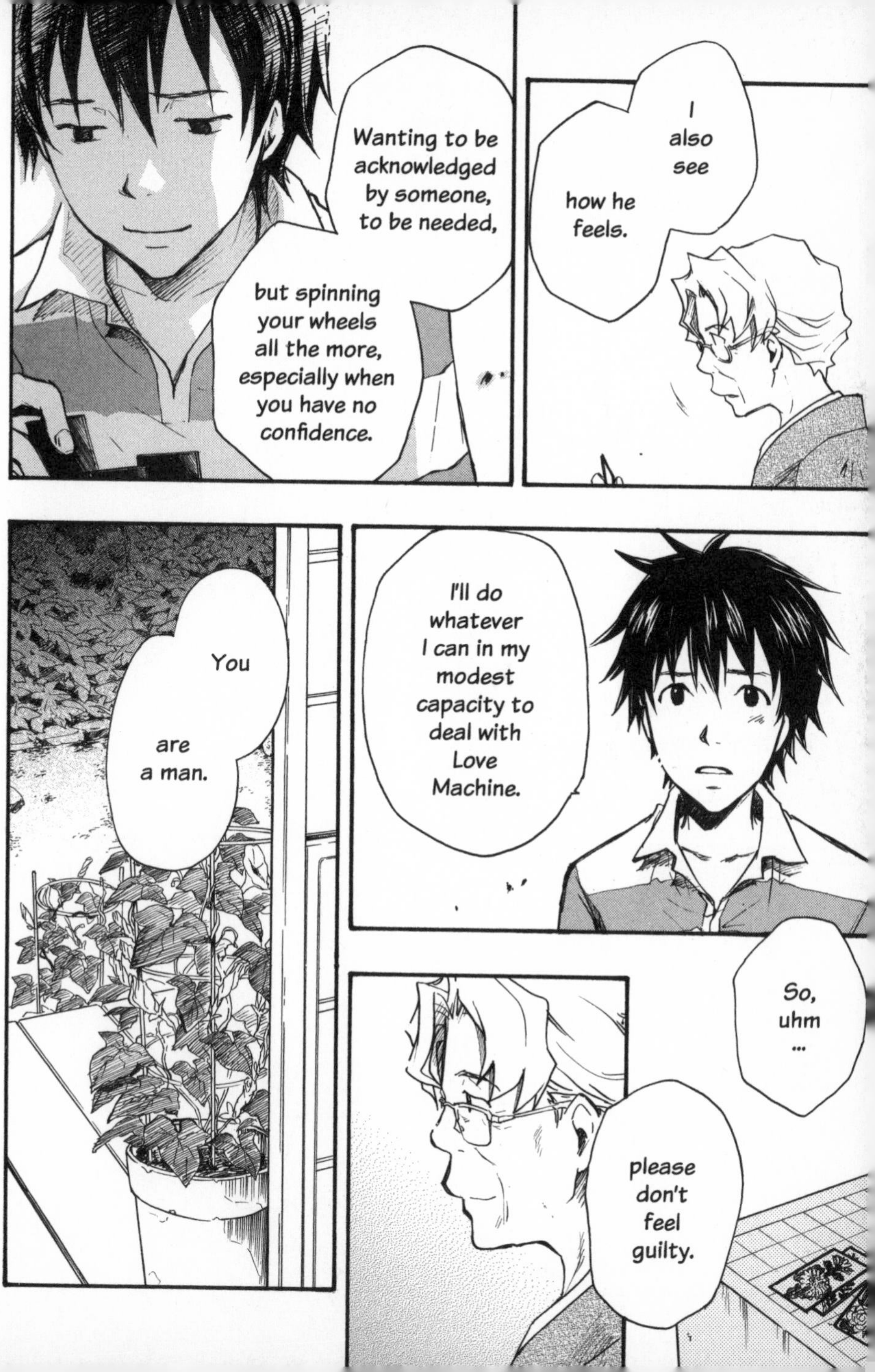
I also see how he feels.
Wanting to be acknowledged by someone, to be needed,
but spinning your wheels all the more, especially when you have no confidence.
I'll do whatever I can in my modest capacity to deal with Love Machine.
So, uhm ...
please don't feel guilty.
You are a man.

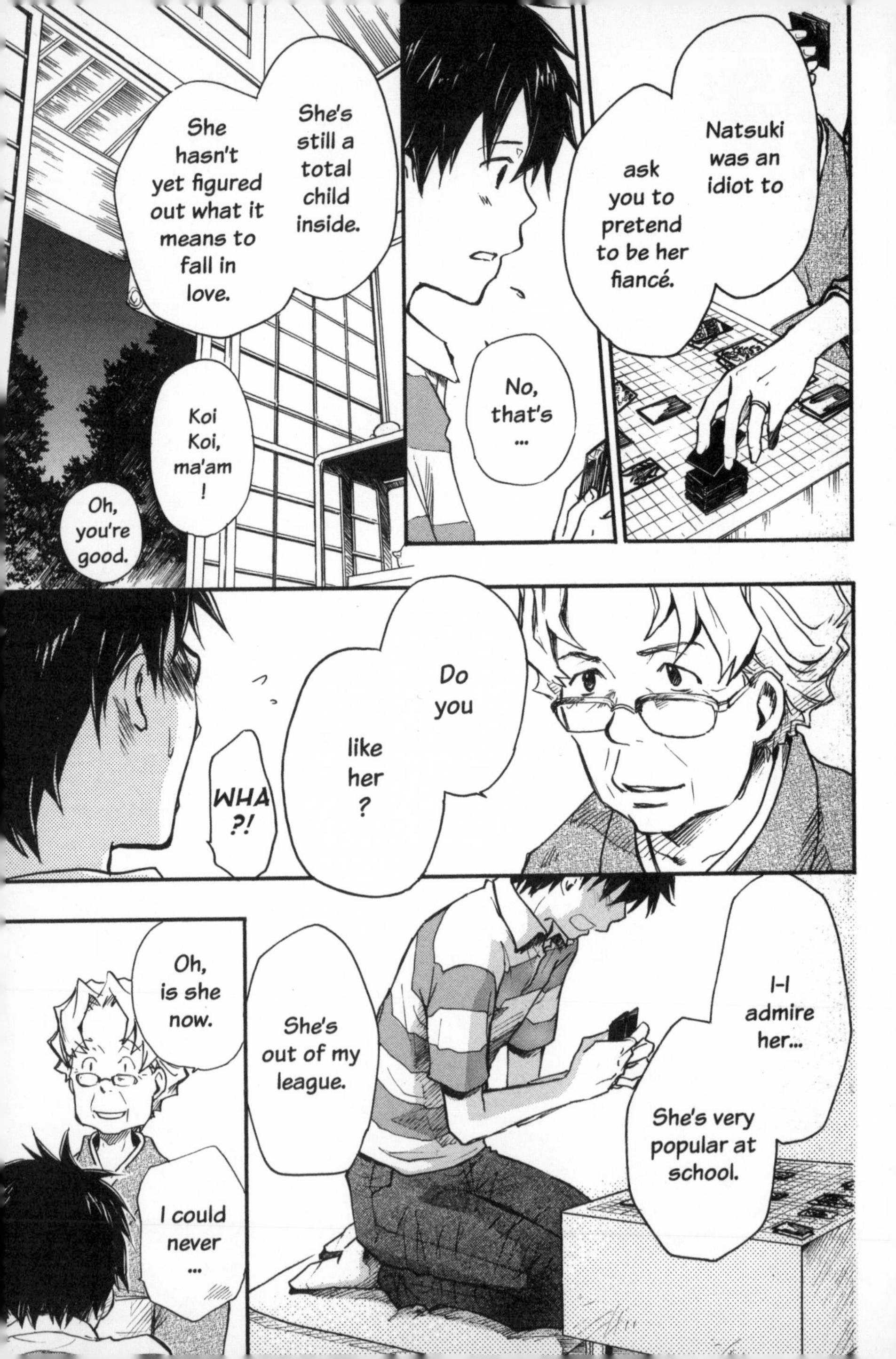
Natsuki was an idiot to ask you to pretend to be her fiancé.
No, that's ...
She's still a total child inside.
She hasn't yet figured out what it means to fall in love.
Koi Koi, ma'am!
Oh, you're good.
Do you like her?
WHA ?!
I-I admire her...
She's very popular at school.
She's out of my league.
Oh, is she now.
I could never ...

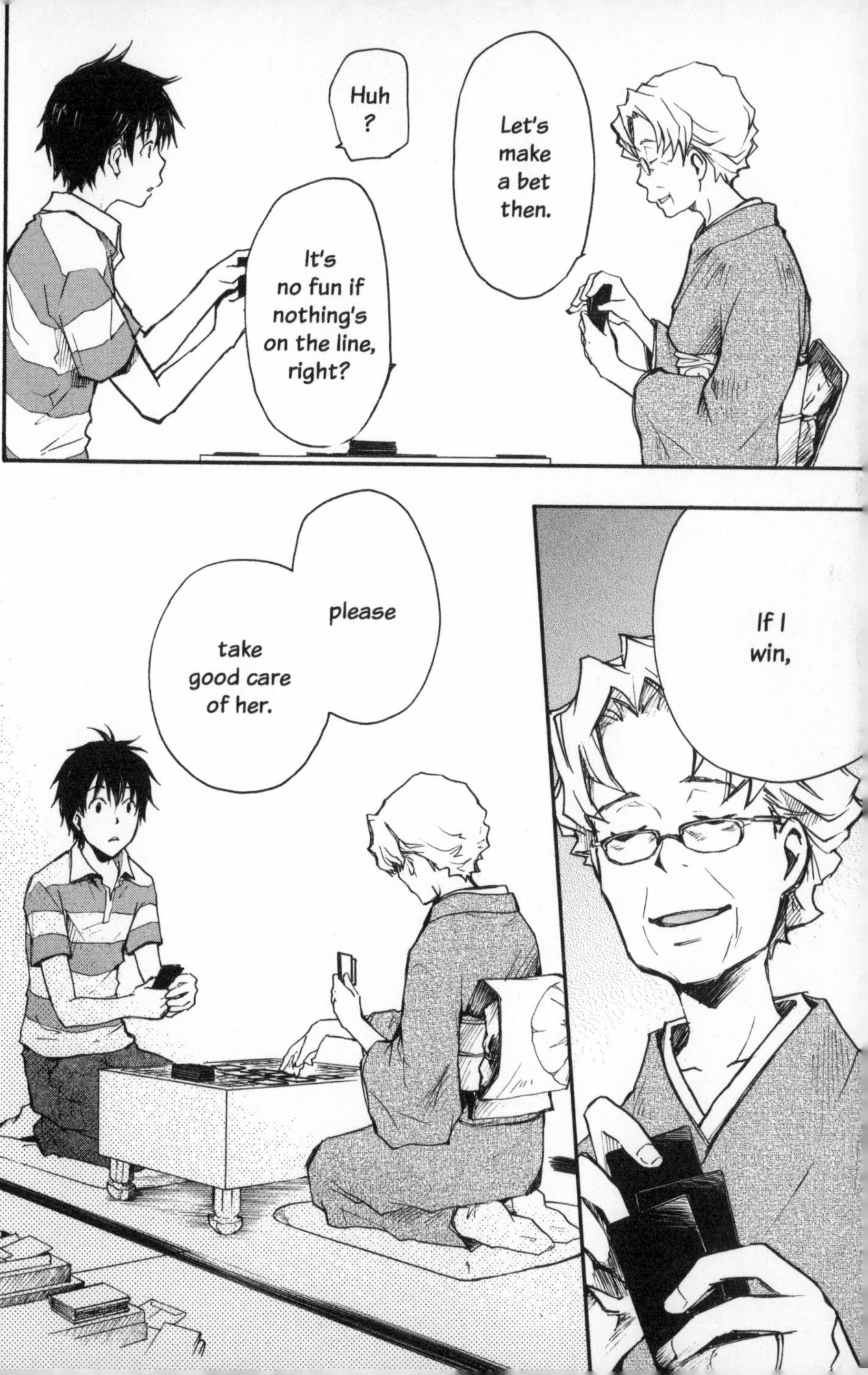
Let's make a bet then.
Huh?
It's no fun if nothing's on the line, right?
If I win,
please take good care of her.

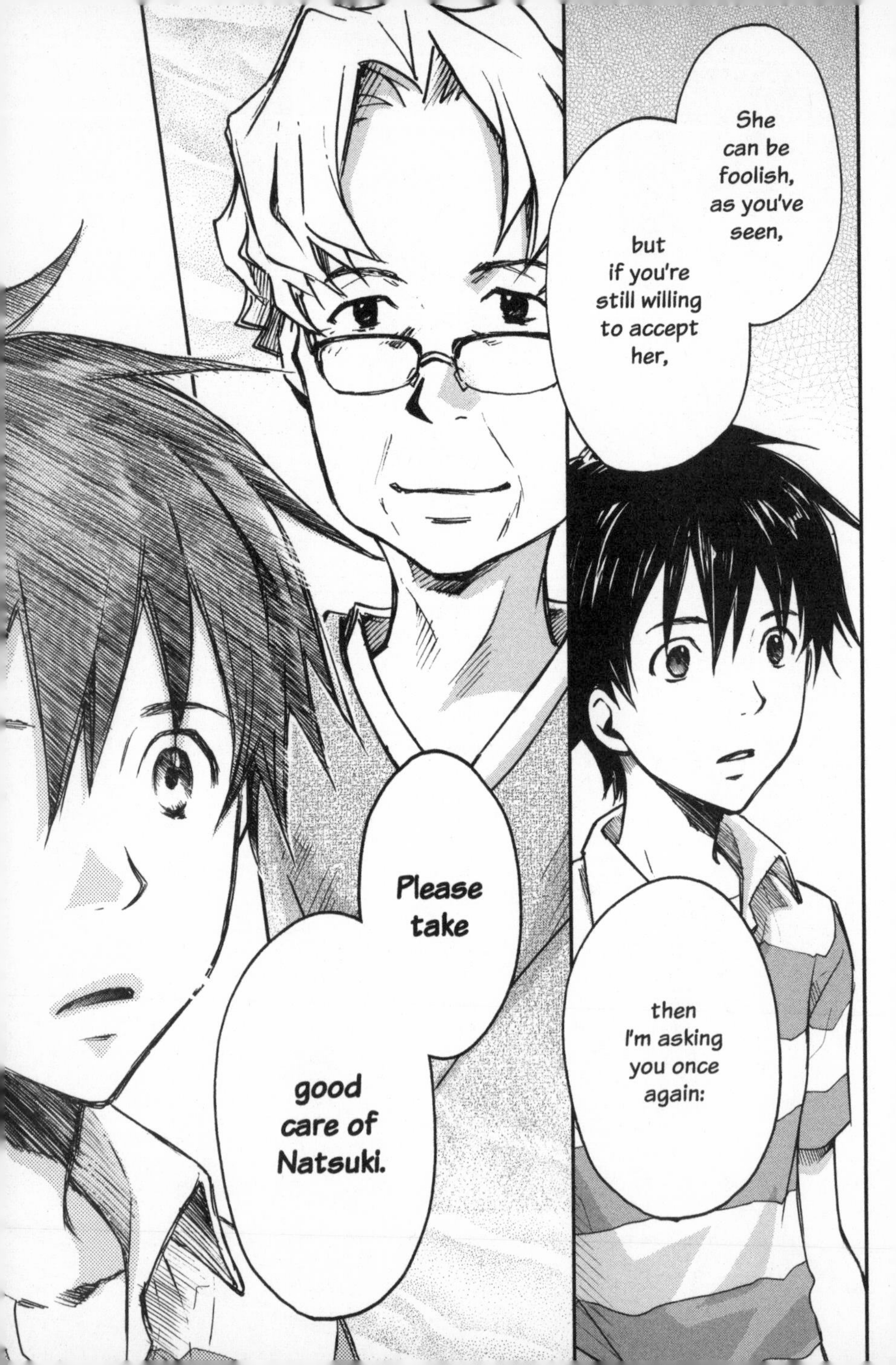
She can be foolish, as you've seen,
but if you're still willing to accept her,
then I'm asking you once again:
Please take
good care of Natsuki.

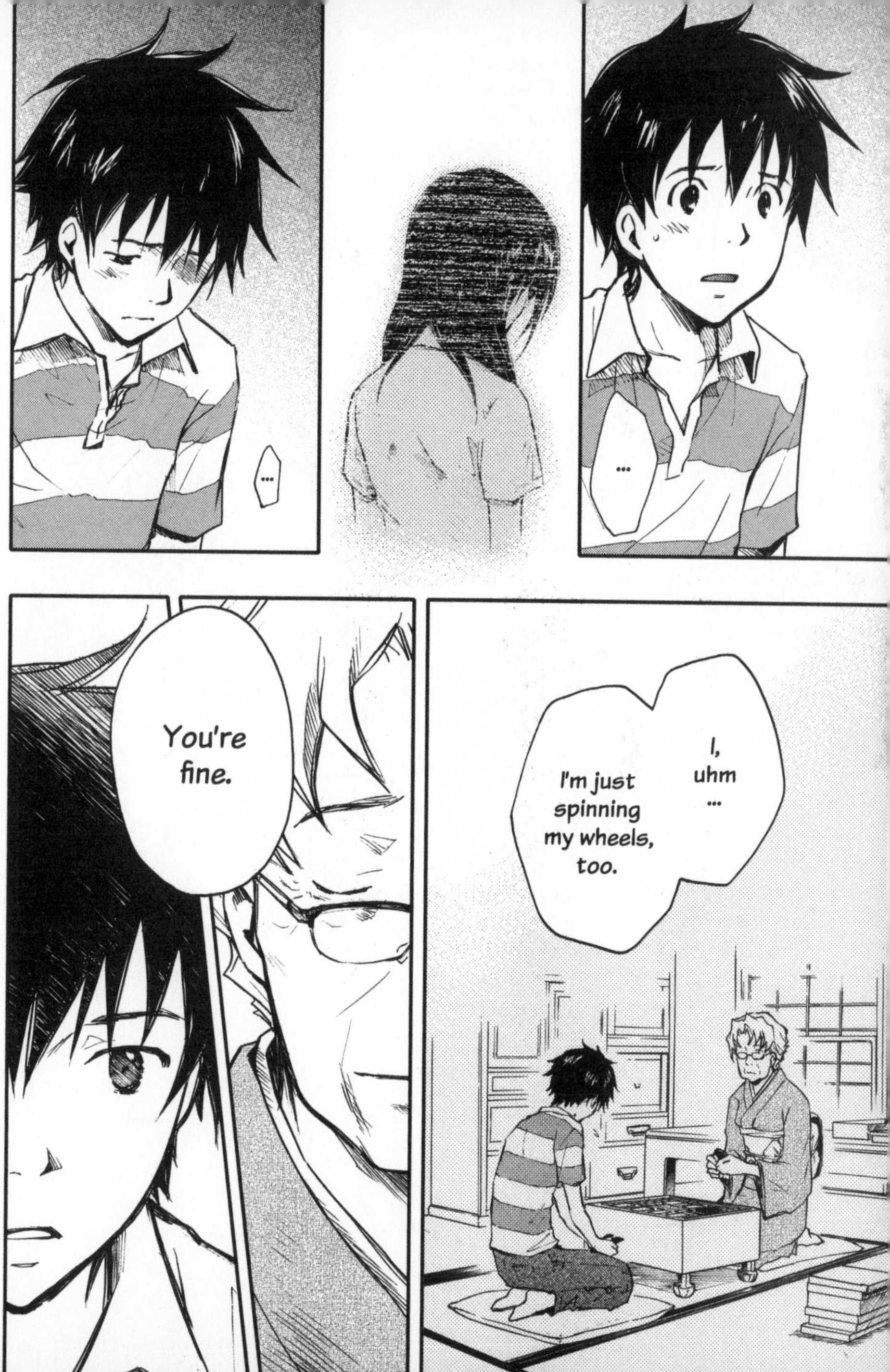
...
...
I, uhm ... I'm just spinning my wheels, too.
You're fine.

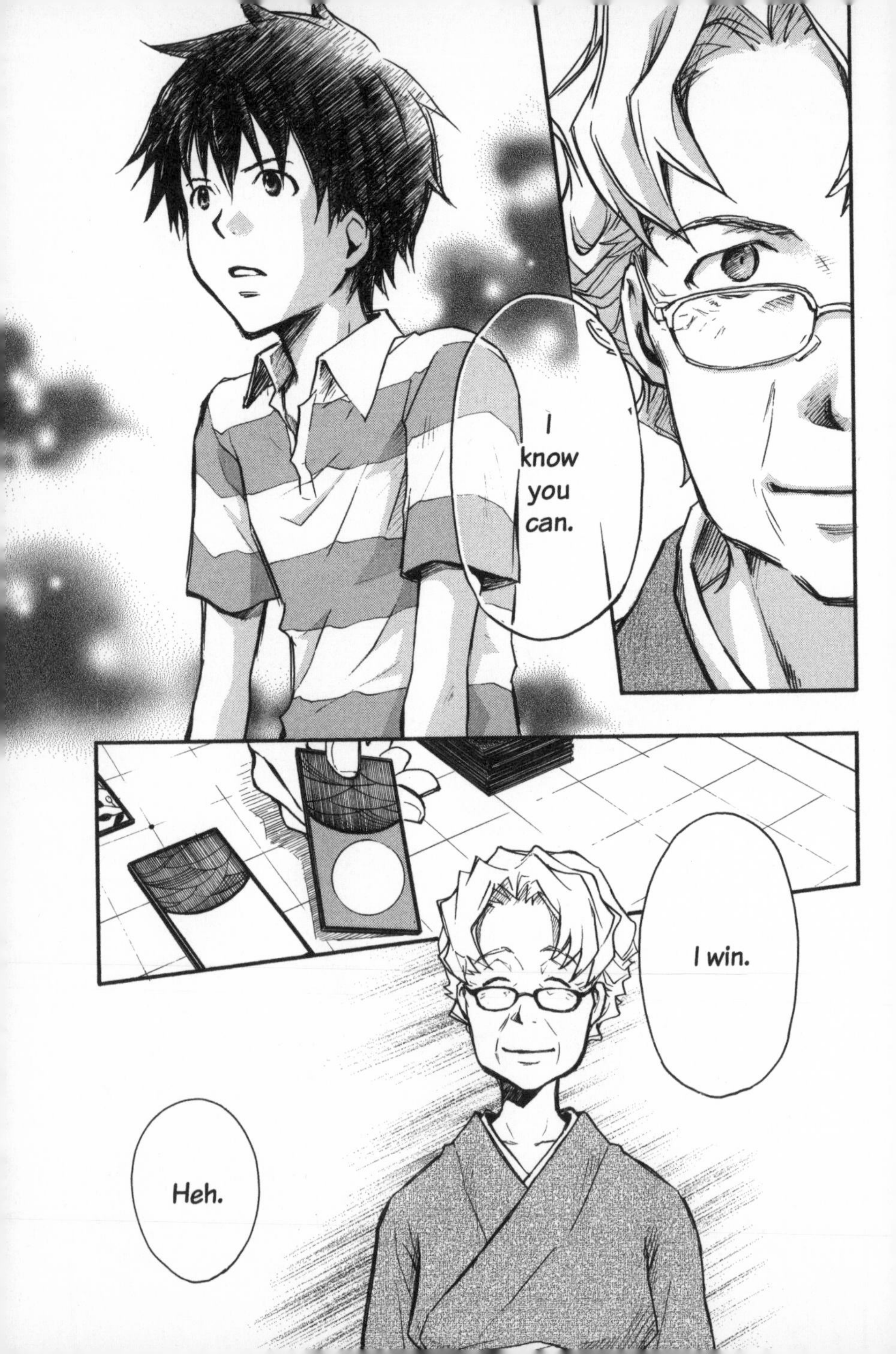
I know you can.
I win.
Heh.

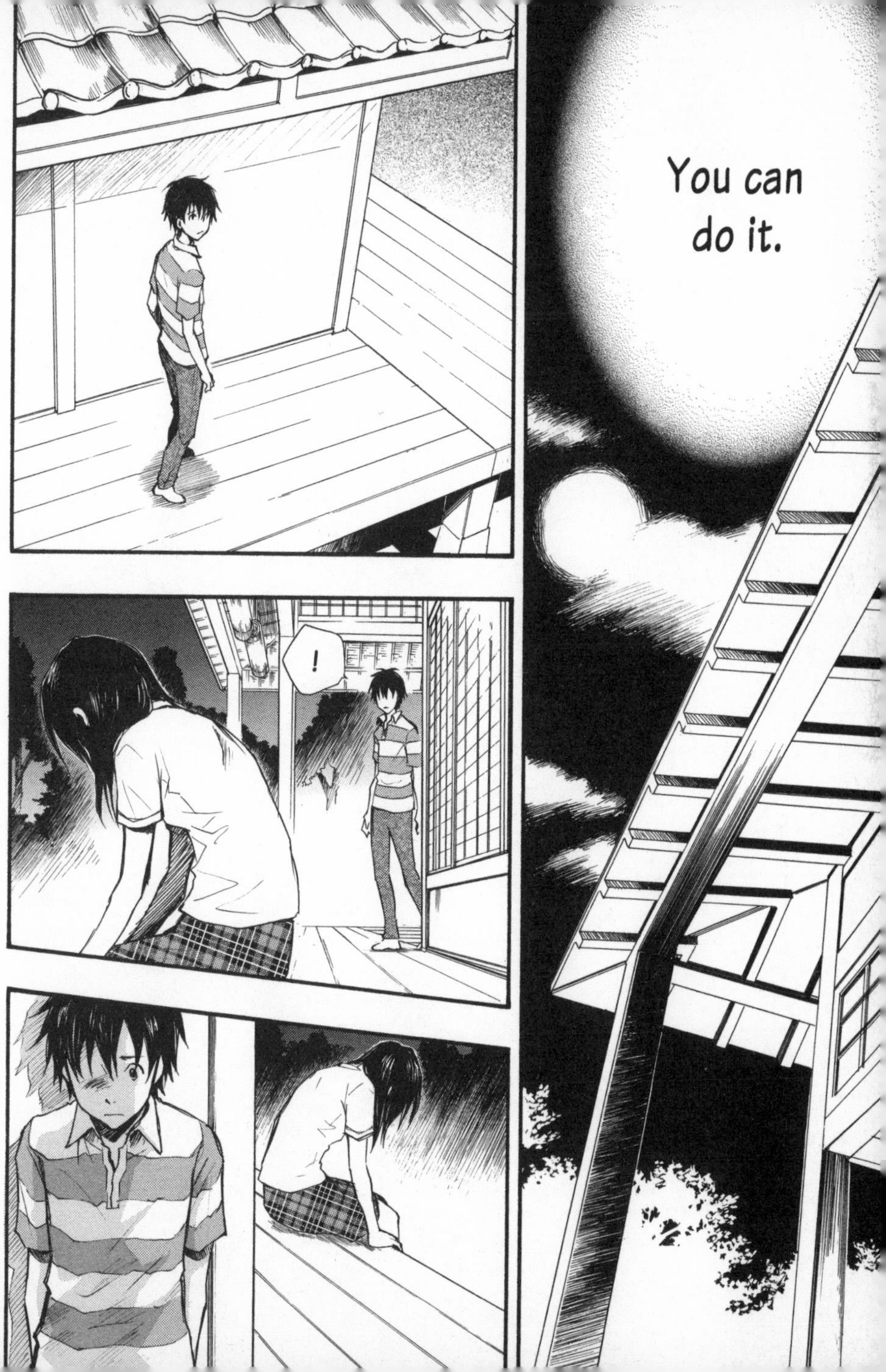
You can do it.
!

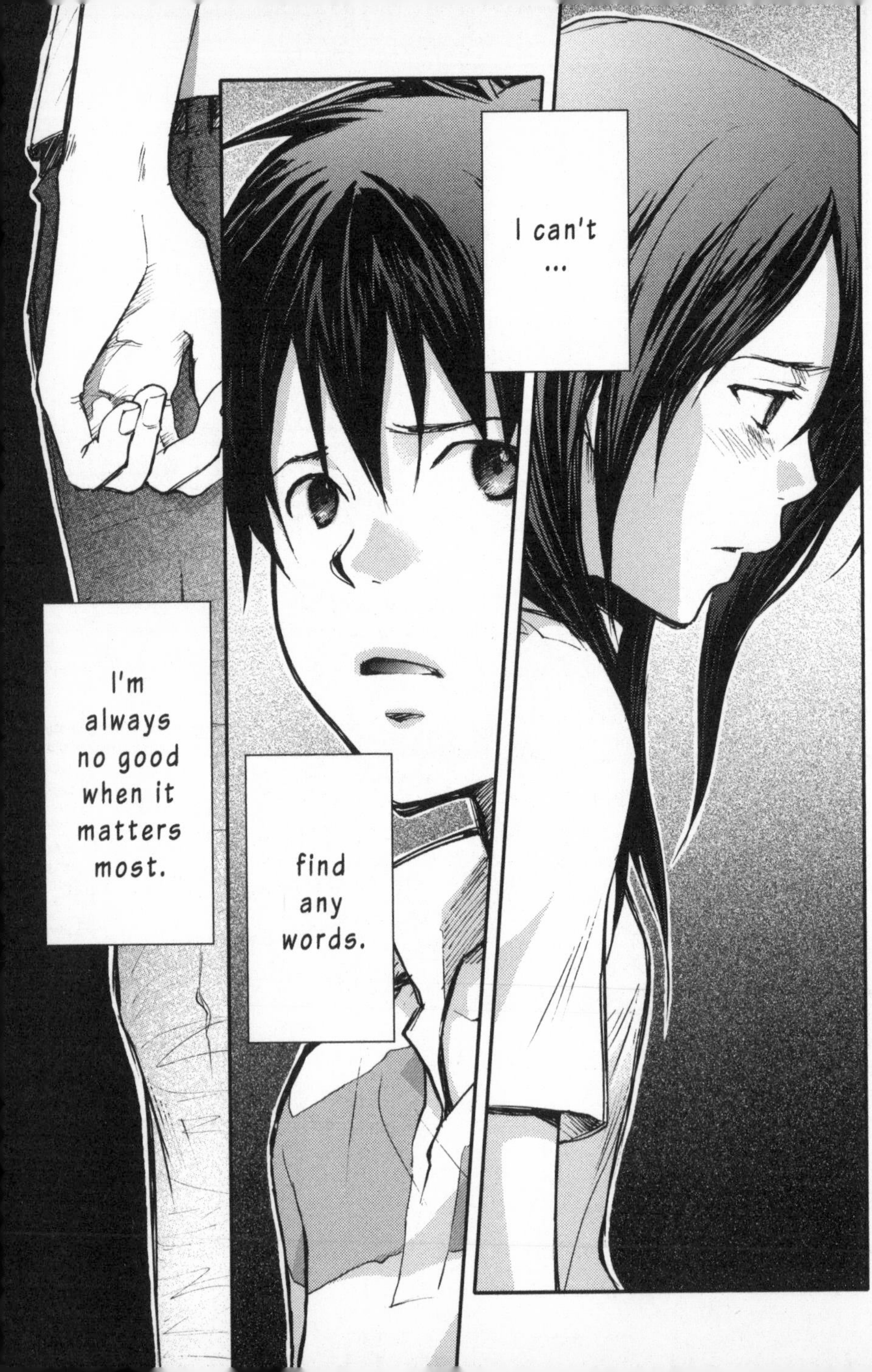
I can't ...
find any words.
I'm always no good when it matters most.

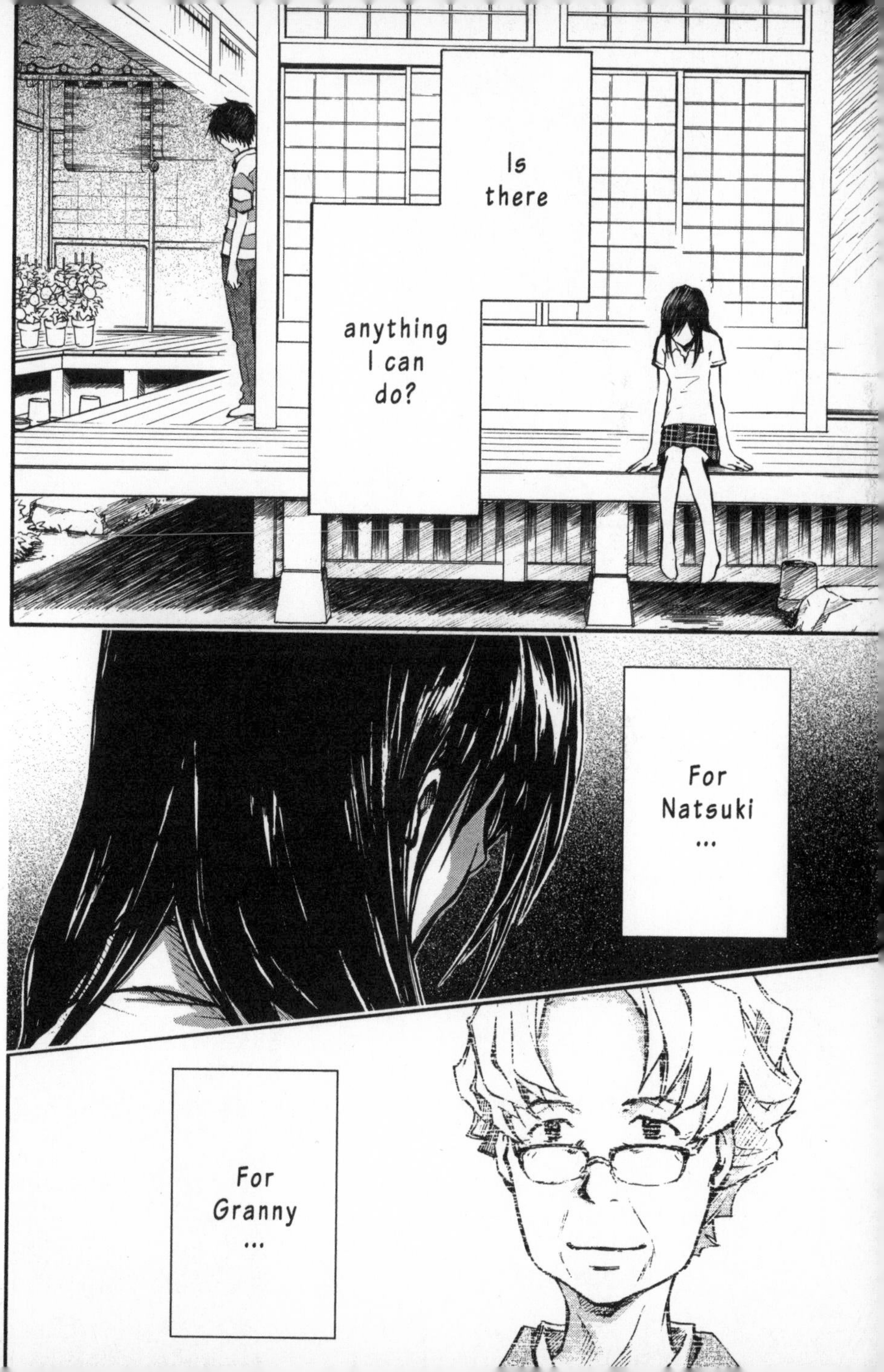
Is there
anything I can do?
For Natsuki ...
For Granny ...

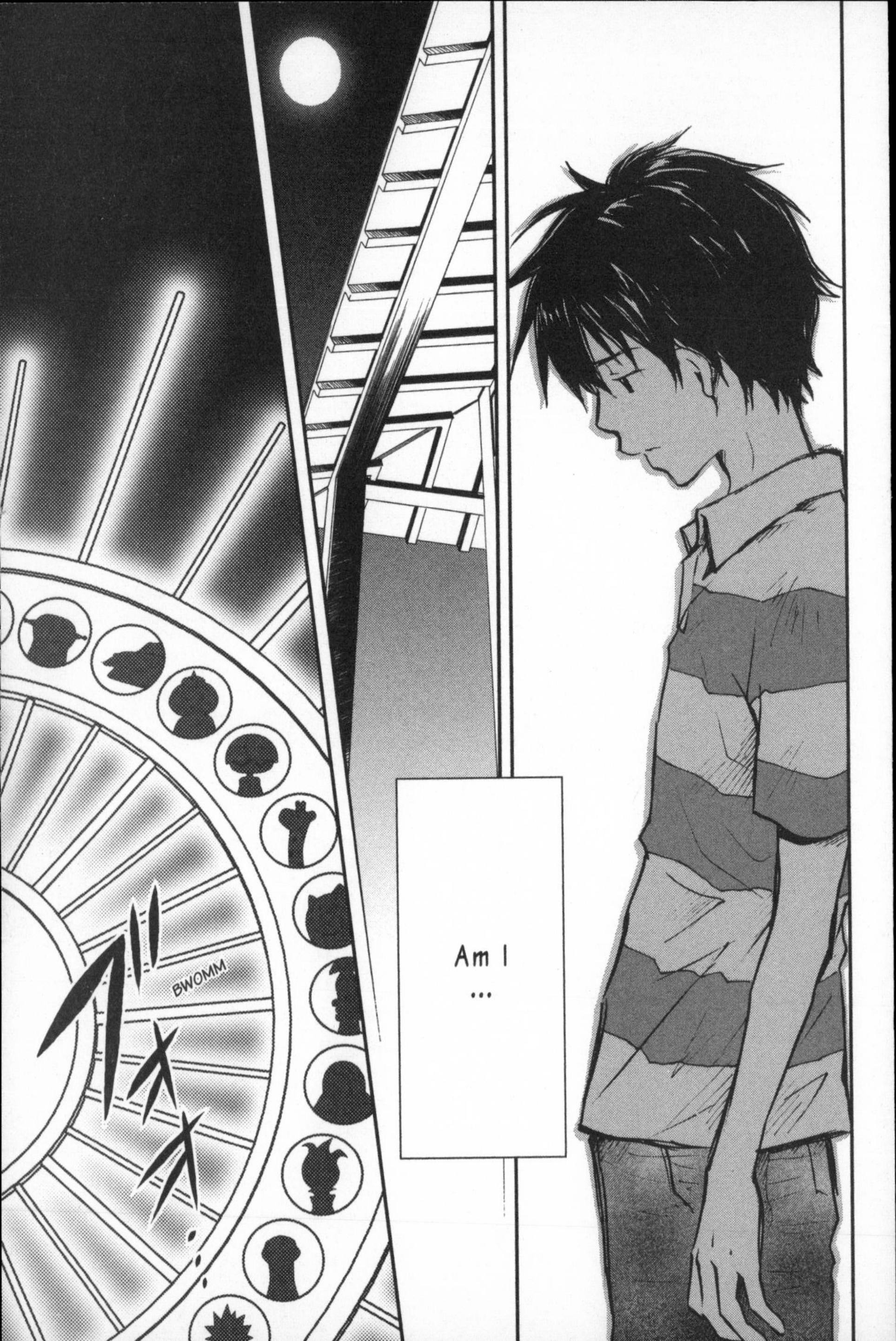
Am I
...
BWOMM

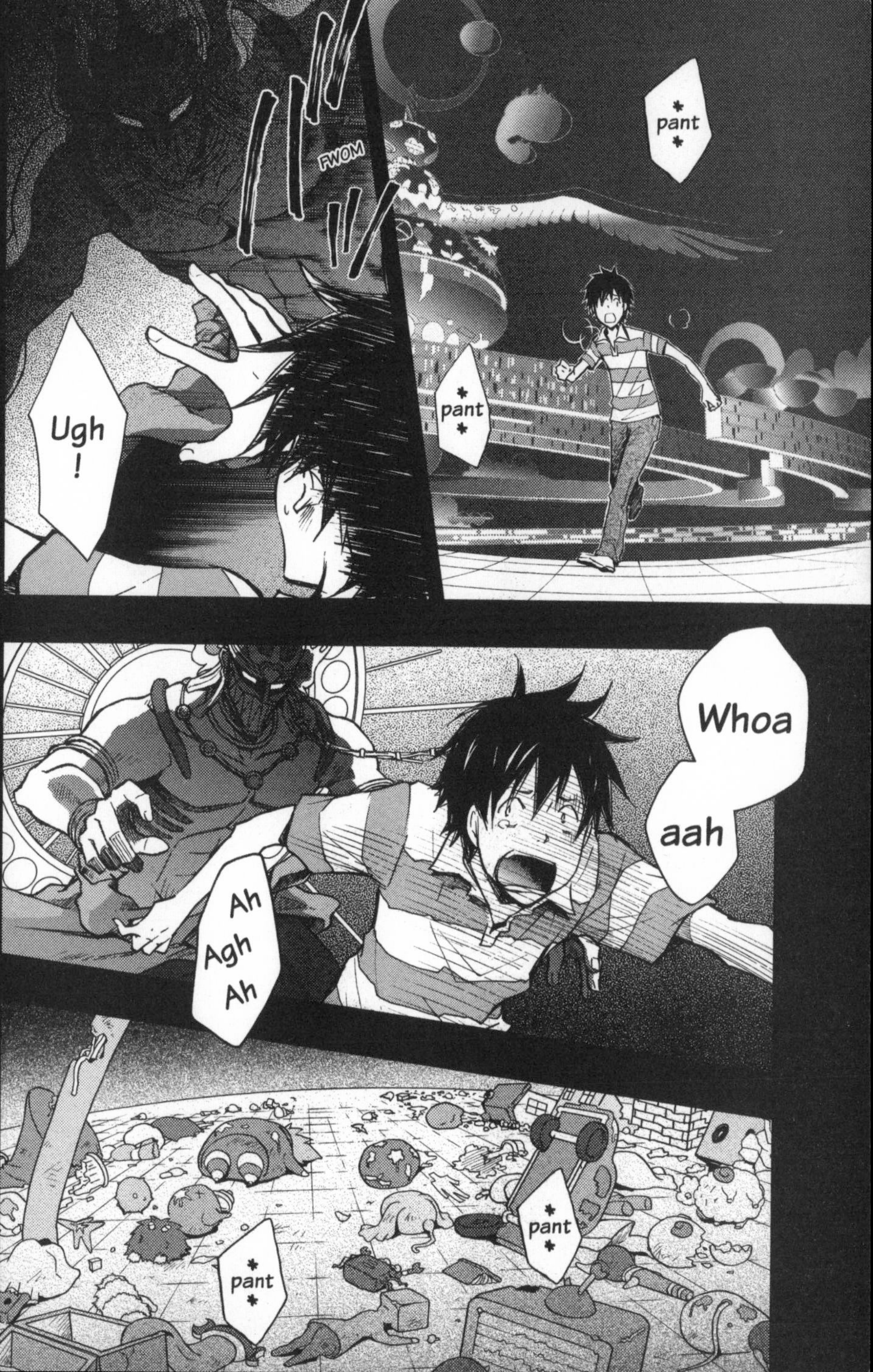

pant
pant
FWOM
Ugh!
Whoa aah
Ah Agh Ah
pant
pant

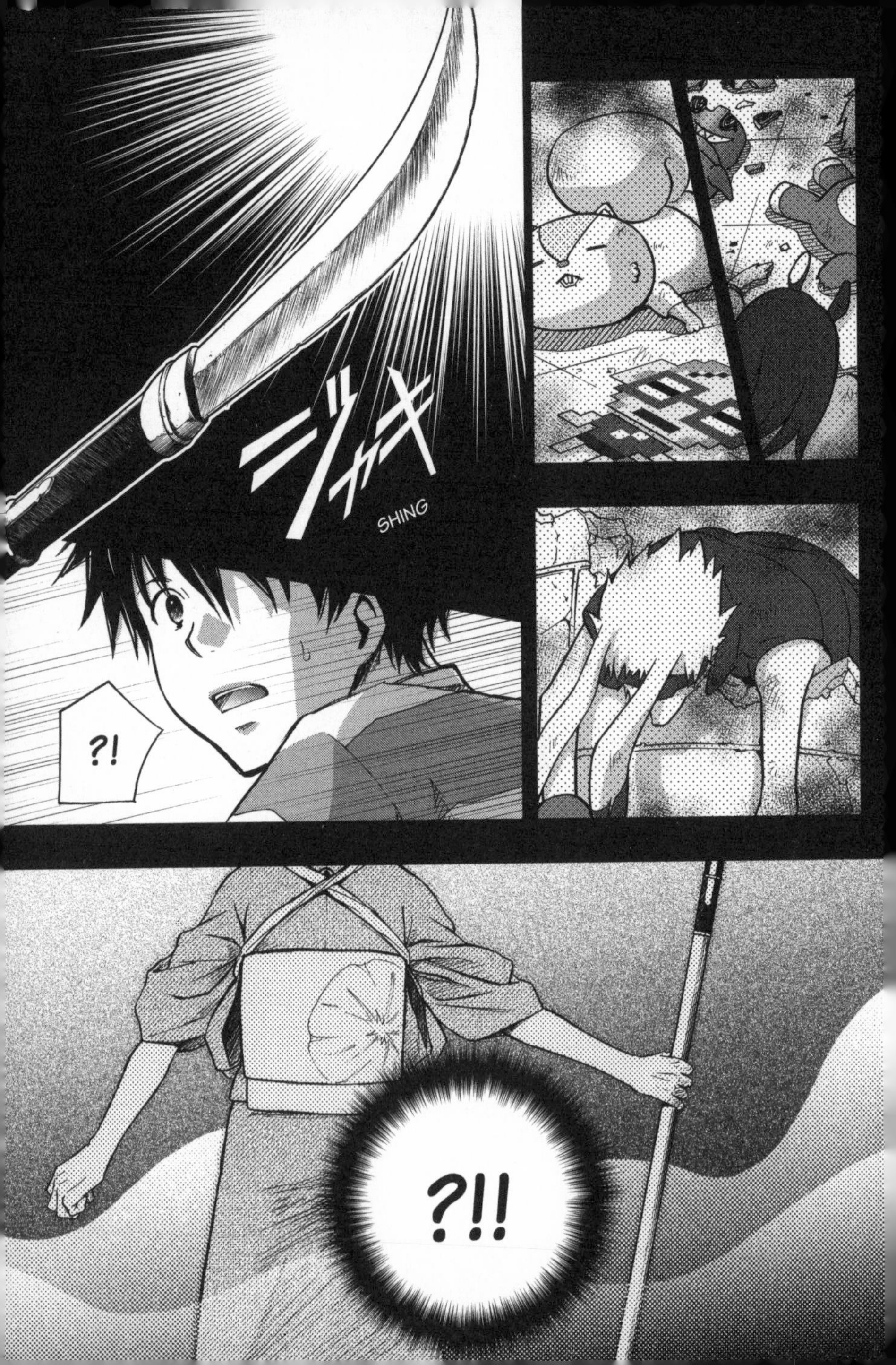
ジャキ
SHING
?!
?!!

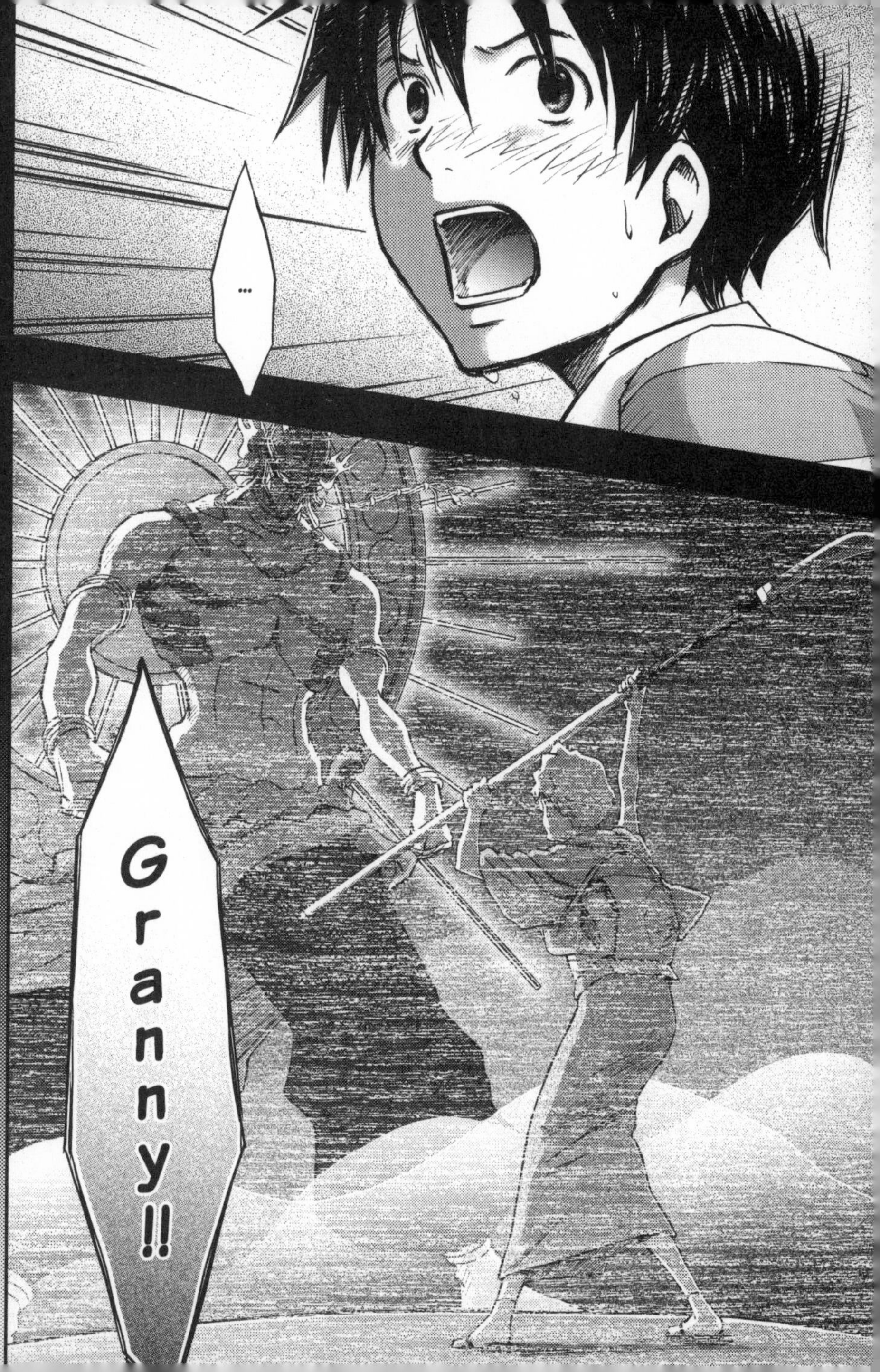
…
Granny!!

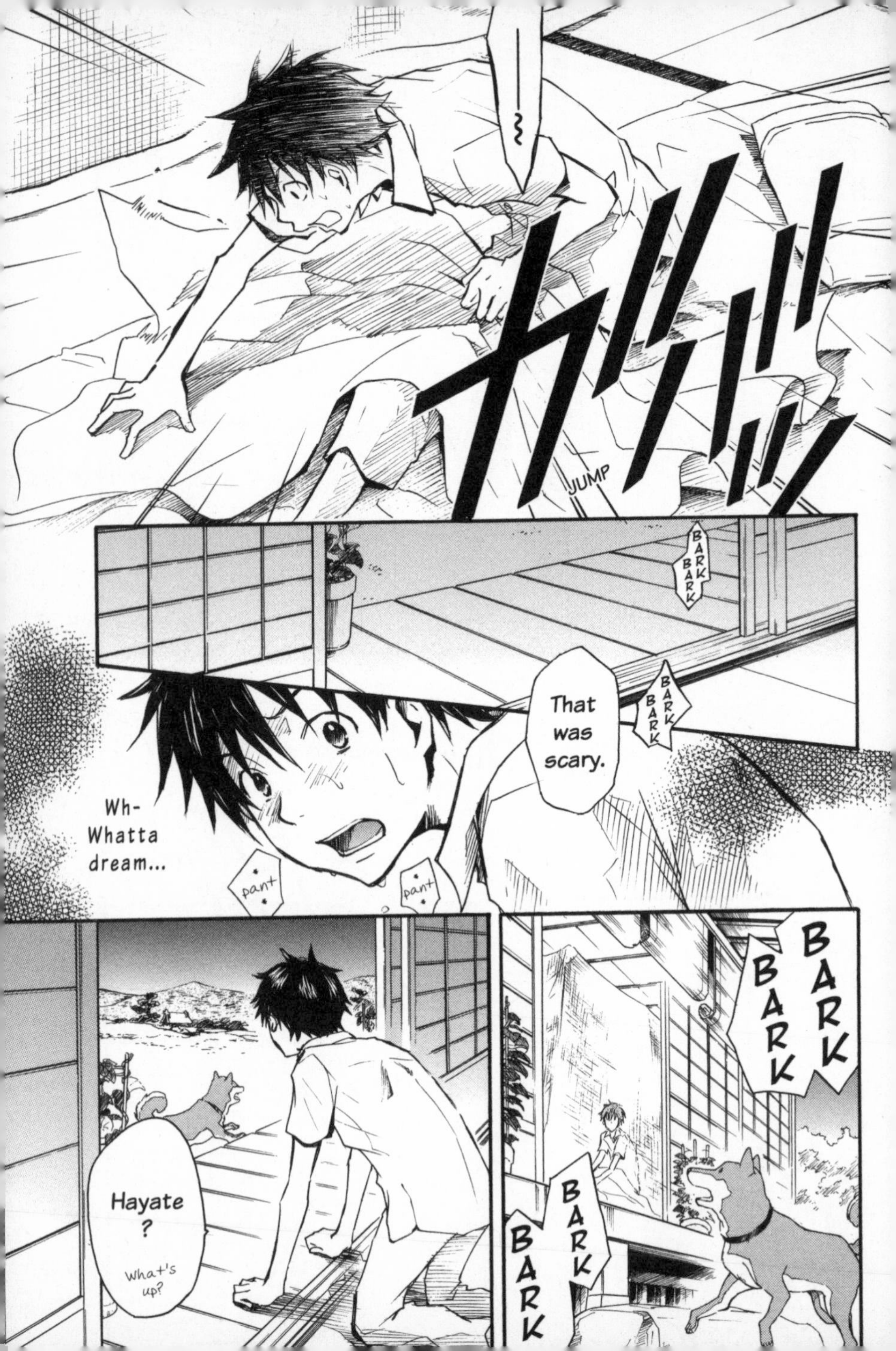

JUMP
BARK BARK
BARK BARK
That was scary.
Wh- Whatta dream...
pant
pant
BARK BARK
BARK BARK
BARK BARK
Hayate?
What's up?

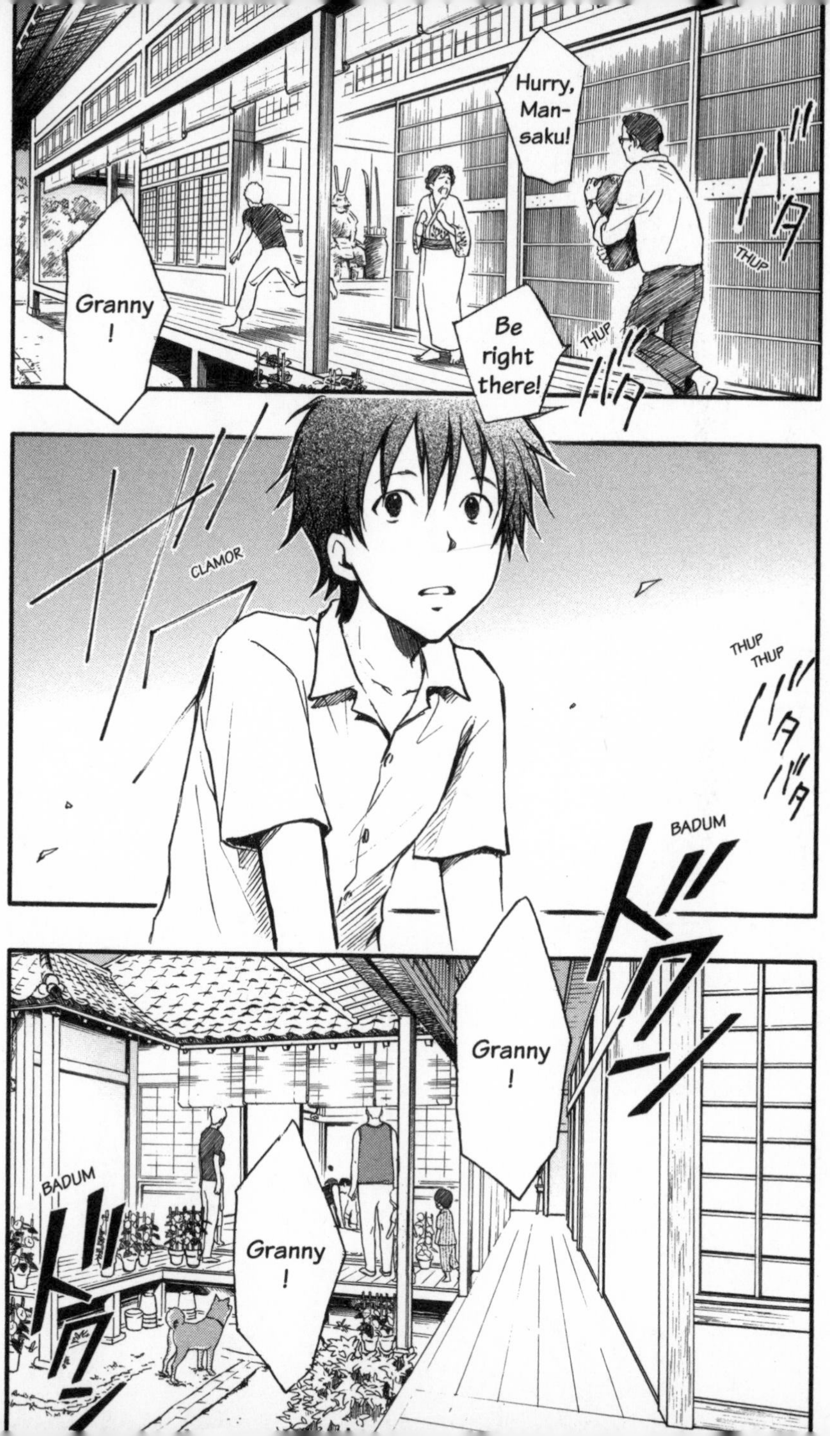
Hurry, Man-saku!
THUP
Be right there!
THUP
Granny!
THUP THUP
BADUM
CLAMOR
Granny!
Granny!
BADUM

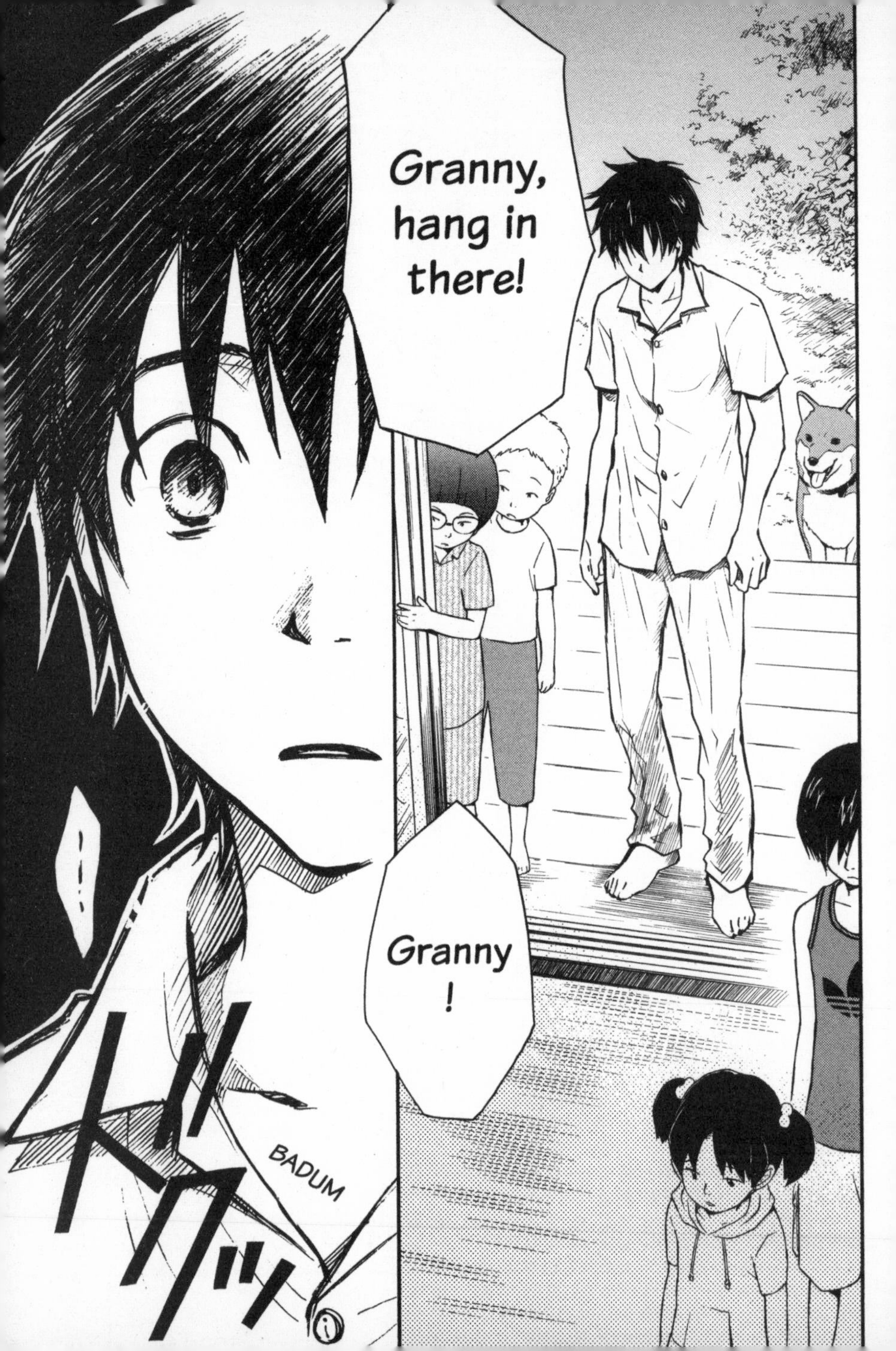
Granny, hang in there!
Granny!
BADUM

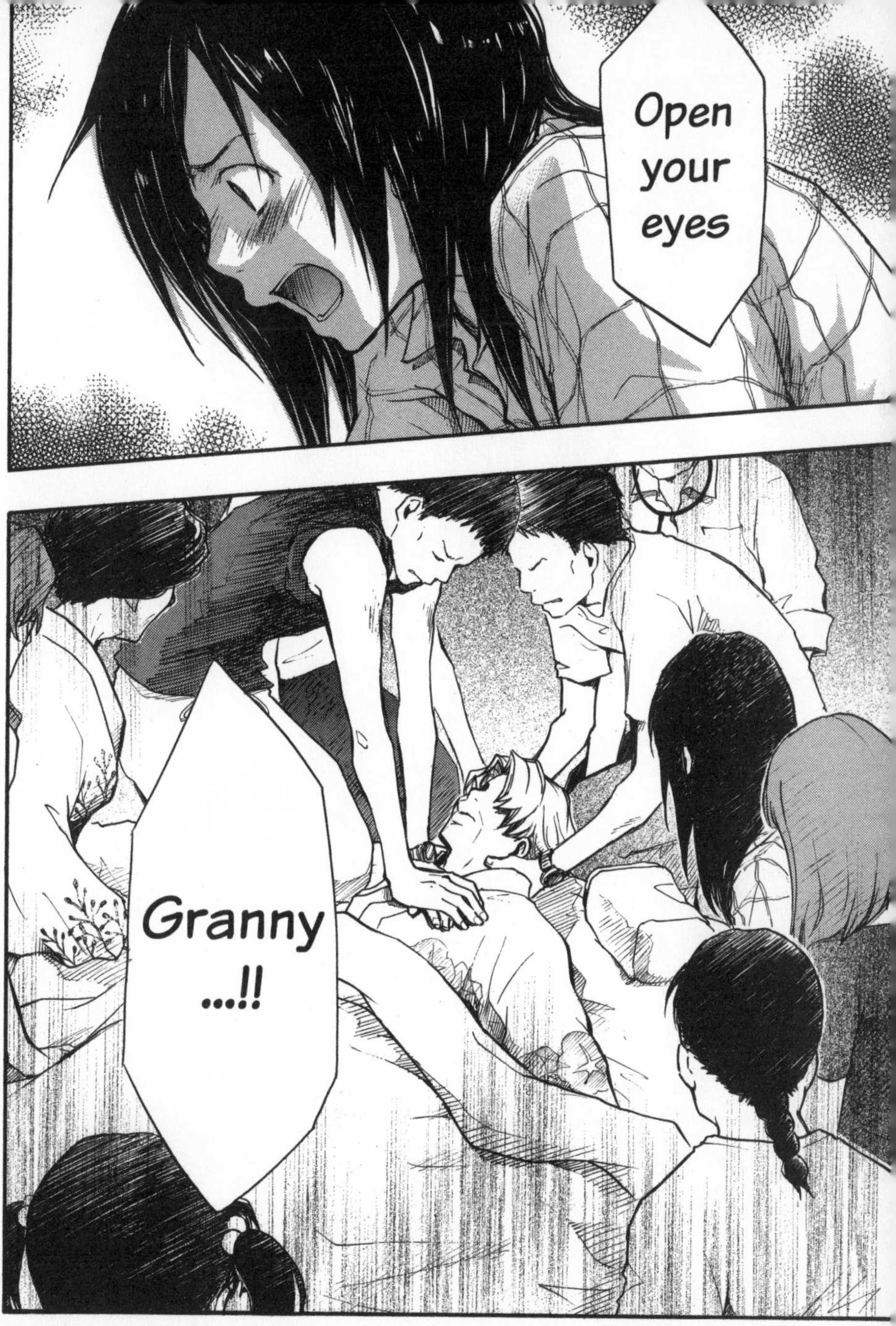
Open your eyes
Granny ...!!

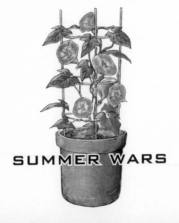

SUMMER WARS

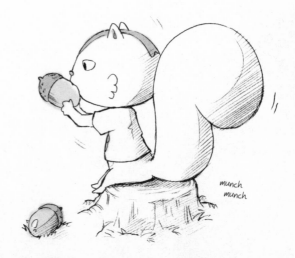

munch
munch

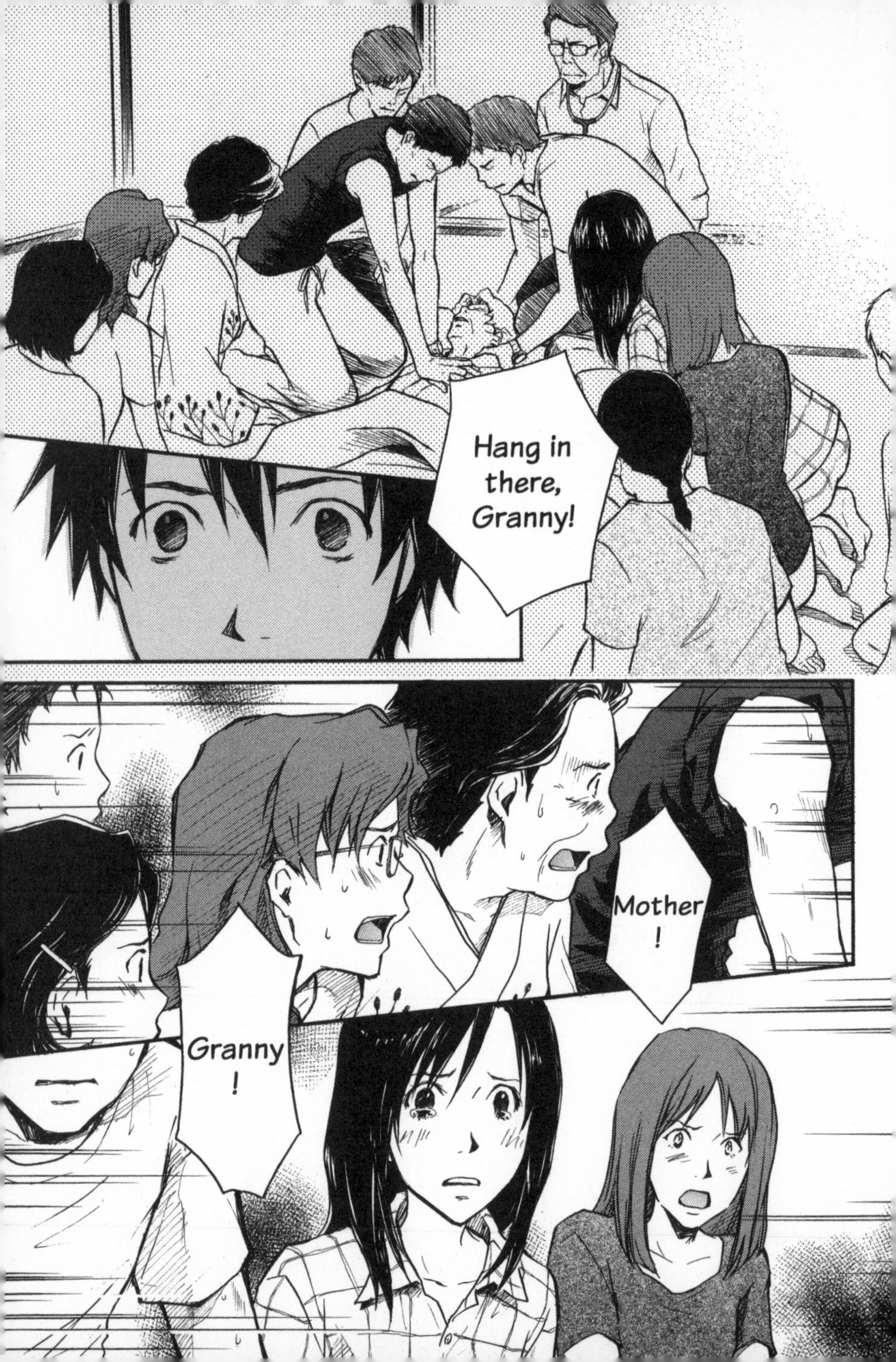
Hang in there, Granny!
Mother!
Granny!

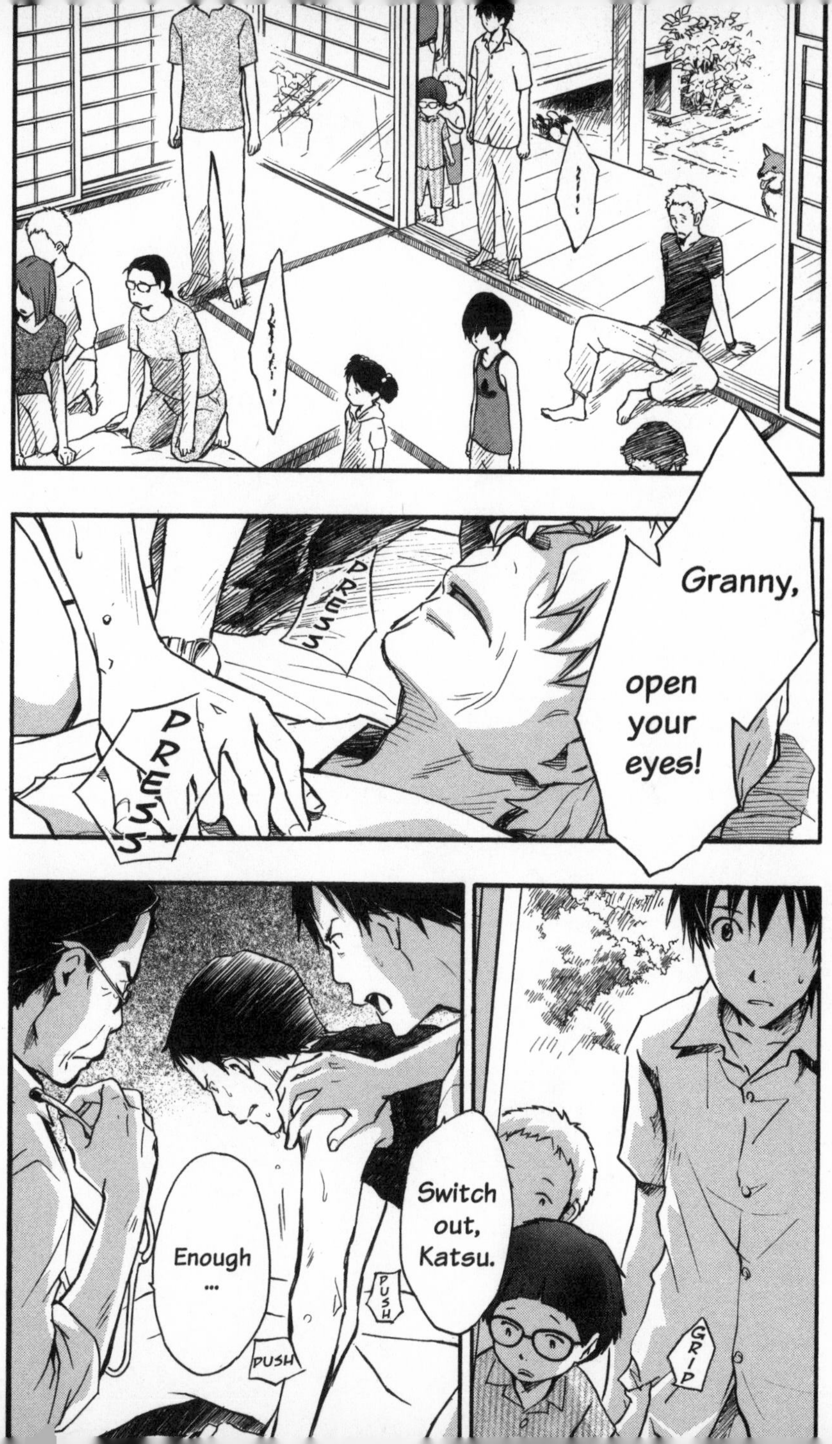
PRESS
Granny,
open your eyes!
PRESS
GRIP
Switch out, Katsu.
PUSH
Enough ...
PUSH

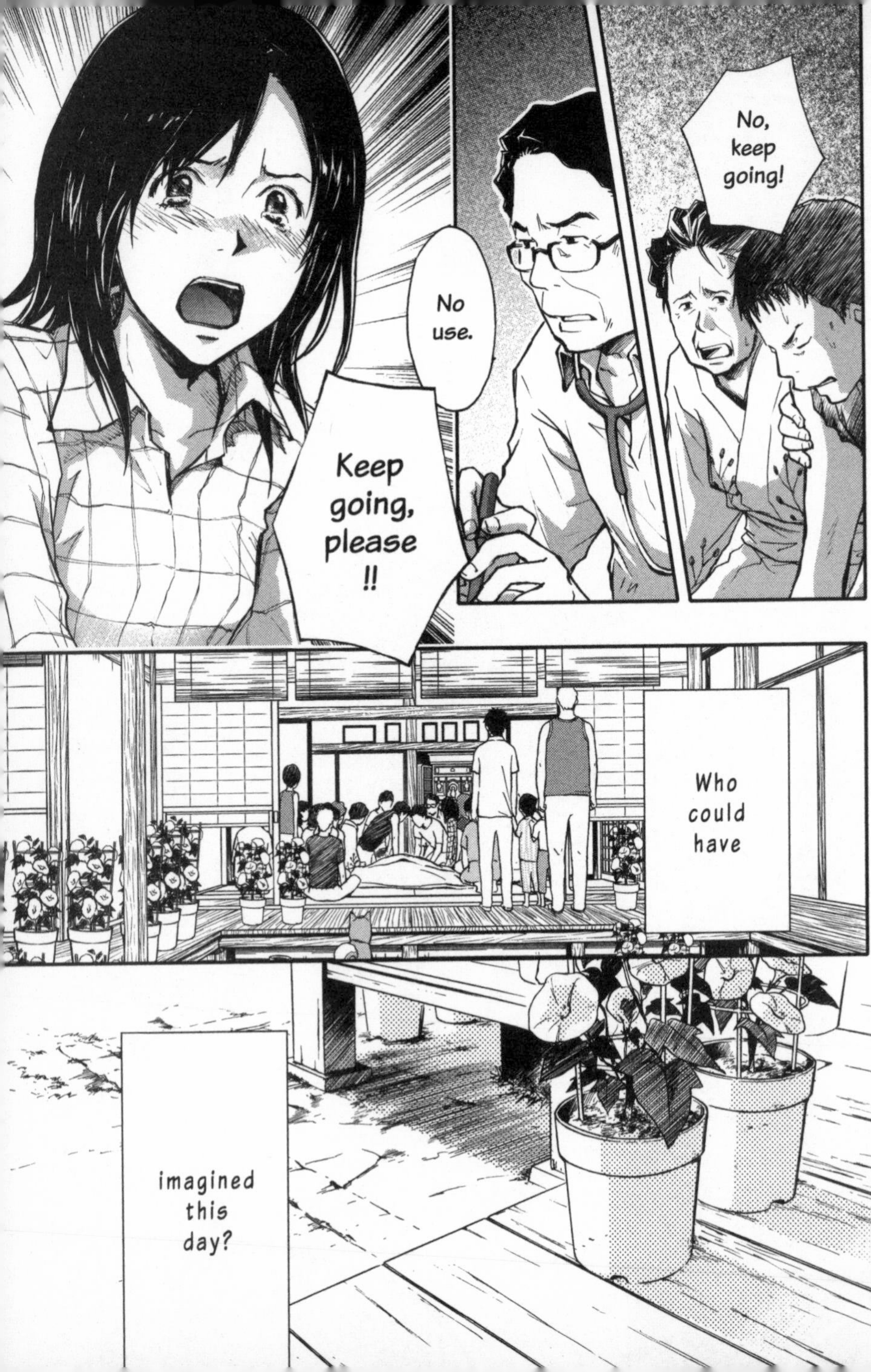
No, keep going!
No use.
Keep going, please !!
Who could have
imagined this day?

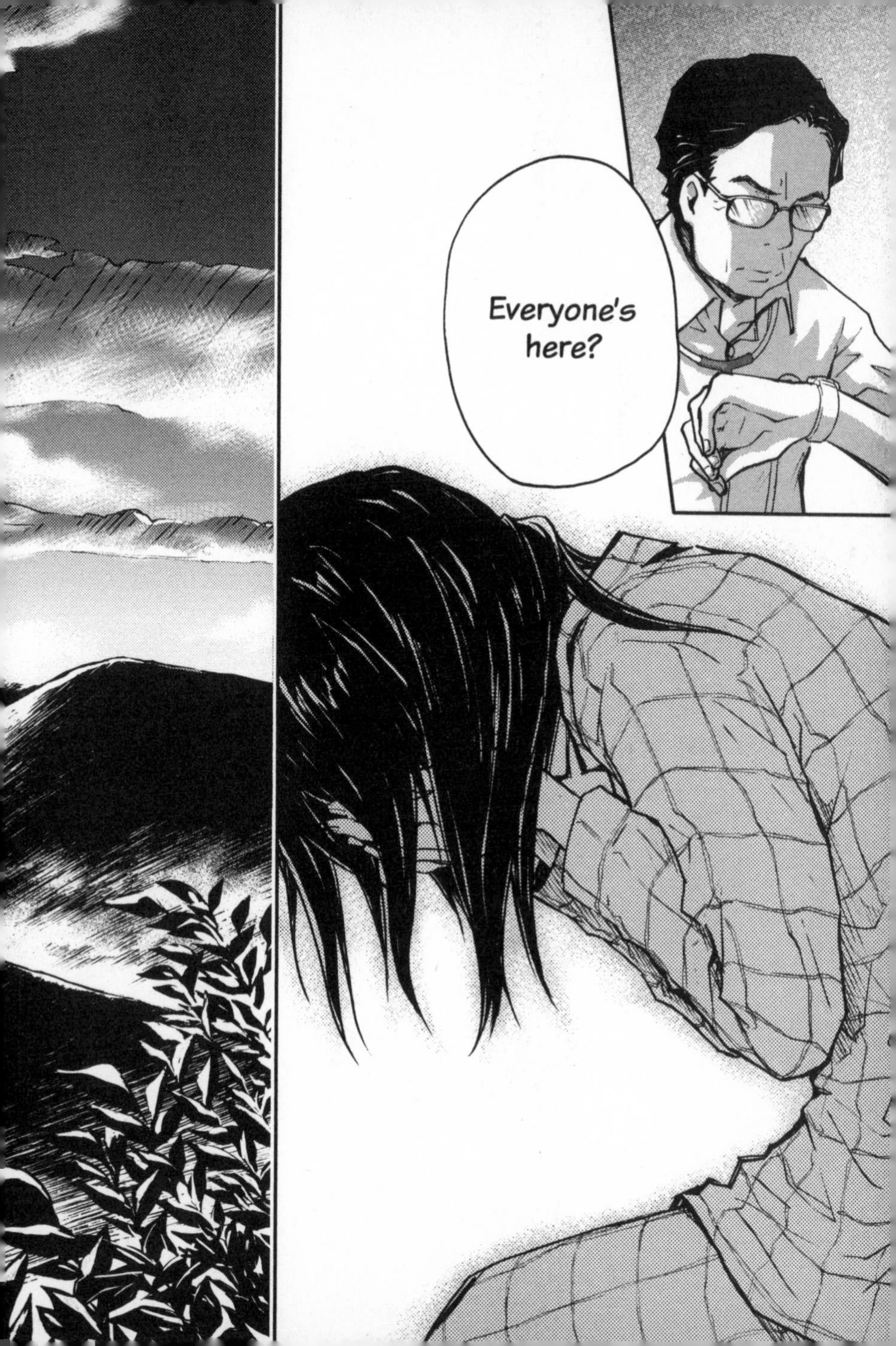
Everyone's here?

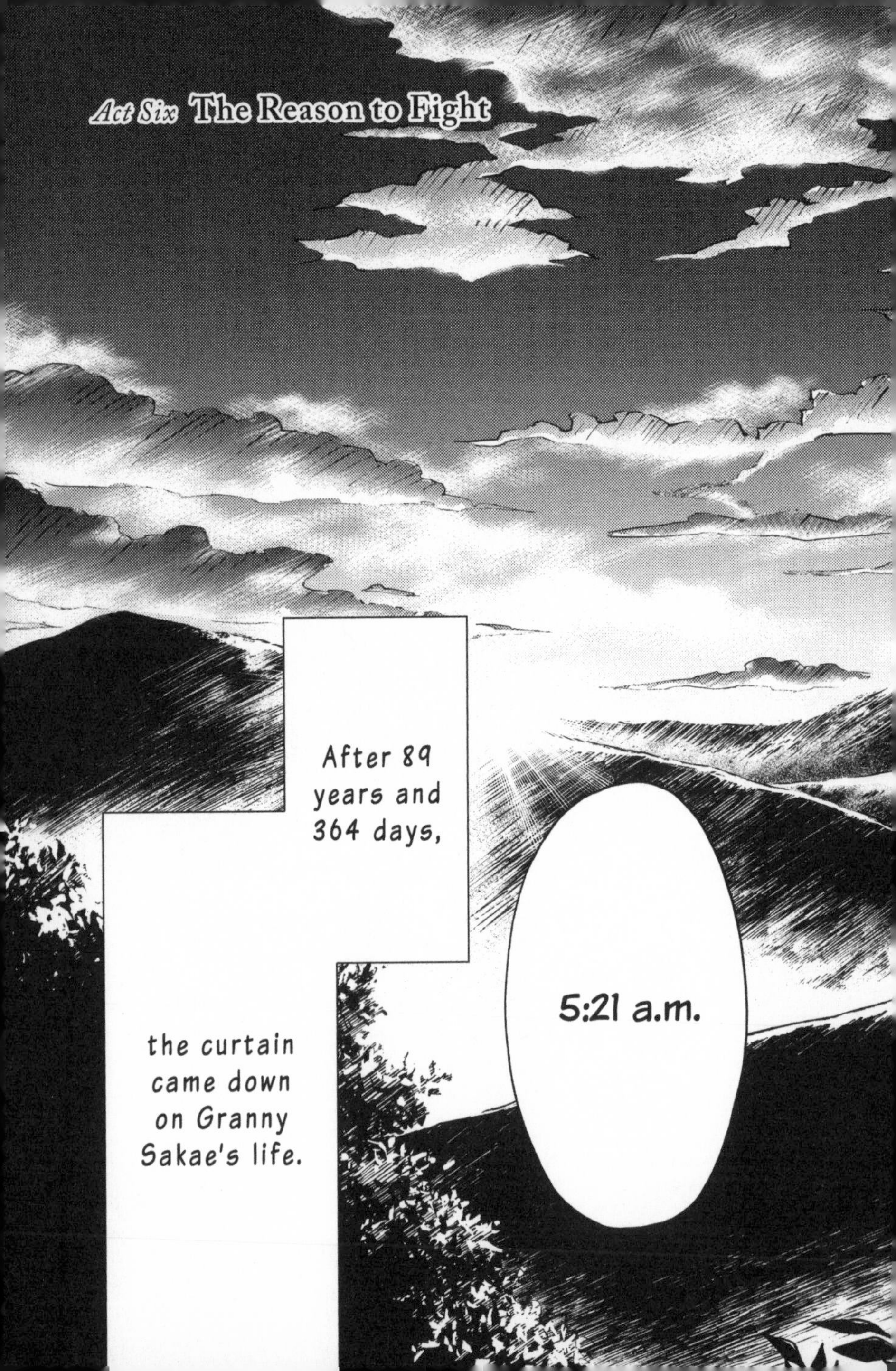
Act Six The Reason to Fight
After 89 years and 364 days,
the curtain came down on Granny Sakae's life.
5:21 a.m.

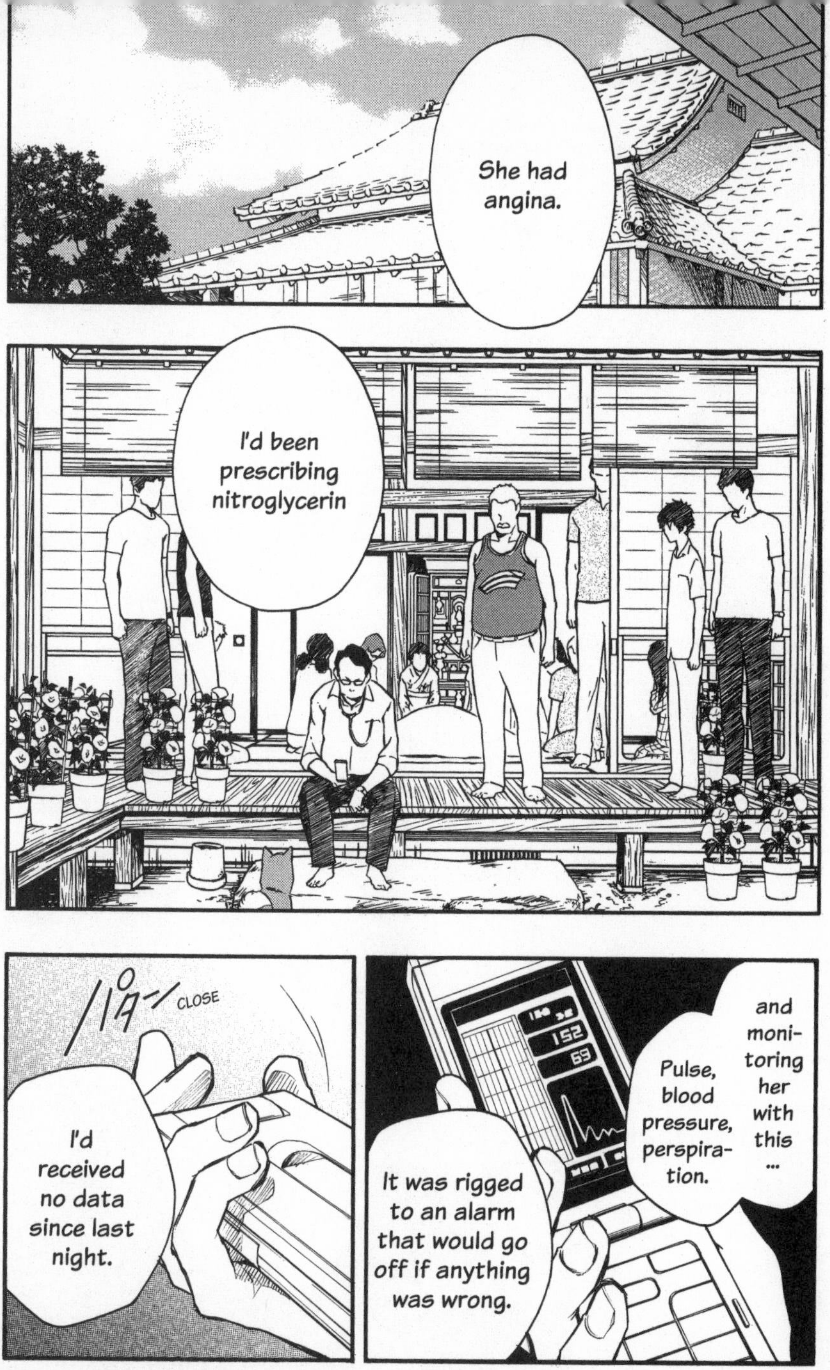
She had angina.
I'd been prescribing nitroglycerin
and monitoring her with this...
Pulse, blood pressure, perspiration.
It was rigged to an alarm that would go off if anything was wrong.
CLOSE
I'd received no data since last night.

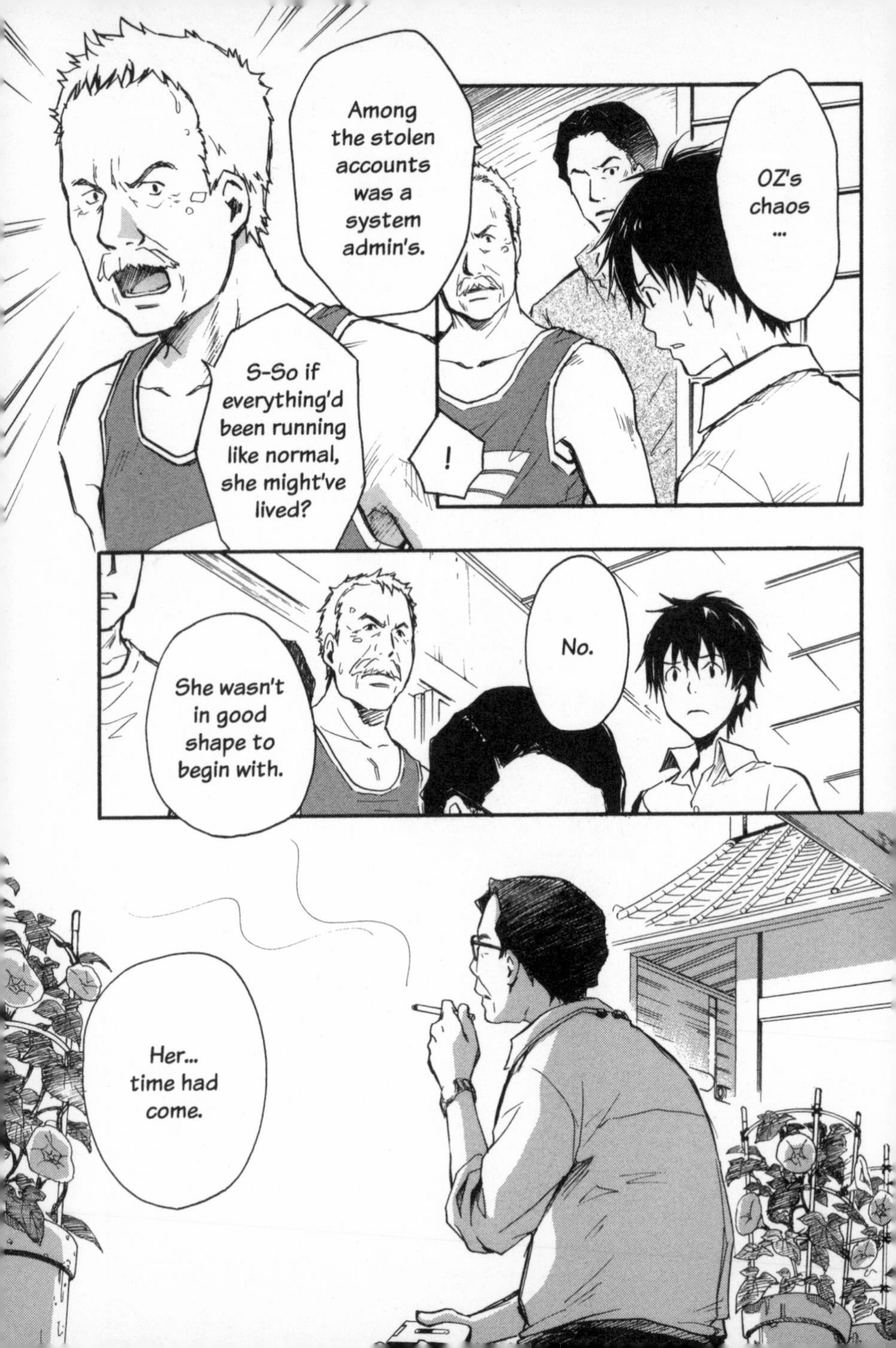
OZ's chaos ...
Among the stolen accounts was a system admin's.
!
S-So if everything'd been running like normal, she might've lived?
No.
She wasn't in good shape to begin with.
Her... time had come.

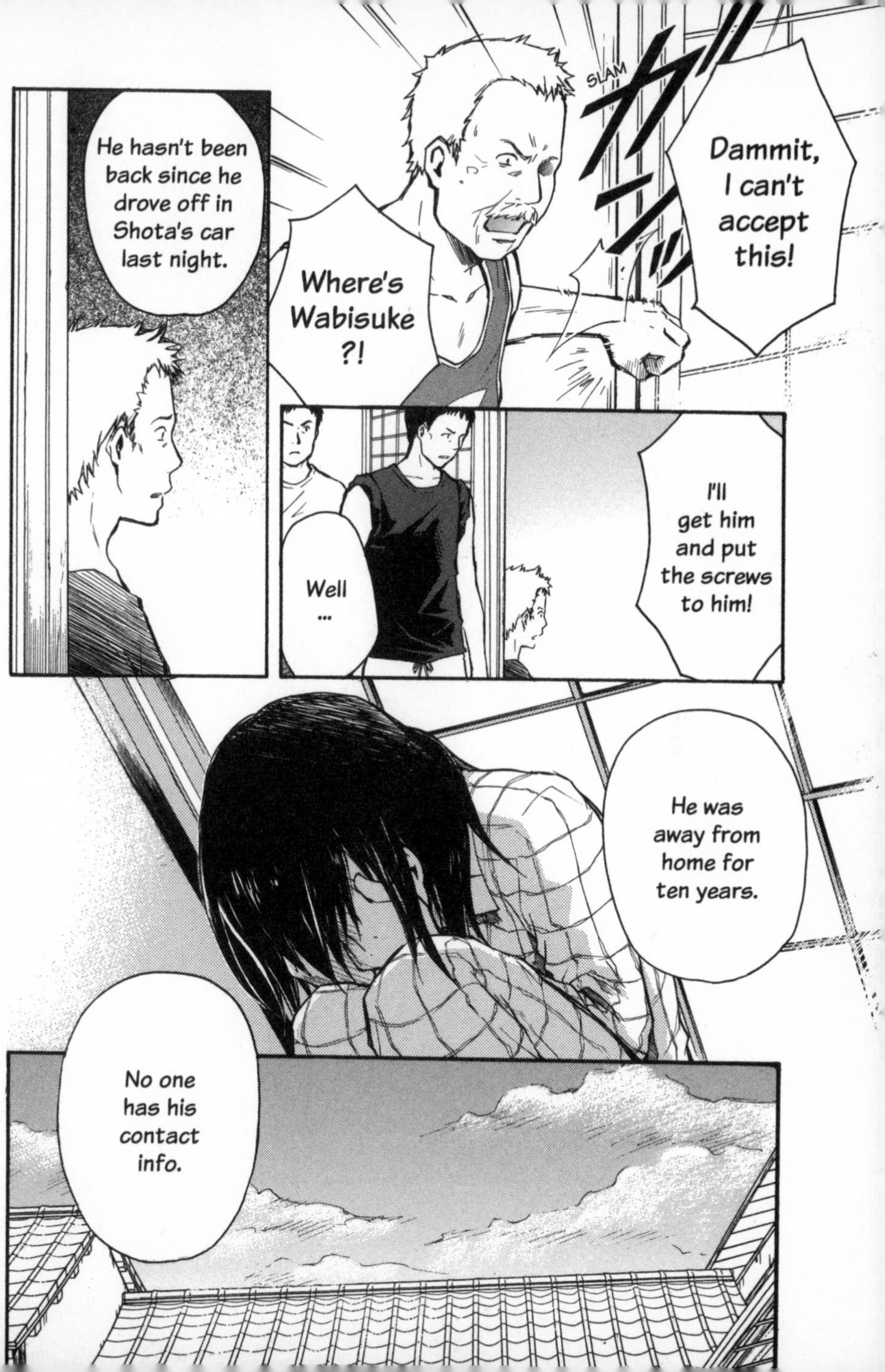
Dammit, I can't accept this!
SLAM
Where's Wabisuke ?!
I'll get him and put the screws to him!
Well ...
He hasn't been back since he drove off in Shota's car last night.
He was away from home for ten years.
No one has his contact info.

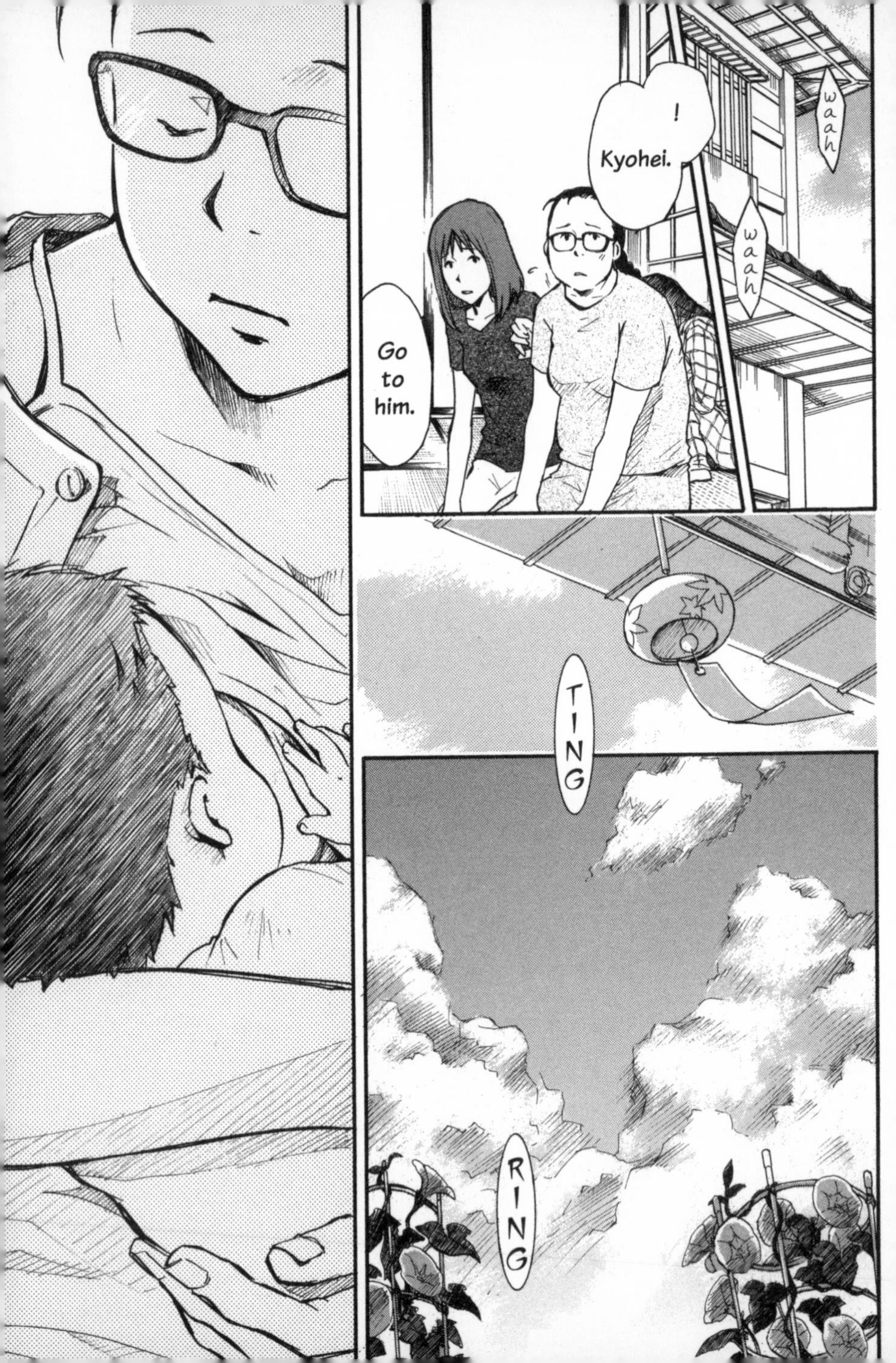
waah
waah
! Kyohei.
Go to him.
TING
RING

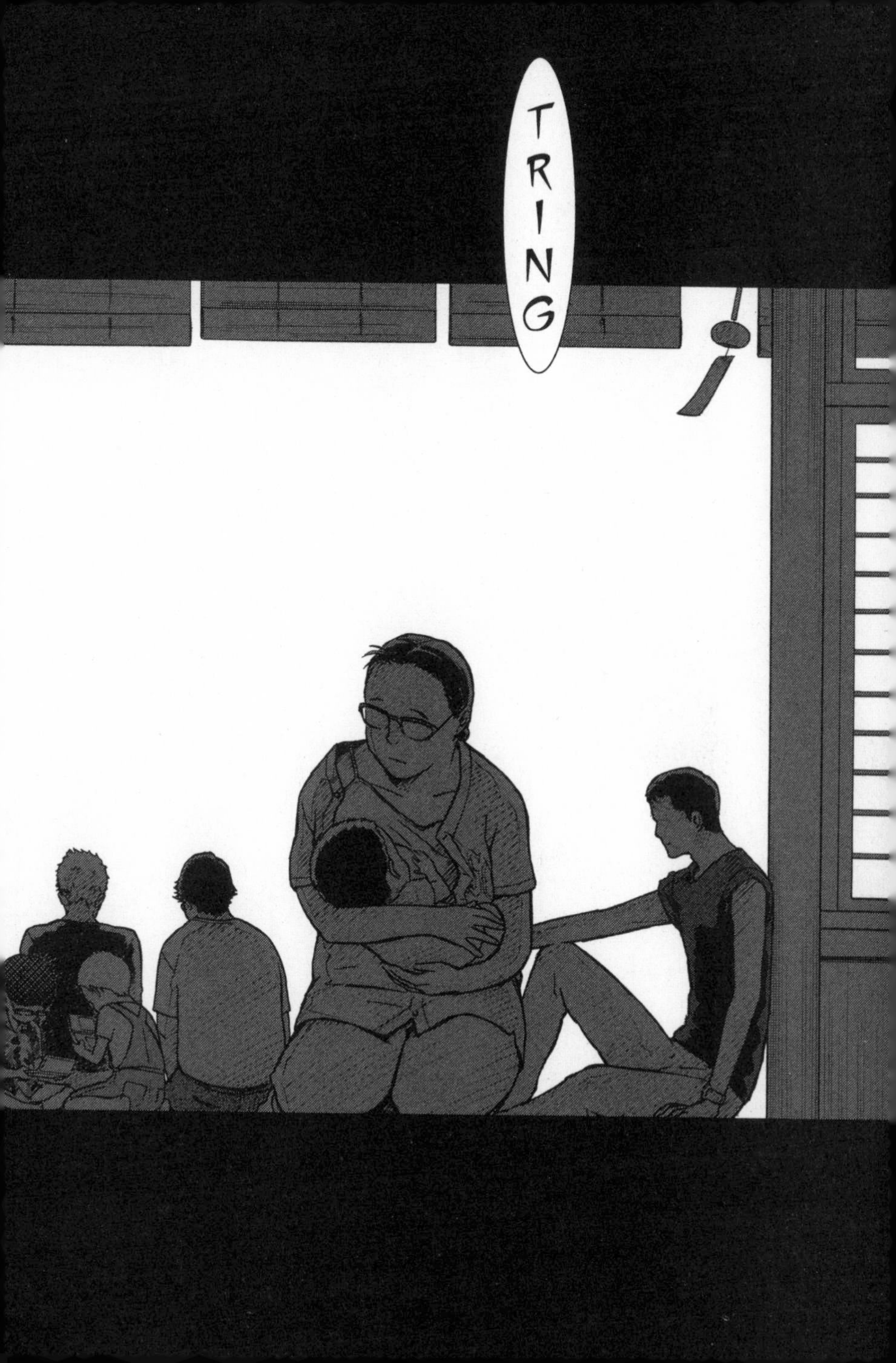
TRING

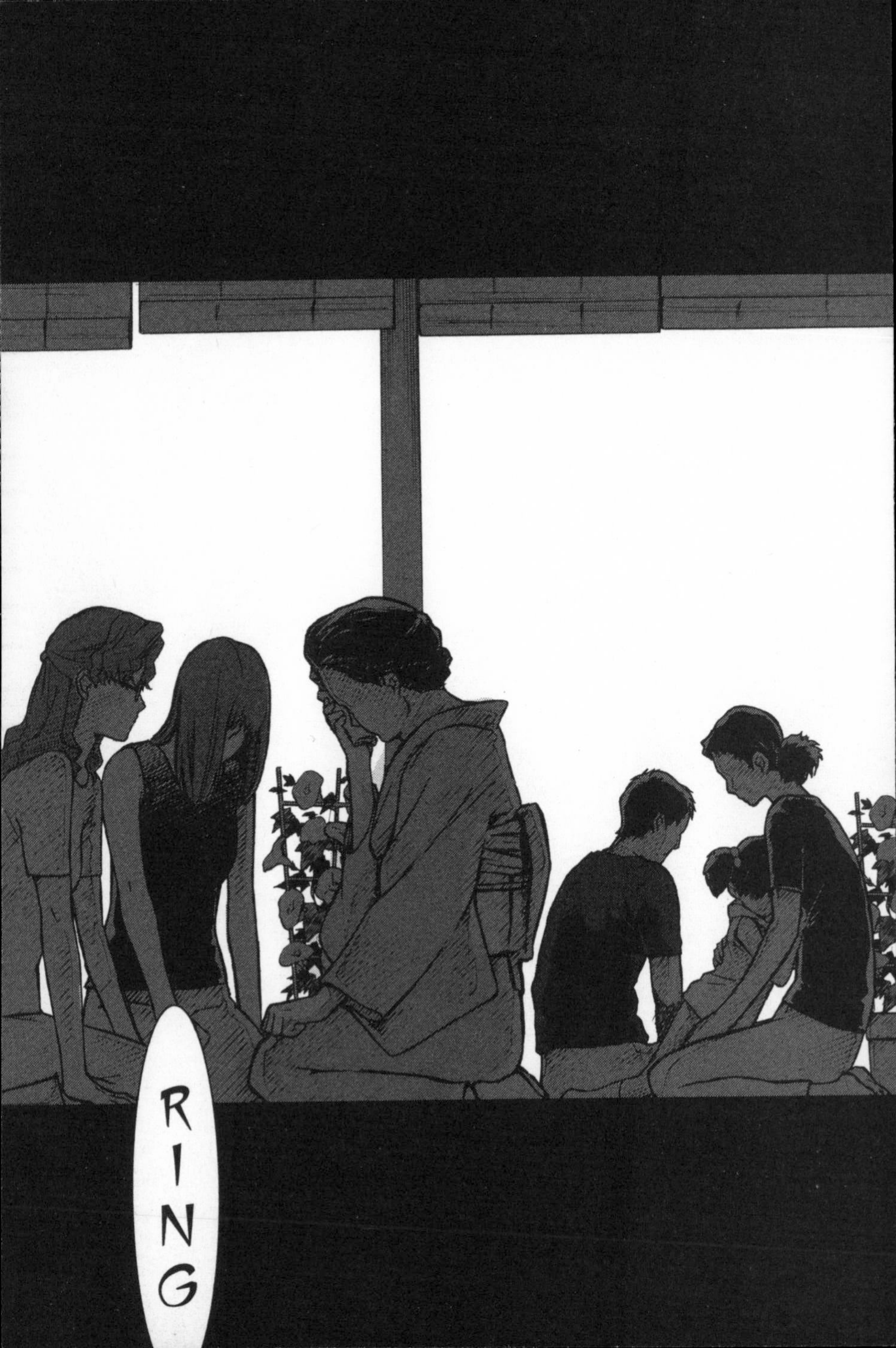
RING

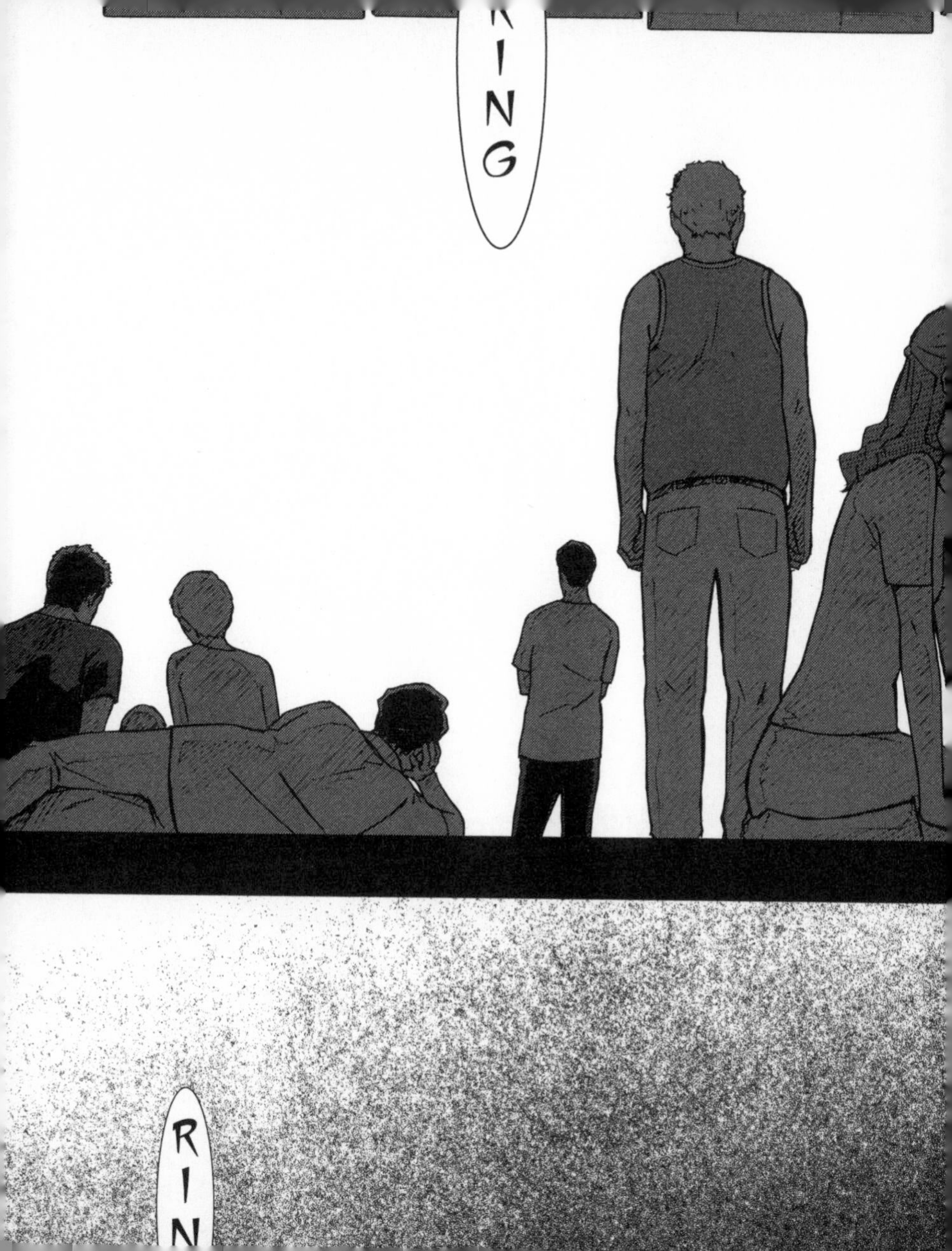
ING
RIN

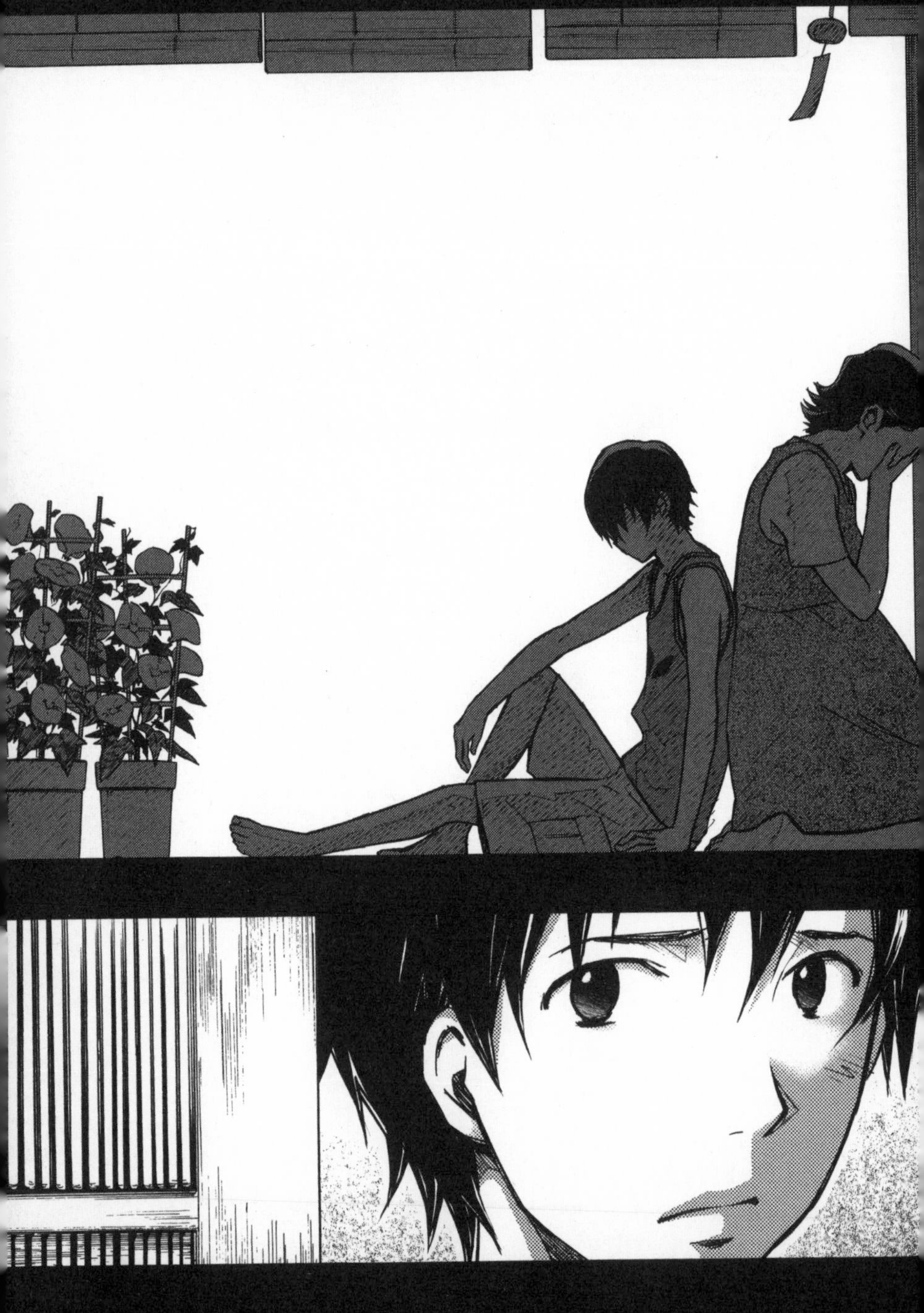

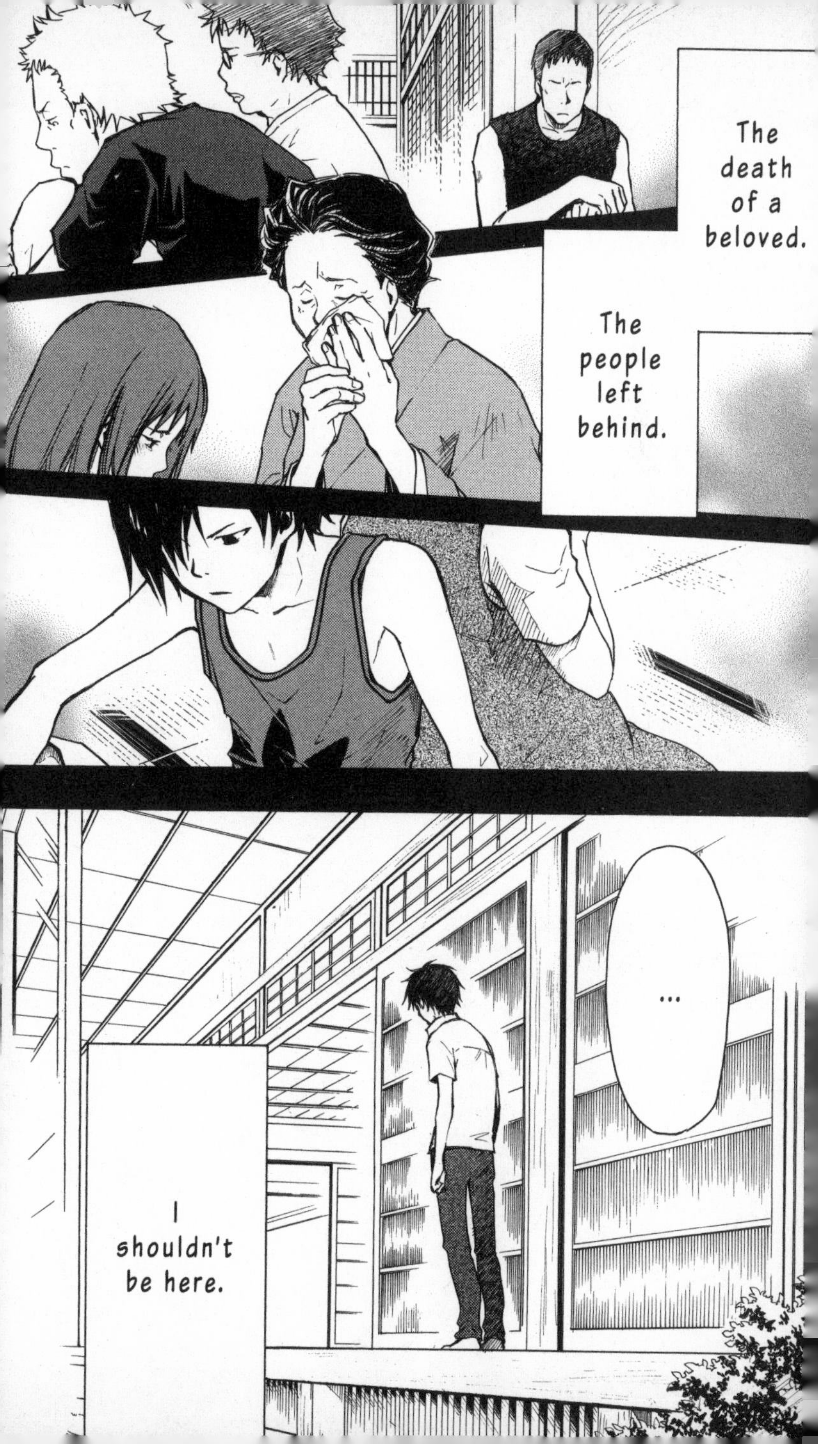
The death of a beloved.
The people left behind.
...
I shouldn't be here.

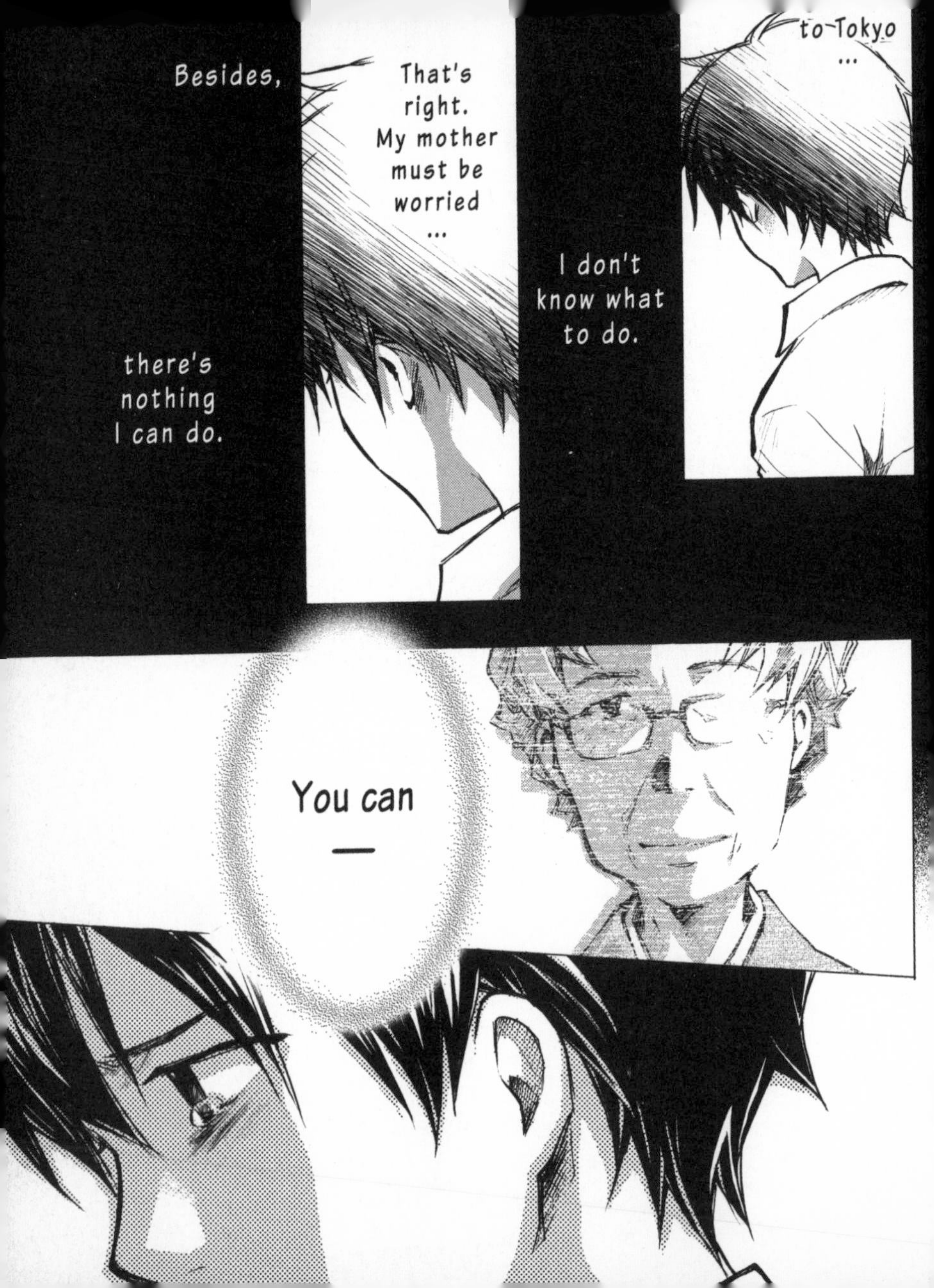
to Tokyo ...
I don't know what to do.
That's right. My mother must be worried ...
Besides,
there's nothing I can do.
You can —

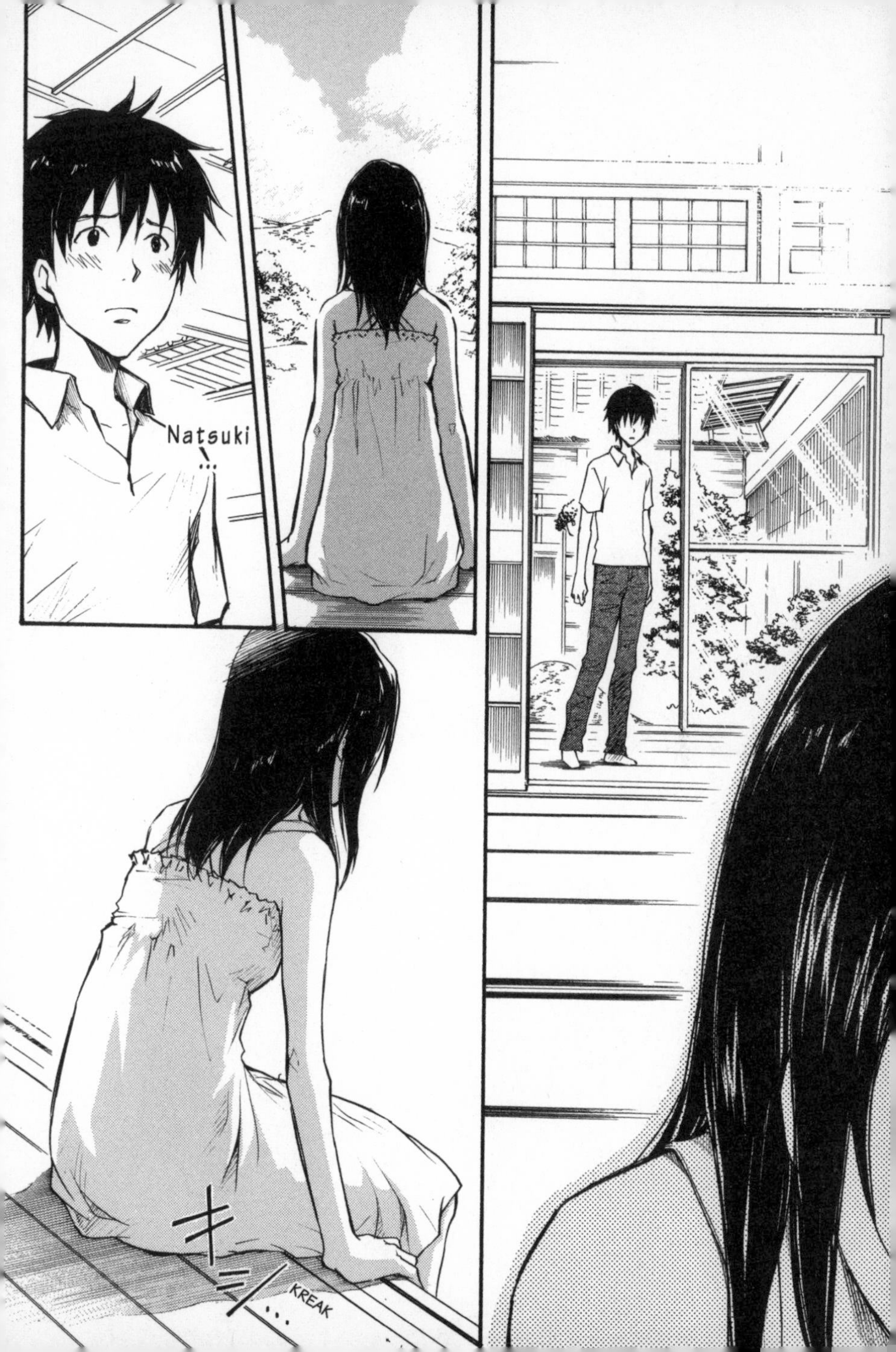

Natsuki
...
KREAK
...

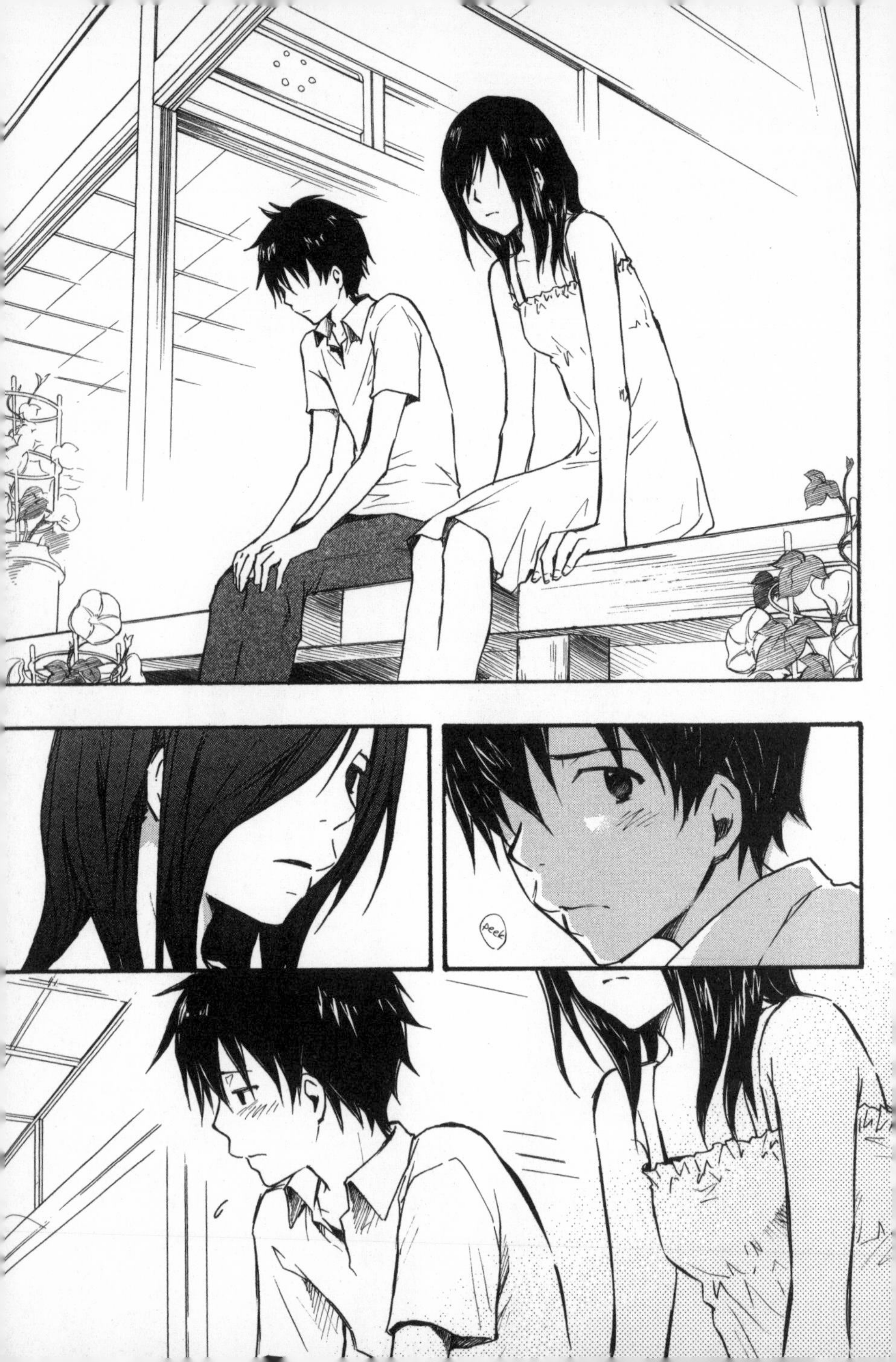
peek

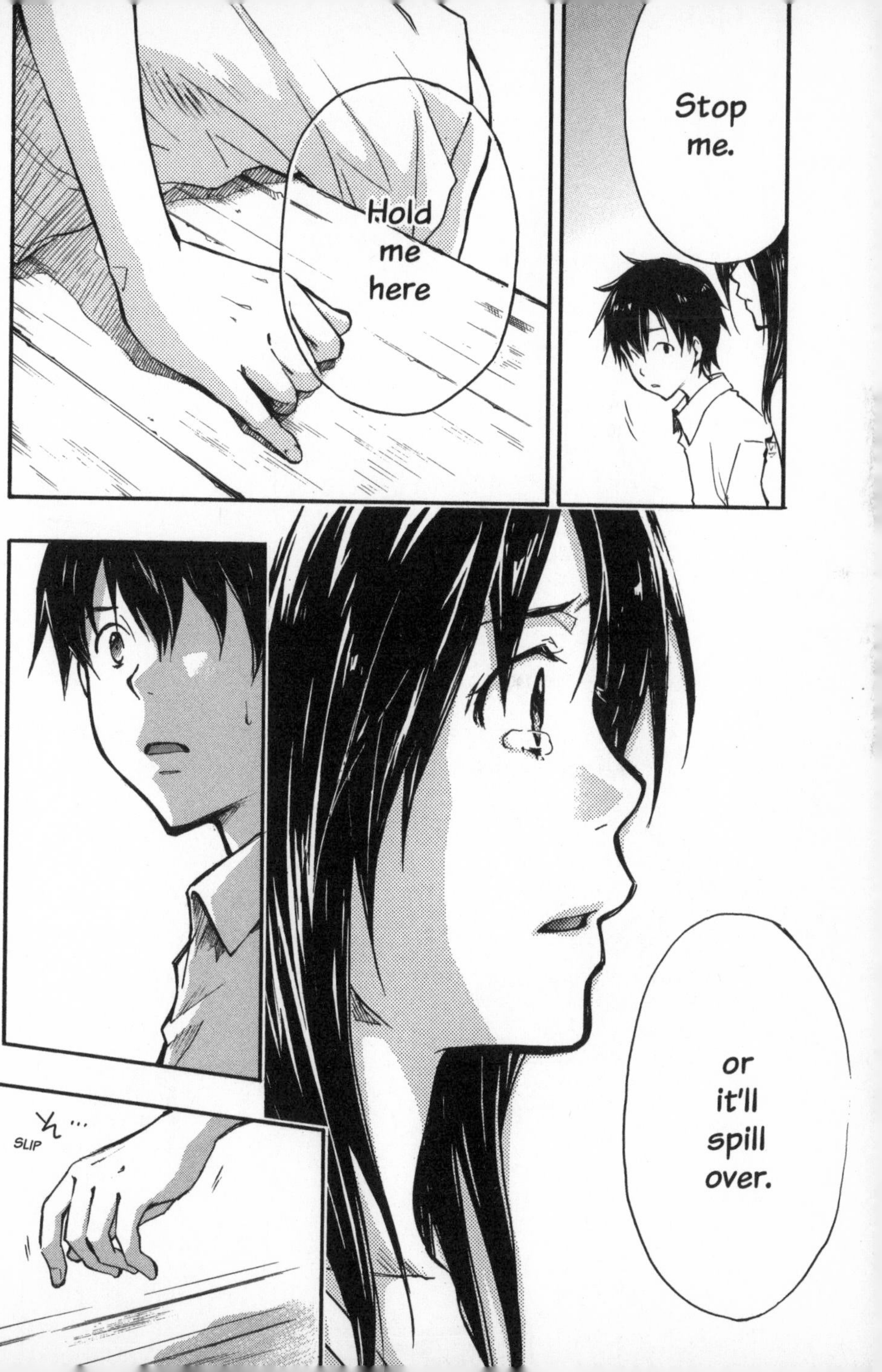
Stop me.
Hold me here
or it'll spill over.
SLIP

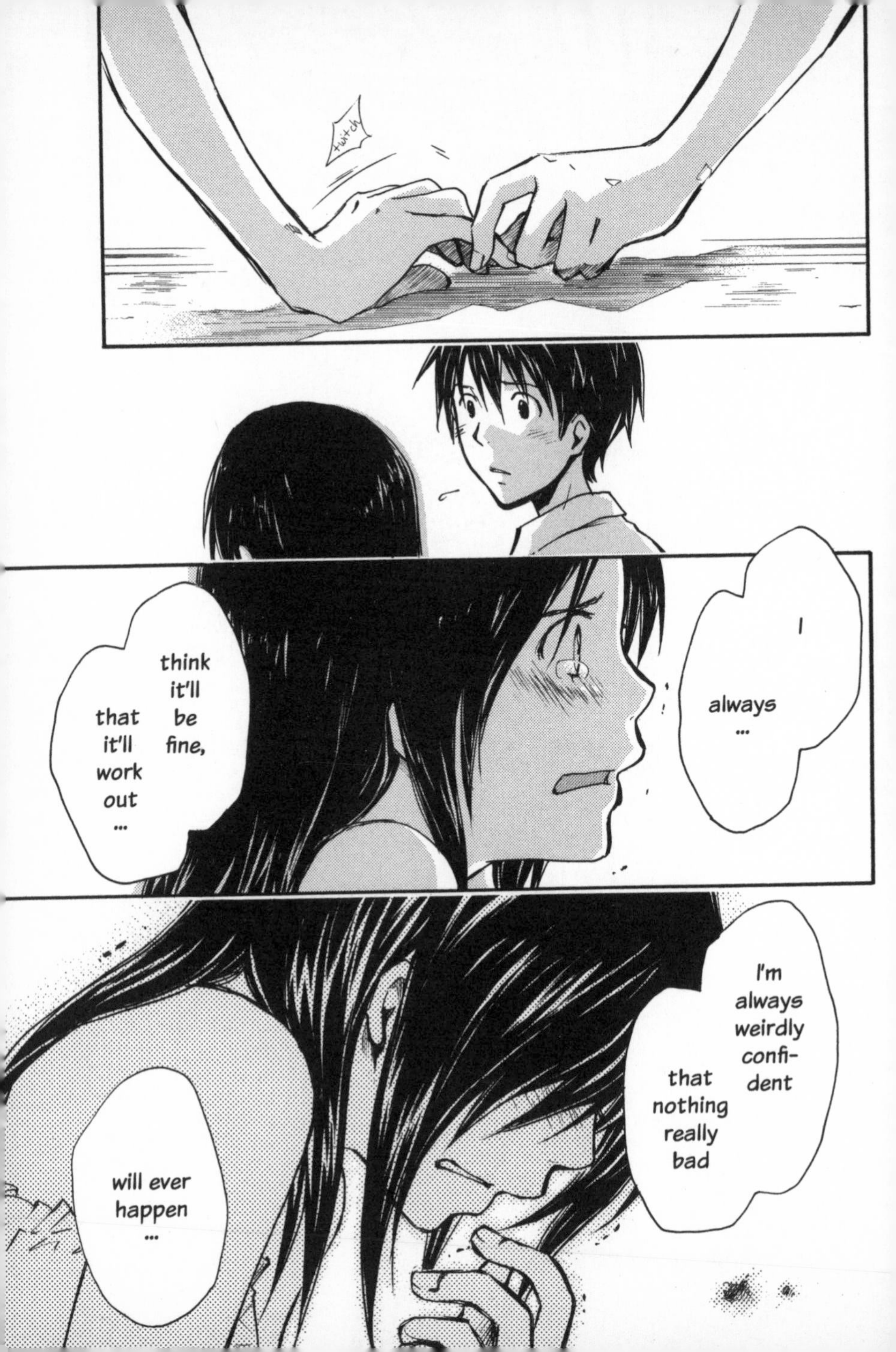
twitch
I always ...
think it'll be fine, that it'll work out ...
I'm always weirdly confi-dent that nothing really bad
will ever happen ...

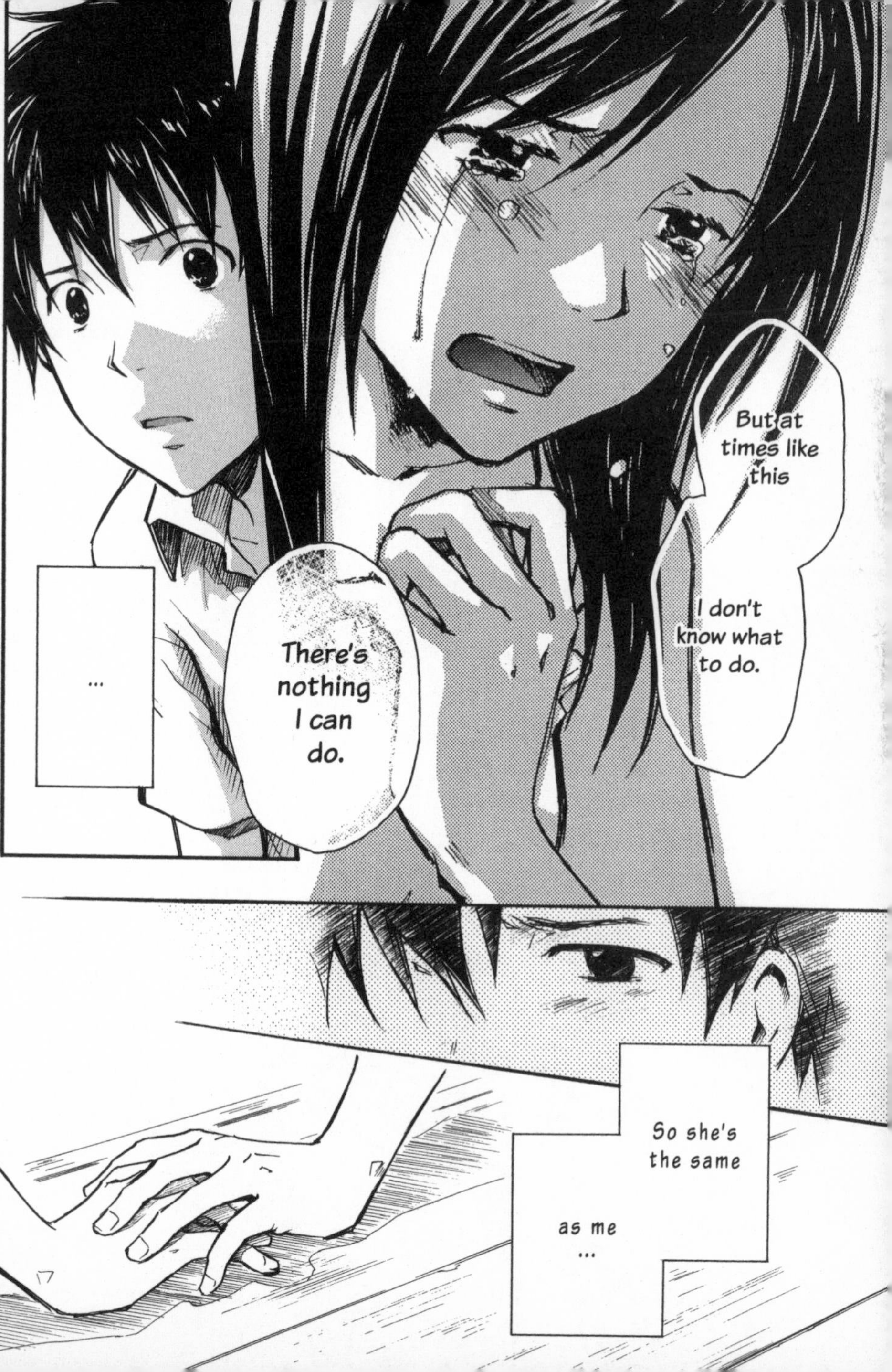
But at times like this
I don't know what to do.
There's nothing I can do.
...
So she's the same as me ...

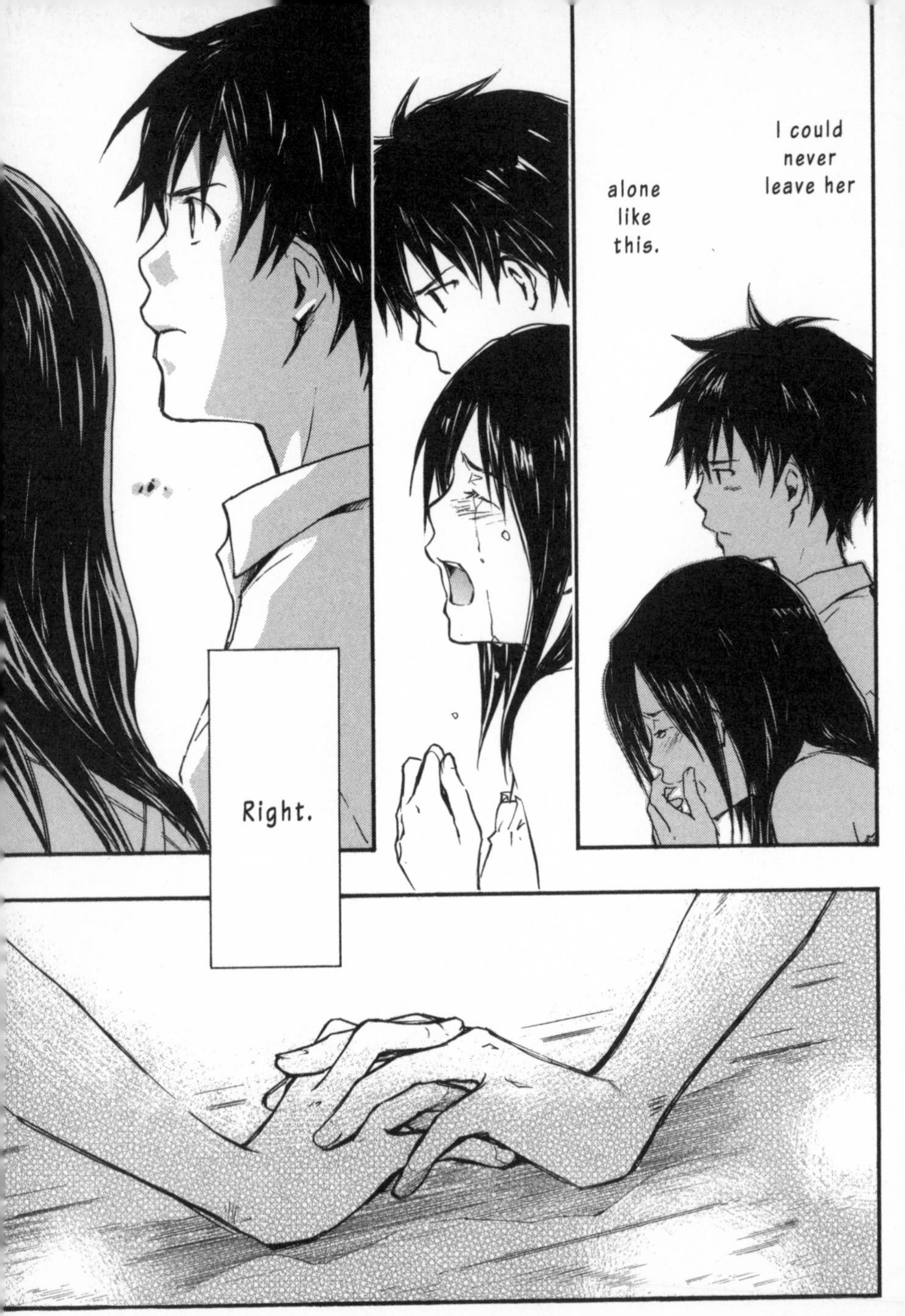
I could never leave her
alone like this.
Right.

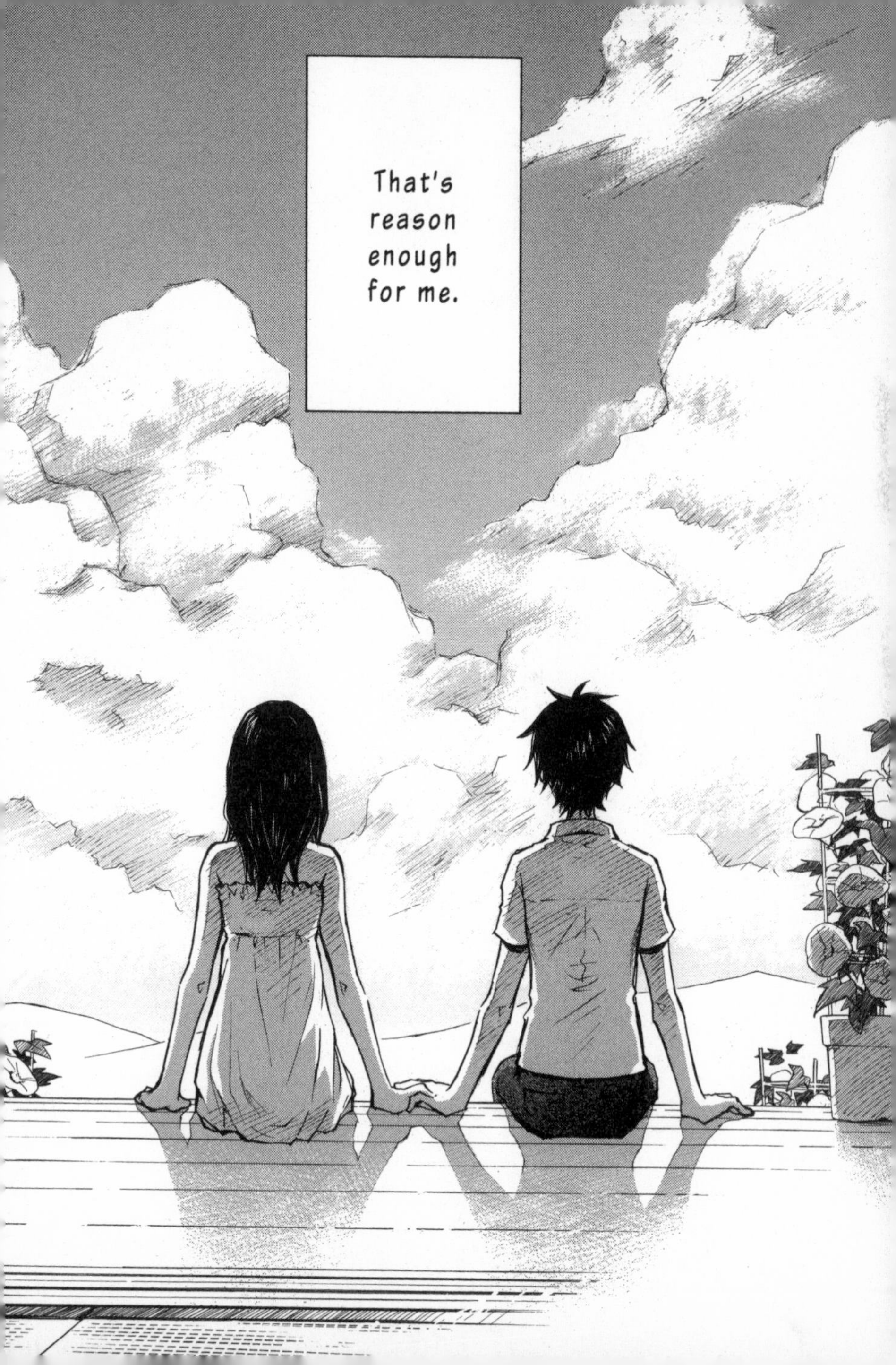
That's reason enough for me.

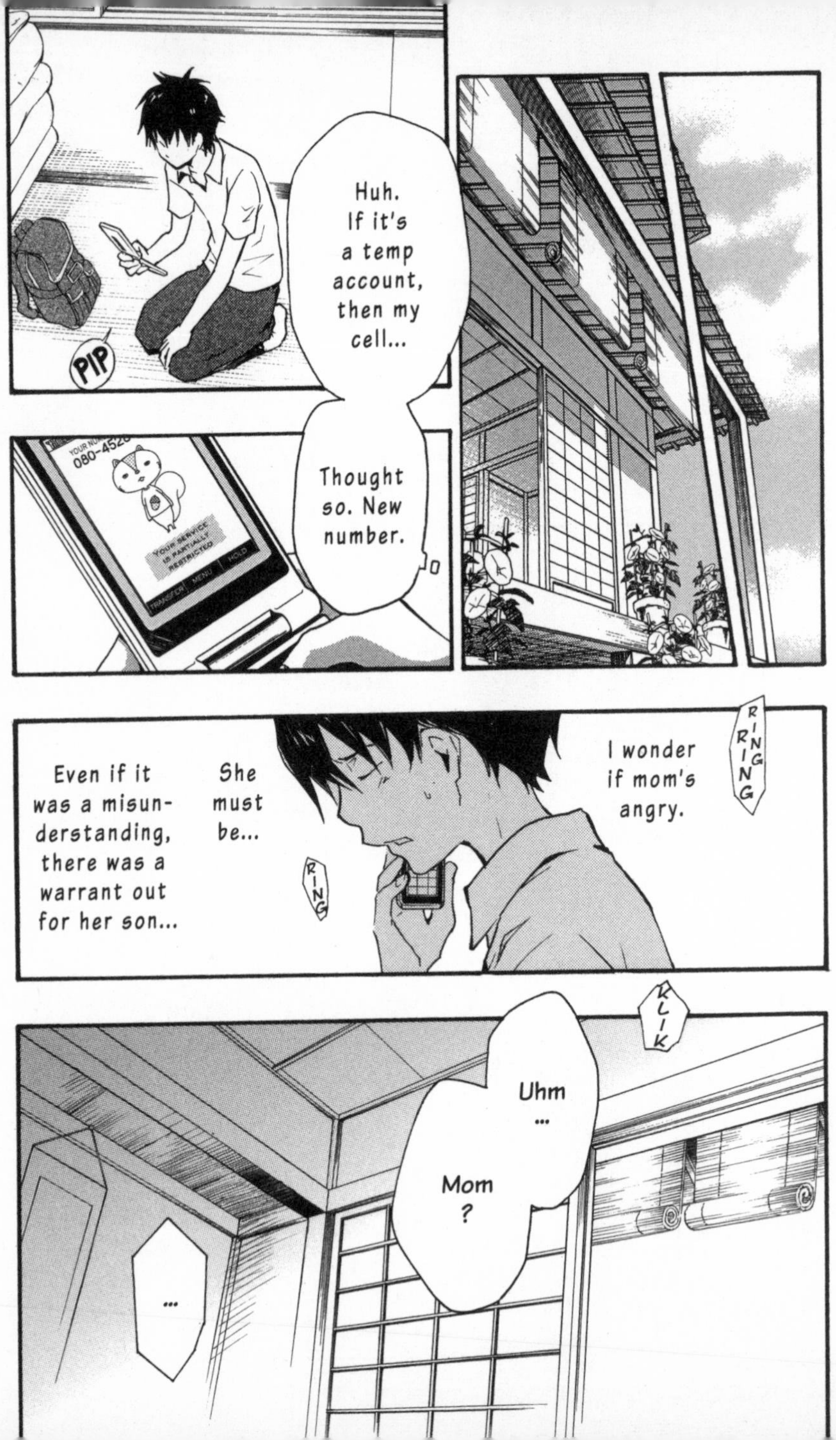

Huh. If it's a temp account, then my cell...
PIP
YOUR SERVICE IS PARTIALLY RESTRICTED
TRANSFER
MENU
HOLD
Thought so. New number.
RING RING
I wonder if mom's angry.
RING
She must be...
Even if it was a misunderstanding, there was a warrant out for her son...
KLIK
Uhm ... Mom?
...

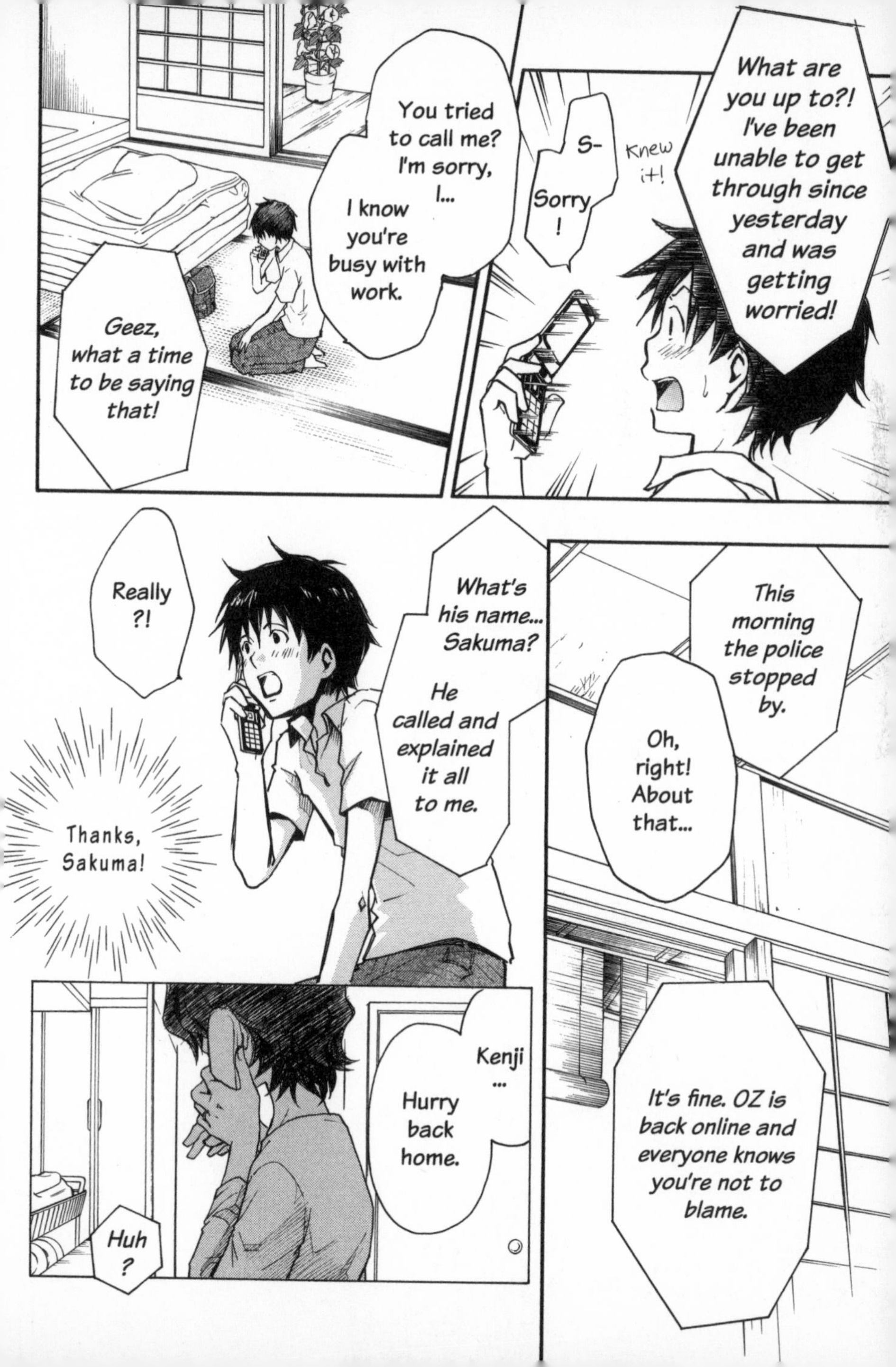
What are you up to?! I've been unable to get through since yesterday and was getting worried!
S-
Knew it!
Sorry!
You tried to call me? I'm sorry, I...
I know you're busy with work.
Geez, what a time to be saying that!
This morning the police stopped by.
Oh, right! About that...
It's fine. OZ is back online and everyone knows you're not to blame.
What's his name... Sakuma?
He called and explained it all to me.
Really?!
Thanks, Sakuma!
Kenji...
Hurry back home.
Huh?

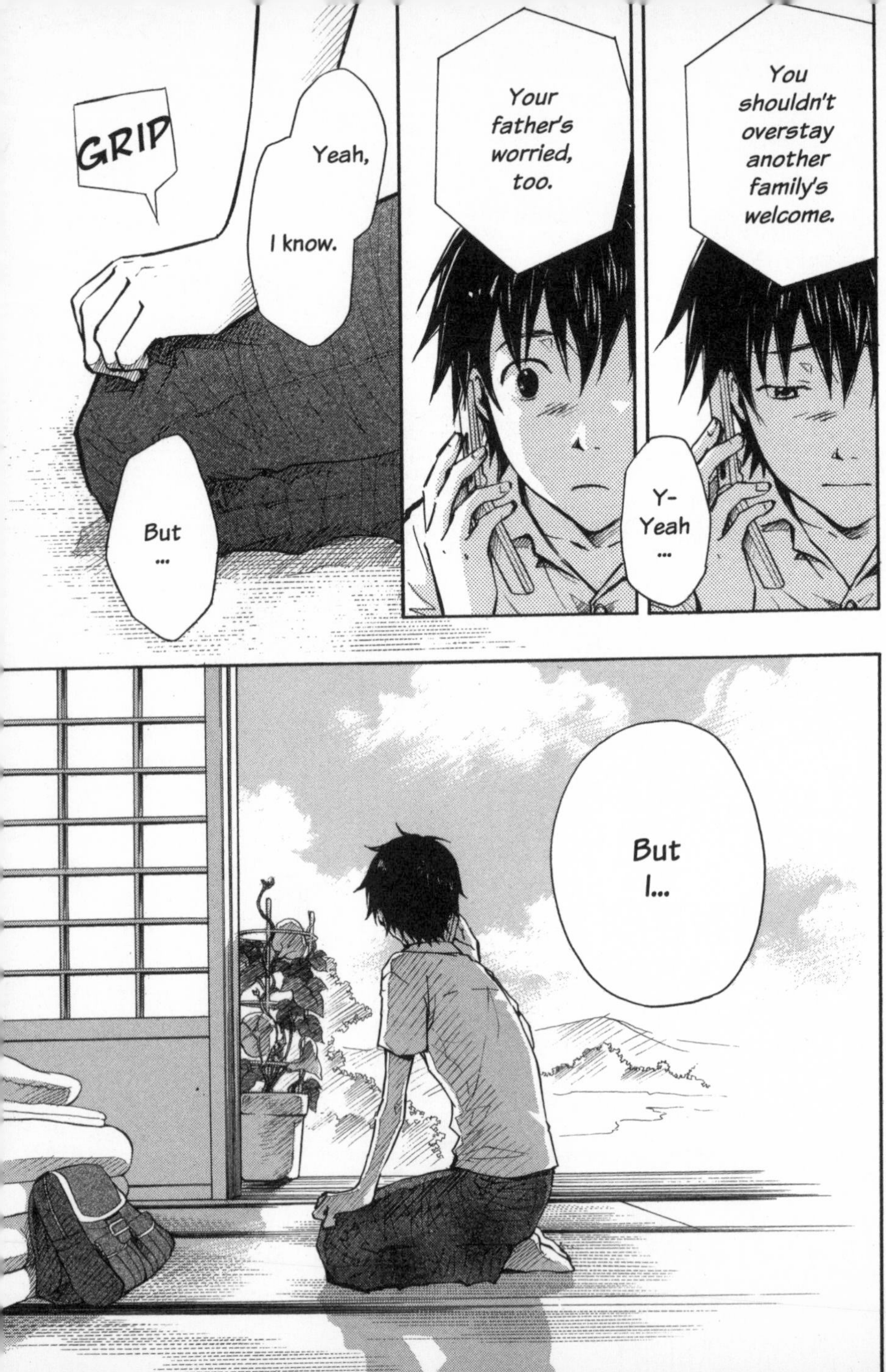
You shouldn't overstay another family's welcome.
Y-Yeah...
Your father's worried, too.
GRIP
Yeah, I know.
But...
But I...

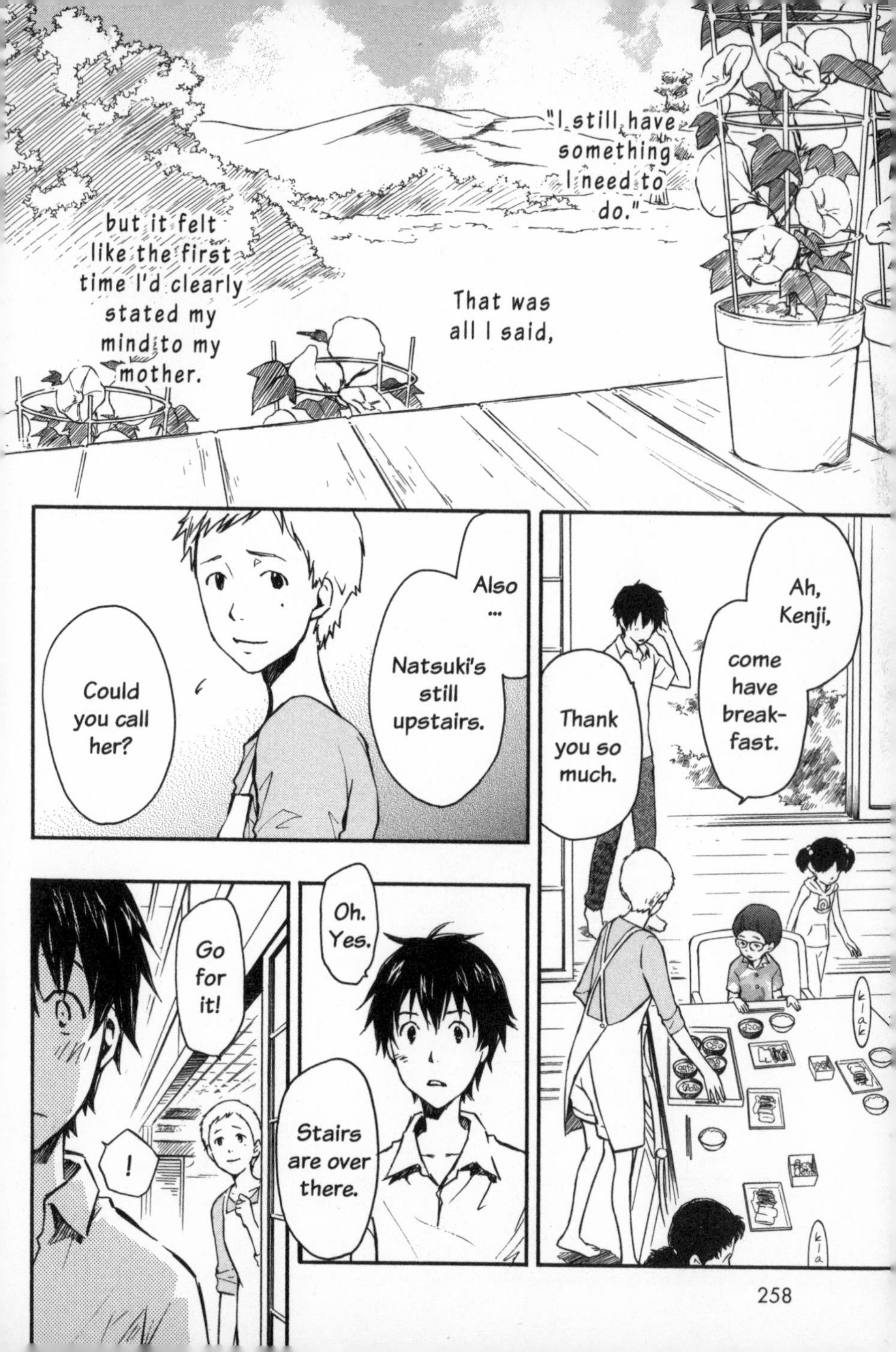
"I still have something I need to do."
That was all I said,
but it felt like the first time I'd clearly stated my mind to my mother.
Ah, Kenji, come have breakfast.
Thank you so much.
klak
kla
Also ...
Natsuki's still upstairs.
Could you call her?
Oh. Yes.
Stairs are over there.
Go for it!
!

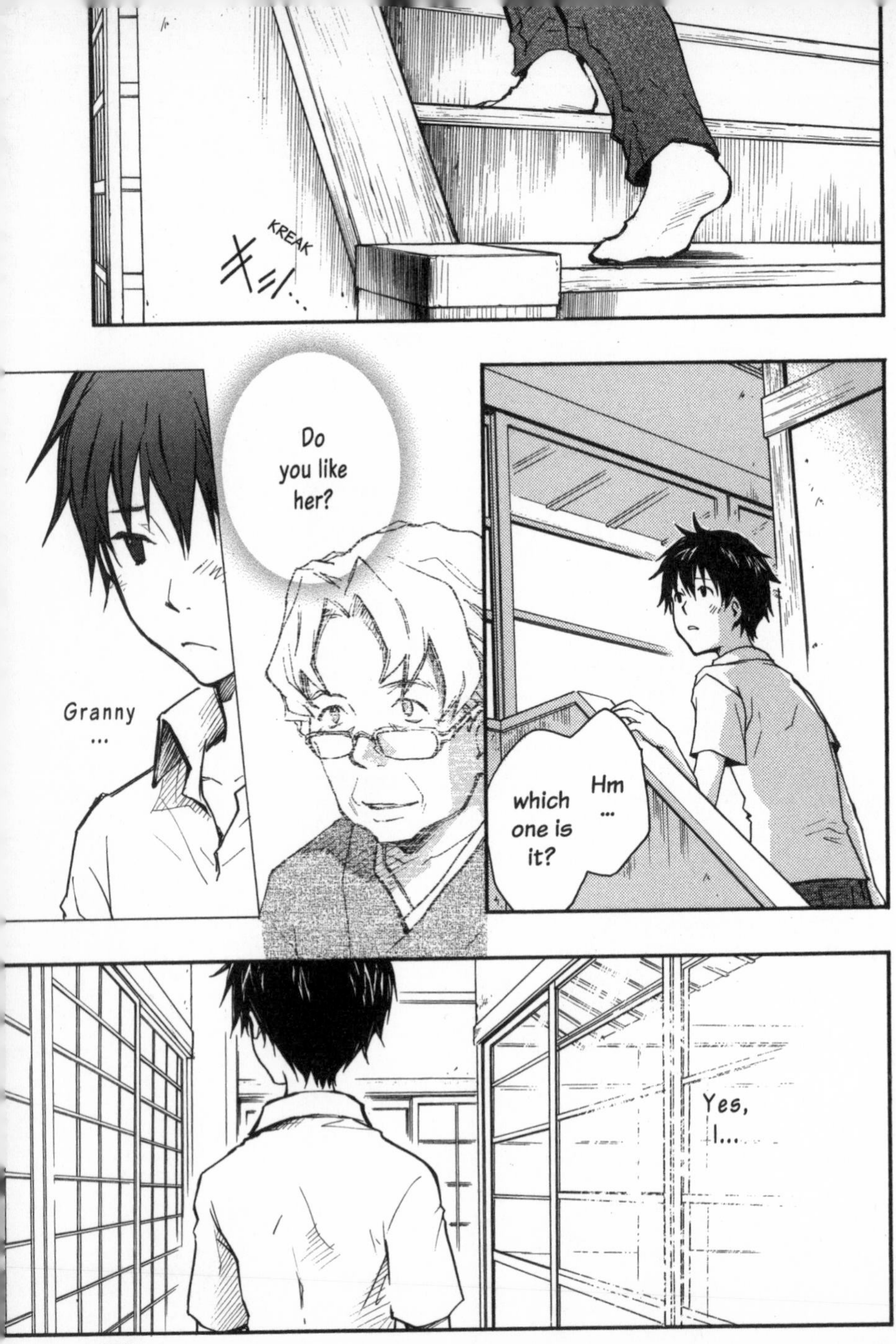
KREAK
Hm ...
which one is it?
Do you like her?
Granny ...
Yes, I...

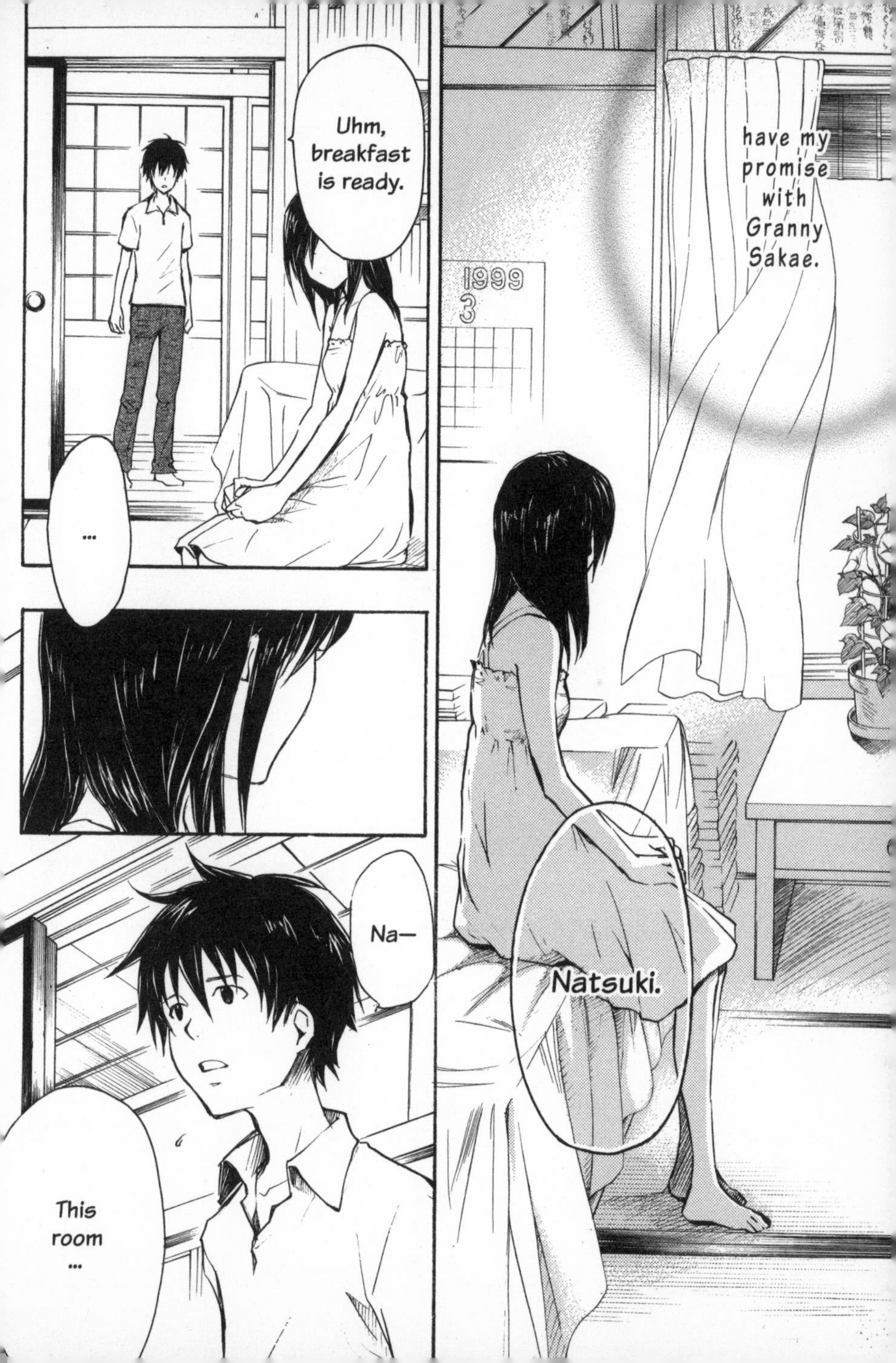
have my promise with Granny Sakae.
1999
3
Natsuki.
Uhm, breakfast is ready.
...
Na—
This room ...

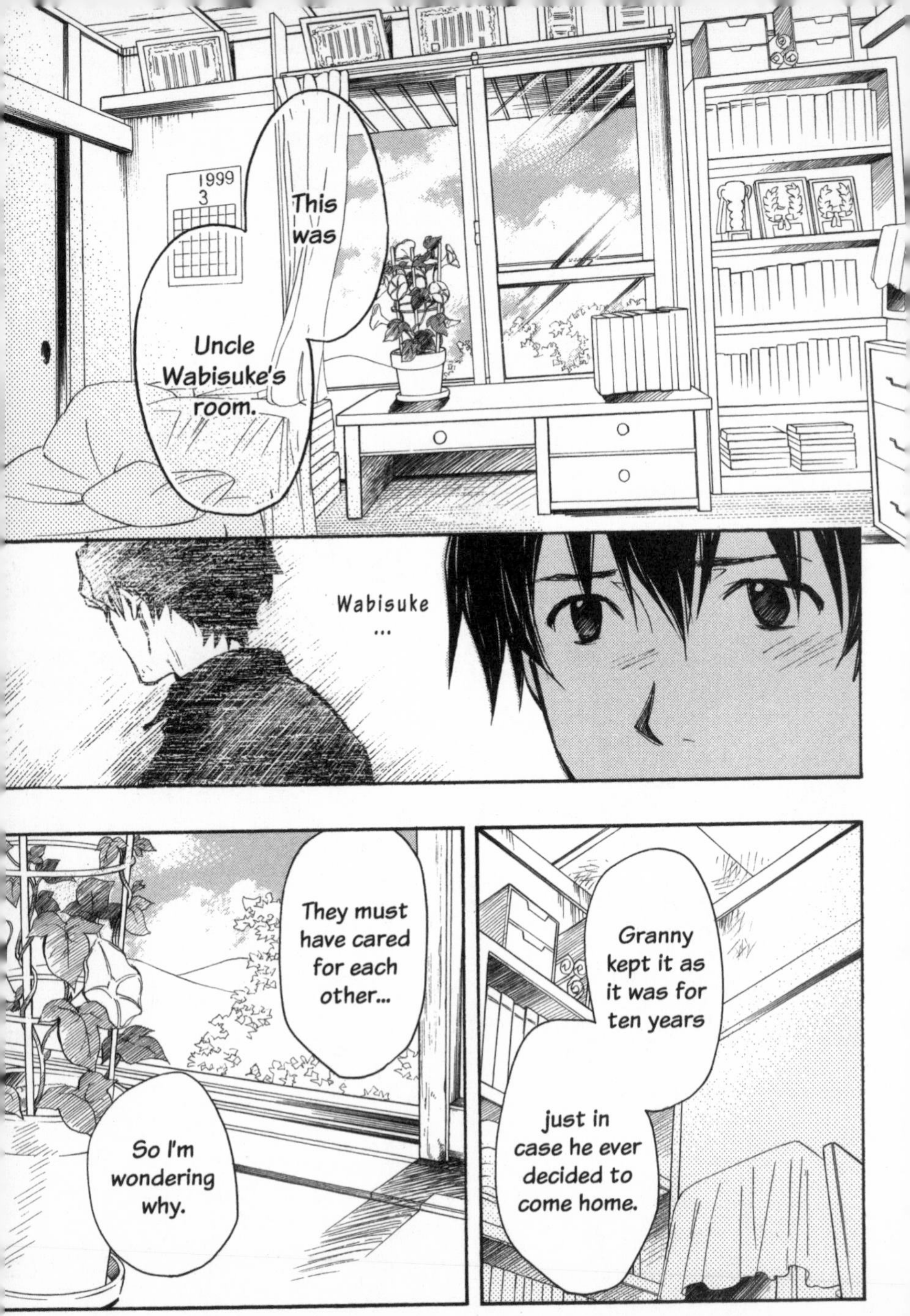
1999
3
This was Uncle Wabisuke's room.
Wabisuke ...
Granny kept it as it was for ten years
just in case he ever decided to come home.
They must have cared for each other...
So I'm wondering why.

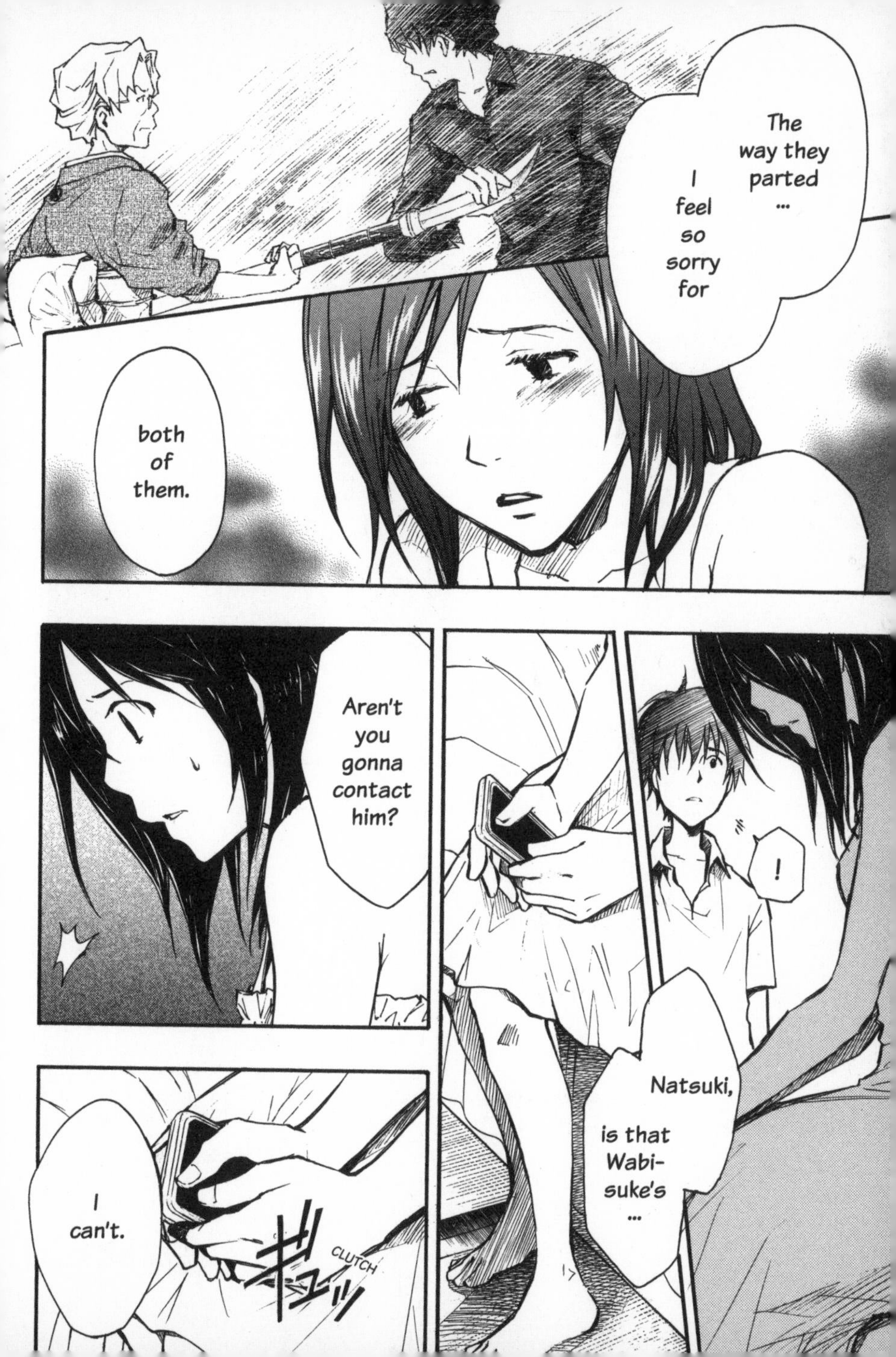
The way they parted ...
I feel so sorry for
both of them.
!
Natsuki, is that Wabi-suke's ...
Aren't you gonna contact him?
I can't.
CLUTCH

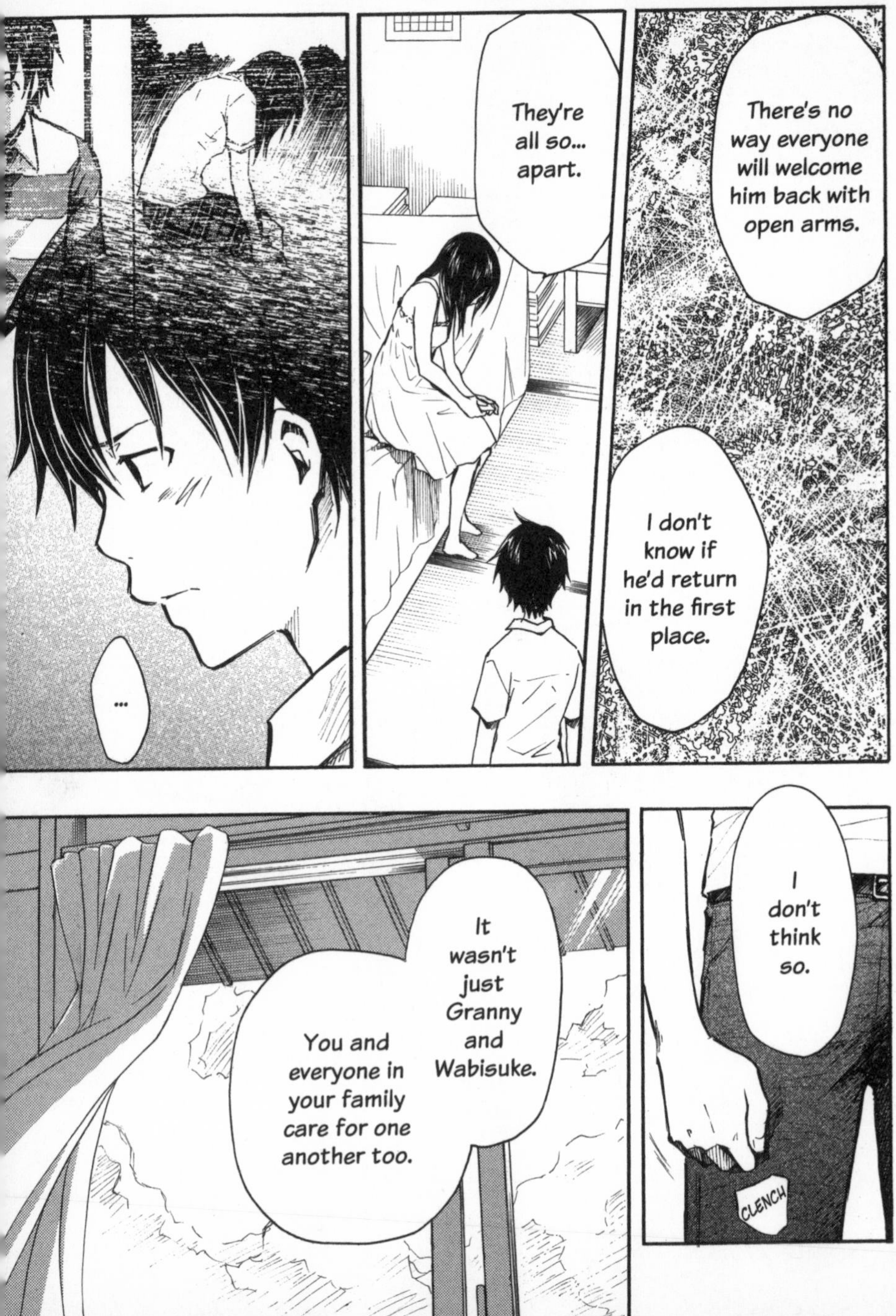
There's no way everyone will welcome him back with open arms.
I don't know if he'd return in the first place.
They're all so... apart.
...
I don't think so.
CLENCH
It wasn't just Granny and Wabisuke.
You and everyone in your family care for one another too.

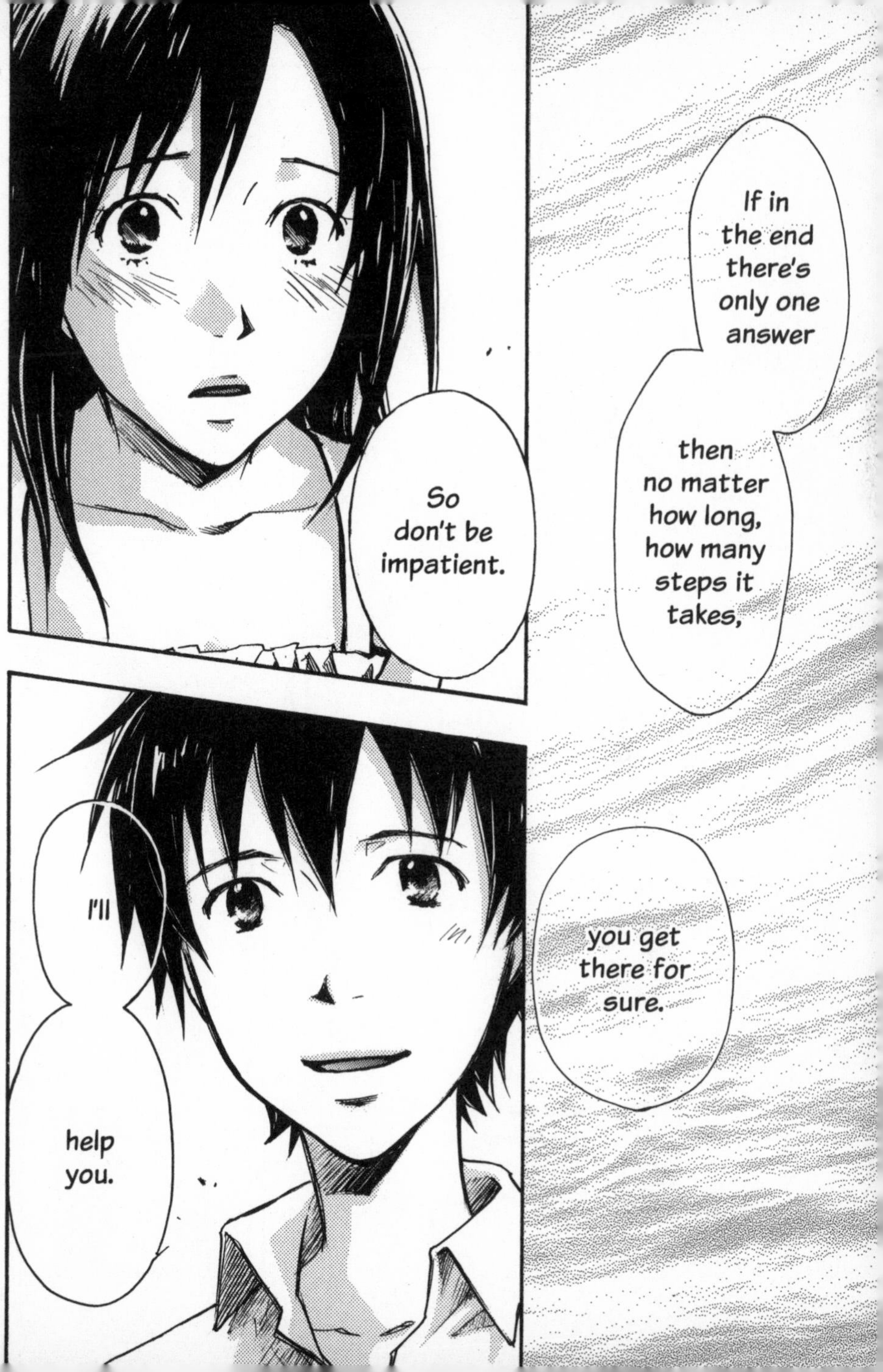
If in the end there's only one answer
then no matter how long, how many steps it takes,
you get there for sure.
So don't be impatient.
I'll
help you.

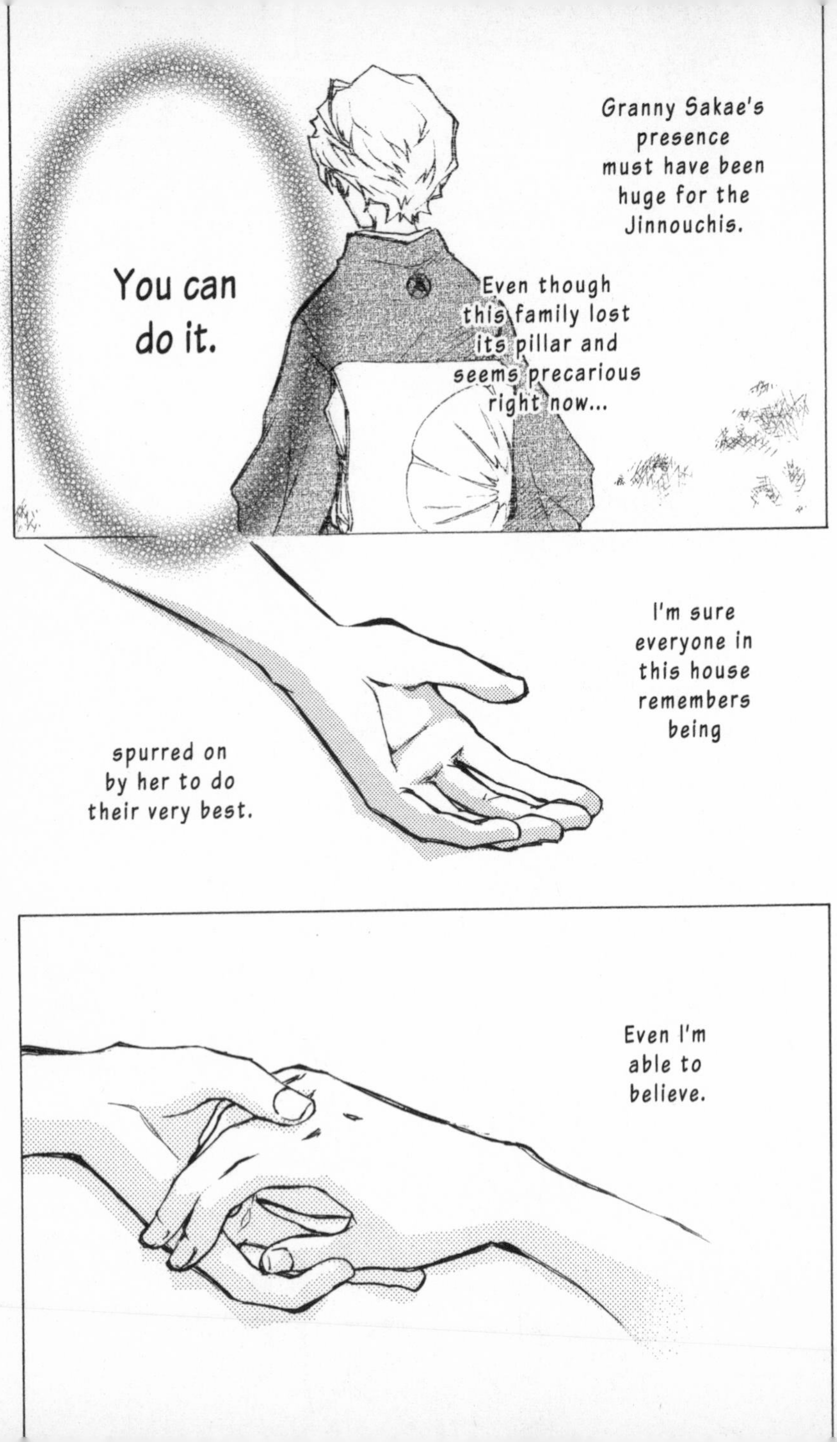
Granny Sakae's presence must have been huge for the Jinnouchis.
Even though this family lost its pillar and seems precarious right now...
You can do it.
I'm sure everyone in this house remembers being
spurred on by her to do their very best.
Even I'm able to believe.

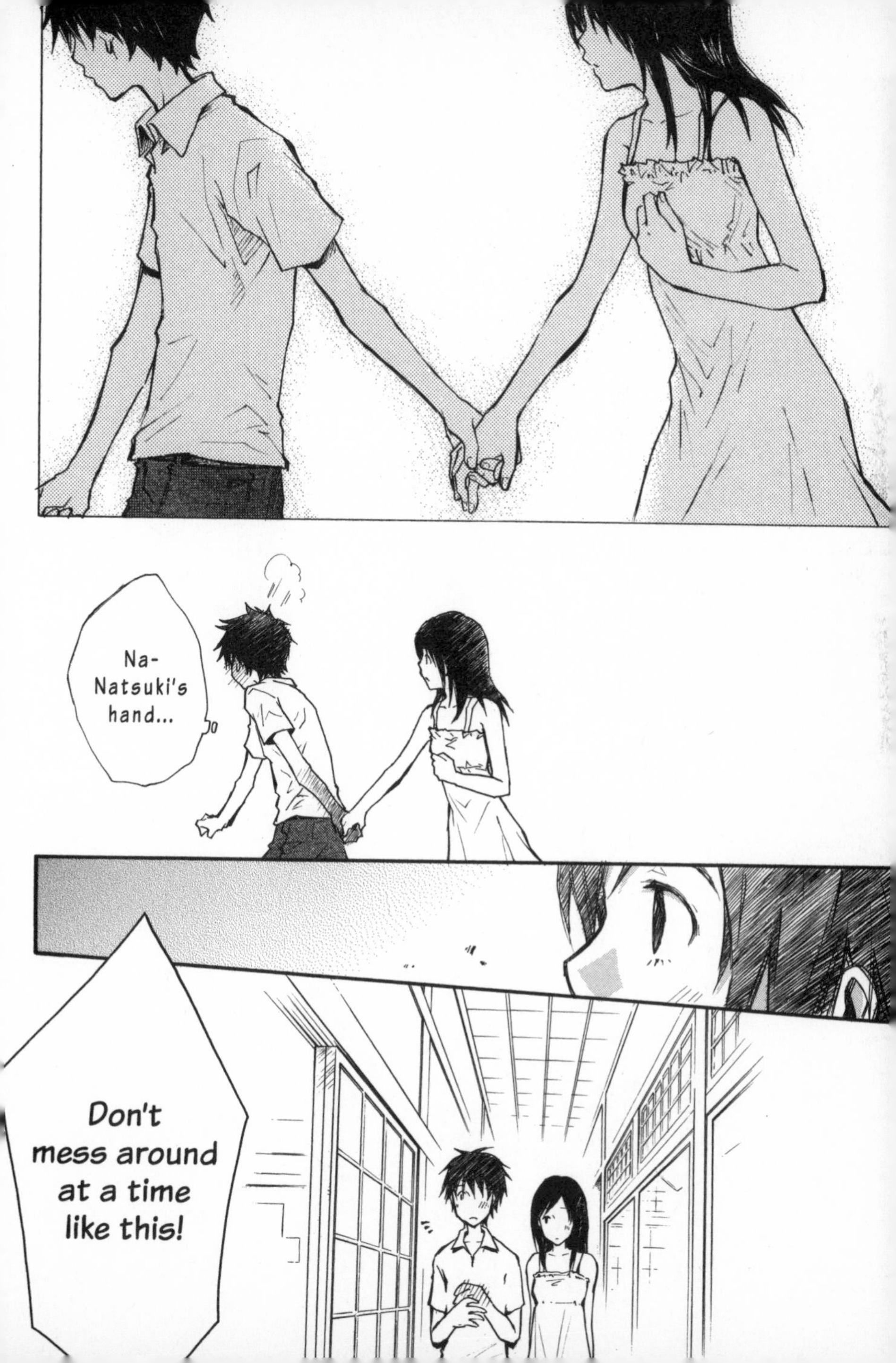
Na-
Natsuki's
hand...
Don't
mess around
at a time
like this!

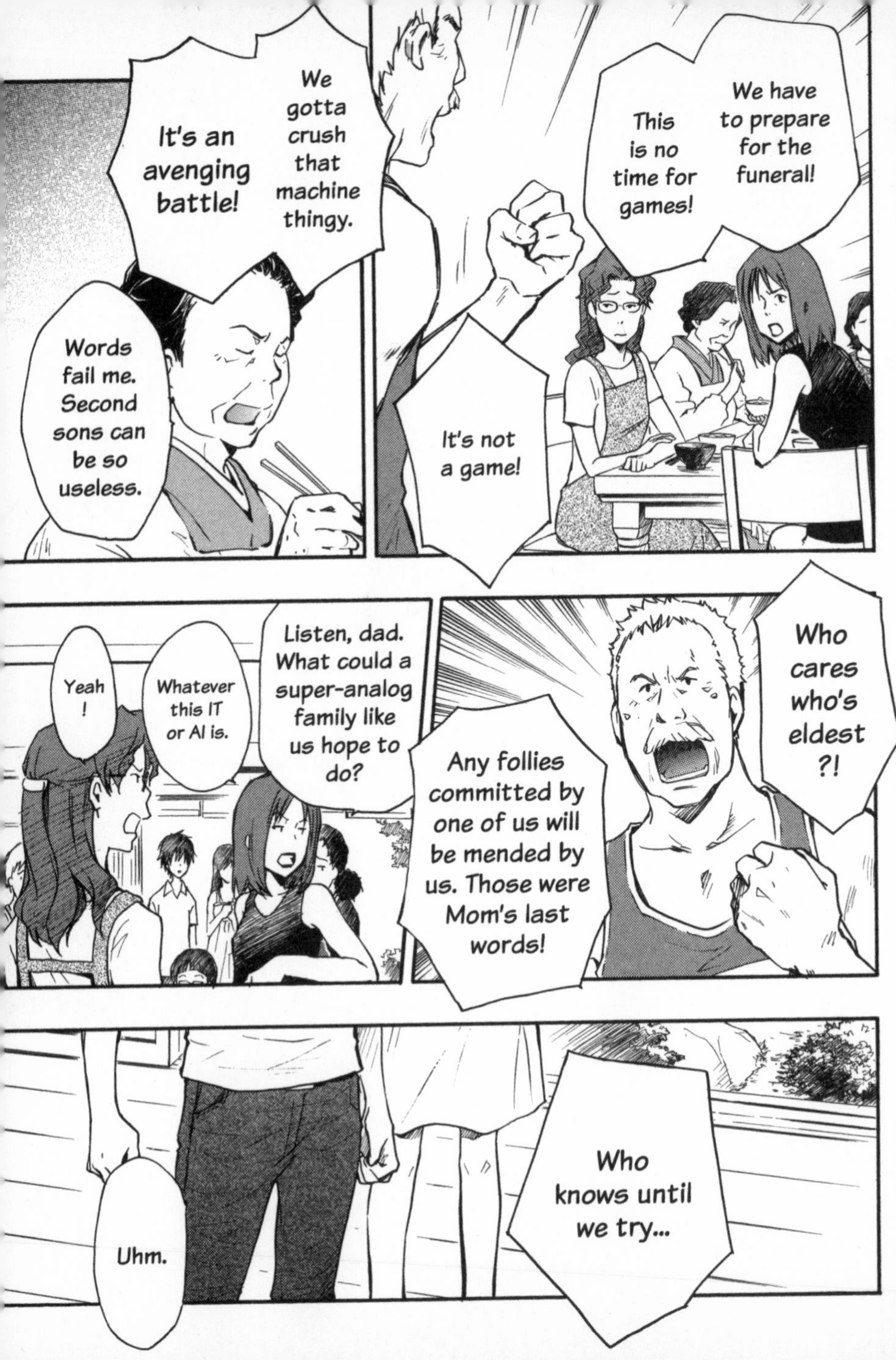
We have to prepare for the funeral!
This is no time for games!
It's not a game!
We gotta crush that machine thingy.
It's an avenging battle!
Words fail me. Second sons can be so useless.
Who cares who's eldest ?!
Any follies committed by one of us will be mended by us. Those were Mom's last words!
Listen, dad. What could a super-analog family like us hope to do?
Whatever this IT or AI is.
Yeah !
Who knows until we try...
Uhm.

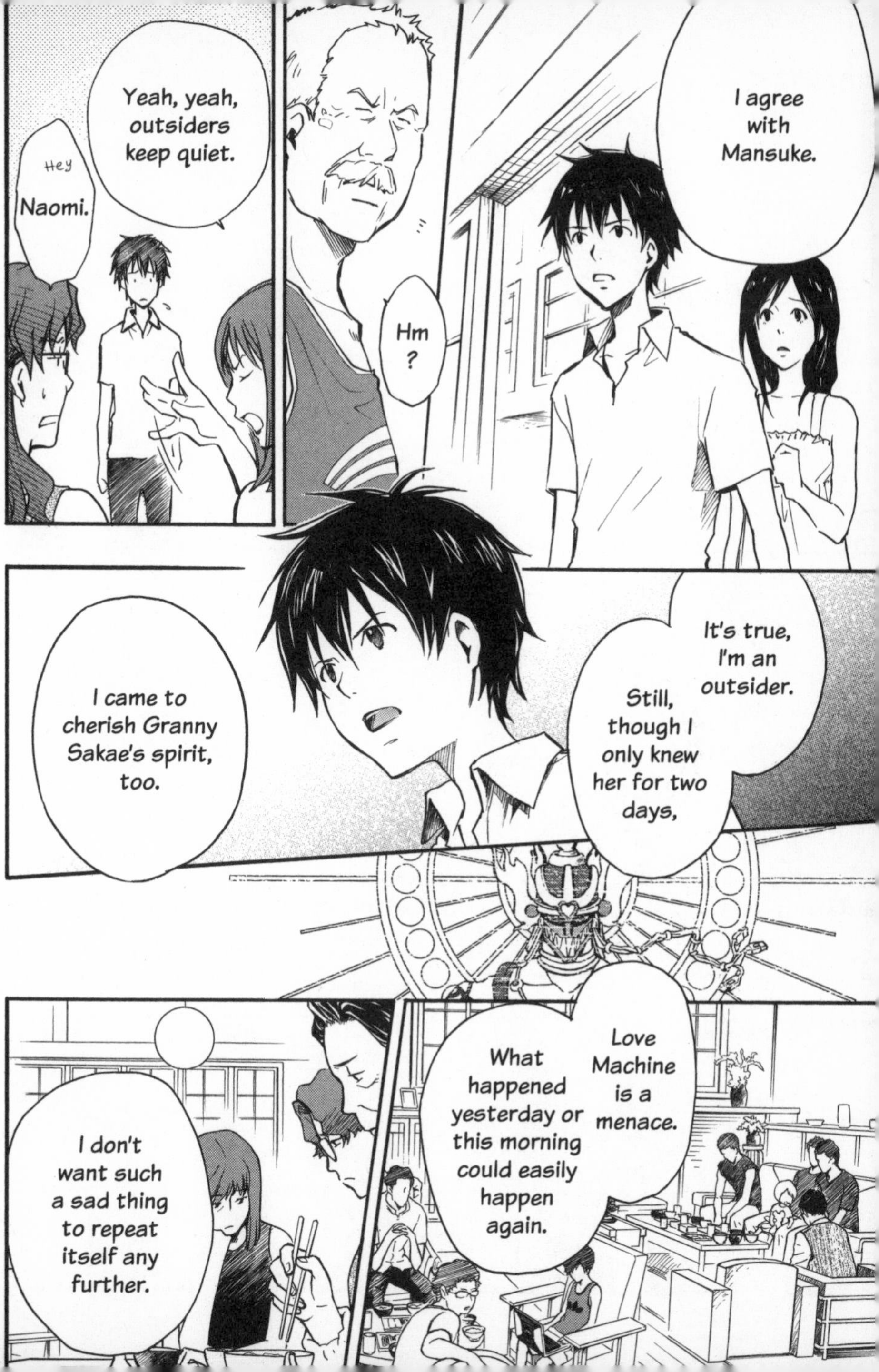
I agree with Mansuke.
Hm?
Yeah, yeah, outsiders keep quiet.
Hey
Naomi.
It's true, I'm an outsider.
Still, though I only knew her for two days,
I came to cherish Granny Sakae's spirit, too.
Love Machine is a menace.
What happened yesterday or this morning could easily happen again.
I don't want such a sad thing to repeat itself any further.

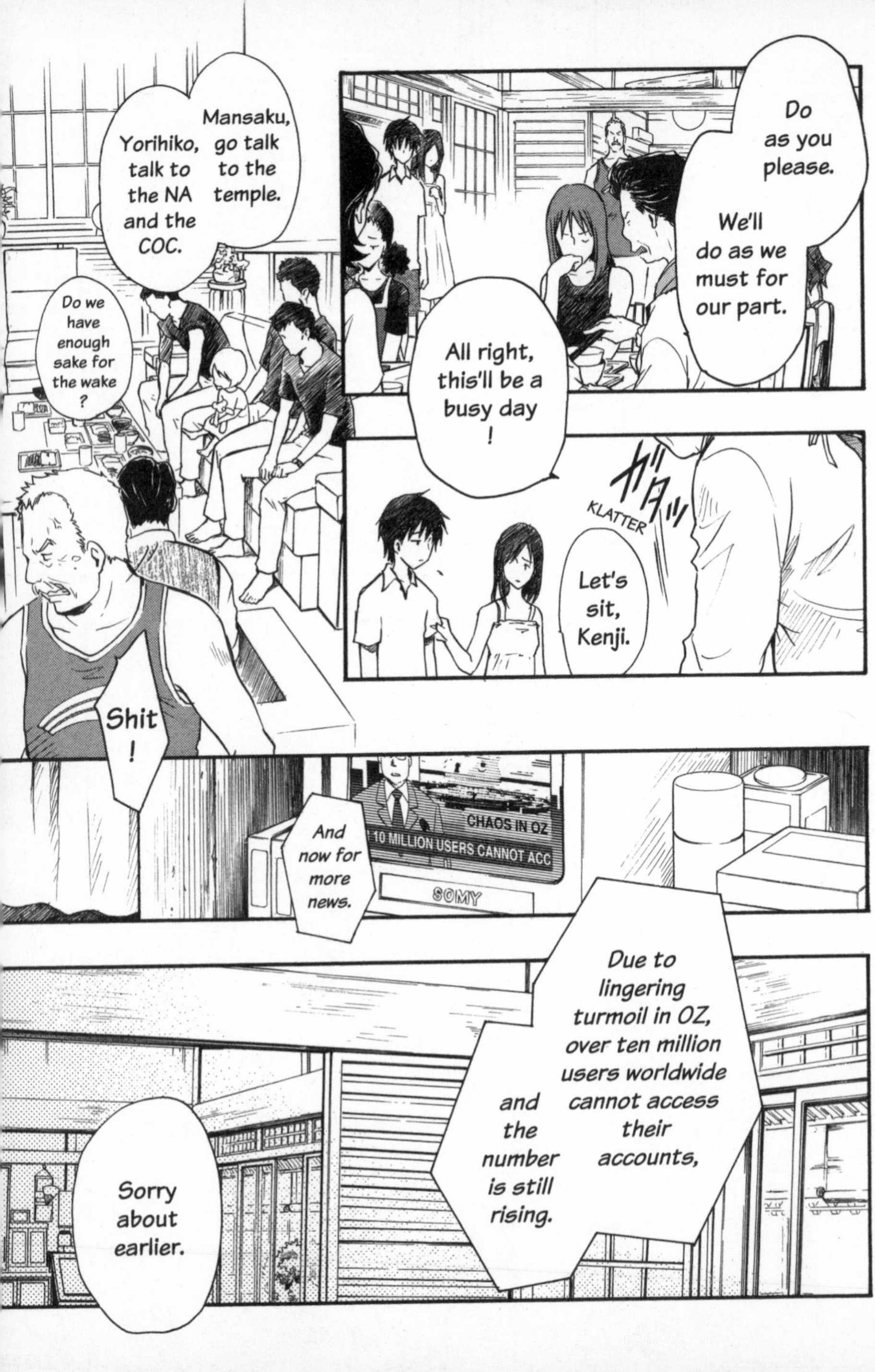
Do as you please.
We'll do as we must for our part.
All right, this'll be a busy day!
ガタッ KLATTER
Let's sit, Kenji.
Mansaku, go talk to the temple. Yorihiko, talk to the NA and the COC.
Do we have enough sake for the wake?
Shit!
CHAOS IN OZ
10 MILLION USERS CANNOT ACC
SOMY
And now for more news.
Due to lingering turmoil in OZ, over ten million users worldwide cannot access their accounts,
and the number is still rising.
Sorry about earlier.

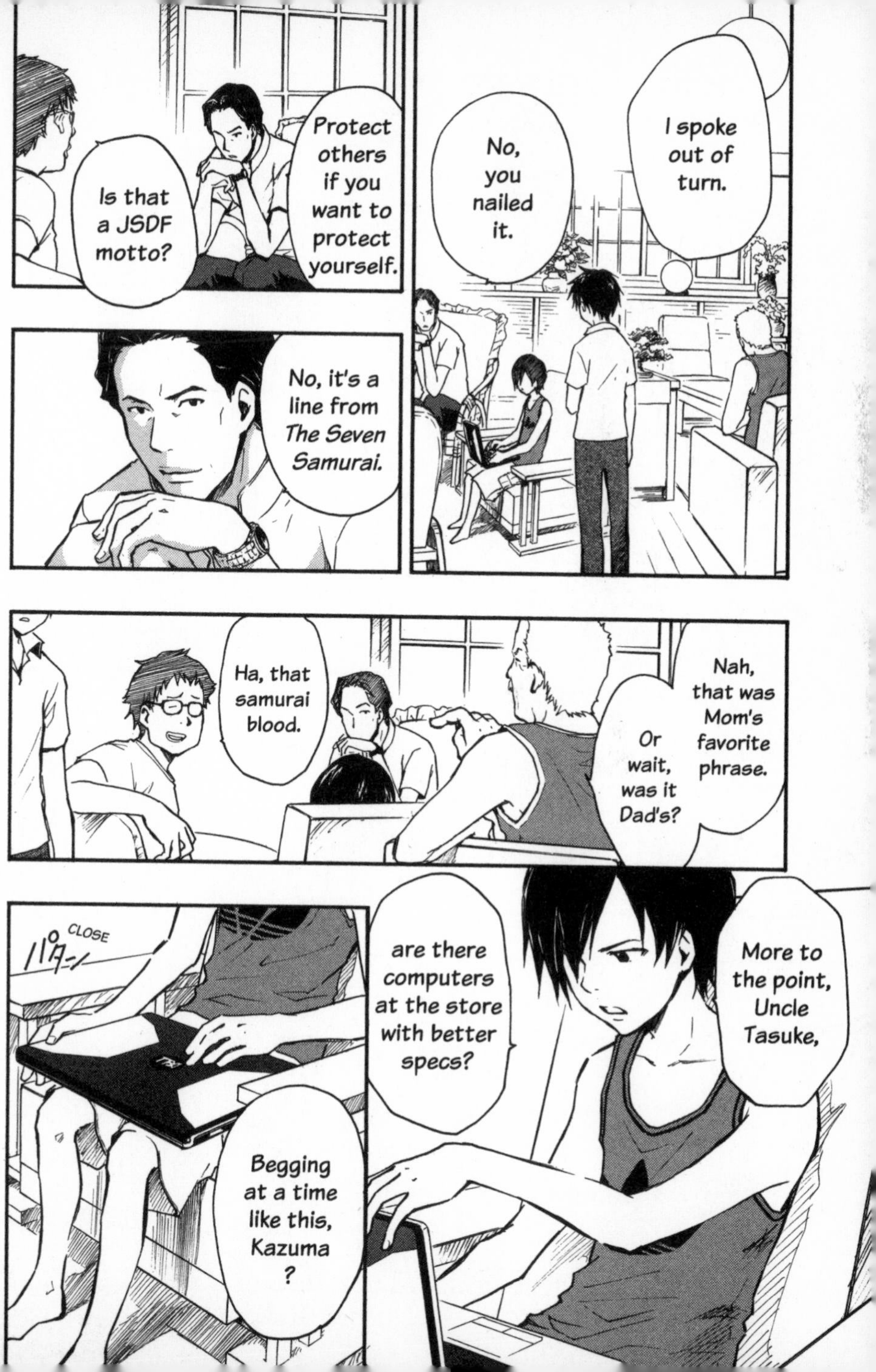
I spoke out of turn.
No, you nailed it.
Protect others if you want to protect yourself.
Is that a JSDF motto?
No, it's a line from *The Seven Samurai.*
Nah, that was Mom's favorite phrase.
Or wait, was it Dad's?
Ha, that samurai blood.
More to the point, Uncle Tasuke,
are there computers at the store with better specs?
Begging at a time like this, Kazuma?
CLOSE

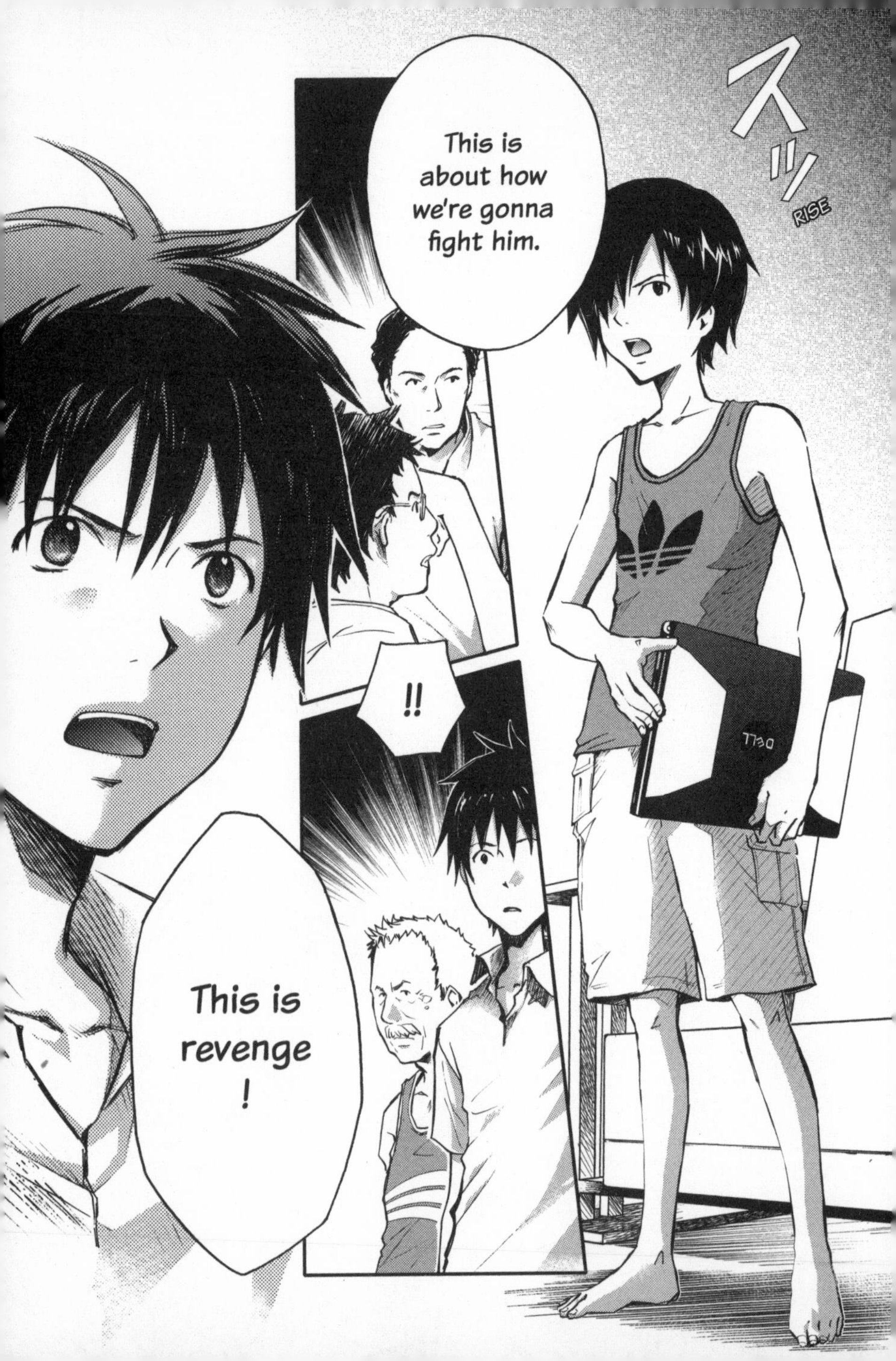
スッ
RISE
This is about how we're gonna fight him.
!!
This is revenge !

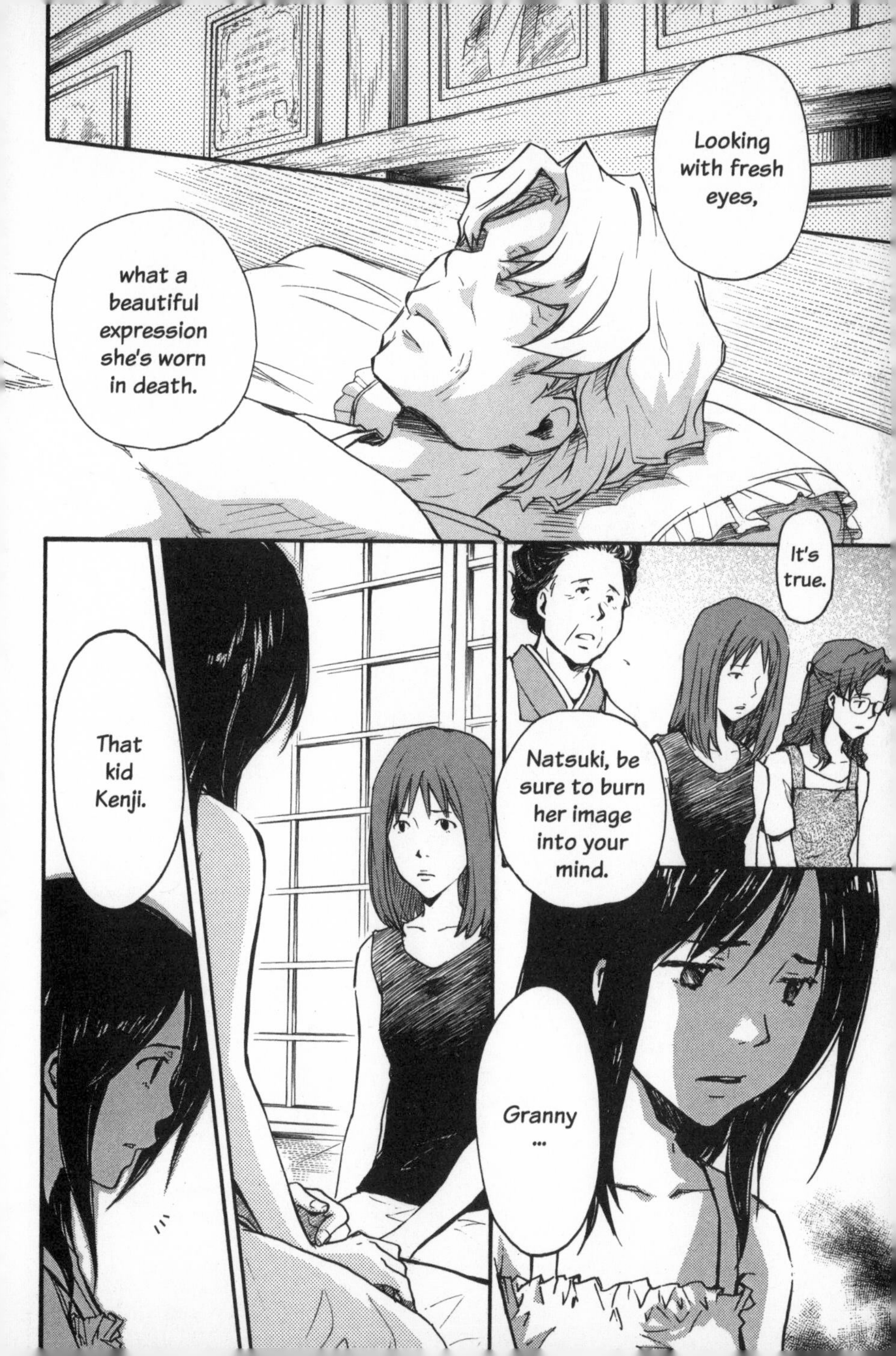
Looking with fresh eyes,
what a beautiful expression she's worn in death.
It's true.
Natsuki, be sure to burn her image into your mind.
Granny ...
That kid Kenji.

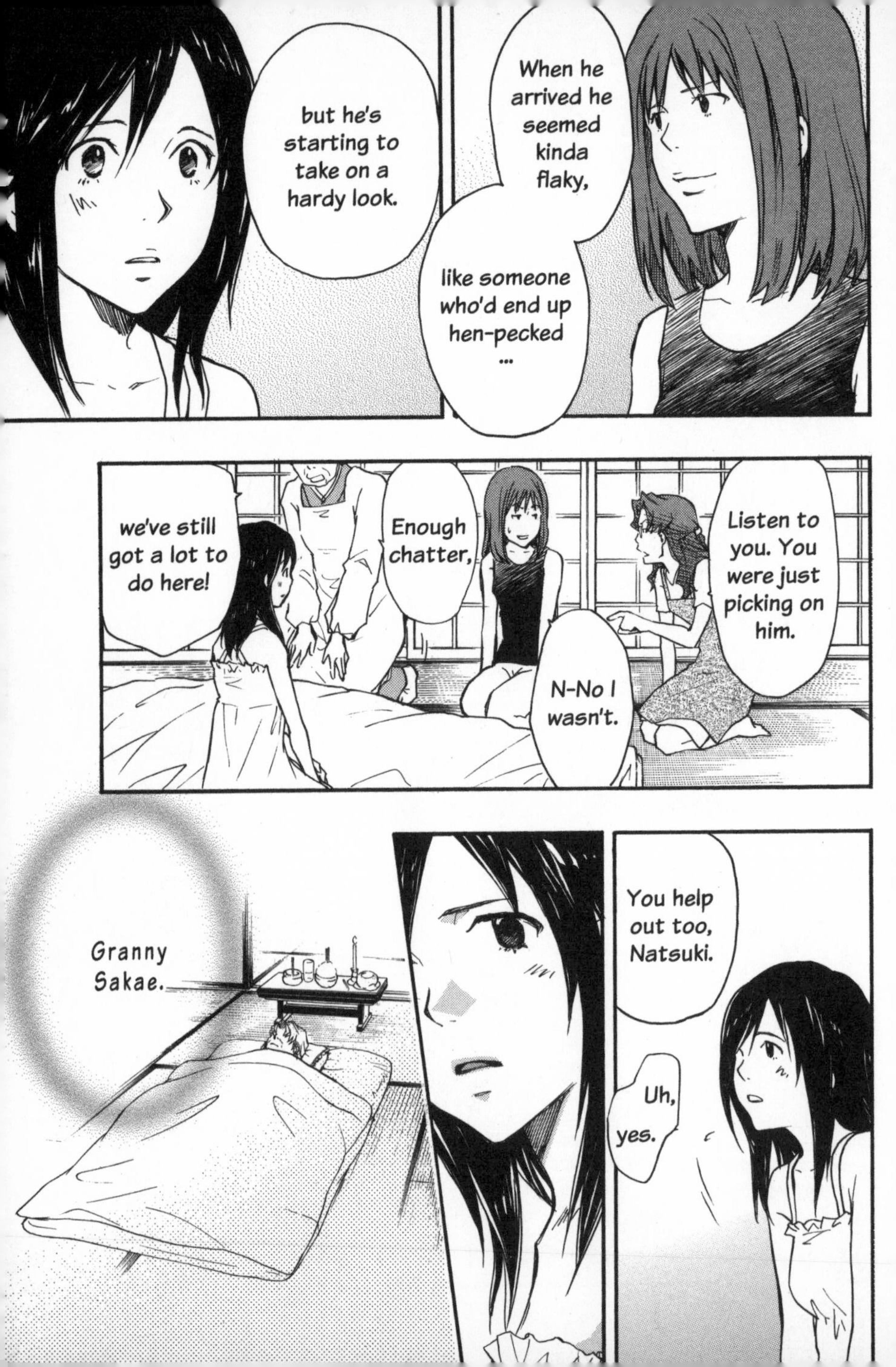
When he arrived he seemed kinda flaky,
like someone who'd end up hen-pecked ...
but he's starting to take on a hardy look.
Listen to you. You were just picking on him.
N-No I wasn't.
Enough chatter,
we've still got a lot to do here!
You help out too, Natsuki.
Uh, yes.
Granny Sakae.

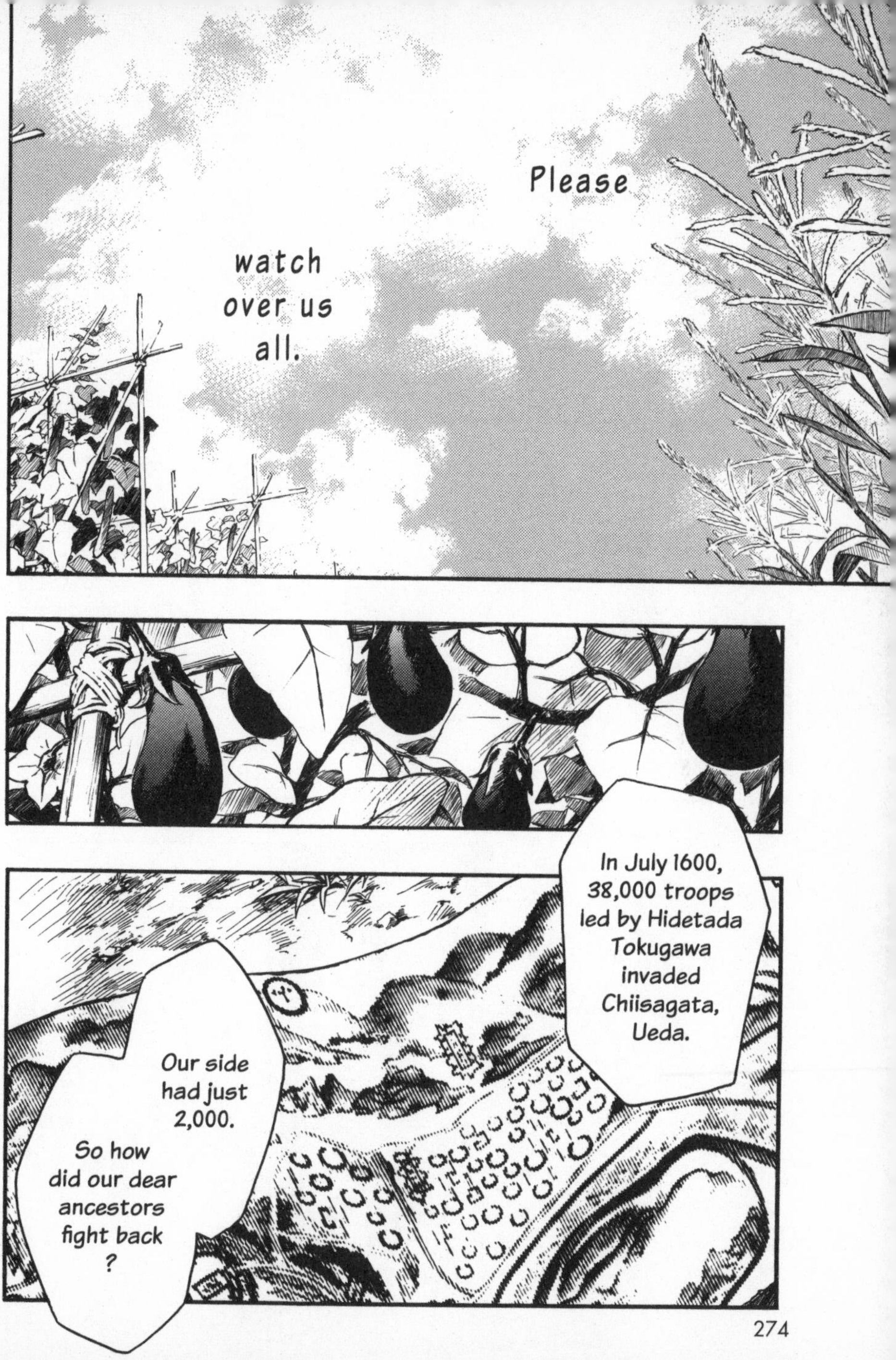
Please
watch over us all.
In July 1600, 38,000 troops led by Hidetada Tokugawa invaded Chiisagata, Ueda.
Our side had just 2,000.
So how did our dear ancestors fight back ?

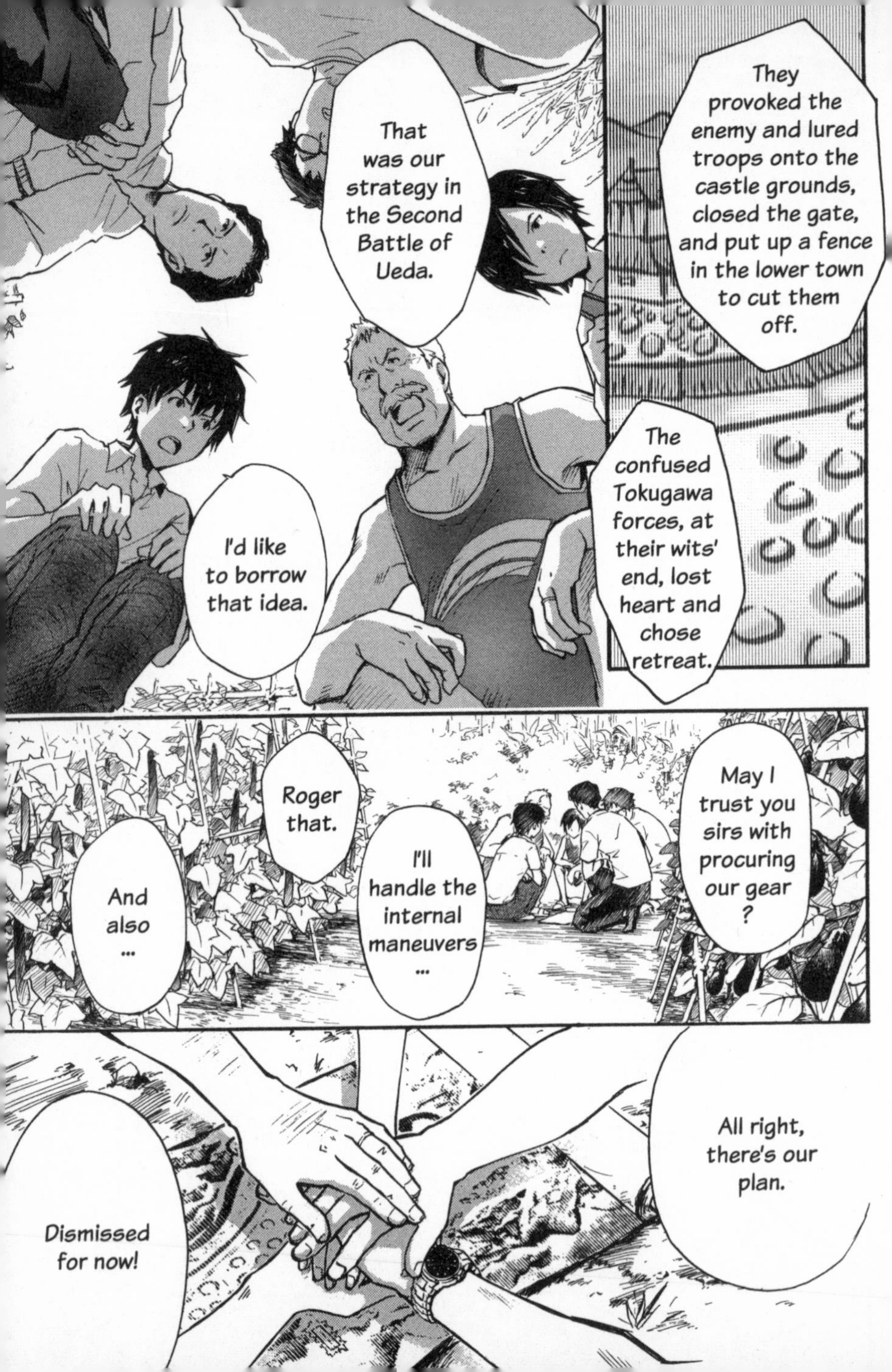
They provoked the enemy and lured troops onto the castle grounds, closed the gate, and put up a fence in the lower town to cut them off.
The confused Tokugawa forces, at their wits' end, lost heart and chose retreat.
That was our strategy in the Second Battle of Ueda.
I'd like to borrow that idea.
May I trust you sirs with procuring our gear ?
Roger that.
I'll handle the internal maneuvers ...
And also ...
All right, there's our plan.
Dismissed for now!

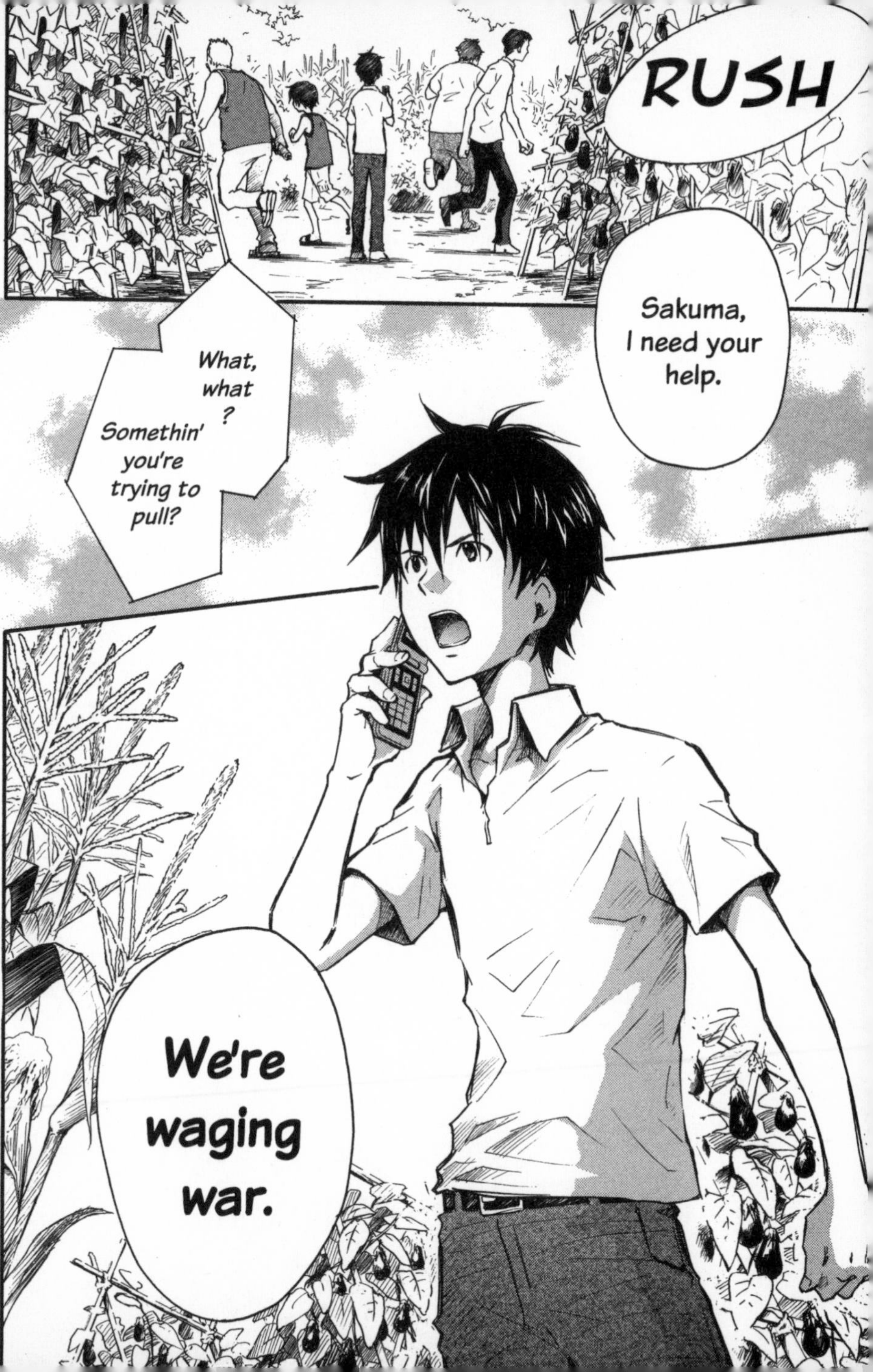
RUSH
Sakuma, I need your help.
What, what? Somethin' you're trying to pull?
We're waging war.

SUMMER WARS

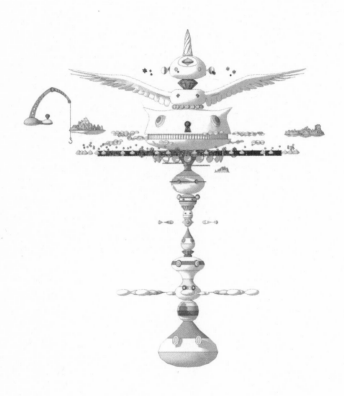

TO BE CONCLUDED
IN PART 2

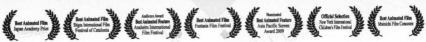
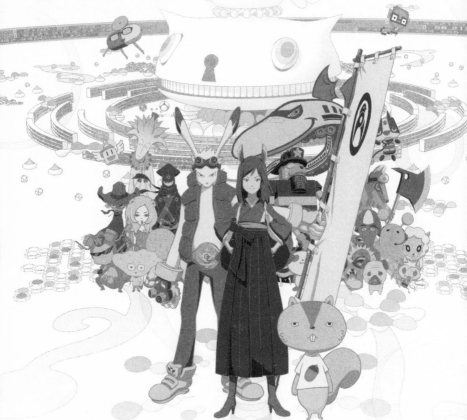

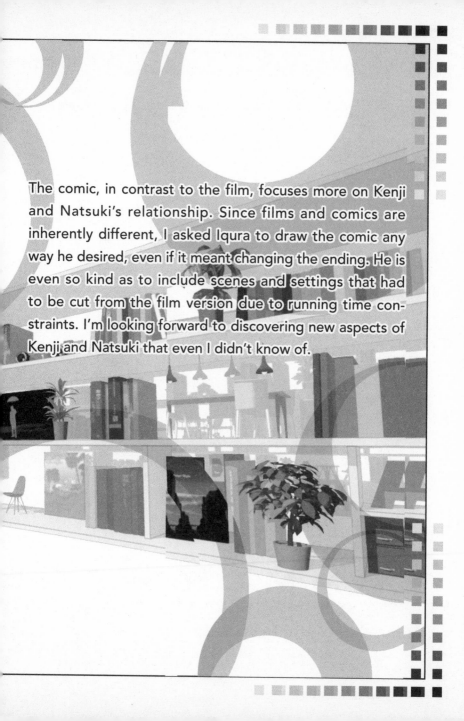

The comic, in contrast to the film, focuses more on Kenji and Natsuki's relationship. Since films and comics are inherently different, I asked Iqura to draw the comic any way he desired, even if it meant changing the ending. He is even so kind as to include scenes and settings that had to be cut from the film version due to running time constraints. I'm looking forward to discovering new aspects of Kenji and Natsuki that even I didn't know of.

Special Message

On *Summer Wars* Becoming a Comic

The first time I saw Iqura Sugimoto's art, I knew at a glance that I wanted him to draw this story for me. The facial expressions of Kenji and Natsuki are so sensitive and charming, aren't they? Kenji is a youth with zero confidence, but his inner kindness and sincerity stems from that lack of confidence. I feel that Iqura grasps Kenji's individuality and draws him with deep affection. And Natsuki is adorable in every panel she's in!

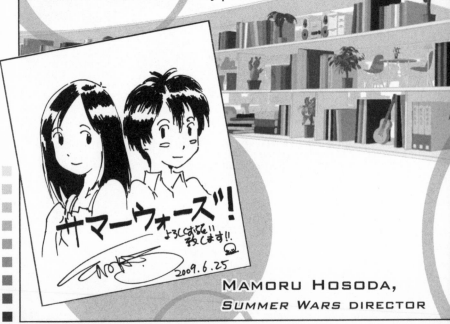

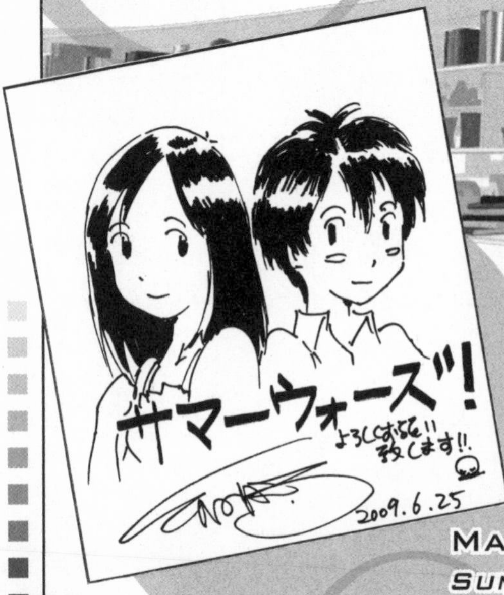
サマーウォーズ!
2009.6.25

Mamoru Hosoda,
Summer Wars director

SPECIAL MESSAGE

ABOUT IQURA SUGIMOTO'S SUMMER WARS

Young Ace, the magazine that serialized *Summer Wars*, started publication at almost the same time the film was released, and I'd been looking forward to seeing the manga version.

At first, I felt that Mr. Sugimoto was very faithful to the original film, but as I continued reading, I noticed that his unique, distinctive characteristics came through and that he was making *Summer Wars* his own.

I'm the type to see a character like Kenji, who seems to be an introvert at first glance, and yell, "Try harder!" (laughs) and the manga captures this aspect of his character very well, allowing the reader to slip right into the story.

So will Kenji be able to show Natsuki the "manliness" I expect from him? And what will happen of their relationship, I wonder? I'm looking forward to reading on.

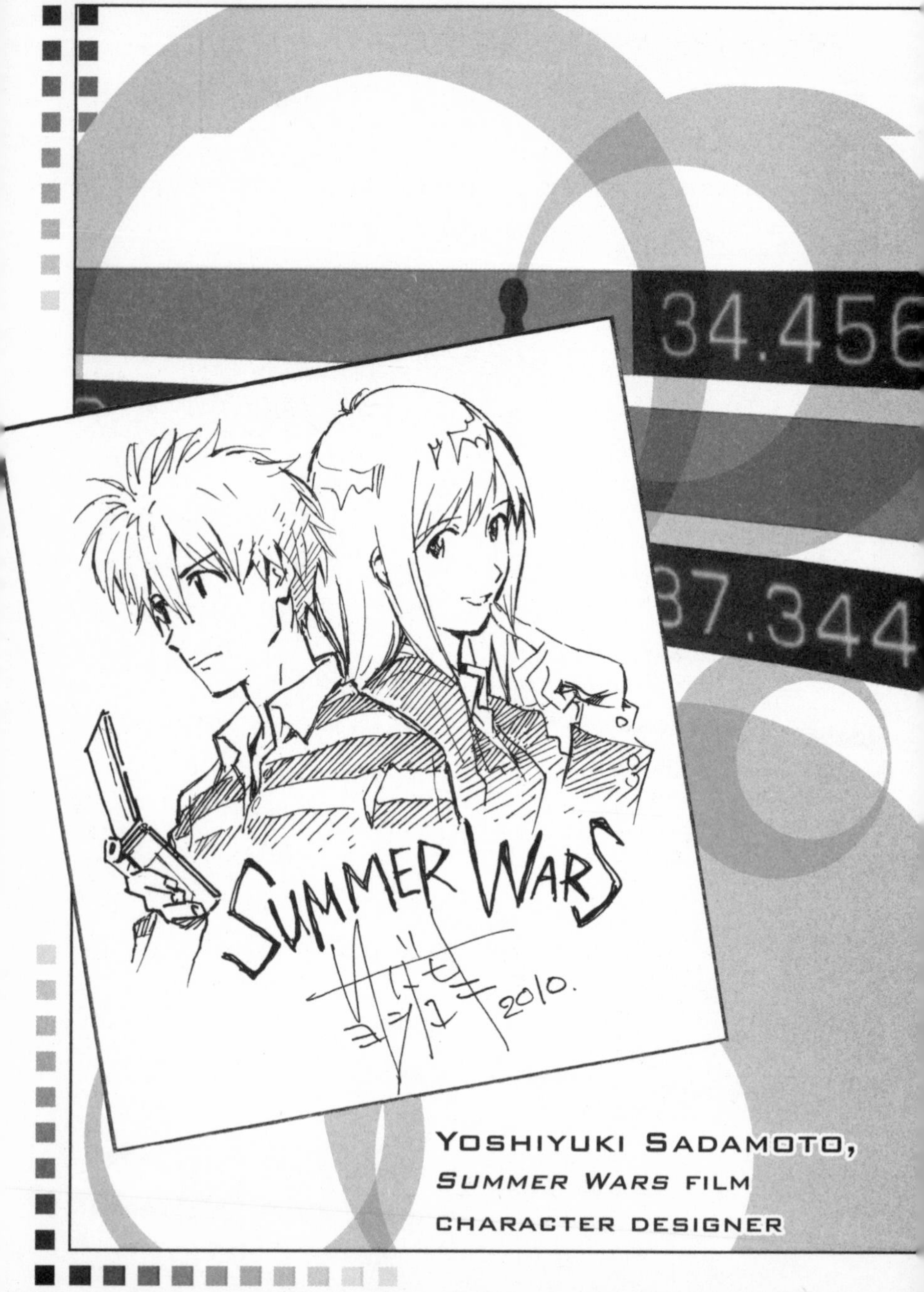
34.456
37.344
SUMMER WARS
2010.

YOSHIYUKI SADAMOTO,
SUMMER WARS FILM
CHARACTER DESIGNER

Summer Wars Character Rough Sketch Collection

Here are the initial character designs by Iqura Sugimoto, with notes from the artist!

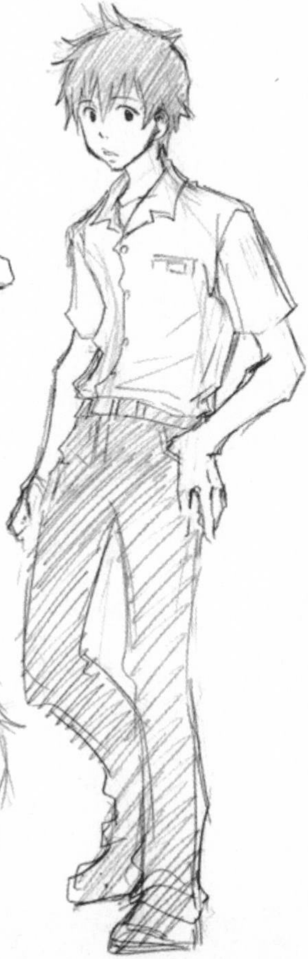

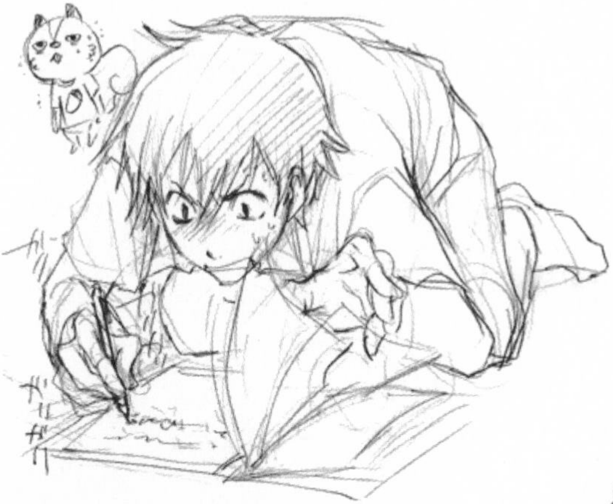

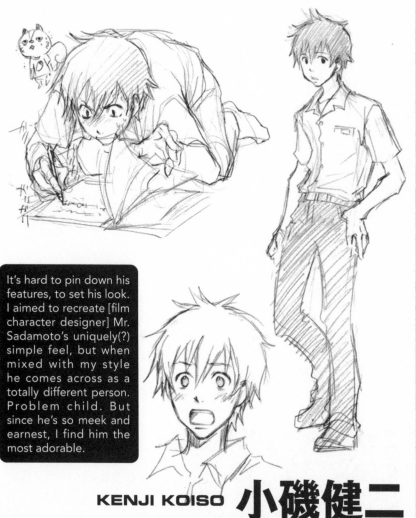

It's hard to pin down his features, to set his look. I aimed to recreate [film character designer] Mr. Sadamoto's uniquely(?) simple feel, but when mixed with my style he comes across as a totally different person. Problem child. But since he's so meek and earnest, I find him the most adorable.

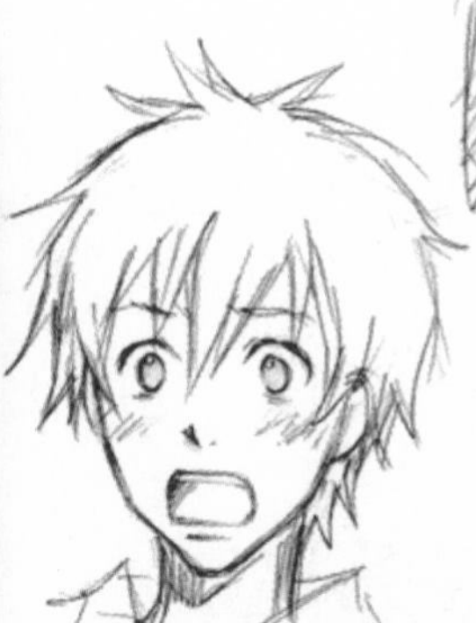

Kenji Koiso 小磯健二

篠原夏希 NATSUKI SHINOHARA

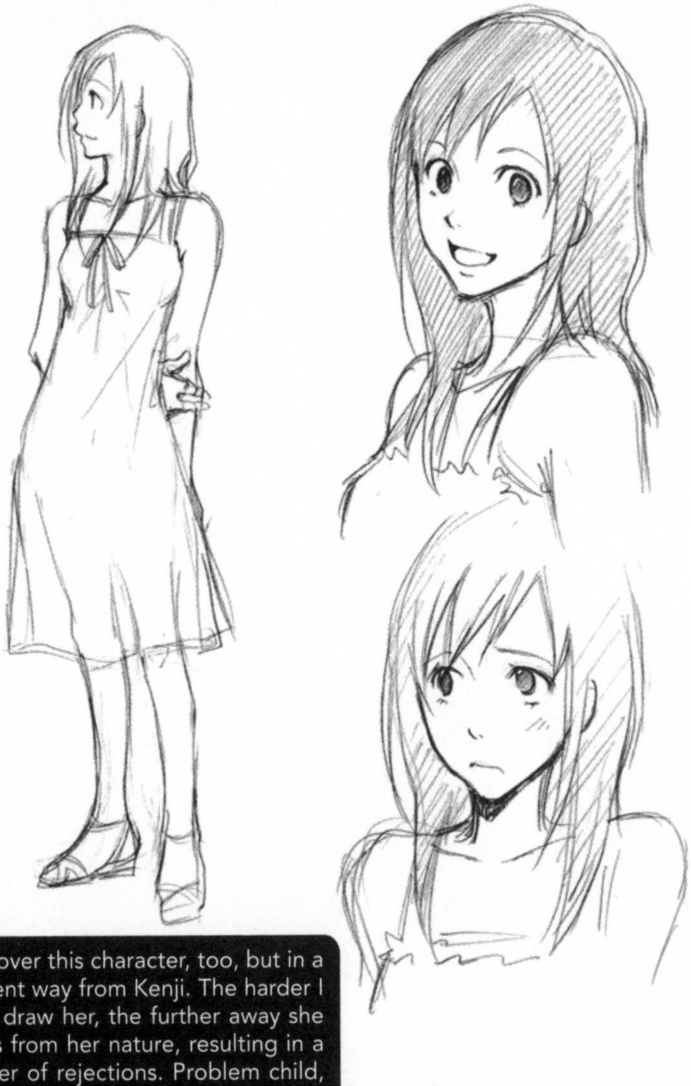

I fuss over this character, too, but in a different way from Kenji. The harder I try to draw her, the further away she seems from her nature, resulting in a number of rejections. Problem child, just like Kenji...

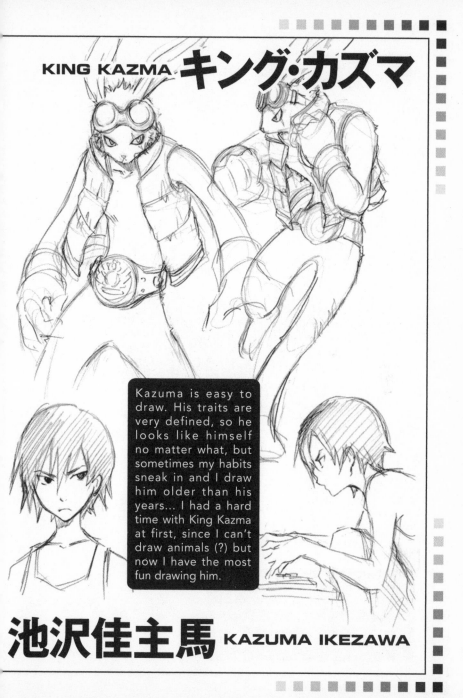

KING KAZMA キング・カズマ

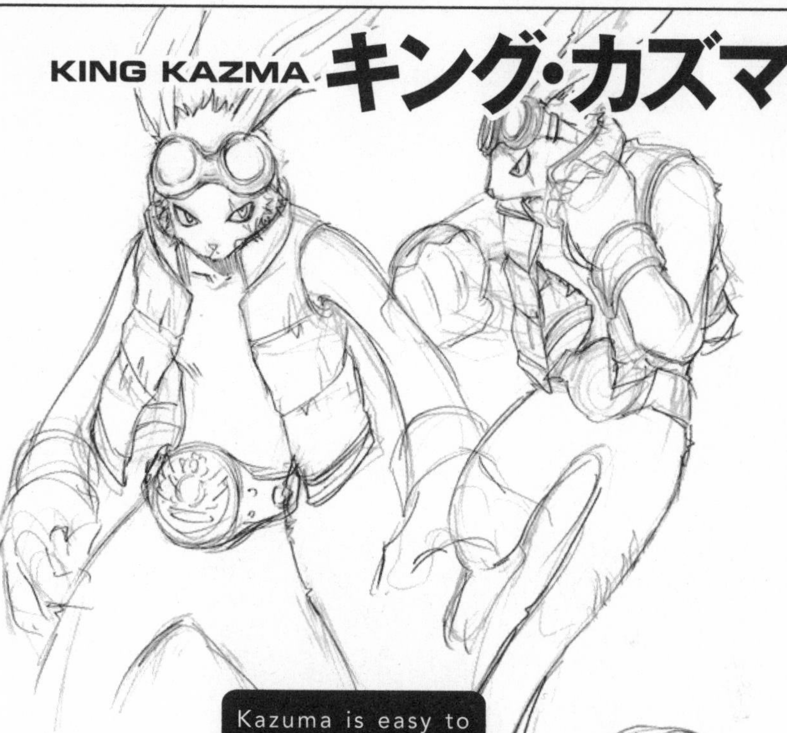

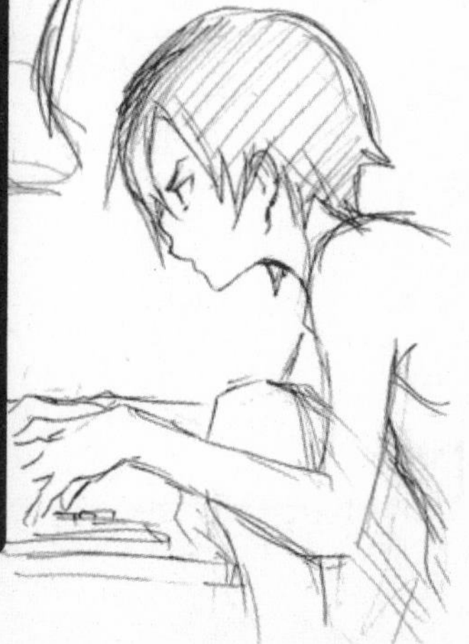

Kazuma is easy to draw. His traits are very defined, so he looks like himself no matter what, but sometimes my habits sneak in and I draw him older than his years... I had a hard time with King Kazma at first, since I can't draw animals (?) but now I have the most fun drawing him.

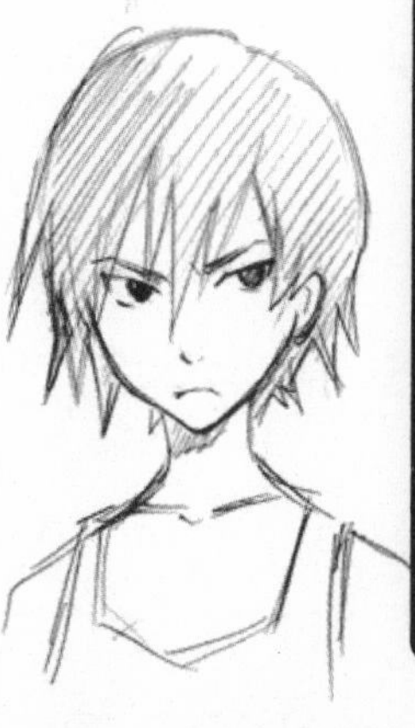

池沢佳主馬 KAZUMA IKEZAWA

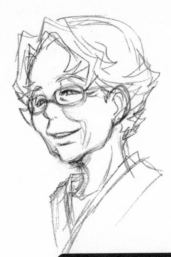

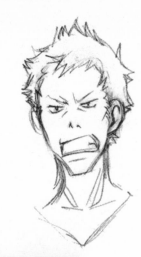

陣内翔太
SHOTA JINNOUCHI

陣内栄
SAKAE JINNOUCHI

Since there are so many characters, it's hard to keep them all straight, especially on pages where the head count is very high. But it's great practice drawing all ages and different character types. I draw them with the intent of learning new things.

佐久間敬
TAKASHI SAKUMA

陣内侘助
WABISUKE JINNOUCHI

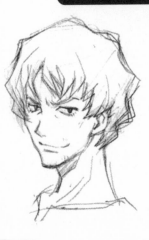

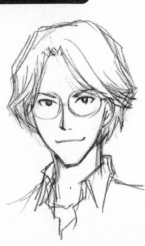

SUMMER WARS

PART 1

Production: Grace Lu
          Anthony Quintessenza

Copyright © 2009 SUMMER WARS FILM PARTNERS
          © Iqura SUGIMOTO 2009, 2010
Edited by KADOKAWA SHOTEN
First published in Japan in 2009, 2010 by KADOKAWA CORPORATION, Tokyo.
English translation rights arranged with KADOKAWA CORPORATION, Tokyo
through TUTTLE-MORI AGENCY, INC., Tokyo.
English language version produced by Vertical, Inc.

Translation provided by Vertical, Inc., 2013
Published by Vertical, Inc., New York

Originally published in Japanese as *Samaa Wouzu 1, 2* by KADOKAWA SHOTEN, 2009, 2010
Samaa Wouzu first serialized in *Young Ace*, 2009-2010

This is a work of fiction.

ISBN: 978-1-939130-15-0

Manufactured in Canada

First Edition

Second Printing

Vertical, Inc.
451 Park Avenue South
7th Floor
New York, NY 10016
www.vertical-inc.com